LORD SELKIRK: A LIFE

LORD SELKIRK
A LIFE

J.M. BUMSTED

MICHIGAN STATE UNIVERSITY PRESS/EAST LANSING

Michigan State University Press
East Lansing, Michigan 48823-5245

Printed and bound in Canada.

15 14 13 12 11 10 09   1 2 3 4 5 6 7 8 9 10

Interior design: Relish Design
Cover design: Doowah Design
Maps: Weldon Hiebert

Bumsted, J. M.
Lord Selkirk: A Life / J.M. Bumsted.
p. cm.
Includes bibliographical references and index.
ISBN 978-0-87013-853-9 (cloth : alk. paper) 1. Selkirk, Thomas Douglas, Earl of, 1771–
1820. 2. Pioneers—Manitoba—Biography. 3. Scots—Manitoba—Biography. 4. Red River
Settlement—History. 5. Frontier and pioneer life—Manitoba. 6. Manitoba—Biography.
7. Manitoba—History. 8. Fur trade—Canada—History. 9. Canada—History—1763–1867.
10. Enlightenment—Scotland. I. Title.
F1063.S47B86 2009
971.27'01092—dc22
[B]
2008031073

Visit Michigan State University Press on the Word Wide Web at
www.msupress.msu.edu

To my youngest grandchildren
Oliver and Joenna

CONTENTS

ILLUSTRATIONS FOLLOW PAGE 254

"The best-laid schemes o' mice an 'men
Gang aft aglay,
An' lea'e us nought but grief an' pain,
For promis'd joy!"

—*Robert Burns*, "To a Mouse, On Turning
Her Up In Her Nest With the Plough," *1785*

PREFACE

Writing a full-length biography of Thomas Douglas, fifth Earl of Selkirk, has proved a far more difficult job than I had initially expected when I first undertook research for it in 1976. I had always conceived of biography as a fairly straightforward business. The subject in effect defined itself, and the events of the life had merely to be chronicled and explained. As I soon discovered, quite apart from the complexity of the chief character, a Selkirk biography was not all that simple. The first problem was a sea change in the nature of biography itself, brought about chiefly by the enormously detailed lives of literary figures. The amount of detail led the biographers to assume that their real task was to explain the subject's inner being, a quest for which they had enormous material.

Unfortunately, there were great holes in the Selkirk Papers. The Public Archives of Canada, as it was known when I began research on the life of Lord Selkirk in 1975, held a great cache of transcriptions from the family papers. The transcriptions ran to more than 20,000 pages. When examined more closely, however, these 20,000 pages contained a vast amount of material on the fur trade and events of the fur-trade war between Selkirk and the North West Company, and not as much personal material dealing with his life as I had expected. I discovered that the transcriptions had been made by the Public Archives at the turn of the century from the vast horde of papers in the family muniment room at St. Mary's Isle in Kirkcudbright. These were subsequently microfilmed on twenty-one reels of microfilm, the form in which researchers now use them. The original instructions to the transcribers, local ladies of the community, were to copy all papers of "Canadian interest." What this meant, I soon found, was that large categories of the earl's personal papers had not been copied. One could see that more personal material had existed, because it kept being cited and quoted by a number of scholars who had visited St. Mary's Isle, notably George Bryce, Chester Martin, and John Perry Pritchett. The Selkirk transcriptions contain one journal kept by his lordship of his North American tour from 1803 to 1804. The citations of other scholars suggested that he kept other journals over the years, perhaps even a lifetime's worth, but because they were not of Canadian interest, they were not transcribed. A tantalizing selection of material from a section of the family papers labelled "Private Correspondence, St. Mary's Isle," was made on behalf of the Hudson's Bay Company (now microfilm reel A27). A lengthy correspondence between Lady Selkirk and the earl's sister Katherine Halkett between 1808 and 1820 survives only in snippets in the books of Martin and Pritchett, as does a lengthy correspondence between the fourth earl and his sons (especially Basil, Lord Daer, and Thomas, the fifth earl). A cache of copies of family papers also exists, associated with the raid of John Paul Jones on St. Mary's Isle in 1778. A number of printed but unpublished pamphlets, most of them authored by Lord Selkirk, was subsequently donated or sold to the Ontario Archives by John Perry Pritchett, who must have obtained them from the family in the course of his research. The family manse and the library at St. Mary's Isle were themselves destroyed in a fire at St. Mary's Isle in 1940. According to local people in Kirkcudbright whom I interviewed in 1976, the fire occurred under suspicious circumstances but was not thoroughly investigated because of wartime conditions. Occasional Selkirk papers have turned up in a number of other repositories, including letters written by Selkirk and kept by the recipients. The most important of these collections consists of letters between Selkirk and Alexander Macdonald of Dalilia, housed in the Edinburgh University Library.

The Public Archives of Canada, which of course was not to know that the family muniment room would be destroyed, thus produced through its transcription policy several important if unexpected complications for a Selkirk biographer. One of the most important results of the fire was that Selkirk's life, apart from his great North American work, was sadly underdocumented. The story of his formative years, in which he was very much under the influence of the Scottish Enlightenment, proved very difficult to uncover, as did any real understanding of his political activities in Scotland

and London, both before and after his election to the House of Lords. I have tried as much as humanly possible in this work to emphasize that Selkirk was not a one-dimensional character with a monomaniacal commitment to North American colonization. He was also a figure of the Scottish Enlightenment and an important, if minor, national political figure during the Napoleonic Wars.

The gaps in the Selkirk Papers have also exacerbated a major feature of Lord Selkirk's personality: his almost pathological reticence to reveal his interior life and thought. Selkirk was not much given to self-confession; his admission to his wife of mistaken actions with regard to Daniel McKenzie and his apology to William Wilberforce were most uncharacteristic. What has survived of Selkirk's correspondence is almost exclusively the business stuff, and such letters are the least likely to allow their author to speak about his emotions, his dreams, his fantasies, and his beliefs. Even the surviving letters between Selkirk and his wife are ones in which communicating information at a distance is usually more important than elaborating private feelings. In any event, the Selkirk papers allow the biographer precious little access into the private world of the subject. We have no idea whether the man had any religious beliefs or any aesthetic sensibilities, much less deep undocumentable feelings about what was happening to him. An earlier biographer, John Morgan Gray, attempted to correct for this absence of interiority by inventing some, apparently assuming that his vast store of knowledge about Selkirk allowed him to enter the earl's thought processes. I am not comfortable with such a *verstehen* approach, not least because after spending twenty-five years with Selkirk, I still would not claim entirely to understand him. I suspect that his emotional life, such as it was, was highly compartmentalized. The modern style in biography is very much to emphasize the interior life, but I believe the biographer has to have better signposts than Selkirk affords before entering such a process.

Yet another challenge that the life of Selkirk presents to the biographer is a logistical one that also militates against an interior life. For most of his career Selkirk is physically in the British Isles, while his enterprises are chugging along in North America—usually doing badly—under the direction of agents. The agents, especially those in Red River, do report to the earl on a regular basis, but those reports are at best months later than the events they describe. Obviously the reader needs to know about what is happening with Selkirk's various overseas ventures, which are clearly a crucial part of his life.

Indeed, most writing about Selkirk tends to be more about the work than the life. Introducing the amount of detail about what is happening thousands of miles from Selkirk—and over which he has absolutely no control—into an account of his life is no easy matter. In a not dissimilar way, Selkirk's involvement with the law courts of the Canadas requires a lengthy discussion of legal proceedings and manoeuvrings, most of which have little to do with the earl personally, even if he were present for the trial being described, which was not always the case. Conscious that the result of their researches was not a biography has led several scholars, notably Chester Martin and John Perry Pritchett, to present their findings as something else than a life study. The question of how and when to integrate this external information into the narrative is also a problem. I have usually chosen to introduce the North American material at the time Selkirk learns about it rather than at the time it happens, for obvious reasons. The result of these limitations is a quite different kind of biography from what I had originally intended when I began my research.

A project that has carried on for nearly thirty years is bound to accumulate considerable debts to a variety of people. I begin by acknowledging the assistance of countless archivists and librarians who have helped me with research over the years. In Scotland, particular thanks go to the University of Edinburgh Library; the Scottish Record Office (and Ian Grant, who shared the results of his research on Robert Brown with me); the National Library of Scotland; the Edinburgh Public Library; the Scottish Catholic Archives; the University of Glasgow Library; the Ewart Library in Dumfries; and the Hornel Library in Kirkcudbright. Professor R.J. Adam of St. Andrew's University not only entertained me at his home, but also allowed me to take away copies of Sutherland family documents that he subsequently published. In Canada I am grateful for the assistance of the Public Archives and Record Office of Prince Edward Island (especially Nicholas De Jong and Harry Holman); the Public Archives of Nova Scotia; the National Archives of Canada (especially Patricia Kennedy and Peter Bower); the Public Archives of Ontario; the McCord Museum, Montreal; the McGill University Library; the University of Western Ontario (particularly Douglas Mackenzie, who shared with me his work on Baldoon); the Public Archives of Manitoba (particularly John Bovey, Peter Bower, and Barry Hyman); the Hudson's Bay Company Archives (particularly Shirlee Ann Smith and Ann Morton); the University of British Columbia (particularly the late Leslie Upton); the Public Archives of British Columbia (particularly John

Bovey); and the University of Manitoba Archives (particularly Richard Bennett, Michael Mooseberger, Shelley Sweeney, and Lewis Stubbs).

I am also indebted to all my colleagues on the Selkirk Papers Project, first established in 1979 at the University of Manitoba to publish the Collected Writings and Papers of Thomas Douglas, Fifth Earl of Selkirk, with the assistance of a grant from the Province of Manitoba. It was the hope of the project to make a successful grant application to the Major Editorial Projects branch of the Social Studies and Humanities Research Council, but unfortunately the branch lost its funding with our application in the pipeline.

The original participating editors in the project were: P.A. Buckner (University of New Brunswick); Philip Wigley (University of Edinburgh); Jennifer Brown Gibson (then the University of Manitoba); Frits Pannekoek (then Alberta Heritage); A.B. McKillop (then University of Manitoba); Sylvia Van Kirk (then University of Toronto); Douglas Sprague (University of Manitoba); and Herbert Mays (University of Winnipeg).

The original editorial committee of the project included Dr. Frances Halpenny (then University of Toronto); Dr. Serge Lusignan (then University of Montreal); Mr. Derek Bedson (then President of the Manitoba Record Society); Dr. Cornelius Jaenen (then University of Ottawa); Professor G.A. Shepperson (then University of Edinburgh); Professor Glyn Williams (then University of London); Dr. F.G. Stambrook (University of Manitoba); Dr. John Foster (then University of Alberta); Dr. John Robson (then University of Toronto); and Dr. David Chesnutt (then University of South Carolina).

At the University of Manitoba, I also received much assistance with the Selkirk Papers Project from President Ralph Campbell and President Arnold Naimark; Vice-president Academic David Lawless; Dean of Arts Fred Stambrook; Provost Walter Bushuk; the several chairmen of the History Department—John Finlay, George Schultz, and John Kendle—and University Research Officer Henry Jacobs.

Student assistants on the Selkirk Project included Wendy Owen, Gerhard Ens, Sharon Babaian, David Hall, Gerry Berkowski, and Joanne Drewniak.

Finally, I am indebted to the office staff at St. John's College (particularly Lesley Cowan and Carla White) for help in assembling the manuscript of this work.

Despite all this assistance, there are still doubtless errors of omission and commission, for which I am solely responsible.

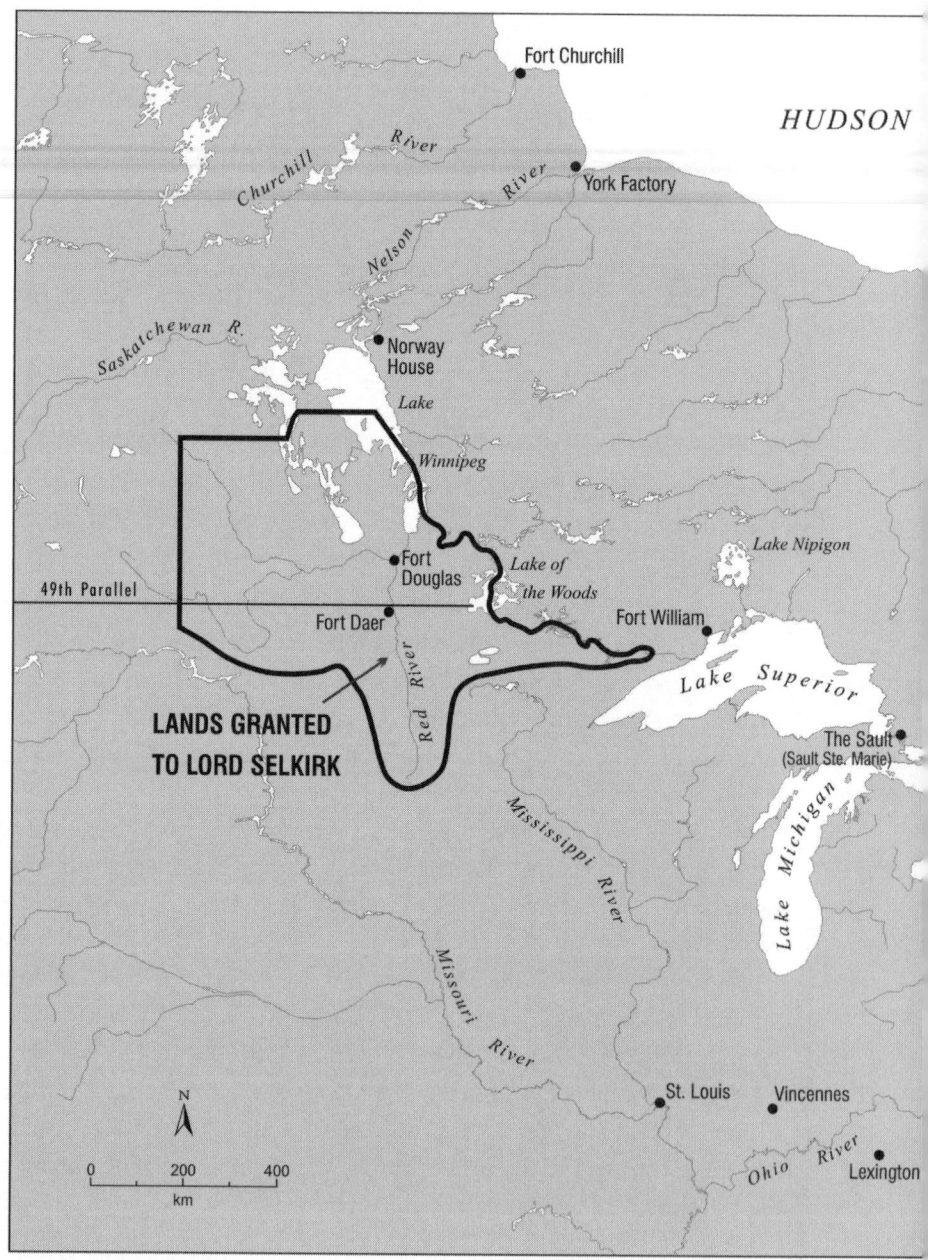

Fort Churchill

HUDSON

Churchill River

Nelson River

York Factory

Saskatchewan R.

Norway House

Lake Winnipeg

Lake Nipigon

Fort Douglas

Lake of the Woods

Fort William

49th Parallel

Fort Daer

Lake Superior

The Sault
(Sault Ste. Marie)

Red River

LANDS GRANTED TO LORD SELKIRK

Lake Michigan

Mississippi River

Missouri River

N

St. Louis   Vincennes

Ohio River

Lexington

0   200   400
km

North America c. 1812

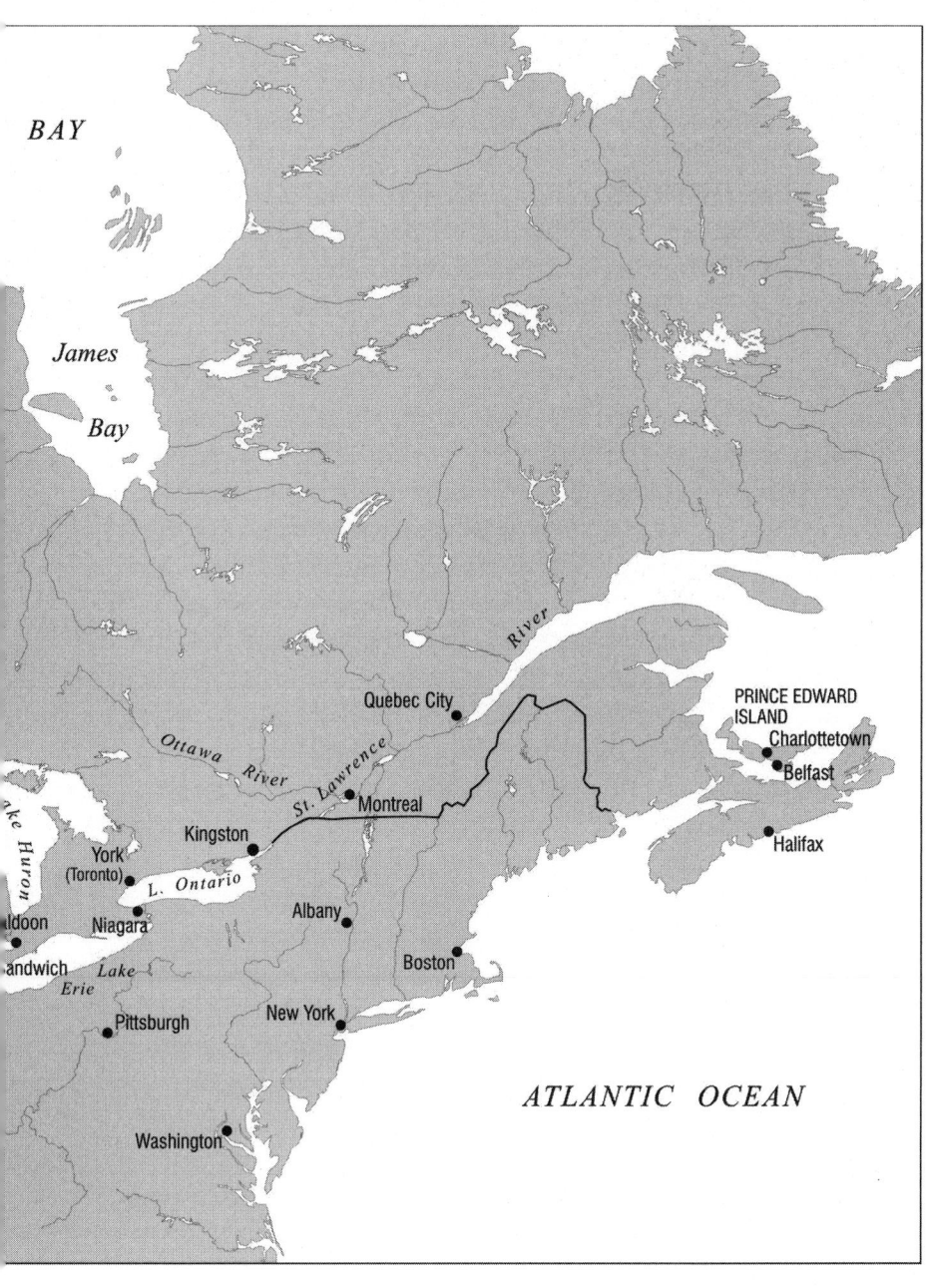

LORD SELKIRK: A LIFE

CHAPTER ONE

Dunbar

Tʜᴏᴍᴀꜱ Dᴏᴜɢʟᴀꜱ ᴡᴀꜱ born at St. Mary's Isle in Kircudbright, Scotland, on 20 June 1771.

Scotland's House of Douglas was not an ancient one. A product of the intermarriage of three families—the Hamiltons, the Dunbars, and the Douglases—it had been ennobled only in 1646 by a beleaguered Charles I, then searching desperately for Scottish supporters. For the period from 1744 to 1799, the House of Douglas was headed by Dunbar Hamilton Douglas, fourth Earl of Selkirk, whose very names commemorated the families who held the lands that supported the title. Although the fourth earl was a fairly obscure member of the Scottish nobility, little remembered today, his career somehow managed to intersect many of the major currents of eighteenth-century Scotland. He was involved with the formative years of the Scottish Enlightenment, exemplified agricultural improvement in his region, was a litigant in the notorious "Douglas Cause," opposed the government in Scottish peerage elections, and subsequently was a critic of the North administration during the war of the American Revolution. The fourth earl became well known as a leading Scottish Whig, and his eldest son, Lord Daer, was a more radical version of himself. Dunbar entertained Robert Burns, who in turn dedicated Scottish nationalist poetry to him. All these involvements would have an influence on his family and on his children, including his youngest son, Thomas, born in 1771, who would unexpectedly inherit the title. Thomas would spend his early years fully immersed in the family preoccupations, but in his later years would turn against some of them, especially the political ones.

THE SCOTTISH ENLIGHTENMENT

Before he inherited the earldom from a grand-uncle in 1744, Dunbar Hamilton Douglas had in 1739 enrolled at the undergraduate college of the University of Glasgow. The college and the university were a late medieval establishment, founded in 1449, with a small enrolment in a city that had grown from a population of 12,000 in 1708 to over 18,000 in 1743. Glasgow's urban growth was based on both mercantile commerce (mainly tobacco from North America) and industrial development (mainly in linen and cotton).[1] The college had recently reformed its system of teaching by a statute of 1727 that abolished an ancient tutorial system (in which one tutor or "master" taught a student everything throughout his career) in favour of a lecture system divided into three philosophical classes in Ethics (or moral philosophy), Logic, and Physics. Badly educated in his childhood, Dunbar had learned Latin and Greek in his later adolescence so that he could matriculate at Glasgow. There he was known as a scholarly recluse and as a pupil of that great teacher of moral philosophy, Francis Hutcheson, who was brought in from Dublin to teach the subject at Glasgow between 1729 and 1746. Hutcheson, who brought a number of young scholars with him, helped reinvigorate the college at Glasgow.

Frances Hutcheson has often been regarded as the Father of the Enlightenment in Scotland, both because of his role in introducing English thinkers like Shaftesbury, Locke, and Newton to Scotland and because of his influence on Scots like David Hume and Adam Smith. The Scottish Enlightenment is usually associated with Edinburgh and the University of Edinburgh during the second half of the eighteenth century, but the development of a Scottish intellectual and philosophical tradition with strong interests in politics and economics had begun earlier in the century at the University of Glasgow.[2] Adam Smith, a pupil of Hutcheson's from 1737 to 1740, had used a subsequent appointment in Moral Philosophy at Glasgow to introduce a generation of students to his version of political economy, which was eventually published as *The Wealth of Nations*. As one of Smith's successors pointed out, "the duties and relations of man, as a moral agent, are so closely connected with those that belong to him as a member of a political or civil society, that it is natural enough to give both [Political Economy and Moral Philosophy] to one teacher."[3]

Hutcheson brought a breath of fresh air to teaching in Glasgow. He insisted on classroom discipline and lectured in English (a major innovation!). He was regarded as one of the master lecturers of his generation. Like many of the great Scottish university teachers of the eighteenth century, Hutcheson served as an out-of-class mentor to his students. He entertained them every Friday evening from 5:00 to 8:00 p.m. in his personal library, and encouraged open discussion. He felt that his life's work was in the moulding of the character of his young pupils. Long after his death, his reputation remained. One of his biographers has admitted that Hutcheson published "nothing of moment while at Glasgow," his influence being based on earlier publications while in Dublin—some reprinted after his death—and, of course, on his teaching. In 1772 one writer exclaimed of Hutcheson, "If ever a Professor had the art of communicating knowledge and or raising an esteem and desire in it in the minds of his scholars; if ever one had the magical power to inspire the noblest sentiments and to warm the hearts of youth with an admiration and love of virtue; if ever one had the art to create an esteem for Liberty and a contempt for tyranny and tyrants, he was the man!"[4] In his writings and lectures, Hutcheson stressed the need to promote the "common good of all" at the same time that he opposed arbitrary government and reserved the right to resist tyranny. Hutcheson opposed large standing armies and much favoured the establishment of a citizen militia. The emphasis on the common good as a goal of the good life was one of the central characteristics of the moral philosophy taught in Scotland in the eighteenth century, and Hutcheson came close in his teaching to emphasizing "the greatest good for the greatest number," that guiding principle of utilitarianism in the nineteenth century. He also emphasized the right of colonists to revolt against a mother country that no longer appreciated them, a principle that made him a favourite of the Americans later in the century.

In religious terms Hutcheson was a moderate Presbyterian, while in political terms he was a major contributor to what one scholar has labelled the "Commonwealthman" or "Real Whig" political tradition of the eighteenth century.[5] "Real Whiggery" was to some extent a political extension of one of the major streams of the Scottish Enlightenment. The Real Whigs were not a political party, but rather a collection of individuals who loosely shared a series of attitudes and beliefs. They were hardly flaming radical revolutionaries. They supported the Revolution Settlement of 1688 (in England) and the Act of Union of 1707 (in Scotland). One of the major achievements of the Scottish Enlightenment was to assimilate the political writings of a number of English thinkers into Scottish political consciousness, and most of the writers so integrated—Harrington, Sidney, Locke, Lord Shaftesbury—were Whigs rather than Tories in political sympathy. The Real Whigs admired the

Americans and even the French; many would support both the American and the French revolutions. They were tolerant of a variety of religious beliefs. They were sympathetic to the people and wanted a government that would respond to intelligent public opinion. They believed in progress and sought reform informed by the existence of natural rights everywhere. They supported mixed government—the balance of the trinity of the King, Lords, and Commons—and were very much against eighteenth-century innovations such as the development of cabinet government and the rise of political parties that in their view threatened liberty. In terms of Scotland, Scottish Real Whigs were highly critical of the way in which the government in London manipulated—in the interest of political power—Scottish elections in the House of Commons and the election of Scottish peers to the House of Lords. It would take many years before Dunbar Hamilton Douglas would nail his colours to the mast and become involved in politics. But when he did so, the colours were unmistakably those of the Real Whig.

The success of the Scottish Enlightenment depended heavily not only on Scotland's universities, but also upon the nation's "clubbability." The eighteenth century in Scotland was an age of masculine conviviality, with clubs and societies of all descriptions meeting regularly for food, drink, discussion, and improvement in the coffee houses, oyster cellars, and taverns of the major cities. The poet Allan Ramsay referred to the "Clubs of Minds that move at large,/With every Glass can some great Thought discharge."[6] Although clubs flourished everywhere in eighteenth-century urban Scotland, they were particularly strong in Edinburgh. As the centre of Scottish political, ecclesiastical, and financial life, as well as the winter home of the landed interest of Scotland, Edinburgh gradually took over from Glasgow the leadership of the Enlightenment. Younger members of the landed families (like David Hume, younger son of the Laird of Ninewells) dominated law, medicine, the universities, and the church. These groups were concentrated in Edinburgh and met together in the evenings in the public houses of the city.

Edinburgh in 1755 had a population of just over 57,000 people. It was dominated by the Castle, a mediaeval structure built on a volcanic rock 443 feet above sea level. From the castle ran the Royal Mile, a street five coaches wide sloping eastward and downwards to the abbey of Holyrood and the palace rebuilt by the Stewarts. The Royal Mile was lined with stone buildings called "lands," as tall as twelve or more storeys, containing hundreds of apartments or tenements heated with coal fires. The "better sort" lived on the fifth and sixth floors. The smoke produced by the fires led to the nickname for the entire city—*Auld Reekie* or "Old Smoky." Around the Royal Mile, the population huddled together in fewer than 7000 houses on twelve streets, twenty-two wynds (through lanes), eight courts, and 260 closes (small court-yards). An English visitor in 1776 found the wynds and closes "so very steep, that it requires great attention to the feet to keep from falling."[7] For places that could not be reached by coach—and there were obviously many—chaises and sedan chairs carried the wealthier inhabitants and their guests to and fro. Sewage and water supply was a serious problem. Slops were still dumped (albeit illegally) into the streets at night and picked up in the morning by scavengers. The city was on the verge of its great expansion out of the "Old Town" north into the "New Town," although much expansion also occurred in the south, beginning with George (or George's) Square, created in 1766 just north of the park called the Meadows, which itself was produced by draining the Burgh Loch.[8]

The clubs of Edinburgh offered an opportunity for philosophers and intellectuals to rub shoulders with aristocrats, merchants, clerics, and professional men of various descriptions. One of the leading clubs was the Select Society of Edinburgh, which dominated intellectual and club life in Edinburgh from 1754 to 1764. The Select Society was founded at the instigation of Allan Ramsay the younger, with the collaboration of Adam Smith and David Hume. Smith explained the purpose of the society at its first meeting on 22 May 1754 as "the pursuit of philosophical inqury, and the improvement of the members in the art of speaking."[9] One of the Select Society's earliest members in the 1750s was the fourth Earl of Selkirk. The Select Society quickly turned from a debating society into one of action, encouraging various aspects of the arts, letters, manufactures, and agriculture through the awarding of premiums, and soon spinning off the Edinburgh Society for Encouraging Arts, Sciences, Manufactures, and Agriculture. In its later years, in the early 1760s, the Select Society turned its attention to a controversial campaign to improve the ability of Scotsmen to read and speak English in place of the "Scotch dialect" that so many in England found offensive and vulgar. The campaign for English, of course, also made it possible for Scots to read the English libertarian political philosophers like Locke and Shaftesbury. The great works of the Scottish Enlightenment were written in English, although the conversation in the clubs was often conducted in Scottish, and "Jupiter" Carlyle reported that "since we began to affect speaking a foreign language, which the English dialect is to us, humour . . . is less apparent in conversation."[10] The Select Society was replaced by other clubs in the 1760s, such as the Poker Society, although by this time Dunbar Earl of Selkirk had largely abandoned Edinburgh for his estates and his family.

AGRICULTURAL IMPROVEMENT

If the growth of the Scottish Enlightenment was the major intellectual and cultural development of Scotland in the eighteenth century, the movement for agricultural change was undoubtedly its major economic development. Here also the fourth Earl of Selkirk was an active participant. Agriculture was still the basis of Scotland's wealth. Traditional Scottish agriculture was inefficient and backward, and there was no single set of agricultural practices. But in general, joint tenancy required a communal working of the land that discouraged innovation, as did partible inheritance, leading to continual subdivision and redistribution. Many fields contained ridges separating long narrow strips of furrowed land; the ridges produced drainage but also concepts of individual property. This "run-rig" system was associated with ideas of shared land and fairness, but was very unwieldy and antithetical to the introduction of new practices such as rotating crops and using fertilizers. Much land was employed for grazing. Most of the land, whatever its usage, was owned by a relatively small number of landlords but worked by a relatively large number of tenants. Traditional agriculture was distinctly uncommercial, and, not surprisingly, the landholders took the lead in change. New legislation in the middle of the eighteenth century allowed longer leases and promoted enclosure. Individual landlords were able to concentrate decision-making powers in their hands and force change in the direction of commercial management.[11]

The new economic movements began in Galloway, the home of the ancestral lands of the House of Douglas, at the beginning of the eighteenth century. Galloway was a region comprising the Shire of Wigton and the Stewartry of Kirkcudbright. Situated in Scotland's southeastern corner, not far from the Lake District of England with which it shares many geological features, Galloway's past had been a turbulent one, with overmighty lairds and constant civil war. King James II and the Eighth Earl of Douglas had carried on their own little war in the middle of the fifteenth century, which had culminated in the murder of Douglas in 1452 by the king himself, who stabbed the earl at Stirling Castle. Beyond its coastline loomed a mountainous region inhabited by semi-itinerant pastoral people that reminded many observers of the Scottish Highlands. Wool was the principal crop. Like the Highlands, the region was famous for its clans and its fierce fighting men; the latter in the seventeenth century were "Covenanters" who supported the Kirk and the Scottish Parliament against the pretensions of the King. Witches were burnt in Galloway until the end of the seventeenth century. In the Stewartry of Kirkcudbright, much ploughing was still done by teams of four horses abreast, with a boy or woman walking backwards in front of the ploughman.[12] Galloway was a land where, by the time of the Union of England and Scotland in 1707, the old and new Scotlands coexisted in uneasy juxtaposition.[13] Modernization, particularly in the form of agricultural reform or "improvement," met with great popular resistance. Indeed, the first large-scale riots against improvement occurred in the region at the beginning of the eighteenth century.[14] Particularly unpopular was enclosure, which led to the consolidation of small farms and resulted in loss of employment. For many years, bands of "Levellers" pulled down fences and at Culquha on one occasion fought openly with soldiers under the direction of the sheriff. Many were killed and hundreds were taken prisoner, some to be transported to the plantations. But improvement was inevitable. Given its physical closeness to an England that had begun improving its agriculture in the seventeenth century, Galloway was bound to take the lead. Whether there was any relationship between improvement and support for James VII in the "Fifteen" is uncertain, but a number of Galloway peers were captured at the Battle of Preston, and a number were subsequently executed.

Soon after his graduation from Glasgow, Dunbar Douglas had to face the Jacobite Rebellion of 1745. Unlike his father—who had supported the Stuart cause in 1715—Dunbar firmly declared his allegiance to the Hanoverian monarchy and helped to raise volunteer forces to fight the Pretender's army should it make its way out of the Highlands. After this brief flurry of public patriotism, Dunbar had travelled for some years on the continent and spent some time in Edinburgh. But he ultimately returned to his estates to marry, raise a family, and engage in the commercial modernization of his property. On 6 December 1758, he married Helen Hamilton, a distant cousin and fifth daughter of the second son of the Earl of Haddington. Helen brought little property to the family, but her connections were extensive. For over twenty years after his marriage, Dunbar Douglas led the life of a minor and obscure

Scottish nobleman. He put his energy into the improvement of his estates, especially a property acquired by the family in 1725 at St. Mary's Isle just to the south of the town of Kirkcudbright. Here on a peninsula of several hundred acres, originally a twelfth-century priory, Dunbar extended an earlier Jacobean manor house. The result was a sprawling brick structure, not very distinguished, obviously mainly Georgian in influence. On the peninsula, lands were marled, trees planted, and livestock (especially sheep) bred to increasingly higher standards. St. Mary's Isle became the centre of a model farm, influential in bringing new techniques of agriculture to Galloway and demonstrating their efficacy. Dunbar's own specialties were horticultural, his heated greenhouses producing plants for ornamentation and experimentation. He planted trees everywhere—for timber, for decoration, and for profit. His extensive orchard of fruit trees was the basis of a scheme to establish an orchard by the house of every tenant on the estate. Dunbar also improved the family estate at Baldoon, in Wigtonshire. Although now largely forgotten, the fourth Earl of Douglas was noted in his own way as one of Scotland's major agricultural improvers. Ultimately, Dunbar's improvements paid off, as estates would be sold later in the century for vast sums of money.[15]

While Dunbar was active in his nursery, Helen was equally busy in hers. An heir, Sholto Basil, was born on 3 September 1759, less than ten months after the celebration of the nuptials. A sickly child, Sholto died within his first year; the Countess was already carrying Isabella Margaret, born 6 September 1760. Seventeen months later another daughter, Helen, arrived, and finally in March of 1763 came the long-awaited heir, Basil William, who as the family's eldest male held the courtesy title of Lord Daer. After Basil a succession of male children followed: John in 1765, Dunbar in 1766, Alexander in 1767, David in 1769 (he died the year following, in May 1770), and finally Thomas on 20 June 1771. The countess had seemingly done her work well, and the family was well supplied with males to carry on the line. As if satisfied with her production of males, Helen shifted back to daughters, with Mary in 1773, Elizabeth in 1775, Katherine in 1778, and finally Anne (who lived but ten days) in 1782. In twenty-three years the Countess of Selkirk had produced thirteen children—seven males and six females—ten of whom, evenly divided between the sexes, survived infancy. The mansion house at St. Mary's Isle would ring with the sounds of children for many years.[16] Who could have suspected at the time of Thomas's birth that the four eldest males would all die unmarried and childless, leaving only Thomas to survive his father and inherit the title?

THE DOUGLAS CAUSE

In the period of virtually continual childbirth, Dunbar Douglas seemed content to improve his lands and enjoy his constantly expanding family. As the record of births suggests, he was not away from home for many protracted periods. Members of the Scottish peerage were already well-known for their military and colonial service, but Dunbar's only major involvement with the outside world appears to have been thrust upon him when because of his family connections he became a principal litigant in the most notorious and complicated civil legal case in eighteenth-century Scotland, the so-called "Douglas Cause."[17] The Douglas case concerned the disposition of the estate of Archibald, Duke of Douglas, who had died without issue on 21 July 1761. The duke had suffered the misfortune of becoming involved in a fatal duel earlier in his life, which had left him emotionally shattered; he lived in retirement and virtual isolation. A last-minute settlement had left the estate to "the heirs of the Duke's father's body," thus designating as heir apparent one Archibald Steuart Douglas, the only surviving son of the Duke's only sibling, Lady Jane Douglas, who had died in 1753. Archibald's tutors (he was a minor) quickly obtained possession of the estate for their client as heir of the Duke of Douglas. But Archibald's inheritance was quickly challenged by other members of the family. Initially, the actions raised against Archibald were by other potential heirs, the Duke of Hamilton and the fourth Earl of Selkirk, who claimed that parts of the estate had been settled upon their families by deeds executed in the seventeenth century. The Court of Session at Edinburgh decided routinely late in 1762 against the rival claimants and in favour of the designated heir. So far so good.

But the case was not so simple. It transpired that Archibald Steuart Douglas had been born in mysterious circumstances in Paris in July of 1748 to a fifty-one-year-old Lady Jane Douglas, who was estranged from her brother and who had two years earlier married Colonel John Steuart, an aged and somewhat feckless Jacobite adventurer. Lady Jane had apparently given birth to twins in Paris, but when the circumstances of the births were later scrutinized carefully, there was some reason to suspect that things were not as they seemed. The chief attorney for the Duke of Hamilton, Andrew Stuart, had become increasingly dubious of the events surrounding young Archibald's birth, and his research in France produced evidence that, at the very least, called into question whether the present Duke of Douglas was indeed the son of Lady Jane Stewart. A surviving portrait of Andrew Stuart shows us a stern man without the slightest trace of humour in his face, a man who would stubbornly pursue to the bitter end what he regarded as chicanery. The new evidence was heard in 1766 and 1767 on the instigation of the Duke of Hamilton; the Earl of Selkirk was not associated with this action. It was absolutely massive in volume and somewhat contradictory in nature. We are told that the sheer bulk of the proofs that had to be printed to be circulated among the participants in the case—1034 quarto pages for the Hamilton case and 1066 quarto pages for the defence—so taxed the printing houses of Edinburgh that several delays ensued. Because of the amount of the material, "short cases," rather than arguments based on the full proofs, were ordered to be drawn up. The pleadings were the longest ever heard in a Scottish court to that time, lasting in all twenty-one days. The subsequent memorials on the pleadings ran to over 800 pages by the Hamilton forces, although somewhat fewer for the Douglas side.

The Hamilton lawyers pointed out that Sir John Steuart and the pregnant Lady Jane moved from boarding house to boarding house and European city to European city in the spring of 1748. The couple ended up in Paris in the house of Madame Le Brune in Fauxbourg St. Germain, where Lady Jane allegedly gave birth to twin sons. The youngest twin was quite sickly and was put out to nurse for fifteen months; the elder remained with his parents. The Hamilton case insisted that there had been no births, or at least no live births, and that the children had actually been obtained on the streets of France, one purchased from his parents and the other kidnapped from a circus. A frequent change of nurses of the older child and the relegation to the country of the younger were both regarded as efforts to obfuscate the truth. Although the question of inheritance had not yet emerged, the couple was in desperate want of money, and clearly hoped that news of the births would soften the heart of the Duke of Douglas. One interpretation of events, by the mystery writer Lillian De La Torre, has argued that there was indeed a substitution by Sir John, but it was the result of his efforts to please his wife, who desperately had wanted the children and not an attempt to defraud the family. The younger child subsequently died, and Lady Jane, in obvious grief, joined him soon afterwards. Her correspondence and other evidence certainly makes clear that she thought the children were hers.

The judgement of the Court of Session was given to much public excitement on 7 July 1767 at a dramatic occasion at Holyrood House in Edinburgh. It was claimed by the *Scots Magazine* that upwards of £100,000 had been wagered on the results of the decision. Each of fifteen judges gave his opinion. The first fourteen opinions divided equally, seven on each side, and the Lord President of the Court, Robert Dundas, provided the deciding opinion in favour of the Hamiltons. The announcement of the decision led to riots in the streets of Edinburgh. The decision was, of course, appealed by the Douglas side, aided by a young James Boswell, to the House of Lords in London. The case was finally heard beginning on 19 January 1769. Again the pleadings were long and arduous. The decision was rendered on 27 February 1769. According to Alexander ("Jupiter") Carlyle, who was present on the day, he was forced to stand from eleven in the morning until nine at night, with no refreshment but a small roll and two oranges while final speeches were made. The meeting room of the Lords was extremely hot, and Lord Mansfield at one point collapsed from the heat in the midst of his speech and was revived only by administration of large quantities of wine. Lord Chancellor Camden concluded by declaring, according to Horace Walpole, that "the whole plea of the Hamiltons" was "a tissue of perjury woven by Mr. Andrew Stuart, and that, were he sitting as judge in any other Court, he would order a jury to find for Mr. Douglas, and what that jury ought to do on their oaths, their Lordships ought to do on their honours."[18] The final verdict was given about 9:00 p.m. in favour of Douglas. It was a popular decision, greeted in Edinburgh by mobs smashing windows of the Hamilton supporters. The army had to be called in to restore order.

The fourth Earl of Selkirk had remained aloof from the attack on Archibald Douglas's parentage. We do not know why he adopted this position, but it seems plausible that he found the Hamilton position an unsavoury one. His silence on the filiation matter did not mean that he would not press his own claims based upon his rights according to the ancient documents. Dunbar went to the Edinburgh Court of Sessions late in 1769 to argue that, according to seventeenth-century deeds, he was entitled to share in Archibald's inheritance. He lost his case, but decided to appeal to the House of Lords, where he would eventually lose again. How the involvement of the House of Lords in his legal claims may have affected Dunbar's political attitudes is not at all clear, but it was certainly the case that he had shown no interest in peerage politics until 1770, the same year he appealed his Douglas claims to the House of Lords.

PEERAGE POLITICS

One of the stickiest issues of the unification of Scotland and England had been the political rights of the large number of Scottish peers, 154 titles on the Union Roll of 1707. In addition there were hundreds of "lairds" counted as nobility by Scottish usage. The English had insisted that to permit all the peers of Scotland into the House of Lords—much less the lairds—would completely alter the character of that House. The real problem, of course, was that the English did not regard a Scottish peerage as worth as much as an English one. A compromise was found. In the *Act of Union* of 1707, the leading Scottish peers were allowed to elect sixteen of their number to represent them at Westminster. This effectively reduced the status of the Scots peerage below that of their English cousins, each of whom held a birthright seat in the House of Lords. At the same time, Scottish peers, unlike Irish ones, were not eligible for membership in the House of Commons. So Scottish peers not elected to the House of Lords found politics closed to them. Not surprisingly, Scottish peers were looked down upon by the English aristocracy. Much opposition existed in England to the elevation of Scottish peers to the British peerage, and a standing order of the House of Lords in 1711 prohibited any Scottish peer who became a British peer from sitting in the upper house.

By 1770 a series of customary procedures and rules had developed for governing elections. Neither open campaigning nor political organization was formally allowed. Peers were permitted to draft circumspect letters to their fellows informing them of a willingness to "stand" (not to "run"), and a few friends of the candidate might meet in an Edinburgh tavern or oyster house before the election to indicate their support. Vote exchanging was permitted. Open voting by the peers for their representatives took place at Holyrood Palace at every general parliamentary election. It was possible to ballot by proxy or to submit signed lists rather than to appear in person in Edinburgh. The very diffidence of the peers to engage in politics had earlier opened the door for political interference by the government in London. Thus there had emerged a "government interest" fuelled by political patronage that turned increasingly to the Scottish peers for parliamentary support.[19] The management of the peerage elections in the first half of the century had been done by the Duke of Argyle, who treated the peers "with respect and delicacy." Then for a period of about twenty years, between the fall of James Stuart Mackenzie and the rise of Henry Dundas as government managers of the Scottish peers, roughly between 1765 and the mid-1780s, peerage elections would prove difficult to manage and there were some stirrings of independence.

Late in 1770 the death of the Duke of Argyle forced a peerage by-election, and the British ministry of Lord North found an opposition developing to its attempts to influence the results. That opposition was led, particularly on that day in January of 1771 fixed for the election at Holyrood House, by the fourth Earl of Selkirk, who declared to his fellow peers that "the ministers of state have, contrary to the rights of the constitution, used undue influence relative to the election." Lord Selkirk was especially incensed that the ministers sought to intimidate "all who have depended on the favours of administration from giving their votes in that unbiased manner which is essential to the existence of liberty and our free constitution."[20] This ringing declaration of Whig rhetoric was the first of many occasions when the Earl of Selkirk and his family would fight for the independence of the Scots peerage and the standing of their order. The problem of the peerage was one inherited from Dunbar by his heir Thomas, and the latter would find it equally vexing. The opposition received 18 votes in 1771. In 1774 Dunbar again battled unsuccessfully to halt government interference with Scottish peerage elections. At this point opposition to management of peerage elections by London had not yet become associated with general opposition to the government.

THE AMERICAN REVOLUTION AND JOHN PAUL JONES

Dunbar publicly opposed the North ministry for political meddling in the Scottish peerage elections, and he was equally critical of the government's policies, particularly toward the American colonies. His Real Whig sentiments, absorbed thirty years earlier from Frances Hutcheson, doubtless played a part in his attitudes. As he would later write, "with regard to the King's Ministers, I neither have nor can have any interest with them, as I have generally disapproved of most of their measures, and in particular of almost their whole conduct in the unhappy and ill-judged American War."[21] In the same letter he insisted that "except having the disadvantage of a useless Scottish title, I am in all respects as much a Private Country Gentleman as any one can be, having a retired life in the country and engaging in no factions whatever."[22] The reference to the useless Scottish title doubtless reflected a grievance over the peerage election.

Dunbar's protestations were accurate enough, yet occasionally the outside world intruded on his privacy and that of his family. Ironically enough, the main instrument of harassment would be an American naval captain named John Paul Jones, whose vessel *Ranger* raided St. Mary's Isle in April of 1778.[23] Contemporary rumours—and later biographers—suggested that Jones was the illegitimate son of the third Earl, a parentage vigorously denied by one of his biographers, who has pointed out that the sea captain had built a monument to his father "John Paul Senior" in the churchyard at Kirkbean.[24] The elder Paul was a gardener near Arbigland, employed on the estate of John Craik, a member of the Scottish gentry. His son went to sea in 1761, and rose to become a merchant captain. Off the Island of Tobago in 1773, the younger Paul had a disagreement over prize money with his crew, ending up skewering the ringleader with his sword. He escaped to Virginia and, as "John Paul Jones," was commissioned a first lieutenant in the American Continental Navy in December of 1775 without having spent any lengthy amount of time on shore in the American colonies. The addition of the "Jones" to the name had probably been done to confute pursuit, since the young man was, after all, technically a murderer. Young Paul may have been a long-time lover of liberty—many Galloway Scots were—but he may also have appreciated that he was unlikely to have much of a chance to advance in the Royal Navy. Within months he was promoted to temporary command of the sloop *Providence,* and a career was under way.

In early August of 1776, John Paul Jones was ordered by the Marine Committee of the Continental Congress to "proceed immediately on a Cruize against our Enemies" in the waters off Bermuda. The *Providence* successfully captured three vessels flying British colours, and Jones fought with Congress to increase his percentage of the proceeds of the vessels' sale. Jones subsequently led a successful raid against the British on Cape Breton in the fall of 1776. Despite—or perhaps because of— his triumph over the prize money, Jones found himself in early 1777 only number eighteen on the Congress's list of captains. Although this rankled with the Scotsman, he was the first outsider in the Continental navy to be placed in command of a new ship, the *Ranger,* in June of 1777. Later that year, Jones sailed for Europe to bring the news of the American victory at Saratoga to Benjamin Franklin, who used the information to encourage the French to support the United States. The spring of 1778 found him in the Irish Sea, where he captured a British sloop of war and carried out a scheme of raiding an English seaport to bring the war to the enemy. The port he chose was Whitehaven, on the western English coast not far from the Lake District. Jones knew White-haven well, having sailed from there for America years before. The result was a bit of fiasco, producing much hullabaloo but precious little damage. But Jones was not done. He now put into effect a planned raid on St. Mary's Isle in Kirkcudbright Bay, not far from Whitehaven, where he hoped to kidnap the fourth Earl of Selkirk, who could be used in exchange for pris-oners held by the British authorities.

John Paul Jones did not realize that the "great laird" of the neighbour-hood of his childhood was not an important national figure, but although based on an erroneous assessment of Dunbar's importance, his scheme was not otherwise a bad plan. That an American naval vessel could raid the Scottish coast with impunity and engage in a political kidnapping would have enormous propaganda value. It would be the eighteenth-century equivalent of a terrorist attack. Jones himself led the initial party of two officers and well-armed sailors. Meeting the head gardener on the path to the mansion, Jones told him that they were a Royal Navy press gang. This story sent all the young men around the estate off into the town to hide, exposing the estate to whatever depredations the Americans chose to inflict. When Jones learned that his prey was away at Buxton "taking the waters," he immediately returned to his ship. But his men wanted booty, and the captain authorized them to take away the family silver so long as they left the family unmolested.

We know a good deal about this minor incident in the war of the Amer-ican Revolution because of the prominence of John Paul Jones, which led the United States Naval Academy to do historical research in Scotland. The result was the copying of extensive family papers from the mansion at St. Mary's Isle before a fire destroyed the building (and its library) in the early days of World War II. The serendipitous survival of such material suggests that there was a lot more that has been lost. In any event, this incident provides virtually our only opportunity to catch a glimpse both of family life at St. Mary's Isle and of the Countess of Selkirk in operation. Lady Selkirk described the entire business in a lengthy letter to Dunbar, written the following day. The household that day consisted of the countess, a number of daughters, and one son, the future fifth earl. His four elder brothers were not present, of course, because they were all away at boarding school. A governess, Mrs. Mary Elliot, was in charge of the children. A family of guests was also present. Mrs. Wood was the widow of the former governor of the Isle of Man, and she had three young daughters, who doubtless provided playmates for the Selkirk girls. A number of male and female servants also made appearances in the countess's narrative. According to her account, Lady Selkirk had acted with great presence of mind. She quickly determined that the best strategy was to give the intruders, who told her they were looking for the household silver—cutlery and plate—exactly what they wanted. She instructed the butler, who was in a pantry attempting to secrete some of the plate, to turn everything over. She even produced an inventory of what had been stuffed into sacks, and ordered the butler to produce a missing coffeepot and teapot. The teapot was full of warm, wet tea leaves from breakfast; it was probably less hidden than still on the breakfast table along with the coffeepot. The total haul weighed in at 250 ounces of silver.

The officers of the party decided they did not want to take the time to track down all of the small items listed in the inventory, and they paid no attention to other possible loot such as watches and jewellery. The countess very nearly got the junior officer, a young American in a marine uniform who was "very civil," to receipt the inventory, but he had only written "This is to cert . . . " when he was ordered to desist. The officers did accept and each drank a glass of wine proffered by Lady Selkirk, and then they and the rest of the armed party departed with the sacks for the *Ranger,* which was standing off shore. Within a day, the British ship *Drake* from Carrickfergus met the *Ranger* at sea, and after a fierce battle of over an hour, the American vessel was the winner. Casualties were heavy.

As for the Douglas family, polite compliance had reduced the damage to the minimum, a loss of property but nothing else. At the same time, young Thommy Douglas, who was in the house but had not actually witnessed the raid itself, later claimed to have been greatly affected by it. He would write in 1813, "This was a momentous moment in my life. I was terribly frightened . . . and when I was but a youth I developed an antipathy for the United States due almost solely to the buccaneering of John Paul."[25] The countess wrote Mr. Craik at Arbigland to report that the man in command of the raid was John Paul, "a great villain . . . born in your grounds and a gardener's son of yours." The Earl of Selkirk received the letter from his countess describing the raid while he was on his way back to St. Mary's Isle. He spurred his horse on and met his wife and children at Annan. The family then joined the Dumfries social circuit and became immerse in "dressing, assemblys, suppers and receiving visits."[26]

The incident of the raid on St. Mary's Isle was not quite over, however. It had several curious aftermaths, the first shortly after the event and the others some years later. In a letter dated from Brest on 8 May 1778, John Paul Jones wrote to the Countess of Selkirk, explaining his intentions at St. Mary's Isle.[27] He wished to use Lord Selkirk as "the happy Instrument of alleviating the horrors of hopeless captivity" by exchanging him for Americans held prisoner by the British, and he had no intention of looting. Jones denied any interest in riches and promised when the plate was sold, he would purchase it and restore it. Ostensibly an appeal to Lady Selkirk's feminine sensibilities to help "effect a general Exchange of Prisoners"—Jones wrote of her "gentle Bosom" and her "soft Persuasive Arts"—the letter was a self-indulgent effort to appear as a sophisticated man of the world and a gentleman. It was so contrived that Jones sent three originals by three different hands to make sure that the recipient received it.[28]

Lord Selkirk actually penned an answer dated 9 June 1778 to this epistle, but he was unable to get the British minister to deliver it to the American captain at Brest.[29] Dunbar's letter pointed out the inconsistency of Jones's declarations of peaceful intent and gentlemanly comportment with his departure "from the established and usual practice of Modern War" by involving innocent civilians. He insisted that neither he nor Lady Selkirk would accept the return of the plate and suggested that any proceeds from its sale be given to the private men under Jones's command "as an encouragement for their good behaviour." Dunbar concluded by acknowledging that Jones had kept his men under good discipline. This would not be the last that the Selkirk family would hear about their plate or from John Paul Jones, who apparently had some vague intention of retiring on the Solway Firth after his military career was over. The hostility to his raid continued unabated—attacking innocent civilians was not regarded in Scotland as good form or honourable behaviour—and perhaps encouraged Jones to keep his promise to restore the plate. He had the silver valued as bullion at Brest after the war, there being no market for such "old-fashioned" British silver. It was said to be worth 3000 livres or $600. After deducting the captain's fifteen percent, Jones paid his officers and crew the balance out of his own pocket. He then sent the plate back to St. Mary's Isle, and Dunbar acknowledged its return in the Edinburgh newspapers.

The John Paul Jones raid on St. Mary's Isle became part of the folk consciousness of Scotland. In his 1882 history of Manitoba, George Bryce quoted one contemporary ballad:

> Ye've all heard of Paul Jones,
> Have ye not? Have ye no?
> Ye've all heard of Paul Jones,
> Have ye no?
> Ye've all heard of Paul Jones;
> He was a rogue and a vagabond,
> He was a rogue and a vagabond,
> Was he no?
> He enter'd Lord Selkirk's hall,
> Did he not? Did he no?
> He enter'd Lord Selkirk's hall,
> Did he no?
> He enter'd Lord Selkirk's hall,
> Stole the gold and the jewels all,
> Stole the gold and the jewels all,
> Did he no?[30]

The final irony of the John Paul Jones story is to be found in contemporary Kirkcudbright. In the local tourist information, the American sea captain is treated as a great hero, although in the American Revolutionary War he was on the enemy side. The raid on St. Mary's Isle is now treated in Kirkcudbright as a great adventure rather than as an act of terrorism. Unmentioned in the literature is the family whose property was terrorized in 1778, although one of the members of that family present on the day—Thomas Douglas–would later become a major figure in Canadian history and the founder of one of its provinces. Lord Selkirk is commemorated in Kirkcudbright by a discreetly hidden plaque placed in St. Cuthbert's Church by the province of Manitoba.

CHAPTER TWO

Apprenticing

THE JOHN PAUL JONES affair was probably the major external event in the life of the young Thomas Douglas until his departure for school in England in 1782. The matter of schooling must have provided something of a problem for his parents. He was certainly kept at home until a later age than either his elder brothers or most of his contemporaries. Although a bright enough lad, he was not physically strong and was far removed from the title and the inheritance. Whether he already had at least a predisposition to pulmonary problems is not clear, but seems likely. Thomas would have to fend for himself in later life, and his parents clearly sought to fit him for a profession. Two of his elder brothers were soldiers, an occupation for which Thomas was apparently regarded as physically unsuited. His failure to enter the military could hardly be attributed to want of interest in military matters. At several points in the 1790s he attempted to convince his father to allow him to become a soldier. He would later serve successfully as Lord Lieutenant of Kirkcudbright, and actually revelled in leading a contingent of mercenaries westward in 1816. Under the circumstances in 1782, a future in the law was probably what his parents intended. Having been kept at home for so long, as well as having a personality that was both retiring and unworldly, he required some exposure to the world rather than the continued cosseted life of private tutoring. But Thomas was hardly ready for the rough and tumble of Scotland's only possible candidate for his education, the Edinburgh High School, widely known at the time for its harshness and vulgarity. "Among the boys," later observed Henry Cockburn, who had attended Edinburgh High School in the 1780s, "coarseness of language and manners was the only fashion. An English boy was so rare, that his accent was openly laughed at. No Lady would be seen within its walls. Nothing evidently civilized was safe. Two of the masters, in particular, were so savage, that any master doing now what they did every hour, would certainly be transported."[1] Cockburn's reference was doubtless to physical abuse, but such an environment would hardly suit a peer's son of delicate constitution, however distant from the title. Thomas could hardly, like his later friend Walter Scott, apprentice at the law to his father until he was ready for university. Fortunately, the English boarding school that elder brother Basil (Lord Daer) had attended was still in operation, and so Thomas was taken there.

PALGRAVE

Palgrave School, named after the town in which it was situated, was on the border of Norfolk and Suffolk, about thirty miles northeast of Cambridge. At the edge of the Fen Country, the climate was a damp one that probably only increased any tendencies to lung problems brought to it by its pupils. Whether Thomas and his elder brother Lord Daer contracted consumption at Palgrave is uncertain, but the climate of the surrounding countryside certainly did not prevent consumption's onset. Palgrave was one of the many dissenting academies opened in eighteenth-century England to train the sons of non-Anglican merchants and professionals, and occasionally the offspring of Scottish peers and lairds, who would also be regarded by the English as nonconformists. Begun in 1774 and closed in 1785, it lasted longer than most such institutions.[2] Like most dissenting academies, it was concerned with education for the present. Its students were not likely to become men of leisure and would not require the classical education needed to attend Oxford and Cambridge, both closed to dissenters. Palgrave and its competitors were the educational outlets for the two main currents of dissenting thought in eighteenth-century England: evangelical pietism and experimental science. From the standpoint of a young Scot, Palgrave would also help eliminate any Scotticisms or Scots accent.

Ostensibly Palgrave was run by the Reverend Rochemont Barbauld, but its real driving force—as contemporaries recognized—was Barbauld's wife, the former Anna Laetitia Aiken. The Aiken family came originally from Kirkcudbright, and this origin probably accounts for Dunbar's awareness of

Palgrave's existence. Anna Laetitia Aiken's father John was a teacher at the famous dissenting academy at Warrington. Mrs. Barbauld, as Anna Laetitia was always known, was a literary figure of considerable contemporary accomplishment and reputation. Her standing in the literary firmament has improved a good deal over the past few years, particularly since the increased amount of attention paid to women writers, and especially those with feminist leanings. Mrs. Barbauld's books for children, worked out during the Palgrave years, were *Lessons for Children* and *Hymns in Prose for Children,* both intended as reading primers written expressly for children at their own reading level.[3] They were extremely popular and were reprinted often until well into the nineteenth century. But Mrs. Barbauld was not simply a children's author and teacher. She was also a published poet; her first volume entitled *Poems* was published in 1773, and gave signs of her later concern for women's rights. For the fourth earl to select Palgrave for his sons marks him as a man of distinctly liberal views.

The Barbaulds were evangelical Unitarians, not so much a contradiction in terms in the English context as in the American. They were hostile to predestination and crisis conversion experiences, but also to undue rationalism. They believed in experimental piety and a genteel Christianity, and were in many ways the precursors of what is today popularly regarded as "Victorian Morality." For young Thomas Douglas, Mrs. Barbauld—who taught him writing and history—was a major influence. She united the notions of moral and intellectual development that he would find so appealing in his subsequent work in Edinburgh with Dugald Stewart. The Barbaulds encouraged leadership as well as scholarship, and their school's rules prefigured the major educational reforms of the English public schools of the nineteenth century. Thomas fitted well into their program, and at one point Mrs. Barbauld commented that he had "grown into a very fine youth & is in every sense one of the first if not the first among his fellow students. He has a well-directed ambition, a sprightly pleasing manner which if I am not mistaken will enable him to make a figure in future life." Revealingly, she added, "he is not one of those however who entertain us."[4] From an early age, Thomas Douglas had little sense of levity or playfulness. His approach to life was enthusiastic, but totally serious.

While young Thom was in England developing his sense of moral responsibility, Dunbar decided to wade into Scottish politics in a much more committed way than earlier. In 1784 a new ministry, headed by William

Pitt, came into power. Its Scottish lieutenants, especially Henry Dundas, who spoke for the nation's gentry and professional classes, were once again arranging the election of Scottish peers.[5] Henry Dundas had first come to prominence in 1774 as the Duke of Buccleuch's political manager. A few months later he became lord advocate (attorney general) of Scotland, and mounted a vigorous initiative to prevent Scottish emigration to North America during the war with the colonials. Dundas also proved willing to bypass Parliament for measures he wished to see adopted, at the same time that he became one of the North government's most active defenders in the House of Commons. When the North ministry fell from power in 1782, Dundas was continued as lord advocate (and political manager of Scotland) under the succeeding Whig ministries.[6] Dundas was not merely a power broker. He also spoke for small and middling Scottish landholders in opposition to the interests of noblemen. The Dundas campaign in favour of the elimination of fictitious votes exercised by the wealthy could be seen as support for the smaller landholder, but it was also a challenge to the great peers of Scotland, most of whom lived outside the country. Dundas was both a member and a patron of an Edinburgh literary society known after 1779 as the "Mirror Club," which was led by Henry Mackenzie (the "Man of Feeling"), a very competent journalist and pamphleteer. The publications of the Mirror Club quietly supported the political pretensions of Henry Dundas.

At the close of the war with America, a liberal Whig government under the Earl of Shelburne had briefly governed Great Britain. Its major accomplishment had been the negotiation of an unpopular peace with America, one that surrendered to the Americans on almost every major issue. The British gave away access to the fisheries and the Ohio territory, while abandoning the Loyalists and their Aboriginal allies to their fates. The fourth Earl of Selkirk had found this government attractive, however, at the same time that he had, in 1782, joined the Society for the Promotion of Constitutional Information, founded by Christopher Wyvill and John Cartwright. This organization was committed to parliamentary reform. During the American war, a good deal of discussion had taken place across the country about political reform. That discussion had come from both the ranks of those who were politically represented in Parliament, notably the independent country gentlemen in England, and from those who had no voice in Parliament, mainly the working-class inhabitants of the burgeoning towns that were flourishing during the beginnings of the Industrial Revolution. In 1780 another stream of political discontent involving opposition to the emancipation of Roman Catholics in Ireland had come to the fore. Lord George Gordon appeared at the House of Commons at the head of a crowd of 50,000 people seeking to present a petition calling for the repeal of the 1776 Roman Catholic Relief Act. The demonstration turned ugly, and for five days the mobs roamed the streets of London, destroying Catholic buildings and public ones indiscriminately. Nearly 300 protesters were killed and twenty-five hanged. The "Gordon Riots" raised the spectre of unleashing unmanageable violence in the course of legitimate public demonstrations. They frightened many of the reformers, but not all.[7]

The Society for the Promotion of Constitutional Information was one of a number of so-called "corresponding societies" that had emerged during the war against America, most of them convinced that only a more democratically elected Parliament could avoid the mistakes being made in America by the North ministry, backed by the King and the establishment. Reverend Christopher Wyvill (1740–1822) was a Yorkshire dissenting clergyman from a landowning family who had organized the Yorkshire County Association in 1779 to attempt to force Parliament to end the expensive American war and to agitate for parliamentary reform, especially for annual general elections and more independent members of Parliament. The Yorkshire Association was closely connected with the Whig faction of the Earl of Rockingham. Cartwright (1740–1824) had written a pamphlet in 1776 entitled *Take Your Choice*, which had advocated annual parliaments, the secret ballot, and virtually universal manhood suffrage. Both Wyvill and Cartwright believed that peaceable reform was possible, at least in the 1780s.

The Whig government's successor in 1784 was a ministry headed by a young William Pitt, supported by Tory elements and increasing amounts of Scottish political jobbery. Henry Dundas became friendly with young Pitt in 1783, and became his lieutenant shortly thereafter. The alliance of Dundas with Pitt worked to the advantage of both; Dundas's Scottish influence helped support the Pitt government, and the Pitt government's allowing Dundas to become so influential built his power base. The satirical poem "Rolliad" would later in the century comment on the Scottish elected peers:

Alike in loyalty, alike in worth,
Behold the sixteen nobles of the north;
Fast friends to monarchy, yet sprung from those
Who basely sold their monarch to his foes:
Since which, atoning for their father's crime,
The sons, as basely sell themselves to him;
With ev'ry change prepare'd to change their note,
With ev'ry Government prepar'd to vote,
Save when, perhaps, on some important bill,
They know by second sight the royal will.[8]

Pitt had been chancellor of the exchequer at the age of twenty-two in the Shelburne government, trading on his father's reputation but obviously possessing some real leadership qualities and a talent for financial administration. The Pitt ministry was the very antithesis of Real Whiggism, however, since its major features included loyal support for the King and a resistance to constitutional reform, at least partly on the grounds that it was too dangerous to let the genie of popular democracy out of the bottle, as the Gordon riots had so clearly demonstrated. This conservative view would be buttressed later in the century by the violent events of the French Revolution.

In the early 1780s, reform without violence was still possible to contemplate. The fourth Earl of Selkirk girded himself to resume battle against political interference from Whitehall in the peerage elections of Scotland. Over the next few years, as the young Thomas Douglas grew to manhood, his family would become increasingly associated with opposition elements to the ruling establishment in Scotland and Britain. Dunbar, in close collaboration with his eldest son and heir, Basil Hamilton Douglas, Lord Daer, would fight fiercely for reform of the political privileges of the Scottish peerage, and eventually for more wide-reaching changes in the political franchise and in representation. In the process, the family's paths would cross those of a number of noted radicals of the day, including Robert Burns and Thomas Paine. The family would also make itself politically and socially unacceptable to most of its contemporaries, a fact that was to prove of enormous importance to the future career of its youngest son when he would unexpectedly succeed his father as fifth Earl of Selkirk.

Nothing really surprising was to be found in the new-found militancy of Dunbar in 1784. It was simply a logical extension of his earlier concerns for the independence of his order. During the 1770s he had opposed the political interference of the ministry in London in the Scottish peerage elections, but had neither attempted to lead those who shared his fears nor endeavoured to organize his colleagues. The American War had demonstrated what went wrong when concerted ministerial policy went unopposed. A purely personal opposition was not sufficient. Dunbar therefore "formed a Plan for a General Union of those who wished for freedom in the Peerage Election uncontrolled by Court Influence, and to his surprise discovered it was not a 'Wild Chimera.'"[9] Others were now prepared to rally to his side. Like most "True Whigs" of his time, Dunbar associated the chief threat to freedom with party. He thus could stand only reluctantly to oppose the government at the head of a faction of opposition. He was at first an unwilling politician who had shown little previous interest in public life and would demonstrate precious little agility in the corridors of power. But, again typically, after involvement he became totally committed. Once engaged, he would not retreat. Each confrontation and each defeat merely strengthened his determination. Such stubbornness was a family trait, built into Douglas genes. It would serve both as advantage and disadvantage for his ultimate heir. Unsuccessful in his declared candidacy to the House of Lords in 1784, Dunbar protested his defeat to Lord Camden in London on the grounds of government interference that had reduced the Scottish peerage to "the most wretched dependence on Ministry."[10]

In his Letter to Lord Camden, Dunbar noted that he could, if he so desired, determine Commons elections in two counties. Instead, he proclaimed self-righteously, more than twenty years earlier, "rather than be dependent on Ministers, I gave up all connection with Politicks & retired indignantly into obscurity and insignificance, and threw away then as good an Interest as any Peer in Scotland had." As Dunbar realized full well, however, the Selkirk "Interest" would make it possible to elect his sons to Parliament, only provided the law allowed them to sit, as was not presently the case. This would eventually become part of the issue. Dispatching Lord Daer, just turned twenty-one, as his emissary, Dunbar worried the government with the prospect of a formal protest to the House of Lords, and it offered him what seemed to be a commitment to reform the peerage elections, assuming that the peers were keen. Selkirk spent the next few months preparing a petition for reform, but as the ministry knew full well, he was not able to obtain sufficient support from his colleagues.[11] This first involvement of the family with Scottish peerage reform was distinguished mainly for the public debut of Lord Daer, who would become increasingly prominent over the next few years. Daer would take up peerage reform in a different context, and twenty years later Thomas—as fifth earl—would again resume the struggle to convince his fellow peers to alter inequitable procedures, with little more ultimate effect on the system.

As for young Thomas, he spent the summer of 1785 in the companionship of the son of a New York Loyalist of Scottish origin. The earl described the young man, the son of former New York governor Cadwallader Colden, as exhibiting "too many of the prejudices of the American Loyalists," but some of these attitudes towards the American States may well have inadvertently rubbed off on his hosts.[12] Certainly it was from the Coldens that the Douglas family acquired the land in upper New York State that would help lead Thomas to his eventual involvement in North America.[13] It seems possible that the Loyalist suspicion of American democracy espoused by young Colden may also have ultimately had its effect.

EDINBURGH

Palgrave closed permanently in the summer of 1785, but it was time for Thomas to move on. In the autumn of 1785, Lady Selkirk took her three youngest children, including Thomas, to Edinburgh, where they were boarded at the house of a Miss Colburn. That the countess dealt with this matter herself indicates that she was still playing an active role in Thomas's education, but whether this was her wish or whether her involvement was by default is not clear. Certainly Dunbar was far too busy with politicking and Lord Daer to devote much time with his youngest son. Nevertheless, Thomas became introduced to the city of Edinburgh, where he would enter the university and spend five happy years maturing. The city in which Thomas was to grow to manhood had changed considerably since his father had been active there a generation earlier. Edinburgh was now at the very pinnacle of its renaissance, the centre of the Scottish Enlightenment and renowned throughout the world—both for its architectural splendours and for its learned conversation—as the "Athens of the North."[14] Architects such as the Adam brothers were busy laying out squares of classical symmetry in the recently developed New Town to the north of the castle, and filling them with houses of equally classical proportions. The New Town was joined to the old by a huge mound, started in 1783 and made up of 1,305,750 cartloads of earth from the foundations dug for new buildings in the city. The man who had designed the New Town, James Craig, laid it out along a ridge running to the north parallel with the Royal Mile. On the ridge, he created a major street, George Street, and at the south and north of the development, two cross streets, Princes Street and Queen Street. Each building on these streets was to be forty-eight feet in height. Public buildings were also constructed. Robert Adam's Register House was the first, begun in 1774.

Classical Edinburgh was not simply a construct of stone and mortar. Its real asset was its people, especially those connected with the university and with learning. Most of the leading intellectual figures—doctors, lawyers, scholars, philosophers, poets—had little connection with the merchants, professionals, and aristocrats of the New Town, but resided in the medieval closes of the Old Town atop the "Mound." Here the university flourished, albeit housed in new buildings, and here were the taverns, coffee-shops, and oyster bars that served as the meeting places for the hundreds of "clubs" for which Edinburgh was justly renowned. There were more clubs by the 1780s than there had been in Dunbar's day, and it was in them, perhaps more than in the lecture halls of the university or even the New Town drawing rooms of the well-to-do, that one could find the giants of the Scottish Enlightenment: David Hume, philosopher and historian; Adam Smith, political economist; William Cullen, medical theorist and reformer; Dugald Stewart, philosopher and teacher; and the young men—such as Robert Burns the poet or Walter Scott the future novelist or Thom Douglas the peer's son— who flocked around them.

Scholars have long debated the precise combination of ingredients responsible for this enormous outpouring of creative energy in a relatively poor, backward, small, isolated, and historically disadvantaged corner of Europe. They have equally disagreed about its bent and its ideological basis. But what has been generally agreed is that the intellectual basis of the Scottish Enlightenment was a questioning scepticism toward traditional knowledge and a rethinking of old questions on the basis of new conceptualizations and even experimentations.[15] A new scientific approach to human nature appeared. "In our universities, what a change has been gradually accomplished since the beginning of the eighteenth century!" proclaimed Dugald Stewart at the end of the century. "The Studies of Ontology, of Pneumatology, and of Dialectics, have been supplanted by that of the Human Mind, conducted with more or less success, on the plan of Locke's Essay, and in a few seats of learning, by the studies of Bacon's Method of Inquiry of the Principles of Philosophical criticism, and of the Elements of Political

Economy."[16] Along with a new and relatively open attitude toward the study of man went a firm conviction that any attempts to improve the lot of mankind through enlightened ideas were not merely beneficial but essential, and such reform was the highest form of moral behaviour possible for the sensitive and responsible individual. Whether such views represented moral idealism or moral pragmatism is irrelevant to appreciating the thrust of the movement. This was the intellectual environment into which Thomas Douglas—barely fifteen—stepped in 1785, and it was the one that would shape his ideas and his life. Important aspects of his thinking would change over time for Thomas Douglas, but not his general commitment to the principle of improvement.

Young Thomas Douglas matriculated at the University of Edinburgh in December of 1785. His intention, or perhaps that of his parents for him, was to prepare for a career in the law, that frequent recourse for the younger sons of the nobility in Scotland. The family apparently never considered the possibility of colonial service, either in America or in India. His courses over the next few years would be the standard fare of the time: classics, mathematics, logic, rhetoric, belles-lettres, natural philosophy, and ethics. There is little evidence that he took many of them terribly seriously.[17] Nor did he have to do so. Attendance at the university was basically unorganized and decentralized. The school year began in mid-November and ended in April, leaving plenty of time for travel abroad or activity in the country. The student applied for a ticket of leave to attend a course of lectures, remunerating the lecturer with a fee for the ticket, and went along to listen and take notes, or not, at his pleasure. No one took attendance, there was no student participation in classes, and there were neither term essays nor course examinations. Those students attending with a view toward eventual certification in one of the professions such as law or medicine might ultimately face some sort of reckoning, and many of the ambitious took detailed lecture and reading notes that still survive today.[18] For a young man like Thomas Douglas, whose family position could be guaranteed to open doors, most of the learning process could be less formal. On the other hand, Thomas was diffident and modest, traits that could be interpreted as an attitude of aloof superiority. For Thomas, making friends would not come easily.

As the youngest male of the Douglas family returned to Edinburgh in 1786 for his first full year at university, he experienced two events in his family that would affect him considerably. His father broke with his kinsman

Lord Morton over peerage politics, the first of many such rifts with the Scottish establishment that would mark the growing gulf between it and the family of the fourth earl.[19] Over the next few years, Dunbar's family would become isolated as one of the few aristocratic ones supporting radical political and social change for Scotland. On a more personal level, Thomas's sister Helen became betrothed to James Hall of Dunglass, a well-known figure in Edinburgh scientific circles.[20] Hall had travelled extensively in Europe and was acquainted with many scientists and philosophers in Germany and France. This alliance would also add to the family's radical connections, since Hall was friends with many of the men who would be leaders of the French Revolution in its early days. The acquisition of Hall as a brother-in-law was of enormous importance to Thomas, for it provided him with an older man who could serve as a mentor and exemplar, a role his father apparently did not fill. Like the fourth earl, James Hall was quite close to and fond of Lord Daer, but unlike old Dunbar, Hall could and did find time for Thomas. The Hall house in Edinburgh provided a centre of family activity in which Thomas could participate.

If Hall provided guidance and example, so too did Professor Dugald Stewart, an old family friend and lecturer in moral philosophy at the University of Edinburgh. Stewart (1753–1828) was the son of a lecturer at the university, who received his early education at Edinburgh High School and the university before attending the University of Glasgow, where he fell under the influence of the Scottish philosopher Thomas Reid, the founder of the so-called "Common Sense" school of philosophy. Stewart would spend the remainder of his long life expounding and expanding on Reid's insights, the chief of which, according to George Davie, envisaged "facts not contained in the sum of the various elementary experiences involved in the genesis of . . . items of the common sense, and this peculiar and fundamental fact of self transcendence is held by Reid and most Scottish philosophers to be an ultimate irrational mystery."[21] Dugald Stewart returned to the University of Edinburgh in 1772 to fill in lecturing for his father, who was ill, and in 1775 he became a professor of mathematics. When Adam Ferguson went to America on government service in 1778, Stewart lectured in his place, offering a set of lectures on moral philosophy that he would spend the remainder of his life expanding and improving. Stewart, like Thomas Hutcheson at Glasgow forty years earlier, gathered around him a constantly changing group of young men for whom he served as patron. Many of them would live in his house while they attended the university. The list of those thus taken under his wing included Sir Walter Scott, Francis Horner, Sydney Smith, Lord Brougham, James Mill, as well as Lord Daer and Thomas Douglas. Stewart was a friend of reform in the 1780s, and he would later— like the family of the fourth Earl of Selkirk—spend time in France during the early years of the French Revolution. In his lectures, Stewart maintained that virtue and morality were epitomized by selfless dedication to the improvement of society. In later years, Thomas would, as fifth Earl of Selkirk, attempt to combine the scientific spirit of James Hall, with its emphasis on careful experimentation, and the philosophical spirit of Dugald Stewart, with its stress on altruistic dedication to others. He would send his first publication to Stewart, doubtless hoping for the older man's approval.

As well as young university students, Dugald Stewart also took under his wing other young men of ability and radical inclination. One of these individuals was the poet Robert Burns. Like John Paul (Jones) the son of a gardener, Burns was born near Ayr on the Firth of Clyde in 1759. Obviously manifesting special gifts of intellectual capacity from an early age, Burns was encouraged by his father to attend school, and he received enough of the rudiments of education to be able to teach himself in later life, often through membership in clubs and societies, including the Freemasons' Lodge. As he grew up, Burns read widely in the literature (poetic, political, and philosophical) of the Scottish Enlightenment. Burns may have been self-taught, but he was extremely well read. A part of his reading was in various Real Whig texts of the eighteenth century, and Burns could hardly avoid in the 1780s becoming involved in the leading political movements of the time: the hostility to the American War, the parliamentary reform movement, and the campaign to abolish slavery.[22] On 31 July 1786, Burns published a substantial volume: *Poems, Chiefly in the Scottish Dialect*. This work was an instant success, selling out most of a first printing of 612 copies within four weeks. It brought Burns to the attention of the Edinburgh literati. Apparently Dugald Stewart was one of the first in the city to read the book and recognize the merit of its contents.

Stewart invited Burns to his country house at Catrine for dinner on 23 October 1786.[23] Another of the guests that evening was Basil William Douglas, Lord Daer. Like many of his contemporaries, the poet was absolutely bowled over by Daer's charm. The result was a poem entitled "Lines on Meeting With Lord Daer." In it Burns exulted on the occasion, "A ne'er to-be-forgotten day,/

Sae far I sprackl'd up the brae, I dinner'd wi' a Lord." And he concluded with his personal reaction to both the meeting and to his Lordship:

> I watch'd the symptoms o' the Great,
> The gentle pride, the lordly state,
> The arrogant assuming;
> The fient a pride, nae pride had he,
> Nor sauce, nor state, that I could see,
> Mair than an honest ploughman.
> Then from his Lordship I shall learn,
> Henceforth to meet with unconcern
> One rank as weel's another;
> Nae honest, worthy man need care
> To meet with noble youthful Daer
> For he but meets a brother.[24]

This would not be Burns's last poem inspired by the Douglas family, but it certainly suggests the public charisma of Lord Daer. The wedding between Sir James Hall and Helen Douglas took place at St. Mary's Isle on 11 November 1786, only a few weeks after the meeting of Daer and Burns.

The fourth Earl of Selkirk was finally elected as a representative peer at a by-election early in 1787, and began spending increasing amounts of time in London, even acquiring a residence there. A "political view" of Scotland written about this time characterized Dunbar as "a very independent man, *attached* to no party, but who has hitherto acted with Opposition from conviction."[25] He became increasingly obsessed with the manipulation of the Scottish peerage by the government in London, writing the Earl of Buchan in 1788: "The Enemy knows . . . how to employ this engine; & is already at work . . . to satisfy the vain, the ambitious & the greedy."[26] Lord Daer often accompanied him, leaving Thomas behind in Edinburgh to begin to make some friends among his fellow students. The "political view" described Daer as "a man of real abilities and ingenuity, and of the most indefatigable industry."[27] In the summer of 1787, Thomas made a number of expeditions on horseback by himself and with his brothers, practising sketching and studying geology with Sir James Hall. The young man also spent considerable time on the Dumfries social circuit, where—as he wrote undergraduate friend William Clerk of Pennicuik—"every body has been dancing like the devil."[28] Most of the dances were probably the reels so popular at the time in Edinburgh social circles. While Dunbar and Daer engaged in various major projects of estate improvement, Thomas built and planned a tree "plantation" seventy feet long by thirty feet broad. Still obviously apprenticing, Thomas attempted to follow in the footsteps of his elders.

THE CLUB AND THE SPECULATIVE SOCIETY

Although a youngest son still unrecognized by the outside world, Thomas was gradually expanding his horizons. By the autumn of 1788 he had begun attending law lectures, coming into contact with many more of his ambitious contemporaries. He also attended public addresses by Adam Smith, who was living in retirement in Edinburgh and was greatly admired by the young Thomas.[29] Chief among his new friends, perhaps met through William Clerk, was a young man exactly his own age slightly lamed by a childhood bout with polio. Walter Scott had attended Edinburgh High School and had moved on to the law school at the university.[30] A small circle of about a dozen young students that included Scott, William Clerk, Adam Ferguson, George Abercromby, and Thomas Douglas formed an informal organization in imitation of their elders. Known as "The Club," it met Friday evenings in a room in Carrubber's Close for discussion and debate. The participants then adjourned to a nearby oyster tavern to—in Scott's words–"doff the world aside and bid it pass."[31] The club's members remained close friends. Throughout their later careers, mainly in law, they dined twice a year, at the close of the winter and summer sessions of the law courts, and marked personal triumphs by allowing the celebrant to host a special dinner for his old associates. Only Walter Scott and Thomas Douglas made their marks outside the Scottish legal community, and while their respective careers as British author and North American colonizer made it difficult for them to remain close friends in later years, there was always a bond of mutual respect and admiration between the two men.[32]

While Thomas was making friends among Edinburgh students, his elder brother Daer initiated the first round in a series of open challenges to the established order of Scotland. On 6 and 13 October 1789, Daer had attempted to enrol as a freeholder in Wigton and Kirkcudbright. He was refused on the grounds that he was the eldest son of a Scottish peer and hence ineligible to exercise the freeholder's privilege of voting for and sitting in the House of Commons.[33] The *Act of Union* of 1707 had stated that none were eligible to sit in the British Parliament who had been ineligible in the Scottish one before 1707, and the last eldest son had sat in Scotland's Assembly in 1558. After the union, eldest sons were routinely disqualified by the Commons, although Alexander Lord Saltoun pointed out in 1788 that these decisions meant that the eldest sons of Scottish peers "were marked out as a distinct and separate body of subjects, to whom *alone* the rights and privileges of Britons are refused."[34] The issues here were extremely complex. The anomaly was a double liability to an able young man like Daer, for his succession to the title would merely allow him to enter the contest for an elected seat in the Lords, while family influence in Galloway could virtually assure him a secure place in the Commons. In an age in which many members of the British aristocracy sought to make careers in Parliament, the liability was a serious one. On the other hand, the smaller landholders of Scotland continued their hostility to the extension of power of the wealthier Scottish aristocracy, and it is likely that Henry Dundas was behind the scenes opposing Daer, who was the son of an important Scottish peer not a friend of the government. Daer appealed the local rejection, with his father's full support.

On 22 December 1789, the Honourable Thomas Douglas petitioned for membership in the Speculative Society of Edinburgh, thus attempting to join brothers Basil, Dunbar, and John within the ranks of the most prestigious Edinburgh debating society of the eighteenth century.[35] Although founded by students at the university in 1764, the society permitted—indeed, encouraged—them to remain active after their departure from the cloistered halls of academe. No restrictions about age applied, and although most members were between the ages of eighteen and twenty-one, many were younger or older. The Speculative Society was an exclusive club, from the first limited to a handful of members elected by ballot (around fifteen) devoted to "Improvements in Literary Composition, and Public Speaking."[36] At each meeting, one member was "to deliver a Discourse on any Subject" he chose, and every other member in attendance was allowed to comment once on the discourse. Afterwards, a debate was held on a separate list of questions, the evening's topic opened by a member in rotation. The society had its own building adjacent to the college, originally built at society expense in 1769 and expanded in 1775, and its own library. The "hall" or main meeting room of the building was twenty-five feet long by nineteen feet wide. The new applicant's petition for membership would have been posted on the wall of the society's room. Here the members would meet each Tuesday evening at 7:00 p.m., a change from 6:00 p.m. voted about the time of Thomas's election. By this time, the society had fallen on hard times, with few new members and many meetings without a quorum, which was nine members. Why the society had run into trouble was a matter of some controversy. Its early historian argued that the arrival of the French Revolution and political troubles in Scotland meant that it was dangerous to assemble weekly for public debate.[37] Certainly the society resolved in 1794 to be "cautious in admitting as subjects of discussion or debate, the political topics of the day." At this time, the height of the political hysteria in Scotland, the Tory members drove the Whigs out of the society. The actions of 1794 suggest under how much suspicion all who questioned the standing order, including the family of Thomas Douglas, could come. But whether there was a self-imposed ban on political topics earlier, as another historian later suggested, seems dubious.[38]

Thomas was easily admitted to the Speculative Society, and he had his first opportunity to speak publicly there on 2 March 1790, when the question of the evening was: "Has the late Revolution in France been equally glorious and will be attended with consequences equally beneficial to that Country that the Revolution in 1688 has to this?"[39] Thomas no doubt weighed in on the affirmative side. By early 1790 the French revolution was well into its first phase. The storming of the Bastille on 14 July 1789 had ushered in the winds of change. A National Assembly grown out of the old Estates-General had begun meeting in Paris, and the passage of revisionist legislation was well underway. The first stage of the revolution was in the hands of the French aristocracy, and the goal was that of a constitutional monarchy with the nobility in charge. At this time the aristocracy had not yet lost control of the National Assembly, there was still no Terror, and as the resolution of the Speculative Society suggests, the French Revolution (described in March 1790 as "late" and thus finished) could still be fitted within the constitutional box favoured by Englishmen when they thought about their revolution in 1688. Revolution could still mean the unleashing of liberty under the constitution. One of the few in Great Britain who was not convinced at this stage that the French Revolution was a good thing was Edmund Burke, who was busy writing his *Reflections on the Revolution in France*. It would finally appear in print in November 1790.[40] Both its publication and the escalation of events in Paris would force many in Britain to rethink their attitudes about what was happening in France.

Thomas spoke with animation and served as teller for the victorious affirmative side on 13 April 1790, when the question was a more pointed: "Will the late Revolution in France have a beneficial effect upon the interests of

Great Britain?" Again the assumption of the question was that the revolution led by the nobility was finished. No record exists of his arguments or those of the debate as a whole, but Thomas probably insisted that the revolt of the French aristocracy against absolutism could serve as an example of further reform within Great Britain, already blessed with a constitution that merely needed improvement. These topics certainly suggest no self-censorship at the Speculative Society in 1790, and also indicate that those favourable to the French Revolution were in the majority in the society. On 27 April, Thomas read his first essay to the society. The subject was "The Territorial Tax." Owing to the paper's great length and to questions put to its presenter, the debating/ discussion topic had to be postponed.[41] This paper has not survived, but it was probably considerably less topical than the debating one that had to be put off. Characteristically, Thomas dealt with the question exhaustively. Equally characteristically, he had chosen a topic that fell within the realm of political economy, that new subject upon which Dugald Stewart was now regularly lecturing at the university.

In the parliamentary elections of 1790, both Dunbar and Daer challenged the establishment without success. No doubt both men saw themselves as acting in the spirit of the French aristocracy. Putting himself at the head of the "associated Independent Peers," the fourth Earl of Selkirk stood for re-election to the House of Lords but was defeated by a government list and government manipulation of proxy votes.[42] He appealed his defeat to the House of Lords itself, which spent three years on the case before finally over-turning the official results and ordering him to be seated. As for Daer, he attempted to stand for the Commons, but was defeated in the election for a seat representing one of the fourteen Scottish royal boroughs.[43] Soon after this election, the events of the French Revolution and the arguments of Edmund Burke's *Reflections on the Revolution in France* led both the government and the Scottish landed aristocracy to come to oppose the sorts of political reform with which the Earl of Selkirk's family was becoming increasingly associated. Burke insisted in his book that the French Revolution was not comparable to the English Revolution of 1688 because the French were moving violently away from their heritage. The French Revolution was not constitutional and was not based on the principle that the good society has to be organic rather than contractual, wrote Burke. His work would, as we shall see, lead to an answer from the great pamphleteer of the American Revolution, Thomas Paine, in which Lord Daer would play a role.[44]

Over the winter of 1790-91, Thomas was back again in Edinburgh. He opened debate on the first question of the season discussed by the Speculative Society: "Have the National Assembly of France acted wisely in abolishing hereditary jurisdiction?" He was also a chief supporter of the petition for membership of Mr. Walter Scott. Individuals like Scott, who lacked the funds to travel abroad, were the mainstay of the organization. He was quickly chosen its librarian and served on most of the important committees as well. We do not know which side Thomas took on the question of abolishing hereditary jurisdiction, since this move struck at the heart of any aristocracy, including his own Scottish order. He may well have taken the negative side. Thomas served on the committee to select new questions for debate and listened to an essay by James Gordon on colonization, perhaps his first introduction to the issue that would become his life's chief work. He spoke, probably in the negative, on the question: "Ought any permanent support to be permitted for the poor?" He was teller for the nays on the question: "Ought the Duration of Parliament to be shortened?"[45] This latter task, on 30 March 1791, was Thomas Douglas's last action with the Speculative Society, for in early April he left the city for revolutionary France in company with his brother-in-law Sir James Hall. He never returned to the university. Enlightenment Edinburgh had given him its sensibilities, and now it was time to be off to revolutionary Europe to observe ideas in action.

CHAPTER THREE

Paris, the Continent, and the Shadow of Daer

SIR JAMES HALL had travelled extensively in Europe in the late 1770s and early 1780s with his tutor, establishing contact with a number of leading intellectuals and scientists. He had formed a particular friendship with the French chemist Antoine Lavoisier.[1] Like Hall, Lavoisier was especially interested in the relationship of chemistry and geology. Like most scientists of his age, his intellectual interests were wide reaching, stretching from agriculture to the manufacture of gunpowder to the improvement of society through the introduction of savings banks. He was also involved with the government in the Fermé General, the hated chief tax-collecting agency of the government, where he had become a principal *financier* on borrowed money. As Simon Schama has observed, "It was not all that unusual in the France of Louis XVI for public men to be simultaneously intellectuals, administrators and businessmen."[2] In 1789 Lavoisier served as an alternate deputy to the States General, and in 1790 he had headed a commission to regularize weights and measures in France; the result was the metric system. In 1791 he became secretary to the Academy of Sciences.[3] He would come under the suspicious eye of the radical leader Jean-Paul Marat in 1792, and as a former member of the Fermé General he would be tried, condemned to death, and executed in May of 1794. But in early 1791 Lavoisier was still in political favour, and Hall could use their friendship to gain access to the upper reaches of the intellectual circles of revolutionary society in Paris. Hall obviously also intended to employ the occasion to provide some direction and tutelage for his young brother-in-law. A tour of Europe and a visit to Paris—

especially in the exciting atmosphere of 1791—would be an essential component of the education of any eighteenth-century British gentleman. Thomas and his brothers obviously looked up to and admired Hall, and so the elder man made an ideal informal tutor.

Hall and Thomas Douglas left Dunglass, the site of the Hall country residence on the east coast of Scotland, on 3 April 1791. The coach journey through England was relatively swift, averaging up to eleven miles per hour, and the pair was in London within four days, greeted at Dunbar's London house in Upper Brook Street by the "whole family." After a brief family gathering, an expanded party of Hall, Lord Daer, John Douglas, and Thomas left on 15 April for France in their own coach. Once in France, the party stopped by the roadside on the way to Paris to talk to peasants about agriculture, to the undoubted astonishment of the local peasants. At St. Omens they saw a new design of plough and Hall actually tried it out. "Daer said that in our country every body held the plough & that we were not aristocrats" like the hated French nobility, Sir James noted in his journal.[4] By 19 April the little group was in Paris.

PARIS

Ah, Paris! Then, as now, the city was a magnet for foreign visitors and French from the provinces. People were drawn to Paris by ambition, by the search for pleasure, and by the opportunity to make cash money. Paris contained nearly ten times the number of people in Edinburgh—upwards of 600,000—and it sprawled across vast expanses of land that not so very long ago had been open fields. Traffic was congested, and everyone wanted to get to where they were going as quickly as possible. The streets were nearly all paved and lit at night with oil lamps. In some districts there were even sidewalks, a new innovation of the 1780s. Increased numbers and constant mobility meant that much of the population could become anonymous residents of the city, their background unknown to anyone but themselves. It was possible to blend into the crowd when walking the streets. Although the gap between the wealthy and the poor remained, contemporaries talked of "a confusion of ranks."[5] The maintenance of proper deference was becoming increasingly difficult at the same time that class consciousness was growing. A broadened consumer culture was spreading rapidly, and elaborate shop signs were springing up everywhere. There had been a veritable explosion of paper in 1789, with over 200 newspapers on the streets and 36 printing shops. The city had not yet lost most of its churches, clerics, and religious institutions—that loss would come later in the decade—but Hall and his family arrived in Paris in the middle of a controversy over the rights of Roman Catholic priests within the city. While some like the comte de Mirabeau sought to fan the flames of religious dissension, the priests had objected to the attempts of the National Assembly to create a national church, and had appealed to the Declaration of the Rights of Man to support their grievance.

Sir James Hall quickly established contact with Lavoisier and other members of the philosophic and scientific community in the French capital, including the Duc de La Rochefoucauld-Liancourt, a descendant of the great seventeenth-century writer of aphorisms and president of the directory of the department of Paris.[6] On 21 April Hall's party were invited to a soiree attended by La Rochefoucauld-Liancourt, the economist Dupont de Nemours (he harkened back to the earlier Physiocrats of the 1760s, who had sought then to free French agriculture from the chains of medieval and feudal conventions), and the Marquis de Condorcet. Of these men, young Thomas would be particularly attracted to Condorcet, whose background was in both mathematics and political economy. Born in 1743 in Ribemont, Marie-Jean-Antoine-Nicolas de Caritat, Marquis de Condorcet, had been elected to the Académie des Sciences in 1769 and was appointed its secretary in 1779. His most important mathematical work was done on the theory of probability. A protegé of Turgot, Louis XVI's Controller General of Finance in 1774, Condorcet was inspector-general of the French Mint, a post he held until 1791. As an economist, Condorcet worked on the public policy of scarcity and the establishment of "true prices" by the marketplace. A "true commercial interest," he would write in 1790, was "the same for all nations; it is the restoration of the most complex freedom," and he added in 1791 that all economic policy had to be abandoned "to the free will of individuals."[7] For Condorcet, the marketplace and individual free will would produce the fastest variety of human progress. Condorcet's influence—rather more than Adam Smith's—can be sensed in Thomas's first publication, an anonymous pamphlet on poor relief in Scotland, appearing in 1799.[8]

After this soiree, Daer left the party to take up lodgings in the Grand Hotel du Vendome, while Hall, John and Thomas eventually ended up in the Grand Hotel de Vauben, Rue de Richelieu.[9] Sir James Hall's journal of his 1791 Paris visit is full of daily doings, mainly with "T" or "T.D." They dined regularly with Lavoisier, heard about the revolution from Condorcet, observed Robespierre and other debaters at the riding academy where the meetings of the National Assembly were held, and attended plays and operas. On 7 May, John Paul Jones called at the Grand Hotel de Vauben, having met Daer the night before at a dinner hosted by William Short, the secretary of the American legation in Paris. The two men had been in the same room for several hours before being formally introduced. Jones was living in Paris, in ill health and drinking too much. He refused to be drawn on the St. Mary's raid. "He seems a sensible little fellow," Daer later wrote to his father. "He acknowledged he was from Britain, but said he was *settled* in America before the war began, and it was then his country. I did not ask him from what part of the kingdom."[10] That same evening Hall and Thomas dined "at home" with the Abbé Sieyès, Condorcet, and Lavoisier. The last took off his coat after dinner to help Thomas with a chemical experiment of some sort.

On 13 May John returned to England, leaving Hall and Thomas together in their lodgings, although they were frequently joined by Daer. A few days later, Thomas entered into a discussion with a dinner guest on Locke's insistence on the relationship of government to the protection of private property. Hall had initiated the subject by remarking that the estate of a man without children should be distributed among the poor, and recorded in his diary, "T.D. supported me in this by saying that to employ a man's estate on his death for the public service was making a present to those who otherwise must have paid for that service, to those who paid the taxes, that is, as we all agreed to the landed proprietors—to the rich and not the poor."[11] The two men subsequently adjourned that evening to dinner with a number of prominent republican leaders, including Brissot de Warville and Achille-François de Lascares d'Urfé (the Marquis du Chastellet). Brissot was interested in penal reform and the abolition of slavery, both subjects of great interest to the Scots. He was also an outspoken advocate of using war to disseminate the principles of the revolution, which may have been somewhat less congenial to the visitors.

The summer months of June and July 1791 passed quickly. The times were exciting and the politics confusing. The Society of the Friends of the Constitution, which had earlier established itself in the library of a Jacobin convent only a short distance from the National Assembly—hence its common name "the Jacobins"—had more than 1000 members and had taken upon itself the role of acting as "great accuser" against the old aristocracy. The

Jacobins were led by Robespierre, George Danton, and Jean-Paul Marat. Their discussions echoed in the pages of the Paris newspapers. In response, the Marquis de Lafayette had founded the Society of 1789, which met at the Palais Royal. This was the home of the moderates, including those committed to King and Constitution. The Society of 1789 included among its members in 1791 the Duc de La Rochefoucauld-Liancourt, Dupont de Nemours, Lavoisier, and Condorcet, who edited a periodical, the *Journal de la societé de 1789.* This little group were *philosophes,* intellectuals united by their interests in science, political economy, and political philosophy. Often politically allied to Lafayette's Society of 1789 during the debates and manoeuvrings of 1791 was another group, the Girondins, so named because most of its members were deputies from the Gironde department. The Girondins, led by Jacques Brissot de Warville, were mainly members of the professional middle classes. They were republicans who wanted constitutional government and who opposed the attempt to control the revolution by the Jacobins and the Paris mob. It was with some of the leaders of this centre faction in 1791 that Sir James Hall and his family enjoyed their closest contacts.[12]

The little party of Scots carried on a constant round of social engagements with the intellectuals among the centrist moderates, as well as visits to the countryside to examine agricultural practice and survey the state of the people during a period of revolutionary change. On one occasion Thomas observed that "the republican spirit of the country" seemed greater than was to be found in Paris itself.[13] Lord Selkirk himself joined them in late June, at about the time Louis XVI tried to escape from Paris and was returned to the city under guard. There were regular visits to the National Assembly to listen to the debates, which were mainly over the future of the monarchy and France's overseas colonies. Within and without the National Assembly a life-and-death struggle went on between the moderates and the radicals, which the moderates would eventually lose in August of 1791 after the Hall group had returned to Britain.

On 3 July, on the eve of the anniversary of the American Declaration of Independence, the little Scottish party dined at home with Thomas Paine as principal guest. Paine had been born in 1737 in County Norfolk, the son of a Quaker. He was deliberately denied an education in Latin and, like Robert Burns, had worked as an exciseman. He emigrated to America in 1774 with a letter of recommendation from Benjamin Franklin in his pocket. In January of 1776 Paine published his pamphlet *Common Sense,* which advocated in simple direct English prose a republican independence of Great Britain on the grounds that monarchy was both wrong and harmful.[14] Unable to settle down in the post-revolutionary United States, he left for France in 1787 with the plans for the construction of an iron bridge of his own design that he hoped to see built across the Seine. He spent the next four years crossing the English Channel between France and England and writing the book that would become the *Rights of Man,* the first part of which was published in England in February of 1791. The publisher took fright at the radical opinions he was circulating and dropped the project shortly after a few copies had been issued. It was picked up by another publisher in collaboration with William Godwin, Thomas Holcroft, and Thomas Hollis, and the fresh edition appeared on 13 March 1791.[15] In person, Paine was full of stories and anecdotes, and admitted his understanding of French was quite imperfect. A few days later the Scots "supt" in Condorcet's rooms with du Chastellet and Paine, talking of the "fable about maintaining bees, emigrants, education."[16] The *Fable of the Bees*, of course, was the famous work by Sir John Mandeville arguing that all men were motivated solely by self-interest, which should be the guiding principle of a modern society. Young Thomas Douglas had absorbed a version of this argument in the lecture halls of Edinburgh with Dugald Stewart. We do not know what was said about emigration that night.

On 7 July Sir James Hall recorded in his journal, "Abbe Sieyès has written a monarchial letter in the Moniteur & Payne who goes to England tomorrow with Daer means to have an answer to it."[17] The exchange between Sieyès and Paine had been cooked up between the two men to highlight the differences between the arguments for monarchy and the arguments for republican government. Paine's letter answering Sieyès appeared in *Le Moniteur* on 8 July, arguing for a "government founded upon the principles of the Declaration of Rights; principles to which several parts of the French Constitution arise in contradiction."[18] The next day Daer set out in his carriage for England with the Swiss-born Étienne Dumont (a collaborator of Mirabeau) and Paine accompanying him. Dumont was not impressed by enforced companionship with Paine, who "knew by heart all his own writings and nothing else."[19] Lord Daer was apparently not quite so put off by the American. Daer and his companions arrived in London only a few days after a series of Church and King riots in London. They were in time to celebrate the second anniversary of the fall of the Bastille. The party was supposed to take place under the auspices of the Society for Constitutional Information at the Crown and Anchor Tavern, but because its proprietor feared the wrath of the British government, it was moved to the Thatched House Tavern instead. Daer and his fellow revellers were put under immediate surveillance by the British government.

Étienne Dumont had complained that Tom Paine's "unbelievable egotism" included a belief that the *Rights of Man* "had set off a new chain of ideas and principles." In this, of course, Paine was proved quite right. As a European, Dumont probably did not appreciate Paine's genius and its influence in Britain—or America. Paine's work answered Edmund Burke's *Reflections on the Revolution in France,* a classic statement of constitutional conservatism. According to Burke, change was useful only if were executed to preserve the existing social structure and to prevent a breakdown of the social order. The French Revolution did not meet these criteria and was, moreover, harmful to the French people in terms of the extent of violence it unleashed. Paine offered what E.P. Thompson has described as a "new rhetoric of radical egalitarianism" replacing an older discourse of constitutionalism.[20] The new discourse was based upon a rejection of monarchical and hereditary principles, an unbounded faith in representative institutions and "right reason," and upon a freethinking rejection of the Bible and the doctrines of Christianity. Paine's rejection of the Bible was regarded by British authorities as a major offence. He scoffed at the Bible, seeing it—in William Blake's words—as "a Poem of probable impossibilities." As far as the virgin birth was concerned, for example, Paine asked, "Were any girl that is now with child to say . . . that she was gotten with child by a ghost and that an angel told her so, would she be believed?"[21]

After Daer's departure from Paris, Sir James Hall and Thomas Douglas were thrown even more closely together. By this time political events in Paris were moving at a breakneck pace, and the two men spent much of their time crowding into public proceedings to observe and listen. They still managed to find time for regular dinner parties with the leading intellectuals of Paris, usually discussing some aspect of political economy. They occasionally dined with members of the British community, including the British Ambassador Lord Gower, who had written to the British government on 8 July warning it of the impending arrival of Thomas Paine in England. Hall and his brother-in-law found Lady Sutherland "remarkably cool," no doubt because they had become notorious as "violent friends of liberty."[22] A Paris newspaper reported that Robespierre was plotting with two Englishmen whose names—M. D'Ark and M. le Chev'r d'Ark—transparently conflated Daer and Selkirk. Such publicity doubtless hastened the departure of Hall and Thomas from France, and they were back in London by 27 July 1791. A few days later Hall and Thom called on Sir Joseph Banks and Josiah Wedgewood, subsequently meeting Mr. and Mrs. Barbauld at dinner, where they "disputed much about French politics."[23]

No written record survives of the reactions of Thomas Douglas to his Parisian visit of 1791, but it must have had a considerable impact upon him, as it certainly did upon a far more urbane and experienced Sir James Hall. For the younger man, it had been largely an opportunity to observe and listen, one given to few Britons of his generation. In a short space of time, he had been exposed to the leading thinkers of revolutionary France, and had at least listened to them discuss economics and politics in an informal setting.

He had also witnessed the turmoil of the French Revolution at first hand, and if nothing else he had been made to appreciate that intellectuals could also be men of action, that ideas were not mere arid academic exercises, and that some sort of reform of society was essential to prevent political chaos. Throughout his subsequent public career, Thomas would insist on the need to translate ideas into action, on the need to test social theories experimentally. The experiences of 1791, combined with the later extreme events of the French Revolution—including the ugly deaths of several of the thinkers he had met in 1791, such as Condorcet and Lavoisier—were also vivid reminders of the dangers of allowing change to go too far too fast. Paris in 1791 would not be his only schoolroom, but it was undoubtedly a critical one, for the city was far more alive with a spirit of adventure, social experimentation, and even danger, than was the staid little Edinburgh which had provided his previous public instruction.

If the Paris visit of 1791 were important for Thomas, it had also an enormous impact upon others of his family, especially his elder brother Lord Daer, whose activities became increasingly radicalized after his return from France in the company of Thomas Paine. In October of 1791 Daer finally managed to become enrolled as a Kirkcudbright freeholder, although this action was immediately challenged in the courts.[24] Daer not only was battling for the rights of the eldest sons of Scottish peers, but also against the increasingly hostile opinion of his politics among the Scottish aristocracy. Lord Selkirk found himself "deserted and avoided by most of his former acquaintances and friends," few of whom would have regarded Daer with as much tolerance as did Sir Ralph Abercromby.[25] That worthy commented of Daer that "unless the opinions of a young man of twenty had a tinge of republicanism he would be sure to be a corrupt man at forty."[26] Selkirk radicalism was more than most members of the Scottish aristocracy could stomach, however, especially after it became associated with popular electoral reform and not merely with changes in the rights of the peers.

Late in April 1792, a well-attended general meeting in Kirkcudbright met to consider proposals for major electoral reform, including the reduction of property qualifications and the sending of delegates to a convention in Edinburgh in July. Lord Daer had written to this gathering supporting reform and requesting "their vote for him as a delegate."[27] He was duly chosen, although the county did not commit itself either to support its delegates or the measures decided upon by the convention. Even this cautious action was more than many could tolerate, one local critic of the proceedings observing that the logical extension of such "levelling principles" involved the question of "why one man should be allowed to be so rich, while another was so poor," adding the inevitable comment that the present state of Europe rendered "all attempts at Innovation more improper now than at any other period."[28] In the view of most members of his order, Daer's support of reform ran against his best interest as a son of a Scottish peer. At about the same time, the London Corresponding Society was organized in the nation's capital. Admission to membership called for an affirmative answer to three questions, including: "Are you thoroughly persuaded that the welfare of these kingdoms require that every adult person, in possession of his reason, and not incapacitated by crimes, should have a vote for a Member of Parliament?"[29] Setting its dues at one penny a week to put membership within the reach of everyone, the society in April 1792 publicly introduced a series of resolutions advocating reform measures. Lord Daer was a member, apparently from the society's foundation. Thomas Hardy, the society's secretary, forwarded Daer his "new ticket at 1d. a week" on 14 July 1792.[30] That same month, a number of distinguished Whigs, including Lord Daer, founded the Society of the Friends of the People, which was intended to be less radical and to introduce debate over parliamentary reform into Parliament.[31]

The government responded to all these actions by issuing a proclamation against seditious writings. Much of Scotland was critical of this proclamation, claiming that it encouraged magistrates to spy on reformers and actually publicized Tom Paine's writings. The editor of the *Bee,* an Edinburgh news-paper, commented that a bookseller in Edinburgh told him that before the proclamation *The Rights of Man* lay on his shelves unsold, but now "the book that was forbidden to be sold" disappeared at twice its previous price. There were riots in "almost every village in the North of Scotland," and a nasty confrontation in George Square in Edinburgh between a mob attempting to burn an effigy of Henry Dundas on 4 June, the king's birthday. Officially this unrest was attributed to Thomas Paine. Unofficially, the sheriff of Lanark-shire wrote Dundas that the real problem was "an almost universal spirit of reform and opposition to the established government and legal administra-tion which has wonderfully diffused through the manufacturing towns of this country, and is openly patronised by many county gentlemen of fortune."[32] Those patrons included members of the family of the fourth Earl of Selkirk.

While his elder brother was busy at politics, Thomas Douglas continued his informal education. He planned a tour of the Highlands of Scotland, his first visit to the region that would become the Scottish centre of his life's work. Why he chose to visit the region at this time is not clear, although he had relations who had married into the leading clan families of the High-lands, notably Clanranald, and he may have been drawn by the popular discontent of the time. In any event, accompanied by a "Mr. Gilmour," he set out in the spring of 1792. The only surviving report of the journey comes in the form of a letter to his father, dated from Perth on 2 May 1792. At Dundee, Thomas reported, "I had the honour of seeing Mr. Dundas carried in proces-sion & to be burnt in effigy immediately for opposing the reform of the boroughs. The people seemed to have a dash of the French *qui vivre.*"[33] Despite the briefness of the comment, it tells us a good deal about Thomas's political views in 1792. He was still supporting Daer and his attacks on Henry Dundas, he was still sympathetic to the Paris mob, and he still approved of the radical ardour of his family.

We know very little more about Thomas's Highland visit in 1792, although he would later often refer to it in general terms. He was by his own account present in Ross and Cromarty in August of 1792 when the popula-tion rose in arms against the introduction of new sheep walks in the area.[34] Lord Adam Gordon, commander-in-chief of Scotland, wrote Henry Dundas privately that "no *disloyalty* or spirit of *rebellion* or dislike to His Majesty's *Person* or *Government* is in the least concerned in these tumults."[35] They were completely motivated by rumours of the letting of land in the region to sheep farmers, "which meant all the former tenants would be ousted and turned adrift, and of course obliged to emigrate." This was perhaps Thomas Douglas's first exposure to the problem of emigration from the Highlands that would soon take over his life. In the short run his visit apparently induced him to learn some Gaelic and his experience remained in the back of his mind for years, until he had the opportunity to do something about the turmoil in the region.

Despite protestations and warning to the authorities that the movement for parliamentary reform was not necessarily a seditious one, the dread of mobs and violence was genuine. Not much was required to persuade the government that reform would soon lead to revolution. The constitutional agitation led to the founding of a number of new periodicals and journals, most of which were critical of the ministry. The result was what one newspaper described as "political madness" in Scotland. "Societies are everywhere formed and clubs instituted for the sole purpose of political debate," argued the *Caledonian Mercury* on 30 September 1792.[36] The new organizations began to vie with one another through the publication of lengthy declarations of their principles. One letter from Glasgow to Henry Dundas argued that discussion of reform was not dangerous when confined to the landed classes, but took on a different appearance when the "lower classes" were invited to join and the mob encouraged. By November of 1792 Dumfriesshire was aflame. Young Thomas Douglas was caught up in the spirit of the times. He wrote his father, "I believe if the reformers could bring about anything like the Irish volunteers everything they ask would be granted at once."[37] Sir William Maxwell reported that Paine's *The Rights of Man* was in the hands of "almost every countryman and could be had for twopence."[38] The meeting of the county delegates for electoral reform had met briefly in July of 1792 and adjourned until December. When it convened on 11 December as the first General Convention of the Delegates from the Societies of the Friends of the People throughout Scotland, it met in the midst of the great political tumult and tension of the day at Lawrie's Rooms, James' Court, Edinburgh.

Thanks to the presence at the meeting of government spies and informers, we have a fairly full report of the proceedings of this meeting, although obviously not an analysis of the manoeuvring of the delegates.[39] The 186 delegates represented eighty societies from thirty-five towns and villages, most of them in the industrial district lying south of Dundee and bounded by Glasgow on the west and Edinburgh on the east. A full listing of those present was given in the minutes. Lord Daer was the only delegate with a title. He represented Portsburgh in Edinburgh. Daer was on his feet from almost the beginning of the meeting, responding to a proposal from Thomas Muir that the convention should elect officers. Muir was the vice-president of the Glasgow Friends of the People, and one of the most militant radicals in Scotland; he would be sentenced by a court to fourteen years transportation in August 1793. Daer addressed the meeting "by the familiar epithet of 'Fellow Citizens'" and maintained that a meeting occasioned by the "great principles of liberty and political equality" ought not to set up men in a permanent situation of power. Moreover, he added, while the government was keeping such a close eye on the convention's proceedings, it would be wise to divide the responsibility of leadership. Although Daer did not say so, most if not all of those in attendance knew that such a proceeding was based on that in the National Assembly in France.

Despite the rhetoric and the references to the French Revolution, Daer was not being particularly radical in this intervention. Reading between the lines, one can assume that he was trying to prevent the convention from being captured and controlled by the radical element. Before the day was out he would rise to oppose establishing a committee to present an address to the King, saying that "immediate and precipitate consideration" of such a business "might ruin the whole cause in twenty-four hours." As Daer explained in a speech early the following day, he was opposed to standing committees because they "threw the powers of the Convention into the hands of a junto." He added that his experience in France had taught him that the best way for the convention to proceed was to table all motions and then adopt the best. His efforts to establish such a procedure were, not surprisingly, totally opposed by Mr. Muir, although agreed to by the delegates. From the outset, therefore, Lord Daer was the leader and chief spokesman of the conservative faction at this gathering, and he was called to the chair on 12 December.[40]

Immediately after Daer had taken the chair, probably to silence him in debate, Thomas Muir presented to the convention a printed address from the Society of United Irishmen in Dublin. Many delegates spoke against receiving this address on the grounds that it contained statements that were at least potentially treasonous, and Daer agreed with them. The address was eventually rejected. Before his departure for another meeting, Daer cautioned members against using the epithet "National Convention" for their meeting, since not all Scotland had sent delegates. The unspoken reason, of course, was the association of the term with France. After Daer had left the gathering, the Muir faction quickly gained control of it. Motions became more radical and the Irish Address was reconsidered although still not accepted. The convention spent several days drawing up resolutions on parliamentary reform, the moderates winning out on all major issues. A few days later Daer, apparently in absentia, was appointed to a committee for drawing up the minutes of the convention and having them printed. As the convention was ready to adjourn, one Mr. Fowler moved that "all should take the French oath to live free or die," and the members rose as one man to take the oath.[41] One of the conservatives at the meeting pointed out that this oath might be interpreted as sedition, and it was not recorded in the printed minutes, although a government informer included it in his report to Henry Dundas. The authorities thought that this oath, the discussion of the United Irishmen address, and the proposal that the Friends of the People should be armed with a "Brown Janet" to help suppress disorder were sufficient evidence of the real intentions of this convention, which agreed to meet again in April of 1793.[42] Lord Daer was not present at this April gathering.

Daer had left Friends of the People convention for another meeting, that of the county delegates for electoral reform. It was a far more distinguished gathering than the one at Lawrie's Rooms, including among its members Henry Erskine, the lord chief baron of the exchequer and the lord advocate of Scotland.[43] Daer had told the Friends of the People as he left that he did not expect much good to come from the gathering of the county delegates. Given the attendance by the supporters of government, the outcome at this meeting was not very extreme. It agreed to reduce property qualifications from £400 to £100 Scots, and submit such alterations to the counties. Daer fought against such minor palliatives in favour of more strenuous change, but the meeting eventually "unanimously came to resolutions expressive of their attachment to the constitution of this country, and their abhorrence of levelling principles."[44] Government spies were not likely to find much to report from a gathering of this sort. Whether the informers managed to convey to the authorities that Daer at the Friends of the People meeting had been a firm advocate of moderation and legal reform, or that he had left the gathering before affairs had turned radical, is another matter. He was himself put under surveillance and was eventually advised to leave Scotland to avoid prosecution.

One of the reasons that the government was suspicious of Lord Daer was because of the sentiments he expressed to Charles Grey (later Lord Grey of the Reform Bill) in a letter of 17 January 1793. Here Daer declared that "Scotland has long groaned under the chains of England."[45] He proceeded to analyze the English constitution "as we Scotsmen see it." For Daer, Scotland had been "a conquered province" from the Union of the Crowns in 1707. Union had done little "except removing a part of the obstacles which your greater power had posterior to the first Union [of the Crowns in 1603] thrown around us." Scotland was governed not by Parliament, argued Daer, but by its law courts in audacious and arbitrary fashion. Because "we have been the worse of every connection hitherto with you, the Friends of Liberty in Scotland have almost universally been enemies to the Union with England." This nationalistic declaration was, of course, highly subversive, as the Convention of the Friends of the People had recognized in its debate over the printed address from the Society of United Irishmen in Dublin. Part of what the Friends of the People wanted, they insisted, was the restoration of original rights and ancient liberties back to the medieval period before any sort of union, when Parliaments in both nations were annual and, as Thomas Muir put it, "every man who was free had a right to sit in Parliament, either by himself or his representative; that in Scotland a free man was even more free than in England."[46] Not all Friends of the People felt it necessary to go back to ancient times. In the Convention a Mr. Aitchison insisted that the English and Scots "as one people . . . are entitled to the same privileges."[47]

His youngest brother was not a witness to the events in Britain with which Daer had become so intimately involved. Whether Thomas Douglas had escaped to Europe to avoid any possible association with Scottish radicalism or merely to continue his education is not clear. Probably a bit of both was involved. In any case, later in 1792 Thomas was again back in France, reporting to his old mentor Dugald Stewart that the people of France anxiously awaited the re-establishment of order, and observing that another insurrection might make the establishment of armed force necessary.[48] Thomas at this point had been in close contact with Condorcet and Pierre Louis Roederer, the former the leader of the constitutional committee of the French convention, the latter the editor of the *Journal de Paris*. It was Roederer who had advised the king on 10 August to take refuge in the Assembly, after which he went into hiding. Thomas appears to have left France either before the suppression of these moderate elements or before his association with them was well known. The destruction by fire of the Selkirk Papers has left the chronicler of the family for the period of the 1790s working with little but shadows and echoes of hard information.

From revolutionary Paris, Thomas seems to have moved on to Naples, where he visited a kinsman, Sir William Hamilton, perhaps best known as the husband of Lady Emma Hamilton. Sir William Hamilton was legally the son of Lord and Lady Archibald Hamilton.[49] But his mother was the favourite mistress of the Prince of Wales (later George II), and William was brought up as a foster brother of the young man who became George III. He was probably an illegitimate member of the royal family. After military service in Europe, he married an heiress with a fortune of £6000 a year, thus providing him with the money to engage in his obsession of collecting art work. An appointment as British minister to the Court of Naples in 1764 fit perfectly into his mania. Shortly after first his wife died in 1782, Hamilton returned to England on leave of absence, where he met the beautiful Emma Lyons, the mistress of Sir Charles Greville. Hamilton fell in love with Emma, wooed her, and brought her to Naples where she became his mistress. The two married in England in 1791. How long Thomas tarried in Naples at Hamilton's villa is not clear, perhaps as long as a year and a half. But the elder man had an interest in vulcanology and science that Thomas could share. The life was pleasant, the company good, and Thomas may well have had a bout of trouble with his lungs that encouraged tarrying in Naples.

Thomas was probably still in Naples in June of 1793 when, on his tour of Kirkcudbright in company with John Syme Robert, Burns visited St. Mary's Isle on a whim, since, according to Syme, "it occurred once or twice to him that the Isle was the seat of a *Lord,* yet that Lord was not an *Aristocrate.* He knew the family a little."[50] Daer does not appear to have been in residence at St. Mary's Isle, but two of his sisters were, and they sang for the poet. Also in the company of around fifteen young people was the musician Pietro Urbani, who sang Scots songs. Burns himself spoke his words to the tune of "Lord Gregory," and "such was the effect, that a dead silence ensued." According to John Syme, almost immediately after the visit with the Selkirk family Burns composed "Scots wha hae," his poem about Robert Bruce's march at the battle of Bannockburn, which later became an unofficial Scots national anthem. The meeting with Urbani, with whom he drank in Dumfries for several days thereafter, may have been part of the spark, although Burns's familiarity with the career of Lord Daer might equally well have provoked a song on what the poet himself described as being "on the theme of Liberty & Independence."[51]   Certainly Burns was familiar with the agitation of late 1792. The subsequent report to the Excise Board (his employer) that he was "disaffected" with the government was apparently the result of various provocative toasts he had made on a number of semi-public occasions in 1792.

Later in 1793 when Lady Hamilton first met Admiral Horatio Nelson, Thomas may well have been present, although they would hardly have noticed him. By his own admission Thomas's "timidity" put him "in company without making me one of the company."[52] His father encouraged him to acquire more worldly experience, writing, "I have known many lads of sixteen, who, as the vulgar saying is, could have bought and sold you in a market."[53] From Naples Thomas moved on to Switzerland, apparently contemplating a military career in Poland. He met the noted North American traveller Count Andreani, whose work he later quoted with approval. Drifting through Europe seeking experience and a career was brought up short in 1794 by news of the death of brother Sandy in Guadeloupe and the serious illness of Lord Daer, who died in Devonshire of consumption in November of that year.

Daer's movements in the last two years of his life are extremely difficult to track down and verify, partly because of his illness but also partly because of government prosecution of the radical nationalist elements with which he was associated. Thomas Muir had been arrested in July 1793. He was soon joined in custody by the Frenchman Maurice Margarot, David Downie, and Robert Watt. The latter two were allegedly apprehended with plans for some sort of seizure of Edinburgh Castle. Watt was a former government spy who had been relieved of his duties in 1793 and had turned to conspiracy. He was hanged and his head cut off, the executioner holding it up to view exclaiming, "This is the head of a traitor."[54] Joseph Gerrald, sentenced to fourteen years transportation in 1794, had told the court that sentenced him that England had robbed the Scottish people of their rights from the time of the Union of 1707, adding "but if that Union has operated to rob us of our rights, it is our objective to regain them!"[55] Lord Daer was apparently an early member of a clandestine group called the United Scotsmen, modelled on the United Irishmen, that emerged after the suppression of the leadership of the Friends of the People. He was reputedly a member of a seven-man secret executive of this organization, although given his illness he could not have been very active, and the United Scotsmen would become prominent only several years after his death. According to an obituary published in the *Gentleman's Magazine* in May of 1795, he had " broke off all connexion with the men he had formerly acted with, as soon as he discovered their motives to be less pure and patriotic than his own; and that, for some time before his death, he had renounced all communications with Democrats."[56] A late conversion to loyalty, if such there was, did not have much effect on the reputation of his family, however, which was well tarred with the brush of republicanism and sedition.

The death of Daer was taken extremely badly by his father, who had made the young heir his constant companion, associate, and confidante. A father's hopes for the future of the family, as well as for the fulfillment of ambitions he himself had never realized, had been bound up in Daer. While the *Gentleman's Magazine* obituary doubtless exaggerated, various other sources, including the poetry of Robbie Burns, suggested that Daer was a wonderful combination of intellectual acuity and sweetness of character. His loss was a crippling blow both to Dunbar and to his surviving sons, who knew full well that they were not regarded in quite the same light. John became Lord Daer, but there was continual friction between the new heir and his father, caused in part by Dunbar's inability to adjust to the new situation. Ill with consumption, John preferred to reside in Florence. In winter of 1795, the young physician Andrew Duncan, junior, had written to his father expressing skepticism about his ability to carry out the assignment, which his father had obtained for him, of caring for an invalid Lord Daer and returning him to Scotland. Duncan had eventually travelled to northern Italy via Germany and Switzerland, arriving in 1797 only to discover that John Lord Daer had died before he had left England.[57]

After the death of his eldest brother was followed by the demise of brother Dunbar at St. Kitt's and the serious illness of brother John at Florence, Thomas had come back to Scotland in 1796. He still had military aspirations, attempting in 1797 to raise a corps of Scottish volunteers. His father opposed the venture. By this time it was clear that Thomas was the family's only hope, and his father's "distress of mind" at the prospect of military involvement held Thomas back.[58] Then with the death of one more brother in 1797, Thomas officially became Lord Daer, heir to the title, a position to which he had never aspired.

CHAPTER FOUR

Finding a Role in Life

FOR A FEW YEARS AFTER 1797, Thomas Douglas as Lord Daer spent much of his time managing the family estates, acting essentially as a "man of business" for his father, who was by this time quite infirm. Thomas engaged in complex negotiations with the Town Council of Kirkcudbright, for example, to tidy up boundary lines on Selkirk lands adjoining those of the town. But the young man had considerable energy, and it would not be satisfied by estate management. He managed to find two projects related to his interests in political economy that could be carried out from the family base in Kirkcudbright.

One of these projects was undertaken for the Board of Agriculture, that curious organization established in 1793 by Sir John Sinclair, an indefatigable compiler of social statistics and research information. The board was a quasi-public agency funded by Parliament but organized as a voluntary society, with noted agriculturalist Arthur Young as secretary. It never really had a satisfactory function, although its creation was related to Scotland's unrest in the early 1790s, particularly the rural discontent in the north. Sinclair convinced the government that the research and dissemination of information about Scottish farming might help assuage public fears about agricultural improvement. Among the Board of Agriculture's more successful activities were the compilation of county-by-county agricultural surveys and reports, many of which were published.[1] The report for Galloway was to be the responsibility of Thomas Douglas, Lord Daer, and he went about the task of collecting information on agricultural practices with his usual enthusiasm, concentrating particularly on sheep husbandry. The introduction of sheep walks into the Highlands, as Thomas had seen in 1792 when visiting the region, was a major item of public discontent. As well, a series of bad harvests and wartime inflation had also contributed to much rural distress in Scotland. By early 1798 the report was in rough form, ready to be perused by Sinclair but "not yet in a state for the public."[2] By this time, however, the Board of Agriculture had lost its government support, the major factor in its existence. The impetus for investigation was apparently lost, and Thomas's volume was never completed, although the rough notes for it remain in the surviving copies of the Selkirk Papers.

Considerable connection existed between agricultural investigation and relieving the Galloway poor. The new Lord Daer undoubtedly became involved in the latter problem as a major landholder, although the question clearly also fascinated him as a political economist and reformer. The late 1790s were a period of great difficulty for the rural poor. Food was in short supply and expensive. As the fourth Earl of Selkirk's old friend Charles James Fox once trenchantly put it, "the great majority of the people . . . an enormous and dreadful majority are no longer in a situation where they can boast that they live by the produce of their labour."[3] Contemporaries saw few solutions. One was enclosure to increase production, especially of grain, or to shift production into more useful channels, such as sheep. Another was the notorious Speenhamland System, by which in England especially low wages were supplemented with public poor relief provided by the parish. The trouble with Speenhamland, charged its critics, was that it artificially kept wages low. Minimum wage laws were an unthinkable solution. They would infringe the sacred right of property—including the right of an individual to sell his labour at the market rate. Regulation of the grain trade ran counter to the "system of natural liberty" preached by Adam Smith and other eighteenth-century political economists. Indeed, the question of the regulation of grain in periods of extreme shortage had been a hotly debated one throughout the eighteenth century. Most economic thinkers preferred an open market, but some drew the line when the poor really suffered. One especially sharp discussion had come in France at the end of the 1760s. It pitted Galiani, Diderot, Voltaire, Necker, Grimm, Linguet, and Mably (for regulation) against Quesnay, Baudeau, Roubaud, Dupont, Mecier, Morellet, and Condorcet (against regulation).[4] A similar debate had also erupted in Scotland in the 1770s, with James Steuart on one side and Adam Smith on the other. In 1798 Thomas Malthus anonymously had published his essay on population.[5] This work had not dealt so much with regulation as with the relationship between food supply and population expansion, gloomily predicting an eventual demographic disaster. Many connected with the Board of Agriculture advocated that the poor consume alternative and less costly foodstuffs than their usual diet.[6]

The efforts of Lord Daer in Kirkcudbright to help the poor in the late 1790s resulted in his first publication, an anonymous untitled pamphlet describing the 1799 relief system obviously implemented at his instigation.[7] The only known copy of this work, without a title page, is in the Dugald Stewart Collection in the University of Edinburgh Library. Its authorship is attributed, in Stewart's hand, to Lord Selkirk, which suggests that Stewart had received it after Thomas Douglas had acceded to the title. Whether Selkirk had this pamphlet printed for public or private distribution is not clear in the absence of a title page. There was no general system of poor relief in Scotland. Instead, responsibility for the poor was in the hands of the heritors (ratepayers) and kirk sessions in every parish.[8] As T.C. Smout has pointed out, "in public statements and private papers alike eighteenth-century landowners reveal themselves as glorying above all else in the paternal quality of their rule."[9] Thomas Douglas certainly fit well into this trend. The only difference between his efforts and those of others was his attempt to articulate some general principles for what he was doing.

What Selkirk described in his pamphlet was the introduction of a system that reduced the consumption of grain. The heart of the scheme was the distribution of meal at reduced prices to those without it, but with the quantities distributed to families calculated "not at their ordinary rate of consumption, but at the lowest to which it was supposed they could by the strictest economy reduce it." The innovation of which Selkirk was so proud was the calculation of the lowest possible rate of consumption. By examining the diet of the "labouring class," he determined that they consumed meal both as porridge and as cakes. Porridge would produce more nourishment than cakes, especially when made not only with grain but also with pot barley. The distribution of larger quantities of pot barley enabled the county to reduce the daily consumption of meal by cottagers and their families from eight ounces per capita to six ounces per capita, with considerable savings to those providing the relief.

The specifics of the Galloway scheme outlined in the pamphlet are in many ways less interesting than the general philosophy enunciated by the author. Here three points stand out. First, Selkirk characteristically approached the problem as an exercise in political economy, attempting to use the occasion to seek "experimental proof" of the efficacy of a particular method.[10] To the modern reader, the dispassionate tone and cold analysis of the pamphlet will strike a discordant note. But Selkirk thought of himself as a social scientist—although he would not have used the term—as well as a philanthropist. Second is the author's sense of the social responsibility of the upper classes. He had no interest in altering the structure of society, but rather a definite desire to draw "closer those bonds of union between the different classes of society, on which the stability of social order so essentially depends." This union was without doubt constructed in terms of a paternal relationship. "The poor," Selkirk wrote, "were sensible they received their aid from the good-will of their superiors, and the relief was administered by those who contributed it."[11] Third, the pamphlet advocated voluntarism and opposed the importation of a Speenhamland-type system of poor relief to the city of Edinburgh. Selkirk opposed taxation for relief of the poor on the grounds that the poor would not feel gratitude if "the only aid they receive is extorted from the rich without their consent." Moreover, such relief would lead the poor "to believe that the assistance given them is their right," and any hardships suffered would be "considered an injustice."[12] A poor rate, wrote Selkirk, "will spread a profligate dependence on it among the poorer classes; the money that would otherwise be laid up for the support of age and infirmity, will go to the whisky shop; poverty and misery continually increasing, will continually add to the demands upon public charity." Such a policy not only undermined the spirit of industry, it also perpetuated the cycle of poverty it was intended to relieve.

The three characteristics of his poor relief pamphlet would remain with Selkirk throughout his life. He would always view his various projects as scientific experiments. His attitude toward the people with whom he was working would always be paternal. And he would insist that his people be as financially self-supporting as possible. At this point, he had not moved much beyond seeing public support as destructive of the morals of the poor and recognizing an obligation—voluntary—to assist them. In later years Thomas would find an alternative way to aid the poor that preserved the principle of self-help. This would come in the concept of emigration to North America.

Such schemes were well beyond the capacity of a mere male heir to a Scottish
estate, but the means for larger endeavours would soon come to hand.

BECOMING LORD SELKIRK

In May of 1799 the aged Dunbar died, and Thomas Douglas became the
fifth Earl of Selkirk. The old man's financial affairs were quite tangled. As
the male heir, Thomas inherited the Galloway property and honoured his
father's last wishes for bequests to his four daughters, although these were
not legally binding.[13] The major stumbling block was the estate at Baldoon,
which had been sold in 1793 to Lord Galloway for £155,000. At the time,
Dunbar had intended to use the proceeds to pay off the family's debts and
provide an inheritance for his younger children. Galloway's offer in 1793
had paid off the debt but provided no surplus. Basil, then Lord Daer,
succeeded in persuading his father to write into the agreement of sale the
condition that the property would be leased to Daer for ten years, at the end
of which time arbiters would decide on the value of the improvements made.
Galloway would make an additional payment of this amount.[14]

The improvements made were not as great as Basil had hoped, for he had
been ill and politically involved for some time, and after his death the supervision of Baldoon had passed from brother to brother in rapid succession in
the 1790s. Nevertheless, the amount of money involved was substantial, and
at Dunbar's death the arbitration had not yet occurred. The family engaged
in considerable internal controversy over the added value to Baldoon.
Thomas insisted, based on his own knowledge and the opinions of the family
steward William Mure, that £60,000 was all the improvements would bring.
Sir James Hall questioned this assessment, and there were unseemly accusations that Mure was not acting entirely in the family interests—he and Sir
James had never gotten on. Thomas stubbornly insisted that he would take
£20,000 and settle £10,000 on each of his sisters. The business would drag
on for years and, unfortunately, would to some extent poison relations
between Thomas and his brother-in-law.

A valuation roll for purposes of the land tax was coincidentally made up for
Kirkcudbright immediately after Dunbar's death, and indicated that the main
estate at St. Mary's Isle was valued for tax purposes at nearly £9,000, a figure
based on the annual rental value of the lands.[15] In addition, Thomas inherited
land in New York State (obtained from the Colden interests and registered
formally in his name in 1800), as well as scattered property elsewhere in the

south of Scotland. The New York property was located in the western part of
the state, not far from the Genesee tract promoted at the end of the eighteenth
century by Charles Williamson for Sir William Pulteney and various Scottish
associates, including the Earl of Hopetoun.[16] Almost a century ago, the Canadian scholar Helen I. Cowan saw this Genesee tract as a model for Selkirk's
later schemes.[17] Certainly Selkirk examined the tract on site on his later American tour. The involvement of Pulteney and the Earl of Hopetoun in American
land speculation and development in the late 1790s does suggest that some
Scots were thinking about overseas investments. Because aliens were not
allowed to hold land in New York state until 1800, we do not know if the
purchase of the New York tract was at Pulteney's instigation or whether a result
of the earlier association between Dunbar and the Coldens. In any case, the new
earl had a gross income of perhaps £10,000 per year, certainly a substantial sum
but not one sufficient to permit the sort of adventurous colonization activities
in which he would subsequently engage, at least not without considerable strain
on the estate. Although he had enjoyed several years to prepare for the previously unexpected eventuality of the title, Thomas Douglas was now twenty-
eight years old and the fifth Earl of Selkirk. He had inherited a considerable
estate and had to decide what he was to do with his life. Managing the lands in
Kirkcudbright, negotiating minor business with local politicians as the heritor
and chief laird of the district, or organizing poor relief for Galloway were obviously not likely to be sufficient outlets for a man with his energies and income.

In December of 1799 the new Earl of Selkirk turned to other matters
beyond his estate. He attempted unsuccessfully to gain approval from his
fellow magistrates of Kirkcudbright for a new scheme of poor relief, probably a version of the one discussed in his printed pamphlet, which he may in
part have published in order to argue his case before a larger audience.[18] The
reluctance of his colleagues to join him in schemes of local reform was joined
that month by the refusal of the town of Kirkcudbright to accept what
Thomas regarded as legitimate and rational arrangements to resolve the
ongoing boundary disputes between the town and the estate. The Town
Council on 28 December 1799 peremptorily rejected all his proposals as
injurious to the town, and added insult to injury by declaring that in some
matters His Lordship was "misinformed as to the nature & extent of their
Mutual Rights."[19]

Thomas doubtless found local attitudes irritating, and they contributed
to other factors leading him to look beyond his immediate environs. His

eldest brother had become a legend in the Galloway region, a figure of mythic proportions whose reputation was only enhanced by his premature death. The memory of "Good Lord Daer," affable, accessible, radical, was not something to compete with easily. Thomas needed to become his own man, not to follow in his brother's shadow. Finding wider horizons would require some time, however. As the fifth Earl of Selkirk he could not sit in the British House of Commons; the path to the House for the sons of Scottish peers had not been opened and was irrelevant to a peer. A political career was severely limited both by the electoral nature of the Scottish peerage system, and by the fact that his family's radical reputation was quite out of step with the opinions of his colleagues and Scottish political realities. If Thomas sat down to survey his prospects in politics, as he must have done, he undoubtedly came to the conclusion that he was relatively young and virtually unknown, except as a member of a renegade family. He needed to bring himself to the attention of his contemporaries in another light were he to be successful in the political arena.

Surviving evidence does not allow us to identify the precise mental process that led the new Lord Selkirk to his projects in emigration and North American settlement, but clearly the schemes he ultimately developed did not come to him overnight as a fully developed vision. Instead, they were worked out over a fairly protracted period on the basis of reaction and adjustment to circumstances. From the time of inheriting the title if not before, Selkirk needed to do something significant, likely something that combined political economy and philanthropy. Even these vague ambitions probably took shape fairly gradually, as he settled into the life of a Scottish peer. When the Highlands of Scotland and North America were added into the equation is another matter.

Selkirk's movements between late 1799 and 1801 are largely a mystery. A tantalizing reference in Dugald Stewart's diary for 1801 reads simply "St Mary's Isle—North of Scotland."[20] The two men probably discussed subjects of mutual interest—moral philosophy, philanthropy, and political economy— in the context of Selkirk's pamphlet on poor relief, a copy of which had been sent to Stewart. It is tempting to speculate that Thomas, in company with his former mentor, again toured the Highlands, great schemes bubbling in his head. If so, it seems likely that Stewart, as his later correspondence indicated, attempted to restrain the younger man's enthusiasm.

Less speculative is the brief tour in company with fellow geologist John Playfair and "Lord S." described in Sir James Hall's diary for October 1801.[21] Playfair (1748–1819) was professor of mathematics at the University of Edinburgh and a distinguished mathematician, but was better known as a geomorphologist and popularizer of science. While laid up with rheumatism in 1797 he had written an *Essay on the Accidental Discoveries Which Have Been Made by Men of Science, Whilst in Pursuit of Something Else, Or When They Had no Determinate Object in View.* Soon after this tour with Hall and Selkirk, undoubtedly a bit of a holiday, Playfair would publish *Illustrations of the Huttonian Theory of the Earth,* on which he had been working since 1797. This work helped establish James Hutton as Britain's first great geologist. The party started at Dunglass and spent four or five days in Edinburgh before travelling via the Dumfries races to the Isle of Annan. There they revisited "the junction of Granite and Schistus formerly discovered and traced by Ld Selkirk (then T.D.) & myself in 1788." From the Isle of Annan the trio travelled through Ayshire, where they found some strata that could not be reconciled with other observations. Hall noted, "Ld S. thinks that much may be ascribed to back draughts taking effect after the first violent action had ceased."[22] Although his geological opinions were very much an amateur's, they were obviously taken seriously by men like Hall and Playfair, who were regarded as experts of the day. This close relationship between gentlemen dabblers (especially members of the nobility) and professionals was a characteristic of the eighteenth-century Enlightenment in Scotland and in France. It was possible partly because so much knowledge was speculative rather than highly specialized, partly because men still deferred to a "noble lord." Selkirk's interest in geology would persist throughout his life, finding expression in entries in his journal of his tour through North America in 1803–04 and later in his collection of geological specimens from western British America. Hall's record gives no indication of any great projects being formulated by his brother-in-law, however. Selkirk apparently spent some time in Ireland in 1801 on some sort of fact-finding expedition.

HIGHLAND EMIGRATION AND ECONOMIC DEVELOPMENT

The controversy over Highland emigration and development that flourished at the start of the nineteenth century was one that must have appealed to a young ambitious political economist looking to establish a reputation. Lord Selkirk must have known of the overpopulation in the

Highlands, of the various schemes of Highland improvement, of the escalating trend of emigration, as well as of the disproportionate number of
Gaelic speakers, often Catholics, who were involved in it. How the idea
had come to him of transporting and resettling emigrants in North
America is not at all clear, however. It is doubtful that he had gotten the
concept from contemporary practice. There were a number of emigrant
contractors in 1801 transporting people to North American destinations
from locations in the Highlands. But none of them intended to plant
settlements as well, and most of them had very unsavoury reputations.
The most notorious of these contractors was one Hugh Dunoon, who in
the spring of 1801 filled two vessels with over 550 male and female Highlanders bound for Nova Scotia. The government had responded to
Dunoon with complaints of exploitation of "a poor ignorant set of
people" and threats to regulate the transatlantic passenger traffic in the
best interests of the Highlanders.[23] Perhaps Selkirk had heard of earlier
emigrations to North America led by natural leaders among the Highlanders themselves, several of which involved Roman Catholics. The
successful transplantation in 1772 of several hundred Macdonalds from
the western Highlands and Islands to the Island of St. John (later Prince
Edward Island) was an outstanding example, although following through
on this model might have led Selkirk to fix on Prince Edward Island
earlier and not as a default location.[24] A more likely starting point—one
that could be mixed with emigration—was the Genesee promotion in
upstate New York of Sir William Pulteney and other Scots.

The "mania for emigration" was in full swing by 1800, and it was much
publicized in the press of the day. Almost exclusively it was confined to the
Highlands of Scotland and had its origins in British policy after the "45."
After the Highland support for the pretender Charles Stuart in 1745, the
second such uprising in thirty years, the region north and west of the Highland fault in Scotland was deliberately and forcibly integrated into Great
Britain and the British Empire. The old clans and the traditional society
surrounding them were broken down at the top, and the Highlands exposed
to the contemporary world. The British government wanted no recurrence
of the raising of a clan army in the North on behalf of Stuart pretenders.
It abolished the chieftain's hereditary rights to hold their own independent
courts, and proscribed the practice of wardholding—the attachment of
the obligation of military service as a condition of tenancy—although the

authorities increasingly used the tradition of military obligation to raise Highland regiments. The old clan chieftains were converted into proper British landed proprietors, and encouraged to modernize their holdings, principally by streamlining their operations and shifting to a money rental. As the reformed chieftains moved into British society, they needed increasing amounts of money, and to increase income from rentals, more rather than fewer tenants were desirable. With the traditional relationship between laird and people under attack, the Highlander found himself without the old security of place at the same time that he was faced with new conditions and opportunities.[25]

The new opportunities were particularly evident in military service.[26] In both the Seven Years War and the War of the American Rebellion, the Highlands provided the British Army with a number of soldiers vastly disproportionate to its population. In both wars the North American theatre was a central focus of British military activity, and many of the Highland regiments served there.[27] The Highlander's first mass exposure to the world outside his glen or island thus involved an introduction to the open society of North America, a wilderness country with vast tracts of land available for the taking and with obvious agricultural possibilities. After both wars, officers and common soldiers in North American service were offered land grants in the New World, including lands in Nova Scotia and the Island of St. John. More Highland officers than common soldiers took advantage of the grants, which for officers were large enough to encourage subdivision for sale to emigrants. Indeed, since land grants to officers were substantial, and because many officers who were younger sons of Highland lairds or tacksmen had little to look forward to at home, it was initially the officer class—part of the traditional Highland leadership elite—that became first involved in North American emigration. Nearly half the Island of St. John was granted to former officers, many of them from Scotland. Much of the region around Pictou was granted to men from the eighty-fourth regiment (the Royal Highland Emigrants) in 1784. Loyalist officers in Upper Canada had land available to settle newcomers in the 1780s. From the outset, former officers with lands to settle were among the most active emigration promoters.

New conditions in the Highlands after the "45" developed most rapidly in the Western Highlands and Islands region, especially in the counties of Inverness, Argyll, and Ross. Most of the Highland emigrants to British America before 1815 came from this region, where increasing population led to intense competition for continually smaller parcels of land inadequate to support a family. While precise population figures are unobtainable, all modern demographic research points to a substantial increase in population in northwestern Scotland in the second half of the eighteenth century. One scholar has recently computed the average annual compounded rate of population growth in the Hebrides during these years at 0.97 percent; the adjacent mainland it was 0.56 percent. Despite emigration, the overall increase of population between 1755 and 1801 was 56.2 percent on the Islands, and 29.3 percent on the mainland.[28] Here, in the region supplying the vast bulk of the early Highland emigration, one finds no eviction for sheep, but a proprietorial encouragement of continued subdivision. As holdings became smaller, those upon them became increasingly dependent upon imported meal for their survival, and bad harvests were catastrophic. The outside meal was financed out of non-subsistence activity: by sale of cattle, by cash remitted to the region by those working in the Lowlands or fighting in the army, and, especially in the Islands, by income from kelping.

Highlanders had been going to America for most of the eighteenth century, often as transported prisoners. Over the last third of the eighteenth century, the Highland pattern of emigration to British America solidified and became family oriented. This characteristic, combined with the relative isolation of the Highlanders, led to a preference for vessels that they chartered themselves or through contractors. Such vessels came directly to the region. Charters were less expensive, and at least before 1803, they offered families special fare arrangements. Since spring was the most favourable time to sell livestock and property to liquidate assets and raise the cost of passage, late spring sailings were common. Departures at this time might actually get the emigrants on to the land in America in time for a bit of planting, although often this was not possible. Migration to British America, therefore, tended to be a late spring/early summer movement of unskilled agrarian Highlanders who on arrival clustered with their families in isolated communities of friends and kin.

Contemporary observers were virtually unanimous in characterizing the potential emigrant population as highly resistant to change. Surveyor John Blackadder wrote of the Uist people in 1799 that they had "a spirit for rejecting new Modes of Improvement, and an independent cast of mind which will not be bound down (as the Farmers in other Countries generally are) by Covenants in leases to do what other people think right for them to

do, if they do not think the thing proposed right themselves."[29] Many agreed
with Blackadder that it was sudden change that had produced emigration in
the Highland districts. When the relatively high incidence of Roman Catholi-
cism and Gaelic language usage among those departing is added to their
other characteristics, it is clear that the early emigration of Scots was of a
traditional and conservative people, singularly well equipped to preserve
their culture in the New World. Almost without exception, the newcomers
resumed their familiar agricultural practices in North America, whether or
not those practices were suited to the new conditions. They grew grain, raised
black cattle, and cultivated the soil with traditional implements.

The rise of the kelping industry undoubtedly accounts to a considerable
extent for the higher rates of population growth on the Islands relative to the
mainland, since the industry provided a regular supplement for those on
inadequate holdings and encouraged both larger families and subdivision.[30]
The profits of the kelping industry to the proprietors in the region not only
deflected them from a policy of clearance, but also led to vocal and active
opposition to emigration, especially in the early years of the nineteenth
century. Kelping was a form of cottage industry in which the landlords
merely acted as middlemen, marketing a crop gathered and processed by
tenants and subtenants on shores where, typically, the laird reserved the kelp
rights to himself in his leases. Kelp making extracted from seaweed an alkaline ash used in making soap and glass. It flourished in the Hebrides in the
period from 1760 to 1815, exactly coinciding with the first Highland emigration era, because normal British supplies of alkalines from the Baltic were
insufficient and often reduced or eliminated by warfare. Some kelp was cast
on shore, but normally the weed had to be cut by hand in tidal waters, the
harvester often standing up to the waist in ice-cold water for hours on end.
Then it had to be hauled to a kiln, where it was reduced by burning to one-
twentieth its original weight. Finally the burnt kelp was hauled by the
harvesters to the point of shipping. Only at this late stage did the laird enter
the operation, collecting the burnt kelp at his wharf for sale to merchants
from Hull or Liverpool.

The price the proprietor received for "his" kelp rose from two pounds
per ton in 1750 to ten pounds per ton in 1800 and twenty pounds per ton
in 1810. Since the laird never paid his tenants more than three pounds per
ton for manufacture (and usually less), and expended but two pounds per
ton for shipping and handling, profits—with almost no direct involvement

or overhead—could be enormous, as much as 400 percent in a year of high prices. Because of the extensive labour involved and the shortness of the season when the weather was sufficiently dry to permit open kiln fires and sufficiently warm to let harvesters withstand the water temperature, few tenant families could make more than four tons of kelp in a year. The system obviously encouraged large families and subtenancy, for having more hands was one way to increase income. Another way to improve income, of course, was to pay less rent and receive better payment for kelp from the landlord, and tenants did try to strike better bargains. But tenant efforts to increase income, in a sense, counterbalanced one another. With a limited supply of land, larger families and more subtenants ultimately meant additional competition for leases, in which the kelp payment was stipulated as an important part of the rental agreement. Overpopulation resulted in a fierce bidding for land and leases, which kept rentals up and kelp payments down. Tenants who demanded better terms could find themselves without lands in the new setts (the process by which entire estates were regularly reallocated to tenants), obviously evicted but hardly "cleared" in the classic meaning of the term. The lairds should have been pleased to get rid of the malcontents, but the constant complaint of the proprietors was that emigration most affected accommodated tenants rather than those dispossessed.

In the continual struggle with the proprietors over land, leases, and kelping contracts, emigration was not merely a possible alternative for those left without land, but virtually the only bargaining counter the settled population could employ for putting pressure on their lairds. An extensive and systematic depopulation of the region through emigration, which would mean that the landlords were no longer in total control of the bargaining situation, was the abiding fear of the great kelping lairds like Clanranald, Lord Macdonald, the Earl of Seaforth, and the Duke of Argyll. In the 1770s and again in the 1800s, when the population not only threatened a mass migration but also actually began one, the lairds and their factors responded with feverish hostility to the exodus. Conditions were improved on the kelping estates while emigration was a serious threat. Although such a bargaining weapon was never systematically organized or planned, it would be a mistake to view the popular response to and use of emigration as anything other than deliberate and calculated. Some people, especially among the Roman Catholic leadership, were prepared to encourage emigration as an intentional device to improve conditions on the Islands, and many tenants threatening to leave were quite aware of what they were doing.

Some alarmists, of course, tended to view any emigration as disastrous, and that of 1801 to 1803, for example—involving fewer than than 10,000 from a population in excess of one million—was often seen as the beginning of a general "depopulation of the country." In part the overreaction was caused by the contemporary view of emigration as an epidemic disease that could easily spread, and in part because a few Highland districts did lose large numbers of people. Arguments against Highland emigration always began by bemoaning the loss to Britain of its "Bravest and most steady Soldiers". After the French Revolution, Highland backwardness even became a positive boon, since they were, as one anonymous writer observed, "The only considerable body of Men in the whole Kingdom who are as yet absolutely Strangers to the levelling and dangerous principles of the present Age, and therefore they may be *safely* trusted indiscriminately with the knowledge and use of Arms." Ironically, the same attributes that had made the Highlanders such feared and detested Jacobites eventually made them attractive Hanoverians, for they were uncontaminated by the "profligacy, sedition, & atheism of modern philosophy."[31] But beyond the military arguments were economic ones. Despite Adam Smith and other free-trade thinkers, late eighteenth- and early nineteenth-century British and Scottish economic thinking was still fundamentally mercantilistic. People were as much a national asset as coal or iron; "labouring hands" were an important natural resource. To permit them to leave for North America, where they might be employed against the mother country, as had happened during the American Rebellion, was obviously bad policy.

For those Scottish economic thinkers who concentrated increasingly on Highland development in their writings, the loss of population was particularly pernicious. Almost to a man those Scots who advocated Highland improvement were anti-imperialists, intensely hostile to the overseas empire. Nor was this attitude surprising. For them, limited resources of manpower and investment had been deflected in the past from one underdeveloped area (the Highlands) to another (North America), and American independence had demonstrated the error of the policy. From their standpoint, British North America could only be settled at the expense of Scotland, and especially the Highlands, for both regions were in contention for the same pool of capital and population. In their perception of a competition between underdeveloped Scotland and underdeveloped North America, the econo-mists and polemicists were undoubtedly accurate. In their conviction that Scotland and the Highlands could be converted into a satisfactory substitute for North America, that proper public and private policies could make the North competitive, they were on far less certain ground. Most obviously, Scotland did not have North America's vast abundance of natural resources. But the confidence of the Highland developers was based on other equally dubious assumptions as well.

One point upon which all Highland improvers and emigration oppo-nents—the two stances became increasingly indistinguishable—could agree was that what the Highlands most needed was full employment. As a result, over the period from 1770 to 1800, a fully integrated program of Highland development was gradually worked out by a number of economic writers, headed by men like James Anderson, John Knox, and John Sinclair. These men attempted to work from realistic principles. They admitted that most of the soil of the region was not prime arable land, and for this reason empha-sized its conversion to sheep pasturage and flax plantation, thus providing raw materials for textile manufacturing. They noted that the waters around northern Scotland were rich in fish, an asset not then adequately exploited. A scattered population teetering on the brink of constant starvation in its semi-pastoral state, dependent on optimum growing conditions often not experienced to feed itself, could be moved into fishing and manufacturing villages on the coasts, and the glens turned over to sheep. Communications were difficult in the North, and gradually everyone became an advocate of road building and obsessed with the need for canals at Crinan (bypassing the Mull of Kintyre) and through the Great Glen between Fort William and Inverness. The building of roads and canals would provide temporary employment, and when completed, the economic boom resulting from the new transportation facilities would absorb the construction force.

LORD SELKIRK AND EMIGRATION

The first real evidence of Selkirk's involvement with emigration comes in a letter dated 20 November 1801 from Roman Catholic bishop John Chisholm, who was in charge of the Highlands district for his church, to his superiors in Edinburgh. The letter was sent by express, wrote Chisholm "on account of a letter I received from Lord Selkirk whom I never saw and with whom I never corresponded."[32] Chisholm continued:

His Lordship's letter was too long in the way and I was determined
to lose no time in answering it. It is the result of views that his Lordship did not communicate to me. But he affirms that they are of
importance and concern my flock. He proposes my going to Edin'r
immediately to have a personal interview which is impossible just
now as I have been very ill. . . . But I promised his Lordship to be
ready for Edin'r on the next intimation from him if I continue to
mend as I do. . . . In the meantime you'll examine into this affair as
soon as you can and find out if possible the meaning of it, without
laying yourself open to any for I suppose as his Lordship has not
been explicit with me he wants to keep his view secret.

The Roman Catholic Church in Scotland was officially proscribed but
informally tolerated by the government, which appreciated "the Loyalty &
Constitutional principles of the Roman Catholic Clergy of Scotland."[33] It
was accustomed to secrecy and clandestine operations, and Bishop Chisholm
was only cautious and prudent, not hostile, to Selkirk's overtures. In January
1802 Bishop Chisholm reported to his superiors, "I continue to correspond
with Selkirk. I cannot as yet give you any proper account of the business, and
it is not quite clear to me yet."[34] At this point, the documentary trail goes
cold, probably reflecting the fact that Chisholm managed to meet with
Selkirk and discuss the "business" with him personally. Chisholm then
reported orally in Edinburgh to the leaders of his church. In view of Selkirk's
activities over the next few months, his business was doubtless some sort of
colonization venture in North America, for which he wanted the assistance
of the church to help recruit potential settlers.

It certainly seems likely that Selkirk received little encouragement from
Bishop Chisholm at this point, for early in 1802 he had opened negotiations
at the Colonial Office to transport at his expense a contingent of Irish rebels
to North America. As far as we know, this was the original transatlantic
scheme as developed by the young earl. In this first embryonic proposal we
can see the main outline of his thinking, as well as the synthesis of earlier
influences and activities. Selkirk advocated a colony in North America specifically for Irish Catholics, which would suit their "Religious & National Prejudices" and drain Ireland of "the most dangerous subjects" most likely to
spearhead future disturbances. He was prepared to recruit and lead the
emigrants if the government would pay their passage. Selkirk did not define
what "leading" meant; his subsequent ventures suggested that it meant
accompanying the emigrants to America and then leaving them in the hands

of agents, but perhaps he had something different in mind for this venture. "Believing that the new colony would need a "favourable Climate, soil, & navigation," and regarding the remaining unsettled and unoccupied territories of British North America as "very unfavourably situated in point of climate," he pressed the government to procure Louisiana from Spain. Here the "most dangerous subjects" likely to lead a future Irish rebellion could be isolated and their discontent channelled in positive directions, an argument that clearly demonstrated Selkirk's desire to be constructive.[35]

The complex chain of events that began with the initial letter to Bishop Chisholm and continued with negotiations at the Colonial Office for an Irish settlement in Louisiana would end with Selkirk's putting three ships of emigrants ashore on Prince Edward Island in the late summer of 1803. It was a long way from Irish rebels at the Bay of Mexico to Highland Scots in the lower provinces of British North America. The story of the shift introduces us to another Selkirk, one whose principal personality traits were impetuosity, obstinacy, and often brilliant improvisation, with the rapid readjustment of hastily conceived plans to new circumstances at the constant risk of inconsistency and misunderstanding. Nothing in Thomas Douglas's early biography prepares us for this aggressive, almost swashbuckling, Lord Selkirk. His early life was sheltered and his personality not particularly outgoing. It was almost as if the inheritance of the title and his need for recognition had released deeply suppressed instincts. In any case, in the new world in which he began playing, there was obviously no firm commitment on Selkirk's part either to destination or to the place of recruitment of settlers. In this sense, the Highlanders were simply objects of benevolence, pawns in a larger game. That larger game was probably connected with the need for some kind of major successful socio-political experiment, preferably one that could be written up in a book. While he got away with improvising as he went along in the Prince Edward Island venture, largely for reasons beyond his control, Selkirk took many of the wrong lessons away from his success. An application of the same principles to Red River would later destroy him.

CHAPTER FIVE

Towards Prince Edward Island

W HEN THE YOUNG LORD SELKIRK in early 1802 had proposed to the British government that he would lead a settlement of Irish rebels to Louisiana, there was no particular reason for the authorities to treat this proposal with any interest. It came out of the blue from an individual who had no obvious vested interest in Irish affairs, such as Irish estates. Nonetheless, Selkirk had a long meeting with the secretary of state for Ireland, Lord Pelham, early in April of 1802. Pelham explained patiently why the government could not accept his offer.[1] Pelham did add that while Ireland was to be left to settle itself down, the Colonial Office people might well be interested in a settlement involving Scots. A day later Selkirk submitted a supplementary document that addressed the problem of the proposed settlement's location but not the source of settlers. He argued that unoccupied lands could not be found on the eastern seacoast of North America, and in order to find "a sufficient extent of good soil in a temperate climate one must go far inland." He therefore proposed a settlement in the territory where the waters falling into Lake Winnipeg united with the rivers draining into Hudson Bay, emphasizing that Indian traders spoke highly of the region, which he compared with some of the Russian provinces in climate and soil. Since trade and transportation would be difficult in this remote area, the settlers would have to produce goods valuable in proportion to weight, and in this respect hemp would be ideal. The Hudson's Bay Company, which held charter rights to the land, could be indemnified by licence fees on those trading with the Aboriginal peoples, an ample compensation since the company did not have an "absolute monopoly"; the Canadian fur traders were rapidly penetrating the country via an inland route. The licence fees would also pay for the civil and military establishment of the colony, and the colony would help pacify the indigenous residents, who could be controlled by shutting off supplies of European commodities.[2]

SEARCH·ING FOR A LOCATION

By April of 1802 Selkirk had shifted the location of his prospective colony to unsettled territory around Lake Winnipeg. Several points about this shift are worth emphasizing. One is that Selkirk offered this change of location virtually overnight, suggesting that he had already the Lake Winnipeg region in mind as a backup if Louisiana were unacceptable. This region had recently been described by Sir Alexander Mackenzie in a book extremely popular in Scotland, and one that Selkirk read with considerable interest.[3] Selkirk had also gone to experts. A former North West Company partner retired in Scotland had been approached for advice on the formation of an inland colony, but had found the scheme "too absurd almost to be mention'd." Joseph Colen, the recently retired chief of the Hudson's Bay Company's York Factory, found the idea far more attractive, however, and much of Selkirk's information undoubtedly came from him.[4] In any event, the North West Company was later not entirely accurate when it charged Selkirk with an interest in the Red River region only because of his subsequent investments in the Hudson's Bay Company. Red River had long been in his head as a possible location for a settlement, remote but apparently containing rich agricultural land. Like many another bright and energetic entrepreneur, Selkirk seldom wasted imaginative ideas, preferring to recycle them in another guise at a later date.

While he was prepared to alter the location of his settlement, Selkirk was less willing to change the place of recruitment of his settlers. On 4 April he wrote again to Lord Pelham answering the argument that the Irish could not be induced to emigrate by a private individual, insisting that his studies in Ireland indicated that many could be induced to emigrate for advantageous wages for a term of years, and while such people could return home at the expiry of their contracts, "after having tasted the sweets of property in Land, there is no probability of their making that choice."[5] Here Selkirk was reading out human behaviour from some of the most typical assumptions of people in Britain about the attractiveness of land in North America for those who did not have any. In truth, he would later be able to recruit Irish servants for North American service, but many of them preferred to return to Ireland at the close of their contracts. Selkirk nonetheless maintained that his opinion was an informed one, based upon "the attention I have paid to Agriculture for a considerable number of years & the particular opportunities I have had of studying it as practised with singular success on a scale of uncommon extent." In explicitly invoking his research for Sir John Sinclair as a qualification, Selkirk both demonstrated that he had no better evidence to offer for his arguments and that he did not understand anything about America.

Lord Pelham finally got rid of a pesky Scottish earl by transferring the whole matter to Lord Hobart at the Colonial Office. Selkirk tenaciously started all over again. He turned to peppering colonial secretary Lord Hobart with requests for reactions to his plans. In the meantime, Selkirk sold some of his lands in Kirkcudbright to Adam Maitland of Dundrennan, perhaps intending to use the £7000 purchase price to help fund his colonization schemes.[6] By June of 1802 he had an agent—William Burn—in Ireland recruiting labourers. Son of a Northumberland farmer, Burn had moved to his mother's native land, Scotland, to become a tenant sheep farmer on property acquired by Lord Selkirk. Burn had a local reputation for reliability and good management of his flock, and Selkirk hired him at eighty pounds per annum. Burn was probably reliable enough, but there was a big difference between an old family retainer—the sort of stewards that Selkirk was accustomed to dealing with on his estates—and a recently hired agent. Throughout his life, Selkirk would expect too much of his hired employees in terms of loyalty and commitment. The employment of Burn does, however, suggest that Selkirk was thinking in terms of a North American sheep farm, probably in Upper Canada. What relationship this sheep farm would have to any colonization scheme was not at all clear. Burn was to seek 100 hands, mainly from the Catholic counties, who were to be engaged for as long as possible, preferably five to ten years. Each man was to have ten to twenty Irish acres or a passage home at the conclusion of his service.[7]

Finally realizing that Hobart was getting unfavourable advice with regard to transporting Irish rebels to Lake Winnipeg, Selkirk shifted his preferred destination to Upper Canada. A conversation with Lord Hobart on 11 June was inconclusive, but on 6 July Selkirk tried again. If his initial proposal was unacceptable, could he obtain from His Majesty a tract of land "in Upper Canada adjoining the Falls of St. Mary between Lake Superior & Lake

Huron, & also of the mines & minerals I may discover along the north coasts of these two lakes?" Observing that Hobart had mentioned the possibility of Prince Edward Island, Selkirk was prepared to take land there as well.[8] In short, Selkirk had no firm plan in mind beyond some vague scheme of creating a sheep farm on wilderness land in North America with hired Irish labour. What he wanted was a land grant, partly as a means of government assistance for his project, but more importantly as a mark of government approval for the project. For his part, Lord Hobart could not be seen to be encouraging emigration, the opposition to which was growing in Britain. He replied that he could find no reason to deviate from policy and make a special land grant to an individual, but he was prepared to write to the governor of Upper Canada to "afford the most favourable consideration which his General Instructions will admit to Your Lordships application." At the same time, Hobart emphasized that the government of Upper Canada would probably object to the arrival of large numbers of Irish, and suggested Selkirk look to "Scotch & German families" at the beginning.[9] His time consumed by his North American projects, Selkirk brushed aside attendance at the 1802 Scottish peerage election, writing one candidate: "I conceive my attendance can be of no use & do not think of taking any part in the Election."[10] He was not yet ready to advance himself as a candidate.

BEGINNING A VENTURE IN UPPER CANADA

On 21 August 1803 Selkirk informed Lord Hobart's secretary that he was sending an American acquaintance, Richard Savage, to the Falls of St. Mary to examine the situation there first hand. He requested official letters of recommendation to the British commanding officers of the western posts in the region.[11] That same day Selkirk wrote a lengthy letter to Lord Hobart, arguing for special consideration in the land grants to be made him, particularly regarding mineral rights. His principal argument was the "peculiar importance to the internal commerce of Canada" of the Falls of St. Mary, through which most of the fur trade passed. Because of its distance from settled regions, prospective settlers required "extraordinary encouragements," and anyone organizing such a colony needed compensation "beyond the usual range." Significantly, the earl agreed that he should begin with settlers "more tractable than the Irish," and while he was investigating the possibility of Germans, "of Scotch I have no doubt of procuring a sufficiency, as great numbers are at this moment about to emigrate from the Highlands." Referring to a "recent visit to that quarter," perhaps to consult with Bishop Chisholm, Selkirk noted the resumption of American emigration by the Highlanders, and added, "I shall offer them such superior terms as I think can scarcely fail to retain these valuable people in his Majesty's Dominions."[12]

The letter to Hobart is interesting partly because of its insistence on the commercial value of the Falls of St. Mary. Selkirk was obviously—and quite naturally—attracted to regions through which traffic would pass, even if that traffic was only that of the fur trade. He as yet had no particular interest in the fur trade himself, however. The Hobart letter is also the first evidence we have that Selkirk had decided to work with Highlanders instead of the Irish. His emphasis on turning them from American to British American destinations was a necessary rationale for his operation, since it meant that he was not leading an emigration but merely redirecting one that was already occurring. But the redirection of Highlanders was not likely to be enough to save Selkirk from criticism in the north of Scotland, as his old tutor Dugald Stewart attempted to warn him. By transporting Highlanders, Stewart wrote Selkirk, he would be seen as promoting emigration and associating with an unsavoury group of recruiting agents, against whom the Highland Society of Edinburgh had undertaken a campaign that would culminate in public regulation of the traffic in emigrants in 1803. Recalling the earlier persecutions of the family, the Edinburgh philosopher recommended that Selkirk do his good at home. He concluded with a warning that Selkirk might well have recalled at the end of his life but patently ignored here:

> The objects you aim at are distant, & of more than doubtful attainment; and should your schemes miscarry, either thro' your premature death, or any of the other numberless accidents by which your benevolent wishes are liable to be frustrated, you would entail on your memory (together with the ridicule which always attends unsuccessful Projectors), the reproach of being the Author of all the disappointments & miseries which might await the companions of your Adventure.[13]

Selkirk paid the older man no heed and pressed on with his schemes.

Planning in the summer of 1802 took the form of recruiting settlers and also preparing in advance for the build-up in America of a substantial herd of sheep for breeding to be taken to the new colony. Given that Selkirk did not yet really have a definitive location in Upper Canada for his colony, this preparation was really quite audacious. True, he realized that putting together a large herd of sheep would take some time, but it was all too characteristic of his operations in North America that finding a location and building a herd were being done at the same time rather than in sequence, thus enhancing the possibility of trouble if anything went wrong. The problems of getting a herd on site would be especially difficult at the Falls of St. Mary, which was his anticipated destination at the time of arranging for the sheep. After much difficulty, Selkirk managed to send William Burn to America to supervise the preparations. Advertisements were circulated in Ireland for "A few young Men who will go to America to cultivate an Estate in Upper Canada, the property of a Scots nobleman and a gentleman of the greatest respectability."[14] The advertisement suggests that Selkirk did not intend merely a settlement, but a personal estate as well. Whether the estate and the site for the settlement would be coterminous was not entirely clear, probably because Selkirk himself did not know the answer to this question.

Burn recruited a dozen Irishmen, who embarked at Tobermory in the *Bess,* a ship chartered by Selkirk. As might have been expected, Selkirk's original plans were soon in ruins. The *Bess* proved unseaworthy, and Burn had second thoughts about leaving for America. He was under considerable pressure from a Miss Bacon—to whom he was "pledged"—to remain in Scotland. Burn finally agreed to go for one winter to "set things agoing." The delay forced Selkirk to revise his original scheme. Burn was sent directly from Liverpool to New York City without Irishmen or animals in order to take over a flock of sheep already collected by Richard Savage at White Creek, near Cambridge in upstate New York. Savage had been charged by Selkirk with buying 1000 ewes and wintering them in upstate New York. Burn departed on 2 October and arrived in New York City on 10 December. He was accompanied by Alexander ("Sandy") Brown, an experienced Scots shepherd, and his dogs. Brown had been hired by Selkirk as a man who would "answer better with a numerous flock than any American."[15] This assertion suggests that Selkirk did not think the Americans were very competent, at least not with sheep. The earl provided detailed breeding instructions for Burn and Brown. The two men reached White Creek on 24 December 1802 and wintered in the area. They as yet had no instructions from their employer about where the sheep were to go.[16] As for Selkirk, he as yet had no land upon which to put either animals or humans.

A VISIT WITH FATHER MACDONELL

Sometime in the late summer or early autumn of 1802, Selkirk called upon Father Alexander Macdonell, a Scottish Catholic priest who was in London attempting to find government support for the emigration of the Glengarry Fencible Regiment of which he had been chaplain. Macdonell had accompanied—indeed, led—his Highland flock from Glengarry to Glasgow in 1792 to work in the cotton mills, and when they had been formed into the First Glengarry Fencibles (a regiment he had helped to organize), he became their chaplain. The Glengarrys had fought in Ireland, mainly against Irish rebels who were also Catholic; the government was happy to have their Catholic presence to suppress the Irish because it was able to insist that putting down the Irish was not a religious but a political matter. With Ireland pacified, the regiment was now disbanded, and neither the laird of Glengarry who had raised it nor the cotton manufacturers who had once employed the men wanted to accommodate the ex-soldiers on sufficiently favourable terms. Macdonell thus sought government aid for their resettlement in British North America, preferably with their friends and relatives in Upper Canada.

The threat of emigration had some impact on the laird of Glengarry. In the autumn of 1801 he had his estate surveyed "with a view of ascertaining the real value of it, and thus from known date to be enabled to fix the reduced price at which it would be reasonable I should let it to my numerous Tenants and Dependents."[17] Then Glengarry offered his lands at ten percent less than he could get on the open market. To his surprise his tenants preferred to surrender their leases and continue their plans to emigrate to Canada. Glengarry subsequently offered life rent tenures and indemnities for all mutually agreeable improvements.[18] But Father Macdonell kept up the pressure. After corresponding at length with Prime Minister Henry Addington on the subject, the priest managed to obtain an interview with that worthy. Addington admitted that the loss of Highlanders to America was of great concern to his administration. He had been impressed with the campaign of the Highland Society of Edinburgh, backed by the great kelping lairds, against emigration. But he was prepared to provide government support for the removal of the Glengarrys to almost any place in the empire except Upper Canada, where the situation of the British was "so slender and so precarious, that a person in his situation would not be justified in putting his hands in the public purse to assist British subjects to emigrate to that Colony."[19]

Addington's reference to the British situation in Upper Canada was undoubtedly to the large numbers of Americans who had settled in the colony, both Loyalists and late Loyalists. Many officials in the colony were understandably concerned about what would happen should war break out again between the United States and Britain, as seemed likely throughout this period.[20] In this context sending a loyal Highland regiment to Upper Canada might have seemed a good idea, but instead the prime minister offered a very attractive arrangement if Macdonell would take his flock to Trinidad, promising free transport, eighty acres of land to every head of family, and cash to purchase four slaves. Father Macdonell refused this proposal on the grounds that the climate was unhealthy, and he also turned down suggestions of land in New Brunswick, Nova Scotia, and Cape Breton Island. Curiously enough, Prince Edward Island apparently never came up in these conversations. For reasons we shall see, Lord Hobart should have been more aware of Prince Edward Island than the remainder of the government. In any event, according to the priest, a number of Scots political figures met privately with him to dissuade the Glengarrys from emigrating, and the Prince of Wales even offered waste land in Cornwall to keep the Highlanders in the British Isles. With Major Archibald Campbell (later lieutenant governor of New Brunswick), Macdonell then proposed "a plan of organizing a military emigration, to be composed of the soldiers of the several Scotch Fencible Regiments just then disbanded, and sending them over to Upper Canada, for the double purpose of forming an internal defense, and settling the country."[21] This proposal would eventually feed into the government's efforts in 1803 to raise a regiment of Highlanders for Canadian service.[22] But for the moment Macdonell continued pressing for some aid to his beleaguered people.

At their meeting in London in 1802, Selkirk offered the priest a position as agent for a proposed colony at "those regions between Lakes Huron and Superior . . . where the climate was nearly similar to that of the north of Scotland, and the soil of a superior quality."[23] This was a perfectly correct statement of the location of the colony that Selkirk was promoting at the time, a matter of some importance since Macdonell's recollection of their conversation was written many years later when his memory might have been fuzzy. According to the clergyman, he refused, saying that private business would keep him in London. That business was probably a lawsuit he was engaged in against Macdonell of Glengarry that developed as a consequence of financial disputes.[24] Selkirk offered to indemnify Macdonell up to

£2000 for "leaving so suddenly," but the priest refused. Instead he asked the earl "what could induce a man of his high rank and great fortune, possessing the esteem and confidence of His Majesty's Government, and of every public man in Britain, to embark on an enterprise so romantic as that he had just explained?" Selkirk was taken aback by the question. He could hardly respond that he did not have quite the esteem and confidence the priest had suggested. He answered instead that given the situation of Britain and Europe, "a man would like to have a more solid footing to stand on, than anything that Europe could offer."[25] Selkirk was a very private man, and he was hardly likely to discuss his innermost thoughts with a man he had only just met. But his statement was likely at least partially true. North America provided an alternative, a way of forging a new career in the New World free from the encumbrances of family traditions and the past. In the context of 1802, a year that provided a breathing space in the unremitting wars between the French and the English, he may also have been thinking about an insurance policy in case the military conflict resumed and went badly. Whether the earl also recognized that Macdonell was suggesting that his rational Enlightenment upbringing was now being invaded by romantic dreams is another matter entirely.

ACQUIRING SETTLERS

Like Father Macdonell, Selkirk still had no lands. But just as he had begun acquiring sheep, so too he began acquiring settlers. As might have been expected, he found his major recruiting grounds in the Hebrides, particularly on the Macdonald and Clanranald estates of Skye, Mull, and Uist. Father Macdonell would have been an ideal agent for this activity. These islands had experienced a substantial growth of population as a result of the wartime boom in kelp. Payments for producing the kelp were small and the pressure on land was fierce. During the autumn of 1802 the most active emigration agents in the Hebrides were those employed by the Earl of Selkirk. The "Big Major," Alexander Macdonald of Keppoch, formerly of the Glengarry Fencibles—who had himself been "deprived of his Farm . . . for a shooting quarter"—was particularly successful among tenants from his former regiment (who were not at the time being successfully served by the efforts of Father Macdonell in London). Dr. Angus MacAulay, previously a Macdonald factor who was both preacher and physician, was also prominent in the campaign for emigrants. Like the Big Major, MacAulay had long been involved in regimental recruiting for his laird.[26]

In November of 1802 the earl himself took a hand in recruiting "in and through the Estates, where discontent was prevalent, where new setts [leases] approached, or where persons were desirous to emigrate, or necessitated to do so."[27] The principal targets were the estates of Lord Macdonald and Clanranald. He made a handsome figure. Tall—he stood well over six feet— and slender, with carroty red hair, Selkirk looked every inch a laird himself, and astounded the local people by conversing with them in serviceable Gaelic. It was difficult to persuade Highlanders to agree to emigrate to a location in British America as isolated as the Falls of St. Mary. According to one hostile contemporary, "his Lordship was most accessible, and affable, and even familiar; and promised everything; offering to gratify any demand or wish they could frame." His proposals were admittedly "tempting, in the present State of this Country and Temper of the People."[28] Anxious to get his project under way, Selkirk did agree to whatever terms were asked of him, thus increasing the suspicion of both the landlords and the prospective emigrants. Despite his visit to the Hebrides, Selkirk did most of his work in Glasgow, where one of his critics observed him holding "his Levee at the Bucks Head Inn."[29] Claiming that Angus MacAulay owed him money, that same critic—one of the kelping proprietors—wrote his factor to "gett a warrant of Search & deprive him of Ld Selkirk's Money & then Lodge him in Inverness," presumably in the gaol. MacAulay evaded his would-be captors. Other recruiters were less fortunate. The authorities complained that the "recruiting sergeants for emigration" succeeded in attracting "a crowd by using the bagpipe and a flag," distributing "vast quantities of spirits," and reading what the ruling classes were always certain were forged letters from America telling of prosperity and success.[30]

According to the final written agreement, at least as reported by Edward Fraser of Reelig, Selkirk offered inexpensive transportation to his settlement in Upper Canada, full provisioning while in transit, and promised either to sell land at fifty cents an acre or to lease 100 acres perpetually in return for a rent of twenty-four bushels of wheat annually.[31] This arrangement was backed by a £1000 fulfilment bond by Selkirk. For prospective tenants who could not afford to pay for passage or land, he reduced transportation costs drastically, agreed to provision them at cost (without cartage fees) for two years or until they could harvest first crops, and threw in a cow per family. The earl even provided a money-back guarantee (including payment for all improvements and transportation home) if the immigrant was not completely satisfied. How he expected to deliver on any of these promises at isolated St. Mary's, hundreds of miles from any overland transportation, remains a mystery. It is possible that Fraser, who was of course extremely hostile to Selkirk, had gotten the agreement wrong. But it was certainly the case that Angus MacAulay would always subsequently maintain that his honour as well as his employer's was pledged to something resembling these commitments, which in the end were not honoured. The way in which MacAulay stated the matter certainly suggests that only honour rather than legal contract was at stake. No copy of the terms offered by Selkirk to potential immigrants in 1802 survives in the Selkirk Papers, so we can never be certain of what was offered. But in addition to the MacAulay testimony there is also some considerable circumstantial evidence that Selkirk had overreached himself.

Certainly a good deal of sales resistance developed to Selkirk's proposals among shrewd Highlanders. The deal was apparently too good to be true. Despite all the inducements, or perhaps because of them, Selkirk was forced to ask Dr. William Porter of the British Fisheries Board to endorse his scheme.[32] By the end of November 1802, however, Selkirk was able to report to Lord Hobart at the Colonial Office that he had signed up 100 families, on condition he accompany them "to see that their stipulations are fulfilled." Most of these families were self-financing, members of the more prosperous possessor class in the Highlands whose movements characterized most emigration in this period. Despite the quality of his people, Selkirk was understandably having second thoughts about the costs of his project, further evidence of his generous promises. He informed the colonial secretary that the expense of his commitment was well beyond his personal fortune; he was therefore pausing until the government informed him what it would do to alleviate his burden or what indemnification he could expect if he undertook it himself.[33] Regardless of the evidence of Edward Fraser and Angus MacAulay, there must have been some escape clause in the agreements.

THE DEATH OF LADY SELKIRK

The pause Selkirk announced to the Colonial Office was probably partly caused by family matters. Early in December Selkirk received word in Edinburgh of the death of his mother in Bath, and so he rushed off for that town to join his sisters, who had accompanied Lady Selkirk there.[34] No evidence exists to suggest that Selkirk was particularly close to his mother, and no comments survive regarding his reaction to her death. He may have mourned her passing, but her death also terminated one more tie to the family estate in Kirkcudbright and to Scotland. In the inevitable family gathering surrounding the death of Lady Helen, the question of the Baldoon estate arose again. The arbitration for the value of the improvements remained unsettled. According to Selkirk's sister, "Lord Galloway & the Law people employed by him (some of them of no very creditable characters) were so difficult to deal with, & did so harass my brother, that he became quite disgusted with the entire matter."[35] The whole family realized that the earl's "mind was wholly engrossed with his project concerning Highland emigration." They feared that he would accept any offer of payment made to him. Sir James Hall continued to insist that the improvements were worth £100,000 rather than the £60,000 Selkirk calculated, and wanted his brother-in-law to pursue the matter vigorously. The earl at first responded "jestingly" that Hall "take it, & make a Kirk & a Mill of it," but later seriously offered to allow Sir James the management of the negotiations while he was away in America. Hall eventually agreed, providing he was given sufficient authority to act independently.[36] The written agreement specified that Selkirk would receive £20,000 of the proceeds, and the remainder would be equally divided amongst his sisters.[37] It was formally registered on 1 February 1803.[38]

PUBLIC HOSTILITY IN SCOTLAND TO EMIGRATION

At the end of 1802, the gathering storm in Scotland over emigration broke forth in full fury. Symptomatic of the furor was the publication in September of 1802 of Alexander Irvine's *An Enquiry into the Causes and Effects of Emigration from the Highlands and Western Islands of Scotland, with Observations on the Means to be Employed for Preventing It*. It would be this book, more than any other, that Selkirk would answer in his own work on emigration in 1805. Irvine was a Church of Scotland missionary in the North who was sensitive to the thinking of the ruling classes. He offered a full-scale defence of the Highland lairds. As "Anti-Plagiarus" would write in the *Farmer's Magazine* a few months later, "The poor and oppressed have no biographers."[39] Irvine rejected the thought that emigration arose from "the oppression, exactions, or harsh treatment of Superiors," defying any reader to point out an action "capable of driving any innocent person from his country." Noting the interest of the northern landlords for Highland development, he asked rhetorically: "Can we harbour the thought, that men, who are capable of such patriotic exertions, should act so inconsistently, as the charge of oppression would lead us to believe? Would they drive from the country those very people whose interests they study to promote?" Criticism, wrote Irvine, came from those who had left discontented or from those who did not understand the Highlands. In the latter category, Irvine placed most foreign, especially English, travellers.

Progress, particularly agricultural improvement, Irvine admitted, could produce emigration. But "to keep pace with the progress of improvement in the south," he insisted, "many sacrifices must be made, and many schemes must be devised, which require all the invention of ingenuity, and all the economy of prudence." Among the sacrifices was the necessity "to deprive some persons of their possessions, to make room for others more industrious or more fortunate." According to the missionary author, the landlord only "removes the lazy and the indolent, to encourage the active and the industrious." When the laird did enlarge his farms to admit a "person of more understanding and more efficient capital [i.e., a sheepfarmer]", he usually provided for those dispossessed by offering them a small croft. "But pride and irritation scorn to accept his provision. Emigration is then the only remedy." Irvine was prepared to admit that some improvers moved too quickly, adding "men have pushed forward with all the precipitation of fresh conviction, with all the bigotry of modern wisdom, and with all the intolerances of ancient usages, till they armed the passions and prejudices of the people against them, rendered themselves unpopular, their measures abortive, and thinn'd the country of its most useful inhabitants." But the reader got the clear sense that sweeping away "custom endeared by a thousand ties, and sanctioned by a thousand years" was impolitic rather than immoral.

The missionary was prepared to allow that uncertainty of tenure was a problem. But he insisted that people "who are dissatisfied, either with the civil or religious establishments of one country, commonly fly to another, in order to remedy an evil which originates more in the constitution of their own nature than in political circumstances, and which a change of place is seldom able to eradicate." The discontent of emigrating Highlanders, in short, sprang "from the perturbations of their own mind" rather than from genuine difficulties. The prospective emigrant deceived himself into thinking that "if he could get once abroad, he would have all his wants supplied, and wishes gratified in a moment," and he naturally turned against his native land. Avarice and the desire for prosperity (which Irvine conceded the average emigrant saw "but a very small prospect of acquiring . . . at home") pressed him on.[40]

Like most of the ruling classes, Irvine became truly virulent when he turned to the "interested persons, who promote the ferment of the people, and go about recruiting for the plantations with the usual eloquence of crimps." Military recruiters could be tolerated, but those signing up civilian emigrants were not acceptable. Not since the 1770s had such a concerted attack been mounted against the promoters of emigration, who

> generally gain belief from the character they assume, their subject, and the dispositions of those whom they address. Their mountebank elocution is wonderfully popular, because suited to every capacity. Their exaggerations and fictions work like talisman's wand, or an electric shock. The poor and illiterate portion of the community have taken it for granted, that all foreign countries are different from their own.

Poor Highlanders might at least have hoped that other countries were different. Most recruiters, argued Irvine, had vacant American lands that they tried to get cultivated by any means possible, especially by taking advantage of gullible common folk, who listened because of a predisposition to delusion. Although Lord Selkirk was never mentioned by name, all of Scotland seems to have understood that he was the biggest promoter of all, using—as Edward Fraser of Reelig angrily complained—money from the sale of good Scots soil" (Baldoon) to finance his activities.[41]

As was so often the case with such rumours, Selkirk's situation was much misunderstood. It may have been true that he hoped to use the Baldoon money for his American ventures, but he had not yet received any payment for the Baldoon improvements, and certainly would not realize a windfall of £60,000, the figure commonly circulated about the Scottish countryside. Selkirk was simply not as well financed as his opponents believed. Not that it mattered. Whatever the truth, the force of public opinion (within the ranks of the "public" that mattered in Britain at the time, those represented in Parliament) made it quite impossible for Lord Hobart to continue his quiet support for Selkirk. The colonial secretary withdrew his offer of lands in Upper Canada.[42] Criticism of Selkirk's recruiting operations continued unabated, only increasing in volume when his name later became associated with emigration among extremist Protestant sectarians in Stratherrick.[43]

Early in 1803, one James Stewart, formerly of the Fraser Fencibles, had written to Selkirk enquiring about a position as North American agent for the earl. Selkirk replied he had no situation available, but he encouraged Stewart to recruit emigrants on his own behalf.[44] By January of 1804 Stewart—with the assistance of his brother-in-law, the schoolmaster at Blair— was advertising for emigrants on the Perthshire estates of the Duke of Athol, claiming his project was to be done under the direction of Lord Selkirk. Stewart was unable to produce any authority for these statements. Over forty signatures of men with families had been obtained by Stewart to a contract for passage, chiefly among those attracted to the revivalistic preaching of a breakaway Presbyterian sect called the "Haldanites." Led by Robert and James Haldane, this movement emphasized the necessity of a personal knowledge and experience of grace, maintained the absolute authority and Divine inspiration of the Bible, and sought a return to traditional Calvinistic doctrine. Perthshire Deputy Lieutenant William Robertson complained to the Duke of Athol and to the lord advocate about the usual "seditious" talk of better times in America and advertisements offering to bring the people from "Poverty and meanness." Robertson was upset that people should think of leaving Scotland when their country most needed them, particularly since all those involved were fully employed or in possession of land. In the Highlands, Robertson observed, "both agriculture & store farming have undergone a rapid change from what accords with the prejudices and circumstances of the people in general. They will readily abandon the scene entirely, than be forced from idleness to labor, or to an alteration of their habits & opinions in the management of their stock."[45]

Robertson's views were fully consonant with the arguments advanced by Alexander Irvine in 1802. Like most ruling-class commentators on emigration at the time, Irvine was certain that neither the unskilled nor the very poor ventured abroad, which only made the loss more dangerous and the development of means to arrest it more pressing. Like most of his contemporaries, he placed his reliance upon the creation of new employment opportunities: "in vain you offer any terms, if the people see no prospect of a competent livelihood." To improvers, the missionary recommended slow change and the offer of small holdings to displaced tenants. He admitted many would spurn the descent from tenant to crofter, but "if a man of this kind . . . refuses any rational accommodation, the country is better without him; he is ripe for emigration. He may be cured by changing his residence. His spirit is not sound." Irvine never explained why the "unsound" could not be allowed to depart unimpeded. When emigration sprang from discontent, he proclaimed, little could be done. But when it came from the instigation of others, "there is a law against kidnapping, or manstealing: and what is instigation, but a species of kidnapping?" Worse still, emigration promoters—Selkirk still never mentioned by name—were responsible for "leading the poor people on to ruin, disturbing their enjoyments, rendering them ripe for a revolt, deluding them by false hopes, and of course inspiring them with discontents of the most dangerous tendency." Alexander Irvine stated the overall critique of emigration by the Scottish ruling classes with considerable cogency. Only the newly founded *Edinburgh Review*, a radical Whig journal, was critical, calling the book a "tedious volume of eloquence." The reviewer thought the subject of emigration important. He summarized it but made no other comment beyond promising some general remarks on the subject if the occasion presented itself "in a more manageable form."[46] The Earl of Selkirk had hardly improved his family's radical image by becoming involved in the emigration business.

If Selkirk had intended to induce the government to acquiesce in his excessive promises in the Highlands, he was sadly mistaken. Instead, the public furore left him with an agreement with emigrants and no lands upon which to fulfill it, as well as with a large flock of breeding sheep wintering on the New York frontier. The earl wrote to Prime Minister Addington and managed an interview with that worthy. He was told in no uncertain terms that his "Interference in the Emigration has given umbrage." To avoid the criticisms, he again offered to return to Red River, this time converting his Highlanders into a regiment for military service there.[47] Quite apart from the impracticality of thinking that men recruited as emigrants could be turned instantly into soldiers, there was considerable military resistance to the concept of a Highland regiment for North American service, as the subsequent history of the "Canadian Regiment" in 1804 and the fate of Selkirk's proposals of 1812 would demonstrate. Furious activity on Selkirk's part in early 1803 led Lord Hobart to allow that the government might be persuaded to look favourably on a settlement that would be located on Prince Edward Island, where lands could be obtained cheaply from private proprietors without involving the ministry in an unpopular project. Hobart's encouraging attitude came because in early 1803 he was as colonial secretary in the middle of a full-scale attempt to resolve the complex problem of landholding on that colony in the Gulf of St. Lawrence, and a settlement led by Selkirk appeared to be part of the answer to the government's needs. In some ways, the shift to Prince Edward Island merely meant jumping from the frying pan into the fire, but Selkirk was fairly desperate and he leapt with alacrity into the tiny opening offered him by Lord Hobart.

CHAPTER SIX

Selkirk and the Island

A S LORD SELKIRK SEARCHED desperately in the spring of 1803 for a North American destination for his settlement, Colonial Office reform of the land system on the former Island of St. John, renamed Prince Edward Island in 1798 in honour of one of the sons of King George III, was in mid-stream. Virtually the entire land surface of the island had been granted—by lottery—to private proprietors in 1767, in return for their assumption of responsibility for its settlement and development, as well as the cost of its administration. Divided into sixty-seven lots of roughly 20,000 acres each by surveyor Samuel Holland in 1764–65 (lot sixty-six of 6000 acres was reserved to the Crown), the island's land was almost completely given away in advance of the establishment of any formal government, a relatively uncommon practice in British colonial history. In marked contrast to Nova Scotia, which had cost the Crown over £600,000 to establish, the island was intended to be completely self-financing from the outset. The private proprietors were to meet two conditions in order to maintain their grants: they were to improve and populate their lots with substantial numbers of foreign-born Protestants or settlers already resident in North America—one person for every 200 acres—and they were to pay a sizeable annual quitrent ranging from six shillings per hundred acres for good lots to two shillings per hundred acres for poor ones. The obvious expectation was that the profits of settlement would provide the proprietors with revenue to pay the quit-rents. While it was not specified in the grants, the general strategy was that the money would come from rental of lands to tenant settlers. Originally

attached administratively to Nova Scotia, the island was permitted a separate government in 1769 on the understanding that the costs of administration would be born entirely by the proprietors, most of whom had signed a
pledge to meet this obligation.[1]

None of these intentions, commitments, and promises had ever been
fulfilled. The proprietors did not produce the requisite number of settlers;
most of those who came originated in the British Isles, and many lots remained
almost totally uninhabited until well into the nineteenth century. Quitrents to
the Crown soon fell badly in arrears, and the cost of governing the island had
to be assumed by the Crown during the War of the American Rebellion. From
the beginning of actual settlement, criticism of the proprietors and the system
of landholding was endemic, and the Land Question—as it was soon called—
became a central component of intense island political and social conflict. The
peace did make possible some efforts by the Colonial Office to deal with the
accumulation of problems on Prince Edward Island. Receiver General of
Quitrents John Stewart sailed to London and on 4 April 1802 submitted to
the British government a plan for bringing quitrent arrearages up to date.[2]
This would raise substantial revenue for paying the officers of the island and
might force more proprietors to become active because they could no longer
hold on to their lands without any expense. Noting that current quitrent
arrearages stood at £59,162.17, Stewart proposed to reduce them to £18,732
by dividing the townships into five classes based on numbers of settlers.
Classes four and five, on which little settlement had occurred constituted
nearly half the land of the colony. This plan offered "ample indulgence to the
whole Body of Proprietors." Its adoption required orders to the receiver
general of quitrents, "who is fortunately upon the spot" in England—where
most of the proprietors resided—and instructions to the island's governor
regarding proportions and terms of grants to be subsequently made. A separate memorandum of "Observations" on the plan emphasized that it would
generate revenue for the island and "throw nearly half of the lands into the
hands of Government."[3]

THE COLONIAL OFFICE REFORM
OF PRINCE EDWARD ISLAND

The Lords of the Committee of Council for Trade and Foreign Plantations
considered the affairs of Prince Edward Island at their meeting of 6 April
1802.[4] They agreed that it would be "inexpedient, and, in some cases,

perhaps unjust, to endeavour now to exact the full Payment" of quitrent arrearages. The Lords instead recommended a "judicious Abatement," and within a few days they had before them a plan virtually identical to that proposed by John Stewart on 4 April. Colonial Secretary Lord Hobart himself proposed a time frame, which required the payment of reduced arrearages within one month of notice for those who held fully or partially settled lots, and gave slightly more time for those with unsettled lots, who would have to pay more. It is not clear whether Hobart thought the serious proprietors could easily find the money, or whether he hoped that the need to pay almost immediately would force many proprietors to put their Island lands on the market, where they could be bought up at low prices by individuals, like the Earl of Selkirk, eager to obtain colonial land. The entire proposal, while superficially plausible, was full of potential inequities. The most obvious was its failure to take into account the plight of the few resident proprietors who had actually invested in the island and had brought settlers. Most of these people lacked capital with which to pay the composed arrearages. These proprietors, including Captain John MacDonald, John Hill, and William Bowley—and later a handful of others—were soon petitioning Hobart for exemptions. MacDonald insisted that the composition scheme rewarded the "least meritorious" and John Hill insisted that there was no circulating medium on the island out of which back quitrents were to be paid.[5] Hobart was not initially sympathetic to such pleas and arguments. A decision had been made and he wanted it executed. To some extent Hobart may have wanted to act quickly before the island's proprietors could organize an opposition based on the usual cry of the "rights of property." There is no evidence, however, that the proprietors ever mounted any coordinated opposition to this particular quitrent composition.

Over the next few months, Lieutenant Governor Edmund Fanning, responding to orders from Lord Hobart at the Colonial Office, assented to two closely related pieces of legislation. One of the acts actually set up a court of escheat. Both pieces of legislation were technically deficient, and both had been passed on the basis of hasty decisions by the British government that Lord Hobart's administration was already probably coming to regret. The British decision to settle the quitrent arrearages and to establish a court of escheat ought to have gone a long way toward resolving the island's Land Question, however. It did not. Instead, the deficiencies of the legislation meant that it was never really applied on the island itself. On the other hand, what the government's quitrent composition for Prince Edward Island did achieve was to frighten a number of proprietors and throw a number of lots on the open market at a reasonable price. In the spring of 1803, hunting desperately for inexpensive land in North America on which to settle Highlanders with whom he had contracted, Lord Selkirk managed to obtain privately lots thirty-one, fifty-seven, fifty-eight, sixty, sixty-two, and fifty-three, roughly one-tenth of the total land surface of the island. With his later acquisitions, Selkirk would ultimately hold about 140,000 acres, one-seventh of the island. Most of the property, which was virtually unsettled and thus potentially subject to substantial quitrent arrearages, was purchased from the Ellice interests who later would oppose Selkirk in Red River.[6] According to proprietor John Cambridge, Selkirk was pleased with his purchases, but refused to buy from Cambridge, whose prices were too high; "he purchas'd his Townships at a very Low Price, " Cambridge reported.[7] No evidence exists that Selkirk had any other interest in Prince Edward Island beyond the availability of the land at bargain prices.

LORD SELKIRK'S PERSONALITY

Not until the winter of 1802 and the recruitment of Highlanders for resettlement in North America did Lord Selkirk embark upon a sufficiently major undertaking in which his dominant personality traits would be clearly in evidence. There were perhaps signs of these characteristics earlier in his career, and the biographer might mark them. But they were, before 1803, to a considerable extent masked by circumstances, and could as well be regarded as evidence of an immaturity out of which he might well grow. He did not outgrow them, however, and the ones exhibited in the North American ventures of 1803 and 1804 were certainly the traits that dominated the remainder of his life. Any appreciation of Selkirk's personality must begin with his restlessness and impetuosity. Despite continual frail health (an obvious family trait, at least among Douglas males), Selkirk was always a bundle of extraordinary nervous energy, usually kept under control by sheer willpower and the conventions of the age. The outward air of reserve with which he faced the world merely served as a front for a man who could never sit still, who revelled in action and in the projecting of new schemes. The adult Selkirk was not a sober and rational man of the Enlightenment, but rather an impetuous dreamer who well belonged to the Age of Romanticism, as Bishop Alexander Macdonnell had suggested. His energy was apparent even as he lay dying of consumption. His attendant physician, who had lived eight months with him, observed that there was something "restless about him, an agitation of mind, evinced by his bodily movements; and a certain decision in his tone, which, perhaps, bordered upon obstinacy. His was a mind which could not remain a moment unoccupied. There was no approach to a state of rest."[8] Selkirk's actions and dealings with people throughout his life demonstrate that Dr William Lefevre was here describing the man, and not the disease, although in some senses the man may well have been the disease. The personality traits of Selkirk described overlap with one of the recognized pathologies of consumption, which Selkirk may have contracted early in life and suffered from intermittently throughout his adult career.[9]

Selkirk's restlessness meant that he could not easily settle down in one place to lead a conventional life supervising a single project or set of projects. Constantly and conspicuously absent from the sites of his various ventures, he would thus become almost totally dependent upon hired agents. Unfortunately, the earl had either bad luck or bad judgment in choosing his agents, probably a combination of both. He tended to be charmed by the promises of men who were appropriately deferential to his schemes, forgetting that when he was no longer around to supervise them they might well have ideas of their own. He understandably did not have much confidence in men who told him the unvarnished truth about the unlikelihood of success of some of his wilder schemes. He could be persuaded to change his agents—or at least the tasks expected of his agents and their position in the overall command structure—if a more persuasive individual were to come along. Selkirk's relationship with one of his first colonial agents, Angus MacAulay, was symptomatic in this regard. He became increasingly less enamoured of MacAulay as agent when the Highlander made clear that Selkirk was not keeping his promises to his emigrants, and he would rapidly shed MacAaulay as a major employee once the settlers were landed on Prince Edward Island.

Moreover, Selkirk could not rest content with simply putting his affairs in the hands of agents; he felt compelled to write them constantly, exploring at great length all the dimensions of the underling's instructions, considering first this option and then that one. Much of the difficulty the earl had with his distant agents, who never seemed quite to get things right, undoubtedly resulted from a congenital inability to leave well enough alone. Furthermore, he never understand that most of the men he employed in North

America—who were not family retainers with lifelong loyalties to him—were merely temporary employees whose fidelity went no deeper than the financial contract between them. Selkirk paid well, but he expected too much from those he hired. He was quite capable of eliciting considerable loyalty from some of his agents through the force of his personality, but almost all of them sooner or later let him down. To make matters even worse, Selkirk constantly thought on his feet, making up plans as he went along. Upon meeting with the Marchioness of Stafford in 1813 to discuss emigration plans for Red River, for example, he obviously distressed the lady by improvising new schemes on the spot. When she raised practical objections to his initial well-considered proposals, he offered an alternative, she reported, "from an idea which he said had at that moment occurred to him on reading a letter I showed him."[10] Throughout his life, Selkirk committed himself to ventures before he had carefully thought them out.

Selkirk's impetuous flexibility was tempered—or perhaps in some ways rendered worse—by the obstinacy that Dr. William Lefevre noted in 1819. Once an idea had taken hold of him, he was unable to let it go completely. He was prepared to drop a scheme temporarily or to alter it instantly to suit immediate conditions, but earlier abandoned projects kept re-emerging under new guises. He first had the notion of resettling poor Celtic peasants in America in the 1790s, and it never left him. Frustrated in taking Irishmen to Red River in 1802, he picked the scheme up again in 1808; he had first suggested recruiting a Highland regiment for service in Red River in 1803, although he did not actively attempt to implement the plan until 1813; the Highland regiment reappeared as the private army of De Meurons in 1816. What seemed like a sudden whim was often merely the reappearance of an old idea. So a certain consistency, a sense of obstinate purpose, did reside in many of Selkirk's schemes, but he never recognized that those not privy to his innermost thoughts were incapable of appreciating the fact. A very private man, he seldom took others into his confidence, and soon developed an understandable reputation for instability. His noble relations in Scotland called him "cousin Whistle-about."[11]

SELKIRK'S INTRODUCTION TO THE ISLAND

Much of Selkirk's information about Prince Edward Island and its potential came from receiver of quitrents John Stewart, the Scots-born son of the former chief justice and the architect of the Quitrent Composition of

1802.[12] Stewart wanted to get somebody to inject new money into Prince Edward Island and rejuvenate the property market. Some idea of what Stewart undoubtedly told Selkirk can be gleaned from Stewart's book, *An Account of Prince Edward Island, in the Gulph of St. Lawrence, North America*, published in 1806. Stewart wrote that the island had enormous agricultural potential. The winters were moderate, and there was no sickness lingering about the place. He did not make much of the fact that the island was quite literally covered with snow and cut off from the remainder of the world for six months every year by sea ice. Like most colonial promoters, Stewart exaggerated the similarity of the climate of the island and that of the Highlands. The truth was that the island winter was both longer and harsher, sufficiently so as to freeze the waters of the Strait of Northumberland to the south of the Island and the Gulf of St. Lawrence to its north. As for the agricultural potential, it was certainly there, but only after the trees had been cleared from the land. Selkirk got a somewhat misleading picture from Stewart. Although in 1806 Selkirk's sister married the other major Scottish proprietor on the Island, Sir James Montgomery of Stanhope, the two men were not acquainted in 1803. They apparently met first in 1805, after the earl's return from North America, when they discovered they had common interests.

From the British government's perspective, deflecting Selkirk's enthusiasm to Prince Edward Island was a positive boon. The island had not flourished and an infusion of new blood was obviously desirable. Government support for Selkirk's island activities could be defended as part of a necessary rescue operation. Thus both Lord Hobart and Selkirk were bailed out by the earl's land acquisitions on Prince Edward Island, which had long been a favourite destination for emigrating Highlanders.[13] Major parties had been sent by Lord Advocate James Montgomery and by John MacDonald of Glenaladale before the American Rebellion, and at least two shiploads of passengers from the Hebrides had arrived on the island in 1790.[14] Over the years, other Highlanders had reached the island singly or in small parties. Thirty years of Highlander experience with the island was a bit of a mixed blessing. On the one hand, it meant that many of Selkirk's potential settlers had relations or friends already in residence. On the other hand, the island had a bit of an unsavoury reputation in the northern islands. Captain John MacDonald's settlers from Uist were still in 1803 without proper leases, and at the beginning of the year the opponents of emigration in the Hebrides were industriously circulating a letter from Charlottetown which began: "This is to let you know that I am sorry for coming here and I dont like it at all and I wish you would do for me to get home again because I wont stay here." The writer, one Donald Steel, complained of the unsettled climate and the lack of employment, requesting his former laird to write his brother "to tell my friends at Uist that they wont do as I did if they can."[15] That this letter was probably at least partly contrived by the Scottish opponents of emigration made its impact no less around the firesides of Uist. The publicity given this epistle was part of a more general campaign to discourage North American emigration, but it had particular relevance at the moment Selkirk acquired his land there.

In a larger sense, the shift to Prince Edward Island forced upon Selkirk clearly worked to his advantage. The Prince Edward Island settlement was the only one of Selkirk's colonial schemes that ever flirted with success, and it probably would have worked even better had Selkirk spent more time on the island cultivating his estates. Selkirk's presence at the beginning enabled him to personally resolve many problems that his agents in other venues could not do. But the earl spent little of his North American time on the island, and other factors were more important in his settlement taking hold. In the first place, compared with Baldoon and Red River, the duration of time at sea was weeks shorter, and even more importantly, the emigrants had no long over-land journey upon disembarkation. The passengers on Selkirk's ships approaching the island could literally see their lands from shipboard. In the second, despite his medical officers, Selkirk's vessels did experience a typhus outbreak, and while shipboard medical care probably had little effect on its incidence, the shortness of passage and the proximity of the land certainly did. The passengers managed to get out of crowded conditions before the disease reached epidemic proportions; the Kildonan settlers for Red River would not be so fortunate. Third, the island was a healthy place, as John Stewart had asserted. Baldoon would be planted in a malarial swamp, but Belfast did not have to face contagious disease. Fourth, the new settlers found many relations and friends already on the island to help them feel at home, and other conditions were favourable as well. Provisions could be obtained in the region with little difficulty, and once the trees were removed, the soil was fertile and easy to work, ideally suited to the cultivation of potatoes familiar to the newcomers. Fifth, Selkirk's settlers of 1803 were for the most part rela-tively well-off Highlanders who brought some capital with them, rather than

becoming almost instant objects of charity on the island. Last, Selkirk's settlement on the island was not complicated by the considerations of large imperial, commercial, or even utopian strategy that so confused his later operations.
As a result of the Prince Edward Island success, Selkirk thought he had learned
something for the future, and he justified his venture after the fact by arguing
that Highlanders were entitled to preserve their traditional way of life, a sort
of utopian outcome. But at the time of its creation, the Prince Edward Island
settlement was simply one of agrarian transplantation, due to circumstances
beyond Selkirk's control—for he kept trying to achieve something more
significant—uncontaminated by larger objectives and issues.

Once he had obtained some land, Selkirk faced the critical problem of
persuading those who had already signed up for Upper Canada to shift with
him to Prince Edward Island under quite different terms, and of recruiting
additional new emigrants to fill up the three ships he had already chartered
for the spring of 1803. Given the general reputation of the island in the
Hebrides, these objectives were not necessarily easy to meet. The Upper
Canadian people were not at all enthusiastic about a new agreement, and
some of those involved apparently took Selkirk to court for breach of
contract.[16] These may well have been the people that Selkirk later moved to
St. Mary's Isle and sent to Upper Canada aboard the *Oughton* in 1804. The
alteration of the conditions originally proposed by the earl was a long-
standing grievance, even among those who eventually sailed with Selkirk to
the island. It was certainly kept alive by Angus MacAulay.

THE PASSENGER VESSEL ACT OF 1803

In the spring of 1803 Selkirk caught another break that would make his
Prince Edward Island venture possible. At this point the British Parliament
saved him by its hasty passage of the Passenger Vessel Act of 1803. The government needed a short-term brake on emigration while the various schemes
of internal improvement were put into operation, thus providing immediate
employment for redundant Highlanders and creating the basis of a new
Highland prosperity. It found this brake in the concern expressed in various
quarters for the health and welfare of the poor emigrants, crammed into
ships chartered by unscrupulous promoters like so many heads of cattle, or
like so many slaves.[17] The result was the passage in 1803 of legislation regulating the emigrant trade, sometimes seen as the beginning of a new ruling-
class attitude toward the welfare of the poor.[18] The act, ostensibly a piece of

humane legislation designed to protect emigrants from exploitation, had strange inconsistencies, as Selkirk later noted in his book *Observations on the Present State of the Highlands*.[19] But despite Selkirk's later exposure of the selfish motives for the passage of the act, it was a godsend in disguise. Scheduled to take effect on 1 July 1803, the act would instantly triple or quadruple the cost of passage to America, and thus drove most emigrant promoters out of business virtually overnight. Many in the Hebrides had already failed to renew their tenancies and had even sold their property in anticipation of moving to America in 1803. Those who had previously signed up with Selkirk had hoped to make alternative arrangements if he could not meet their terms.[20]

Suddenly the earl was left as the only emigration promoter in town. His project would survive the stringencies of the new legislation because Selkirk was not trying to make money so much as to accomplish other goals. Moreover, his ships were exempted by Order in Council from the new passenger regulations; Lord Hobart wanted new settlement to succeed. Both old recruits and new ones flocked to his banner. Selkirk himself assiduously circulated rumours that emigrant ships destined for the United States would not be allowed to clear customs. The resultant three ships—the *Polly*, the *Dykes*, and the *Oughton* were full with over 800 passengers mainly from Skye, with others from Ross-shire, northern Argyle-shire, parts of Inverness-shire, and the island of Uist. A blacksmith had been recruited at the last minute, and the passengers included a number of former schoolteachers and at least one Gaelic bard.[21] Presumably there was also a piper, although he was never mentioned by name. As the new parliamentary legislation required, there was a medical officer on each of the vessels. Except for Angus MacAulay, who was acting as one of Selkirk's agents, no clergyman was part of the emigrant party. This *lacuna* was not unusual but, rather, typical of Selkirk's settlements. He obviously did not regard clerics as terribly important, probably reflecting his own lack of interest in organized religion.

Selkirk himself was accompanied by a manservant and valet named Jilks, who got only one brief mention in the earl's diary and was one of those invisible but ubiquitous servants so common at the time. The earl even acquired fifty impoverished families from Uist at the last minute who helped fill the last ship. Selkirk carefully met all the conditions of the legislation, convinced that it was directed against him personally. But without the legislation, he would not have succeeded in obtaining anywhere near the number of substantial emigrants he transported in 1803. Those emigrants had deposited at least £4163.7.3 in cash with Selkirk's agent at Portree, and probably more at other ports of loading.[22] Moreover, the government did in the end manage to assist him in a positive way, by cutting red tape and making it possible for him to sail in advance of harassment under the act and ahead of the burgeoning military recruiting in the Highlands connected with the resumption of the war with Napoleon.[23] There were obviously some advantages to the informal deal Selkirk had made with Lord Hobart and the Colonial Office.

SELKIRK ON PRINCE EDWARD ISLAND, 1803

What survives of Selkirk's own account in diary form of his venture begins on 3 August 1803, while his vessel the *Dykes* was still at sea.[24] The first landfall was made on 8 August on the south side of the island near Belfast. Selkirk was not much impressed with the quality of the soil here, and his vessel moved on to Hillsborough Bay and Charlottetown, where he called on Lieutenant Governor Edmund Fanning and met up with another one of his ships, the *Polly*, with a party of emigrants headed by Dr. Angus MacAulay. It was MacAulay who had to deal with the "disadvantageous stories of the country" that Selkirk's settlers had already begun hearing. According to Selkirk, who probably got his information from John Stewart's brother Charles, the stories were circulated by "people who have set themselves down on the lands under the idea that they would revert to the Crown, & then they would have a claim of preference by their occupancy:—these are now sour at finding themselves turned out."[25] There was also some grumbling from those on neighbouring lots who collected hay on Selkirk's lands. This was probably Selkirk's first introduction to the popular discontent against the landed proprietors that had been seething for years on the island. His informant, Charles Stewart, was arguably the principal "man of business" on the island at the time. By 1803 Stewart, a younger son of the former chief justice, had obtained a large number of minor offices, including acting clerk of the Council, coroner of the Crown, clerk of the errors, registrar at Chancery, receiver of inland duties, and assistant acting engineer. According to one hostile observer, Stewart "had a share" in "all the disputes in the island," generally as "the Governor's Agent and Messenger, when any particular plan was to be set on foot, in which the Governor did not care to appear himself."[26] Astounded by the high price of provisions, Selkirk determined to import his grain from New York. Nevertheless, he was forced to buy some grain locally, paying cash for whatever his agents could find.[27]

Anxious to get out among the settlers, Selkirk found himself delayed in Charlottetown by the importunities and hospitality of Lieutenant Governor Fanning, who invited Chief Justice Robert Thorpe to dinner and to remain for the night. Selkirk was impressed with neither official. A Loyalist officer during the War of the Rebellion, Fanning had been in charge of the island since 1786 and had managed to remain in office despite several efforts to remove him. By 1803 he may well have been experiencing a loss of mental sharpness, as his actions during the quitrent business described earlier in this chapter suggest. Thorpe had only recently arrived on the island, and would soon leave it for Upper Canada to cause much trouble there. The next day, most of the officers of the government and principal inhabitants of Charlottetown managed to call on the governor and his guest. The list of guests given by Selkirk in his diary indicates that virtually all the colony's elite were in attendance. After all, it was not often that a member of the British aristocracy visited the island, much less one who was investing substantial sums of money in it. He also gathered that one of the reasons for the popular dislike of the proprietors was their refusal to sell small holdings to settlers; "they are all anxious to let, & keep up the impracticable idea of getting a Tenantry like that of Europe," Selkirk noted.[28] Old settlers opposed even perpetual leases, he was told, and were willing to abandon rental lands upon which they had made considerable improvements in order to purchase "wild land." The earl was doubtless pleased that he had already agreed to sell his land in small parcels with small down payments, as well as letting it to those who had no capital whatsoever. His willingness to make the land available to the settlers themselves was perhaps the aspect of Selkirk's settlement that was most often favourably remarked upon and remembered on the island. The earl was astonished to discover that there was no regular postal service from the island, and generalized from this fact that the island needed "a man of activity & ability at the head who would set others agoing—this is not to be found here."[29] He was quite accurate about the lack of leadership, but his comment—clearly referring to Fanning—in no way suggested that he should fill the role himself. Selkirk was equally disturbed to find that the colony's records were "at present . . . tossed about the private house of the Register in no sort of order—great part in loose sheet."[30] Perhaps paying too much heed to Robert Thorpe, who was certainly a troublemaker, Selkirk ended up placing the blame for the island's problems at the door of Lieutenant Governor Fanning, who from timidity and fear of losing popularity let everybody go their own way.

Continued concern over the obvious lack of coordination and cooperation among the people accompanying him he had hoped might be leaders—even Jilks was being difficult, allowing "nobody to do anything but himself"—confirmed Selkirk in his previous decision to appoint "a man with a head of arrangement, to be over them all—constantly at hand, & ready to lay out what is next to be done."[31] That this role really needed to be filled by Selkirk himself apparently did not for an instant occur to him. The importance of his physical presence ought to have been suggested by his almost miraculous ability to resolve disputes among the settlers, especially over the location of their lands. Whether Selkirk had in mind Charles Stewart or James Williams—a Kirdcudbrightshire man who had worked for the Selkirk family for many years—is not clear, but it was probably the latter. Williams had come as some sort of agent to manage the passengers from Uist during the voyage.[32] Selkirk left Stewart in charge of the overall real estate situation, but gave Williams the detailed wintering instructions for the settlements. Williams had not been expected to depart for North America with the settlers, his wife being seriously ill with consumption, but he was on board the *Oughton*, which reached the island on 27 August with a contingent of Roman Catholic passengers from North and South Uist. With Williams available, Selkirk was able to indulge his impatience to be away from the island to tour North America. The earl always found it difficult to concentrate on one thing for very long, and a combination of primitive conditions and the press of people soon did him in. He was pleased that he had managed to use his tent and camp cot, but would not be able to do so for very many nights in the cool of the late Maritime summer.

Selkirk was not entirely happy with the Uist people. Most of them were extremely poor and had large families, he reported. James Williams complained not that they had been badly behaved on the voyage, but that they were dirty and lazy. Fortunately, Selkirk wrote, he had little obligation to most of these arrivals beyond their passage. Equally fortunately, many of these people, who were Roman Catholics, "dispersed & were called for by their friends."[33] They would head for the Catholic lands on the north shore of the island, especially around Tracady. Both because of their religion and because they would require "more to be done for them than for the Skye settlers," Selkirk sought to keep the two groups of settlers separate. He proposed taking those Uist settlers who would settle with him to lot ten, on the west side of the island, but was unable to execute this plan because of the lateness of the season.

Ominously, even before he left, Selkirk had been forced to resolve several disputes between Angus MacAulay and James Williams, whose feuding would continue to simmer over the ensuing winter. MacAulay, who was one of Selkirk's medical men as well as a recruiting agent, had already assumed his future role as both aggrieved employee and man of conscience.[34] The *Passenger Vessel* legislation insisted that each vessel engaged in the immigrant trade carry a qualified medical person. MacAulay always stridently insisted that neither he nor the settlers were being treated in accordance with the initial agreements. For his part, Selkirk always maintained that equivalents had been offered and that no one had been forced to emigrate to the island against his or her will. Selkirk would later comment to Captain John MacDonald that MacAulay's "abilities are unquestionably great & he is also a man of great plausibility; but I have too certain experience, that no reliance can be placed on anything he says: I have also seen in his conduct symptoms of a temper so diabolical, that in justice to human nature I can only describe them to a touch of mental derangement—which may perhaps account equally for his violence and his inconsistency."[35] Selkirk obviously had been hurt deeply by MacAulay's criticisms and he refused to consider him as the individual to be left in charge of the settlement.

Selkirk's diary entries of his activities on the island in August and September of 1803 are symptomatic of both his strengths and his weaknesses. With enormous energy he travelled widely, observed much, and interrogated at length every one he encountered. He demonstrated a real ability to separate the wheat from the chaff in what his informants told him, and the careful reader could find in his scattered observations—almost all of them perspicacious—a fairly reliable picture of the promise and problems of Prince Edward Island in 1803. Selkirk was especially sharp in his observations about farming and agricultural potential on the island, perhaps not surprising given his earlier work for Sir John Sinclair. He almost intuitively recognized the importance of marshland to the early farmers and sought to distribute marshland equitably to his settlers. Also recognizing the value of using fire to rid the land of trees (not yet of much value as timber) and the dangers of out-of-control forest fires, he "directed a cut to be made thro the woods (for stopping the communication of the fire) & to cut off about 100 or 150 acres on Pt. Prim to be burnt & pastured" as "a trial."[36] Having been informed of the cost of constructing chimneys, he recommended the construction of stoves "on the Swiss plan," which would cut the number of days' labour in building from five days to one. He even placed a diagram in the margin of his journal. Selkirk also recognized the difficulty of constructing proper roads and predicted that overland transportation would not happen for many years.

At the same time, the diary also displayed much evidence of haste and impatience, especially in placing the Highlanders on their lands and getting housing started. One surveyor was criticized for wasting his time "in fiddle faddles" and another of those settlers Selkirk hoped would be a leader "daudles about." Both because of the lateness of the season and because he wanted to depart the island, Selkirk pushed matters harder than was advisable when dealing with the stubborn Highlanders who were his settlers. The result was that some of the Mull party, disappointed with their locations— or lack of them—decided to press on to Quebec, although they later took lands on the island from a Major Holland. As Selkirk recognized, this was one of the many discouragements against proprietors transporting settlers to Prince Edward Island, since other landholders would offer better deals. He also discovered that the Uist people resolutely refused to settle inland, having spent their entire lives by the sea. All in all, Selkirk concluded that instead of bringing initially a large number of settlers of mixed ages, a smaller party of young people to prepare the way would have worked better. He would attempt to implement this conclusion later in Red River.

Not surprisingly, between Selkirk's departure from the island in September 1803 and his return a year later, relations between Angus MacAulay and James Williams went from bad to worse. Acting as spokesman for the settlers, MacAulay complained that Williams had not seen to it that enough houses were built quickly enough before winter had set in. The houses were to be log cabins put up by the settlers under the supervision of several local residents. There were further complaints that Williams had not obtained sufficient quantities of provisions, and was both slow and unfair in the allocation of land. Most of all, however, MacAulay insisted that Williams spent far too much time in Charlottetown and not enough with the settlers. Moreover, he had become far too familiar with the elite of the colony. Selkirk was forced to forbid Williams to involve himself in local politics by running for the House of Assembly, although he was prepared to countenance an appointment to the council that was never made. Despite his continued jostling with

Angus McAulay, James Williams was active in the first years of his agency. Recognizing the need for an off-island market for surplus produce, Williams obtained a schooner for the Newfoundland trade. He also began to build a series of mills at Pinette: a grist mill, a shelling mill, and a sawmill intended to cut 600,000 board feet of timber per year. He managed to draw nearly £3450 against Selkirk's bankers in London in 1803–04.[37]

If Williams had drifted into an alliance with the island's official "cabal," Angus MacAulay increasingly found himself acting the part of the servant and tribune of the people, a role he would take on more fully after the arrival of Lieutenant Governor Desbarres in 1805. At his own expense MacAulay erected a chapel near his house on the 1100 acre lot on Point Prim granted him by Selkirk there for his services. He preached regularly in Gaelic and also taught school at this "chapel of ease." In addition to preaching and teaching, MacAulay (who had studied some medicine in preparation for the emigration to North America) served as physician to his neighbours. Far more than most other members of the Highland tacksman class who made their way to Prince Edward Island, Angus MacAulay had found a home. Unfortunately for himself—and perhaps for the island as well—the fifth Earl of Selkirk had not joined him. Perhaps the outstanding impression the earl left of his relationship with Prince Edward Island was the haste with which he departed it.

CHAPTER SEVEN

Touring North America

L ORD SELKIRK SPENT only a little over a month on Prince Edward Island
organizing his settlement, and then, in company with his manservant
Jilks, headed south towards Halifax. From the Nova Scotia capital he sailed
for Boston and travelled across Massachusetts by carriage and horse to
Albany, New York. His ultimate intention was to rendezvous with William
Burn in upstate New York and to search for suitable land in Upper Canada
for his sheep being pastured in New York. Burn had learned in the spring of
1803 that his fiancée would not join him in Canada. The news changed his
plans, and he plunged energetically into Selkirk's business. Burn was
instructed to keep the flock of sheep in New York over the summer of 1803.
Not until June was Selkirk able to send an impatient and uncomfortable
Burn further instructions. The earl now had from the Colonial Office the
promise of a land grant in southwestern Upper Canada, obtained just before
he had departed for North America. Burn was to scout the country between
the Niagara and the Detroit rivers for a proper location for both a settlement and a sheep farm, on which Selkirk intended to pasture a flock of
1000 first-class breeding ewes.

We have a detailed account of Lord Selkirk's journey in the form of a
continuation of the travel diary that began on 3 August upon arrival at
Prince Edward Island.[1] As with almost all of Selkirk's papers, the original of
this diary was lost in the fire at St. Mary's Isle. What survives are handwritten transcripts made by Kirkcudbright ladies hired by the then Public
Archives of Canada. The instructions to these ladies were apparently to

copy all material of Canadian interest but only that material. Other evidence suggests that Selkirk kept more diaries, but this is the only one that survives, albeit only in a transcribed form. It is impossible to tell from the transcript whether the original diary actually began on 3 August or whether only the transcript begins on that date.[2] Both because it was obviously a travel diary and because of Selkirk's reluctance to commit his private thoughts to paper, the diary tells us a good deal about what he did and what he observed, but precious little about the inner workings of the man himself. At the same time, this diary provides our most protracted continuous personal and auto-biographical record of Selkirk's life, virtually on a day-by-day basis, and from it we can glean some considerable further understanding of his person-ality, which was compulsively private and introspective.

Selkirk's diary entries sometimes took a good deal for granted. He was, for example, apparently accompanied for over a year by his manservant, Jilks, who was totally invisible and was never mentioned in the diary. It is entirely possible that he was also accompanied on his journeys around North America by a medical person, a "Dr. Shaw," who was a medical attendant on one of the vessels to Prince Edward Island. It is equally likely that Shaw was a companion only some of the time; he certainly was part of the group that arrived at Baldoon in early June of 1804. In any event, the invisibility of Selkirk's "servants" in the diary was not necessarily a mark against him; most aristocrats took servants for granted. But it was not a mark for him either, since he clearly did not humanize those who looked after him. In this respect he was quite different from his deceased elder brother Lord Daer, who had so favourably impressed Robert Burns so many years ago by his easy familiarity.

By mid-September of 1803, Selkirk was ready to leave the island. He travelled from Charlottetown to Point Prim with a number of local officials who would accompany him across the Northumberland Strait to Nova Scotia. The little party was forced to camp out under the stars, protected with great coats and blankets. Selkirk himself had a hammock and a canopy. When rain began around one a.m., the group decamped and headed for the Wood Islands, from which they rowed across the strait, landing initially in uninhabited territory that was earlier part of the grant to the Philadelphia Company. The suggestion is that others besides Selkirk were the uncomfort-able ones. This north shore of Nova Scotia had been settled by a number of parties of Highlanders since the early 1770s, and Selkirk was anxious to investigate their progress. He continued his habit of interrogating extensively everyone he met. Outside Pictou he questioned two newcomers building a stone house, who told him—"if my Gaelic did not deceive me"—that they had bought 100 acres for 100 guineas.[3] This brief comment was one of the few times in the diary that Selkirk's competence in Gaelic was mentioned, and the remark certainly sounded like that of a man less than fully comfortable in the language.[4]

IN NOVA SCOTIA

His observations around Pictou confirmed Selkirk's earlier ones on the island regarding the preference of all settlers (including Highlanders) for water lots. The settlers who had been in this region since the 1770s came chiefly from Galloway, with a fair mixture of Highlanders, and they were extremely prosperous and contented. "The general appearance of the Settlement," Selkirk wrote, "strongly recalled some Scenes in Swisserland."[5] Even those more recently arrived in the Emigration of 1801 had experienced decent crops.

Closer to Halifax, Selkirk was quite impressed with the settlement at Truro of Scots-Irish from New Hampshire, begun before the American War. Prosperity here was based on the raising of fat cattle for the Halifax market, he wrote. The locals informed the earl that the Nova Scotia government made no proper land grants, but instead issued licences of occupation to actual settlers. The visitor arrived in Halifax on 23 September and remained in the Nova Scotia capital until 7 October, occupied during his entire stay with "a continual succession of dinner parties."[6] When not socializing, Selkirk continued his routine of questioning everyone. In Halifax he even did some research, studying the abstracts of the customs books for the province and reporting the results in his diary. He also copied the latest militia return for the province, which showed smaller numbers than official estimates but gave some idea of the distribution of the population. Finally, the earl spent much time with a Father Burke pouring over maps of Upper Canada and discussing the best place to locate a settlement there. His informant was Edmund Burke, a Roman Catholic priest who had spent some years in Upper Canada before moving to Halifax.[7]

Selkirk heard from the governor, Sir John Wentworth, and others, a good deal of retrospective criticism of the Loyalist settlement of Nova Scotia. The governor now regretted that the disbanded soldiers had not been better employed, and other informants told Selkirk that most of the Loyalists had been sent to harbours on the seacoast where the land was useless, rather than to more promising locations inland that had not yet been surveyed. Although people talked about the freezing up of Halifax harbour, one of the local judges showed Selkirk his diary kept around 1780, which made clear that vessels arrived and left all through the winter. The earl sailed from Halifax on 7 October.

IN BOSTON AND MASSACHUSETTS

On his arrival in Boston a few days after leaving Halifax, Selkirk was almost immediately whisked off to the theatre, housed in a building larger than the King's Theatre in Edinburgh. The earl found "the acting tolerable—music detestable."[8] Selkirk commented on how few ladies were present. His remarks do not suggest a man much smitten with matters theatrical. Not surprisingly, he found that, at least in the upper circles of society entertaining him, strong Federalism and friendship for Great Britain prevailed. Boston reminded him of "an English country town," although the gardens here were better. The diary entries displayed no particular theme or interest, although Selkirk continued his practice of recording a good deal of what he was told, even in casual conversation. He devoted a page of notes to Harvard College, although he does not appear to have been much impressed with that venerable institution. In general, Boston produced no strong response of any kind from the Scottish visitor.

Selkirk left Boston on 19 October in "my own carriage."[9] The diary's discussion of the difficulty of obtaining horses on hire to pull the carriage make it quite clear that Selkirk had not purchased a carriage in Boston but had instead brought one across the Atlantic that was considerably heavier than the local standard. Six months later, Selkirk would record in his diary that the American carriages were quite "ingeniously constructed for lightness and cheapness."[10] Since no mention was made of the carriage earlier—he had travelled by horseback in the Maritimes—it had apparently been shipped directly to the Massachusetts capital. By carriage he journeyed across the state of Massachusetts, paying particular attention to the geological features of the landscape and agricultural practice, especially regarding the raising of livestock. A lengthy entry on sheep was made while the earl was staying at Williams's tavern in Marlboro.

Selkirk found no appearance of a town between Boston and Worcester, but "at every meeting house a small collection of 6 or 8 houses."[11] He stopped travellers on the road to ask them questions, but appears to have received most of his information from innkeepers, at least at the inns in which he stayed. He apparently astonished the "Country people" at Belchertown "when I sat down to take a sketch of Country."[12] Like most aristocratic travellers of the time, Selkirk was a tolerable artist who worked in pencil and in watercolours. The few sketches surviving—none from this journey—indicate that he was capable of producing a decent likeness of the landscape. At Cheshire Selkirk learned of a great cheese of 1200 pounds that was produced in the community and sent to Thomas Jefferson. The visitor seemed even more impressed with the information that a house "2 Stories & garret 40 by 28" could be built for about $1000.[13] In western Massachusetts and eastern New York, Selkirk's carriage travelled on a turnpike road on which tolls were charged. He was told that more than 500 families travelled each autumn via this route into the west. As he pointed out in his diary, the presence of a decent road not only was an advantage in carrying produce to market but also in bringing purchasers to the farmer's door. Increasingly his recorded comments about the countryside related to good and bad settlement practices.

ALBANY, GENERAL HAMILTON, AND THE GENESEE COUNTRY

On his first night at Albany, the earl found in his hotel "a party of wild young aristocrats worthy of London or Edr." The resultant merrymaking "made us very thick," he reported.[14] Selkirk did not drink to excess, but as this entry suggests, he was not averse to the odd evening of heavy conviviality; like most occasional drinkers, he probably felt quite proud of himself for getting "thick." This was the first occasion in the United States where Selkirk indicated that he had fallen among congenial spirits from his own social class, and he was generally quite impressed with the Albany aristocracy, whose position was based—as in Britain—upon large landholdings. The young bucks he had fallen in with truly were connected to the great landholding families of the region, and Selkirk quickly found himself invited to dinner with the Van Rensselaers, arguably the richest and most aristocratic of their ilk. Selkirk used his letter of introduction from a London Huguenot merchant to Alexander Hamilton, but probably could have met the great man through his accidental aristocratic connections.[15]

Alexander Hamilton had been born in 1755 in Nevis in the Caribbean islands and had come to New York in 1772.[16] His father James Hamilton was one of the many Scottish merchants who resided in the Caribbean region in the eighteenth century.[17] He had begun living with Alexander's mother Rachel Fawcett Lavine in 1752, although she was not divorced from her husband until 1758. James had subsequently deserted his family, forcing young Alexander to become a clerk for two New York merchants at the age of eleven. Hamilton was obviously a prodigy, so brilliant that people on his island financed his education in the American colonies. Before he was twenty, he was writing revolutionary pamphlets that displayed a firm grasp of politics and political theory. During the war he served as George Washington's confidential secretary, and he later was the principal author of *The Federalist Papers* (with James Madison) that argued for ratification of the constitution drafted at convention in 1787. Hamilton served as the first American secretary of the treasury, where he introduced an entire system of public credit and an economic system based on protective support for infant industries that was discussed in his 1791 *Report on Manufactures.* He was also an early leader of the Federalist Party. By 1803 he was out of office and living in semi-retirement in upstate New York. Hamilton's wife was the daughter of General Philip Schuyler, one of the grandees of New York. He had served as a military commander at the battle of Yorktown in 1781 and still used the military title.

Selkirk was literally blown away by Hamilton, who was about twenty years his senior. The earl wrote in the diary that he had seldom "met with a man of whom I formed a higher opinion—the clearness of his ideas, & the readiness with which he brings forward a solid reason for every opinion he advances combine with his very extensive information in giving an uncommon zest to his conversation—and to this he joins a degree of candour in discussion very rarely to be met with."[18] Selkirk had sent Hamilton his letter of introduction the day after his arrival in Albany.[19] Hamilton had called on Selkirk at his hotel the following day, and the earl had subsequently spent an entire day with the American at the home of Hamilton's father-in-law, General Philip Schuyler. Selkirk did not report at length at this point in his diary about the conversations between the two men, but he would subsequently use them, as we shall see, as part of the basis—along with his own observations—for a full-scale analysis of the polity of the United States. A single day's meeting was probably too short a period of time for Hamilton to remake completely Selkirk's perceptions of the United States, and it appears more likely that the older man mainly rather helped confirm impressions that Selkirk already had, as well as perhaps providing him with a conceptual framework in which to operate. In the short run, Selkirk's diary while he was in Albany seemed rather more concerned with linguistic than political considerations. He noted that the Dutch were losing their original language, as were some of the Irish, and concluded "every language which is not spoken by a Govt must it would seem wear out."[20] Selkirk would return to the language question later.

For some unknown reason, the earl appears to have abandoned his carriage in Albany and continued on his journey "in a Coach or Stage Wagon & 4 Horses which engages to go to Niagara."[21] On this leg of his travels he devoted most of his attention to observations about the Scottish settlers, both Highland and Lowland, of upstate New York. This was not surprising, given that he was heading westward toward his Genesee lands, which were connected to the landholdings earlier acquired by Sir William Pulteney and a number of Scottish speculators in the region.[22] At Geneva, Selkirk could not find Pulteney's agent, but he did speak with several other informants at the local land office. From these and other sources, he managed to put together a picture of the Genesee speculations upon which the British investors, through the agency of one Charles Williamson, had spent hundreds of thousands of pounds. Selkirk found the situation different from what had been feared by some in Great Britain, who had apparently spoken of fraud. Pulteney had paid too much for the initial land purchase, then was encouraged by Williamson's sales on credit to impecunious settlers to buy more. As for Williamson, he spent profligately on improvements that developed the country—including hotels, theatres, and race tracks—but did not particularly benefit Pulteney's investment. On the other hand, the locals spoke highly of Williamson and did not think that his motives were evil. Selkirk did not offer a final judgment, but recorded that he thought the business as bad as reported, although for different reasons. As he travelled west, he encountered and commented on other similar large-scale land speculations in the region, concluding that most would eventually be successful if they did not have to compete with the Mississippi region when it opened for settlement.

ON THE UNITED STATES AND AMERICANS

At Buffalo Creek, Selkirk sat down to collect his thoughts and observations on land speculation and the political climate in the United States. This essay in his diary is one of the first pieces of Selkirk political speculation remaining to us following his student days, although it would not be the last. He began by discussing a local dispute between settlers and a land company based in Pennsylvania, particularly in the context of the inability of the courts to protect land titles against squatters. The essay quickly turned to more general analysis, although still within the context of the question whether the United States had a government capable of providing social order and protection for investment. These were issues of considerable interest to Selkirk as he attempted to decide where to locate his sheep.

Selkirk took his larger theory from the arch-Federalists, headed by Alexander Hamilton. He began by commenting on the "great feebleness" of the American government to enforce the law when it went against local interests. The military establishment was too weak to support constituted authorities. The American Constitution was a "patched work." The introduction of monarchical principles by the founding fathers to give the government energy produced "a jumble of contradictory principles." The presidency was close to an elected monarchy, and was such a political prize that it served as the basis for partisan party politics—"the bane of America." The partisan politics in turn produced a government by patronage, which extended even into the military.[23] The Federalists sought to correct this problem by introducing the notion of a President and Senate for life—even the hereditary principle—but General Hamilton and others in Albany thought there was too much opposition to heredity to advocate it openly. Hamilton insisted that the political division of Federalist and Anti-federalist was both local and blended with the conflict between commercial and agricultural interests. Thomas Jefferson, argued Hamilton, held theoretical views about the incompatibility of a republic and commerce. The Republicans had won less in 1800 than the Federalists had lost, because their measures were not popular.[24]

Alexander Hamilton also claimed that the rivalry between Virginia and Massachusetts had shifted in a way that virtually isolated New England, which might lead to a total separation. Such separatism was totally opposed by Hamilton, who insisted that after a division new and equally contentious parties would appear. The preservation of the unity of the American Empire, Selkirk thought, seemed to be Hamilton's ruling principle. "The Evils of democracy," Selkirk wrote, "are less in proportion to the extent of Empire, as the division of different districts prevents the mob uniting & their contradictory prejudices & sentiments prevents the precipitate measures that would be likely in a smaller state." Whether this generalization was Hamilton's or Selkirk's is not entirely clear. What is certain is that Selkirk reported on Hamilton's wholehearted support (against the Federalist Party generally) for the Louisiana Purchase. The general's only complaint was that the administration had not acted sooner. But the purchase had contributed to the popularity of the Jefferson government. Hamilton admitted, reported Selkirk, "that as *Territory* Louisiana is of no value to the U.S. & thinks they ought to exchange the Western bank of Mississippi for the Floridas."[25] Curiously enough, nowhere in General Hamilton's analysis of American politics was the subject of black slavery mentioned.

One of the major points that Selkirk gleaned from his Federalist informants was a fear for the future of large property holders in America. The earl thought that the problem, at least in New York, was less a "disregard of property" than the presence of several great landed proprietors. But he seemed to accept the principle that "except as an article of speculation in which the capital value only is thought of . . . no rich man would think of vesting money in the purchase of Land as in Europe to produce an annual revenue."[26] This reality led to another: the "almost total want of a Landed Aristocracy," which was perhaps responsible for the American "sordid attention to money." From Selkirk's perspective, the Americans had compounded their problems by copying England in so many things rather than striking out on their own—or perhaps copying from other jurisdictions, including Scotland. He gave as examples the "servil" replication of the English Poor Laws and the English common law, both of which were not to be found in Scotland.

The earl did not attempt to comment much on "the manners of the people," beyond noting that this probably had little to do with the American government. He did report that every gentleman with whom he had consulted spoke disgustedly about the moral character of the backcountry people, who exhibited "litigious cunning" and a general propensity for drink. Selkirk blamed the litigiousness on the universal diffusion of education, which got only to the point of destroying the "simplicity of ignorance" without substituting "the correctness of principle." He reported that Alexander Hamilton even maintained that universal education made the people presumptuous about their own judgements and "therefore more liable to be misled by demagogues." At the same time, Selkirk himself insisted that he found no surliness, incivility, or disrespect among the Americans he had met on his travels, providing he addressed them as an equal.

If Selkirk had entertained any notions of developing his Genesee holdings, he was doubtless disabused of them by what he been told in Albany and what he had discovered at the scene. The United States was not a particularly good place for a Scottish nobleman to attempt to build an estate. Perhaps British America would be more welcoming. At the same time, his diary did not demonstrate any evidence of the deep-seated anti-Americanism that Selkirk would subsequently demonstrate. By mid-November of 1803, in any event, he had crossed the Niagara River and entered Upper Canada on horseback. He soon encountered Niagara Falls.

BRITISH AMERICA

Like most early visitors to Niagara Falls, Selkirk was bowled over by its splendour, writing: "The great falls goes indeed beyond imagination, & exceeded every idea I had formed of its grandeur." In Niagara he visited with Thomas Clark, a native of Drumfries-shire who had come to Canada in 1791 to work for Robert Hamilton, his cousin.[27] Hamilton was the major military supplier at Niagara, and Clark followed in his footsteps. He had built a wharf and storehouse at Queenston in 1799, subsequently founding in 1800 a firm with several other Scots arrivals that traded mainly in flour. By 1803 Clark, Hamilton, and John Forsyth controlled local commerce, their position based on a government contract. Selkirk was much impressed with Robert Hamilton whom he described as a "very respectable & intelligent man, & of very liberal ideas." The earl made a number of diary entries about commerce and prices on the Great Lakes.

From Thomas Clark and Robert Hamilton, who had spent several years in the western fur trade, Selkirk had his first glimpse of that trade. Their descriptions were of the Michilimakinac fur trade, carried on by independent traders quite apart from the North West Company. His extensive notes on this trade and the traders emphasized the extent to which Lowland Scots competed with the Highlanders of the North West Company for western furs. For the moment, however, the earl was perhaps more interested in the reports from Sandy Brown, the shepherd who had the year before successfully brought Selkirk's flock of sheep west from Albany. William Burn had sheared the sheep and sold much of the wool. Selkirk was told that the flock, while mixed, would serve as the basis of a "good breed." He also learned that sheep could be profitably driven to Upper Canada, where both wool and sheep would bring a good price.

Near Niagara, Selkirk also had a first encounter with a recent American settler to Canada. Asked how he reconciled an oath of allegiance to two governments, the settler "answered that the Oath to each only applied while resident within their territories—he could never take an Oath to be otherwise understood." Selkirk observed that everything he had heard about the Americans indicated "that they are merely induced by the facility of getting land, and that loyalty is a mere pretext." He also met Colonel Thomas Talbot, one of the few landholders in Upper Canada who had begun developing a private estate on the western frontier. The Irish-born Talbot was returning from York to his land near Dunwich. Selkirk's Scottish hosts thought Talbot's plans to offer small fifty-acre allotments to actual settlers would not work because of their size. Although Selkirk and Talbot would be often linked together in the later secondary literature as early developers of Upper Canada, apart from their positions as non-corporate individual landholders, their operations would really be quite different in philosophy.[28] Talbot intended to be the squire of his estates, living in residence and interacting with the people settled on his lands, many of whom were tenants, in traditional English aristocratic fashion. Selkirk, on the other hand, planned to be an absentee developer, more interested in philanthropy and investment than in any feudal standing in the New World. Part of the difference was that Selkirk already had an established Scottish estate, while Talbot had nothing in Britain. As early as 1803, however, Talbot was promoting his intentions to favour British over American settlers in order to control "the growing tendency to insubordination and revolt" in Upper Canada.[29] Although Selkirk did not mention any conversation on the subject with Talbot at this time, he may well have been influenced by the Colonel in his political attitudes.

Selkirk had hoped to make direct contact at Queenston with his agent William Burn, but was forced to sail on the last vessel bound for York (later Toronto) on 20 November without so doing.[30] Burn had left White Creek, New York, for Queenston, Upper Canada, in early September 1803, and would spend much of the winter of 1803–04 with a surveyor exploring lands on Lake Erie and the Thames River. The schooner on which the earl took passage was literally towed to York by a group of Mr. Forsyth's voyageurs who were heading for Montreal as passengers and who pulled the vessel with rowboats the last few miles. York was hardly very prepossessing. Selkirk described it in his diary as a community of sixty or seventy houses, scattered on lots varying between one and one-quarter of an acre still "very ragged from the Stumps." The only public building was a two-room structure that served as the home of the various agencies of the government, and the ground was marshy, thus encouraging fever and ague.

Governor Simcoe had moved the capital of Upper Canada from Niagara to York in 1794. The decision was a very "slap dash" one, Selkirk reported, with officials forced to abandon comfortable houses for "an absolute wood where people were sometimes losing themselves between one hut & another."[31] Simcoe had chosen the York site partly because of its harbour and partly because the land around it was unpossessed by Europeans and thus could be taken over by his "friends." Selkirk was not much taken with Simcoe's contribution to the development of Upper Canada. He quoted the Mohawk leader Joseph Brant as saying, "Gen S. Has done great deal for this province, he has changed the name of every place in it."[32] He added that Simcoe's general system was to ape England "without regard to the circumstances of the country." This was particularly true in the decision to adopt English law in its entirely, although its intricacy was totally unsuitable to an infant country without professional men. The inability to staff all the courts actually thwarted justice.

If Selkirk were not much taken with York or Governor Simcoe, he was equally unimpressed with Upper Canada's current officialdom and especially with the venial public culture of the colony. He might have found the same veniality in Prince Edward Island had he stayed long enough to discern it. He did there meet Sheriff Alexander Macdonell, who would become his Upper Canadian advisor and agent, beginning a protracted and somewhat unsatisfactory relationship with the Macdonell family in North America. For some unknown reason, Selkirk was always partial to Highland Catholics. Macdonell had some military experience in the American war, had been a client of John Graves Simcoe, and was fluent in French, English, Gaelic, and several Aboriginal languages. In 1803 the sheriff was a prominent member of the small bachelor elite in the tiny capital, dining in the mess, drinking tea and wine in great quantities, and playing whist in the evening. He was also quite politically ambitious.[33] Lieutenant Governor Peter Hunter tried to warn Selkirk of Macdonell's weaknesses, but was not heeded.[34] The earl's careful investigation of land-granting procedures in Upper Canada soon led him to conclude that the system had many difficulties and was subject to much abuse. Much confusion remained from the earlier granting of land to both Loyalists and soldiers, and the surveyor general had enormous power to assist or hinder those seeking land. Nevertheless, he felt that he had established a good relationship with Lieutenant Governor Hunter, and was sufficiently confident about land grants to write in late December to an American acquaintance about his plans of bringing a "settlement of High-landers to a Township near Lake Erie" and his desire for a "few of their countrymen who have long been in America" to "instruct the newcomers in the methods of the country."[35]

At York, Selkirk also eventually had an opportunity to meet with his agent, William Burn. With additional input from Burn, who had spent the autumn scouting for land in western Upper Canada, the earl more or less decided on the Chenail Ecarté on the north shore of Lake St. Clair, not far from Detroit, as the site of his future settlement. The land there was marshy, and would not require much clearing to be suitable for sheep. It would also prove to be malarial, of course. After drafting detailed instructions for William Burn about the exact locations for his lands, Selkirk set off on 4 January 1804 for Montreal, travelling by horse along the north shore of Lake Ontario.[36] Burn headed west to the northeast corner of Lake St. Clair, where he laid claim to two adjoining unoccupied half-townships because he could not get enough land in a single township. Selkirk eventually petitioned for, and received, 1200 acres personally and another 200 acres for each of fifteen heads of families coming from St. Mary's Isle to Baldoon.[37] He then proceeded to give fifty acres of the 200 acres to each of the heads of families and kept 150 acres for himself.

As he journeyed to Montreal, Selkirk continued to make detailed obser-vations of the settlements and their population, paying particular attention to the occasional pockets of ethnic communities he found along the way. At Presqu'isle he found a Yankee settlement peopled by Americans from New England attracted by Governor Simcoe's proclamation of free land in 1796. The earl admitted that the appearance of this settlement seemed to confirm the superiority of New Englanders as settlers, since the community was materially as far advanced as the far older Niagara River ones. Selkirk found Kingston much more impressive than York. He then moved on to Glengarry, in southeastern Upper Canada, visiting at the Osnabrook farm of Captain

Miles Macdonell, Sheriff Alexander's brother-in-law. Selkirk approved of what he saw and heard regarding Miles, who was "much of a gentleman in manners & sentiment" and was "so popular that he could get work done when nobody else could." These qualities Selkirk regarded as important, and he filed Miles away for future reference. For his part, Miles was equally impressed with Selkirk, and later reported the visit at length in a letter to his brother John.[38] In the course of this letter Miles commented, "mere farming will hardly support my family in the manner I could wish," a sentiment that he had probably indicated to his visitor and that certainly would leave him receptive to Selkirk's subsequent offers of employment. In Glengarry Selkirk found a thriving Highland community, with houses which, while poor by American or English standards, were "a wonderful advance from the Hovels of Glengarry [in Scotland]" and equal to those of "farmers of 100 or 150£ a year in Galloway."[39] The Highlanders of Glengarry had adjusted well to American conditions, while maintaining their own traditions. Selkirk was suitably impressed.

Selkirk liked the look of French Canada, especially "the appearance of old settlement & thick population," which was quite European. In Montreal he was royally entertained by the "grandees, nabobs of the N.W.Co. etc," most of whom were Highland Scots. He learned a good deal more about the economics and politics of the fur trade, which he recorded at length in his journal. He recognized Simon McTavish as the leading force behind the old North West Company and an element of coercion as the way in which French Canadian employees were managed. He thought that, because of the discipline the Canadians could produce, they would easily triumph over the Americans in the west. McTavish was quite open about his plan to challenge the validity of the charter of the Hudson's Bay Company in order "to force the H. Bay Co. to a compromise."[40] The Nor'westers would later accuse the earl of imposing on their hospitality by accepting their confidences without indicating his direct interest in their affairs. The charges were only half-true. Selkirk did allow himself to be wined and dined at the Beaver Club, the private lair of the fur barons in Montreal. He did listen to their boastings of their plans and their summaries of their business activity, and he undoubtedly did not broadcast any information about his attempts to interest the British government in settlements in Red River or at the Falls of St. Mary. These were both areas of pivotal concern to the North West Company, of course, in terms of their extended transportation and supply system. But there is no evidence that at this time he had any interest in the Hudson's Bay Company or in the fur trade itself. The careful observations that he recorded in Montreal were no different from those he made everywhere in North America. Fascinated by everything he saw and was told, Selkirk was quite prepared to accept information from any source, and most people in North America—including the Montreal fur traders—were quite happy for the opportunity to impress a British Lord.

Selkirk's Scottish experience enabled him to grasp the problems of French Canada quite easily when he was in Quebec City for the opening of the legislature, although his expression of them was a bit awkward:

> The English at Quebec & Montreal cry out in the true John Bull style against their [the French's] obstinate aversion to institutions which they [the English] have never taken any pains to make them understand—& are surprised at the natural & universally experienced dislike of a conquered people to their conquerors & to every thing which puts them in mind of their subjection.[41]

Selkirk had earlier recorded with some astonishment the efforts of the Lower Canadian legislature to force the universal adoption of American sleighs, which were wider and longer than the French variety, noting that "the Canadians prejudiced against everything English & as much wedded to old habits as the people of an old country, were obstinate, & evaded every attempt to enforce the law.[42] He was struck by the English absence of "system in dealing with Canada," observing:

> the only chance of reconciling the people would have been either to use every effort to change them entirely in language & institutions & make them forget that they were not English— for keeping them as French to give a Government adapted to them as such, & keep every thing English out of sight—neither of these plans had been followed, & the policy of Govt. has been a kind of vibration between them.[43]

The result, thought the earl, was confusion and contradiction. Fluent in a French polished during years in the drawing rooms of Paris, Selkirk observed that "even in private society the English & Canadians draw asunder."[44] He clearly did not approve.

BACK TO THE UNITED STATES

On 21 February Lord Selkirk left Montreal in a hired American sleigh, with a second for his "Servants."[45] He did not record who was in the other sleigh, although presumably it included the redoubtable Jilks and perhaps Dr. Shaw. He travelled through Burlington, Vermont, to Albany, New York, where he again met General Hamilton. At Albany a Colonel Troup blamed the failure of the Genesee Speculation on Charles Williamson's overextension, claiming that Williamson had been infected with Land Mania and had not kept regular accounts. "Probably too coming from a narrow situation to the command of a very heavy purse his head was a little turned," Selkirk added.[46] He did not yet have enough experience with North American agents to know how common this syndrome was, nor did he learn anything useful from this particular debacle. The earl did get to hear Alexander Hamilton make several speeches on legal matters, which impressed him greatly. The New York legislature was in session, giving Selkirk an opportunity to see American democracy in action. He found every issue influenced by the forthcoming contest for the governorship of the state in which Aaron Burr was the leading candidate. Burr would be supported by most Federalists, who were not fielding a candidate, as the least dangerous man, although Alexander Hamilton disagreed.

As Selkirk travelled toward New York City, he found the gubernatorial election "the universal subject of discussion." Aaron Burr was, he found, generally regarded by Federalists "as a man of no principle." After a personal interview with Burr, Selkirk came away convinced that he was "one of the most guarded & reserved men I ever conversed with," capable of talking for hours without revealing his opinions. From Alexander Hamilton, Selkirk again heard speculation that New England was on the verge of separation from the Union. "He thinks Burr if at the Head of New York may come into the measure as more easy to acquire an entire ascendancy in the divided than in the entire field."[47] Hamilton also feared the prospect of anarchy, given the escalating virulence of parties, and insisted that the military was useless in the event of a war between the North and the South. Selkirk himself suspected that separatism would not extend beyond New England unless supported by Burr. These, in any event, were the rumours and speculations floating around New York City in March of 1804. Selkirk was not to know that out of them would come only a few months later a duel between Burr and Hamilton, and the death of the latter.[48] On 24 April 1804, Selkirk left New York in a sloop heading north along the Hudson River, ending his journey by walking ten miles to Albany. His mind was now beginning to focus upon the settlement he proposed to found in Upper Canada.

BALDOON

When his employer had earlier visited in Albany on his way to New York City, William Burn had been ordered to proceed immediately from Queenston to Baldoon to clear land and sow Indian corn, potatoes, and timothy in anticipation of the earl's arrival there in early May. With ten oxen, Burn departed Lake Erie on 4 April and arrived at Baldoon on 9 May. He hired local labour and began to clear and plant, while Selkirk worked his way westward on his return from New York City. The earl was now interested in the best way to get settlers and sheep to Canada, and determined through local enquiry that boats were the most feasible form of transportation. Along the way he agreed with a Colonel Walker to take charge of his New York lands, which were to be sold on credit, a process that meant that the agent needed constantly to visit the settlers to make sure that they were progressing. The agent would get a percentage of the proceeds. Thus Selkirk needed to make no further investment. By 20 May 1804 the earl had reached Queenston and checked on his sheep. He paid Richard Savage the travelling expenses awarded him by Messrs Hamilton and Clark—there obviously had been a disagreement over the amount—and noted the settlement was "final."[49] Sandy Brown reported twenty dead sheep. Selkirk ordered the flock sheared and arranged to turn over management to one Lionel Johnson for the summer. He then set off to go around the lake to York, riding "thro' horrible roads," mainly unsettled.

The diary does not indicate precisely what brought Selkirk to York, but it appears to have been to offer Sheriff MacDonell the management of his settlement, to be called Baldoon, in Upper Canada, which he did on 27 May. The notation in a supplementary diary (apparently brief notes for further elaboration in the full diary) is sketchy: "Salary 200L—Sheep—Distillery—Settlement etc. (Burn, Brown, Wright) —he did not answer positively but seemed inclined—quere if could keep Shirriffdom wd. marry at S[andwich] —comes journey, notwithstanding Election." Selkirk thus offered MacDonell a princely salary of £200 per year for supervision of all aspects of the new settlement, including subordinate personnel. Wright was Archibald Wright, who had been promised a place in Upper Canada by Selkirk. Burn was receiving eighty pounds per annum less eighty pounds deducted for his mother in Scotland, and Alexander ("Sandy") Brown was getting thirty pounds per annum.[50] From the beginning, however, MacDonell himself introduced the problems that would bedevil his agency: first, the question of residing at the settlement; second, the question of holding onto the sheriff's appointment, which would require his absence; and third, the question of his continued political involvement, which again would militate against residency on the Chenail Ecarté.

Selkirk left York on 29 May by boat. Although he does not say so in the main diary, he was accompanied westward by Sheriff MacDonell and apparently also by Dr. Shaw. He was soon at the head of the lake (what is now Hamilton), where he was visited by Joseph Brant. The earl and his prospective agent arrived at Baldoon on 8 June. William Burn in his journal recorded that Selkirk arrived with "2 Gentlemen or sumthing like Gentlemen," a reference apparently to Alexander MacDonell and Dr. Shaw. Burn's entry suggests that Selkirk's two companions were not very prepossessing in appearance. It is difficult to determine whether Burn was more upset by the fact that the size of the party put a strain on the settlement's limited sleeping facilities or by the earl's failure to order a day's drinking to celebrate his arrival. Moreover, it gradually became clear that Burn would have to work under MacDonell's supervision, for the sheriff would eventually accept the appointment as Selkirk's agent in Upper Canada. The earl and the sheriff had conversed about the appointment continually on their way to Baldoon. At the settlement Selkirk made clear that MacDonell would have to reside at Sandwich if not at the settlement, and would have to give up the sheriffdom. In the end, Selkirk offered to try to get another appointment for MacDonell to replace the one he would have to surrender, and MacDonell in his turn "understood that in accepting my agency he would take to it as his personal employment & that he relinquished every idea of applying personally or by friends for Govt. promotion, & if offered would not accept it till I be acquainted & had time to provide another in his place."[51] On 2 July MacDonell spoke of the appointment as settled and desired to return to York to sort out his affairs.

Selkirk's notes while at Baldoon indicate his usual flurry of activity in organizing material for construction at the settlement and supplies of imported food for the incoming settlers. He planned construction of a barn and fourteen houses. On paper the preparations were quite impressive. But he left Baldoon at the end of July before sickness struck and the major party of 101 Highlanders—most of whom had been recruited in the Hebrides in late 1802, housed at St. Mary's Isle over 1803, and transported in 1804 aboard the *Oughton* to Quebec—had arrived. A few of this party had left St. Mary's Isle later in 1803 bound for Prince Edward Island, but had been turned around by wartime conditions on the Atlantic. The list of passengers survives in the Selkirk papers labelled "Passengers, Labourers for the Earl of Selkirk's Settlement in North America."[52] Not all of these people were indentured labourers; most were settlers who had earlier paid for their own passage. These settlers, many of them ill, appeared on 5 September in the midst of an epidemic.

During the late summer of 1804 increasing quantities of local grain whisky had been shipped to Baldoon, and Selkirk's hired workmen, including William Burn, turned increasing to the readily available alcohol. Eight barrels containing thirty-nine gallons each of whiskey were on hand at Baldoon on 1 July to disappear between late July and early September.[53] The small party of workmen was ravaged by fever, probably malarial, beginning in late August. The arriving settlers quickly began dying of diseases probably contracted on their long journey to Baldoon. William Burn died on 15 September after two weeks suffering from a fever acquired locally. Alexander MacDonell would later blame Burn's demise as much on the "effects of excessive intemperance" as on the "prevailing fever." In any event, the settlement lacked winter provisions and the housing Selkirk had ordered constructed, while Burn's books and papers were in complete disarray. Selkirk was never able to put Burn's affairs sufficiently in order to determine whether his aged mother in Scotland was entitled to any back pay. As years of expenditure and correspondence with his estate managers would demonstrate, Baldoon would always be a problem. Planning on paper was not the same as planning on the spot.

Selkirk returned to York with an offer for the government of the province. He wrote General Hunter on 30 August that he was willing to open a road at his expense in the western region fifty feet in width and free of stumps and roots for twelve feet of the width, with bridges and firm surface. In return, he was asking for a grant of land representing three concessions on either side of the road. This land was presently without much value because of the absence of transportation.[54] The Upper Canada executive council rejected this proposal on 18 September. According to its calculation, Selkirk would get 600,000 acres of land in return for building the road, and the board did not think construction would cost anywhere near that amount.[55] According to the earl's calculations, based on American figures he had gathered, roads in Upper Canada would cost between $600 and $1000 per mile. The road from Grand River to Chatham would cost at least $100,000, the road from York to Amherstburgh would cost a minimum of $200,000. Selkirk's was a classic developer's offer, suggesting the sort of arrangement that later built most of Canada's railroads. He valued the land at its pre-improvement price, while the Canadians preferred to make their assessment of value on post-improvement rates. Both evaluations could be defended. While at York he had tried to get another government appointment for Sheriff MacDonell as he had promised, but was unsuccessful.[56]

What are we to make of Baldoon?[57] Selkirk named it after the family estates sold in Scotland, thus suggesting that it had some personal meaning for him, perhaps in the nature of a replacement in the New World of something lost in the Old. He spent much time writing careful and detailed instructions for its management.[58] Unlike Prince Edward Island, with which he had become involved to fulfill his commitments, Baldoon seemed to represent on paper both a public and personal vision for Selkirk. On the public side, Baldoon was intended both to demonstrate the efficacy of planned resettlement of Highlanders and to serve as an illustration of Selkirk's dream of "National Settlements" of people non-English in culture and language who could help preserve the heartland of British North America from the pernicious influence of American culture. On the private side, Selkirk seemed ready to carve out a major North American estate for himself and his heirs, based upon scientific techniques of agriculture and careful settlement planning not commonly practiced in North America. He sought to utilize the same improvement techniques in Upper Canada that had worked for his family in Kirkcudbright. The problem was that Upper Canada was not the south of Scotland. Finding loyal agents would be much more difficult in North America than in Galloway, and more to the point, Selkirk would be thousands of miles away and unable to supervise them.

Obviously the acceptance of the agency by Sheriff MacDonell had enabled Selkirk to leave Baldoon in his supposedly competent hands. But given all this, why did the earl not wait for his settlers to arrive, ensuring personally that all was well? One possible explanation is that because many of these settlers were the ones who had refused to shift destination to Prince Edward in 1803 and had even threatened court action against Selkirk, he was fulfilling his obligations without feeling any real sense of responsibility for them. Whatever the reasons, the fairly precipitate actions of departure, first from Baldoon itself and then from North America, suggest that Selkirk had no intention of remaining in the New World any longer than absolutely necessary. Selkirk's diary offers no further hints of an explanation for his behaviour beyond detailing his return to Prince Edward Island via York and Montreal. He arrived on the island on 2 October. This date was fairly late in the year for travel to and from the island. In a whirlwind of activity he attempted to resolve problems that had emerged in his absence, particularly a conflict between James Williams and Angus MacAulay, which would continue to simmer for many years. A number of disputes with Selkirk had emerged among the settlers as well. Dr. MacAulay insisted that Selkirk's terms for settlers had been so favourable to the emigrants "as to give rise to suspicion of more distant views—on Fur Trade—or Copper Mines." MacAulay wanted matters settled to the settlers' satisfaction. The earl recorded in his diary that "these ideas are probably the result of his own imagination rather than what he has heard from others—but attend."[59] There is no evidence that Selkirk ever did understand McAulay's point, although the earl also consulted with a number of individuals in the region regarding future emigration to the Gulf of St. Lawrence, for he intended to send more settlers to the island.

Overall, Selkirk's North American tour, and especially his diary record of it, demonstrated that he was still basically operating in the Enlightenment mode—asking questions, collecting information, and relying on detailed advance planning. He was still a man of reason rather than a man of action. By 20 November Selkirk was back in New York, awaiting passage to England. The last North American entry in his diary was a highly favourable character reference for Miles Macdonell, and the only entry after his return to Britain was a sketch of brother Daer's shrine at Exeter Cathedral, at which he had obviously stopped.[60] The visit to Daer's final resting place was probably something of an exercise in exorcising ghosts. Daer, his memory, and the family traditions had hovered over Thomas Douglas for many years, but Thomas was finally free. He had now established his own career path, quite apart from Daer and the family. North America had liberated him. Unfortunately, he would never quite free himself of the past, and the next few years would see him increasingly drawn back into the long-standing concerns of his family.

CHAPTER EIGHT

Observations on the Present State of the Highlands

T HE SELKIRK PAPERS are virtually silent about what the earl was doing
upon his return from North America, although we can surmise that he
quickly began serious work on drafting his book *Observations on the
Present State of the Highlands*. He undoubtedly spent much of his time in
the first half of 1805 on this, his first major publication. Its composition
took place against the backdrop of rapidly shifting developments in British
(and Scottish) politics and of correspondence from his agents in Prince
Edward Island and Upper Canada.

On the public front, the news was encouraging. The Tory administration
that so disliked Selkirk's family had gotten itself into serious political difficulty, and Henry Dundas, the government's Scottish political manager, was
personally under a heavy attack that would soon turn to impeachment.[1]
Dugald Stewart would consider the fall of Dundas "an event . . . synony-
mous with the emancipation and salvation of Scotland," and most opponents of the government would have agreed.[2] Since he was a major opponent
both of Selkirk's family and an independent Scottish peerage, the fall from
political grace of Dundas must have spurred Selkirk's pen. A possible political career as a representative peer of Scotland was the prize if the earl could
bring his name before the public without creating an excess of hostility.

On the private side, Selkirk's position was much less favourable. He
learned early in January of 1805 from Alexander MacDonell of the Baldoon
disasters of the previous autumn. The situation became worse in every
successive letter.[3] The earl wrote to General Hunter looking to exchange his

lands on the Chenail Ecarté for property less exposed to the marsh, but that was hardly a short-term solution.[4] Neither was limiting Alexander MacDonell's line of credit.[5] Indirect information from James Williams on Prince Edward Island was more encouraging, but there were hints that all was not well in the Garden of the Gulf either. Williams had sought a market for the settlement's anticipated produce in Newfoundland, even buying a schooner for the trade. He successfully established additional emigrants sent by his employer. In response to the demand for timber in Britain, he began to build a sawmill at Pinette, intending to cut 600,000 board feet of timber per year, at least partly for export. But despite continued drawings for cash upon Selkirk's account, he had not yet written a word to the earl, an omission that suggested that something suspicious was going on. Were Selkirk to be able to boast of any success in his colonization ventures, he needed to do so quickly, before the settlements he had established ran into serious difficulties. He wrote quickly, producing a work less of scholarly reflection than of large-scale pamphleteering.

One of the few interruptions Selkirk permitted himself from his writing on Highland emigration was for the preparation of a proposal to govern-ment, sent to the Earl of Camden, for the settlement of Mohawk lands on the Grand River in Upper Canada.[6] The plan itself had probably been first sketched out on shipboard sailing back to England. On one level, this scheme was merely another speculative and promotional attempt by the earl to obtain large amounts of North American land through government grants, offering to exchange settlement (which would make land more valuable) for property. But the reasons he assigned for the promotion were of more than passing interest. One of the Canadian developments that had bothered Selkirk on his American tour was the number of American settlers who had moved into Upper Canada. The colony was being populated by "Adven-turers from the American States, lawless & restless characters who have been tempted to migrate into Canada" by easy access to land. Many of these newcomers had posed as Loyalists. This movement of Americans was dangerous because it tended "to corrupt the principles & undermine the Security of the Province in general." In the long run, a European population uncontaminated by American principles would be the best to introduce, but so long as government opposed emigration, Selkirk suggested recruiting settlers from among Scottish settlers who had gone to the United States and become anti-Democrats. Such settlers could be placed on lands on the Grand

River, where the Mohawks were already in the process of bargaining their lands away to "vagabond Americans." The bargains needed to be annulled and the lands granted to someone like himself prepared to settle loyal subjects there. The Grand River scheme was Selkirk at his most inventive, spinning something of possible substance out of a fine web of interlocking assumptions. Only a handful of dozens of these proposals would actually become acted upon. In Grand River we can see some of the persistent themes that excited the earl's imagination: imperial advantage, especially vis-à-vis the United States, and the acquisition of large amounts of waste land in North America. A hasty addendum to the original letter to Camden, penned on 14 February, insisted that the government needed to prevent the Mohawks from completing their land deal.[7]

Even though Selkirk's book on the Highlands was prepared in haste, it was a major contribution to the debate over emigration and the clearances, the first serious attempt in many years to re-examine the exodus of Highlanders to North America. Scottish public opinion, as reflected in newspapers, journals, books, and the proceedings of the Highland Society of Edinburgh, was convinced that no genuine economic or social need existed for the departure of the Highlanders to the New World. They left because they were capricious or misguided. Selkirk had spent a good deal of time on horseback and on shipboard thinking about the Highland problem. To his credit, he attempted to write in the broader context of political economy, facing the larger issues of his subject directly. His work addressed a specific regional problem, but it had larger implications. In a very real sense, the earl was the first British theorist of North American immigration. He offered an explanation of why people were departing their homeland and why they should be encouraged to continue to do so. The book was in page proofs by May, for an Edinburgh attorney wrote to Clanranald factor Robert Brown that he had by accident seen the proofs, which made "most infamous mention" of Brown without actually naming him.[8]

OBSERVATIONS ON THE PRESENT STATE OF THE HIGHLANDS

From the outset of his book, Selkirk concentrated his attention on the inconsistency of the opponents of emigration, who simultaneously sought to improve the Highlands in ways "most conducive to the pecuniary interests of its individual proprietors" while offering no real solutions to the dispossession of the ancient inhabitants and the inexorable economic changes that were occurring. It was clear, he maintained, that the process of agricultural improvement had already gone too far to be reversed, and with that improvement "in no part will cultivation require all the people whom the produce of the land can support." Proprietors could not be expected to concede to a population possessing land at a rent much below its potential value, and therefore most of the Highlanders would need a new means of livelihood. Clearances for sheep were only the most spectacular dispossessions and were not the root cause of the difficulties in the Highland region. But since dispossession was inevitable, what options did the Highlander have? He could join the labouring force in the manufacturing towns, often outside the region, or he could continue his traditional pastoral ways by emigrating to America. Emigration, Selkirk maintained, was "most likely to suit the inclination and habits of the Highlanders," since it promised land and outdoor labour. Sedentary labour under firm discipline in a factory would not suit the bucolic Highlander, and he had few skills to bring to the labour market.

Selkirk then turned to deal with the various objections that had been raised against emigration. Although he was concerned with a specific region in a specific time, he was raising issues that were far more general than perhaps even Selkirk would have recognized. The Highlands was a remote, underdeveloped area undergoing inevitable, if long delayed, economic change. The change would require fewer people. Highland development was not a legitimate argument against the removal of population to America, he insisted, for development in the form of major public works projects would less alter "the essential circumstances of the country" than provide temporary employment for those near the various construction sites. The loss of a supply of soldiers was a real danger to the nation, but compulsory measures against emigration would not "add a single recruit to the army." The real threat to the Highland nursery of soldiers, to the continued recruitment of hardy peasants loyal to their clan leaders and well-behaved because serving among friends and neighbours, was the change occurring in the Highlands independent of emigration. With change the Highlands would become no different from any place else in Great Britain, and regiments composed of the region's manhood would be "no longer composed of the flower of the peasantry collected under their natural superiors."

As to the argument that emigration carried off able-bodied labour essential for agriculture and manufacturing, the earl asserted that, paradoxically enough, production was increased by the exodus of excess people from the region. In the north of Scotland, the traditional Highlanders existed as "intrepid but indolent military retainers," good only for drudge labour so long as they remained landless and degraded. While the state was certainly entitled to regulate the loss of skilled labour, "there is perhaps no precedent of regulations for obviating a deficiency of porters and barrowmen and ditchers." Moreover, the manufacturers of Paisley and Glasgow were not the men responsible for attempting to restrict emigration. Those restrictions, even if successful, would not prevent the depopulation of the Highlands. Manufacturing in the Highlands could never succeed, Selkirk wrote, because excess population and low wages were the only advantages the region could offer a manufacturer, and none would attempt an enterprise under such circumstances.

A point at which Selkirk hit hard was that the same interests that had been responsible for the regulatory legislation of 1803 were also implementing the changes underlying emigration. This argument was one that impressed the reviewers. It was quite unfair to deny to their tenants the same rights they themselves were demanding. If public welfare were truly the issue, why not a restriction on the proprietors to dispose of their lands, instead of a brake on the population to dispose of their bodies? Selkirk allowed that the popular exodus could be avoided by returning to the old ways, but if the old ways were not acceptable, then the consequences must be followed to their logical conclusion. Attempting to be sympathetic to the lairds—after all, he had to live with them—Selkirk speculated that the landlord's aversion to emigration sprang partly from the unjust criticism levelled against him for making improvements. Instead of defending their just actions, the proprietors had turned to lashing out against their people and those who had allegedly deluded them. The earl then examined the activities of the Royal Highland Society and Parliament regarding emigration regulation, and was extremely skeptical and critical of the published reports of both bodies. But he reserved the full force of his fury for the legislation itself, the inconsistencies of which he well and truly exposed.

Selkirk had read the minutes of the Highland Society, still available today in manuscript at the society's headquarters in Edinburgh, and in *Observations* pointed out that the basis of the legislation—the supposed abuse of the emigrant—was not well documented by either the society or by the Select Committee of Parliament that had recommended the emigration act. He noted that the food allowance bore absolutely no relationship to the normal living standards of the Highlanders when in their own homes. Moreover, Selkirk implicitly questioned one basic assumption of those who hoped through legislation to price the passage to America out of the reach of the typical Highlander: that he was extremely poor. Selkirk argued that the increased cost of passage resulting from the new Act could in most cases be met by emigrants, but out of the cash reserve that they needed to be able to settle at their destination. He added,

> What is to be thought, however, of the superabundant humanity of the Highland Society, of which this is all the result—which to save the emigrants from the miserable consequences of being as much crowded on ship-board as the King's troops themselves, and of living there on the same fare as at home, reduces them to land in the colonies in the state of beggars, instead of having a comfortable provision beforehand?

The Highland Society, Selkirk wrote, represented "one class of men, for whom they appear as advocates at the bar of the public." Such a comment, while legitimate, was hardly designed to increase his popularity among the Highland lairds.

When Selkirk eventually finished his analysis of the Scottish situation and moved to that in North America, he offered two related propositions regarding Highland emigration: first, the presence of Highlanders would help prevent British North America from falling to the Americans; and second, the newcomers (and other ethnic groups) should be concentrated in what the earl labelled "national Settlements" in order to help preserve their language, culture, and manners and take full advantage of what Highlanders offered. In his various colonization ventures, Selkirk was always concerned to preserve the old culture, but he did not here elaborate much on the concept of national settlement, moving on quickly to describe his efforts on Prince Edward Island as an illustration of how Highland settlers could best be assisted so as to increase their chances of success in a strange environment.

Observations was initially greeted most enthusiastically by the reviewers, who unanimously recognized the force of his arguments. Unfortunately, most reviews at the time were published anonymously, and for the most part we do not know who were their authors. Most of them were particularly impressed by the critique of the passenger legislation. *The Critical Review,* for example, commented: "We think that he has combated the prejudice and censured the weakness of some leading movers of the late transactions of the Highland Society with considerable success, and that his publication will have a powerful effect in removing such embarrassing and untoward obstacles to the adoption of a just system of policy."[9] The *Scots Magazine,* traditionally hostile to Highland emigration, acknowledged that Selkirk "certainly appears to us to be guided by such sound and enlarged views of policy, and has explained these in a manner so clear and forcible, as to leave hardly any room for contesting the important conclusions which it is his object to draw." Moreover, added the reviewer, "of all the persons affected by the present state of things, the Highland proprietors are certainly the last that have any title to complain, since it is their own work."[10]

Hearty applause came also from the recently founded *Edinburgh Review,* which thought the question so well handled that the work merely needed to be summarized. This anonymous reviewer was one of the journal's founders, Francis Horner, one of the major luminaries of the later Scottish Enlightenment and a leading Whig thinker of the nineteenth century. Horner was a native of Edinburgh, a graduate of the local High School, and like Selkirk, a protegé of Dugald Stewart at the University of Edinburgh. A few years younger than Selkirk, Horner also shared a keen interest in the debates of the Speculative Society. Horner was impressed with Selkirk's book, concluding that political economy must not mistake "as symptoms of decay and devastation, the movements actually occasioned by the growth of wealth, enterprize, and industry," and adding that Selkirk had "contributed a new article, very nearly finished in its form, to the general elements of political administration, and . . . cast light on one of the most intricate parts of the science of oeconomy, that in which the theory of wealth and the theory of population are examined in connexion." In private correspondence, Horner added that the book was "a valuable piece of description history, as well as political economy," noting that the critics had experienced a "concurrence of opinion" on its importance.[11]

Even the *Farmer's Magazine* was impressed. Its reviewer wrote: "We hope that every Highland proprietor will peruse this work; not that we wish it to have the effect of inducing them to drive their tenantry from their estates, but of persuading them to adopt prudent measures in the management of their properties, that the people may have time to prepare, and may leave them without shewing any discontents."[12] Not surprisingly, the Highland lairds also read Selkirk's book with care. They tended to be considerably less enthusiastic about the argument. Some were defiant. The Marchioness of Stafford wrote to her husband in July of 1805—she had probably just finished reading the book—that "in spite of Lord Selkirk" she expected the Sutherland estates to preserve most of their population through improvements.[13]

Despite the obvious attention and approval excited by the appearance of *Observations* at the time of its publication, posterity has not followed the lead of the contemporary reviewers in regarding Selkirk's book as an important item either in the canon of political economy or in writing on the Highland Clearances. These two areas must be distinguished, for the problems are distinctive to each.

As far as political economy is concerned, one of the major problems with *Observations* was that the immediate issues addressed by Selkirk rapidly shifted, altered to some extent by the force of his own arguments.[14] When Selkirk wrote, hostility to emigration from the British Isles was almost unanimously exhibited in both Scotland and Great Britain. The work's pioneering quality was soon forgotten, however, and it came to be seen as a tract for the times rather than as a general statement of theoretical principles, an assessment encouraged by the nature of subsequent attacks on it by spokesmen for the Highland lairds. Equally important, Selkirk himself did not pursue his ideas further in print, at least not in ways that gave his thinking any coherence. Selkirk's later publications were occasional and issue oriented, and many of his ideas were communicated in unpublished correspondence with and memorials to the British government, thus helping perhaps to disguise his own emphasis on the need for system.

A perfect example of the problem of appreciating Selkirk's thinking came in terms of the elaboration of his thought about the strategy of settlement. Instead of including this material in his book, Selkirk pursued it only after *Observations* had gone to the printer. Correspondence from Sheriff MacDonell had made clear not only that Baldoon posed a serious health problem, but also that there were difficulties in obtaining land concessions from the government in Upper Canada. In personal interviews with and written representations to Prime Minister William Pitt, the earl attempted to gain government support for his settlement ventures in that province. The result was a lengthy unpublished document entitled "Outlines of a Plan for the Settlement & Security of Canada," which reflected Selkirk's American thinking as of the summer of 1805. He submitted his ideas, he wrote, on the basis of "an attentive & pretty laborious investigation of the local circumstances" of the Canadas, he wrote to Pitt.[15] An earlier letter observed that the "Outlines" was indeed the document the earl had spoken about with Pitt. It also noted that the 4 February proposal to Lord Camden had been deemed "inadmissible," although Selkirk still thought the general principles on which the Camden proposal was grounded were good ones.[16]

The chief problem of the Canadas, Selkirk insisted, was the constant influx of American settlers into the region, ultimately endangering British interests. The Americans were encouraged by easy land-granting procedures and low prices, and the entire land system of the Canadas needed serious overhauling. He advocated discouraging Americans while encouraging Highlanders, Dutch, Germans, and Welsh, "in short any who speak a different language from the English." The earl maintained that if the Canadian provinces were divided into four or five districts, "each inhabited by Colonists of a different nation, keeping up their original peculiarities and all differing in language from their neighbours in the United States, the authority of Government would be placed on the most secure foundation." He even suggested some guidelines for national settlements. The Dutch could be placed in townships below Kingston in Upper Canada. The Highlanders could go to those parts of Upper Canada west of Niagara in sufficient numbers "to preserve themselves from the contagion of American manners," and Highlanders could be attracted from the United States to this enclave. Americans around Lake Ontario should be moved further north.

Selkirk wanted not only national settlements, but also a natural aristocracy. He recommended entails on larger grants to assure a landed aristocracy so much needed, particularly in Upper Canada, and in general a land policy less favourable to common settlers. Clergymen from the national groups should be encouraged regardless of denomination, and of course, the regulations of the *Passenger Vessel Act* of 1803 should be reconsidered since "Gov't appears to have been taken by surprize when they consented to the measure." The British government did not take Selkirk's proposals at all seriously, and the scheme remains important only as evidence of the further elaboration of the earl's thinking on the subject of national settlement. These ideas ought to have been included in his book, however. In future negotiations with the government, Selkirk would drop his insistence on non-English speaking settlers and would concentrate entirely on land-granting practices.

An equally critical factor, along with his limited publication record, in Selkirk's failure to achieve prominence as a political economist was inherent in the principles he was attempting to combine and reconcile. At first glance Selkirk appeared to be expounding the standard liberal notions of the Scottish Enlightenment, arguing for freedom from restraint and the encouragement of natural and inevitable processes of change and modernization. This was the context in which the contemporary reviewers applauded the work. But Selkirk was not simply a *laissez-faire* liberal, for he was committed not only to positive intervention in the emigration process by private and public interests, but also to paternalistic intervention to preserve what were to him important human values. Unlike most of the political economists of his time, Selkirk recognized that human nature had to be taken into account in the process of change and, moreover, that human nature was simply not as adaptable as the marketplace or the economy. Undoubtedly the most interesting new feature of Selkirk's book on emigration was his insistence that traditional Highland culture and personal psychology were inimical to modernization, and that the Highlander had a legitimate right to evade progress. For Selkirk, the traditional way of life could be in large measure preserved by emigration to land-rich British North America, and he even offered a series of arguments that found strategic advantage for the colonies in the perpetuation of cultures such as that of the Highlander. The earl was not the only contemporary who concerned himself with the human cost of progress, but he was one of the few Enlightenment figures who both accepted the inevitability and even desirability of change at the same time that he sought practical alternatives for its victims. He may have embraced the demographic ideas of Thomas Malthus, but he did not share Malthus's fatalism. He recognized that the vaunted schemes of Highland development would not work, at least not in the ways that their proponents advanced. It would appear that few readers of *Observations,* either at the time of publication or subsequently, recognized Selkirk's ingenious reconciliation of progress and tradition.

In terms of the Highland Clearances themselves, Selkirk had failed to appreciate sufficiently the peculiar reasons for the opposition of the kelping lairds to emigration. The economy of the western islands was not the same as the rest of the Highlands. The principal factor was the manufacture of kelp, from which an alkaline ash was derived that was in short supply in Britain during the Napoleonic Wars. Kelping made possible the maintenance of a much larger population than would have been possible in ordinary agricultural terms, and its demand for labour explains why the kelping lairds were so hostile to emigration. Selkirk did not focus on the unusual nature of this region in his book, and as we shall see, the opponents of emigration from this area were in no position to emphasize the point. They, like Selkirk, preferred to argue in more general terms.[17]

DEVELOPMENTS IN LATE 1805 AND EARLY 1806

By late 1805 rumours of the downfall of the Tory government of William Pitt, who was seriously ill, were endemic in Britain, and Selkirk exposed his political ambitions. He obviously felt sufficiently established to begin to think about a Scottish seat in the House of Lords. He began writing the obligatory letters requesting support from his fellows in October, long before the elections had been formally called.[18] The Ninth Earl of Keltie commented to a correspondent: "Your Lordship will have had a circular from Lord Selkirk, who has a mind to be in time!"[19] The earl became involved in Presbyterian Church politics as well.[20] In the meantime, the news from his American agents continued to be unfavourable. Alexander MacDonell reported another outbreak of malaria at Baldoon, and added, "when well, the settlers are discontented, violent & rapacious—now they are unfit for any exertion."[21]

A few days later, in a letter Selkirk received on 18 October, a desperate MacDonell had penned: "For Heavens sake, my Lord, lose no time in instructing me how I am to proceed. You will find that your views will be frustrated & that you cannot effect a permanent settlement at Baldoon . . . eventually your Lordship will be under the necessity of giving up the idea."[22] MacDonell pressed for a removal of the settlement to lands elsewhere in the province. Selkirk replied in early November by observing that MacDonell's letters had given him a "distress of mind" that was "more than I can express," but insisted that the possibility of removing the settlers had been delayed by the failure of the Upper Canadian government to cooperate with him in providing alternate grants of land. "I trust you will take good care that the public throughout Canada shall understand how the case stood," he wrote self-righteously, "& that it was my anxious desire & positive instruction to remove the people from Baldoon before the unhealthy season." The responsibility for "the calamities which have befallen the settlers" were on the shoulders of General Peter Hunter, he insisted.[23] The earl did not consider the possibility that his absence thousands of miles from the settlement had anything to do with the problem. Blame was arguable. What would be indisputable was subsequent information from Selkirk's New York bankers that he owed them $10,809.11.[24] As for Prince Edward Island, Selkirk attempted desperately through intermediaries to gain some information on the progress of his settlement, because he had not heard from James Williams since his departure from the island in October 1804.[25]

The North American situation was obviously deteriorating rapidly for Selkirk. Alexander McDonell's letters made plain that the man had panicked, perhaps legitimately, and as for James Williams, he was simply not communicating with his employer. Selkirk could do little more than answer McDonell with firm words and sentiments of affection; there seemed little point in writing Williams at all. Williams still existed, for Selkirk received in late 1805 a copy of a letter he had written to Lieutenant Governor Edmund Fanning of Prince Edward Island. But the letter was not very helpful about the present state of Selkirk's settlements.[26] Beyond the problems with his agents lurked other issues. Selkirk was convinced that the Upper Canadian government was unsympathetic to his projects, and on Prince Edward Island, the House of Assembly, in a "Jacobinical temper," was arguing for public seizure of lands where the quitrents authorized in 1767 had not been paid and the conditions of settlement of the original grants had not been met. The earlier attempt by the Colonial Office to resolve the quitrent business had obviously failed. Selkirk recognized that the original conditions of settlement on Prince Edward Island had never been observed, having been "devised by some theorist, devoid of experience in Colonization."[27] These conditions had called for the establishment of large numbers of settlers, who had to be "foreign Protestants," and could probably never have been met. But he blamed the legislative demand for forfeiture of the lands on the fact that "a considerable proportion of the inhabitants of the Island are natives of the older Settlements in America & inherit the levelling spirit of the New Englanders."[28] This statement was not terribly accurate and tells us more about Selkirk's attitudes to Yankees than it does about Prince Edward Island. Whatever the reasons, however, it was clear that the American projects were not going well.

Around the end of 1805, the wedding between Sir James Montgomery and the earl's sister Lady Elizabeth was announced. Montgomery and Selkirk met in London in 1805 and got on together very well. The marriage in 1806 would ally the two families with the largest landholdings on Prince Edward Island, totalling almost one-fourth of the total land surface. If they could cooperate together to "improve" the island as they had their estates at home, the island might begin to prosper. Had either or both of them chosen to move to the island, their energy might have been transformational. What the island needed, arguably, was the presence of a major landowner such as Selkirk, both to provide leadership for the settlers and to cut through the resistance of the colonial governments to new initiatives. Despite his American visit, Selkirk still had not learned that men and governments could not be manipulated very successfully at long distance.

The opening months of 1806 saw a chorus of three full-scale critiques of Selkirk and his book *Observations on the Present State of the Highlands* appear in print. One attack was by Clanranald's factor Robert Brown, and two were by anonymous writers.[29] Brown was a member of one of the most influential and powerful classes in Highland society, the men who actually ran the great estates for their employers. For the most part, these factors operated out of offices in Edinburgh. They became especially important in the event of minorities and absences of the lairds, often for military purposes. In these cases they often became members of the trustees running the estate. Like most factors, Robert Brown was devoted to maximizing income for his employer. As indicated by its title, one of the critiques collected letters that had originally appeared in one of Edinburgh's newspapers. All three responses were characterized by *ad hominum* arguments and a reiteration of the optimistic sentiments always characteristic of the opponents of emigration. All also indicated a hostility to the overseas empire. Selkirk was accused of romanticizing the culture of indolent Highlanders, of the outsider's ignorance of "true conditions" in the Highlands, and of pecuniary self-interest. All three authors insisted that there was room for even more people in the Highlands, by opening waste land for cultivation and shifting much of the population to crofting on very small landholdings. Maintaining that America was not really a land of opportunity, they advanced the arguments that Highlanders were required at home as soldiers and in the south as labourers. A stronger case could have been made against Selkirk by admitting the peculiar conditions prevailing on the kelping islands and insisting that kelping was necessary to the national wartime economy. Instead, the critics attempted to refute the earl's generalizations about the inevitability of economic change and its corollary of the need for fewer people. The reviewers were relatively unimpressed with these responses.[30] Events in Upper Canada and Prince Edward Island might well also have undermined Selkirk's position—had the critics known about them. Selkirk's arguments, after all, relied not only on the population surplus in the Highlands but also on the presumption that life was better in the New World.

If developments both in Scotland and at his settlements in British America caused Selkirk some distress in the winter of 1805–06, there seemed some hope for better days. On 23 January 1806, William Pitt died, and his ministry was replaced by one headed by William Wyndham Grenville (Lord Grenville), with Charles James Fox having particular concern for foreign affairs.[31] This ministry was a coalition of three factions in Parliament—the followers of Grenville, of Fox, and of Lord Sidmouth—and was the only Whig government that served in Britain between 1783 and 1827. This brief ministry, usually known in a derogatory sense as the "Ministry of All the Talents," would be best remembered for its bill for the abolition of the slave trade.[32] Fox and Selkirk's father had been friends, sharing in the Whig battles against the ministry associated with the early days of the French Revolution. By March of 1806 it was widely rumoured in Britain that Lord Selkirk would replace Anthony Merry as British minister to the United States, and the American government was so informed.[33] On the surface, this appointment appeared to make a good deal of sense, for Selkirk had recently travelled widely in the United States and obviously had a lively interest in American affairs. On the other hand, his American acquaintances were mainly among the Federalist forces out of power in Washington, and many of his views of the United States were hardly designed to win much favour with the administration of Thomas Jefferson. As if to demonstrate his assessment of Americans, Selkirk submitted a new position paper to the government in late March of 1806. It was entitled "Suggestions respecting Upper Canada," and was personally delivered to William Wyndham by his parliamentary secretary.[34]

The eastern part of Upper Canada, Selkirk began, was settled by Loyalists. But most of the western part of the province was peopled by Americans eager for cheap land, and "they are by no means a safe or desirable population." The presence of too much land on the market depressed the prices and encouraged "wild & restless" Americans to cross the border. The result was that "the dependence of the Province on Britain must hang by a thread." What was required was an alternative population to the Yankees. In this respect, Selkirk argued, Highland emigrants would be ideal. Their language and culture was different from the Americans. If simply allowed to mix with the Upper Canadian population, the Highlanders would soon lose their distinctive manners and language. They might become better farmers, but they would lose their "sturdy dependence." Instead, the Highlanders had to be settled where their language could be maintained "as the prevailing & established dialect" and where they could maintain their "national peculiarities." Southwestern Upper Canada was an ideal place for the Highlanders. The existing Americans could be moved north of Lake Ontario, and Highland Scots in the United States encouraged to come to Upper Canada.

The appointment as minister appears to have been offered and accepted, but was never implemented. Thus the earl never got the opportunity to get back to North America on public business. Selkirk waited around for months to learn of his fate, writing an old university friend that he had been "put off in a teazing manner" and found the suspense disagreeable.[35] Whether Washington had objected to Selkirk or whether the rapid deterioration of the health of Charles James Fox—reaping the price of years of hard living— played crucial parts in the delay is not clear. Probably Fox's illness did matter, and events moved quickly beyond anyone's control. Fox died in September and Parliament was dissolved soon after. It is also possible that Selkirk's continued barrage of position papers on American affairs to the ministry while his appointment hung fire either annoyed those in power or provided evidence that he was simply not the right man for the job. Whoever was appointed needed to placate the Americans on a variety of vexing issues. As Selkirk made plain, he did not regard friendship with the United States as the only aim of British policy in the New World, and he was full of unworkable ideas and grandiose schemes.

In one position paper, Selkirk threw his support behind a comprehensive effort to liberate the Spanish colonies of Latin America, partly to restore British honour and partly to prevent them from falling into the hands of the French.[36] South American military adventures had been discussed and entertained by the Grenville ministry throughout 1806. Lord Grenville had opposed South American activity in the 1790s, but now was on the verge of becoming an enthusiast, and Selkirk was thus probably attempting to win favour with the prime minister. He argued that such an enterprise would be the basis of "lasting friendship" with the United States. It would allow the Americans to obtain Florida, which they coveted. "Some secret stipulation in this subject would effectually secure them to our interests and render them more pliant upon all the other subjects we have to discuss with them." True to his Scottish heritage, Selkirk argued, "*The Isthmus of Darien* [Panama] *is the Key to the whole trade of South America,*" and control of this region should be Britain's only territorial concern.[37] In a subsequent paper Selkirk counselled against the acquisition of Latin American territory. He insisted:

> where the people have not the tie of a common origin and language with us, where their religion and their laws are so different, as those of these Colonists are from ours, it is almost unavoidable, that in time jealousies must arise, that the affections of the people will be alienated, that they will feel the control of a distant foreign country to be irksome, and that sooner or later we must resolve, to abandon the dominion, or to maintain it be a Severe and ruinous Struggle.[38]

Although an expansionist, the earl tried not to be an indiscriminate imperialist.

If Selkirk bombarded the ministry with ideas about South America, he also continued to offer advice about British policy within the North American colonies as well. His major statement of early 1806 was "Granting Lands in North America," sent both to the colonial secretary and to the Board of Trade.[39] In fairness to the earl, he knew a good deal more about colonial land policy and procedures than he did about Latin America; he had probably done as much on-the-spot research on the subject as anyone else in either Britain or America, and his views deserved a hearing.

Land policy must be adapted to local circumstances, Selkirk insisted, with the main point to give each family a farm to cultivate by distributing land among actual settlers. At the same time, he was not opposed to extensive grants to large proprietors, for land was essentially useless until it was improved. In an interesting line of argument, the earl maintained: "From the principles so clearly laid down by Mr. Malthus, it will be easily understood that in a Colony where an original nucleus of population has been planted, that population increasing at a certain rate, will be capable of carrying forward the improvement of the country with a proportional degree of rapidity—a rapidity increasing like the population in a geometrical proportion." From this colonial extension of Malthusianism, Selkirk concluded that large grants did not hinder development if a base population was already in place. Major proprietors could afford to improve their lands in a way not given to ordinary settlers. Turning to proprietors in a new colony, Selkirk argued that the lack of success in Nova Scotia and Prince Edward Island of experiments with large proprietors should not prejudice the government against extensive grants. He opposed an absence of policy, as well as one of giving lands away to actual settlers. These approaches only attracted American squatters, "a set of lawless vagabonds, straggling upon the frontiers of our provinces." Far better to give the land to leading people. Free lands diffused and perpetuated a "levelling spirit among the people," and a system of agrarian equality ran counter both to British principles and the "experience of ages." A "respectable landed Aristocracy" was the basis of political stability. Selkirk laid down as a dictum: "Where land is of no value no Aristocracy can be found," adding that the absence of a distribution of ranks was "the greatest defect in the political system of our Colonies, as well as of the United States." These arguments were far removed from Selkirk's much earlier support for the French Revolution and notions of "equal agrarians."

What the British government made of these submissions is quite unclear. They certainly gave evidence that Selkirk was interested in American affairs, that he had much first-hand information at his disposal, and that he was constantly thinking about New World problems. They also suggested that he was critical if not hostile to American democracy, more than hinting at a patronizing condescension that many Jeffersonian Americans would have found offensive. At the same time, his policy papers of 1806 also demonstrated that Selkirk's views were hardening, particularly in response to his American experience. His views on the importance of a landed aristocracy in the preservation of social stability had been first expressed in his pamphlet on poor relief, but he was coming increasingly to insist on these principles and even to seek their extension in the free air of the New World. Whig aristocrats in Britain had always maintained an uneasy tension between their commitment to equality and the preservation of a stability essential to their own social order. For Selkirk the scales had certainly tipped in favour of the latter concern. In many ways, the subsequent break with family political tradition was being prefigured in the development of Selkirk's thinking.

The spring of 1806 saw Selkirk actively involved in politics, simultaneously breaking with his family's past and in other ways extending it. The forthcoming parliamentary election would be a hard-fought battle, and unlike his father, Thomas was prepared to use his local power on behalf of Whig candidates. He was even willing to take steps that his father had always opposed and criticized, by creating artificial voters through fictional transfers of property within constituencies. The practice was, of course, common throughout Scotland. Thomas defended his behaviour on the simple grounds that his opponents were already doing it.[40]

While old Dunbar would not have applauded the creation of fictional superiorities by his son, he would doubtless have applauded Thomas's concerns for the position of the Scottish peerage. The occasion arose because of the uncertainties surrounding the elevation of the Earl of Eglintoun to the British peerage. This elevation gave Eglintoun a hereditary seat in the House of Lords. Eglintoun had been elected a representative peer of Scotland, and many, including the Earl of Selkirk, had assumed that the change of status had created a vacancy among the Scottish peers. The government failed to act on this assumption, however, and a petition to the House of Lords was drafted and circulated among the Scottish peers, winning some approval.[41] Selkirk himself met with "a noble Lord, very high in administration" (Lord Grenville himself), who was rumoured to be opposed to reopening the question of the privileges of the Scottish peerage. As in 1784, an irate Earl of Selkirk was deflected from protesting the system on the grounds that government would accept reform "if the Peers of Scotland should unite" in seeking it. Selkirk was encouraged by the prime minister to take the lead in organizing his colleagues, and he would later do so in 1806 and 1807.[42]

In addition to dealing with leaders of the ministry on a variety of topics and engaging in political activity in Scotland, Selkirk also in early 1806 saw a second edition of *Observations on the Present State of the Highlands* through the press. The new edition was rather more of a reprinting than a substantial revision. Type was reset, providing a number of minor differences of capitalization, punctuation, and page numberings from the first edition. The only major additions were in the footnotes and appendices, particularly an updating of the progress of the Prince Edward Island settlement, based on second-hand information since the earl still had not heard from island agent James Williams, and a new Appendix V dealing with population data and changes in the Highlands. If more details on Prince Edward Island had been available, they might have induced the author to make more substantial changes, especially to his chapter on the island. But the absence of information, combined with the failure of the critics of the book to force Selkirk to rethink it, led him to reissue it virtually unaltered.

With the publication of the second printing of *Observations*, Selkirk brought some sort of tentative conclusion to a phase of his life that had begun with Highland projects and continued with his American tour. The development (or lack of development) of the settlements would continue to disturb him for a number of years, but after early 1806 the bulk of his attention was turned away from British America and his settlements and toward British politics. With his usual zeal, Selkirk threw himself into peerage politics and several movements of reform.

CHAPTER NINE

Joining the Establishment

By THE BEGINNING OF JULY 1806, Selkirk had learned that he had no immediate chance of returning to North America in any official capacity. His settlements cried out for hands-on management, but Selkirk attempted to deal with them at long distance. He was at the same time moving successfully toward one of his cherished ambitions: membership in the British Parliament through election to the British House of Lords. Achieving the goal would not be easy.

For Prince Edward Island, Selkirk wrote to an old acquaintance in Halifax, James Stewart, asking him to investigate the situation. He was particularly concerned to learn news of his settlers, noting: "I don't know if you have seen any of the replies that have come out to my book, but they all attempt in a very malignant manner to insinuate doubts on the veracity of the relation I have given to their progress, & pretend that no account from the Colonies is to be trusted—I would wish to be able to refute this vile aspersion in a manner that could admit no reply."[1] As for James Williams, the earl admitted to Stewart that he could not be certain that the agent had turned "rogue," but thought there was sufficient evidence to fit with other examples of the "malignant effect of the American Climate on the honesty."[2] He wanted Williams to allow Stewart to examine the books in Halifax, to report to Stewart monthly, and to clear all bills of exchange with him. Williams managed to defer the ordered visit to Halifax, however. Throughout his long connection with British America, Selkirk could never bring himself to admit that he asked too much of his agents. Their failures were never couched in terms of his own responsibility. Failures were theirs, not his. In fairness to the earl, James Williams clearly turned out to be a bad apple.

More publicly, Selkirk assumed the leadership of the landed proprietors of Prince Edward Island, pressing upon the ministry a bill (for passage by the island assembly) adjusting lines and boundaries of the lands there. This bill had been apparently drafted by John Stewart, whose book on the island appeared about this time with many kind words for Selkirk. The bill and his assumption of leadership would involve the earl in island politics and personal conflict in an unfortunate way, as we shall see.[3] Selkirk also transmitted to the government with his approbation a proposal from Miles Macdonell for the creation of a Highland Fencible Corps in Upper Canada. Because of the disastrous Canadian Regiment experience of the government a few years earlier—in which large parts of a Highland fencible regiment recruited for service in Canada had risen against their officers while garrisoned in Glasgow—there was no enthusiasm in ministerial circles for such a proposal.[4] Selkirk apparently did not appreciate the extent of government hostility to colonial fencible corps, and would make proposals of his own in 1813.

As for the earl's affairs in Upper Canada, he continued to solicit alternate land grants to make it possible to provide new lands for his Baldoon settlers.[5] While Selkirk continued to chaff at the absence of news from Prince Edward Island, he did receive correspondence from Alexander Macdonell that sounded at least superficially more promising in 1806. The people at Baldoon, despite sickness, had decided to remain on the site Selkirk had selected for them, and the shepherds were extremely enthusiastic about the quality of the grass there.[6] Although Macdonell continued to have trouble with the Upper Canadian government, noting with his enclosures: "Your Lordship will perceive how little disposed this Government is to accomodate [sic]," Selkirk was more sanguine. He advised his agent: "The change of administration, alters very materially my prospects & views in U.C. as I can now depend on every reasonable accommodation & a fair interpretation of my original grant, & moreover the Gentlemen who in Council have shewn so *fair* a regard for the spirit of their Sovereigns orders, may expect a haul over the coals for their pains."[7] The earl wrote that he had "full confidence in the fairness & liberality of the present government" and was preparing once again to become active in Upper Canada. Selkirk's belief in the ability of a government in London to influence a government in the colonies was touching, if totally misguided. Like most contemporaries, the earl gave entirely too much credit to the possibility that colonial bureaucracies would respond to political winds more than three thousand miles away. If he wanted to change policy in York, Upper Canada, he would have been much better advised to be on the spot.

PREPARING FOR THE PEERAGE ELECTION

Autumn of 1806 saw Selkirk in the midst of political preparations for the forthcoming parliamentary election. He still regarded himself as a Whig, and he was active in support of Whig candidates for the House of Commons, employing his considerable influence in Galloway to good advantage. Anxiety about a seat for Henry Erskine, lord advocate for Scotland in the Whig government and a personal acquaintance, led Selkirk to work behind the scenes to obtain for Erskine the nomination of the Dumfries Burghs.[8] Selkirk was equally active on behalf of his own order, serving as one of the leading lights of a concerted effort to gather the peers of Scotland and their heirs apparent to consider "what steps it may be advisable to take with a view of obtaining for our Order certain advantages granted by the Union of Ireland to the peerage of that Kingdom."[9] The principal advantage enjoyed by the Irish peerage, of course, was the right of younger sons to sit in the House of Commons.

At the same time that he was pressing for Scottish peerage reform, Selkirk was also concerned that he himself be chosen as a representative peer. Another round of letters from him circulated in late October to the select electorate, announcing his candidacy and hoping for support, which if received he would "ever esteem it the most distinguished obligation."[10] On 27 October Lord Grenville sent to the Scottish peers a list of the names of "those Peers whom I understand the friends of Government are likely to support."[11] This was the government list, and Thomas's name was on it! His father might well have been horrified at the thought of his son's name appearing on one of those hated attempts by the ministry in London to influence the independent votes of the Scottish peers. But Thomas might well have answered his father that he was attempting to implement a reform of the Scottish peerage system that would permit those not elected to the Lords to serve in the Commons, as was the case in Ireland. In any case, a serious political career for a Scottish peer was possible only by playing according to the existing rules.

Whether or not immediate political concerns were foremost in Selkirk's mind as he prepared yet another position paper on the New World in early October, the exercise—which involved personal meetings with Lord Grenville and George Canning at the Foreign Office—undoubtedly helped keep his name and claim to expertise before the government. The main thrust of the submission was to reiterate his earlier arguments on the need for British involvement in the inevitable attempts of Spanish colonies in Latin America to liberate themselves from their colonial yoke. Selkirk's advocacy of an active British military role to prevent these territories from falling into French hands was an argument of the moment, but it was on this occasion cast in terms of British policy toward the United States. Selkirk emphasized that Alexander Hamilton had earlier advocated an "Anglo-American partition of the Spanish American Colonies in the western hemisphere," and although Hamilton was dead, his killer Aaron Burr was adventuring in the Spanish territories and might be useful to the British.[12] Burr sought to establish an independent territory under his control in the trans-Mississippi area, mainly using part of the Louisiana Purchase, and he was certainly willing to deal with the British. Selkirk argued that Thomas Jefferson could probably be won over to a campaign of colonial liberation in Latin America, noting that under Jefferson the United States was "an ambitious young nation with great potentialities."[13] Canning's response was noncommittal, but Grenville observed that it would be difficult "to ally the United States of America with us in the liberation of the Spanish territories in the Americas" given Jefferson's lack of friendliness to Britain and the present state of Anglo-American relations in general.[14]

In an edited version of the foregoing document published in 1943 in the *Canadian Historical Review,* American scholar John Perry Pritchett referred in a footnote to entries in Selkirk's diary for 1806–07 in which Selkirk minuted a meeting with Lord Grenville about the Spanish colonies in America and four conversations with George Canning. He also made entries on 21 and 22 December 1806 about the possibilities of the Spanish American situation. This represents one of our few glimpses of one of the diaries that were apparently lost in the fire at St. Mary's Isle, which Pritchett had seen on a research trip to the family home in the late 1930s. Unfortunately none of the material cited or quoted by Pritchett adds anything substantial to our knowledge of Selkirk. But it does suggest that we would know a good deal more about the inner life of the earl had we access to this material. The prime minister was certainly dubious about the schemes of Aaron Burr. Once again Selkirk had demonstrated his imaginativeness and his intimate knowledge of American affairs, but combined these attributes with support for hare-brained schemes (such as Burr's western conspiracy). The ministry may well have found in this exchange further substantiation for the wisdom of not appointing Selkirk to the American post. Selkirk certainly found the attitude of the Grenville government "perplexing and dilatory," and blamed it on Canning. This incident certainly suggested that Selkirk's Enlightenment reputation for rational thinking was occasionally being modified by attacks of romantic overimagination; the plans of Aaron Burr were clumsy fantasies at best.

A few weeks later, in November of 1806, Selkirk was again memorial-izing the government, arguing that the Irish would soon join the Scots High-landers in a major flow of emigration to North America, pushed out by the usual culprits, overpopulation and agricultural improvement. These Irish, especially the Roman Catholics among them, Selkirk maintained, needed to be redirected to British colonies. Selkirk recommended amalgamation of the Irish and the Highlanders. He insisted: "A National settlement, speaking their original & favourite dialect will be equally attractive to the Irish as to the Highlanders; & it will be of use to preserve among the Settlers, those national customs & peculiarities, which are associated in their minds, with the traditions of the ancient greatness of their race."[15] Naturally he recom-mended Upper Canada as the ultimate destination. The need for cooperation between Gaelic-speaking Scots and Gaelic-speaking Irish would become one of Selkirk's major assumptions in the early planning for the Red River Settle-ment a few years later. Unfortunately, for a variety of historic reasons, Irish and Scots did not get on very well and Selkirk's hopes would be thwarted.

Peerage politics heated up in the autumn of 1806, as the election called for 4 December at Holyroodhouse in Edinburgh came closer. There were problems with the government list, and Selkirk worked actively behind the scenes to ensure his own support. When the day arrived a much larger assembly than usual appeared in person, and all but nine absent peers had actually submitted proxies. Selkirk was sufficiently concerned about his own prospects to vote for himself, but he was easily elected.[16] A day later, the earl was in the chair at a meeting of the Peers of Scotland held at Fortune's Tavern in Edinburgh, called to consider peerage reform. The gathering was an informal rump of those earlier present at Holyroodhouse, but it included more than twenty peers and heirs apparent. Not all present were enthusiastic for change; a motion for adjournment by Lord Napier and Earl Morton was defeated by only fourteen to eleven votes. Those assembled then debated another proposition, probably drafted by Selkirk: "Would it, or would it not, be advantageous to the Peerage of Scotland, that their Representatives should be chosen for life, provided the Peers not elected should have the same privileges of eligibility to the House of Commons as enjoyed by the Peerage of Ireland?" It was decided that Selkirk as chairman should send the proposition to every peer and heir apparent, requesting an answer by 1 December 1807, following which another meeting should be called as quickly as possible.[17] Such a conclusion was probably as much as Selkirk could have expected at this point. As he departed Edinburgh for London, where he would take the oaths associated with his entrance into the House of Lords, he could feel relatively pleased with the course of events. He had managed to enter politics in the only way available to him, he was moving his fellow peers in the direction of reform, and he was achieving some measure of success.

IN THE HOUSE OF LORDS

Although Selkirk did not immediately throw himself into the middle of proceedings in the House of Lords, he attended assiduously and made his maiden speech in the midst of a spirited debate on the second reading of the second bill to abolish the slave trade, the Grenville-Howick Bill for Abolition. This was the major piece of legislation of the Grenville government and called for total and unequivocal abolition.

The first shot in the formal campaign for abolition of the slave trade in Britain had begun in 1776 when David Hartley of Hull presented a bill for abolition. This effort met little support, but within a few years a small group of evangelical Anglicans (popularly called "the Clapham Sect") led by William Wilberforce had managed to get the matter taken seriously by Parliament. The first legislative step in the process was the prohibition of the actual trade itself. In May of 1789 Wilberforce made his first speech in the House against the trade, concluding: "Sir, when we think of eternity and the future consequences of all human conduct, what is there in this life that shall make any man contradict the dictates of his conscience, the principles of justice and the law of God!" Abolitionism was one of those great moral questions that stirred up British public opinion to an extent that few other issues could do. Wilberforce's early efforts for abolition were failures, but the government-sponsored bill for prohibition met with very little resistance in Parliament. Quite apart from its moral virtue, the bill was favoured by the "West India Party" of British slave owners of the West Indies—the principal opponents of the elimination of slavery itself. This was because the British slave owners calculated that by abolishing the trade, they would make it harder for the French sugar islands to compete with them. The slave owners, in anticipation of abolition of the trade from Africa, had stocked up on slaves in the decade before the legislation was passed.[18]

In the House of Lords debates, the Earl of Westmoreland had argued that if Britain abandoned the slave trade, others less humane might take it up, adding that the trade was an economically valuable one and abolition would endanger the rights of property.[19] Lord Selkirk rose to answer his colleague, insisting that moral offence took precedence over property. In some ways, Selkirk's involvement in the debate over the slave trade had its ironies, since the principal point that most contemporaries took from his book on emigra-tion was that parliamentary interference with the immigrant trade, often compared to the slave trade, was a bad policy. But characteristically, Selkirk used the bulk of his speech to lecture on the demography of the West Indies, concluding that abolition of the trade would improve planter treatment of their Negroes and hence would increase the population of the region.[20] William Wilberforce, listening intently to the debate on his precious reform bill, thought Selkirk's remarks "sensible and well-principled."[21] Selkirk was one of a number of young peers and heirs who spoke in favour of the bill. At one point, the House of Lords spontaneously gave Wilberforce, who appeared to observe the proceedings, three hurrahs. In the end, the vote was 283 to 16 for abolition.[22]

Wilberforce was twelve year's Selkirk's senior, the son of a wealthy merchant of Hull who had been converted to evangelical religion through reading William Law's *A Serious Call to a Devout and Holy Life*. Selkirk, on the other hand, appears to have had no visible religious beliefs whatsoever. One searches his surviving papers and writings in vain for any comments about God, Christ, religious doctrine, or church attendance. Nevertheless, the two men were prob-ably acquainted before Selkirk's speech. The connection would have been through Selkirk's old teacher, Anna Laetitia Barbauld, who had published a poem entitled "Epistle to William Wilberforce, Esq. on the Rejection of the Bill for Abolishing the Slave Trade," in 1791 and subsequently become a good friend of the abolitionist, with whom she shared many reform sentiments. After 1807, Wilberforce and Selkirk would become close friends and occasional legislative allies.

To a correspondent, Wilberforce wrote that the earl had spoken in the House of Lords with "so low a voice that he could scarce be heard."[23] Nobody expected a maiden effort in Parliament to be outstanding, but from the very beginning Selkirk had demonstrated two principal failings that would hold him back as a political figure in an era where the cut and thrust of parliamentary debate was one of the places where an aspiring young man could make his mark. In the first place, he was a terrible public speaker, lacking volume, animation, and any sense of humour. Fellow-Scot Archibald Constable, the publisher, reported a few weeks later, after attendance at the House of Lords, that "whatever may be his merit as a writer," Selkirk was a "most wretched speaker, and I think will never be a good one."[24] In the second place, Selkirk had a tendency to lecture rather than to debate, droning on endlessly with carefully prepared arguments full of good points lost on his audience.

If Selkirk began inauspiciously in the public glare of the House of Lords, he was still working hard behind the scenes. The ministry, already in its dying days, received several new submissions from Selkirk early in 1807. One was directly concerned with his own affairs, in which he observed that since 1802 he had expended more than £30,000 (£35,000 with interest) upon North American colonization, and had in the process acquired property that could not be sold for more than £10,000. While he recognized that he had no legal right to compensation, he argued that his losses, plus the suffering of his "patrimonial affairs" while he was away, deserved indemnification, since he had performed a public service.[25] He suggested that he would be prepared to accept a large grant of waste lands in Upper Canada for his efforts. Since Selkirk must have known that Grenville would soon be out of office, this memorial was probably not to have been taken very seriously. More important business was probably another document about the Passenger Vessel Act of 1803, with Selkirk suggesting revisions to parts "particularly objectionable." He argued here that two passengers for every three tons was a more reasonable standard than the present regulation, and suggested changes in the amount and kind of provisioning more in keeping "with the actual habits of the peasantry of Scotland."[26] Nothing ever came of either of these initiatives, the government falling soon afterwards.

Perhaps the most interesting of the position papers Selkirk churned out for government perusal in early 1807 was one entitled "Bounds of Louisiana." Noting that the British government was negotiating with the Americans over unresolved boundaries, Selkirk called attention to the question of Louisiana, an enormous territory possessing many advantages of soil and climate that should not be given away gratuitously to the Americans. Arguing that territorial rights rested on treaties, and where these were silent on occupancy, the earl pointed out that the 1783 treaty with the United States did not refer to territory west of the Mississippi and that the Americans had only acquired Spanish rights through purchase from France. The northern boundaries of Louisiana had not been fixed, Selkirk argued, and Great Britain had a strong claim to territory through its conquest of French Canada and through occupancy. While Selkirk was prepared to concede to the Americans the Mississippi region, he maintained that the British could claim territory above the 47th latitude, partly through the French and partly through the British traders of the Hudson's Bay Company, which France certainly could not have ceded away to anyone.[27] He would return indirectly to these considerations in 1811 when negotiating his vast grant of territory from the Hudson's Bay Company, a grant that studiously ignored any demarcation between British and American territory in the West.

REFORM OF THE SCOTTISH PEERAGE

The early months of 1807 also saw Selkirk hard at work in his study, drafting his arguments for reform of the Scottish peerage. The resultant pamphlet was completed on 19 February with the Ministry of the All the Talents still in control of Parliament, but by the time it was printed a month later, political circumstances had altered dramatically, a point alluded to by the author in a brief preface.[28] In the end, the Irish question, and particularly pressure from Irish Catholics, did the Grenville ministry in. The government felt it had to make concessions to the Irish Catholics, and it decided to open all ranks in the army and navy to individuals regardless of their religion, thus in effect repealing one of the main purposes of the *Test Act*. The king in early February stated that he could not support such a concession, and the government spent a number of weeks attempting without success to find a formula that would allow the king to accept its policy. In the end Grenville surrendered the seals of office and became the main leader of those politicians opposed to the subsequent administrations of Lords Portland, Perceval, and Liverpool, all of whom were generally regarded as Tory in character.

Following the meeting of the peers in Edinburgh that Selkirk had chaired in December of 1806, he had circularized an account of the proceedings. Replies he had received suggest that reform would not have an easy ride. The Earl of Morton described the proposal that Scots peers not elected for life to the Lords be eligible for the House Commons as "degrading, and consequently disadvantageous beyond all possibility of compensation to our order," while Lord Torphichen produced a more lengthy and more reasoned response.[29] Those peers not elected for life would be reduced, argued Torphichen, to "absoloute Insignificance, almost Non-Existence." The elections would not necessarily produce a representative group, he insisted, and those eligible for the Commons who had once sat in the Lords would feel reduced in status. Perhaps more critically, Torphichen pointed out the importance of money for Commons electioneering, observing: "That Ingredient, Some of us *have*, but most, certainly many, *have not.*" This financial consideration was obviously one that did not bother Lord Selkirk, but for many of those of his fellow peers who had to watch their pence more carefully, the reform proposal would leave them with no political role whatever. The plan was dangerous, said Lord Torphichen, both because it was unconstitutional and because it set a dangerous precedent for altering the terms of Union of Scotland and England. Behind all his arguments lurked Torphichen's concern, doubtless shared by others, that the scheme was "calculated only to distinguish a few of our Order to the "absolute Humiliation of the remainder."[30] Why the meeting in December 1806 had coupled lifetime election to the Lords with eligibility for the Commons for those not so elected is not at all clear. What this pairing meant was that peers were given two quite different issues that could produce hostility.

Thomas Douglas was an intensely private man, and he did not often expose his thinking on personal matters to public scrutiny. *A Letter to the Peers of Scotland* was something of an exception. Here Selkirk wrote from personal experience, obviously extrapolating from his own situation to that of his order in general. As such, the pamphlet gives us an unusual opportunity to examine Selkirk's own assessment of his political future at the start of his public career. The present system, Selkirk insisted, excluded many capable men from public life and the pursuit of "honourable ambition." Probably thinking of his own father, Selkirk pointed out that the practice of party voting had excluded Scottish men of talent from the Lords in favour of lesser figures, who were supported by the prevailing party. "From such exclusion, my Lords," he warned, "none of us, in the present state of our elections, can flatter himself with being exempt: today the vindictive *ostracism* may fall on the head of our adversaries; to-morrow it may light on our own."[31] Men defeated by party machinations in Commons elections could normally find another seat, but Scottish peers had no alternative, being the only individuals in Britain who "in spite of the most distinguished and acknowledged merit, may be sunk in oblivion and condemned to obscurity." Moreover, he noted that some peers and heirs might find the Commons a preferable theatre for the display of their talents. As for the question of degradation, surely each peer could judge the question for himself.

Selkirk insisted that only by enlarging its political opportunities could the Scottish peerage be true to its traditions: "It is no longer the ferocious valour of the feudal chieftain that leads the highest honours of the state, but the talents of the statesman and the orator. The senate, in short, is now the *arena*, in which individuals have to struggle for personal consequence and distinction." This observation was not entirely true, for there were other arenas such as church, army, colonial administration, and university. But given the assumptions of the early nineteenth century, it was probably the case that politics was the principal goal. Having chosen to contend in the political arena, Selkirk must have often been conscious during the next few months of the force of his analysis. What Selkirk's arguments did not take into account, of course, was that many of his order were not so much ambitious for distinction as content with status.

THE FALL OF THE GRENVILLE MINISTRY AND SOME ADROIT MANOEUVRING

As Selkirk's involvement in British affairs increased, the level of his interest and concern for his North American settlements commensurately declined. His recent political successes put any notion of starting afresh in America well into the background. A North American career had clearly been a fall-back position from the outset. The fact that neither of his settlements did particularly well assured that they did not tempt him to consider further their personal supervision. Although the earl had still not heard from agent James Williams on Prince Edward Island, a Pictou attorney sent to the island in October 1806 on Selkirk's behalf had reported that the settlement appeared to be flourishing. James Williams was still in charge, appearing to be—said the reports—"very attentive to your interest but . . . rather *hard* in his Dealings."[32] That Williams had supposedly received a good deal of revenue in cash and produce, and that the mill he had built earlier had plainly "turned out to good advantage," cast considerable doubt on the agent's continued failure to communicate with an employer who had thus far received no return from his investment. As for Baldoon, it appeared to have reached some sort of stability, and no more news of fresh disasters emerged from that quarter. Alexander Macdonell was able to fill his letters with gossip, both about Upper Canadian politics and about the settlers themselves.[33] An attentive reader might have wondered how an agent supposedly located in a remote corner of Upper Canada could know so much about the goings on in the capital, but Selkirk was not reading carefully. He continued to complain to Macdonell about the expenses of Baldoon, which were "frightfully great," and pressed for continued work on drainage of the marshlands.[34] The comparative briefness of the letter was Selkirk's own demonstration of his level of involvement in colonial affairs while he manoeuvred around the political crisis of the fall of the Grenville government.

The fall of the Ministry of All the Talents and its replacement with a more Tory-oriented government meant that there would be another parliamentary election, including another voting for Scottish representative peers. The situation facing Selkirk was exactly the one he had attempted to explain to his fellows in the pamphlet on peerage reform. Like any member of the House of Commons, Selkirk would have to stand for re-election, and at first glance his chances did not seem very good. Although formally an independent, he had been associated with the reform Whigs. He would have to overcome ministerial support for other candidates and the natural predilection of the Scottish peers to vote for known Tories. Having tasted the excitement of the public arena, however briefly, the earl understandably did not look forward to losing his elected seat in the House of Lords, especially given the peculiar lack of options for alternative entry into political life inherent in his Scottish title. Some hope was unexpectedly held out when the Duke of Buccleuch, who was managing the government interest in the forthcoming peerage election, approached Selkirk with the suggestion that the ministry might well manage to include him in its approved list. What prompted Selkirk to accept this offer was simple. The alternative was political rustication. His critics would label this decision sheer opportunism, although it must be emphasized that in many respects, particularly in terms of social attitudes, Selkirk had been drifting increasingly in a Tory direction. In any event, he insisted to both Buccleuch and his fellow peers that he was staunchly independent, admitting to the Duke his awareness that many would find his scruples "over-refined." But, he insisted, "It is a matter of feeling."[35] The reference to "feeling" is one that Buccleuch would have understood. It came from the title of the well-known 1771 novel by Henry Mackenzie entitled *The Man of Feeling*, and referred to a consistently held and well-nuanced set of emotional values.

Selkirk did indeed appear on the subsequent government list, and despite his declaration that his own votes would be given in accordance with his conscience, he would "vote with fewer exceptions to our list than I expected," as Buccleuch observed.[36] Some resistance developed among the older peers to Selkirk, partly because of his peerage reforms, and there was a good deal of discussion of his inclusion in the government list. Lord Napier commented, "I hope he will not be a wandering planet, though I doubt much that he will ever become a fixed Star."[37] Lord Haddington called Selkirk "cousin *whistle about*," adding "why they took him up I know not, except that all Ministers in one only instance follow the scriptures, 'that there is more joy in Heaven for one sinner who repents than in 20 just men.' Which in plain English is, that they always court their enemies & neglect their friends."[38] This comment is perhaps the best explanation of Buccleuch's courtship of Selkirk available, although it is also possible that his lordship sensed a young man of substantial talent and wished to bring him into the fold. In any event, at the election at Holyroodhouse on 9 June 1807, Selkirk received forty-three of sixty-two votes, and was easily re-elected a representative peer. As Buccleuch had anticipated, most of his own votes were cast for government candidates.[39] The earl's acceptance of an essentially Tory government's support was a calculated gamble. He might well lose credibility by this political shift, but the alternative was to return to the political wilderness, a condition that his American projects could not at the time ameliorate. Whether the risk would be justified by success was a question only the future could answer.

Selkirk's agreement with the Duke of Buccleuch had one other major immediate consequence besides its assurance that he would be able to remain within the House of Lords. In March of 1807, the earl was appointed Lord Lieutenant of Kirkcudbright, a traditionally ceremonial military position that during the years of the Napoleonic Wars actually brought with it responsibilities and authority.[40] The lords lieutenants were civilians of county importance who were charged with home defence for their counties. They supervised not only the militia within their jurisdiction but also the various volunteer companies organized through local initiative and accepted as part of the military by the War Office.[41] Since the French had more than once seriously threatened an invasion of Britain, the organization of home defence was an important matter for any coastal county. Kirkcudbright, located as it was on the west coast of Scotland within easy sailing of Ireland, had been the earlier target for John Paul Jones. It had to be prepared. Home defence, and particularly the organization of local militia, had been a constant concern of Selkirk's father, particularly after the *Ranger* raid of 1777. Whether Selkirk's appointment was the result of interest he had expressed in such matters or simply a mark of approbation by government is not clear. Certainly the Whig government of Lord Grenville had been concerned with army reform. William Wyndham's advocacy of new enlistment periods and his criticism of the volunteer movement that gave the local squirearchy a chance to play soldier had produced a good deal of disquiet.[42] Selkirk had always maintained a desire for military involvement, and would more than once include military command in subsequent American activities. In any event, Selkirk threw himself into his new role with characteristic energy. Equally characteristically, his first instinct was to produce some general principles and system for home defence.

AN INTEREST IN DEFENCE

As part of the Whig military reforms, William Wyndham had also proposed to train each year 200,000 militia soldiers chosen by ballot to assist in times of invasion. This scheme was cancelled as part of one of the new Castlereagh government's first actions. In its place was put a new militia transfer bill, which proposed to raise 44,000 militiamen across Britain by use of a ballot.[43] On 10 August 1807, Lord Selkirk rose in the House of Lords to deliver a long and carefully argued speech on home defence, the text of which he subsequently had published as *Substance of the Speech of the Earl of Selkirk, in the House of Lords, Monday, August 10, 1807, on the Defence of the Country.*[44] The short duration between his appointment as Lord Lieutenant of Kirkcudbright and a speech exhibiting great familiarity with the militia question suggests that the subject was one he had long contemplated. It is even possible that he had discussed the matter with his father in the 1790s. The speech occurred at the point of Napoleon's greatest success, the victory at Freisland and the announcement of the Anglo-Russian alliance at Tilset. The British naval victory at Copenhagen would ease the crisis, but for the moment Britain seemed in great danger of a mobilization of all the fleets of northern Europe against it. In this speech Selkirk protested that the proposed legislation was insufficient, for French invasion was a distinct possibility and preparedness the only deterrent. "It is not to the Channel that we must look for security," he proclaimed, "but to the hands of Englishmen fighting for their liberties, for the glory and independence of their country." If there were to be an adequate defence force, it required a "permanent system." The earl thus called for the creation of a well-trained reserve army, led by "the principal landed proprietors of the county," insisting that "in the process of time the whole people will have gone through a course of discipline; we shall become, like our enemies, a nation of soldiers; and then England will assuredly be invincible." Particular criticisms of the existing arrangements were accompanied by references to "the valuable speculations of Mr. Malthus," as Selkirk used demography to argue his case for the creation of a general citizen army. From his reference to Malthus to his insistence on system, Selkirk demonstrated in this speech that he was still very much a child of the Enlightenment.

MARRIAGE

Involvement with his political career and his militia proposals contributed to a growing lack of interest on Selkirk's part with his American settlements. For once, his agents were the ones complaining about lack of communication.[45] But Selkirk's time was also increasingly taken up with personal matters. He was by now a thirty-six-year-old bachelor, the last male of his family. The time had come to marry, settle down to domesticity, and produce an heir. In the course of his attendance at the London social soirees of 1807, Selkirk had met a vivacious and eligible potential partner in the person of Miss Jean Wedderburn, by all accounts one of the great beauties of the season. The two were instantly attracted to one another. Miss Wedderburn was twenty-one years old, the daughter of a distinguished Scottish lawyer. One of her elder brothers (Alexander) was a rising London merchant, another (James) was married to the daughter of Whig potentate Lord Auckland. Through brother James, Jean had become not only the sister-in-law but also the close friend of Lady Mary Louisa Auckland, and it was at the Auckland home in London that Thomas and Jean had first met. We know virtually nothing about their courtship. The only contemporary evidence is in a letter from Lord Auckland to Lord Grenville in November of 1807, commenting that "Lord Selkirk is not much to be admired either for his political conduct or for his eloquence, but he is amiable and good in private life, and therefore I am glad that he is to marry Miss Wedderburn.[46] Auckland added, "Lady Auckland has the great responsibility of buying the wedding clothes and laces." The wedding took place at Inveresk, the bride's home, on 24 November. It was a quiet and private affair, announced discreetly in the press.[47] The new Lady Selkirk would bring the earl domestic happiness, a supportive help-mate, an heir, and a number of relations who would become his friends and allies throughout his future North American peregrinations.

CHAPTER TEN

Settling Down

T HE BEGINNING OF THE YEAR 1808 found Lord Selkirk more settled (and perhaps more satisfied) than he had ever been before in his life. His marriage had provided him with a basis for domestic tranquility. His involvement with peerage revisions seemed behind him, and he had found a new "cause" to champion, that of militia reform. The news from America, moreover, was good for the first time in years.

Halifax merchant James Stewart had consulted with the chief justice of Prince Edward Island about a possible replacement for James Williams, but had had been told that possible candidates "taken in the Aggregate . . . are a sad lot on the Island." A "confidential, steady, and honest Manager" was almost impossible to find.[1] To his pleasant surprise, someone to investigate on the island drifted onto the scene in the person of Lieutenant Basil Hall, the son of Selkirk's sister Helen and Sir James Hall of Dunglass, who was posted to Halifax with the British navy in the spring of 1807. Hall had visited Prince Edward Island late in 1807 and had sent back a personal report of progress in Selkirk's settlements. He had also induced James Williams to provide reports and some accounts. He would subsequently make a career as an international travel writer, producing a constant stream of books describing various parts of the world to eager readers in Britain. Attempting to delineate the physical features of the places he visited as well as the ethnography of the people, he wrote successful books that covered many obscure parts of the world. His most controversial book was an account of travels in the United States, where he joined his uncle in social criticism of the Americans. At the time of his Prince Edward Island visit, he was a young naval lieutenant stationed at Halifax under Sir George Cranfield Berkeley. His mother subsequently complained to a friend that Basil was not well suited to the assignment: "You see he has mismanaged matters in the first outset, for by blabbing his intentions all over Halifax, openly before he set out, he infallibly spread the report of himself."[2] Lady Helen obviously suspected that her son had issued the alarm to Williams, who was thus prepared for his arrival. Mothers are often our severest critics.

The accounts James Williams showed Hall appeared to indicate that Selkirk's lands were being successfully settled and were even generating a revenue, although it was not yet reaching Scotland.[3] Attempting to estimate the financial situation from the information available is an absolutely hopeless task. Selkirk would claim that he had spent over £30,000 on his American ventures and had sold only 16,000 of the 143,000 acres he held on the island. The remaining land in 1807 was worth, he estimated, about £10,000. As Lucille Campey points out, this shortfall added up to a substantial deficit, perhaps £1 million in modern money. Not all of it was lost on the island, however; the Upper Canadian deficit was probably even larger.[4] One of Williams's letters to Selkirk provoked by the Hall visit was "written under much emotion."[5] Vigorously defending himself from the suspicion of fraud, Williams insisted that he had worked hard on Selkirk's behalf, and denied that the sawmill had been profitable, although much effort and money had been spent on it. "Your Lordship must not expect every twenty shillings your Agent receives will produce the same to you." Williams was here referring to the fact that payment was often in kind, and the produce hard to market. This continued to be a problem until the Selkirk estate disposed of its holdings over fifty years later. Williams's letters offered some explanation for the lack of communication, and a fairly detailed justification for the absence of cash remittances: expenses were high, and any surplus was being ploughed back into the estate. James Stewart seemed well pleased with the effects of Basil Hall's visit, and, as a result of his recommendations and further explanations from Williams, Selkirk agreed to accept his agent's explanations.

Were Selkirk in a suspicious mood, or were he contemplating a serious American operation, he might have found some of the responses of Williams most unsatisfactory. But Prince Edward Island had apparently served its purpose, and so long as it did not continue to be a drain upon his income, he was apparently content. As with Baldoon, Selkirk's chief concern was to minimize further outlays of funds rather than to expand his commitment, although he was happy to receive land grants to compensate him for his efforts.[6] Williams was ordered to return to Britain to justify his conduct in person—as he himself in his letters had insisted must be done—but not until he had accommodated another party of Highlanders coming to the island in 1808. Nothing more is known of this 1808 party, which had not been recruited by Selkirk but was apparently being steered to his lands. In any case, it would soon become clear that Williams was neither willing to return to Britain nor to provide regular reports.

MILITIA REFORM

Prince Edward Island was not the only area of past Selkirk activity that now seemed less important. He was now prepared to accept that the peerage proposal "is now completely asleep—there is no probability that the Dundas's will ever countenance it or the present ministry suffer it to pass." Although he was prepared to fight on if any possibility of success existed, he wrote Lord Leven, it seemed pointless to carry on further.[7] While his marriage and new-found domesticity undoubtedly contributed to his relative lack of concern for matters that had once seemed crucial, so too did his current involvement in military reform. January of 1808, he reported to Lord Leven, found him "in the midst of what one of my literary friends calls 'the agonies of the Press.'" This was a phrase that his father had several times used in his correspondence many years earlier. Such work was, Thomas confessed, "a species of torture which makes me forget every thing external."[8] The publication upon which the earl was engaged was a revised and greatly expanded version of his speech on home defence. It appeared under the title *On the Necessity of a More Effectual System of National Defence, and the Means of Establishing the Permanent Security of the Kingdom*. It appeared under the imprint of J. Hatchard in London and of Constable and Company in Edinburgh. These were both commercial publishers, and it would appear likely that the work had been commissioned by them. In the extensive pamphlet that resulted, the author attempted to enlarge upon his earlier proposals for a local militia, "rather for the purpose of illustrating the general principle, and of showing its practicability, than with any idea of exhibiting a perfect system." But as this rather defensive statement suggested, the proposal was an elaborate one that encouraged disagreement with its particulars.

Once again Selkirk demonstrated his preoccupation with demography by carefully calculating the number of young men who would be affected by his scheme of required national military training. His true social attitudes were on open display. He wrote enthusiastically of the "internal energy, resulting from that happy connection which subsists between the different orders of society," a Tory observation if ever there was one. Selkirk went even further, insisting that what needed to be imparted to his citizen soldiery was less experience in the use of arms than "habits of strict obedience." He justified his proposal in a variety of ways, including the argument that such military service would "operate in an indirect manner in favour of the whole body of manufacturing labourers, by withdrawing the competition of a large portion of the younger workmen, and throwing the employment that remains into the hands of those who are more advanced in life, and more generally burdened with families." He recognized that Ireland was different and suggested a separate system, explaining it carefully. Selkirk accepted that the internal state of Ireland made compulsory military service impossible to enforce, and proposed instead a levy for raising a body of fencibles, to be composed of Catholics recruited in Catholic areas.

In his conclusions, Selkirk emphasized the importance of the principle of universality. Although he was clearly no democrat, insisting as he did on the replication of the natural order of society in the command structure of his citizen army, he also recognized that his plan would be totally subverted by "any exemption in favour of the higher ranks of society, or any which can be purchased by pecuniary sacrifices." Going further, he wrote: "To lay the burden of compulsory service upon the poor, and not upon the rich, would be contrary to the spirit of that constitution which it is our ambition to preserve." But in the last analysis, what Selkirk most demonstrated so graphically was that curious combination of accurate vision and utter impracticability of details that characterized so many of his proposals. In the matter of universal military training, Selkirk was, as has often been noted, "ahead of his time." But as was typical of his vision, such universal training was expressed as an over-elaborated concrete scheme designed for a specific purpose.

SIR ALEXANDER MACKENZIE AND NORTH AMERICA

In the spring of 1808, Selkirk continued his communications with his American agents, showing slightly more positive interest than he had displayed for several years past.[9] As early as 1807, Alexander McDonell in Upper Canada had suggested that he would like to be relieved of his agency. Selkirk now replied, "It has appeared to me for some time past that your avocations are now so multiple that it is impossible for you to devote your individual attention to my affairs as constant residence at Baldoon would require a sacrifice of other objects more important to yourself." But he did not actually yet move to replace McDonell. Nevertheless, neither his American letters nor other surviving evidence offer any indication that his energies were seriously engaged in American projects, or that he was contemplating any new initiatives. Thus, it is very difficult to explain Selkirk's associations over the summer of 1808 with Sir Alexander Mackenzie, the noted fur trader and explorer, in the purchase of shares of stock in the Hudson's Bay Company.

Mackenzie had left North America in 1799 to return to Britain, after a number of bouts with severe emotional stress. Two years later, in 1801, he had published his *Voyages from Montreal . . . to the Frozen and Pacific Oceans*, ably assisted by the English journalist William Combe. How much of the book was actually written by Mackenzie remains uncertain, but it was a best-seller. In 1802 Makenzie proposed to the Colonial Secretary Lord Hobart a scheme for cooperation between the North West Company (NWC) and the Hudson's Bay Company (HBC), but he was not trusted by the fur trade nabobs in Montreal and nothing ever came of the proposal. After a brief spell in Lower Canadian politics, Mackenzie had returned to England in 1805, and apparently had become restored to the confidence of the merchants who ran the North West Company. In any case, in 1808 the Hudson's Bay Company stock was selling at bargain prices in London. The company had suffered greatly over the years from its rivalry with Canadian fur-trading companies, and then had been devastated by Napoleon's closure in 1807 of its major market for furs in the Baltic. The HBC had been forced to cancel its fur auctions in England.

Only a single tantalizing piece of evidence of the connection between Selkirk and Mackenzie survives, and it exists as a transcription of a letter from Mackenzie to Selkirk dated 27 June 1808 in the Selkirk Papers at the National Archives of Canada.[10] The letter suggests that the two men were collaborating in some scheme of buying up undervalued shares of Hudson's Bay Company stock. Several of Mackenzie's biographers have suggested that Selkirk and Mackenzie, although appearing to cooperate at this period, were really in deep conflict over the acquisition of the HBC. Mackenzie wanted to use the HBC charter to support the NWC operations, while Selkirk wanted a land grant in the west based on the charter to establish a settlement at Red River. While Selkirk had certainly earlier been and would later be interested in a Red River colony, there is no evidence that such a venture was on his mind in 1808. The Mackenzie biographers have extrapolated from earlier and later interests on the part of both parties to this particular year, when Mackenzie apparently sought to use Selkirk as a front man in his negotiations with HBC stockholders.[11] It is not clear what role the earl thought he was playing. Mackenzie, who was a vain man, was doubtless pleased to be "using" Selkirk for his own purposes, and like most such operators, would have been thoroughly offended to think the reverse might also be the case. It likely was not. At this stage, the venture with Mackenzie was probably merely an incidental speculation made possible by Selkirk's knowledge of the actual value of the depressed HBC stocks, rather than—at least in 1808—some deliberate policy of re-entrance into North American colonization activity.

More important in 1808 than his dalliance with Sir Alexander Mackenzie and the Hudson's Bay Company was Selkirk's continued active attendance at the House of Lords, and the execution of his duties as Lord Lieutenant of Kirkcudbright. On 1 July Selkirk was elected a Fellow of the Royal Society, a recognition by his contemporaries of his commitment to scientific investigation; the honour no doubt pleased him enormously.[12] Selkirk did find it necessary in the summer of 1808 to turn his attention at least briefly to Canadian affairs, responding to an 1807 report by the Upper Canadian authorities that had been less than enthusiastic about the earl's settlement ventures and his requests for future land grants. Selkirk defended himself against the charge that he was asking for more land than he was entitled to and, as evidence of his sincere desire for equity, offered to relinquish to the Crown 25,000 acres of land in Prince Edward Island—which was not waste land—in return for land in Upper Canada that, until improved by someone like himself, was useless.[13] The offer, in its assumption that land grants in North America were interchangeable between one province and another, demonstrated that Selkirk did not really understand how North America was administered in practice.

The argument that land had no value until it was improved was equally dubious. But this response, while defending his position, was not really that of a man eager to acquire more land. The basis of his rising reputation was in Britain, not in America.

A letter from Alexander Murray to Archibald Constable, the publisher, dated 3 August 1808, gives us a very favourable picture of Selkirk at the time. Murray described at length St. Mary's Isle, the surrounding countryside, and Selkirk's place in his community, writing, "A more beautiful spot that he inhabits I think you have never seen. His house and *policy* (you know all Scottish peers have some, but he would rather have his *in his head* than about his house) are upon a peninsula, once the seat of a Priory, but just as profitable when occupied by a young man and woman of great merit."[14] Describing the town of Kirkcudbright, Murray noted:

> This town is also the grand arena of county politics. The Earl of Selkirk is now at the head of one party, the Earl of Galloway directs the other. I am inclined to think that the Earl of Selkirk, if he choose, may at last preponderate. But this will not arise so much from his own merit, which is very great, as from his skill in buying and selling, this being a grazing county. You must feed your *beasts* well, and then you may lead them to the slaughter.[15]

Murray reserved his highest praise for the library at St. Mary's Isle, which, he wrote, "consists of a capital collection of well-chosen useful books. It is particularly rich in what are called books in Political Economy. It contains an excellent set of the higher Classics; not so many Greek, however, as Latin; nor is it deficient in books in Antiquities; but these have not been a primary object. In short, it is a statesman's library, but that statesman seems to be a philosopher."[16] Much of this library had doubtless been collected by his father, since there is no evidence that Selkirk had any competence in Latin. But Selkirk's public image had never stood higher than with Alexander Murray.

Throughout the fall of 1808 and the early spring of 1809, Mackenzie and Selkirk continued to acquire small amounts of Hudson's Bay Company stock. This business was apparently not accompanied by any enquiries on Selkirk's part about the Canadian West, nor by any writings on the subject. Since both of these lines of action usually accompanied any major shift in his interests, it seems likely that the stock dealing continued to be a relatively incidental business, albeit a curious one. In the spring of 1809 Selkirk did draft a lengthy statement of Upper Canadian affairs in the form of a letter to Lieutenant Governor Francis Gore.[17] The letter continued his defence of his actions criticized by the Upper Canadian committee of council in 1807. He argued that his requests for land grants were justified and legitimate, given his colonization efforts in the province. At about the same time, Selkirk began searching for a new and larger London house, one commensurate with his present domestic situation.[18] He found one in Portland Place.

REPUDIATING WHIGGISM

Early in 1809 Major John Cartwright, the doughty reformer who had in 1780 founded the Society for Constitutional Information (which had included as members Selkirk's father the fourth earl and his eldest brother Lord Daer), laboured to obtain a number of respectable sponsors for a dinner in London in support of parliamentary reform. The dinner was to be held at the traditional dining spot of the reformers, the Crown and Anchor tavern. Naturally as the brother of Lord Daer the present Earl of Selkirk was invited to participate, but he chose to respond—with Cartwright's permission—with a pamphlet disassociating himself from the public object of the occasion.[19] The earl had apparently been waiting for such an occasion to make a public explanation of his political shift from the Whigs to the Tories. He wrote away at Blackheath while he waited for Jean to give birth. Not being present at the birth was quite common for fathers at this time, but it still suggests a distance in Selkirk's personal relations, even with his beloved family. The heir, Dunbar James—Lord Daer—was born on 22 April 1809. The pamphlet was finished three days later. As usual, the surviving documentation gives us no glimpse into Selkirk's response to the birth of his son. The resultant *A Letter Addressed to John Cartwright, Esq., Chairman of the Committee at the Crown and Anchor; on the Subject of Parliamentary Reform* marked Selkirk's formal break with the political tradition of his family.

In the pamphlet, the author admitted that in his early years he had supported reform to correct the obvious abuses of the political system and to remove the influence of corruption. While he still abhorred corruption and venality, he wrote, his experience in the United States—which had a system of representation approximating that sought by the reformers—had turned him against the reform movement. Despite popular representation and a general diffusion of property in the United States, the Americans still exhibited much public misconduct. They had not elevated the management of public affairs. Indeed, the American abuses were often more "infamous and bare-faced" than those in England. Referring to the events of the French Revolution, Selkirk noted that the reformers had always sought to go further, displaying an "improvidence, which led them to despise every reform, short of complete regeneration: and pursuing "a phantom of ideal perfection" that threw away "the substantial good which was in their hands." Reform might threaten the good, Selkirk insisted, while not necessarily introducing "an additional portion of virtuous principle." One of Selkirk's principal concerns was with the rise of demagogues in a popular democracy, an issue he had reported on at length in his journal/diary of his tour of North America in 1803–04. What he did not admit was that he found the Americans far too bourgeois and money-conscious. As he had noted in his travel diary in Albany in 1804, however, Americans were not able "to feel that absolute *insousiance* about money from which the character of a *Gentleman naturally* arises."[20]

Selkirk referred in his pamphlet approvingly to the comments of "Peter Porcupine" (William Cobbett) on American politics. Cobbett had spent six years in New Brunswick in the British army from 1785 to 1791, and then a number of years in the United States, where he wrote under the pseudonym of "Peter Porcupine," attacking extreme republicanism and demagoguery. *Porcupine's Political Censor* was published in Philadelphia from 1796 to 1797, and *The Life and Adventures of Peter Porcupine* in 1798. In 1802 Cobbett began his *Cobbett's Weekly Political Register,* in which he issued diatribes against commerce and nostalgic glimpses of earlier times. Although superficially quite different, deep down Selkirk and Cobbett had much in common. Both men were committed agrarians, and both sought to return to simpler agrarian values, Cobbett in England and Selkirk in his new settlements in North America. Both men also instinctively believed that political and social unrest were caused more by industrialization and economic change than by subversive writing. In his conclusion, Selkirk argued that constitutional reform would deflect the public's attention from other more important matters, such as economic reform.

The little publication sold well enough to be reprinted in a second edition. It also unleashed a considerable public controversy. Cartwright himself responded to the earl in the *Sunday Review,* and J.C. Worthington also prepared an answer. But the major attack came in a brief pamphlet from Cartwright's close associate John Pearson, one of the more obscure

reformers of his age. Pearson chided Selkirk for betraying "a tone of superiority beyond what the writer of it is perhaps warranted in assuming," but
he was particularly incensed at the use of the American example, insisting
that conclusions could not be transferred from one nation to another, for
"the political constitution the best adapted to one of them, might be pernicious, in an extreme, to the other."[21] Selkirk's disappointment with the
United States was a result of his "having too lofty expectations of mankind"
and was essentially irrelevant to the British argument over political reform.[22]
None of his critics challenged Selkirk's sincerity. Indeed, his disassociation
from political reform was a position toward which he had been slowly but
inexorably moving for a number of years.

If Selkirk had hoped to use his pamphlet to raise his parliamentary profile,
the strategy did not appear to work. Selkirk's political position was considerably less secure than it might appear to the outside world. Although in 1807
he had won re-election to the House of Lords as a representative peer for
Scotland, his future was not bright. His failure to achieve a reform of the
political rights of the Scottish peerage, to make possible either a lifetime seat
in the Lords or the right to stand for the Commons, meant that he continued
to be totally dependent upon government favour for his position. His forensic
limitations made it impossible to achieve much reputation as a speaker or
debater whose value to government would be recognized, and he was far too
independent to be prized for his political loyalty and reliability. Even in the
early nineteenth century, many did not like politicians who crossed the floor
of the House or who refused to comply with party discipline. Selkirk was
unlikely to achieve ministerial office under any government, much less one
that still tended to associate his family with hated Whig reform tendencies.
Even his declaration of personal opposition to parliamentary reform had not
totally removed the stigma.

The earl's considerable public reputation as a proponent of emigration to
North America and as a maker of colonies was a mixed blessing. Government policy would not be able to reflect his arguments until after the wars
with Napoleon were concluded, and his own settlements on Prince Edward
Island and Upper Canada had in truth been costly ventures that had little to
show for them. Selkirk had no desire to invest more time or money in these
areas. His interest in military reform had perhaps contributed to his selection
as Lord Lieutenant of the Stewartry of Kirkcudbright in 1807, but had not
created much of a buzz in either military or political circles. One of Selkirk's

biographers paints a cozy family picture of the new house in Portland Place, but in truth, in 1809 Selkirk was probably very much at loose ends, ready to cast about for some new project upon which he could expend his considerable talents and energy.[23]

MARY COCHRANE

Before he could move ahead, the earl may have needed to close down the past. The Cartwright pamphlet can be seen as part of an effort in this direction, as was probably another move he made in 1809 that appears to have dealt with his earlier personal life. In the summer of that year Selkirk summoned a certain Thomas Halliday, a stonemason on his way to Prince Edward Island with whom he had not been previously acquainted, and negotiated a bargain with him. Halliday was to carry with him to the island a young red-haired girl named Mary Cochrane. According to a later letter from Halliday to the earl, the stonemason was to "Maintain, Cloath and Educate her the Same as I did to my own Childring, for which I was to have a Hundred Acres of Land and her another along Side of mine." These terms were spelled out in a letter to James Williams. Halliday was to clear both lots and Mary was to have her choice when she came of age. Neither the subsidy nor the eventual inheritance was particularly munificent. Young Mary was said in the settlement to remind folk in physical appearance of the earl himself, and she would later be described on the island as "Mary Douglas, Only daughter of Lord Selkirk." Even if she were a daughter, she would not be the only daughter, of course, since Lady Jean would give birth to one as well. In any case, Halliday had trouble getting his (and Mary's) land from James Williams, and Selkirk would in 1815 write an angry letter to Williams's successor as agent complaining, "I am extremely disappointed that any just claim on me, should have remained so long unsettled, and I must request that these transactions be brought to a conclusion without further delay." This instruction did not acknowledge any commitment to Mary, but only to Halliday, although another letter to Halliday himself did mention the land for Mary Cochrane.[24] In 1818 Thomas Halliday would write Selkirk again, still looking for his land. He added to that letter in his inimitable spelling,

> Dr McCally your Lordships Bitter Enemy told me in public that the Red headed Girl that was with me was not my Daughter to which I told him that I got all my childring in the Dark and had no other

surty But the word of my Wife for them he then went on with Long-winded Storey that he said Williams told him your Lordship was her Father, and her Mother was a woman near Kirkobrough and that her name was Nelly Cownche and that he Williams did want her that he might get the Land that was for her and me for his own Childring and that Strumpet that was with him.[25]

This evidence was pure hearsay twice removed, but the existence of a specific name for the mother suggests it may have had some substance.

In the absence of DNA testing or other documentary evidence besides Halliday's 1818 letter and other Selkirk letters to Halliday and the agent, the business can remain only a curious speculation that raises more questions than it answers, a subject of island gossip but little more. For Selkirk to send an illegitimate daughter, possibly born to a local serving girl, to the colonies in 1809 makes perfectly good sense. His wife had recently given birth to an heir, and he was in the process of tidying up his earlier life. Given the conventions of the time, however, there was no reason for Selkirk to be ashamed of producing an illegitimate child before his marriage, particularly to the extent of providing for her quite so shabbily. If he was trying to keep the girl a secret, sending her to Prince Edward Island, where he was well known and a major landholder, was hardly a very promising strategy. Certainly Halliday and James Williams were both convinced they understood the circumstances, responding with nudges and winks. But would Selkirk have employed an ill-educated stonemason whom he did not previously know if there were deep secrets to be buried? In many ways we want Mary to be a daughter born on the wrong side of the blanket. In his early years especially there was little warmth and humour about Lord Selkirk, and fathering an illegitimate child would provide at least a small measure of common humanity. But he never acknowledged that inadvertent act of paternity.

AN ASSESSMENT OF SELKIRK IN 1809

On first glance, Lord Selkirk in 1809 appeared to have turned himself into a rather dull fellow. He had repudiated his radical past and perhaps buried an earlier personal mistake. He was not expanding his investments or his interests in either Prince Edward Island or in Upper Canada, and, indeed, seemed more than likely to shut them down. Election to the Royal Society in July 1809 certified that he was a product of the Scottish Enlightenment, but there was little other evidence that he was actively continuing his earlier intellectual interests. Certainly becoming a member of the Alfred Club— which one of its members (Lord Byron) once described as "pleasant; a little too sober and literary . . . upon the whole a decent resource in a rainy day, in a dearth of parties or parliament, or in an empty season"—hardly represented much imagination or willingness to flaunt convention.[26] The Alfred Club was at 23 Albemarle Street. It was a recent foundation, having begun in 1808 and would have a waiting list of 354 in 1811. Most London clubs offered young Regency gentlemen a chance to gamble, gossip, and show off new styles in their fine new clothes. The Alfred featured a library and a splendid collection of bishops and their gaiters. The Earl of Dudley called it "the dullest place in existence." Selkirk doubtless consciously believed that the decent sobriety of the Alfred Club was what he craved. But such a desire was belied by his subsequent behaviour.

Had Selkirk's career ended at this point, he might have been commemorated as a minor figure of the Scottish Enlightenment—a man of science and reason, whose activities had fizzled out like a damp squib with the Enlightenment itself—and little more. But Selkirk was on the verge of a second career, one that would move him in an entirely different direction. Just as the mindset of his society was imperceptibly shifting from Enlightenment Reason to Romantic Adventure, so too was Selkirk's public life. He would cease to be a man of reasonable behaviour, and gradually become instead a man of action. Selkirk would turn himself into an individual with an impossible dream that he would attempt to realize with every sinew of his body and every penny of his fortune. The result was that he would become a full-fledged tragic hero, doomed by his own flaws to fail in his self-selected life's work. The break in his life plainly came around this time and at this point.

CHAPTER ELEVEN

Taking over the Hudson's Bay Company

LORD SELKIRK AND ALEXANDER MACKENZIE had become involved together in Hudson's Bay Company (HBC) stock activity in 1808. Their reasons were initially probably quite different one from another. Mackenzie and his various Canadian associates and rivals had been extremely successful interlopers in the fur trade. They had been so triumphant that they came to see the British firm less as a troublesome competitor than as the possessor of legal advantages and an alternate route into the fur-bearing regions. These advantages would be worth taking over. For his part, Lord Selkirk had been merely dabbling in a company in a region that had long fascinated him. He had shown interest in land development, but had no previous record of activity in the stock market. Nevertheless, the dynamic of the market drove him forward.

The Hudson's Bay Company was in serious difficulty by 1809, with the value of its shares of stock constantly declining on the London market. The company had found the competition from its Montreal-based fur-trading rivals extremely expensive to meet, involving the need not only to pay higher prices for furs for which it had no market but also to increase salaries and other expenses to protect its limited share of the trade in the north. In 1805 the HBC had become involved in negotiations with the reorganized North West Company (NWC) (which had emerged from a period of intense local rivalry and competition as the major North American fur trader through a merger of the old North West Company and Alexander Mackenzie's XY Company) to "concert arrangements for the better regulating of the Indian

Trade in America." Although they held most of the trade, the Nor'westers were interested in two aspects of the Hudson's Bay Company's operations. For the long term, they were covetous of the charter, which gave the HBC a putative monopoly of trade and government in the entire drainage basin of Hudson Bay. The Canadians had ignored the charter's monopoly and got away with it, but realized their position would be much stronger with it on their side. Both sides in 1805 knew that the charter rested upon the slim foundation of the royal prerogative making the first grant in 1670. Such prerogative would better support the HBC's land claims in the region than its trading claims, said the lawyers consulted by the London Committee.

In the shorter term, the North West Company was also interested in the direct connection between Europe and the fur-bearing regions of the North American interior provided by the Hudson Bay route. It had already begun to interlope in Hudson Bay itself, particularly at Charlton Island, where a vessel had been sent to test the charter. One of the company's lawyers had opined that "the Northwest Company may navigate the Hudson's Bay and carry on their trade as they please, without any fear of legal molestation. . . they may act as if no such Charter existed."[1] The London firm in 1805 nevertheless balked at allowing the Canadians use of the transit route through Hudson Bay without any guarantees that its own trade would not suffer. The HBC's directors had instinctively recognized that despite the decline in their share of the North American fur trade, the charter privileges they still claimed from the British Crown were a valuable asset not to be squandered.[2] Moreover, the HBC remained convinced that its trade goods remained superior. The London Committee did not seek a trade commensurate with its charter, but merely a decent return on the goods it shipped to North America. It was in 1805 prepared to deal, provided a good bargain could be made that the opposition would keep. Negotiations were broken off between the two companies in February 1806, chiefly because the HBC believed that once the Nor'westers were officially allowed in the bay, the company would soon be annihilated.

After closure of the Baltic by Napoleon in 1807 had cut off the principal market for furs in eastern Europe, however, the company had been forced to suspend auction sales rather than risk low prices. It relied heavily on its credit standing with London bankers, especially the Bank of England, to continue its operations in North America. Dividends could no longer be paid out of profits, and while initially they were only cut during the heavy competition of the period from 1800 to 1808 from late eighteenth-century highs of eight percent to a more modest four percent, they were totally suspended beginning in 1809. By the end of 1808, the HBC owed the Bank of England £50,000 and had a paltry £101.1 in its current account.[3] What buoyed the company up was the realization that apart from the question of its share of the fur trade, its trade in North America was once again increasing and would be very profitable—when the Baltic market was again opened.

THE FUR TRADE

The business of the Hudson's Bay Company depended on the North American beaver (*castor Canadensis*-Kuhl), the continent's largest rodent, weighing from thirty to sixty pounds. Its amphibious body was covered with a soft felt-like underfur one inch thick and protected with an overlayer of coarse guard hairs roughly two inches in length.[4] The beavers lived in the forested regions of lakes and rivers, constructing dams for their lodges in the watered areas—usually slow-moving streams—and gathering construction materials from the adjacent woodlands. One family (two adults and young) inhabited a lodge, although the lodges often gathered together in colonies. The thickness of the beaver's fur depended on the length and coldness of the winter, and the number of beaver depended on the richness of the habitat. This meant that the furs got thicker and the number of beaver greater as one headed north and west across the continent, with the greatest centre for these fur-bearing rodents in the drainage basin of the Mackenzie River—the so-called "Athabasca country." Because the beaver lodges were so substantial and time-consuming to build, the beaver was not a migratory animal and was easily trapped. The pressure of trapping upon any local beaver population was severe, and thus the need for new supply drove the fur traders constantly west into the northern regions, where they found the skins increasingly superior.

From the very outset, the European intruders discovered that Native practice with beaver skins provided an element of processing that made the skins especially desirable in Europe. The Natives skinned their catch and sun-dried the beaver skins before stitching several skins into a robe that they constantly wore, often immediately next to their body. Beaver skin was not only warm, but also water resistant. The act of rubbing the skin against an oily human body over long periods had the useful effect of eliminating its guard hairs and reducing the skin to its felt component. It was possible to get rid of the guard hairs in other ways, but they were not quite as efficient or satisfactory. *Castor gras* (greasy beaver), or coat beaver, was always the most valued commodity in the fur trade. Skins that had merely been sun-dried (parchment beaver) were acceptable but not as valuable.

Initially the furs were made into coats, but Europeans soon discovered that North American beaver felt could be processed into hats. These became the principal end-product of the beaver trade. Fashion in hats came and went, although the beaver always provided the preferred felt because of its thickness and water-shedding capacity. In the seventeenth century, French policy drove the hatters (who were mainly Protestant craftsmen) out of that country. They settled down in London, where the best furs were soon being auctioned. By the end of the eighteenth century, the felt stovepipe or "top" hat was assuming principal prominence. It consumed a fair bit of felt. Most beaver skins (or pelts) had to be stripped of their guard hair and turned into felt in European factories, employing a complex process of combing and beating and shellacking and dying. The use of intoxicating chemicals (chiefly mercury) in this process affected the minds of those employed in the process; hence the phrase, "mad as a hatter."

Other commodities could also be traded with the First Nations and collected off the land by the fur traders. There was some market in Europe for the skins of other fur-bearing animals such as marten and lynx. Down feathers (for pillows and coat linings) from ducks, geese, and even swans were also shipped by the HBC to Europe in some quantity. The skins of the buffalo (or bison) did not until later in the nineteenth century become an important trade item. They were too bulky to move and ship in any quantities. As for the wool of the buffalo, to the chagrin of the people of Red River, it turned out that the buffalo wool was quite impervious to bleaching and dying. One could have it in any colour, as long as it was almost black. The chief value of the bison before the later nineteenth century, when it was killed for buffalo robes, was as meat, consumed fresh and dried by Native people and fur traders alike. When cut into strips, cooked, pounded into flakes, mixed with berries, and packed into ninety-pound bales, it was turned into a high-energy, easily portable ration called pemmican. This ration served as a basic food of the voyageurs on their canoe journeys. An acquired taste, one trader described it as tasting like dried blood. Whatever its taste, pemmican along with beaver fuelled the conflict among the great trading companies of the northern half of the continent.

The fur-trading system that the Hudson's Bay Company had developed at the bottom of the Bay was highly institutionalized and ritualized. The institutionalization occurred to enable the company to conduct a barter trade in a manner that could be reflected in an accounting system. The basis of the system was a value unit called the "made beaver," set by the company within the "Official Standard of Trade" (for local trade goods) and the "Comparative Standard of Trade" (for European goods). Both units were set by the London Committee of the company annually, and they fluctuated very little. Some flexibility occurred within the system, however, and the English factors usually managed to mark up the terms of exchange beyond the official standards. This informal markup was called the "Overplus." The London Committee scrutinized the books carefully and complained if the overplus at any given factory did not measure up to the norm. The factor's job was not an easy one. He had to keep the overplus up and satisfy the Aboriginal people at the same time. Much depended on the state of competition at any point in time.

Ritualization reflected the Aboriginal need for ceremony as part of a gift-giving and gift-exchange arrangement that carried on practices probably begun long before the Europeans had arrived. The complex trading ceremony began when the Aboriginal trading parties arrived at the trading post, led by their trading captain. Whether trading captains had existed before the arrival of the European is not clear. The position probably reflected the new demands of the fur trade. At the height of the system's prominence, in the mid-eighteenth century, many captains had been given red military coats (the "captain's outfit") as marks of their status. They also got other gifts, most of which would be subsequently distributed among their followers. The trading captain had little real power among his fellows, but he knew how to speak ceremonially with the European traders and how the system worked so that his people would not be totally out traded.

The ritual began with the smoking of the peace pipe or calumet before the beginning of trade. The captain would "harangue" the traders, emphasizing how hard his people had worked, how far they had come, how much they loved the English, how much they wanted to be treated fairly. He would then make a gift of furs to the factor based on a levy against his people. The HBC factor would respond by stating how much the English loved the Aboriginal people, how generous they would be, how necessary it was for the Aboriginals to trade only with them. The factor would then return the captain's gift, usually in the form of brandy and tobacco. Both of these commodities could be and usually were adulterated. Then, with the captain looking on from inside the warehouse, the trade would be conducted with each individual Aboriginal person through a "hole-in-the-wall" or open window. Native wants were fairly limited given the nomadic way of life of the bands. After the trading was completed, the captain would distribute the gifts he had received to his fellows, and a feast would be held. Then the Aboriginal people would go away for another year.[5]

SELKIRK'S INVOLVEMENT WITH THE HUDSON'S BAY COMPANY
After his initial involvement in the stock market, Selkirk was likely influenced by his brother-in-law Andrew Wedderburn (who through family inheritances would change his name to Colvile in 1814) and his future brother-in-law John Halkett, who probably helped enlarge his thinking. Wedderburn and Halkett were both members of an extensive and powerful Scottish legal family headed by Alexander Wedderburn, first Baron Loughborough, who served as lord chancellor of England in the early years of the nineteenth century. Andrew Wedderburn was a highly successful London sugar merchant, senior partner in the firm of Messrs. Graham, Simpson, and Wedderburn, who had for many years supplied the Hudson's Bay Company with rum. John Halkett had served as secretary to his cousin Alexander, and had subsequently received several colonial appointments to Caribbean sugar islands—as governor-in-chief of the Bahamas in 1801 and of Tobago in 1803. In 1809 he was serving as first chief commissioner of West Indian accounts for the British government. Both men were plugged into the city, and they quickly grasped the business implications of Selkirk's dabblings in Hudson's Bay Company stock. Alexander Mackenzie hoped to gain control of the Hudson's Bay Company through a relatively small investment in devalued stock. He was chiefly concerned to acquire the company's privileges, which would be folded into the North West Company's assets. Others might use the HBC for different purposes, however. A few enquiries around the city doubtless told Wedderburn that the HBC had been very conservatively managed for generations, and might easily be turned around by new and aggressive policies and tactics. The company was presently trying to diversify into the timber trade and to acquire government assistance, but these efforts were not likely to show much return for years. In short, the

HBC was ripe for takeover. Selkirk and his relations began acquiring stock and proxy support on their own behalf in 1809.

Selkirk made his first appearance at the Hudson's Bay Company's General Court in November of 1809, having purchased £2000 of stock from a Mrs. Merry the previous March during the period of his involvement with Alexander Mackenzie. His opponents claimed that he had borrowed the money for the purchase, and this may well have been true. Although neither he nor his relations at this point actively intervened in company affairs, Selkirk was by this juncture apparently beginning to think imaginatively about the affairs of the company. On 6 December 1809, he wrote to Captain John MacDonald of Prince Edward Island about island business, concluding in a postscript with mention of a proposed military expedition that he hoped MacDonald would lead. The invitation was hardly very specific, but the choice of MacDonald as a recipient of such an overture was suggestive of his intentions.[6] In the early 1770s, Captain John had successfully led a party of Highlanders to settle on the Island of Saint John (later named Prince Edward Island), and he had spent the war of the American Rebellion serving in the British army. MacDonald himself replied to Selkirk's overture, "I have read over and over your Lordship's postscript, which I am unable to conceive, unless it points at establishing a Settlement of Highlanders, whose type I am sorry to think is materially altered, by way of advanced post or barrier in the upper Country." In any event, he was not interested in such a position, writing in answer, "My diffidence is mostly in myself 68 years of age—rather unwieldy—constitution fled—courage departed—memory impaired—impractised in the official and superior walks—Activity gone—Wishing only with submission to the Almighty Disposer for five or Six more years of life in order to put my Children, who are young, so far more forward."[7]

Further hints of Selkirk's thinking occurred in a letter he wrote on the same day as the one to Captain John, this one to Miles Macdonell in Upper Canada:

> I have lately heard ... of an agency, which will probably suit you, not in the regular army, but in a service which would be attached with permanent advantages. The employment to which I allude, having been mentioned to me confidentially, I am precluded from entering into an explanation at present, further than to express my conviction, that if I can succeed in obtaining it for you, it would be more advantageous than that which you were desirous of obtaining last year.[8]

The reference to an earlier appointment probably refers to Macdonell's efforts to raise a corps of Glengarry Fencibles for service in Upper Canada, for which he had sought Selkirk's support. Miles was to remain in readiness for a summons to London if and when the plans matured. The heavily veiled references in Selkirk's letters to his North American correspondents hardly point to leadership of a full-scale colonization venture organized by Selkirk. What they do suggest is an employment by a private trading company such as the Hudson's Bay Company, perhaps heading a squad of armed men to protect company traders as they expanded into the Athabasca region and began to compete actively with the North West Company.

At the time of Selkirk's letters to North America, the HBC had begun deliberations on the proposals of fur traders William Auld and Colin Robertson to reinvigorate its trade. Auld had served for many years for the company at the bay, rising to chief factor at Fort Churchill.[9] He had recently returned to London from a wintering expedition to Reindeer Lake that had been met with much opposition from the North West Company's Robert Henry. Colin Robertson had spent a number of years with the North West Company, but had resigned in 1809, partly because of slow promotion prospects and partly because of a long-simmering feud with his superior, John McDonald of Garth.[10] William Auld lent Robertson the money to come to England, and introduced him to the London Committee of the Hudson's Bay Company. Auld and Robertson both believed that the HBC should abandon its defensive position and go on the attack. The company needed to push its way into the rich Athabasca country, according to Robertson by hiring unemployed Canadian fur traders as the advance guard. It also needed to diversify into the timber trade now that Baltic timber was in short supply. Command of a military contingent to protect such ventures seems the most reasonable explanation of Selkirk's feelers to MacDonald and Macdonell. The London Committee at first seemed favourably disposed to the proposals of Auld and Robertson, but became less enthusiastic at about the same time that Andrew Wedderburn purchased the stock of Thomas Neave on 3 January 1810.[11] Wedderburn announced his intention of standing for election to the committee of management not long after obtaining his stock, and he was quickly accepted.

The committee had gotten cold feet about an aggressive program before Wedderburn's election, and had decided on a much more limited new policy. No longer would it attempt to compete directly with the Canadians, but instead it would serve as an agent supplying trade goods to inland traders who would operate on their own accounts. The major company effort would be put into the supposedly lucrative timber trade. This shift in policy, associated with long-time director George Hyde Wollaston, quickly became known as "Wollaston's Plan." It had been suggested by Wollaston as early as April 1809. It was not only opposed by Auld and Robertson, but also met with little favour from Lord Selkirk, who commented both upon it and what he regarded as a better arrangement in papers written in February of 1810, at about the same time that he was writing to Miles Macdonell. He told Macdonell that while his proposals had "not yet taken such shape as to leave me at liberty to enter into fuller explanations," they had matured sufficiently to make Macdonell's presence in London essential.[12]

The Wollaston Plan, Selkirk argued, would lead the inland traders to detach themselves from the company, either decamping to the United States with the trade goods or entering into competition one with another. Because the right of the company to exclusive navigation of the Bay was legally suspect and possibly to be contested, a single lawsuit by an independent trader might open it to all. Only the continued trading presence of the company maintained the monopoly, and under active management it could outbid interlopers such as the Canadians. Referring to the earlier struggle between the XY Company and the North West Company, Selkirk observed it was a "contest of Capital—the question was which had the heaviest purse." He continued, "Such is the Contest, for which the Company must be prepared, when they determine to make a vigorous & effectual effort to obtain a footing in Athabasca."[13] As Selkirk undoubtedly understood, in the wilderness of North America far removed from the sort of law and authority available in Britain, commercial competition would not stop short of violence. Not merely capital but human lives would be thrown into the fray, and the appropriate analogy was probably not to commercial rivalry but to war.[14] His thinking on this point was connected somehow with his overtures to Captain John MacDonald and to Miles Macdonell and the subsequent request that Miles make his way to London as quickly as possible.

Better ways existed for opening the interior than the one suggested by Wollaston, insisted Lord Selkirk. He expanded on these in another memorandum that became part of Andrew Wedderburn's counterproposal, the "Retrenching System" or "New System," submitted to the committee on 7 March 1810.[15] Even before the unveiling of his detailed proposals,

Wedderburn had apparently suggested the recruitment of personnel from the western islands of Scotland to put some backbone in the company's struggle with the Canadians. He had been authorized to recruit such men and to offer them land in Red River upon the expiration of their contracts.[16] Nor was this the first time that a colony at Red River had been talked about in HBC circles. William Auld had been earlier advised to recruit from the Western Isles of Scotland, offering land at Red River after the expiration of three years of service. Plans had also been discussed for a settlement at Red River of retired servants.[17] While the final scheme had obviously not been originally fashioned in the fertile brains of either Wedderburn or Selkirk, it makes some sense to see Selkirk's hand here rather than that of the cautious sugar trader. Combining features of the Wollaston Plan and the Auld/Robertson proposals, thus transcending difficulties with a vigorous prosecution of policy, the plan had the mark of Selkirk's energy stamped all over it. Wedderburn contributed to the partnership an insistence on sound business and accounting practices, more honoured in the breach than in the observance over the next few years, but the boldness and willingness for confrontation suggested the persona of his brother-in-law. The new system offered a profit-sharing arrangement with the company's servants plus an orderly plan of inland expansion based upon newly recruited Highlanders. As we have seen, to lead the Highlanders Selkirk had been in contact with Captain John MacDonald and Miles Macdonell, obviously in anticipation of some version of this proposal. Colin Robertson's scheme to compete with the North West Company by recruiting Canadian fur traders had been set aside, and the HBC would attempt, for the next half decade, to use Europeans inexperienced in the North American wilderness as its shock troops. The mystique of the military Highlander was being stretched to its ultimate limits. Wedderburn's scheme reinvigorated the company, but whether at this point it was intended in the short run to establish a new settlement is not entirely clear.

For the moment, the Retrenching System offered little new or useful to the company's servants dealing on the spot with Canadian competition, and it has often been criticized for its sublime ignorance of the realities of the fur trade.[18] But what Wedderburn and Selkirk apparently envisioned was a long-term reorganization of the company's activities in the West, based upon the monopolistic advantages granted in the Charter of 1670. As Selkirk himself explained in an undated memorandum written at Fort William over the winter of 1816–17, "If the trade had come to a stand, the Indians would have been left completely at the mercy of the North West Company, and the influence of that unprincipled association would have been so completely confirmed that the Hudson's Bay territorial rights would not only have become a mere dead letter, but it would have become utterly impracticable ever at any time to recover them."[19] Such reorganization could not take place overnight, and what would transpire demonstrated that more cautious and incremental building rather than sudden innovation was what was really required. The opposition certainly caught a whiff of a new spirit within HBC ranks, and it began another round of negotiations in November of 1810, again offering to partition the fur-trading territory and divide the trade. Again the HBC refused to accept such an arrangement.

As for Selkirk himself, little evidence survives of his activities and movements in the year 1810. This may mean that the earl had not yet entered actively into the fur-trading game, but was still collecting information. He was in Ireland in the summer, visiting with his old friend the novelist Maria Edgeworth.[20] The two may well have compared notes on estate management, since Maria was at the time running her father's estate. She was also much interested in Irish emigration, and during this visit Selkirk could have begun making the contacts in Sligo that would be activated over the next few years. He continued his routine political, military, and estate management activities in ways that left little mark on official records and none in the Selkirk Papers. Developments in his North American settlements occurred beyond and outside his control, and he did not show much interest in them. Baldoon agent Alexander Macdonell was effectively replaced by Thomas Clark of Sandwich. As for Prince Edward Island, Captain John Macdonald gave James Williams a rousing endorsement, writing:

> I am happy in believing him to be a man worthy of your Lordship's confidence. He appears to be very capable: He is universally allowed, as far as I can hear, to be supremely Zealous for your Lordship's Interest, and what exceedingly surprises me considering he has to do with Highlanders, whom I know to be the most peevish, impatient, Suspicious ungrateful sett in the world, when they find themselves in a Situation to take advantage; I have hitherto been unable to hear of so much as a single whisper of their dissatisfaction with him, one man excepted.[21]

Captain John wanted Selkirk to take a lead in proprietorial opposition to the local government of the island, but the earl showed no signs of involvement.

The doughty old Highlander advised Selkirk to hold on to his island property, since he was convinced the corner had been turned there. James Williams began to forward the first cash returns on Selkirk's island investment, although he continued to make excuses for his failure to account for his stewardship with complete records.[22]

While Andrew Wedderburn, with the somewhat perverse assistance of Northern Department superintendent William Auld, succeeded in cutting company expenses to the bone, Selkirk was quietly doing research in preparation for a major new settlement project, particularly by consulting with former Hudson's Bay Company employees retired in Scotland. Substantial amounts of geographical information about the territories claimed by the Hudson's Bay Company were available to anyone willing to seek it out, not least in the mounds of records accumulated over the years by the company and in the first-hand recollections of retired servants.[23] In January 1811, his wife Jean gave birth to a second child, a daughter named Isabella. A few weeks later, on 6 February 1811, a formal proposal from Selkirk apparently burst upon the committee of management quite suddenly. The minutes reported with no further introduction:

> Resolved that Mr. Wedderburn be desired to request Lord Selkirk to lay before the Committee the Terms on which he would accept a Grant of Land, within the Territories of the Hudson's Bay Company, and specifying what restrictions he is at present prepared to consent to be imposed on the Settlers: And what Security he sees fit to offer the Company, against any Injury that may eventually arise to the Trade of the Company or any of their Rights & Privileges.[24]

The reason for the secrecy before the actual unveiling of the proposal was doubtless partly to prevent the North West Company from learning of the new plans, partly to prevent opposition from organizing. At the same time, we are unable to follow in detail the gestation of this scheme in either the surviving Selkirk papers or in the records of the Hudson's Bay Company. Most historians have assumed that Selkirk had been working privately on the idea of a Red River settlement for many years. Some have even seen his earlier interest in the fur trade on his North American tour in 1804 as evidence of his advance preparations. Many have argued that his involvement in the Hudson's Bay Company was a product of his ambition for Red River. It is equally likely, however, that his growing commitment to the HBC and Andrew Wedderburn led Selkirk back to Red River at a fairly late point in the proceedings. The earl himself later insisted it was the HBC that had initially wanted a settlement at Red River, mainly as a refuge for retired and redundant fur traders and their Native families. The problems of re-energizing the Hudson's Bay Company had led the London directors to approach Selkirk about taking over the plans for the settlement, which could be combined with the need to recruit more vigorous employees from Ireland and the Highlands of Scotland.[25] Selkirk certainly had some experience at transatlantic settlement and at recruitment. This scenario actually makes more sense and fits better with the surviving evidence than one that sees Selkirk fulfilling a long-standing vision in 1811. Selkirk's first interest was in the Hudson's Bay Company and its reform, and Red River colonization was imposed upon him as a neat and tidy solution to a whole series of problems. In any event, the proposed grant was discussed again on 13 February and tentatively approved by the committee a week later, subject to revisions and to the ratification of the company's shareholders meeting in General Court. On 6 March 1811, the committee formally approved a draft of the final arrangements and of the conveyance of land.[26] The earlier legal opinions that the HBC charter could not sustain a trade monopoly but did justify land claims were now turned to advantage.

Selkirk was back in the colonization business, and he plunged himself headlong into the affairs of the company as well. In April he was negotiating with Christie & Co. of Birmingham for a ten-horsepower steam-driven sawmill for the bay, and that same month saw the appearance of an advertisement in the *Inverness Journal* calling for a "few young, active stout men" to join the employ of the Hudson's Bay Company, chiefly for a settlement. "The Company have resolved to encourage ... in a part of their territories, which enjoys a good climate, and favourable soil and situation."[27] If the establishment of settlements at Baldoon and Prince Edward Island had both been marked by many unexpected difficulties caused chiefly by transportation and communications breakdowns, these settlements would be mere child's play by comparison with the audacity of Selkirk's new scheme. He was proposing, with HBC cooperation, to plant a British colony in the very middle of the continent, nearly 1000 miles beyond the normal communications and transportation facilities of the company. A rival company—the North West Company—had a complicated interior canoe route into the territory, but one that was quite extended and that required considerable time to traverse. The Hudson's Bay Company did have a route into Hudson Bay, but it involved one single passage per year, with a ship leaving England in June and returning in the autumn. To reach the region proposed as site for the new settlement would require an overland journey, perhaps using rivers and lakes but certainly a difficult one, of yet another thousand miles. Even in the twenty-first century, this journey—when undertaken by a team of experienced wilderness people for a television series and executed with the current from the Red River to the Bay rather than the reverse—was extremely problematic. Because only one vessel per year was sent to the Bay, leaving in June, it was necessary to begin recruiting for it before the final approval had been placed on the project by the HBC's General Court. Some of the men to be recruited would be sent by Selkirk to locate a site for the proposed settlement and begin preparations for the arrival of colonists in subsequent years, but others would be employed by the company as shock troops to help protect its servants against intimidation and violence by the North West Company. Selkirk's undoubted impatience to begin combined with a concern to catch the North West Company off guard. Miles Macdonell was already in London eager to undertake his new assignment, and William Auld had made clear the need for reinforcements if open conflict with the Canadians was to be begun.

When examined rationally by any of the standards of the Scottish Enlightenment, this settlement scheme set under foot by Selkirk in 1811 was sheer and unadulterated madness, even before a concerted opposition from the North West Company was added into the equation. A biographer can readily recognize this reality, but explaining his subject's willingness to become involved in such folly is quite another matter. Perhaps the best explanation that can be offered is that Selkirk became somewhat offhandedly involved with a project in which he did not fully understand the monumental difficulties he was facing. He mistakenly thought he had surmounted similar difficulties in Prince Edward Island and Baldoon, and truly believed that careful planning and a willingness to expend money could make anything work out. The sheer magnitude of the enterprise was so awesome as to blind its promoter to its realities. Moreover, as was usually the case in such promotions, one thing led to another. It was easy to believe that one was the victim of constant unpredictable misfortune, and also at various points to become persuaded that it would be easier and better to press forward than to give up or fall back. The fifth Earl of Selkirk was a man who both minimized difficulties and was extremely stubborn. The extent of the opposition from the Canadian fur traders did not put him off, but instead impelled him forward.

Any interest Selkirk may have retained in his estates on Prince Edward Island was negated by developments there. Dr. Angus MacAulay, the preacher-physician-schoolteacher who had helped Selkirk recruit his original settlers and accompanied them to take up residence on the island, had not only joined the anti-proprietorial faction that would be called "the Loyal Electors," but also went openly about supporting vague charges that Selkirk had purchased island lots for "a mere trifle" and peopled them with Highlanders "at their own expense." Moreover, there was talk that the earl had abandoned his emigrants on the beach to fend for themselves. Selkirk realized that MacAulay himself had expected in 1803 to be named the earl's agent, and much of his hostility could be attributed to disappointment that James Williams had been given the job instead. But since the earl was unable to gain full reports from Williams, he was frustratingly incapable of being certain that MacAulay's accusations did not have some validity.[28] Third-party reports reassured Selkirk that his people were prospering and were contented, but the estate was not producing any income. Worse still, after years of procrastination, James Williams not only positively disobeyed a direct order of Selkirk to return to Scotland to make a personal report, but also proceeded to contract with a timber merchant named Spraggon to remove all the valuable timber on Selkirk's lots on terms very unfavourable to the earl.[29] To add insult to injury, when Williams was finally replaced, his successor Charles Stewart was unable to take legal action to recover the earl's assets and could not prevent the merchant from suing Selkirk in the island's Chancery Court for attempting to go to law.[30] This legal business would continue for years.

THE NOR'WESTERS

The fur-trading enterprise with which Selkirk and the HBC were proposing to compete was an operation in almost every sense antithetical to the traditions of the old chartered company.[31] The North West Company was initially founded in 1779 as a joint-stock company by a number of independent trading partnerships active in the western fur trade. Its intent was to provide an organization for raising capital, as well as providing a lobbying presence with the government of Quebec. The corporate being of the company was

very diffuse and decentralized, later leading to Selkirk's lawyer Samuel
Gale's complaint that there was something disturbing about an organization that could "wield the force of thousands of men while it is scarcely
possible to fix responsibility upon an individual partner possessed of funds
in the concern."[32] From the outset, the strength of the company was in the
hands of its traders and the voyageurs who manned the canoes that headed
west every spring for the *pays d'en haut*. The traders were, for the most part
Highland Scots. The voyageurs were French-Canadians. The NWC flourished partly through its flexible organization and the exploring thrusts of
some of its intrepid partners. It also flourished because its traders could be
absolutely ruthless when the situation required. Eventually the company
became overextended, both in terms of investment and geography, which
led it to seek some sort of understanding with the HBC to avoid unnecessary competition.

The leading French traders who had been in the west during the French
Regime were rapidly replaced after 1763 by Americans and especially by
Scots Highlanders, many of whom had spent some years in America. Highlanders proved especially adaptable to the fur trade. One aspect of Highland
culture that suited them to the fur trade was their clannishness, which led
them in the wilds of North America to work together, reinforce one another,
and recruit kinsmen. The second feature of Highland culture that made these
Highlanders successful fur traders (and explorers) was their familiarity with
hunting, the bush, and rough living. The men who ran the NWC were not
sons of crofters, but sons of Highland tacksmen who had entered the British
army as officers or had immigrated to America because of the disruptions to
the clan system after Bonnie Prince Charlie and the "45." For such men, the
wilderness of western Canada was not intimidating. Most were, like Alexander Mackenzie, surprisingly well educated and multilingual. They soon
added Native languages to their arsenal, even introducing some aspects of
Gaelic into fur-trade patois in the process. Those who made careers in the
west took Native wives and, like the French, began raising families in the
country. Most were "wintering partners," who remained among the Native
peoples for years on end. Bold, adventurous, utterly ruthless, the Highlanders
soon totally dominated their competition. Whatever the Highland fur traders
were, they were not gentlemen in the European sense of the term. For some
members of the Selkirk family, notably Lady Selkirk, the conflict between the
Nor'westers and her husband took on the nature of a class conflict among

Scots of differing social origins. Selkirk was a noble "man of honour," while his opponents were unprincipled products of the old clan system of the Highlands.

Clannishness was both an advantage and a disadvantage to the NWC, which was increasingly dominated by the McTavish and McGillivray families. After 1800, no fewer than fourteen members of these two families were involved in the NWC. Such family dominance on the one hand helped provide solidarity of direction. On the other hand, it made new directions difficult. The NWC in 1811 was headed—as it had been since 1804—by William McGillivray, a native of Dunlichty in Scotland and a nephew of Simon McTavish, one of the early spirits in the Montreal fur trade.[33] The company's Thunder Bay depot had been named Fort William after him in 1807. McGillivray operated out of Montreal, was a member of the Scotch Presbyterian Church, and had important political links to the government of Lower Canada. In 1814 he would be appointed to the Legislative Council of Lower Canada, which meant that he had the ear of the governor of the colony. McGillivray was responsible for putting his brother, Simon McGillivray, in charge of McTavish, McGillivray and Company, the London agents for the NWC.

The NWC was able to flourish because of its flexible organization and the local initiative of its partners. Over the period between 1779 and 1811, a number of Montreal-based firms provided short-term competition in the western fur trade. Almost without exception, they were first opposed and then swiftly incorporated into the NWC partnership. Competition from the so-called XY Company, which broke away from the NWC in 1798, lasted the longest, for about six years. Equally important, inland exploration was actually encouraged by the company, on the grounds that it would eventually lead to new sources for furs and to the Pacific Coast. As early as 1792, the NWC had engaged in trans-pacific commerce, initially through American merchant firms. The company found the cost of shipment through the East India Company (EIC) to be prohibitive and the trade permitted by the EIC quite restricted. As a result, it proved less expensive to ship its furs to an east-coast American port and have them trans-shipped in an American ship to Canton than to deal around the Horn with the East India Company. The shipments averaged 36,822 pelts per year between 1792 and 1796, and over 20,000 per year between 1804 and 1808. The NWC was anxious to be able to ship west-coast beaver directly to China, although the Oregon furs were not prime and would have to be used for felt rather than for coats.

Prime beaver came from the Athabasca. Dealing with the Athabasca region via a canoe route of several thousand miles was inefficient and expensive. The Athabasca was believed to be close to the Pacific, and it theoretically could be supplied less expensively from a coastal depot. This same thinking led the NWC to attempt its negotiations with the HBC to gain access to its coastal outlet. Thus, Alexander Mackenzie explored first the Mackenzie River, then the Peace River, and finally reached the Pacific Slope overland. Thus in 1808, Simon Fraser successfully completed the navigation of the treacherous Fraser River to its mouth at the Gulf of Georgia. Thus, David Thompson, who left the HBC for the NWC in 1797, explored the headwaters of the Mississippi and, in 1811 ascended the Columbia River to its source before traversing it to its mouth at Fort Astoria. In 1811 the NWC petitioned the British government for a charter giving it exclusive rights in the region between the Rockies and the Pacific slope. The NWC's expansion was not only to the west. In 1802 the partners also had purchased the stock of the King's Domains (the Tadoussac Posts) originally held as a monopoly by the King of France in the Saguenay River country of what is now Quebec and continued by the British conquerors. The monopoly was leased for twenty years. The chief products of the relentless expansion of the territory in which the NWC traded were in the short run greatly overextended supply routes, which required great organization and coordination (as well as large amounts of capital) to support. But the overall effect of the system of partnership was an active competition among the partners themselves for success, one that the Hudson's Bay Company could only hope to emulate.

Without doubt the NWC could be extremely ruthless in dealing with its own employees, with competition, or with uncooperative Natives. In 1816 Lord Selkirk devoted his book *A Sketch of the British Fur Trade in North America* to cataloguing the excesses of the company in the west. Selkirk observed that the absence of any institutions of law and order encouraged disorder, because the traders believed "the commission of almost any crime would pass with impunity."[34] Selkirk also insisted that most of the intimidation was effected through the agency of the Aboriginal and mixed blood peoples, whose role in the violence was distinctly misunderstood in Europe. William Coltman, who prepared a report on the fur-trade war for the government in 1817, agreed with Selkirk that the business activities of the NWC were rooted in violence and intimidation. The company did not always treat its own employees generously. Much hostility prevailed between the winterers and the Montreal merchants who supplied them. The company certainly dispensed summary justice to Indians who were judged guilty of violence or bad behaviour. It reserved its roughest treatment, of course, for its competitors, particularly the Hudson's Bay Company.

By 1811 the NWC was on the eve of its maximum extension, for in 1812 it would actually take over the administration of the fur trade on the Pacific Coast. It had formally schemed for this extension since 1810, when it requested from Whitehall a twenty-one-year monopoly on trade in those parts of the British West not claimed by the HBC. It also asked for permission from the East India Company to export furs straight to Canton. An NWC agent in London arranged a meeting in March 1810 with the secretary of state for war and colonies, Lord Liverpool, who failed to respond to the request. The British government eventually sent word to its ambassador in London to investigate the American plans for the Northwest. In November of 1810 Simon McGillivray wrote to Lord Liverpool calling for a British warship to be sent to the Columbia to prevent an American takeover of the region. McGillivray insisted that what was at stake was "the ultimate right of Possession of the whole Northwest coast of America." In the summer of 1811, the NWC decided to act unilaterally, voting at Fort William to send a brigade of sixty men west to the Columbia to compete with the Americans.

The NWC expansion to the Pacific would be a very mixed blessing. Extended transportation lines stretching virtually across the continent required the use of more extensive personnel simply to maintain communications. These men had to be paid and supplied. Along with them came larger numbers in dependent entourages. In 1806 the company at its annual meeting at Kamanistiquia (Fort William) discussed the proposition that "the number of women and Children in the country was a heavy burthen to the concern." It attempted to reduce the number of women maintained by the NWC, particularly at various provisioning posts established along the lengthy route into the lucrative trading region of the Athabasca. One of the principal provisioning regions was at the junction of the Red and Assiniboine rivers, the very site at which Lord Selkirk hoped to plant his colony. Extended transportation lines also meant that it took years for the capital invested in an "outfit" of trading goods sent west to return east in the form of furs to be sold in the European markets. While all commerce in this period took long periods for investment to come to fruition, the five-to-seven-years delay the NWC incurred seemed excessive by anybody's standards. Certainly the NWC went constantly deeper in debt to London bankers, a problem that would eventually help sink the company.

THE GRANT TO SELKIRK

The London agents of the North West Company threw down the gauntlet from the beginning, seeking to oppose the grant to Selkirk through the General Court of the HBC. The Nor'westers probably expected to fail here, but perhaps hoped that they could cast sufficient doubt on the feasibility of the scheme to make possible some deal with the HBC. Instead, overcoming their opposition became part of the very reason the venture clumsily lurched forward. Twenty-one stockholders, the most in years, attended the General Court in Hudson's Bay House in Fenchurch Street on 22 May 1811. No business was concluded on that date, for the opponents of Selkirk forced a delay until 30 May, to give those present time to examine the proposals in detail. According to Miles Macdonell, anxiously waiting outside the door of the meeting room, Sir Alexander Mackenzie had stormed out of the court insisting that the scheme "struck at the root of the NWCo. of Canada which it was intended to ruin" and maintaining to anyone who would listen that one Canadian interpreter could set the Natives of the region against the settlers at any point.[35] Mackenzie's response could be interpreted by Selkirk and his supporters to mean that the scheme was proving its effectiveness. The threat of violence would become a continual part of the opposition to Selkirk, an example of the NWC's bullying tactics. Such threats would merely strengthen the earl's determination to proceed.

At the meeting of the General Court on 30 May, again heavily attended, a memorial prepared by six shareholders, including Nor'westers Edward Ellice and Alexander Mackenzie, was read to those assembled. The memorialists realized that they lacked the votes to stop approval of the grant to Selkirk—several of them had not held stock long enough even to vote formally on the subject—but they were going on the record. Given that fact, one might have expected something more thorough, even allowing for the complaint of lack of time to prepare objections. Of the eight points made, four concentrated on the procedures involved in making the grant and on Selkirk's motives, concluding, "Your Memorialists cannot perceive for the said grant, any other motive than to secure to the posterity of the said Earl at the Expense of the Stockholders of the said Company an immensely valuable landed estate."[36] A failure to appreciate the complex motives behind Selkirk's actions always characterized the Nor'westers, just as he was unable to see their opposition in anything other than the most simplistic terms. The critics noted briefly the difficulty of populating a wilderness 2000 miles from a seaport (obviously thinking of Montreal rather than York Factory) and asserted that the inhabitants of the settlement would compete with the company while gravitating to the Americans. "It has been found," they asserted pontifically and without evidence, "that Colonisation is at all times unfavourable to the Fur Trade."[37] Selkirk and Wedderburn must have heaved a sigh of relief at this weak performance, which did no justice to the issues. Simon McGillivray would do much better a few weeks later, in the pages of a Highland newspaper, and it is a pity his trenchant comments were not heard on Fenchurch Street that day in May.

The reading of the Selkirk arrangements that followed the minority memorial was anticlimactic. Only Sir Alexander Mackenzie among those present had any real notion of the vastness of the 116,000 square miles of territory on both sides of the present Canadian-American border that Selkirk was being granted in return for a nominal rent and a few services to the company, chiefly in recruiting up to 200 effective servants annually for ten years. After discussion, the matter was put to the vote: £29,937 worth of shares voted in the affirmative, and £14,823 in the negative. Selkirk and Wedderburn between them voted only £8,561.13.4 of stock, and the largest single voting shareholder—William Thwaytes with £9,233.68 of stock—voted in the negative. The Selkirk forces did not hold a controlling interest in the company in 1811, although they may have dominated its council chambers. Neither side could possibly have imagined the length or intensity of the conflict that would be touched off by this historic vote. For Lord Selkirk, the whole business would end in public rejection and virtual bankruptcy. He would die in 1820 the tragic victim of his excesses and inadequacies.

CHAPTER TWELVE

Starting up Red River

WITHIN A FEW DAYS of the final approval of Selkirk's grant by the HBC General Court, apparently as a result of the open discussion surrounding it, the London agents of the Canadian traders again approached the Hudson's Bay Company with an offer for the better regulation of the fur trade. The Canadians obviously thought it possible that the grant to Selkirk was part of a carefully calculated plan to put pressure on them to make concessions in a division of the fur trade. Their letter to Governor William Mainwaring was a good deal franker than their earlier critique of the Selkirk grant. They admitted a concern to avoid "a violent competition in the trade of a Country so far removed from the protection of Justice" and a desire "to curtail expense in the Competition for a trade for which the Circumstances of the times are particularly unpropitious."[1] The Canadians were sincere enough in their ambition to avoid expensive and violent competition, although they often expressed themselves in terms of open threats rather than conciliatory invitations. The Nor'westers also operated on the assumption that their *de facto* position of dominance in the West, particularly in the rich Athabasca region, deserved some recognition by their rival, however much the Hudson's Bay Company claimed a trading monopoly throughout the region based on a royal charter. The Canadians wanted to negotiate on the basis of both legal equality with the HBC and of a recognition that they controlled the bulk of the trade. From their perspective, to recognize the HBC charter would be to admit that they were interlopers. For its part, the British concern could hardly recognize the Canadians as legitimate competitors without admitting the irrelevance of the charter. These two mutually incompatible positions made negotiations impossible in 1811, as they had done in 1805 and would again in 1815.

THE STORNOWAY FIASCO

The enterprise envisioned and planned by Lord Selkirk—reinvigorating the fur trade while establishing a settlement in the middle of the continent—was from the beginning a chancy proposition. Some confidence in the scheme might have been generated by an early success in the planning and execution of the first expedition to Red River, which was to assemble in the Scottish Highland port of Stornoway. Instead, this expedition was from beginning to end a fiasco. It began the settlement entirely on the wrong foot, while demonstrating quite obviously that when matters went wrong in an excessively ambitious and complicated schedule, the result was fairly disastrous. Selkirk and his agents always blamed the origins of the problem on local opposition to the project stirred up by the Nor'westers, thus transferring responsibility for the troubles to their rivals rather than recognizing that the real problem was an excessively tight and interlocking schedule in a complex transatlantic business.

It was true that Nor'wester Simon McGillivray had produced a hostile letter signed "A Highlander" addressed to the editor of the *Inverness Journal*. This letter was published on 21 June 1811 and freely circulated among the recruits gathered by Selkirk's agents at the Highland port of Stornoway. The letter insisted that settlements could never be successfully established in the western interior of British America, which was an infertile region subject to an intemperate climate and 2,000 miles from the nearest "settlement of civilized inhabitants." Moreover, McGillivray warned, the settlers would be surrounded by "warlike savage nations . . . which subsist by the chace [sic] and will consider them as intruders come to spoil their hunting ground, to drive away the wild animals, and to destroy the Indians, as the white man have already done in Canada and the United States." The colonization venture, moreover, was not sponsored by the Hudson's Bay Company, as the recruiting advertisements had implied, but by a private individual who had already exerted himself to depopulate his native land by deluding immigrants into becoming "victims of their own rashness and credulity."[2] This linkage of the new project with Selkirk's earlier activities was an inspired addition.

Selkirk doubtless smarted under the personal attack of "A Highlander" and regarded this letter as flagrant misrepresentation, particularly in its invocation of a hostile and warlike Native population. But most of the confusion among the prospective immigrants at Stornoway was the result of hasty recruiting practices and considerable overstatement by Selkirk's agents of both the attractions of the prairies and the conditions of service. Even without the insinuations and veiled threats of Simon McGillivray, Miles Macdonell would have had considerable difficulty in embarking the more than 100 men he had waiting at Stornoway. They had been gathered in Scotland and Ireland under a variety of terms and conditions, and had been given no clarification as to whether they would be employed by the Hudson's Bay Company in the fur trade or by Selkirk for his colony. There were complaints of broken promises and the unsightly spectacle of men going over the side of the ship when customs officials insisted on informing them of their rights.[3]

Delay piled on delay, and the most crucial result of the Stornoway business was that the new recruits were not actually on their way to the Bay on time. They did not depart until the end of July, making it virtually certain that they would have to winter at the bottom of the bay rather than being able to work their way down to the site of the proposed settlement before freeze-up. A less than propitious beginning, it was symptomatic of the sorts of problems that would bedevil this venture. Simon McGillivray had overstated the particulars, but was quite accurate in the general thrust of his letter. Selkirk had not taken proper stock of the difficulties inherent in attempting to transplant settlers to so remote a region as the Red River. Canadian opposition did not create the difficulties, but merely made them worse. As was so often the case in Selkirk's projects, little room was left for the sorts of mishaps that ought to have been anticipated in such a complex operation conducted so far from normal channels. While Selkirk would have denied the charge vigorously, it remained the case that the lives of people were at stake and that the dangers were not being sufficiently taken into account.

The rival companies engaged in fruitless negotiations over the summer of 1811 and the controversy over recruitment persisted in the pages of the *Inverness Journal*. Meanwhile, Miles Macdonell and William Hillier (who had been hired to head the party of roving shock troops) sailed with 105 men for York Factory. Their voyage to the Bay, having gotten off to a delayed start, was "the longest ever known & latest to H Bay," reported Miles to

Selkirk, not arriving until 24 September.[4] Despite the sixty-one days at sea with little to do, none of the young men had made any progress in learning either Gaelic or Irish—Selkirk hoped the ancient tongues would unify the colonists and protect them from American influence—and not a single one had any familiarity with a gun. Although William Auld at York Factory was most cooperative, wrote Miles, it would be necessary to winter the parties on the north side above the Nelson River above the factories. "I was aware of considerable difficulties in prosecuting this Scheme, which a desire to forward your Lordship's views led me to undertake," concluded Macdonell, but "the troubles attendant on it have already exceeded my expectations."

As Miles's comments suggested, one of Selkirk's principal demands of subordinates was a willingness to pass lightly over the obstacles which the earl's ventures usually entailed, in favour of promising to do the impossible. An inability to listen to and heed sincere and oftimes well-informed negative criticism of his plans was not the least of Selkirk's failings, although it was in many ways the reverse side of his ability to reconceptualize problems by cutting through hitherto insurmountable obstacles. Unfortunately, as his critics would frequently point out, the price of the miscarriage of plans that sounded feasible on paper was borne by his employees and dependents, many of whom had no notion of what they were getting into at the outset.

From William Auld at York Factory, both Andrew Wedderburn and Selkirk received some unsolicited negative comments written in the autumn of 1811. Auld was an old hand in the bay who was well set in his ways. He often seemed incapable of giving anything new or different a fair trial. His lack of enthusiasm for the projects that Miles Macdonell and William Hillier were to lead was transparent, but his comments probably deserved a better hearing than they received. Unfortunately, much of what Auld had to say cut against some of Selkirk's most cherished ideas. From the outset, Auld warned against mixing Scotsmen and Irishmen, a combination that stood at the very root of the earl's plans for his settlement. Auld was equally concerned about the lack of experience with local conditions exhibited by both Macdonell and Hillier, illustrated by Miles's plans to use flat-bottomed boats to traverse the rivers to the south, and by promises made that could not be honoured in the rough conditions of the wilderness. The boat business was as much an example of Auld's inflexibility as Macdonell's inexperience, for the boats worked well and became one of the main influences upon the renowned "York boat" of the nineteenth century. To Selkirk Auld was brutally honest.

He began by emphasizing, "To a mind ardent and intent on vast & important plans of Colonization like your Lordships I am well aware of the presumption as well as incompetency of my own very imperfect ideas being at all worthy of your notice." This opening was patently insincere. He continued, he was in "one sense . . . pleased at the present frustration of your designs," since he had no experienced men to convey the new arrivals inland.[5] Auld was not concerned with the First Nations, denying vehemently that the Canadians could stir them up to serious aggression, but he seemed singularly unfamiliar with the mixed blood population in his territory, partly because he had never actually visited the prairies. Selkirk and Wedderburn may later have overemphasized the extent to which Auld was an "enemy within," yet Auld's letters made clear that not everyone among the company's servants on the bay was enthralled with the new policies represented by Miles Macdonell and William Hillier.

OTHER BUSINESS

Selkirk had other matters on his mind in the autumn of 1811 besides the troubles on the bay experienced by his new venture. The mental instability of his young nephew William Hall, who would require medical supervision, took up a good deal of his time.[6] Some form of schizophrenia would prove endemic in the Hall family, eventually leading to the institutionalization of both Sir William Hall and his son Basil. On another front, the earl also spent a good deal of time considering a sheep-breeding program, producing a long set of instructions to agent Thomas Clark for Baldoon.[7] More worrisome, a former agent on Prince Edward Island—Angus MacAulay—was making "defamatory statements" about Selkirk as part of a general campaign of criticizing the island's administration associated with the "Loyal Electors," the first formally organized opposition political party in British North America. MacAulay sought to associate Selkirk with the other oppressive absentee landlords on Prince Edward Island by emphasizing that he had not kept many of his promises to his settlers. Many of those being attacked by MacAulay and the other Loyal Electors wanted Selkirk to protect their interests at the Colonial Office.[8]

Selkirk also began the process, at least on paper, of distributing land in Red River, initially to those supporting his scheme but ultimately to those who would privately subscribe money in return for land. The subscription money would be vested in trustees, who would receive land themselves but were not involved in the administration of the settlement. The three trustees who agreed to serve—Sir Benjamin Hobhouse, Bart., William Smith, MP, and Zachary McAulay—were all well-known Evangelicals and humanitarian reformers. Selkirk had worked with them during the campaign for the abolition of the slave trade and subsequently on other reform ventures connected with Africa and the blacks. The creation of this trusteeship provided an aura of British respectability for his settlement that Selkirk desperately needed.

THE 1812 RECRUITING

The Hudson's Bay Company had ordered 200 men for the upcoming season, and Selkirk set his agents in motion in the Highlands of Scotland and in Ireland. Recruiting went slowly, and in some ways, the earl was relieved to learn in March that the company would be sending only two ships in 1812 and would therefore need only 120 men; if Selkirk required additional tonnage, another vessel would have to be chartered.[9] Later that month he wrote to Miles Macdonell, from whom he had not heard since the arrival of the 1811 ships at York Factory, that while enough men would be obtained in Ireland, "in the Highlands we have met with so much obstruction, that I doubt whether it will be effectually overcome, unless I go out myself which I have serious thoughts of doing next year." The reference was undoubtedly to the reluctance of Highlanders to agree to emigrate if the recruiter did not personally lead the party. Selkirk consoled himself with the thought that Macdonell was not yet ready for a party of the size that the earl would bring himself. He hoped that Miles could handle fifty to sixty men, plus some boatbuilders.[10]

In the spring of 1812, Selkirk unexpectedly came precariously close to joining the ministry and sitting on the government bench in Parliament. Irish questions were to the fore in Parliament, and Selkirk not only had strong opinions on Irish matters but also some first-hand experience to back them up. He was sympathetic to Catholic emancipation, not a popular position with Tories such as Lord Sidmouth, but otherwise he and the government were in considerably more agreement than usual. According to Lady Selkirk, Sidmouth regretted "that he had it not in his power to offer him [Selkirk] a seat in the Cabinet," but the earl was "too much wrapt up in his Transatlantic schemes to give in to any such idea."[11] In the same letter, Lady Selkirk commented on her awareness of her "inability to alter in any degree the direction of his mind . . . far less the course of events."[12] The remark was probably made not to suggest her lack of influence so much as her husband's single-mindedness, once he had fixed on a course of action. While his wife might have preferred that Selkirk become a cabinet minister, she recognized the unlikelihood of such a happenstance, particularly while he was involved with the Hudson's Bay Company and Red River.

In the end, Selkirk was forced to ask the HBC to grant him a licence to send out an additional ship to carry the colonists he was recruiting, the company agreeing to supply a cargo of timber and deals at Moose Factory for the return voyage.[13] He also had to request a licence from the king in Council for the export of military stores to defend the company's factories and settlements in Hudson Bay.[14] Great Britain was, after all, still at war against France. Selkirk had considerable difficulty obtaining a satisfactory vessel at short notice.[15] He continued to be concerned about the leadership of his new settlement, and even suggested to Alexander Macdonell—his former Baldoon agent who was in London to settle his accounts in the spring of 1812—that he might "go to Winipique."[16] His Irish agent B.H. Everard had decided against crossing the Atlantic, and young Archibald McDonald, whom he had hoped would be a leader of this party, was apparently still too immature to be trusted with a position of responsibility.[17] "Archie," as he was called, was held back and sent off for medical and accountancy training. Given Sheriff Macdonell's failures at Baldoon, Selkirk's suggestion indicates how desperate he had become. Macdonell had, of course, worked his way back into some semblance of favour by his willingness to report personally on his agency; if only James Williams in Prince Edward Island could have done the same! Selkirk would have been even more concerned with leadership had he been aware of what had transpired at York Factory over the winter of 1811–12 or had he been able to read the letters being penned by Miles Macdonell on the bay at the end of 1812.

In a letter dated 31 May 1812, Miles had described at length the events of the winter past. It was a sorry tale. All his party were in log and clay houses before the beginning of November, and had physically survived the winter very well. Food was not in short supply, and frostbite was not a serious matter despite temperatures often fifty degrees below zero. The onset of scurvy was easily corrected by drinking spruce juice. The non-physical side had not gone so well. Cabals had formed among the men. This was probably not surprising given their relative lack of activity, but on New

Year's night the Irishmen in the party had attacked the Orkneymen with shil-lelaghs. Subsequently one of the Orkneymen refused to drink his spruce juice, and was summarily confined to a separate hut, which his compatriots burnt to the ground the first night of his confinement. Thirteen men in all—nine from Glasgow and four from the Orkneys—refused to submit to authority, and spent the remainder of the winter in isolation. In the spring they refused to enter HBC service and insisted that they were not being treated in accordance with the promises made to them on recruitment. The problems at quayside in Stornoway the previous year had obviously not resolved themselves. The troublemakers could only be sent back home, "there being no controlling power in this country to manage them, "Miles emphasized strongly the need for a proper judicature in the settlement, suggesting a military establishment based upon martial law. A strong power was necessary to keep order, he insisted, lest "we may be all overturned by the tumultuous onset of our own people." Macdonell concluded by observing that William Auld had told him that according to British statute (43 George III, c 138, the so-called *Canada Jurisdiction Act* of 1803), all legal matters in the country were cognizable only in the courts of the Canadas.[18]

The problem of legal jurisdiction was a serious one, and both Selkirk and the HBC began attempting to deal with it. It plainly should have been considered earlier. But in the short term, the problem appeared mainly to be Miles himself.[19] His decision to sail across the Atlantic with a boatload of men as discontented as those who landed at York Factory in 1811 was obvi-ously a miscalculation. He probably should have winnowed out the worst of the malcontents, even if this had meant fewer numbers. Moreover, Miles was also displaying other weaknesses that would only become more pronounced with time. One was a moralistic censoriousness against the established employees of the HBC, mainly over their sleeping and living arrangements with Aboriginal women. Another was a difficulty in cooper-ating with others. Finally, he had a distinct tendency to paint himself into corners over minor matters to which he responded with harsh disciplinary measures. Discipline was the traditional military way of dealing with anything smacking of insubordination, but in the isolated wilderness of western Canada, men who had not expected to be governed by martial law needed to be inspirationally led, not heavily disciplined. Miles's stiffness and inflexibility—and especially his obvious preference for martial law—were

not encouraging signs in a man who was to become governor of a settlement several thousand miles from the nearest authority.

Lord Selkirk was himself present in Sligo, Ireland, for the embarkation
and departure of the 1812 contingent of men he had recruited for his own
service and for that of the company. He could not blame any problems
involving this contingent upon other recruiters. Many of the party came
from Ireland and the remainder from scattered districts in the Highlands of
Scotland. The earl hoped they would serve as a basis for further recruiting.
This year's overseers spoke fluent Gaelic. To William Auld, Selkirk emphasized his plan for a large emigration in 1813. It was first necessary to restore
the affairs of the company, for "we have a sufficient basis of unquestionable
legal rights if we had physical strength to enforce them for ourselves." He
hoped to come out himself in 1813 "at the head of such a body of men, as
will overawe any attempt to resist the lawful authority of the Co–for that
purpose I must bring out not less than 4 or 500 men."[20] To William Hillier—
the man who was already at the bay to lead a small paramilitary force
intended to confront the Nor'westers—Selkirk stressed the need for moderation and the observation of the principles of the laws of England on self-
defence "engraved by nature on the hearts of Englishmen." The Irishmen in
Hillier's party should not be trusted with firearms, for "the Shillela is their
proper weapon, with that they cannot do much harm; & the occasional
application of that implement may probably teach the messieurs voyageurs
to keep a respectable distance." All Nor'westers were to be treated as
poachers. "We are fully advised of the unimpeachable validity of these rights
of property, that there can be no scruple in enforcing them, whenever you
have the physical means."[21] Selkirk's attitude toward the use of force in the
fur trade was obviously ambivalent at best, and the fine distinctions hard to
communicate to his servants in North America. The bottom line, however,
was an apparent willingness to employ force if necessary.

As his letters to William Auld and William Hillier from Sligo suggested,
Selkirk regarded successful confrontation with the North West Company as
a high priority. He recognized that superior manpower was the best solution,
but he had not yet really worked out any strategy beyond sending large
numbers of new recruits. By this time it was clear that war with the United
States was pending (indeed, it was declared by the Americans against Britain
on the very day of the correspondence with Auld and Hillier), but Selkirk
had few comments on a possible war that day beyond the hope that the two

companies would cooperate for their mutual defence and an insistence that Miles Macdonell as an experienced military man should be commander-in-chief of any joint operation.[22] To Miles a few days later, Selkirk added that war seemed inevitable, adding, "I doubt that Canada will make but a feeble resistance, & our situation in the N.W. will then become very critical. Yet I do not despair of holding our ground, even tho' Canada should be conquered." If the west were invaded by the Americans, Miles should leave his settlers and head with his young men for the plains, joining up with the First Nations. The earl promised to come to his assistance: "it will go hard with me, but I will have a share in your adventures."[23] As Selkirk fully recognized in his rational moments, his duties in Britain made adventuring in North America difficult at the best of times, and certainly almost impossible in a time of actual war with the Americans. But as we shall see, he would do his best to get free.

The letter to Miles Macdonell from Sligo was full of enthusiasm and suggestions for projects. The earl really let loose his fertile imagination, virtually free associating on the problems Miles faced in America. The difficulty of a shortage of meat for making pemmican, for example, could be eliminated "by a method . . . where the meat has been kept frozen thro' the whole summer in an ice house." The shortage of settlers could be partly resolved by encouraging the disbanded North West Company and Hudson's Bay Company servants with Aboriginal families who wandered the interior to settle in the colony. They could be given 100-acre lots at reasonable prices, but not mixed with the immigrant settlers. Such a policy had been earlier discussed by the Hudson's Bay Company but never implemented.[24] Neither Selkirk nor the HBC obviously knew very much about the existence of the people of mixed descent. They simply never paid sufficient attention to this population in their thinking. Selkirk emphasized to Miles in this letter that collision with the North West Company should be avoided at all costs until the question of charter rights and numerical superiority was settled. This caution was quite at variance with what Selkirk had written two days earlier to William Hillier, but Selkirk was not being inconsistent. Hillier's job was to confront the Nor'westers, while Miles's job was to build a settlement. Selkirk elaborated on his own desire to cross the Atlantic, writing, "It would not do for me to come in person till I can come accompanied by such a body of followers as may effectually put down all attempts to resist the authority of the Co'y within their own Territory, & perhaps 500 would not be more than enough for that purpose."[25] Jurisdiction and numbers were key problems with which Selkirk felt he had to deal in the summer of 1812.

THE WAR OF 1812

Resolving the jurisdictional question was no easy matter. In the first place, the British government had to accept the monopolistic privileges of the Hudson's Bay Company charter, as well as the interpretation of that charter by which those privileges had been transferred to Selkirk within the area of his grant. Moreover, such official acceptance had also to reinterpret the meaning of the *Canada Jurisdiction Act* of 1803, or formally repeal it, since that legislation quite plainly put the jurisdiction for criminal justice in Hudson's Bay Company territory under the control of the courts of Upper and Lower Canada. A draft proposal for a judicial system and a legal code (both criminal and civil) prepared about this time survives in the Hudson's Bay Company Archives, annotated by several English lawyers.[26] It was a far-reaching and forward-looking document, never implemented because larger jurisdictional issues intervened. In the end, the inability to establish a clear legal jurisdiction over Red River was both symptomatic of the problems of Selkirk's settlement and responsible for many of them.

Selkirk did not confine himself to organizing Red River in the summer of 1812. He produced a whole series of memoranda for cabinet ministers on various aspects of British policy, often combining his proposals with his own interests. Selkirk was and always had been an unabashed imperialist, and war with the United States provided a focus for his imagination. To Lord Liverpool, at the head of the British government in 1812, Selkirk advocated deflecting Irish immigration from the United States to British North America, arguing that "to form in this way an addition to the resources of the empire, out of materials which would otherwise be destined to swell the strength of an inimical state cannot appear a subject of indifference to the national interests." In Nova Scotia or Canada, large numbers of Irish would be "turbulent & troublesome," he admitted, but a new colony suited to the temper and habits of the immigrants would be different.[27] Selkirk did not mention Red River, but it was clearly lurking around this proposal. Lord Liverpool did not rise to the bait, however.

A few days later, Selkirk tried again, this time expanding on his earlier Irish scheme. The Irish might prefer a colony with lands on easy terms, "a Catholic settlement, formed of their own countrymen, & in every respect constituted, so as to meet their prejudices and flatter their national pride." The earl did not elaborate on how prejudices and national pride would be met, but he did propose to open a subscription that would entitle subscribers to a share of the land granted him by the Hudson's Bay Company and provide a small fund to assist initial settlement. At the outset he did not expect government to take an active part, but it could assist by instructing the Irish government to facilitate immigration, by instructing customs officers not to obstruct passage, and by passing an act of Parliament exempting Hudson's Bay Company vessels from the *Passenger Vessels Act* of 1803. Government should grant a Crown commission to the governor of the colony, and finally, assist in forming a small armed force "to serve as a police guard, and to support the authority of the Governor."[28] What this proposal tells us is that Selkirk appreciated full well that he did not have the support of government for the establishment of Red River. Liverpool understandably ignored the last two items on Selkirk's shopping list, but was apparently willing to cooperate in terms of the first three requests, including legislation exempting the HBC from parliamentary regulation. From our modern vantage point, it is easy to dismiss such sweeping proposals for North American settlement as those made here by Lord Selkirk as ill-conceived and ludicrous, deserving of instant dismissal by the authorities. The record for planned settlement was universally dismal; nothing ever worked out as the planners intended. Contemporaries did not agree, however. While Lord Liverpool did not accept the key components of Selkirk's shopping list for Irish resettlement in 1812, a British government would institute a similar scheme for the Irish in 1823. Not the overall intention but the particulars were what Liverpool objected to, especially in granting a Crown commission to the governor.

While Lord Selkirk memorialized the government, the Americans massed invading armies on the borders of Upper Canada. In the early days of the war, the British achieved an outstanding if unexpected victory in the West, thanks in part to the North West Company. A small contingent of American troops, occupying Fort Michilimackinac on Lake Huron, had not in early July 1812 received word that war had been declared. Captain Charles Roberts, the British commander at Fort St. Joseph on the St. Mary's River, had already learned of the opening of hostilities, however, in a letter from General Isaac Brock ordering him to attack Fort Michilimackinac if possible. Roberts had already been offered the assistance of the North West Company in the region, which had quickly provided him with nearly 200 voyageurs and several parties of Indians (Sioux, Menominee, and Winnebago led by Robert Dickson) totalling about 400 effectives. This force set off for Michilimackinac on 16 July in an NWC schooner and a number of canoes. The subsequent attack was a complete surprise. The American commandant, Lieutenant Porter Hanks, readily agreed to surrender, concerned mainly that his troops might well be massacred even if they capitulated. However, as soon as they heard the capitulation was signed, the Indian parties all returned to their canoes. Roberts decided to use the fort as his western base. Robert Dickson led his warriors on to Detroit, where news of their coming helped General Brock capture the town in August.

Michilimackinac was virtually the only good news for the British in the early summer of 1812. But it was an important victory, not merely on the morale front. In the short run, it secured the West to Great Britain and exposed the Americans to Aboriginal depredations on their western flanks. Equally important from the standpoint of the fur trade, it sealed a long-standing alliance between the Canadian authorities and the North West Company. Even before the triumph, Captain Roberts had been instructed to assist the North West Company in every way possible. The Nor'westers had obviously responded in kind. In September of 1812 a corps of voyageurs was formally embodied in the West, which provided many Nor'westers with military uniforms, including those red coats that so impressed the First Peoples. It would prove very difficult for the Hudson's Bay Company to break up this cosy arrangement between the NWC and the Canadian governments, especially in Lower Canada, in years to come. The uniforms would be eventually employed against the Red River settlement.

As for Lord Selkirk, he displayed no further interest in 1812 in military affairs in the western reaches of British North America after his letter to Miles Macdonell of 20 June. In August he did send a memorandum to Lord Sidmouth on British policy in Spain, reflecting recent victories in the peninsula. Selkirk advocated a *levy en masse* in territory not held by the French, one that promised land allotments out of estates of traitors supporting Napoleon. He also insisted that the British should pay more attention to the lower orders in Spain and less to the aristocracy, suggesting a ruling junta instead of a regency.[29] A few days later he offered a proposal for reform of the Irish Catholic Church to Nicholas Vansittart, recently appointed chancellor of the exchequer, that he insisted would eliminate foreign influence on the church. Patronage should be taken out of the hands of the priests and prelates. Most landowners and merchants in Ireland, Selkirk argued, wanted property protected and civil privileges extended to Catholics, and would not oppose parliamentary action that included such boons.[30]

What led Selkirk to this flurry of government activity is not entirely clear. One possible explanation is that an election was in prospect, and Selkirk needed the support of the ministry were he to remain a Scottish representative peer. Another explanation is that Selkirk was attempting to overcome the problems in Red River by surrounding them with other issues. It may also be that the early Liverpool administration involved men and ideas that Selkirk found particularly congenial, and he thought he might be able to have some effect on government policy. Perhaps he—or at least Lady Selkirk—had not yet given up on the idea of a cabinet position. In any event, Selkirk's name did appear on the "Proposed List of Sixteen Peers for Scotland" prepared in early October by the government's Scottish political manager, Lord Melville.[31] Despite the presence of a government list, tradition demanded that peerage candidates pretend that they were thoroughly independent. They were permitted a discreet solicitation of votes, but no active campaigning. To lords Leven and Melville, Selkirk wrote diffidently, "We are again at the work of vanity & vexation of spirit—I am almost sick of it, but not being *quite cured,* I must needs send you the within." The enclosure was a formal request for the noble lord's support in the election. On this letter, the recipient added his own comment in the form of a short poem:

> So Selkirk says with Solomon
> And yet he wont be cured:
> The work he will not let alone,
> All fruitless tho' assured![32]

The earl was also forced to intricate explanations in order to balance his continued insistence on independent stance in peerage elections with his need for government support.[33] The manoeuvring was successful, for when the government counted up its support in early November, Selkirk had sufficient votes to guarantee re-election.[34]

His successful re-election to the House of Lords represented the high point for Selkirk in the second half of 1812. His North American ventures certainly were not going well. The sheep farm at Baldoon in Upper Canada was ravaged by an American raiding party in the first months of war.[35] At the beginning of July in 1812, Miles Macdonell had still not left York Factory for Red River. He had only a handful of men left from the previous year's "importation," but wrote resolutely to his employer, "a man of one nation is prejudiced against going with one of another—I shall go on with any number—take possession of the tract & hoist the Standard."[36] As for Selkirk's 1812 party, it had experienced an attempted mutiny at sea amongst the steerage passengers and a nervous breakdown a few days later on the part of the man handpicked by the earl to lead it.[37] The Scots and Irish proved totally incapable of getting along with one another.

Miles Macdonell had still not reached the site for the settlement in mid-August of 1812 when he wrote to Selkirk. He was at that point in time sailing down Lake Winnipeg. His boats had proved effective, but the delay obviously meant that the year would pass without any crops being planted or any other serious improvements undertaken in preparation for the 1812 party about to arrive at York Factory. Miles could probably not have done very much with the nineteen effective men he brought with him from the bay, but he was being optimistic in writing Selkirk that he could handle fifteen more families and twenty single men in 1813. More honest was his closing remark that more time would be required to establish the colony than he had at first calculated.[38] In early September, Owen Keveny reported from York Factory on the safe arrival of the party from Sligo. He was now unquestionably in charge of the 1812 settlers. Despite the problems on the voyage, he was ready to take the newcomers inland, but was facing a shortage of both experienced hands and boats. Keveny warned Selkirk not to expect more than half of the promised fifty boats for 1813. Believing that to have another party winter at York Factory would be bad for further recruiting, Keveny was determined to press southward to join Macdonell, who had only just arrived in Red River himself and had enjoyed no opportunity to prepare for fresh arrivals.[39] Owen Keveny had already acquired a reputation for hard driving. Donald Gunn would later write in the *Nor'-Wester* of the oral tradition in Red River:

> Mr. O'Caveny has been represented as uncommonly severe and cruel in his treatment of those under his authority. It has been currently reported, and not doubted, that for the most trivial offence he would order the offending party to be put in irons; in other cases the unfortunate culprit was made to run between two lines of men drawn up fronting each other, and each man prepared with a cudgel to

commence the strange, and to one party concerned, unpleasant operation of belaboring the object of their chief's resentment as soon as
he entered between their ranks.[40]

But any other strategy on Keveny's part in 1812 besides pushing on to the
settlement would probably have produced a complete disaster.

As for William Auld, he continued to insist that most of the problems
resulted from Selkirk's excessive optimism and refusal to listen to the advice
of those experienced in the country. Typically, the earl would pay virtually no
heed to the criticisms when they finally reached his desk. Auld had nothing
good to say about Miles Macdonell, whom he found "not conciliatory."[41]
Selkirk may not have wanted to listen to William Auld, or take any advice,
but the mounting evidence should have seemed fairly clear. The cumulation
of delays and instances of unforeseen circumstances ought to have signalled
the lack of viability of the Red River project, at least as presently conceived.
Certainly nothing had happened to encourage any expansion of numbers
such as Selkirk had talked about earlier. Instead of pausing to take stock,
however, Selkirk pressed ahead with new initiatives as though nothing
untoward was occurring on the North American side.

In early January of 1813, the committee of the Hudson's Bay Company
authorized Selkirk to recruit and send to Hudson Bay "a few Swedes accustomed to the practice of Agriculture in the Northern Parts of Sweden; and a
few Laplanders with Two Brace of tame Rein Deer."[42] Obviously this initiative was an experiment intended to provide additional northern expertise
and perhaps introduce a new beast of burden into a rugged country. The
committee also attempted to limit Selkirk's enthusiasm for Irishmen, noting
"some unpleasant disturbances on the Bay by the Men sent out from Ireland"
and requesting that in future Selkirk recruit "Scotch or Orkney Men, who
are more orderly."[43] Selkirk was not chastised, however. He had already
dropped his grand scheme of Irish resettlement in favour of a proposal to the
government to raise a Highland regiment for the defence of Canada.

CHAPTER THIRTEEN

The Highland Regiment and the Kildonan Immigrants

FROM HIS FIRST INTEREST in the country around Lake Winnipeg, Lord Selkirk had entertained two visions, not necessarily mutually supportive. One was of the settlement of the country as a safety valve for discontented Irishmen. The other was to people the region with Highlander soldier-settlers. Indeed, he had made both proposals to the British government as early as 1803. A Highland regiment, of course, would not only provide protection for British interests in North America, but, equally significantly, would also provide settlers financed at government expense. From the time of the Seven Years War, the British government had found Highlanders serving in Highland regiments to be the perfect shock troops of empire, and several such units had served with distinction under James Wolfe at the Battle of Quebec. Other Highland regiments had subsequently served in the War of the American Revolution and in Ireland in the 1790s. Several Highland lairds, including the Earl of Seaforth and Lord Macdonald, had organized personal regiments in the 1790s, although such behaviour by this time was regarded by the accountants who ran their estates as nothing but an expensive self-indulgence. The most recent British experience with a regiment recruited in the Highlands for North American service had clearly been an unfortunate one.

THE EXPERIENCE OF THE CANADIAN REGIMENT

In 1803, the War Department responded favourably to a recommendation by the Duke of York to form a colonial regiment for service in North

America from those stranded by the sudden passage of the *Passenger Vessels Act*. Whether the government was influenced by Lord Selkirk in 1803 is not clear, but what happened to the regiment it authorized would have enormous impact on Selkirk in 1813. The subsequent tale of the "Canadian Fencible Regiment"—to give the unit its full title—was a sad one. Fencible regiments were normally raised for service at home, but this one was from the beginning designed for North America; presumably its use within the empire made its "fencible" designation acceptable. Recruitment was based on the assumption that in the Highlands of Scotland men were readily available and eager to enlist, especially in the Gaelic-speaking areas. But none of the earlier officers responsible for recruitment of the regiment understood a word of Gaelic, and the reputed pool of unemployed Highlanders proved a myth invented by the opponents of emigration. Most of the poor people who had been unable to leave for North America had been accommodated at home by a variety of public works programs. Recruiting proved much more difficult than expected, and the prospective recruits drove a hard bargain. Many insisted on passage for their wives and children, and the recruiters were pleased to oblige. The wave of protests from the Highland proprietors against what was turning out to be a government-sponsored emigration scheme reached new heights, and new recruitments were cancelled in April of 1804. The recruits and their families gathered in Glasgow, where rumours spread that the regiment was in some sort of disrepute. The delays in embodying the regiment made it impossible to conceive of sending it to Canada in 1804, and the government decided to winter it on the Isle of Wight, also the standard point for shipment of military units to the Indian subcontinent. Again the rumour mill worked overtime, and many men of the regiment refused to obey their officers by heading for these winter quarters. The short-term result was the dissolution of the Canadian Regiment in September of 1804 and a court martial of the leading mutineers, who were let off because the regiment was not under proper organization and discipline. The longer term result was an ongoing memory among British army leaders, including the Duke of York, that Highland regiments recruited for North American service were highly troublesome.[1]

Given the fate of the Canadian Regiment in 1804, it is in some senses surprising that the authorities should allow Lord Selkirk to resurrect such a scheme in early 1813. But politicians sometimes have shorter memories than soldiers, and the military situation for Canada was at the time fairly desperate. A few thousand British regulars—supported by a relatively small number of colonial militia—were attempting to defend British America against much larger American forces of volunteer citizen-soldiers. The British had held out against invasion in 1812 only because the American generals were so hopelessly inept. But the British government had little available manpower to send to Canada, and any new sources for soldiers had to be taken seriously. In any event, on 23 January 1813 Selkirk wrote to his Highland friend Alexander MacDonald of Dalilia that all previous plans for Red River were in abeyance, as the earl was intending to propose to government that he raise and lead a corps modelled on the Canadian Fencible Regiment for "service in America, during the present hostilities there." A stipulation would be added, he wrote, that the men should settle in Red River at the close of their service and their families would be transported there at government expense.[2] A week later he reported to MacDonald that Lord Bathurst, the secretary of war, had approved the plan in general principle. By 13 February he had assembled a list of prospective officers, and four days later he forwarded the outlines of a proposal to Bathurst. Selkirk himself would lead the regiment of 1,000 men as colonel with temporary rank, thus fulfilling a longstanding military ambition and also getting himself physically to North America during wartime without appearing to abandon his responsibilities as Lord Lieutenant of Kirkcudbright or as a member of the House of Lords.[3]

Although his regiment consumed most of Selkirk's attention in early 1813, he did find the time to draft a revision to the 1803 emigration legislation (*Passenger Vessels Act*) exempting the Hudson's Bay Company from the most onerous of its provisions.[4] Had Selkirk gained government support for this revision and for his Highland Regiment, he would have gone a long way toward bringing Red River within the ambit of official approval. Any hope that Selkirk and his officers entertained of the ready acceptance of the regiment, however, was summarily dashed by the army's commander-in-chief, the Duke of York, whose negative observations on the scheme were returned to the earl at the beginning of March.[5] This was the same Duke of York who had been forced to disband the Canadian Regiment in 1804. Characteristically, Selkirk took these criticisms not as the diplomatic but complete rejection of his scheme that the Duke of York no doubt intended, but as objections that could be met with counter-argument, revision, and further negotiation. He responded with a lengthy memorial to Lord Bathurst defending his proposals and suggesting possible modifications.[6] At this point Selkirk was presented with what he chose to regard as a marvellous windfall opportunity.

A PROPOSAL FROM SUTHERLANDSHIRE

The windfall arose out of the profound changes occurring in Sutherland-shire in the northern Highlands. These were part of the changes that Selkirk had predicted and written about in his book on the Highlands. They involved cheviot sheep, introduced into the country in 1794 and growing rapidly in number in the early years of the nineteenth century. The wool produced by the sheep was a far more valuable commodity than the small rentals paid by the existing inhabitants. Pasturage for the sheep pushed out families living on the barren glens of the county and removed them to the seacoast, where they might at best receive small plots of land and become crofters. The estate of the Countess of Sutherland (who became Lady Staf-ford after her husband in 1803 became Lord Stafford) was slow to adopt the strategy of introducing sheep, but in 1809 she became involved with two entrepreneurs from Morayshire—William Young and Patrick Sellar—who had a variety of schemes for Highland improvement that could be adapted to the Sutherland estate. Young especially had improved large tracts of previously uninhabitable coastal Morayshire, making possible the orderly settlement of 200 people on previously useless land. He was later characterized by Lord Stafford's English agent as "a very first rate High-land improver, a strong-headed intelligent Scotchman."[7] In 1809 he and Sellar proposed to the countess a project similar to Morayshire on her lands. They would simultaneously make money and improve the lot of the tenants on the Sutherland estate, who they claimed could not produce their own subsistence and who relied on the bounty of their landlord. They offered a wonderful vision of improvement:

> If your Ladyship can lead the people from destroying the Soil, and from starving every creature on it, to settle in villages; if you can introduce a few Mechanics and manufacturers among them; induce the farmers to the cultivation of flax; set a woollen manufacture such as we have at Elgin, agoing; and get the sons and daughters of the present generation into the employment of those who can teach them industry and which considering the pliability, and acuteness too, of the people, seem no very Herculean undertaking, the present

enchantment which keeps them down will be broken, and Sutherland may enjoy as many comforts and pay as fair rent as any of her
neighbours.[8]

The notion that the existing population could be easily re-educated was one
that Selkirk had questioned at some length in his book, and was of course
denied by the Sutherland's chief factor, Cosmo Falconer, who observed of
the tenants that "only a determined plan . . . will drive them to change,"
adding that they were being stirred up by "some disaffected people."[9]

Young and Sellar soon became aware that improvement would not be
easy in this remote part of the world. The tenantry survived, they discovered,
less by their labour on their virtually useless lands than by working in the
south in the summer or by the remittances they received from relations who
had gone to America. They maintained, however, that one of the reasons that
earlier clearance had produced so much resistance—such as the Ross-shire
riots witnessed by young Thomas Douglas in 1792—was because the people
had simply been removed from the sheep pasturage and "crammed . . . into
hamlets . . . without *any new tract being pointed out for their industry;* and
wanting, we fear, the full supply they formerly enjoyed on their boundless
pastures."[10] The new philosophy for clearance involved the provision of new
holdings for those dispossessed. In 1810 the old Sutherland factor Cosmo
Falconer was replaced by William Young, assisted by Patrick Sellar, who
would collect the rents. A concerted transformation of the Sutherland estates
was undertaken, in which new villages (for fishing on the coast; for wool
processing in the interior) were projected and transportation infrastructure
implemented. The Countess of Sutherland in 1811 wrote to Sir Walter Scott:
"I have great hopes at present, from the abilities of this Mr. Young, of considerable improvements being effected in Sutherland and without routing and
destroying the old inhabitants, which contrary to the Theories respecting
these matters, I am convinced is very possible."[11] The countess was not
specific about the theories about improvement that she hoped to be able to
disprove, but it is certainly not fanciful to think that the arguments advanced
by Lord Selkirk in 1805 were somehow mixed among them.

Despite some understanding of the theoretical problems of clearance,
neither William Young nor Patrick Sellar were really very sympathetic to the
common people with whom they were dealing. Tenants were to be presented
with a non-negotiable alternative, and if they did not like it, they would have
to be coerced "at the point of the sword."[12] Not surprisingly, by February of

1813 the people of Kildonan were up in arms against improvement. Young had intended to move seventy families from a remote part of the interior of the county to the north coast where the sea would supply fish and the crops would properly ripen. This population—smugglers to a man, Young insisted—"rose in a body and chased the valuers off the ground and now threaten the lives of every man who dares to dispossess them."[13] Furthermore, Young saw this challenge as part of a power struggle, writing "if Lord and Lady Stafford do not put it in my power to quell this banditti we may bid adieu to all improvement."[14] The response of the improvers has become part of the folklore of the Clearances, involving as it did the burning of cottages with the tenants still inside them.[15] The threat of troops and their eventual appearance in March 1813 understandably led the resistors to petition Lord and Lady Stafford for forgiveness. But not before they had met in several large assemblages, which the Stafford people saw as "riots," and which appointed one of their number, a retired recruiting sergeant of the 93rd Regiment, to take their case to London.

The people of Kildonan did not intend merely to plead abjectly for mercy, but they were prepared to bid high for the land. They undoubtedly did not fully understand the dynamics of the current situation. The Staffords were not trying to extract larger rentals from their tenants, but rather to revise completely the basis of their estates and their revenues. Nevertheless, Sergeant Macdonald was authorized by the tenants of Kildonan to offer the Stafford family more rent for their lands than the incoming sheep farmer, William Young, had agreed to pay. Moreover, hearkening back to the days of personal regiments, Macdonald was also authorized to offer leave to the Duke of York to raise 700 effective men in the region—very nearly a regiment—to be "at the Comander in Cheif's Disposal in aney part of his Majestys Dominions at Home or North America, provided their aged Fathers and Mothers and Wives and Children cane with propriety keep their Native home."[16] The Staffords were at first politely receptive, having been told by their agents not to inflame public opinion, but Lord Stafford rejected the petition out of hand, claiming "all the signatures were in one handwriting."[17] This was quite likely, but did not necessarily mean that the signatures of illiterate Gaelic speakers were necessarily forgeries. As for the Duke of York, he refused to grant Macdonald an audience. On the other hand, the Earl of Selkirk learned of the sergeant's mission, and was soon listening to him with mounting excitement. The opportunity seemed heaven-sent. Here was the bulk of the manpower for his regiment! Perhaps equally importantly, however, the people of Kildonan were in a very real sense acting in terms of the theoretical arguments Selkirk had advanced in his book on the Highlands. Given this realization, the earl could hardly fail to respond to their entreaties. Quite a lot of evidence exists for Selkirk's subsequent behaviour. It documents Selkirk at his inventive and improvisatory best—or worst.

Soon after his meeting with Sergeant Macdonald, Selkirk visited the Marchioness of Stafford in her London mansion. The Kildonan lands were part of her inheritance and she supervised their management. He sought to explain his project for a North American regiment. According to her account, "He said a plan was in agitation to raise a Corps for service in Canada, that it was to consist of married men, and that those who enlisted were to obtain land and settlements for their Families there." Selkirk asked questions about folding the Kildonan people into the plan. If he enlisted Kildonan men, could the estate accommodate their families until the war was over? Lady Stafford recounted to Selkirk the offers of new land made to the Kildonan people. He thought the offers were "fair and handsome," but "doubted if they [the Kildonan people] would take to habits of Industry at home." The Marchioness found the thought of relocating the families "impracticable," for "leaving the Families without the men to assist in settling them would only increase the difficulty."[18] Despite this rejection and the Duke of York's criticisms, Selkirk continued to negotiate with Sergeant Macdonald, going so far as to prepare a jointly initialled series of queries and answers that Macdonald took back to Kildonan.[19] Selkirk's responses were based on official approval being obtained for his Highland regiment. He was proposing to send the families of the soldiers on ahead to Red River, provided they could obtain government transportation and allowance, although surely he must have recognized what a dubious proposition this was. In any case, when Macdonald returned to Kildonan to report on his mission for London, he took with him no more than an authorization from Selkirk to collect a list from which recruits could later be taken.

As for the earl himself, he submitted to the government a modified version of his earlier proposal. He now wanted to transport (at government expense) the families of the soldiers to Red River at the outset. He also met most of the objections of the Duke of York.[20] A week later, Selkirk once again turned up at the door of Lady Stafford. He had seen an advertisement in the *Inverness Journal* obviously directed at people from Sutherlandshire, he said, offering conveyance to America. Lady Stafford was surprised at this news, since she had been told that her people were reconciled to her plans, and in any event, Selkirk's scheme would not work. Desperately improvising, Selkirk offered—on the basis of a document shown him by the Marchioness—to become a tenant of Lord Stafford at Strathy "on which he would arrange these people and assist in promoting a settlement there." Lady Stafford was not very encouraging, but she did not totally shut the door on this proposal. She said that Lord Stafford would have to consult with his managers in the Highlands, and she and Selkirk "calculated how many days this would require." She added that the people had not behaved very well. More to the point, "if our Agents were to make any proposal to them with a view to sending them to America they would suspect they had not fair play and that it would defeat its own purpose."[21] Selkirk went away promising a proposal on paper, which he apparently never sent. To his chagrin, the commander-in-chief rejected his revised regimental scheme a day after his meeting with Lady Stafford, this time categorically and unconditionally.[22]

Not quite beaten, Selkirk had in anticipation of this decision already written to Lord Bathurst offering to create a corps for service on the northwest frontier composed of resident fur traders supplemented by a few disciplined soldiers. The British soldiers would be conveyed to North America at government expense and settled in the Hudson's Bay territories after the war. The earl offered his own services to lead this corps and to govern "those parts of North America which lie beyond the limits of Canada a Territory not now included in any regular Government."[23] This scheme was more practical. It was approved in principle by Bathurst and endorsed for consideration by the Duke of York.[24] It is of interest because it suggests the points Selkirk most wanted to salvage from his grandiose plans. He wanted to get to North America. He wanted not only government assistance for Red River, but also government assumption of authority over it. A few Kildonaners would probably have constituted the soldiers conveyed there. Useful as this plan might have been, nothing more was heard of it.

SALVAGING HONOUR AND CREDIBILITY

In the end, the only outcome of Selkirk's concerted and frenetic efforts to combine the war in North America with Red River settlement was a commitment of sorts to Sergeant William Macdonald and the people of Kildonan, based upon an assumption of government sponsorship that had been very quickly denied. Unfortunately, William Macdonald had returned to Kildonan from his meetings with the Earl of Selkirk in high spirits. He had quickly acquired a large list of over 1300 recruits and dependents based upon his discussions with and memorandum from Selkirk. While the earl had emphasized the provisional nature of his plans for the regiment, Macdonald operated as if they were definitive. Whether he had misunderstood Selkirk or simply intended to force him to act is not clear. To make matters worse, many Kildonan tenants refused relocations within the Stafford estate, instead selling their stock and effects in anticipation of their imminent departure for North America "with Lord Selkirk." Informed by the Staffords of this development, Selkirk was forced to a desperate series of last minute improvisations to recover something from what had become a shambles. Both his honour and credibility in the Highlands were at stake. To do something for the Kildonan people who had jumped the gun, he would have to return to his previous pre-regiment plans for Red River settlement and combine them with the Hudson's Bay Company requirements for the service of young clerks and traders. And he would have to act quickly. He did not hesitate for a moment, although as so often happened, his hastily conceived plans were likely to convert a bad situation into a worse one.

Late in April, Selkirk wrote to the Marquis of Stafford explaining and justifying his new plan, which did not involve the government at all but was carried on through his personal fortune. The people of Kildonan were the unfortunate victims of a great change for the general good, he argued, but they would never be happy set upon small crofts. How much better such a "bold and hearty peasantry" should people British colonies! The scheme Selkirk intended to propose involved sending able-bodied men the first season to Red River to prepare the way, followed by the remainder of the families over the ensuing few years. Still looking for temporary accommodation for those not immediately transported, Selkirk hoped the prospective emigrant families could be left temporarily on their own lands, or alternatively, relocated for the interim on lands that the earl was prepared to lease from the Staffords for the purpose.[25] The Staffords were prepared to countenance the latter option, although nothing ever came of it. As it became clear that Selkirk had not got his regiment and was planning a settlement at Red River on his own account, factor William Young wrote to a correspondent that the earl "has brought himself in to an awful scrape, and us to a world of trouble, for what can the people now do for themselves, without proper aid from Government and certain pay to the people?"[26] A few days later Selkirk sent his own agent to Kildonan to inform the people of the altered arrangements and to select first recruits.[27]

The Kildonan tenants were told there would be no regiment. Selkirk, however, was prepared to take to Red River sixty to eighty young men who "could proceed without their families on the usual terms of paying their passage, who would on their Arrival either get a *Feu* [a rental holding] on easy terms, or a certain number of Acres to purchase from his Lordship."[28] In addition, the Hudson's Bay Company wished another sixty young men. Such a proposal was a far cry from the arrangements discussed with Sergeant Macdonald. This was little more than an ordinary emigration venture restricted initially to the young and able. As William Young exclaimed, "how the others are in consequence of what Macdonald has held out to replace their Corn and Cattle which they have sold off . . . is more than I can divine."[29] In fairness to Selkirk, Sergeant Macdonald had exceeded his mandate and wilfully misunderstood the terms discussed with the earl. Both the sergeant and the Kildonan people he represented wanted desperately to be saved from crofting, and they believed whatever was necessary to make that possible. Misinterpreting their "betters" was always a favourite tactic of Highlanders to get what they wanted.

In a sense, the result was an excellent opportunity to compare the crofting opportunities in the Highlands with the promises of the New World. The landlord insisted that the estate's offer would mean that the Kildonaners "should live in new houses in place of old, that they should occupy farms which will produce corn in place of farms fit only for sheep, and that they will become industrious subjects in place of continuing vagabonds and breakers of the law."[30] For his part, Lord Selkirk was offering unheard of (to Highlanders) quantities of cheap land at the Forks of the Red and Assiniboine rivers in a land "flowing with milk and honey."[31] The earl headed north himself at the end of May, personally concluding agreements with the prospective emigrants and giving many receipts for their passage money in his own hand. John Strachan would later use these documents as evidence of Selkirk's duping of the Kildonan folk in an angry pamphlet published in 1816.[32] Many of those signed up were to be sent out in 1814. But the disparity between the final terms and Sergeant Macdonald's earlier reports undoubtedly explains much of the subsequent lack of loyalty to Selkirk exhibited by the Kildonan people, as well as the angry tone of

Donald Gunn's later account of the recruiting conducted in Kildonan by the earl.[33] In the end, Selkirk was forced to take thirteen of the most importunate families in 1813; they would have had no place to go in Sutherlandshire. They left Thurso by sloop in May. According to Donald Gunn, "the fore part of the hold [of the sloop] was formed into a huge bin filled with oatmeal; the after part of the hold was occupied by two splendid quadrupeds of the bovine tribe (a bull and a cow), which his Lordship had purchased at Ball'n'Ghobhainn in Rosshire, and which had travelled so far on their way to the new colony."[34] The passengers were taken from Thurso to Stromness, where they were billeted in the village while they waited for the Hudson's Bay Company ships to arrive from England.

On 29 June the Kildonan party sailed with thirty-seven single emigrants (mainly young males) aboard the *Prince of Wales* from Stromness. Of the total of ninety-four emigrants, sixty-eight were under the age of thirty. The passenger list included twenty-one Sutherlands, fourteen Gunns, thirteen Bannermans, five McBeaths, six McKays, and six McDonalds. Among the passengers was young Donald Gunn, who was signed up for Hudson's Bay Company service, and would later produce a detailed and bitter memoir of the voyage and subsequent experiences of the emigrants. Accompanying the passengers was William LaSerre, a young surgeon from Guernsey, who was in charge of the party and was intended to become the doctor at Red River. His assistant was the equally young Archibald McDonald, who had earlier impressed Lord Selkirk and had been kept behind in the 1812 embarkation as a sort of protegé for special training.[35] As might have been expected from a venture conceived amidst such confusion, the Kildonan emigration of 1813 would not prosper. Indeed, not much more could have gone wrong than actually did.

Along with the settlers, the *Prince of Wales* carried a large bundle of letters and instructions for Selkirk's agents in North America. Perhaps the most important document was a letter for Miles Macdonell regarding the thorny matter of legal jurisdiction in Rupert's Land. Legal opinions had established that the charter was valid and unaffected by the *Canada Jurisdiction Act*, wrote Selkirk to his "governor," but he added that "any violent overstretch of authority would be extremely pernicious to our cause" and lead to the abrogation of charter rights by act of Parliament. Particular caution was required in dealing with the North West Company, which would seize on any pretext to cause trouble. Selkirk emphasized to Miles:

Means will be found of bringing our legal rights to a fair Trial before
the Supreme Tribunal in England, and in the mean time any exercise
of Jurisdiction on the part of the Company must be confined to that
which is strictly necessary for preserving the peace & good order of
the Settlement, avoiding carefully any step that might give a handle
for misrepresenting those proceedings as directed to any sinister
object, & particularly to the invidious purposes of monopoly.[36]

The North West Company might be bound by **HBC** jurisdiction, but efforts
to subject it to such jurisdiction could be undertaken only with great
caution.

In a separate letter, Selkirk explained about the Kildonan settlers, noting
that the introduction of sheep had been "pushed on with considerable harshness and has excited very general discontent." The Kildonaners had "so much
of the Old Highland Spirit as to think the land their own," and had acted
with "a great deal of the old Highland pride & warmth of feelings." The earl
thought they were quite pleased with his offer for emigration, and the Sutherland males "seem to be both in person and in moral character a fine race of
men: there are great numbers among them who have property enough to pay
their passage, and settle themselves with little or no assistance and many
capable of paying cash for their lands." He added, "According to the ideas
handed down to them from their ancestors, and long prevalent among high
and low throughout the Highlands, they were only defending their rights
and resisting a ruinous, unjust and tyrannical encroachment on their property." Selkirk worried a bit about whether these Presbyterian sectarians
would accept the leadership of a Roman Catholic like Miles, but hoped they
would do so if their feelings were treated with delicacy.[37] Finding them a
clergyman of their own persuasion was another matter entirely, which Selkirk
did not deal with at this point, although he would later recruit such an individual—who refused to go to America at the last minute.

THE SITUATION AT RED RIVER

Selkirk appreciated the difficulty of his communication links with the bay
and the settlement, noting in another letter to Miles, "the distance at which
we are placed, and the long period which must intervene between our
communications, leaves a sort of melancholy impression of uncertainty in
our correspondence."[38] Letters written to Selkirk over the summer of 1813
by his principal people in Red River did not suggest that anyone was
doing very much to alleviate the uncertainty. Miles Macdonell was clearly

unpopular in many quarters, and there was much pettiness in the complaints.[39] Miles himself reported that he suffered much from "mean artifices & machinations of those by whom I was surrounded," adding, "I have been interfered with & opposed on all sides." Although he admitted that the country "exceeds any idea I had formed of its goodness," crops had been disappointing.[40] According to William Auld, admittedly no friend of Miles, the governor had alienated virtually everyone in the settlement, and had not the faintest notion of how to begin farming. "He is not the Lord of a Stalk of Corn," wrote Auld, adding "to send him the Story of Robinson Crusoe would be vain & useless." Even by mistake, Auld insisted to Andrew Wedderburn-Colvile, Miles had succeeded in doing nothing right. "If Lord Selkirk had advertized for a fool of the first magnitude he never could have better succeeded than he has done with the present man."[41]

Whether William Auld was accurate or fair in his assessment of the reasons for Miles's failure was, in one sense, irrelevant. What mattered was that a full two years after his departure from Scotland, the settlement was still almost totally undeveloped, and agriculture had barely begun. The settlers were still almost completely dependent upon the natural produce of the country, chiefly the buffalo, and Selkirk now had another hundred colonists on the way, with more promised for 1814. The settlers would probably have done far worse had they not received considerable assistance from the fur traders of the North West Company stationed at the Forks, who had greeted their arrival with mixed feelings but had supplied them with provisions, including wheat, barley, potatoes, and some farmyard animals. Miles Macdonell was concerned about the shortage of food before he even realized that he would have extra mouths to feed. That shortage led Miles Macdonell to a potentially fatal decision: "in consideration of the number of people for whom I have to provide subsistence," he wrote to Selkirk in July of 1813, "I shall be fully justified in laying an Embargo on all provisions within our territory except what may be necessary to bring out the parties. Should I be able to enforce this matter they [the North West Company] may not perhaps be induced to continue the fur trade here, provisions being their chief object in this part."[42] This letter, written within a month of Selkirk's warning not to exercise excessive jurisdiction against the Nor'westers, was a perfect example of the communications gap. Miles reiterated his intention in September, when he reported on the arrival of the first Kildonan settlers at Fort Churchill (where they had landed instead of at York Factory) and the subsequent need to feed them at Red River. "I am now determined that the N.W.Co. shall not take more provisions from there, than what will carry out their people who winter in Red R & when they find themselves subjected to this they may not perhaps think it an object to continue there." At the time of this writing Miles had not yet received the packet with Selkirk's letter warning against just such a step. It had gone to Fort Churchill with the settlers, and he had to head back south, unable to wait any longer for the correspondence.[43] The packet was opened by William Auld after Miles's departure.[44]

Although the news that development had been slow at the settlement distressed Selkirk—"not one symptom of existence" there, wrote William Auld, "neither ploughs, carts, nor horses"—and the threats of Miles to embargo pemmican would prove ominous, such matters paled into insignificance in comparison with word of the problems experienced by the Kildonan people aboard the vessel the *Prince of Wales*. The dreaded typhus fever was brought aboard the ship, and five emigrants as well as William LaSerre, the young surgeon hired by Selkirk to lead the expedition, died on shipboard. Another thirty were weakened by the disease, some to die later. To make matters worse, the epidemic meant that the captain of the vessel refused to transport the settlers as far as York Factory, where Miles Macdonell was waiting for them, and peremptorily deposited them instead at Fort Churchill without proper provisions for a winter they could not avoid. The settlers were in a "very melancholy & very distressed condition," reported William Auld, and were probably stuck at Fort Churchill until the following July. "What will become of these miserable people & ourselves the God in Heaven alone can know. I look forward with horror to the long dreadful winter." He would winter at Fort Churchill himself to supervise them personally, wrote Auld, since Selkirk's protegé young Archibald McDonald, who had been forced to take command upon LaSerre's death, "is quite a cypher among his country people and has managed them in a highly reprehensible manner."[45] Owen Keveny, who had visited the settlers at Fort Churchill, reported to Miles Macdonell that they were totally lacking in order and subordination, as might well be expected given their experiences aboard ship. He added, "They are so wedded to their own opinion & so extremely tenacious of admitting any right of command (especially those that paid for their passage)" that he feared for their survival.[46] Stubbornness had gotten the Kildonaners to Hudson Bay, and it would remain one of their main characteristics for many years.

By November of 1813, Selkirk had received the first letters of the 1813 season from the Bay, and he could begin trying to come to terms with the extent of the disaster they represented. No comments from him about Red River survive for this time, perhaps in itself a commentary on his reactions. More than two years after receiving his grant and sending his first part of settlers, Selkirk had virtually nothing to show for his investment and the labour of his agents on the scene. What could have gone wrong went wrong, and the situation for the Kildonan emigrants would only get worse. Increasingly apparent was the reality that the development of a settlement in the remote Canadian West would be a slow and laborious process at best, even were it not exposed to serious external threats.

CHAPTER FOURTEEN

The Pemmican Proclamation

WHILE MILES MACDONELL HAD BEEN at York Factory in September 1813 awaiting the Kildonan settlers, he held discussions with William Auld and others of the Hudson's Bay Company about policy toward the North West Company at the tiny settlement of Red River.[1] At this point the governor had not seen Selkirk's instructions to go slowly, especially where suggestions of monopoly were concerned; and certainly overall, the earl's correspondence was full of a general spirit of bellicosity toward the Nor'westers, if the manpower were available to enforce it. Understandably, Auld and the traders at York Factory favoured action whenever necessary. From their perspective, the North West Company was a trading rival to be put down wherever possible. Receipt of Selkirk's warnings, which finally came into Miles's hands in December, was too late to change his course of action, if indeed he properly understood their nuances. Miles thought he had the authority to control the trade in pemmican, and he was certain that he had the superior military position. While the latter assessment was probably true in the short run, it was quite misguided. As for the former, Miles's employer understood that his authority as governor of Red River had limited legal standing, but it is doubtful whether his subordinate had the same perception. In any event, the so-called Pemmican Proclamation has always been viewed as the opening event in the great war that erupted between the two fur-trading companies in the Canadian west and that ended only with their merger in 1821. The commission of investigation headed by William Coltman held Miles's action to be the first shot in the conflict. Wars have to start somewhere, and someone has to declare a beginning. Selkirk could claim that he had not ordered the proclamation, but given his correspondence with Miles, that would have been somewhat disingenuous. He made the claim anyway.

THE PEMMICAN PROCLAMATION

In his capacity as governor of Assiniboia, Miles Macdonell on 8 January 1814 issued a proclamation that emphasized, "in the yet uncultivated state of the Country," food was in short supply for the families at the settlement. Therefore, no persons trading furs or provisions within Selkirk's grant (employed by either the Hudson's Bay Company or the North West Company) could take any provisions out the territory for the next twelve months "except what may be judged necessary for the trading parties at the present time within the Territory to carry them to their respective destinations," and only by application to Macdonell. All provisions thus seized would be paid for at customary rates in British bills, and anyone disregarding the proclamation would be prosecuted, with goods and conveyances seized and forfeited.[2] Following the forms laid out in a law book that Selkirk had sent to Macdonell, the governor attempted to "publish" the proclamation at the gates of the various North West Company posts. At the post near Brandon House, John Wills refused to acknowledge "an authority in that district capable of executing such a Proclamation," and threatened to "bring down the Brigades from Fort Dauphin and Swan River."[3] Wills's own letter to Macdonell was somewhat less bellicose, observing potential scarcity of provisions and adding, "I should be very sorry to part with any . . . if there is a possibility of avoiding it." Describing the restriction as a "piece of inhumanity unheard of, admitting you had a right to do so," Wills wrote he was consulting with other partners in the region and in the meantime could not acknowledge Miles's authority to issue such a proclamation.[4]

At this point, Miles was convinced of the ultimate success of his action. In a letter to William Auld dated 4 February 1814, he noted that while crops had not been munificent, by comparison with the previous winter, "I feel myself transported into a terrestrial paradise." As for the proclamation, he added, "I have sufficient force to crush all the N Westers in this river should they be so hardy as to resist openly my authority." While he expected some opposition in the spring, "we are so well armed & I have a parcel of fine active stout fellows that will execute any order they receive."[5] So long as

Miles could maintain military superiority, his assessment was correct. But military advantage was not so easy to uphold on the plains, particularly given the presence of a floating population of large numbers of young men of mixed descent, armed and on horseback.

SELKIRK AND THE MINISTRY

Meanwhile, back in London, Selkirk continued to bombard the British ministry with position papers on a variety of subjects, ranging from the abolition of the slave trade to the reconstruction of Europe to the prospective treaty with the Americans. He blamed the existence of the slave trade on the petty needs of African leaders, arguing "in countries destitute of a regular and efficient government, there can be no security of persons or property, and where the labourer is not assured of reaping the fruits of his labour, it is in vain to expect industry." The former argument certainly suggested that the earl had been thinking about the North American West as deficient of government as Africa. His solution was a confederation of African nations, brought about by the British, "a civilised people, actuated by disinterested views," whose superior knowledge should be able to dominate that confederacy. [6] In a not completely unrelated vein, Selkirk insisted that more than the restoration of the *status quo ante bellum* was required in Europe after the final defeat of Napoleon. He suggested the creation of a united Germany under the house of Austria and a Prussia made powerful east of the Oder by the destruction of the Ottoman Empire, "that standing reproach to Europe." All changes, he insisted, should be acceptable to a majority of people living in the states involved. [7]

The papers on Africa and Europe may well have been part of a smoke-screen to disguise the extent of Selkirk's interest in his final paper on a prospective American treaty and its effect on the Aboriginals. This piece contained his most ingenious and best informed suggestions. Not surprisingly, Selkirk saw great similarities between Africa and the North American West. He feared abandoning to the Americans those Aboriginals between Detroit and the Mississippi who had served the British, and returned to the earlier notion of an Indian territory, free from both British and American control. As in Africa, the British should impose a confederacy, which of course they would dominate. Whether he realized the extent to which the Aboriginals themselves had been working toward such a goal is unclear. [8] But Selkirk was particularly concerned to provide a buffer zone between the

United States and British North America along the western boundary, and he was adamant that no opening should be left to the United States to claim the northwest as an extension of Louisiana. The country north of the height of land dividing the Mississippi from the waters of Hudson Bay, he insisted, was as British as Canada or Nova Scotia, and should not be a topic for discussion with the Americans.[9] Such open and aggressive imperialistic views—often involving political reform brought about by Britain in the best interests of the underprivileged and untutored whom Britain would naturally dominate through its superior "civilization"—were part of the assumptions with which Selkirk was attempting to colonize western Canada. This sort of imperialism is perhaps even more unfashionable today than naked self-interest, but we cannot understand Selkirk's commitment to Red River without taking such views into account.

CONTESTING WITH THE NOR'WESTERS

While his employer was concerning himself with higher affairs of state, Miles Macdonell was attempting in his corner of the world to maintain his control over the North West Company without violence. In a letter to the Nor'westers, Macdonell insisted on his authority in the country and hoped for an amicable settlement of the issue.[10] The Pemmican Proclamation was not mentioned, but was certainly implicit in the background. From Jack River, William Auld wrote that although he had reservations about Miles's procedures, he would acknowledge Miles's jurisdiction and support the principle that provisions should not be taken from the territory without licence. He added that much of the illness of the Kildonan people was caused by their "abominable filthy habits" and observed that he had introduced naval discipline to prevent them from being "smothered in their own excrement."[11] Nevertheless, Auld warned Macdonell that he would get no support from William Hillier in enforcement of his proclamation, since Hillier had not been properly consulted in the affair. To Hillier, Auld subsequently confessed, "We are but poor Matches for the Canadians either in cunning or unjustifiable aggression."[12]

Although given the glacial speed of transatlantic communications involving the Bay, it would be some time before the decision had much effect on events: William Auld had been replaced. The instructions from the London Committee to his successor Thomas Thomas emphasized two points: the first was the need to end the "blind adherence to antiquated customs," which meant that "the quantity of work done by our people both labourers & tradesmen bears no proportion to the days work of a man in any part of Britain." Thus, three-quarters of the staff were to be cut. The second was the need for militancy, "as you are opposed to a set of people who proceed upon a systematic plan of violence to prevent the Indians from trading with us, and to deter our people from protecting them when attempting." Thus, "it is evident that no success can be expected untill you are enabled to repel force by force."[13] While at first glance, to cut the workforce and still expect a concerted opposition to the Nor'westers might seem paradoxical, the view of the directors was that most of the excess employees were over-indulged and—Orkneymen as they were—lacking in backbone. The new recruits Selkirk had sent and was continuing to send were supposed to be better, particularly if put under tighter discipline, and the new system was to be in operation by the winter of 1815-16. Perhaps equally to the point, William Auld had not been a friend to either the new reforms or to the settlement.

By the same mail as the new instructions to Thomas Thomas came a lengthy letter from Selkirk to Miles Macdonell, one which dealt with almost every possible contingency except what had actually happened, and about which the earl was ignorant: the Pemmican Proclamation of January 1814. The letter was critical of Miles but not unfriendly in tone. Selkirk wanted more concrete results and better accounting practices. He did attempt to deal with the mounting complaints against Miles, noting "I cannot help entertaining an apprehension, that there is too little of the *Sauviler in Mode* in your behaviour, to those who are placed under you." He recommended close cooperation with other Selkirk agents such as Owen Keveny, and chastised Miles for his acceptance of cooperation from the Nor'westers, which would give enemies of the settlement an opportunity for misrepresentation. But basically, the letter and instructions could not be read by Miles as hostile.[14]

A few days later Selkirk wrote another briefer but more pointed epistle, observing that in his earlier letter

> I have omitted mentioning that Notice should be given to the Partners or Servants of the NWCo at the Forks to Quit Possession—in the manner pointed out in Burn's Justice—Article "Distress—Tenant holding over"—considering them as Tenants at Will—This should be done in writing, & verbally also, before enough of witnesses to prevent any question as to the Notice being received—the same should be done at all the other Posts of the NWCo. within the Territory of Ossiniboia.[15]

In view of the later criticisms of Miles Macdonell for the Pemmican Proclamation, both by Selkirk and by subsequent historians, it is worth emphasizing that Selkirk himself sought to confront the North West Company and
had ordered Miles to do so in no uncertain language. Selkirk wanted the
Nor'westers evicted as unwanted tenants at will—ironically enough, the
same procedures followed by many an improving landlord in the Scottish
Highlands. Such procedures were questionable enough when carried out by
a Scottish laird—for one could wonder how that laird had obtained his title
to land held for centuries in traditional tribal fashion—and required a
similar presumption of ownership on Selkirk's part. Just as the Highland
tenants would have denied the landlord's right to evict from traditional
land, so too the North West Company would have insisted that they had a
claim of prior occupancy. Miles's proclamation was something more than a
barefaced assertion of authority, however. It also had the merit of offering a
humanitarian justification for that assertion. Food for the settlement was in
short supply, and the proclamation could be defended on those grounds,
particularly as it was directed against all fur traders. But in the end, in the
Pemmican Proclamation, Miles was following exactly the procedures that
Selkirk had recommended. Selkirk might have riposted that merely giving
warnings to the Nor'westers was less provocative than actually seizing
pemmican, as Miles would shortly do. But Miles might have responded that
he had succeeded in seizing the pemmican, and thus completely asserted his
authority. In reality, the extent of the victory was probably the greatest
problem. Miles had been successful in dominating the North West Company
traders in 1814, and for this he would never be forgiven by them.

On the very day that Selkirk was instructing his agent in Red River to
warn out the Nor'westers as tenants at will, William Auld was reporting
to Miles on the North West Company response to the Pemmican Proclamation. According to Auld, John (le Borgne) McDonald had meant to
oppose Miles with force, but other partners in the region had accepted the
force of Miles's argument. The senior Nor'wester at Fort Gibraltar, John
Wills, had been asked by Auld "what the opinion of people would be if
you permitted Strangers (*not to call his association by a worse term*) to
carry out provisions from your own lands when you must purchase
English provisions either in England or here from the HBC's Stores to
subsist?" Wills, who was very sickly and would die soon after, had made
no response. According to Auld, "I don't think either we or the Canadians

will lose a drop of Blood; the *Bourgeois* will bluster & Strut a bit & that will be all." Moreover, Auld added, "you have but to beckon with your finger & every Canadian servant who is free this year will repair to your Standard." Fortunately, the new arrivals at Red River were not from the western islands but "superiorly spirited people coming from the Highlands." Auld had experienced trouble with the Kildonaners, but he recognized their spirit. The Nor'westers were bullies as part of their religion, concluded Auld, but he did not expect serious trouble.[16] Miles concurred, responding that "all our men here have lately been taught the manual & Platoon exercise" and "are in a tolerable state of discipline."[17] A month later, Auld produced another paper supporting and justifying the pemmican embargo, chiefly in terms of the need to provide for the settlers.[18] There can be no doubt that Auld and the Hudson's Bay Company were keen on the proclamation, for the only canoe brigades affected by it were those of their arch rivals.

Rumours of North West Company resistance came to Miles Macdonell from all directions, and he wrote to John Wills at Fort Gibraltar, emphasizing, "being the government party here, we shall not submit, to the threats of any armed body."[19] Wills responded that he never thought Macdonell considered "any of the North West Company's servants as your subjects," but he denied any menace. He could not act on his own, Wills insisted, but would keep the recently delivered pemmican he had received until a "free discussion," expected in June, could take place with the wintering partners.[20] Miles answered that it was his "indisputable duty to endeavour to secure to the British Empire this part of the Country," justifying the pemmican embargo in terms of both of the needs of the settlers and his legal authority.[21] A day later, Wills met with Miles for a private conference. The two men walked together in the spring lushness along the river banks. Wills continued to deny Miles's authority, claiming that he needed a commission from the Privy Council rather than from Lord Selkirk to issue such a proclamation and adding, "You are too weak altogether to attempt the establishing of regular law in this country." It was one thing as a justice of a peace to "give a fellow a few stripes," he maintained, but something quite different to attempt to regulate trade.[22]

Here, on the banks of the Red River, the two antagonists had clearly set out their positions. While Macdonell and his Nor'wester neighbours were debating the issue of authority in the region of the Forks, the Hudson's Bay

Company had begun its major offensive against the Montreal traders, by setting in motion the establishment of a large trading presence in the rich Athabasca territory to the far northwest of the Red and Assiniboine Rivers. The two matters were not, of course, unconnected, for the North West Company's fur-trading brigades were dependent upon Red River provisions for their activities in Athabasca. Former Nor'Wester Colin Robertson had been sent by the London Committee to Montreal to recruit Canadian traders, with the intention of setting out in the spring of 1816. The company issued detailed instructions for the maintenance of reports and journals, emphasizing particularly that full accounts must be kept of any violent aggression by its rivals or any other incident "which may be likely to cause judicial investigation."[23] As the Wills-Macdonell debate and the concern for the record clearly demonstrate, both sides clearly understood what was at stake.

While the HBC was proposing a major expansion that would require the loyalty of each of its employees, it continued its niggling treatment of them. At a committee meeting held the same day as the issuance of the instructions about record keeping, the following entry was made: "Read Letter from Peter Sinclair late of York Factory requesting his Feather Bed might be sent to him. Ordered that he be inform'd that all Feathers received from the Bay are the undoubted Property of the Company."[24] This entry reminds us that furs were not the only produce of the country prized by the Hudson's Bay Company. Such uncaring attitudes would have to be altered were the Canadians to be successfully confronted.

THE KILDONAN PASSENGERS

By late May of 1814 Archibald McDonald was able to report some good news to Selkirk, perhaps the first the earl had received from North America in several years. "Archie" defended the Kildonan people from the many criticisms levelled against them by Hudson's Bay Company employees but, more to the point, wrote that a party of the fittest settlers had left Churchill single-file for York Factory on 5 April. "The piper," McDonald added, "took his station in the centre of the line." Learning to manage snowshoes as they went, the little party had arrived successfully at York Factory and prepared to head south for the settlement.[25] As the remainder of this letter well outlined, the experiences of the Kildonan settlers since their recruitment by Selkirk in May of 1814 had been quite horrific, often almost beyond credence.

The Kildonan passengers on the *Prince of Wales* had sailed across the Atlantic accompanied by a raging typhus fever epidemic, which infected more than sixty settlers and most of the crew of the vessel. The young Guernsey surgeon, Dr. LaSerre, who had been hired by Selkirk to lead the party and accompany it to the settlement as medical attendant, was one of the casualties. The ship's captain, eager to be rid of the infectious passengers, dumped them at Churchill, where no preparations had been made for their arrival. The York Factory surgeon, Abel Edwards, did travel to Churchill with William Auld, helping Archibald McDonald, who was left in charge, to prepare the settlers for the winter. A number of log houses were hastily constructed. Edwards deferred his own passage back to England to remain to care for the people. They required a good deal of attention, reported Edwards. "The greater part of them seem to be much like children," he wrote, "not capable of being trusted a moment out of sight," particularly in the harsh climate for which they were not prepared. As the temperature reached for fifty below zero, Edwards was eventually forced to post orders about proper clothing: "Every man & boy on leaving his residence to go to the woods or elsewhere to have his waistcoat & jacket buttoned closely about his neck & breast, over which he is to wear his toggy or great coat."[26] McDonald and Edwards visited the settlers every morning to ensure that they washed themselves and took their anti-scorbutic.

In fairness to the Kildonaners, conditions were primitive. As Donald Gunn later reported:

> Logs had to serve for chairs; the mud flooring had to supply the want of beds, sofas, tables, &c. We can easily fancy that these habitations were of the most simple construction, and very ill-adapted to defend the inmates from winter frosts, so often accompanied by heavy gales of wind, while Fahrenheit's thermometer ranged for months from 35 degrees to 50 degrees below zero, and many times in the course of the winter fell as low as 55 degrees or even to sixty degrees. To the above we may add, that they had to drag on flat sleds the scanty rations dealt out to them from the company stores, and in order to receive the same and return with it to their families they had every week to perform a journey of thirty miles on snow-shoes."[27]

In November the fort at Churchill was set alight and burned to the ground, destroying all the possessions of the company's officers and much of the food supply to boot. William Auld blamed the settlers for the disaster. In the spring, after the fit ones had snowshoed with great difficulty to York Factory, they still had to wait in tents for spring, when they could be led 800 miles south to the settlement.

POWER STRUGGLES CONTINUED

The same day that Archie McDonald wrote good news from York Factory, Lord Selkirk in London prepared a long litany of instructions for Miles Macdonell, including directions for the construction of Scandinavian stoves and even a book about the stoves published in Swedish. How Miles was to get this work translated in the wilderness was not clear. But as so often happened in the planning of Selkirk ventures, the minor details were handled much more thoroughly than the major issues. Perhaps the most important point in this missive for Miles was buried toward the bottom, where the earl noted that the company had not yet completed arrangements for the administration of justice under the charter, although there was no doubt about its ultimate authority.[28] This position was about to be put to its first real test, of course, and it was not one likely to survive any serious challenges.

On 25 May 1814, Sheriff John Spencer of Red River went to the White Horse Plain where, with the assistance of several freemen, including Jean-Baptiste Lagimodière (the grandfather of Louis Riel), he seized ninety-six bags of "artfully concealed pemmican."[29] Spencer was an orphan educated at Christ's Hospital in London who had been recruited for the Hudson's Bay Company in 1806. In 1814 he had on recommendation of William Auld been appointed sheriff of Assiniboia, little appreciating how the appointment and his subsequent attempt to enforce the Pemmican Proclamation would affect his life.[30] Lagimodiére had been born in Quebec and was employed by the North West Company before he had moved to Pembina and struck off on his own. His Quebec-born wife, Marie-Anne Gaboury, had joined him in the west. She was arguably the first European woman to settle in what is now Manitoba.[31] An exchange of seizures by the respective antagonists followed, the Nor'westers complaining of the taking of two canoes at the foot of Lake Winnipeg, which should be released "unless you mean to declare War against us."[32] Miles responded by freeing the crews of the canoes but keeping their arms, adding "you cannot suppose yourselves possessed of any civil or military authority here."[33] The Nor'westers responded that they would send Deputy Sheriff Joseph Howse, whom they had captured, to Montreal for trial on a burglary charge, insisting, "The Laws of our Country will determine which of the two parties, that took up arms first."[34] Miles stood firm, insisting that there was "no Tribunal at Montreal competent to try" Howse.[35] Once again, the documentary evidence plainly indicates that this was no inadvertent confrontation, but a deliberate effort on both sides to orchestrate incidents dramatizing the ultimate issues to authorities in Canada and in London.

The North West Company partners in the Red River region—John McDonald of Garth, Duncan Cameron, John McDonald (le Borgne), John Wills, and J. Duncan Cameron—wrote on 18 June 1814 to Miles Macdonell from Fort Gibraltar, describing themselves as "British Loyal Subjects." The question of Miles's authority must be settled by a higher tribunal, they maintained, but in the meantime they were willing to meet him "on the most liberal plan." They admitted that the American war put them in a difficult position, since the British government had granted the North West Company permission to ship their goods through the Bay this year to avoid possible trouble with the Americans on the normal western canoe routes. This concession would obviously require the cooperation of the HBC. The writers concluded that it was equally "necessary for the existence of your infant Colony that a perfect understanding & an intercourse of mutual good offices should exist between us & you."[36] In his reply, Miles struck the same note of conciliation. He was pleased to be able to make an amicable settlement, for "we must make mutual sacrifices for the exigencies of the times."[37] He released substantial amounts of fat and pemmican, and promised to release more in return for Nor'wester commitments to help feed his people over the next winter. The Nor'westers agreed to this understanding with alacrity.[38] And so Miles seemed to have won his point. The lesson to be learned seemed to be that if the Nor'westers were met with sufficient firmness, the "bullies" would back down. That the American war had presented special circumstances and that the partners in Red River lacked sufficient military superiority over Miles in 1814 did not, for the moment, seem important.

Neither Lord Selkirk nor the Hudson's Bay Company would learn about this victory, if such it was, for many months. But William McGillivray and the other leaders of the North West Company were far closer to the situation, and for them, the agreement between Miles and the Red River partners was a complete disaster. McGillivray was writing from Fort William asking pointed questions about the Pemmican Proclamation and the Nor'wester response as early as 23 July.[39] Even Miles Macdonell was not entirely convinced that he had won, and used a series of petty squabbles as an excuse to write his employer: "I beg . . . that your Lordship be not permitted by any delicacy to send a suitable person to take my situation—as I find myself unequal to the task of reconciling so many different interests."[40] In fact, Selkirk had already appointed James White as new colony surgeon (to replace La Serre, deceased) and placed him second-in-command, emphasizing to Miles "the advantage of discussion & comparison are so great, that on general principles, I wish all important questions to be considered in Council."[41]

THE ARRIVAL OF THE KILDONAN PEOPLE

The Kildonan settlers finally arrived at the Forks on 22 June 1814, over a year after they had embarked from Thurso for Stromness. Not surprisingly, the party had complained all the way south about the roughness of the river and the continual obstacles that had to be overcome. As Donald Gunn would subsequently explain:

Seven hundred miles of difficult and dangerous navigation lay between them and Red River. For miles, in the lower rivers, the boats had to be towed by men against a swift current, besides many discharges or landing places where part of the cargo had to be carried over on men's backs, the boats taken out of the water and launched over dry land. Besides lesser bodies of water, they had to pass over Lake Winnipeg, a distance of three hundred miles. Some "old hands," (Company's servants) who understood working the boats in the rapids, and over the lakes, were put in each boat with the colonists, who had to work as common laborers on the passage; to take the tow rope by turns, to tug at the oar from morning to night, and to carry the freight over the portages, and all this labour without any compensation.[42]

In reporting that the Kildonan people had arrived at the Forks and were settling in, Archie McDonald observed that most people in the country disapproved of the Pemmican Proclamation, but not because of its assertion of authority. The complaint, he wrote, was that in the end Miles had not kept the pemmican and had merely aggravated the Nor'westers. In Miles's defence, however, McDonald added that the governor had little support from either the Hudson's Bay Company or his own officers. Selkirk's personal presence for at least a year was absolutely essential, he opined, were the settlement to survive.[43] The need for Selkirk's personal supervision was a recurrent theme from his agents, and perhaps should have been better heeded in this case as in others.

In his own report to Selkirk, Miles Macdonell emphasized the enormous advantages in manpower enjoyed by the North West Company, despite their capitulation. According to his reckoning, they had 120 voyageurs, twelve bourgeois (trading officers), and between 200 and 300 freemen and men of mixed descent at their disposal. Miles had a mere twenty-eight men, and was not supported by William Hillier. The newly arrived Kildonaners provided some reinforcement. According to Donald Gunn, "in the course of a few days [after arrival] His Excellency mustered his men, servants and settlers. All were treated to a glass of spirits and furnished with muskets and bayonets and ammunition. Two of the settlers refused to take these weapons of war. The Governor, at the same time, telling them, that according to the law of the land the strong dictated to the weak."[44] Miles waxed enthusiastically about the crops and, for the first time, seriously drew Selkirk's attention to the presence of the Canadian freemen (like Jean-Baptiste Lagimodière) and their families, although he made no proposal for enlisting their support or settling them at Red River on favourable terms. As for the North West Company, "it will require more force than we yet have to dispossess them forcibly."[45]

THE NORTH WEST COMPANY RESPONDS

Although Selkirk could not know it, the annual meeting of the partners of the North West Company at Fort William in early August was an unusually spirited affair. The subject of the pemmican was on everyone's mind, and the post, as was usually the case in mid-summer, was visited by brigades and parties travelling both east and west. In addition to the usual North West Company brigades, the summer of 1814 saw the arrival of a party of fur traders from the west coast that included Gabriel Franchère, and another from Astoria headed by James Keith, with the latest news from the Columbia River. Franchère was suitably impressed with the fort, built on a drained marsh at the mouth of the Kaministiquia River. It looked "more like an attractive village," he wrote in his journal, and was absolutely heaving with voyageurs, fur traders, and Aboriginals, who spent most of the night partying in their big summer blowout of the year.[46] Officially, the compromise with Miles Macdonell was endorsed, but those who had permitted the pemmican to be seized were censured at a special meeting, and "a full determination was taken to defend the Property at all Hazards."[47] By this time the Nor'westers (though not Selkirk's people at Red River) were aware that the war with the Americans was over. The censures against those who had compromised with Macdonell stung deeply, and Alexander (Greenfield) Macdonell, made a partner despite his role in the pemmican business, subsequently reported to John McDonald of Garth:

You see myself and our mutual friend Mr. Cameron so far on our
way to commence open hostilities against the Enemy in Red River. . . .
Something serious will *undoubtedly* take place—nothing but the
complete downfall of the Colony will satisfy some, by fair or foul
means—a most desirable object if it can be accomplished—so here is
at them with all my heart and energy.[48]

This letter was among documents subsequently captured by Colin Robertson
at Fort Gibraltar. Although the North West Company would always maintain that Greenfield and Cameron carried on their subsequent campaign
against the settlement without instructions from the company—a point that
Macdonell's letter does not contradict—the letter does indicate how he had
responded to the censures and ridicule he had endured at Fort William over
his failure to stand up to Miles Macdonell. It is difficult to believe that—
whatever official action was or was not taken—Greenfield and Cameron
were not returning to Red River with a fairly clear idea of what was expected
of them: the destruction of the settlement by whatever means possible. The
Pemmican Proclamation would turn out to have quite a sting in its tail.

THE NERVOUS BREAKDOWN OF MILES MACDONELL AND
OTHER PROBLEMS

On his annual visit to York Factory in the late summer of 1814, Miles
Macdonell showed the strain he had been operating under for some time.
He suffered what amounted to a nervous breakdown. The problem was
probably not directly related to the potential threat from the North West
Company, but rather to his continually deteriorating relationship with
William Auld, combined with an inability to keep the colony's accounts in a
satisfactory manner. Miles was a soldier, not a bookkeeper. He had probably
never previously been required to be organized on paper.[49] His letter to
Selkirk at this time was a rambling and incoherent one. Problems with Auld
were rehearsed, and Miles acknowledged great disappointment that Selkirk
had not himself come with the year's a shipment of settlers, who were not a
prepossessing lot and were likely to cause trouble.[50]

According to William Hillier, who was also at York Factory, Miles in his
emotional state had exclaimed, "I am a villain—the Colony will be ruined all
by my fault &c."[51] This might suggest that Miles was feeling guilty about the
Pemmican Proclamation, but the reference is not at all clear.

A few days after Miles had penned his report to Selkirk, Thomas Thomas
wrote to the earl that Miles was quite incapable of continuing in his position.

Thomas was not certain of the extent to which the opposition from the Canadians had contributed to the problem, but he emphasized that Macdonell had been disturbed emotionally for some time.[52] In a separate letter, Thomas attempted to deal with some of the loose ends that Miles could not handle. The contingent of Norwegians sent to accompany the shipment of reindeer (which Selkirk and the company hoped to breed and use to pull sleighs in a winter transportation linkup between the colony and York Factory) would be sent to Playgreen Lake. Thomas added some thoughts about the route he would prefer for the winter express.[53]

Selkirk received other letters written in the autumn of 1814 that were menacing. One was from Colin Robertson in Montreal. Although quite enthusiastic about his recruitment of men, mainly from the North West Company, it suggested that there could be little secrecy about Robertson's mission in Montreal; the Nor'westers clearly knew that the Hudson's Bay Company were planning a major thrust into the Athabasca.[54] Even more disturbing was a letter from Miles Macdonell's brother, retired from his partnership in the North West Company and living on a farm on the Upper Canadian side of the border with Lower Canada. John Macdonell reported rumours he had heard of the plans of the Nor'westers against the settlement, chiefly by using the Aboriginals against it. "The strongest argument I have heard used to raise a jealousy in the Natives is by inculcating upon their minds a belief that they are Robbed of their Lands without any indemnification." John could see no particular justification for this fear, but added, "Self preservation may justify acts that in other situations would be criminal."[55] When Selkirk saw this correspondence he became alarmed for the safety of his settlement. But terminology and lack of complete understanding of the social structure in Red River led him astray. Whether by "natives" John Macdonell meant the local First Peoples tribes or the mixed-descent children of the fur traders who often worked with the North West Company, supplying them with pemmican is not clear. Perhaps Macdonell had his information correct and his terminology confused. But it is equally likely that he, like Selkirk and others in London, was truly concerned about the First Peoples rather than the mixed bloods. In any case, it was clear that trouble was brewing.[56] Former Nor'wester John Pritchard informed Colin Robertson that Selkirk was being accused of violating "the true principles of British liberty" in his Highland recruiting practices.[57] Colin Robertson reported in November to Selkirk that hostile accounts of the pemmican business had been appearing in the *Quebec Mercury*, adding that he had recruited John Pritchard and sent him back to Red River to purchase land for a farm. Robertson wondered how Selkirk would feel about sending American deserters still in Canada to the colony. He enclosed a letter from Miles's brother John offering to help Miles but asserting an unwillingness to jeopardize his North West Company interests by open meddling.

Although James White was now present at Red River as second-in-command, and Miles apparently had recovered from his emotional problems, the long-term prognosis was not good. The governor returned to the settlement on 19 October to learn that Sheriff John Spencer had been arrested in September on a Canadian warrant; he was shipped east to Fort William in a canoe. Those in charge of the settlement had failed to protect Spencer, and Nor'wester Duncan Cameron refused to replenish any of the provisions Miles Macdonell had allowed the Nor'westers to have over the summer. He went further, and positively forbad the free Canadians to supply the settlement with any meat. Despite this unfriendly act, Miles served notice to quit to the North West Company posts in the region in October of 1814, thus fulfilling Selkirk's orders.[58] This assertion of ownership and authority was probably unnecessary after the Pemmican Proclamation. It was bound to irritate the Nor'westers, and was meaningful only if Selkirk could convince the British government to support him. Miles was no longer obviously distraught and distracted, but he continued to behave strangely over the winter of 1814-15. He seemed unable to relate to the settlers, and spent much of his time alone on the prairies.

The year 1814 had been one of indifferent and occasionally ill health for Lord Selkirk himself. Surviving evidence makes it impossible to be certain that the problem was the consumption (the nineteenth-century term for tuberculosis) that would eventually kill him. But he was clearly quite sick, often confined to his house, and there is little sign of much activity—even writing letters—during much of the year. Consumption is a strange disease, often allowing long periods of remission. Selkirk's health improved greatly in the autumn, and he travelled north to Scotland, attending a ball at Kelso and riding with Sir James Hall across the countryside.[59] Unfortunately, Hall did not comment on the state of his brother-in-law's health.

At the close of the year, the earl was still attempting to gain some first-hand information about his little settlement at Red River, querying recently returned HBC surgeon Abel Edwards about affairs there.[60] The first real evidence that Selkirk had been given any real notion of the state of affairs in his western settlement came in a letter to Colin Robertson written at the end of the year, acknowledging earlier letters to himself and Andrew Wedderburn that had included clippings from the Canadian newspapers. Selkirk found the threats to use the Native peoples worrisome—it was not clear just what group he thought the "Indians" were—but doubted that the Nor'westers would "risk infamy" by following through on such verbal intimidation. He continued to insist that London's most eminent lawyers supported his authority and denied that of the North West Company, although he admitted that in the Athabasca region both trading companies were well beyond the charter. Only here could the Canada Jurisdiction Act of 1803 apply. The earl also noted that "mutual benefit must arise from my judicious & temperate publications to expose the true motive" of the North West Company actions, the first indication that he was again writing for the public. He was probably working on the manuscript of *A Sketch of the Fur Trade*, but he was also preparing the prospectus entitled "Ossiniboia," as well as a pamphlet on First Peoples education. The letter indicates that at the end of 1814, Selkirk still had formed no clear picture of the situation in the West. He was still holding to his assumption that informal legal opinions about the strength of the Hudson's Bay Company charter (and thus his grant under it) would be sufficient to stay the hand of the Nor'westers.[61]

The pamphlet called "Ossiniboia" was in many ways an extraordinary production. Whether it was actually circulated is not clear. The pamphlet exists only in a copy lacking a title page and is housed in the Ontario Archives. Its final page listed the printer as J. Brettel, who usually printed Selkirk's writings, but there was no date of publication. The pamphlet itself describes the last advice from the settlement as dated in July 1814, at which time crops were "luxuriant and promising."[62] This pamphlet was not the prospectus for Red River answered in 1816 by John Strachan in *A Letter to the Right Honourable the Earl of Selkirk*. Strachan was responding to an earlier piece written in 1811, when Selkirk's familiarity with the Red River region was rather primitive. The 1811 piece was never publicly distributed, and Strachan's use of it was in many ways unfair. "Ossiniboia" was a much more difficult piece to attack.

On one level, it enunciated the earl's mature views on how best to settle a wilderness, based upon his experience in various parts of North America, particularly Prince Edward Island, and his thinking about North American land speculation and colonization. The pamphlet offered townships of at least 10,000 acres to proprietors at 400£ each. One-half of the money received from the sale of townships was to be vested in Trustees and set aside for the improvement of the colony. The pamphlet pointed out that "in most of the British colonies, where settlements have been carried on by the proprietors of large grants of land"—read here Prince Edward Island—proprietors who actually brought out settlers from Europe were sabotaged by their neighbours, who "seduced away" the tenantry by offering them a better deal. In Red River, all arrangements for transporting settlers would be recorded before a magistrate, so that a settler could not shift his lands without fulfilling his obligations to his initial patron. The impracticability of this provision certainly became obvious in 1815, when the Nor'westers lured away most of the population of Red River. "Ossiniboia" reiterated Selkirk's insistence that if land were placed in settlers' hands at too low a rate, they would form no "local attachment to their property." It also repeated his belief that in America, the value of landed property depended less on an annual revenue received from it than on the profit to be gained from selling it at an "advanced price." In this context, a tract of uninhabited waste land would eventually become valuable, as cultivation encroached on the wilderness. The principle of land speculation was so well understood in America that the opportunities for entering the game were relatively few, with capitalists occupying most prime property. Red River offered an opportunity for speculation simply because it was so distant from other settlements.

On yet another level, the pamphlet was a reiteration of Selkirk's views on emigration, particularly from the Highlands of Scotland. As far as the Highlands were concerned, Selkirk not only repeated his arguments from his 1805-06 book, but also updated them in terms of the rapid rise of sheep clearance in the region since *Observations* had been written. In this context the Kildonan experience was emphasized. Selkirk pointed out that on the great estates turned over to sheep, the previous tenants were given small plots of land called crofts upon the seacoasts. The problem was that the people had no experience with either fishing or farming. A croft with a single cow and a few acres was a discouraging prospect "to a man who has been accustomed to a large range of mountain pasture, and to look upon his cattle as the only desirable source of riches."[63] If the dispossessed tenantry would only be unhappy on a croft, their qualities—"hardy, frugal, and persevering, of sober and steady habits, and strong impressed with religious principles"—made them ideal settlers for places like Red River.

On a third level, "Ossiniboia" was a speculator's prospectus attempting to persuade outside investment in Selkirk's Red River settlement by the most artful and imaginative means possible. As well as making a virtue of the remote location in terms of land speculation, the author was particularly inventive about the question of marketing produce from the remote and inland situation of Red River. He spoke about improving the Nelson River—"a stream not much inferior to the St. Lawrence in magnitude, but interrupted by several falls and rapids"—and argued that when prices were high enough in the European market, flour, beef, pork, wool, and hemp could all "bear the burden of a considerable charge for carriage."[64] Later appendices discussed the practicability of some sort of winter transport and the possibilities of large-scale sheep farming on the prairies.

Finally, on the fourth level, the pamphlet provided a calculated response to a letter originating in the *Quebec Mercury* in October 1814 and reprinted by a number of English-language newspapers. Selkirk insisted here that the settlement had not been left to starve. From 1 November 1812 to 17 March 1813, he emphasized, nearly 30,000 pounds of meat had been distributed to the one hundred settlers at Red River, or more than two pounds of fresh meat per person per day. In addition nearly 5,000 pounds of pemmican had been distributed over the winter. During the winter of 1813-14, the settlers got 24,000 pounds of fresh meat, 7,800 pounds of pemmican, and had considerable quantities of potatoes they had raised as well. Some of the settlers may have managed their allowances badly, but there was no overall scarcity. As for the climate and the soil of the country, "Ossiniboia" reprinted letters from several fur traders who had experience of Red River. John Pritchard, a former Nor'wester who had resided at Red River, insisted that the climate was little different from that in the Canadas, and both shorter and milder than those in Quebec. Crops matured quickly on soil that was already cleared. Donald M'Kay agreed that the winters were milder than in Canada. The Red River broke earlier than the St. Lawrence, and there was much less snow. This was (and is) true, but did not make the climate less harsh than in Montreal. Other testimony came from Miles Macdonell and Archibald McDonald. The pamphlet reprinted a climate chart of the region kept by Anthony Henday in 1755-56. The general tenor of the piece emphasized what would be done to make the settlement viable. Many of Selkirk's ideas were eventually carried out, although in 1814-15 they sounded like sheer fantasy, difficult to fit into existing conceptions of the prairie west. The sheer bravado of the piece was quite impressive, but it was a romantic speculation rather than a statement of accomplishment.

William Auld, returned from York Factory after being replaced, wrote a conciliatory letter to Selkirk at the end of 1814, arguing that Selkirk's bad opinion of him was the result of the reports from Miles Macdonell. Auld offered to explain the true state of affairs at Red River "so as to enable you to drive into the very abyss your agent's foolish and unprincipled mismanagement."[65] Auld was quite inaccurate in ascribing Selkirk's hostility to Miles Macdonell; Auld's own foot dragging and refusal to implement change brought Selkirk's ire. In any event, on 21 December the earl again wrote to Colin Robertson, re-emphasizing that the Canada Jurisdiction Act did not extend to Hudson's Bay Company territory, a contentious point. He also opposed the introduction of American settlers, "as their political attachments must be dangerous."[66] That same day he wrote to Miles Macdonell, observing that while the Pemmican Proclamation was within Miles's legal powers, it was contrary to the earl's instructions. But given the imprudence of the first step, Selkirk approved what ensued, particularly the compromise with the North West Company.[67] The letter was a substantial vote of confidence in Miles, given the information about his emotional state that Selkirk had been receiving from York Factory. The earl had a tendency not only to make bad choices of his principal agents, but also to support them loyally long after events had made clear their unsuitability. Despite all the warning signs, Lord Selkirk at the end of 1814 plainly had no real conception of the gathering storm of opposition to his settlement brewing in North America.

The Selkirk home at Saint Mary's Isle, Kirkudbright in 1911. Selkirk family papers and memorabilia were lost when the house was destroyed by fire at the beginning of World War Two. (PROVINCIAL ARCHIVES OF MANITOBA)

The crest of Thomas Douglas, the fifth Earl of Selkirk. (PROVINCIAL ARCHIVES OF MANITOBA)

We are not well supplied with authentic images of Lord Selkirk. Here are the three most common images. The two portraits (PROVINCIAL ARCHIVES OF MANITOBA) are later reproductions from paintings that have been lost, probably in the house fire. The bust by the British sculpture Francis Leggatt Chantrey is available only in a photograph in George Bryce's *Lord Selkirk's Romantic Colony* (1911). Of all of the images we have of Selkirk, this is likely the closest to life.

Jean Wedderburn-Colville, Lady Selkirk. (PROVINCIAL ARCHIVES OF MANITOBA)

Ein Wilder von den Saulteux Indianern
am rothen Fluss.
Gezeichnet nach dem 12 ten Theil seiner natürlichen Grösse.

Peter Rindisbacher's portraits of two Saulteux First Nations men, 1822. The sketch opposite is sometimes referred to as a possible portrait of Chief Peguis, although the painting above seems more likely as an image of Peguis. (NATIONAL ARCHIVES OF CANADA)

Fort Douglas on the Red River, 1817, taken from a sketch by Lord Selkirk. (NATIONAL ARCHIVES OF CANADA)

Images of the multicultural mix of settlers who eventually came to Red River, sketched by Rindisbacher in 1822. Entitled "Types of Lord Selkirk's Settlers in 1822," they are, from left to right, a Swiss colonist and his family, a German colonist from the De Meuron regiment, a Scot, and what is identified as a "colonist from French Canada." (NATIONAL ARCHIVES OF CANADA)

Two views of Fort William in 1816, believed to be drawn by Lord Selkirk. (ARCHIVES OF ONTARIO).

The Forks of the Red and Assiniboine rivers in the winter of 1821. (Rindisbacher, "Winter fishing on ice of Assynoibain and Red River," NATIONAL ARCHIVES OF CANADA)

CHAPTER FIFTEEN

The Settlement Dispersed

A S WAS TRUE WITH MOST remote settlements, swift communication between Red River and the centres of authority was virtually impossible. This was not uncommon within the British Empire in the early nineteenth century. The Cape Colony in South Africa and the prison colony in Australia were at least as remote as Red River, although the problem in North America was that Red River was surrounded by uninhabited land, not accessible by sea after a long and tedious voyage. In any case, Lord Selkirk never had enough current information at his disposal to offer intelligent advice to his agents, particularly given the speed with which events could move. What little information he did receive and respond to tended to run between six months and a year behind the current state of play. The solution was obvious and one that Miles Macdonell had been advocating for several years: Selkirk would have to remove to North America to take personal charge of his settlement as well as the Hudson's Bay Company's venture into the no man's land of Athabasca. He was unable to do so. In addition to his obligations in Britain during the wartime emergency—Selkirk was still Lord Lieutenant of Kirkcudbright and a member of the House of Lords—he had suffered a lengthy bout of ill health that doubtless made an ocean voyage seem virtually impossible. As a result, the situation in Red River in 1815 got quite out of hand for want of steady direction at the tiller.

OPENING MOVES

The North West Company partners resident in the Red River region, chiefly Duncan Cameron and Alexander (Greenfield) Macdonell, had returned from the 1815 general council meetings of the company at Fort William determined to make amends by a more active policy for their inactivity regarding the Pemmican Proclamation. Their intention was clearly to eliminate Selkirk's settlement, although not necessarily by violence. They had a good deal of raw material at their disposal in the persons of freemen and young people of mixed descent loosely employed by the North West Company. These young men had never been cultivated by Miles Macdonell and the leadership of the settlement, but had instead been treated with some disdain. Moreover, many of the settlers at the tiny settlement had found conditions much more difficult than they had expected and the government of Red River unable substantially to improve them. Selkirk and his agents may have done their best to keep their promises, but from the standpoint of the settlers, they had failed miserably. Selkirk, in his pamphlet "Ossiniboia," may have been accurate in asserting that no one had starved over the winter of 1813–14, but what the founder did not write (and perhaps did not know) was how hard the settlers had to work to get their winter food. Buffalo meat may have been relatively available. But ill-garbed Scots who were unaccustomed to the cold and the snow were expected to drag freshly killed meat from the plains, where the hunters left it, to the fort by sledge.

Even before the end of 1814, Duncan Cameron had received a letter from one disgruntled settler, asking the fur trader to help relieve a "poor distressed people" by transporting them to Montreal in the spring. The context surrounding this correspondence makes clear that Cameron himself had already suggested the possibility of transportation, but he had plainly a receptive audience for his hints and suggestions.[1] Cameron took the offensive with the malcontents early in 1815, writing to Donald Livingston and Hector McEachern that their greatest enemies were Lord Selkirk, William Auld, and Miles Macdonell. Miles was "made a fool of" by Selkirk and Auld, and he in turn "made fools of all those who were under him." Cameron promised that he would lead all the settlers "out of bondage," as Selkirk would never take them back to Scotland.[2]

At about the same time, in London, Andrew Colvile (formerly Wedderburn) was attempting to deal with the jurisdictional problems in Red River. He wrote to Messrs Maitland, Garden, and Auldjo, a firm of Montreal merchants that had been employed by Colin Robertson to help supply the proposed Athabasca expedition, that "in case the North West Com'y should endeavour to bring any of our Servants to trial before the Canadian Courts we request that you will free the most respectable Counsel to defend them & instruct him to demur to the Jurisdiction of the Court only the Opinions of the most eminent Counsel here it appears the Canada Act does not extend to the Hudson's Bay Co's Territories, they having Jurisdiction therein both Civil and Criminal by the Royal Charter."[3] As Colvile must have known full well, despite the confidence in their jurisdiction proclaimed by both the HBC and Selkirk, both realized that it had never been tested in a court on either side of the Atlantic. Whether Colvile also appreciated that Canadian courts were not likely to be sympathetic to the Hudson's Bay Company pretensions is another matter.

By the beginning of 1815, rumours of the North West Company strategy were rampant throughout the western territories. From Middle Winnipic, HBC trader George Holdsworth wrote to Miles Macdonell in January 1815 that the presence of adequate food supplies for the settlers was a definite blessing, since he had heard that the Nor'westers hoped to use food scarcity to induce the settlers to leave in the spring. Holdsworth doubted the rumours of a North West Company "grand coup" over the winter, but he himself was putting pressure on the Canadians. He appreciated both that the North West Company was becoming increasingly desperate and that a confrontation was in the making. Lord Selkirk and the Hudson's Bay Company were also gaining some awareness of the volatility of the situation in the West. They did what they could to strengthen their hand, although manoeuvring in London would obviously have precious little effect on events in Red River.

In early February of 1815, the governor of the Hudson's Bay Company, Joseph Berens, wrote officially to the minister in charge of the colonies— Lord Bathurst—forwarding a letter from the Earl of Selkirk alleging that his settlement at Red River was "in imminent danger of being destroyed, through the machinations of certain persons who are endeavouring, by malicious misrepresentation, to inflame the minds of the Indians against the Colonists." The evidence was not conclusive, wrote Berens, but surely sufficient to call for precautions to prevent the "horrible consequences" of such an attack.[4] A few days later, Selkirk penned another letter to the HBC. He had now received a copy of the letter from Miles Macdonell's brother about Indian menace in the west, and offered its vague hearsay as evidence that the threats against the settlement were serious. The earl spent much of the letter denying that the Aboriginals had been mistreated by Miles Macdonell, and his examples made plain that when he thought of "Indians," he thought first of Assiniboines, Cree, and Saulteaux, rather than individuals of mixed descent. On the other hand, while he had earlier thought the Nor'wester threats an "idle menace," he wrote, he now realized that some of the partners "have lived from early youth at a distance from the restraints of civilized society" and believed that the remoteness of the country would shelter them from the law.[5]

The possibility of Aboriginal difficulties had already led the Hudson's Bay Company Committee, at its meeting in earlier February 1815, to take up seriously the suggestion that a school be established "for the Instruction & Civilization of the Native Indians" in the company's territories.[6] This action would later enable Selkirk to claim in his *Sketch of the British Fur Trade* that while the North West Company was solely concerned with the exploitation of the Aboriginals, the HBC was interested in "civilizing" them as well. It additionally enabled Joseph Berens to send to Lord Bathurst a "Statement of the Circumstances under which the Settlement at Red River has been formed and the Views of the Hudson's Bay Company in its establishment."[7] This statement insisted that the company wished to provision its people in North America, and thus encouraged "an experiment, which independently of other advantages promised to have the most beneficial effects of the civilization of the Indians."[8] Such action demonstrated that while the London leadership of the HBC was alive to the menace to the settlement, both they and Selkirk still did not have an accurate picture of the nature of the danger. Both were still thinking in terms of "Indians" rather than Aboriginal people of mixed descent as the principal threat.

In its February deliberations, the HBC committee may well have had before it a copy of a pamphlet on Aboriginal education by Lord Selkirk, although that work was probably prepared in the wake of the discussions on that date.[9] The single surviving copy of this work in the Ontario Archives is a small fifteen-page pamphlet without a title page. While attribution of this work to Selkirk is not certain, there are some good reasons for assigning its authorship to him. In the first place, the watermark on the paper is 1814, indicating a publication date coinciding with the company discussion of this question in its governing committee. In the second, the printer was J. Bretell, Selkirk's favourite printer and the man responsible for most of his work. In the third, the style is perfectly consistent with Selkirk's. In the fourth, the proposal is very much in keeping with Selkirk's philosophy, since it emphasizes the need for education without total acculturation and seeks to preserve the essentials of the Native way of life within the framework of schooling, a relatively unusual position for most works of this sort at this time. Finally, this pamphlet is one of several unattributed items acquired by the Ontario Archives about the same time, all of which were printed by J. Bretell and one of which (its opening lines are: "Though I am little disposed at any time to be the hero of my own tale") is unquestionably by Selkirk. If the earl was not the author of this little work on Aboriginal education, he was almost certainly responsible for its printing, an act endorsing its arguments.

The author of this pamphlet attempted to establish some general principle from which a course of action could be developed. While he clearly favoured the process of moving the Aboriginal people from "savagery" to "civilization," he recognized the failure of previous attempts at acculturation. Instead, the author understood the difficulty of enforcing changes that ran against the grain of a culture and a way of life. He therefore insisted that a school be established that would inculcate European skills and values without requiring the pupils "to forget those accomplishments of savage life, without which they would be despised" by their families and friends. Interestingly enough, the author also suggested that the "half-blood" children of the company's European servants could be employed as interpreters and monitors while attending a separate school connected with the Aboriginal one. While this recommendation distinguished the separate existence of the mixed-blood people, the pamphlet did not provide any further details. If this pamphlet were by Selkirk, as seems likely, it suggests that he was quite capable of fresh thinking on thorny North American questions as well as on Scottish ones.

Selkirk himself wrote to Lord Bathurst in early March of 1815, correcting, he said, any misapprehension that might have arisen in a conversation the two men had conducted a few days earlier about Red River. At this point, Selkirk and Bathurst were obviously still talking informally. What had led Selkirk to fear misunderstanding was not clear. In any event, the earl insisted that there was no question of serving the pecuniary interests of one party in a commercial rivalry, but rather one of protecting innocent British subjects from massacre. The intention was not to incriminate the North West Company, but to demonstrate the danger. Selkirk did observe, however, that usually in preventing an impending breach of the peace, "the persons who may be suspected, are the very last who are consulted," a reference presumably to discussions that Bathurst must have held with representatives of the North West Company. He denied that the conduct of the two companies was similar, a point to which he would return at great length in his *Sketch of the Fur Trade* and that could be taken as its larger thesis. The Hudson's Bay Company was responsible for its employees and its board was "composed of gentlemen, who have too much regard for their character, to give any instruction, that is even of a doubtful nature." Unlike the partners of the North West Company, the leadership of the HBC could not escape justice by disappearing into the interior of the country. The North West Company could evade responsibility for any acts of any partner simply by disavowing them, but such disavowal was not the same as protection.[10] This sort of class patronization drove the Nor'westers up the wall.

In this letter Selkirk outlined the main themes of the book he was already working on and attempted to answer the major arguments of the opposition. The problems with the government were clear. Bathurst was unable completely to separate the interests of the settlers at Red River from the overall commercial rivalry between the two fur-trading companies, and try as Selkirk might, he was never quite able to convince Bathurst or the world at large of the distinction. As we have seen, the major reason for the confusion was that Selkirk had, indeed, allowed his colonization activities to become too closely connected with the HBC and the fur-trading rivalry. By his own account, he was colonizing because of the fur trade. He was equally unable to persuade any one that the leadership of the North West Company in Fort William or Montreal or London should be held responsible for the local actions of its employees. Not surprisingly, moreover, the suggestion that the Hudson's Bay Company leaders were "gentlemen" and the North'westers were not was undoubtedly counterproductive and would help contribute to Bathurst's later response to Selkirk when the earl deliberately defied the government.

THE SITUATION IN THE SETTLEMENT AND HBC ACTION

While Selkirk continued to recruit labourers for the company and emigrants for Red River in the spring of 1815—partly in Kildonan and partly in Strathnaver where Lord Reay and his agents had agreed to promote Red River among those they were displacing—the situation in the colony was rapidly beginning to deteriorate. Alexander (Greenfield) Macdonell was at

Swan River organizing for the forthcoming "campaign." He wrote to John Siveright, "We in this quarter assault the Colony in the rear, and to make safe work, we intend to draw some of their own men to our side; when we have got a sufficient number we will then make them face about and fight the Battle. I intend to make myself their General."[11] Miles Macdonell attempted in February to make peace with the freemen encamped near the Turtle River. His emissaries were surrounded by a group of North West Company servants, freemen, and young men of mixed descent, all well armed and some with painted faces. The leader of the freemen, "Bostonais" Pangman of the North West Company, refused to listen to the messengers, held them captive for six days while settlers hunting on the plains were seized, and attempted to lure Miles himself into camp where he threatened to kill the Red River governor. The freeman party painted their faces daily, sang Indian songs, and beat Indian drums, reported John McLeod.[12]

As for Duncan Cameron, he continued to write to discontented settlers, offering to free them from bondage, adding that the surest way to obtain what was due them "is to get whatever you can out of their store & I will take any article that can be of use here off your hands & pay you in Canada for them."[13] A few days later, Alexander (Greenfield) Macdonell reported to J.D. Cameron from Qu'Appelle that "you will see some sport in Red River before the month of June is over." Over 100 "halfbreeds" would be at the Forks, he claimed.[14] The commitment that Selkirk received from Lord Bathurst in March of 1815 "that instructions have been given to the Governor of Canada, to give such protection to the Settlers at Red River, as can be afforded without detriment to His Majesty's service in other quarters" would come too late, even if it had been implemented in Canada.[15] Bathurst's promise meant that the warnings of Selkirk and the Hudson's Bay Company had produced some effect on the government; that nothing could be done in time was not at this stage the government's fault. Given the British reluctance in 1815 to acquire new colonial responsibilities via the back door, Bathurst had made a considerable concession. As John Siveright of the North West Company put it at about the same time, however: "This spring must decide the entire ruin of the Colony—or the expulsion of the N.W. Co. from Red River."[16]

In letters written on the same day—22 March 1815—Lord Selkirk and Duncan Cameron demonstrated that they might indeed have been inhabiting different planets. The earl wrote to the Hudson's Bay Company's

Montreal agents pressing for a small party of artillery men and a few light cannon for Red River, adding that he presumed the governor "would not think of allowing less than one Company of Infantry for the protection of Red River."[17] In Red River itself, Duncan Cameron indicated that the cannon already in the possession of Miles Macdonell was a major factor in the assessment of military superiority, adding that "the Damned Colony" was "a Rascally Republic that neither respects Law nor Rights," but that he had prevented Miles from taking a single point despite his armament.[18]

A day after the letter to Montreal, Selkirk wrote a long letter to his governor full of instructions. Threats from the North West Company had led to successful applications for assistance, "probably a Company of Infantry." The earlier presumption had overnight become at least a probability. The trouble with the Pemmican Proclamation, the earl pointed out, was that it allowed the opposition to argue to the Indians that the colony would destroy the trade in provisions. The interdict should be continued no longer than necessary, for "the legality of the proclamation rests upon the apparent necessity of the case; not (as Mr. Auld seems to have imagined) upon my rights as Proprietor, but on the duty of every Gov'r of a Colony to stop any proceedings of individuals which would occasion famine among the inhabitants of the district under his charge." This statement moved the legal justification for the proclamation a very long way from a direct linkage to the charter. It now seemed to depend on Miles's responsibilities as a colonial governor—of a proprietorial colony based on the charter but not officially recognized by the British government. Coming to join Miles in 1815 were 150 new settlers, mainly Sutherlanders. Selkirk was very hard on arguments based on tradition. "I cannot tolerate the principle," he wrote, "of never trying any operation except with people, that have been trained to it from their infancy." Only the uncertain news from France (where Napoleon was once again on the loose) prevented him from promising that he would be in the settlement by the following spring, but he certainly intended to leave for Montreal in the autumn of this year.[19]

Despite the assurances of government assistance mentioned in his letter to Miles, Selkirk was now genuinely worried about the settlement's future. The shift in the legal justification for the Pemmican Proclamation that he now suggested must have come as a result of consultations with the lawyers in whose opinions he had previously been so confident. The lawyers were obviously suggesting some very real limitations to the authority of the charter.

Moreover, a sense of restlessness in the London Committee of the Hudson's Bay Company had doubtless communicated itself to Selkirk, as major confrontations were developing over which they had no control and had not anticipated. As he had earlier pointed out to Lord Bathurst, the HBC leadership were too gentlemanly to give illegal orders to their employees. Moreover, William Auld, now in London, was doing his best behind the scenes to undermine Selkirk's authority and policies, in part by insisting that the earl was not himself much of an honourable gentleman. "The Earl of Selkirk's influence," Auld wrote to one correspondent, "is as you know quite paramount—he attends regularly at the board every Comm'ee day and nothing is too minute for his inspection or too trifling for his employment." Selkirk and Wedderburn (Colvile) were "utterly destitute of honour & honesty," and not as wealthy as everyone imagined. Selkirk, for example, "borrowed the money which he paid for the stock he holds of the Company's funds."[20]

Certainly an increased interest in the West appeared among the Hudson's Bay Company directors. A committee vote in early April ordered large-scale copies from Arrowsmith's manuscript map of those parts of the company's territories where it was desirable to gain further information for "completing the Topography of the Country." That same committee meeting resolved to appoint a new governor of the company's territories in North America in the person of Robert Semple.[21] No indication of why Semple received the appointment appeared in the minutes. Perhaps the relevant fact was that he was a client of the Earl of Reay in whose territories Selkirk was hoping to recruit new settlers for Red River. Born in Boston in 1777, Semple had joined his parents in Loyalist exile in England after the American Rebellion.[22] He had been a merchant who travelled extensively around the world, and was the author of several of the sorts of travel books so popular at the time; Selkirk's nephew Basil Hall would become the doyen of these travel writers. While more than a hint survives that Semple had served as a spy for the British government in wartime Europe, using his American birth to gain entry to places a Briton could not go, he was nevertheless far more English than American. He had never visited North America in the course of his travels, and he had no known administrative experience, much less familiarity with the workings of colonial government. On the other hand, Semple's background was fairly typical for a colonial appointment at the time. What mattered most was who you knew, not what you knew.[23]

The appointment of Semple did not mean that Miles Macdonell was being replaced, for Miles was governor of the Red River settlement (and a Selkirk appointment) rather than governor of the company territories. Indeed, it was not at all clear what relationship to Miles the new governor was to have, or exactly what authority he would have in the settlement—which Selkirk ought to have been keeping quite distinct from the Hudson's Bay Company for its own protection. As for Miles, he spent most of the winter of 1815 on the plains, apparently trying to work out whatever emotional problems he was experiencing in isolation from his people and his governing responsibilities. He returned to the settlement in April, only to find that Duncan Cameron's supporters among the settlers had broken into the storehouses and taken to the North West Company post at Fort Gibraltar the field pieces upon which Miles relied so heavily for defence. On 18 April, Miles had attempted to secure some support from the servants under limited contract to Selkirk. He issued a proclamation "To Loyal Servants of the Red River Settlement," offering on Lord Selkirk's behalf that if any were hurt or maimed in defending the settlement, they would receive a pension equal to that given in the British service.[24] This proclamation was read to the whole settlement and posted at the fort. The servants and settlers ignored it, although it would become an issue in 1818 when the widow of settler Charles McLean tried to invoke its provisions on her behalf, claiming that her husband had served under its provisions.[25] Led by George Campbell, the settlers were "authorized" by Cameron to take possession of the armaments, "not with a view to make any hostile use of them, but merely to put them out of harm's way."[26] Without the cannon, of course, the entire military balance of power in Red River had been more than subtly altered, because the Nor'westers and especially their friends on the plains had an abiding fear of the armament.[27] Miles wrote desperate letters to the nearest trading posts of the HBC asking for assistance, but not much manpower was available.[28]

In Upper Canada, the leaders of the North West Company were making their own preparations for confrontation with Selkirk and the Hudson's Bay Company. Archdeacon John Strachan of York (Toronto), who had married into the McGill family of Montreal and was close friends with the Montreal fur-trading elite, was preparing a public letter attacking Selkirk for his emigration schemes. Strachan was concerned that Selkirk's emigrants were being gulled, particularly by being sent into the remote wilderness of Red

River rather than being brought to more promising locations in the Canadas. Whether the proposed pamphlet originated with Strachan or with the Nor'westers is not clear, but certainly the clergyman was being supplied with information—including a prospectus for Red River that Selkirk had probably prepared in 1811 but never issued—by William McGillivray.[29] Strachan's proposed intervention suggests some of the wheels within wheels involved in Highland emigration to North America at the time. Not all Scots were on the same side in such matters.

The Hudson's Bay Company Committee, at about the same time that Strachan was penning his pamphlet, resurrected the law code earlier prepared for its North American territories "for the more effectual Administration of Justice in the Colony of Ruperts Land, Hudson's Bay," obviously as part of the changes associated with the appointment of Robert Semple.[30] And from Lower Canada, Colin Robertson reported that, despite North West Company interference, he was departing for the west with a party of fur traders recruited for the Athabasca region.[31] This expedition meant that the Hudson's Bay Company was for the first time directly competing with the North West Company for furs in the rich territory of the far northwest. From the Nor'wester perspective, it represented a major escalation of the rivalry.

On 19 May 1815, the General Court of the Hudson's Bay Company met for an unusually momentous occasion. From the chair, the governor explained the "necessity of a more regular form of Government being adopted in the Company's Territories in Hudson's Bay," and submitted resolutions appointing a governor-in-chief and a council, competent "for the Administration of Justice." The General Court also extended the same power to the governors of Ossiniboia (i.e., Red River) and Moose Factory. Sheriffs were appointed, one for Ossiniboia and Moose, and one for the remainder of the territories "for the execution of all such process as shall be directed to them according to law." The resolutions were separately voted upon by the proprietors (all in the affirmative), and then individuals were nominated to fill the various posts and councils. Robert Semple was named governor-in-chief and Miles Macdonell was officially named as governor of Ossiniboia.[32] These resolutions had the effect of providing a political and especially a judicial structure for the territories within the HBC's charter. They also legitimized after the fact what Miles had done in the course of the Pemmican Proclamation, as well as made Red River a part of the HBC political system. The company then sent Lord Bathurst a copy of the proposed ordinances to be executed by the new system of justice, adding its anxiety that "such Ordinances should receive the sanction of his Majesty's Att'y and Sol. General, before they are acted upon."[33] A subsequent letter to Bathurst, drafted by Lord Selkirk, rehearsed the company's claims and rights under the charter. It emphasized that the company had always exercised jurisdiction "as far as circumstances required," but with the increasing population of the country, "new rights & varied interests have arisen, which call for a more regular & effectual administration of Justice." The company had its own legal opinions, but since the royal prerogative was involved, it sought confirmation from the Crown's legal officers. Nevertheless, since immediate action was required, the company had instructed its newly appointed governor and council to administer justice in the territory.[34]

Had Selkirk been aware of developments in North America in the summer of 1815, he would have realized that the actions of the company were too little too late. The time to resolve the jurisdictional questions through unilateral action by the Hudson's Bay Company was past, if ever it had existed. In Quebec, for example, Governor General Sir Gordon Drummond had received the instructions from Lord Bathurst to protect Red River from Aboriginal menace. Drummond's response was to order his aide-de-camp, Colonel John Harvey, to write to William McGillivray of the North West Company "that some of the Servants of the North West Company are suspected of being concerned in the Diabolical Plot" against Red River. Drummond wanted to know from McGillivray "if there exists in your opinion any reasonable ground" for suspicions for the safety of the settlement from Indian atrocities, adding that if anything did happen, the North West Company would be "considered responsible in the eyes of the world." This appeal, Drummond felt, would be a more useful response to the Bathurst instruction than anything else in his power to do.[35] He was probably right, and the appeal might have worked had McGillivray been a more reasonable man. The Hudson's Bay Company's local agents themselves approved of Drummond's approach to the problem, admitting that the notion of a military force for Red River in the short run was totally unworkable.[36]

William McGillivray responded by noting that a copy of Bathurst's orders had already been transmitted by Henry Goulbourn (the colonial secretary's second-in-command) to the North West Company in London and had been fully answered there. The Selkirk camp would subsequently suspect that Goulbourn was partial to the Nor'westers, with some of whom he had a social relationship, but consulting with the North West Company was, under the circumstances, a sensible response to a complex business, however peculiar it might seem to be asking the accused for their opinions on the allegations. In any case, McGillivray's view was not at all defensive. Selkirk had been enticing people to Red River with "golden but delusive promises," McGillivray argued, and the North West Company could not be held responsible for any hostile actions against Selkirk's people or the Hudson's Bay Company by the indigenous people of the region. Citing the Canada Jurisdiction Act, McGillivray held that "individuals in the Indian country are primarily responsible for their own criminal acts." Moreover, Selkirk was the aggressor, for "under the guise and cloak of Colonization, he is aiming at and maturing an exterminating blow" against North West Company trade. Miles had acted in the capacity of a "Bashaw" in his proclamation, and, McGillivray concluded, "In all such attempts hereafter, the North West Company would assuredly be justified in repelling force by force."[37]

While the Hudson's Bay Company was attempting to legitimize its authority (and that of Miles Macdonell) after the event, the residents of the Red River settlement had been drawn into a confrontation, and Lord Selkirk's forces had suffered a serious defeat. As would so often be the case in these matters, the confrontation was not simply the result of North West Company aggression. Most of the action had been led by mixed-descent residents of the region, but a fair proportion of Selkirk's own people had colluded and cooperated in it. This latter factor would be particularly galling for Selkirk to accept, but it certainly weakened his case against the Nor'westers. The disenchantment of the settlers, including most of the Kildonan party, was plainly a key factor in the events of 1815. Perhaps Selkirk could not be held directly responsible for most of the unfortunate series of events experienced by his settlers, but the Nor'westers were in a very real sense correct in asserting that the planting of a settlement in such a remote region was bound to lead to suffering.

The events of June 1815 at the settlement have often been described in considerable detail.[38] The Nor'westers, dressed in military garb left over from the War of 1812, had recruited the bulk of the freemen and individuals of mixed descent to their side, forming a camp at Frog Plain not far from the settlement. Many of mixed descent rode around the area singing Aboriginal war songs. The contracts of many of the Irish at the settlement, "servants" recruited to prepare the way for settlement, expired on 1 June 1815. They quickly joined the Nor'wester party at the camp. Those of mixed descent, led by Cuthbert Grant and Peter (Bostonais) Pangman, were clamouring for compensation for their Aboriginal rights to the soil that were supposedly pre-empted by the settlement. Horses were stolen and isolated houses were plundered. On 11 June, firing of small arms and of a small field piece earlier taken from the settlement frightened many settlers who had not yet agreed to take up Duncan Cameron's offer of removal to Canada. In the general melee, settler Charles McLean was wounded when a cannon exploded. Miles found his advisors useless, and they offered no counsel except that he surrender to the enemy. On 16 June he lost heart and did so, and was immediately arrested under a warrant issued under the *Canada Jurisdiction Act*. The people of mixed descent then ravaged the crops and burnt many buildings to the ground. Most of the settlers agreed to depart for Upper Canada in the North West Company canoes, and the remainder left the settlement, ultimately arriving at Jack River.[39]

The North West Company partners on the scene had orchestrated the events of June 1815, but accepting their involvement and leadership does not explain what had happened or satisfactorily apportion responsibility. These matters would be debated for years in the controversial literature generated by the various participants, in the Canadian courts, and in the works of modern historians. Was this dispersal of the settlement the first open act of violence in the fur-trade war between the two companies, or was it a legitimate response to previous acts (especially the Pemmican Proclamation and its subsequent enforcement) originating in the settlement? Answering such a question is about as simple as deciding on where to begin the history of the more recent conflicts between the Arabs and Israel. The dispersal of the settlement was plainly an escalation of physical confrontation by the North West Company, complicated by the uncertain roles of those involved who were not employees of either side.

Lord Selkirk and the Hudson's Bay Company were always convinced that those of mixed descent (the "bois brûlés") were completely under the influence of the North West Company partners, and that their demand for land rights was merely a concoction of the Nor'westers to turn these people into the "Indians" whom the North West Company had always insisted would oppose the settlement.[40] The evidence is simply not available to ascertain the extent to which those of mixed descent developed such demands and grievances on their own, but it is certain that these people had grievances against the settlement, that Selkirk had not taken their presence sufficiently into account, and that his local agents, especially Miles Macdonell, had treated them harshly. Indeed, Miles himself admitted that his attempts to interfere in the local provision trade and to "restrict the freemen and half-breeds in running the buffalo on horseback" had produced a bad effect on these vital players.[41] Miles might be able to justify these actions in terms of the requirements for food of the settlement, but he had made little effort to enlist the positive support of the freemen and those of mixed descent, preferring instead to regard them as mere interlopers in the region.

The response to the crisis of 1815 by the settlers in Red River, particularly those arriving in the Kildonan party of 1813–14, was a complex one. Without the support—active or passive—of most of the settlers, Duncan Cameron and the North West Company could not have dispersed the settlement quite so easily. Settler grievances may have been exploited and manipulated by Cameron, but he had a firm foundation of discontent on which to build. The settlers had experienced a far more difficult physical journey of transplantation than they had been led to anticipate, and despite their difficulties, Miles Macdonell had not been either helpful or generous with supplies and implements, apart from the guns he insisted the newcomers take. To require that the newcomers immediately become part of the defensive structure of the settlement was unreasonable; for as Donald Gunn would later emphasize, the only people to be defended against were their countrymen and friends in the North West Company. Miles carefully marked down each item handed out in the settlement account book as Lord Selkirk had insisted he must do. The presumption had to be that the settlers would ultimately have to pay for them. Significantly, the Nor'westers would ostentatiously cancel these accounts before disembarking the settlers for the east.[42] Equally significantly, as we shall see, Lord Selkirk would attempt to collect the amounts owing from the settlers in their new homes in Upper Canada.

Selkirk always maintained that it was a bad policy with Highlanders to give things away, because it made them dependent and took away their pride; but in the case of the Kildonan settlers, this insistence on accountability was clearly a mistake. If Selkirk really intended to plant a settlement at Red River, he should have been prepared to subsidize it totally for the first years, instead of constantly worrying and complaining about the expense. If Selkirk could not personally afford the expense, he should not have begun the operation, and he particularly should not have tried to hold the Kildonaners accountable. He could and should have obviated his concern that his agents were not responsible by residing personally at the settlement, as Miles Macdonell and others had always advocated.

Some good reasons existed for Selkirk's failure to appear to take personal charge of his settlement. One was his health, which was at best indifferent. But as it turned out, whatever his previous physical condition had been, his health flourished during the time he spent in Canada, and especially during his period in the West. A second problem for Selkirk involved his responsibilities during the wartime crisis, particularly his office as Lord Lieutenant of Kirkcudbright and his membership in the House of Lords. He would have had to turn his back on these privileges in order to get away during wartime, and this was not a step he was prepared to take. Selkirk was undoubtedly right in thinking that leaving Britain during the war would have removed any chance he had of government approval for his settlement, but government support was always a chimera and he would probably have been better off not seeking it. One has to suspect that one of the reasons that Selkirk did not initially come to supervise personally his settlement was because he had no particular desire to live—with or without his family—in the backcountry of North America. His record with his remote settlements in Prince Edward Island and Upper Canada suggests that he rode away from them at the earliest possible opportunity.

William McGillivray in Lower Canada brought to the attention of government Miles's attempts to issue ejection notices against the North West Company posts, adding that such procedures "must produce serious results, and I am very apprehensive that unfortunate consequences will follow any attempt on his part" to possess forcibly company property. At the same time, those Nor'westers closer to Red River were exulting that "the Colony has been all knocked in the head by the N.W. Co."[43] As a result of Harvey's correspondence with McGillivray, the Canadian agents of the Hudson's Bay Company would learn that all unfavourable impressions of North West Company conduct had been removed from Drummond's mind. Instead, Drummond was now convinced that any trouble "will arise principally from the conduct of Mr. Miles Macdonell," who had asserted "powers which cannot possibly in His Exc'y's Opinion have been rested in him or in any Agent Private or Public of any individual or of any Chartered Body."[44] If the Hudson's Bay Company had sovereignty in the West, then Canada did not. Although the legality of Miles's proclamation could only be settled in an

English court, Drummond had certainly decided which side in the matter he would back.

Despite their exultation over events in Red River, the McGillivrays recognized that the party being led west by Colin Robertson pushed still further the threat to the North West Company begun by the establishment of the settlement. As an ex-employee of the Nor'westers, Robertson understood how they operated and had no hesitancy about responding in kind. On his way west in the summer of 1815, Robertson heard the news of the settlement's dispersal from North West Company canoes. It was confirmed at Lac la Pluie (Rainy Lake) by Miles Macdonell himself, under arrest and accompanying the party of colonists heading east. At Jack River, Robertson was asked by the settlers loyal to Selkirk to lead them back to Red River, and after several weeks of deliberation, he agreed. A charismatic leader, Robertson soon had the settlement humming again, and even managed a decent harvest with what remained of the crops that had not been trampled.[45]

By mid-August of 1815, William McGillivray in Montreal had received news of the events of June in Red River. He issued what amounted to a primitive press release, in which he put the North West Company case. Selkirk had received his grant from the Hudson's Bay Company, in which he was a "great stockholder," without sanction from government or the approval of resident Indians. He had recruited settlers without adequate explanation of the remoteness of the location. The North West Company had sought to assist the infant settlement, but Miles Macdonell had quarrelled with the resident population, especially "the Half Breed Indians, a daring and now numerous race sprung from the Intercourse of the Canadian Voyageurs with the Indian women and who consider themselves the Possessors of the Country and Lords of the Soil."[46] This was the first time that the Nor'westers had described in detail the particular Indians they had long insisted would attack the settlement. These Indians were obviously not the traditional residents of the region everyone had assumed would be involved. In any case, Miles had issued the Pemmican Proclamation, assuming powers greater than those enjoyed by the governments of the Crown in North America. According to McGillivray, "The disorder excited in the Country by these acts of violence, the disgust given to the Settlers by the extensive disadvantages of the Country, as well as the Violence and Tyranny of their leader, and the dread of the Natives, Indians and mixed Breed, all contributed to break up the colony." The settlers had thrown themselves on the compassion of the North West

Company, who had removed them to prevent an Indian war in which all white men would be victims. But, McGillivray emphasized, the North West Company had promised the settlers nothing beyond transportation to Canada, and no further responsibility for them once they had arrived.

Were the situation described not so personally disastrous to him, Selkirk might well have been amused by the comments of J.D. Cameron, written from Upper Canada about the Red River settlers when they first arrived in the colony. They had complained all the way, Cameron asserted, especially about "pulling at the oar like slaves" and eating Indian corn, "a food that was not fit for animals." Cameron concluded, "In short I am not able to write all their complaints were I to write all night." However much they had been trouble in Red River, "I believe they were thrice more here."[47] Selkirk might also have appreciated the irony of the response of Upper Canada's Lieutenant Governor, Francis Robinson, to the arrival of the Red River people. Robinson dashed off a letter to Sir Gordon Drummond, demanding to know why these folk had been removed from the west by the North West Company, adding, "It is to be regretted that We had not been consulted before they were put in motion, and it appears at present very like bringing Paupers to our door, and leaving them to our mercy."[48]

In London, Lord Selkirk was obviously unaware of the dispersal of his settlement. Nevertheless, he was busy writing the indictment of the North West Company that would become his *Sketch of the British Fur Trade*, and with Napoleon finally defeated, he was also preparing to depart for North America to deal in person with his settlement in Red River. The "Advertisement" at the beginning of his book apologized for its incompleteness, which he explained as a result of the attention he had been forced to give to Red River before departing for "a remote part of the British dominions" to try to protect it. Selkirk spent no time on the French system. He took his historical account of the early British fur trade from Alexander Henry and Sir Alexander McKenzie. From the outset, he emphasized, the system of admitting the successful traders into the partnership had the effect of assuring dynamism and *esprit de corps*. But the fur trade lacked the check of the civilized world in remote situations without the restraint of law. In a piece of prescient analysis that well summarized his own later experiences, Selkirk wrote:

> When a plaintiff has to travel thousands of miles to find the court from which he is to seek redress, and when witnesses are to be brought from such a distance, at a vast expense, and to the total

interruption of their ordinary pursuits, it must be a case of extraordinary importance, which would induce even a wealthy man to
encounter the difficulty of obtaining it.[49]

The earl recognized the important service rendered to Britain by the North
West Company in the War of 1812, although he pointed out that the Voyageur Corps enabled the company's employees to be paid by government for a
protracted period. He was less impressed with the company's treatment of
either its own employees or the First Peoples, citing Count Andreani's travels
to America in 1791 and the Duke of Rochefoucould Liancourt's travels in
America in 1795–97 upon the former point. Exclusive possession of the trade,
to which the company had no right, was maintained by force, especially
against the servants of the Hudson's Bay Company. Much of the latter half of
the book was devoted to an unremitting catalogue of the violence committed
upon the HBC and protestations of the contrasting "moderation" and
"honourable views" of the English company. The HBC, Selkirk insisted, did
not exploit its own employees and sought "to preserve moral and religious
habits among their people."[50]

The inevitable conclusion of Selkirk's analysis was that the British Parliament needed to interfere in affairs in the fur-trade country. The so-called
Canada Jurisdiction Act (43 George III, cap. 138) was most unsatisfactory
as a legislative solution. This legislation allowed crimes in the Indian territories to be tried in the courts of Upper and Lower Canada on the assumption that these districts had a natural connection to Canada. Instead, Selkirk
argued, the law benefited only the Canadian traders who controlled the
inland navigation. He described in detail the cases heard under 43 George
II, cap. 138. These only provided more evidence of the abuse of employees
of the Hudson's Bay Company. The statute, he insisted, had been enacted
only upon consultation with the partners and agents of the Montreal trading
companies, and it confirmed and augmented "the despotism of a trading
company." The "national interest" was not served by the North West
Company's system of trading and justice. At this point the reader probably
anticipated a well-thought out alternative proposal. Instead, Selkirk was
quite brief and incomplete. He advocated that the First Peoples be given "a
permanent tenure of their hunting grounds" and that a better system of
justice, based on local magistrates, be instituted. Doubtless the sketchiness
of this closing section was one heavily affected by the events Selkirk had
mentioned in his opening Advertisement.

This work was finally published by James Ridgeway in London early in 1816. A second edition followed. An American edition was published in New York in 1818, and a French translation in Montreal in 1819. These later editions were obviously part of the print war conducted between the Selkirk faction and the Nor'westers in the later years. If Selkirk had hoped to repeat his success with his book on the Highlands, he would be disappointed by the reviewers' treatment of *Sketch of the British Fur Trade*. Indeed, as we shall see, the reception of this book was considerably less enthusiastic than Selkirk might have expected because, given the course of events in North America, it was seen as too partisan. It had been written too quickly and did not provide the depth of analysis of his earlier work.

Apart from the *Sketch of the British Fur Trade*, the first evidence of the earl's decision to attend personally to his affairs in the New World came in August, when he organized the shipment of a number of personal articles to Quebec.[51] At about the same time, the London Committee of the Hudson's Bay Company authorized Selkirk to negotiate with the North West Company, giving him full and complete powers so to do.[52] While the packers were preparing Lady Selkirk's grand pianoforte and harp for shipment to Quebec, the Hudson's Bay Committee was carefully instructing Selkirk on the guidelines for negotiating with the North West Company.[53] The committee offered nothing new and was not in the slightest conciliatory. The major point in any agreement, the committee stressed, was "the preservation of the Chartered rights of the HBC, avoiding any concession which can fairly be construed into a Imbition of our priviledges." The committee hoped an offer to the Nor'westers of long-term access to the territories of the HBC would have some appeal, since "it seems possible that they will prefer their immediate advantage to any remote interest which they might have to contest our rights at the expiration of the agreement." The Montrealers would have to acknowledge the charter and property rights of the Hudson's Bay Company, however. Only then could negotiations proceed on pulling out of Athabasca and Canada, although in the end these territories could be conceded on peppercorn leases. Selkirk could also grant right of transit through Port Nelson; although if such transit rights were really valuable, he should receive concessions for them. The London Committee was quite willing to negotiate exclusively with the North West Company to the exclusion of other fur traders. Even if what he would hear in Lower Canada upon his arrival had not disposed Selkirk to oppose any deal with the North

West Company, his instructions had made it almost impossible for the two rival fur-trading concerns to come to any amicable agreement. The North West Company was not likely to recognize the charter, and without that recognition there could be no further discussions.

By early September Selkirk was in Towcester on his way to Liverpool, writing a quick letter to his Inverness agent with instructions for the recruitment of new settlers for Red River and for handling the claims of the earlier Kildonan emigrants against their former landlord. He added, "It is necessary that I should obtain justice for those who have thrown themselves on my protection."[54] This notion of responsibility would be oft repeated by Selkirk in the ensuing months. He left Liverpool a few days later. The departure opened a new phase of his career, a phase of direct action. That action was simultaneously exciting and distressing. Selkirk would end up leaving his mark on the history of Canada, but whether that mark was one flattering to him was another matter entirely.

CHAPTER SIXTEEN

Trying to Gain Control

IN THE THREE YEARS FOLLOWING his departure for America in September of 1815, Lord Selkirk was in an unusual situation. For most of his previous career, especially when dealing with his settlements in North America, he had issued the bulk of his orders to his agents from afar. His personal visits to Prince Edward Island and Upper Canada had been brief ones, and he had never managed to get to Red River. As a result, Selkirk was never dealing with current conditions and his orders were typically out-of-date at the time they were issued. From late 1815 until the end of 1818, Selkirk would be personally in command, not merely of the efforts to save his settlement at Red River, but of the entire Hudson's Bay Company attempt to confront directly the North West Company, at first in the field and then in the courts of Canada. This opportunity for personal leadership brought out the best in Selkirk. As a field commander he had a real gift for improvisation. In much of this improvisation, he paid little attention either to niceties or to ultimate consequences. Ironically, even his many friends and supporters—then and since—have been highly critical of much of his behaviour during this period, especially in the late summer and early autumn of 1816. In these months he dealt with the North West Company on its own less-than-scrupulous terms. This approach, while extremely successful, seemed totally out of character for a British gentleman of honour and integrity. To some extent, its very inconsistency with his overall image helped account for its success. The opposition was taken utterly by surprise and was defeated before it could rethink its response.

At the same time that Selkirk was able to take personal command of the situation in North America, he significantly complicated his lines of communications. Not only was he removed from Red River, but he was also removed from the British Colonial Office, the Hudson's Bay Company London Committee, and his economic base in Scotland. There were now serious time lags on information from both the Indian Territories and the centres of power and money. Selkirk resolved this problem by plunging ahead without much regard for the current state of play in either Red River or London. He also threw all financial considerations—about either his own fortune or the HBC's balance sheet—out the window. Telling the story of this period is particularly difficult, given that information about much of importance that was occurring on both sides of the Atlantic was not available to Selkirk as he went about his business. Events in Britain, Canada, and Red River progress along parallel tracks with what was happening in the other places unknown to the participants in any one of the story lines.

THE ARRIVAL OF GOVERNOR SEMPLE

At about the same time that Lord Selkirk sailed from Liverpool for New York, Governor Robert Semple arrived at York Factory with a fresh contingent of settlers. He attempted to formalize the arrangements made earlier by Colin Robertson, who was officially put in charge of the settlement.[1] The new arrivals were, of course, surprised to discover that most of the friends and relations they had expected to join were now back in Upper Canada. They petitioned for the return of the departed and also for representations to Selkirk of "their conduct in the late disturbances in the Colony in as favourable a light as possible."[2] Semple was impressed by these new recruits with whom he had voyaged to North America. He observed that "they were the mildest people, in their manners, I have ever met with."[3] Their indolence was balanced by sobriety, honesty, patience, obedience, and good nature, he wrote. Semple also prepared a statement of observations regarding the settlement, at which he did not intend to reside until the following April. He thought 100 British soldiers sufficient to protect Red River, which would have livestock cultivation as its agricultural base. As for attitudes in the settlement, there were many ingrained prejudices that would have to be overcome. The new arrivals were much influenced by news of the earlier troubles—reported in gloomy letters home, in newspaper accounts, and in oral testimony at York Factory—and it would be difficult to obtain new settlers until these unfavourable reports could be undone.[4] In Red River itself, Colin Robertson was extremely impressed by the harvest, noting that he had twelve months' provisions for 100 families.[5] Those of mixed descent were still active, drafting a petition to the King as the "Free Halfbreeds of Red River" under North West Company supervision.[6] Robertson studiously ignored both them and Duncan Cameron, who was still riding around in his regimentals.

In a formal letter to the Hudson's Bay Company, Governor Semple reported the dispersal of the settlement, adding that "if this be permitted to pass unpunished by the British government it will in fact be desiring us to seek redress at our own hands and to make use of whatever means we may possess according to the natural laws of retaliation & self-defence."[7] The disputes with the North West Company, he insisted, were no longer dependent upon forms of justice that might be introduced in Rupert's Land. "Should our Government refuse immediately to interfere the inevitable consequence will be that Two great Trading Companies of the same nation will be reduced nearly to the State of Two Indian Tribes at War." The North West Company had, by arming those of mixed descent, disclosed "to that lawless race the dangerous secret of their own strength," and "this mischievous Engine" would render every regular establishment insecure. The establishment of a European population in HBC territories, Semple concluded, was "no longer unfortunately as a matter of Speculation or choice but as likely to be absolutely necessary to the future security of all the Posts connecting the Countries above & below the Winnipeg." Such a prognosis could hardly have been based on first-hand experience, and most of the sentiments in this letter must have reflected what Semple was being told at York Factory. Before the HBC could even receive such a report, it learned from the British government that there would be no troops for Red River, partly because such protection was impracticable and partly because the settlement had already been dispersed.[8]

On the very same day that Colonial Office undersecretary Goulburn wrote to the HBC, a newly appointed commissioner and emigration agent of the British government wrote to Goulburn's superior, Lord Bathurst. With the war in Europe finally over, the British government had decided to encourage Scottish settlement to Canada. Advertisements appeared in Scottish newspapers in late February 1815 offering passage to Canada, land grants of 100 acres to each head of family, agricultural implements at cost, and a minister and schoolmaster publicly supported. The prospective emigrant had to provide a character reference and a deposit. The scheme offered no redress if the emigrant were not satisfied. Many of those who took up the offer came from the Edinburgh and Glasgow areas, although perhaps half came from the Highlands.[9] The government agent in charge of the project, John Campbell WS, found the emigration legislation of 1803 to be a serious hindrance. He gratuitously offered to Lord Bathurst his opinion of Lord Selkirk's book on the Highlands and emigration, observing:

> I am so much satisfied with the interesting remarks made by his Lordship that it entirely supersedes many observations that are obviously just in regard to the Highlands as it respects both the state of proprietors, & of the tenants and cottages. His book was received at the time with some prejudice & excited considerable opposition. But it has been found that it contains much truth.[10]

Campbell was quite familiar with the earlier opposition to Selkirk's book, since as kelping laird Lord Macdonald's Edinburgh man of business, he had been responsible for much of it.

SELKIRK IN NORTH AMERICA: THE NEGOTIATIONS WITH THE NORTH WEST COMPANY

As for Lord Selkirk, he had landed in New York to discover that his settlement had been dispersed. He learned the news from a young Irishman who had been an early servant in Red River and had apparently come east from the settlement with the other settlers. From the beginning, Selkirk was convinced that the North West Company was behind the destruction. He was equally certain that the government would have to act. In Lower Canada in early November, he penned a letter to Governor Sir Gordon Drummond attempting to resurrect the idea of military protection for Red River. Of Scots parentage, Drummond had been born in Quebec but educated in Britain before entering the army. In 1813 he had been sent to Upper Canada as Sir Isaac Brock's successor, and despite a lack of military success late in the war had—in typical British fashion—been rewarded for his incompetence with a promotion as temporary administrator of Lower Canada and commander of troops in the Canadas. Drummond was a highly experienced if unsuccessful soldier unlikely to be intimidated by Lord Selkirk. In his letter, Selkirk maintained that a decision not to protect Red River could hardly be taken "upon the mere *ex parte* statement of those from whom the danger was apprehended." Enclosing narratives of recent events sent to him by his people on the scene, he insisted "it would surely be most disgraceful to the British government, if these lawless ruffians should be suffered to make open war upon their fellow subjects." The earl added that the outrages had been committed by "Canadians, mixed with the bastard sons of others, who had thrown off the restraints of regular society, & cohabiting with Indian squaws have formed a combination of the vices of civilized & savage life."[11] Selkirk had by now recognized the existence of a mixed-descent threat to his settlement, but he clearly had not accepted the legitimacy of the opposition. He had absolutely no real understanding of the background of those of mixed descent or of their point of view. If Miles Macdonell had acted improperly, Selkirk continued in his letter to Drummond, the correct recourse was to the Privy Council. Finally, Selkirk noted that there were now 150 persons at his settlement who would require military protection. On a related front, Selkirk had also induced John Macdonell, Miles's brother, to write to the United States enquiring about the possibility of obtaining young Irishmen from the Boston area willing to enlist for a Red River expedition.[12] This particular scheme was not further pursued, but it suggests that from an early date Selkirk may have had in the back of his mind some notion of a mercenary army.

Maitland, Garden and Auldjo—the agents for Lord Selkirk and for the Hudson's Bay Company—had found Selkirk a house in the old town of Montreal. It had formerly belonged to Sir John Johnson.[13] A few days after his arrival in Montreal, Selkirk drafted a letter to Joseph Berens, outlining his position at this stage, particularly with regard to negotiations with the North West Company. The news of the dispersal of the settlement dampened his expectations for a successful negotiation, he began. The Nor'westers' natural arrogance had been enhanced, and he doubted they would compromise until the Crown backed HBC jurisdiction, or the efforts for redress alarmed them. Athabasca had to be "vigorously supported," for it must have been the fear of its commercial success that had induced the North West Company to attack the settlement. This was wishful thinking on Selkirk's part that the HBC's larger strategy was working; more immediate causes existed for what had happened in Red River. "A signal punishment of this aggression is therefore of vital consequences to the [Hudson's Bay] Company," Selkirk argued. He did not expect a fair investigation, however, because the North West Company had a "strange ascendancy" over Lord Bathurst through Henry Goulburn, and the governor of Lower Canada shared the prejudice in favour of the Nor'westers. Surely someone at the HBC, Selkirk exclaimed, must have enough weight "to prevent an undersecretary from throwing aside our representations as waste paper."[14] Although he would carefully explain in *Sketch of the Fur Trade* why the North West Company was so powerful in Lower Canada, Selkirk never admitted the possibility that their position had any legitimacy that governments might prefer to support. Selkirk concluded his thinking at this point by expressing his uncertainty about the future of his settlement. He had sought "the prospect of obtaining an adequate return for the outlay, within a reasonable space of time," he wrote in this letter to Joseph Berens. Only some arrangement with the North West Company could achieve this end. He would not act, therefore, until he had reached some concrete understanding about the fur trade.

In the wake of Selkirk's letter, the governor of Lower Canada had consulted his military advisors about the practicability and expediency of protection for Red River. They had been quite negative. The country was too isolated, wrote W.H. Robinson, and moreover, what "would the Officers become, exiled in a Country where they can have no society, employment, or amusement?" Robinson had less facetious and frivolous objections as well. The presence of warring factions so close to the American border could produce a jurisdictional nightmare in which the army might become enmeshed. "The lives of men are too precious," he concluded, "to be sported with in such Experiments."[15] Not for more than a generation would the British government relent and order a military force to Red River in 1846. Selkirk's settlement would in the meantime be on its own.

To his surprise, Selkirk found himself in early December meeting with John Richardson of the North West Company to discuss an arrangement between the rival fur-trading concerns that both parties agreed was extremely desirable.[16] The Scots-born Richardson had been in North America for more than forty years and was an elder statesman of the fur trade, head of the firm of Forsyth, Richardson, and Company that dealt with the overseas part of the trade. He was also a shrewd merchant who could see the writing on the wall for fur trading. He had already begun diversifying into grain and timber. Selkirk stressed that he had been instructed that any agreement had to be consistent with the "interest, the rights, & the honour" of the HBC. Richardson's response was to query whether Selkirk's instructions extended only to some sort of partition of the trade, or whether they included the possibility of union. Selkirk responded that union had not seriously been discussed by the London Committee, and he could but present a proposal. Since a

continual theme of a series of earlier negotiations between the two companies had been the possibility of union, the failure to consider the possibility
at this stage strongly suggests that the HBC was not really very interested in
negotiations. Selkirk said he could discuss partitioning arrangements. Richardson replied that complete union was the best and only solution to the
conflict. With union not on the table and Selkirk insisting, as he had been
instructed, upon prior recognition of the charter, there was precious little
chance of an agreement emerging from these talks.[17]

The North West Company subsequently proposed a partition of trading
areas "to prevent collision" and to enable the trade to be carried on with
"order and economy," but it refused to concede anything in the Athabasca
and wanted the region around Red River held cooperatively. Red River was
essential to both parties since it produced the provisions "to furnish the
Depots necessary for carrying on the General Trade."[18] As an alternative, it
offered a joint-trade arrangement for the period from 1816 to 1822, with
management under the direction of North West Company agents at Montreal,
on a basis of one-third HBC and two-thirds NWC sharing of profits. Neither
party was to regard the arrangement as affecting the charter issue. Selkirk
riposted that he could allow the North West Company to manage the western
trade only were the HBC allowed to control the trade in its chartered region,
and the question of the charter submitted to binding arbitration by "eminent
legal characters at London."[19] While negotiating so soon with the Nor'westers
was a bit surprising, he reported to Andrew Colvile, "you will be much less
surpriz'd to hear that it has ended in nothing."[20] Indeed, given the constraints
placed upon Selkirk's freedom to negotiate, the wonder would have been if
anything had been accomplished. In principle he thought the proposed territorial division "preferable," even to the "exclusive possession of our own
Territory." But he was apprehensive about the legal effects of a joint venture
with a company of such limited liability. In the end, the key was the Athabasca, and were the HBC thrust into that region pursued actively, "I have no
doubt that in another year, they will hold a different language."[21] As for the
settlement, he was preparing actively for the spring, having ordered twenty
canoes. He was hoping to head west himself to re-establish Red River "in
respectable force."

At about the same time, Governor Robert Semple reported hopeful
news from Fort Douglas. He and the settlers accompanying him had
reached Red River in early November: "The Colours were hoisted, the

guns were fired, at night we laughed, and drank and danced and now the serious Calculations of the Colony Commence." He was heartened by the presence of 400 bushels of wheat and 200 of barley, while buffalo and partridge were plentiful. The "miserable system of treachery and ingratitude" on the part of the Highlanders in 1815, so contrary to their character, could only have been caused by gross mismanagement at the top, especially given such "miserable opponents" as the "Half Breeds and Old Worn out Canadians" presently being "kicked about" by Colin Robertson. Semple's enthusiasm was commendable, but his total misreading of the local opposition augured ill for the future.[22] Semple exhibited all the worst instincts of British Imperialism abroad.

The discussions between Selkirk and the Nor'westers concluded on 27 December 1815, with the Canadians rejecting any agreement based on charter recognition. They had hoped, they wrote Selkirk, to found an understanding on "the practical pecuniary Interest of both Parties," leaving "abstract pretensions and theories, to remain either wholly dormant" or inoperative. Selkirk's insistence on principle over substance would mean great losses, for the two parties would have to return to a "pecuniary Contest."[23] Just as Robert Semple underestimated the opposition at Red River, so the North West Company misjudged Selkirk as a man hampered by useless principles. It was true that he would not sacrifice everything to immediate economic advantage, but he would prove more than the library-bound Man of Honour his opponents implied. In his conflict with the Nor'westers, Selkirk would receive no assistance from the British government. Although the government officially proclaimed the need for both companies to cease violence, it took a hands-off position that really meant that only force would decide the context. The party with the strongest private army would emerge the victor.[24] Neither Goulburn nor the North West Company seriously believed that Selkirk's side would prove superior militarily or that Selkirk would personally lead the HBC into such a contest.

To Andrew Colvile, Selkirk reported early in the New Year on the negotiations with the Nor'westers. He was not impressed with the legal opinion obtained by the North West Company regarding the charter, he wrote, and thought their refusal to accept binding arbitration "in plain English . . . amount to this, that it is not for their interest, to have the rights of the HBC, brought to a decision, & that they will therefore stave off the question as long as they can." The earl then turned to the crux of the matter:

Thus our legal rights will remain an empty name, till we can obtain such a decision, as we can expect to see supported by the public forces, unless we can in the meantime obtain a superiority of force in our own hands, so as to give effectual support to the jurisdiction & drive those who question it to become the appelants.[25]

At this point in the letter to his brother-in-law, he moved no further along this line of reasoning than to suggest that the HBC Committee might consider organizing company servants into a small military force if government were not forthcoming with support. Selkirk was still thinking along the lines of a small mobile force of well-armed and well-disciplined men who could be moved to any quarter "to face down all the bullies." This was William Hillier's squadron of 1811 resurrected. But Selkirk's analysis of the situation meant that in his mind the response to the Nor'westers need not stop there. All the arguments against force had been removed by the opposition, who previously might have aroused public opinion

against the employment of a private military force, instituted, (as they would have said) for the purpose of enforcing an odious & illegal monopoly. But their own outrageous conduct seems to me to have removed this ground of scruple—after the occurrences of last summer, it must be sufficiently evident, that we have to defend ourselves against every species of violence, & that for our own security we are under the necessity of organising what force we have, in such a manner as to be effective.

Selkirk was clearly gearing up to meet force with force.

SELKIRK AND THE USE OF FORCE

In the concluding paragraphs of his letter to his brother-in-law, Selkirk demonstrated the ability to seize the opportunity at hand that would serve him so well over the next months. While contemplating the need for force, he wrote, he had learned of a large body of soldiers who would be discharged in early spring. These men, survivors of European campaigns that had weeded out those not of a robust constitution, would make an ideal private army and first-rate settlers. Selkirk suggested that he would defray half the expense of recruiting these soldiers from the regiments of De Meuron and Watteville "for our mutual defense."[26]

Colvile was already attempting desperately to provide the evidence the government required "as to the persons really guilty of the disturbances" in the West, but he was not likely to be successful.[27] John Halkett reported, after examining the exchanges of letters between the company and the government, as well as the available documentation that could be laid before the colonial secretary, that it appeared unlikely that Lord Bathurst would change his mind.[28] Halkett was a cousin of Lord Selkirk and had earlier been involved with the Selkirk interests in the Hudson's Bay Company, but his family position had changed in 1815 with his marriage to Selkirk's sister, Lady Katherine Douglas. For the next few years, Halkett would take upon himself the management of Selkirk's relationship with both the government and the public.[29] In a separate letter to J.H. Pelly of the HBC, Halkett at this point expressed his dissatisfaction with the government's behaviour and the difficulty of dealing with Bathurst "on a subject in which his Department appears so hostile."[30] In writing to Selkirk, Colvile merely reported the difficulties he was already experiencing in separating Selkirk's accounts from those of the company, adding that John Halkett and he had agreed that Selkirk should have no commission from the HBC as governor in the West. The cautious Colvile explained, "It would be open to animadversions if the Co. were to invest with the powers of a judge the person who is directly & principally interested in the question at issue & from the tone taken by Ld Bathurst it is necessary to be cautious & respect appearances."[31] Given this careful attitude, recruiting a private army and using it against the opposition was not something that Andrew Colvile was likely to greet with much enthusiasm.

Late in January of 1816, Selkirk visited York in Upper Canada, where he interviewed nearly thirty of the settlers who had been brought down from Red River. From them he learned that many had not liked the country from their first arrival. They complained less of the passage and the trip to the settlement than the absence of facilities when they arrived. Most of their hostility was directed against young Archie MacDonald, who had accompanied them across the Atlantic and to Red River. Miles Macdonell was a distant figure often away from the settlement, while Archie was the man who dealt with them on a daily basis. A substantial number of the settlers Selkirk spoke with thought the Pemmican Proclamation had been important, but not the key event. The turning point, argued the settlers, was the arrest of John Spencer. The officers of the settlement had refused to rescue Spencer because he had been taken under a legal warrant issued under 43 George III c. 138. This regard for Parliament suggested to the settlers that, contrary to what they had previously been led to believe, the law was not on their side. Selkirk knew that the confusion over the law in Red River was a serious problem. But he had probably not understood the legal realities on the ground. As Colin Robertson much better appreciated, in the remote areas of legal jurisdiction in the West, it was always best to act as if the law were on your side. This insight may have contributed to Selkirk's conversion to less scrupulous legal behaviour in his subsequent western adventure.

Clearly the settlers resented being caught in the crossfire between the North West Company and the Hudson's Bay Company, and being expected to bear arms in such a struggle was completely beyond their comprehension.[32] Selkirk might have also discovered from these settlers something of his own responsibility for their discontent, but that he even contemplated trying to collect some of their indebtedness to him suggests that he learned nothing of this sort. Instead, what he was told apparently merely confirmed his earlier insight that civilian settlers could not battle the enemy; experienced soldiers would have to be recruited to do the fighting. He was already negotiating with officers from the regiments to be disbanded.[33]

In a typical feverish whirl of activity, Selkirk organized his westward expedition in the late winter and early spring of 1816, at the same time that his attorneys pursued the ringleaders among the disloyal settlers of 1815. On 11 March 1816, he wrote to Sir Gordon Drummond, seeking to complete arrangements for an officer and a few soldiers to escort him into the interior. He was prepared to pay a young De Meurons officer and a few men as a subaltern's guard to protect himself from the wrath of the North West Company's wintering partners. This matter was quite separate from that of the protection of the settlement, he emphasized.[34] Drummond reluctantly agreed to the request, offering to detach a subaltern, two sergeants, and twelve men to be provisioned, conveyed west, and returned to Canada at Selkirk's charge. The soldiers were, he emphasized, to be used only to protect Selkirk against assassins or robbers.[35]

ESCALATING EVENTS AT RED RIVER

While Lord Selkirk was arranging his journey west, at Red River Colin Robertson had been especially active. Robertson visited Duncan Cameron at Fort Gibraltar at the end of February and warned him against alarming the settlers. Robertson wrote to Governor Semple, who was at Brandon House, that some danger was to be apprehended. He advised Semple that in the spring the settlers should not be placed upon their lands or allowed to farm them. Instead, they should remain within Fort Douglas until the period of danger had passed.[36] Settlers reported to Robertson that Duncan Cameron was openly boasting that he had driven them away once and could do it again. Robertson decided to seize the Nor'wester trading post at Fort Gibraltar as "a preventative measure," in the process imprisoning Duncan Cameron and seizing his papers. Robertson did not hesitate to read Cameron's correspondence. Robertson later insisted that he found in Cameron's room an open letter in the Nor'wester's handwriting inviting Aboriginal people to pillage in the spring. This letter led Robertson to seize the remaining papers at Fort Gibraltar and ship them to Fort Douglas for careful scrutiny. Among these papers were a number of earlier letters written between HBC people, which had been opened and obviously read. Robertson also found a circular letter from Cameron and Alexander Macdonell written from Qu'Appelle in February of 1816 saying, "The spirit of our people particularly the Halfbreeds will require to be roused, and we think that the appearance of a few of their color from the nearest posts would again have the desired effect."

What Robertson found in the material encouraged him to detain and open the current letters in the North West Company's eastbound express, which arrived while he was occupying the fort. On 18 March, John Siveright, a clerk of the NWC at Fort Gibraltar, had asked Robertson whether he intended to stop the winter express as it passed the Forks. Robertson replied that he had three men ready to seize the express, but if it were not concealed he would be satisfied with examining the letters from Qu'Appelle, Swan River, and Fort des Prairies. If these contained no evidence of plans against the settlement the express could proceed. Otherwise, he would detain it until Semple's arrival. In the mail packet, he discovered evidence that he was certain demonstrated "a diabolical plan on the part of the N.W. Co. to destroy the Colony of Red River."[37] The letters certainly evinced a clear determination on the part of the Nor'west wintering partners to continue the struggle with the Hudson's Bay Company and the colony, although, as James Hughes wrote, the sooner both companies united the better, "for if we go on & contend one with the other we can but loose our time & get indebted."[38] A letter from Alexander (Greenfield) Macdonell at Qu'Appelle read: "A storm is gathering to the Northward ready to burst on the heads of the rascals who deserve it; little do they know their situation last year was but a joke. The new nation under their leaders are coming forward to clear their native soil of intruders and assassins." This letter did not say that the "new nation" was being stirred up by the Nor'westers, but in another letter Macdonell wrote: "Sir William Shaw is collecting all the Halfbreeds in the surrounding departments, and has ordered his friends in this quarter to prepare to take the field; he has actually taken every Halfbreed in the country to the Forks from Fort des Prairie, it is supposed they will when collected altogether form more than one hundred, God knows the result."[39] According to Peter Fidler's later account, the arrival of the express at Qu'Appelle before Robertson's seizure had seen the hoisting of a "halfbreed flag," which he described as "about 4 1/2 feet square, red & in the middle a large figure of Eight horizontally of a different colour."[40] The flag had been earlier displayed the previous fall for Alexander (Greenfield) Macdonell. Rumours circulated within the region about the gathering of those of mixed descent and their intentions to destroy the settlement. Those of mixed descent were assembling, and the leadership of the settlement was becoming increasingly nervous about what James Sutherland described as "something desperate" to be undertaken by the North West Company and their allies.[41]

In Red River, Governor Semple arrived back at the Forks from a western tour of his territories at the end of March. His immediate instinct was to allow the detained express to proceed, but when he had read some of the opened correspondence he decided to retain it as evidence of the NWC intentions. Semple prepared a series of charges against the captured Duncan Cameron, including the accusation that the latter was planning to renew atrocities this year.[42] Colin Robertson advocated sending Cameron and the intercepted letters to Hudson Bay and thence to England, but Semple insisted "that he did not see any harm the said Cameron could do as a Prisoner."[43] This disagreement appears to have marked the opening of the quarrel that would end with Robertson's departure from the settlement in early June. From Robertson's perspective, Semple (whom Robertson persistently referred to in his writings as "Mr. Simple") placed too much trust in both friends and enemies in a place that was "a hotbed of Hypocrisy, desertion, and party spirit."[44] Robertson did not approve of the release of all the traders arrested except Cameron, despite their solemn promises not to disturb the tranquility of the settlement. He continued to advocate the dispatch of Duncan Cameron and the captured express to England. He also recommended that forts Douglas and Gibraltar be consolidated in order to make their defence easier.

Robertson also insisted that all the settlers should reside at or near one of the forts and should not be placed on their farms until the menace was over. Although he and Colin Robertson were not getting along together very well, Semple wrote a note of approval to Robertson for his aggressive treatment of the Nor'westers. The treatment was demanded by the conduct of the Nor'westers, the governor wrote, and the seizure of the express "was a step arising out of the former and which has happily furnished its own justification to the fullest extent."[45] This letter temporarily covered the growing rift between Semple and Robertson, but the two men were temperamentally at opposite poles. Semple was a gentleman of honour, while Robertson was a realist without scruples. One of the many mysteries of this period is the discrepancy between the swashbuckling Robertson of 1815–16 and the man so easily crushed by George Simpson in the later 1820s. For some reason, Robertson lost his edge over the years.

Hudson's Bay Company men in the region became more shrill in their warnings of potential trouble. Peter Fidler wrote to Semple of rumours that the settlement would be attacked by 150 men in the spring. He warned, "*The Forks is the Key to all.*" James Sutherland reported from Qu'Appelle that alarming stories were frightening his men, and he desperately needed reinforcements.[46] Fidler emphasized to Semple that some of the freemen and those of mixed descent were temporarily neutral, only waiting to see who "should be Masters of the Territory."[47] Semple sent a party of reinforcements to Brandon, instructing its leader to avoid acts of hostility, but to regard those people of mixed descent as part of the North West Company.[48]

SELKIRK TURNS TO FORCE

The day after James Sutherland's warning was written in the west, Sir Gordon Drummond attempted to dissuade Selkirk from his journey to the interior, again emphasizing that the military escort was for his personal protection only.[49] For his part, Selkirk attempted to establish whether the Nor'westers were entitled to the military commissions they had allegedly employed earlier at Red River.[50] Warnings of the danger of the journey he was undertaking came to Selkirk from all directions, including one from his agent at York, who was preparing the supplies and boats for the expedition.[51] But Selkirk continued with his preparations. Selkirk felt considerably heartened by the latest intelligence from Red River, writing to Thomas Vincent that Robertson had not only re-established the settlement, but had also "found means to reduce his antagonists to submission."[52] At the end of March Selkirk wrote to Colin Robertson that he hoped to arrive at the settlement sufficiently accompanied to prevent trouble. Three or four "fully manned" canoes would be dispatched under the command of Miles Macdonell, who was on bail after being taken east in 1815 by the Nor'westers. Robertson was to arrest the ringleaders of the destruction of the colony in 1815, using warrants that Selkirk was forwarding. The earl realized it would be necessary to evict the North West Company by force, but wanted it done regularly under a legal warrant from the governor.[53] This crucial dispatch and its enclosures were entrusted to Jean-Baptiste Lagimodiére, who was returning to Red River overland.[54] Lagimodiére was a Quebec-born ex-employee of the North West Company who in 1806 had married a Cana-dian wife and settled in the west as a freeman.[55] He had worked for Miles Macdonell as a buffalo hunter in 1812–13 and was one of the few freemen to support the settlement. In 1815–16 he had made a legendary journey overland from Red River to Montreal, mainly on snowshoes, to bring Lord Selkirk information about the state of the settlement. According to the oral traditions of the family, Lagimodiére had arrived at Selkirk's house in Montreal in the middle of a Hogmaney party, bursting into the festivities with his melancholy news.

As part of his strategy of protecting Red River, Selkirk in early April opened a correspondence with Bishop Duplessis of Lower Canada about a missionary presence in the region. Selkirk offered to support a priest to minister to "Vagabond Canadians" who, "having renounced all idea of returning to their native places," were really in need of spiritual guidance.[56] The earl had probably gotten the idea from his conversations with Jean-Baptiste Lagimodiére, who was undoubtedly the first live freeman he had ever met. To Sir Gordon Drummond, Selkirk sent a request for a repudiation of those in the West claiming to be Voyageur officers. He reassured Drummond that the presence of royal troops as a bodyguard would prevent the North West Company from attacking him, and argued that the Nor'Westers had no influence over the local Aboriginal people, whose support of the settlers at Red River in 1815 "experimentally proved" his point.[57] For the first time, Selkirk was distinguishing between Aboriginal people and those of mixed descent, although at this point those of mixed descent were reducing the distinction between the two peoples with their insistence on land claims based on the First Peoples heritage.

Although Selkirk would not receive the letter for some time, HBC head Joseph Berens from London was now advocating that Selkirk press a legal confrontation in Canada against the North West Company, using the arrests of Miles Macdonell and John Spencer as the issue.[58] Berens himself admitted that his position was based on an English jurist's understanding of English laws, anticipating the same principles in Montreal. When Selkirk eventually did take the North West Company to court, he would find that the same legal principles could be quite differently interpreted in Canadian and English courts. Berens concluded by observing that Lord Bathurst's neutrality was angering the Nor'Westers as much as Hudson's Bay Company members. This was an acknowledgement that—at this point in the situation—the English government was not necessarily favouring the North West Company, although neutrality undoubtedly worked to the advantage of the side with the better position on the scene, both in the Canadas and in Red River. At this point, that side was the Canadian company.

Meanwhile, Nor'wester John Mure entered into what he himself acknowledged as an unauthorized attempt to resolve the conflict between the two companies.[59] The Glasgow-born Mure had been a major Quebec merchant since the 1780s, and his involvement in the fur trade was always a secondary part of his investment portfolio. At the end of the War of 1812, he took steps to reduce his firm's role in the fur trade. Mure's firm in 1816 was serving as a shipping agent for Selkirk, and this business connection undoubtedly encouraged his intervention in the corporate conflict. As his earlier actions suggested, Mure was not happy with the ruinous cost of competition in the fur trade. He saw the simple solution in North West Company purchase or lease of Hudson's Bay Company rights. This solution would have involved acknowledgement of the HBC charter, which was why Mure's intervention was unauthorized. At the same time, Mure realized that the settlement at Red River might impede such a resolution, writing, "Your Lordship will I think admit that much greater profits would arise to all concerned by a unity of management & I presume that profit is the object with every man interested in either Co'y unless it be your Lordship with whom it can be but a secondary object." Without some arrangement, however, Mure insisted, "one or the other must ultimately go to the wall."[60] Mure was one of the few Nor'wester leaders who recognized that Selkirk's motives were not simply the bottom line. Had his colleagues also understood this, the dispute might have taken a different turn. The McGillivrays certainly failed to appreciate the extent of and reasons for Selkirk's commitment to Red River.

In mid-April of 1816, Selkirk's relations with Sir Gordon Drummond, never very cordial to begin with, started deteriorating badly. Drummond had plainly bridled at this British "Milord" dropping into Lower Canada as an important protagonist in the fur trade. The key issue was the armed escort that Drummond had agreed to provide and about which he was now having sober second thoughts. He accused Selkirk of intending to employ the escort to protect his servants and followers, adding that the North West Company partners had already requested military escorts, to which they claimed they were as entitled as Selkirk.[61] Selkirk had already insisted that he was not planning to extend the protection of his escort to his followers. At the same time, he pointed out to Drummond that if the escort did not defend his dependents, they would themselves have to be armed. The earl refrained from noting that the real problem was the absence of legal authority in the West.[62] Drummond accepted the assurances for the moment, but was clearly not happy.[63]

Although Selkirk would not have the letter for some weeks, John Halkett reported from London on the results of an interview with Lord Bathurst that he had arranged between the colonial secretary and independent members of Parliament friendly to the earl. Bathurst had insisted that government could not place blame in the fur-trade struggle and therefore could not interfere in it. He thought the issues could be solved in the Canadian courts. But ominously, Bathurst strongly objected to Selkirk's involvement in the whole business and especially to the Red River settlement, saying the scheme was "a *wild and unpromising* one."[64] Although he did not say so, John Halkett must have realized that Lord Bathurst understandably did not wish to be forced to assume British authority over half of North America to protect one small settlement established by a private proprietor. In the nineteenth century, the British government was often a most reluctant imperialist, forced to take action to safeguard the lives of its reckless citizens. As far as Red River was concerned, Halkett warned Selkirk not to suppose that ultimately there will be support from government, for only opposition and hostility were to be found in Downing Street.

Despite the unpromising tone of Sir Gordon Drummond's correspondence, Selkirk continued to press him as if he were favourably disposed. News from Red River had led Selkirk to write again to Drummond. The earl learned that the settlement had been re-established by Colin Robertson and Robert Semple. He offered to pay for additional soldiers himself. If Drummond did nothing, Selkirk argued, "many lives may be lost."[65] The only response Selkirk received was a brief note observing that Drummond had a new dispatch from Lord Bathurst about "mutual outrage" in the West. The governor requested that Selkirk convey to the Hudson's Bay Company people the necessity of refraining from violence.[66] Two days later, he complained that Selkirk was urging him to action on points he had already dealt with, adding that he hoped his letters to Selkirk and the Nor'westers would prevent "a repetition of the mutual proceedings and outrages."[67] Selkirk could only deny that the outrages were mutual.[68]

John Mure had to be handled with even more care than Sir Gordon Drummond. In a measured response to the Montreal merchant, Selkirk protested that he had no intention of attempting to ruin the North West Company. All he sought, he insisted, was to confirm his own legal rights and those of the Hudson's Bay Company. He added that the directors of the HBC were not willing to give up management of their affairs or the superintendency of their territories, and he would regard abandonment of his people and the inhabitants of the territory to the Nor'westers as a dereliction of moral duty. Even should the HBC decide to come to terms, he emphasized, he controlled Red River as a "separate and independent property," and was operating it apart from the company except insofar as it introduced law and order "into a Country where force has hitherto been the rule of right."[69] Despite his protestations of independence, however, the activities of Selkirk's settlement and those of the Hudson's Bay Company were increasingly becoming intertwined, especially since the earl was in North America commanding both ventures. As the company's Montreal agents explained to the London Committee, "the operations of Lord Selkirk appear to be so much blended with those of the company, that we cannot at the present moment more accurately determine the proportion of expense." Only Selkirk himself could sort out the responsibility for expenditures upon his return to England.[70]

John Mure could only reply to Selkirk that he hoped the earl's opinions about the North West Company were founded on misrepresentations. It was certainly the case that Selkirk was mistaken about the "undeniable legal title" of the Hudson's Bay Company, and the North West Company merely sought equal rights until the matter was decided by a proper legal tribunal. Perhaps a personal visit to Red River would change Selkirk's opinions.[71]

At this point Sir Gordon Drummond was relieved of his governorship by Major-General John Wilson. Drummond had earlier asked to be replaced as quickly as possible—citing health and family reasons for needing to return to Britain—because he knew his appointment was not permanent. He had not realized that these excuses would prevent him from being appointed to Nova Scotia. Already in a bad temper, he was further aggravated by Wilson's tardy arrival and an "extremely unpleasant" altercation over the exchange of authority with his successor. Not surprisingly, therefore, one of the final acts of his administration was to rescind the official armed escort he had previously agreed to provide to Lord Selkirk, on the grounds that the De Meuron regiment was to be disbanded and he had no other troops available.[72] Drummond may have thus hoped to keep Selkirk from venturing into the Indian Territories, but his decision not to provide the small contingent of soldiers was more than likely merely a result of general ill temper. Life often works that way.

Lord Selkirk did not try to deal with Drummond's successor, beyond forwarding documentation about the North West Company's actions in the west, requesting that it be kept secret until his return from the Indian Territories, since the government seemed determined to misconstrue his motives through "unwarrantable insinuations."[73] The earl did write Lieutenant Governor Gore in Upper Canada that he would soon appear in York to take magistrates' oaths for the Indian Territories.[74] He would head west with proper legal powers. The problem here, of course, was that both of the contending parties in the West could hold commissions under 43 George III, cap. 138, ultimately leading to an unseemly and almost fatal conflict of legal authority. To replace his cancelled guard, Selkirk acquired soldiers from the disbanded Swiss regiments. All the soldiers were recruited as settlers. To common soldiers he offered lands ready for cultivation in the settlement and $8 per month to get there. Making clear his intentions, Selkirk wrote Captain Steiger of the de Watteville regiment that he did not expect long service from his "settlers," but merely a year's employment. The numbers were to be substantial, as many as eighty men from each of the De Meuron and De Watteville units.[75] Drummond's action of cancellation of the guard had not deterred Selkirk from heading west, but instead put him at the head of a large contingent of mercenaries without any possible government complaint. Drummond had not reckoned with Selkirk's determination and flexibility. The addition of substantial numbers of disciplined troops into the fur-trade conflict would, at least in the short run, make an enormous difference to the struggle between the contending rivals. Whatever the moral and legal implications of the recruitment and use of the mercenaries, it was a brilliant stroke.

THE "NEW NATION" GATHERS

While Selkirk was dealing with preparations for his expedition, including provisioning and armaments, Peter Fidler was warning Robert Semple from Brandon House to stay close to the settlement, as the governor might be captured as an "equivalent" for Duncan Cameron by an ever-increasing number of people of mixed descent gathering in the region.[76] Fidler could only hope that the Canadians "will consider their own Interest & not rouse the old Lyon again."[77] More than pious hopes would be required to prevent the impending confrontation. By the time of Fidler's letter, those of mixed descent—under the leadership of Cuthbert Grant—had already swung into action. Cuthbert Grant was not typical of the Métis, but his background does suggest some of the complexities of the origins of that people.[78] He had been born in 1793 in what is now Saskatchewan, the son of a Scots fur trader employed by the North West Company and a Métis woman. Brought to Montreal by his guardian, he was educated there and baptized in the Scots Presbyterian Church. When he returned to the west, he was fluently bilingual. Grant was one of four men—three of them of Scottish origin on their fathers' side—appointed by Duncan Cameron as "captains of the Métis" in the autumn of 1814. By 1816 he was "Captain-General of all the Half-Breeds" and the commander of the local cavalry. In early May the HBC trader James Sutherland set out with his furs from Qu'Appelle for the bay, having been assured by Alexander (Greenfield) Macdonell that he could proceed unmolested down river. Sutherland and his party of six bateaux were subsequently stopped in a crooked and rapid part of the river below Qu'Appelle by a large party of Canadians and those of mixed descent.[79] According to Peter Fidler, the attackers had "their faces all painted in the most horrid & terrific forms & dressed like Indians and all armed with Guns, Pictols, Swords & Spears, & several had Bows & Arrows; and made the War-whoop or yell like the Natives in immediately attacking their Enemies."[80] The cargo of furs and provisions was seized. Sutherland and his party were forced to sign an agreement not to bear arms against the NWC before they were released, after having been kept prisoners for a week. Upon learning of this incident, Governor Semple decided finally to send Duncan Cameron and the captured evidence to York Factory to be shipped to England. Cameron was never brought to trial in England, and after his return to Canada in 1820, he sued Colin Robertson for false imprisonment.

The settlers had returned from their winter haven at Pembina at the end of April, and Governor Semple had immediately sought to locate them on their land. They were assigned separate lots, given seed, and encouraged to plant extensively. At the end of May, a number of settlers placed on their lands came to Colin Robertson, still in charge of Fort Gibraltar, and asked him to shelter them until the dangers being rumoured in the region had passed. Robertson answered that they must apply to Governor Semple, who told them to remain on their lands. The "differences of opinion" between Robertson and Semple had reached breaking point, and Robertson debated leaving the settlement "if he could not concur in the expedience which he doubted, of the measures to be taken for their [the settlers'] common protection.[81]

SELKIRK'S FIRST PARTIES OF REINFORCEMENT

While Robertson and Semple were disagreeing about strategy at the settlement, Lord Selkirk's people had begun heading west. The first to depart had been Jean-Baptiste Lagimodière with documents and dispatches for Colin Robertson. Although he was an experienced bushman, Lagimodière was not a very discreet messenger. As he travelled west, he told whoever would listen to him in the drinking places of Upper Canada where he stopped of the importance of his mission. Word soon got out to the Nor'westers, who sent orders for his capture and the seizure of his dispatches. Lagimodière was eventually captured near Fond du Lac (now Superior, Minnesota) on 16 June 1816. No pretence of legal warrants was offered for this action, which was in fact a kidnapping. Lagimodière's dispatches were read eagerly by the Nor'westers at Fort William, who reached new heights of anger at the thought of being summarily "evicted" from the Forks. Excerpts from the captured documents were later used in NWC polemics as evidence of Selkirk's intentions. In addition to Lagimodière, two separate expeditions departed west to relieve Red River. One left York in early May. It consisted of both men and draft animals. It was headed by Miles Macdonell, still on bail from charges filed against him in

Lower Canada. Miles had been feeling guilty about surrendering in 1815, and Selkirk had given in to his importunities to be allowed to help in 1816, partly because he still held a formal commission of appointment as governor of Assiniboia. From Nottawasaga, on the southern shore of Georgian Bay, Miles reported in late May that "this is the most disagreeable service I have been employed in," with men selling their provisions and equipment along the road for liquor, and the teams slowing down the party.[82] Meanwhile, Captain Frederick Matthey, formerly of the De Meuron regiment, was bringing another party from Lower Canada to join up with Selkirk at Sault Ste Marie.

In late May Selkirk reported to the Hudson's Bay Company London Committee and to Joseph Berens on his activities. To Berens he wrote that he was planning to press a conspiracy case against the North West Company partners for the dispersal of the settlement in 1815, as Berens had earlier requested. He hoped to collect more evidence on his trip to the interior. Regardless of the results, he was persuaded that the publicity generated by a lawsuit would help with both the Colonial Office and the public.[83] He apologized to the committee for failing to distinguish sufficiently between company and Red River accounts, adding that he had no time at the moment to straighten matters out.[84]

At virtually the same moment, William Mure, the manager of Selkirk's estate in Kirkcudbright—which remained the basis of his income and fortune—ominously reported that the coming of peace had brought a general decline in agricultural prosperity in Great Britain. According to Mure, cattle prices had fallen, grain prices were down, and a severe winter had taken its toll. Although most of Selkirk's lands had been let to tenants, they were offering lower rents than expected and rental arrearages were building. To make matters worse, paying the interest on Selkirk's accumulated debt in Edinburgh had not been easy, and he doubted he could transfer large sums of cash to Andrew Colvile in London to pay for the costs of the settlement. He was sorry to send "so deplorable an account of our situation," concluded Mure, but the financial difficulties were likely to continue.[85] Not surprisingly, Thomas Coutts and Company, the earl's London bankers, would shortly thereafter refuse to accept another large twelve-month bill from Selkirk, citing lack of funds and company policy.[86] How much Selkirk knew of his financial situation at the time he headed west is not clear, but he must have had some inkling that all was not well. The large costs of establishing

Red River had been born in part from inflated wartime estate revenues and in part from extensive borrowings in the money markets. The post-war collapse of the economy, as much as Selkirk's increasingly manic expenditures to resurrect his settlement and bring the North West Company to book for its dispersals, would bring him to the brink of financial ruin.

SEVEN OAKS

While Colin Robertson and Governor Semple were in disagreement but still talking to one another, Brandon House was attacked on 1 June by a party of those of mixed descent, Canadians, and First Peoples. Postmaster Peter Fidler later described the scene: "A little after noon about 48 Canadians, half-Breeds, & Indians, but most half-Breeds appeared in the plain all in horse back with the Half-Breeds flag flying, this little army marched in regular order in an oblong square; one was near the middle beating an Indian drum & accompanying it with an Indian Song, the greater part of the rest bearing Chorus."[87] The party galloped to a point opposite the NWC fort on the opposite side of the river, then turned their horses and charged suddenly into the HBC fort, manned by only a few under-armed HBC servants. They ransacked the post and celebrated for days, while residents of the post—most of whom were fur-trade families living in buildings outside the fort itself—moved out on to the plains to take shelter with the First Peoples. The attackers eventually moved down the river toward the Forks. No one was seriously injured in this incident, although Brandon House had been stripped of its rum, tobacco, and ammunition. The "new nation" had intimidated fur traders and settlers alike. It had destroyed property but not actually killed anyone.

Word was brought to Fort Douglas of the destruction of Brandon House on 9 June. The Aboriginal person who reported this news also claimed that Alexander (Greenfield) Macdonell—with Canadians, people of mixed descent, and First Peoples—was heading down the Assiniboine River publicly proclaiming an intention to destroy the settlement. Governor Semple finally decided that at least one of Colin Robertson's long-expressed views was justified. Two forts could not be defended. He marched to Fort Gibraltar, still occupied by Robertson, to order its destruction and the movement of its palisades to help protect Fort Douglas. Although Semple had now accepted the amalgamation of the forts, he still did not want to keep the settlers within Fort Douglas. Robertson later argued that he did not want to remain in Fort

Douglas with Semple while the two men were still at loggerheads.[88] He requested permission to depart from Red River for the Athabasca. The request was granted. Robertson allegedly dramatically left with the parting words, "the Colony is nearly ruined— time will show who has been the cause of it."[89] At Lake Winnipeg he had second thoughts, and he returned to within fifteen miles of the Forks. Here he paused and wrote Semple offering his services. The governor declined, writing back that Sheriff Alexander Macdonell had already replaced Robertson, who then resumed his journey west. On 16 June an Aboriginal man named Moustache arrived at Fort Douglas, claiming to have escaped from the invaders, who were encamped at Portage la Prairie. He said that the heavily armed party would arrive at the Forks in a day or two. The chiefs of the local Saulteaux generously offered to assist the settlement, but Semple—in the first of several fateful miscalculations—said it was not necessary.

While the forces opposing the settlement were gathering strength, and those at the Forks were engaged in disagreement, Lord Selkirk was still in Canada waiting for his hastily assembled party to come together. At the end of May, he learned to his surprise that in the end the government would manage to find a small contingent from the troops stationed at Drummond's Island at the Sault to serve as a personal escort.[90]

In mid-June he wrote a last-minute series of letters. To the English evangelical William Smith, he emphasized his pleasure at the support of friends "amidst the harassing circumstances with which this contest has been accompanied," and the hope that men like Smith and William Wilberforce would help in preventing the British government from acting prematurely on affairs in the Indian Territories before the full facts were known.[91] This letter sounded as if Selkirk had already decided to defy Lord Bathurst. To Lord Melville, Selkirk reported his imminent departure for the interior, "out of reach of all communication with the civilized world."[92] A lengthy letter to incoming governor Sir John Sherbrooke made another plea for a "small military party" to "repress or rather to overawe such attempts" as had been made by the servants and dependents of the North West Company to break up his settlement.[93] Sherbrooke was a career soldier who had served in India and against Napoleon before being appointed lieutenant governor of Nova Scotia in 1811.[94] He was commissioned governor-in-chief of British America on 10 April 1816. In constant ill health and known as a man with a passionate temper, Sherbrooke would later be as supportive of Selkirk as was possible given his instructions. But at this point he had not yet arrived in Lower Canada from Halifax, and he was unlikely to understand fully Selkirk's arguments. Admitting that he had taken advantage of the disbanding of regiments to augment the number of his settlers, Selkirk insisted that he was now less anxious about the problem of protection. But he still wanted his settlement's treatment by the Nor'westers investigated and his own position vindicated. Red River, he maintained, was in the national interest, since only "an agricultural population, having a permanent interest in the Country, can render it a valuable & secure possession of the British Empire," while protecting the west from American encroachments.[95]

After many delays, Lord Selkirk and his party finally departed for the Indian Territories on 18 June 1816. A day later, the Battle of Seven Oaks would be fought on the banks of the Red River. Selkirk had waited too long.

CHAPTER SEVENTEEN

Seven Oaks and
Fort William, 1816

L ORD SELKIRK FINALLY LEFT Montreal for Red River on 18 June 1816. To avoid being ambushed by the North West Company somewhere around Fort William, he planned to travel to his settlement via the old voyageur route along the proposed international boundary. This route is known today as the "Border Lakes Route." It leaves Lake Superior at the mouth of the Pigeon River at Grand Portage, extends 200 miles west through Gunflint and Basswood lakes, and rejoins the later route west at Lac la Croix.[1] Despite the impression left by much of the writing on Selkirk, he did not travel into the west accompanied only by voyageurs, although he would not pick up his military escort of a sergeant and six men from the 37th Regiment until he reached Drummond's Island near Sault Ste Marie. The earl was accompanied, probably in his own canoe, by his manservant William—we never do learn his surname—and by Dr. John Allan, a Royal Navy surgeon who was his personal physician. Both had been with him since he had left Liverpool in 1815. Allan would become more than a doctor; he would serve as confidante and right hand man to Selkirk, turning extremely partisan in the later legal struggles in the Canadas. In his North American tour of 1803–04, Selkirk had travelled with a personal manservant but not with a doctor. The presence of such a medical figure here suggests that Selkirk was still in somewhat uncertain health.

A large party of additional companions also headed west with Selkirk in 1816. Three of these men started from Montreal. One was Archibald McDonald, who was returning to the West after a voyage to England, where he had prepared an account of the dispersal of the settlement for publication in 1816. Another was Captain Jean-Baptiste Chevalier de Lorimier, a soldier of mixed descent (his mother was an Iroquois from Caughnawaga) who had spent much time in prisons during the War of 1812 that had damaged his health. He was made a captain in the Embodied Indian Warriors in 1814 and had been seconded by the government to Selkirk as a guide and interpreter.[2] Also part of the group with Selkirk was young William Laidlaw, a young Scots farmer who had been taken on by the earl at his father's behest in 1815. He was to run the settlement farm on shares. At the Bay of Quinte, the little group was joined by Lieutenant A.B. Becher of the Royal Navy, who had been ordered by Captain William Fitz William Owen (who was then surveying the Great Lakes for the British government) to travel west with Lord Selkirk to make observations and sketches. Allan, Lorimier, and Becher formed a triumvirate of "gentlemen" later joined at Fort William by Captains Frederick Matthey and Proteus D'Orsonnens of the De Meuron Regiment. These men became quite close to one another and to Selkirk during their adventures together over the next few months. They all passed well beyond being neutral observers to becoming active partisans on behalf of Selkirk and his settlers. The way in which all these individuals became willingly co-opted by Selkirk is a measure of his attractiveness as a man and a leader.

Selkirk left behind in Montreal his wife, Jean Lady Selkirk. She was in charge of his Canadian business in a more than nominal sense. Like many female members of the Scottish upper classes, Jean Wedderburn Douglas had been well educated and prepared for a life of managing the business of an aristocratic household. She was not only loyal, astute, and thoroughly conversant with her husband's affairs, but she was also a skilled hostess blessed with great beauty who charmed most of the males who came in contact with her. It is likely that more than one of Selkirk's associates was secretly in love with her. From her base in Montreal, Lady Selkirk directed her husband's Canadian enterprises. She dealt with the merchants supplying the fur trade and the settlement, as well as with the lawyers defending Selkirk's position. As the sister of Andrew Wedderburn-Colvile, she was able to inform her brother of what was happening in Canada in the course of what were ostensibly chatty family letters. When Selkirk subsequently put himself at risk through his behaviour, Lady Selkirk travelled to Quebec to plead his case with Sir John Sherbrooke, the governor of Lower Canada. Jean became immediate friends with the Sherbrookes, and remained close to

Lady Sherbrooke for many years.[3] The friendship with Lady Sherbrooke was particularly crucial, because it supplied Lady Selkirk with inside information about the thinking and actions of the governor.

The journey westward was initially uneventful. At Drummond's Island, the British military outpost to the south of Sault Ste Marie in Lake Huron (now on the American side of the border), the Selkirk party on 22 July attended a public council with the local First Peoples and the Indian Department. Here Catawabety, a Chippewa chief from Sandy Lake, told the gathering that the North West Company people at Fond du Lac had offered him rum and other presents if he and his people would make war on the Red River settlement. He had refused, said the chief, because the Nor'westers admitted that they had no military orders for such action. Catawabety further testified that James Grant (the NWC partner at Fond du Lac) had offered him a reward if he would send his young men after some Hudson's Bay Company messengers who were heading west earlier in the spring. This was Selkirk's first intimation that Jean-Baptiste Lagimodière might not have gotten through with his dispatches to the settlement. When asked by the earl about the First Peoples at the Forks, the Chippewa chief assured Selkirk that they were quite pleased that the settlement had been established.

Two days later, the Selkirk party was packing up to depart from Drummond's Island when Miles Macdonell burst into Charles Ermatinger's house at the Falls of St. Mary to report that he had been within a day of arriving at Red River when he learned of the incident at Seven Oaks. Miles had written on 7 July from Lac la Pluie, on the Winnipeg River, with news of the disaster, advising Selkirk—whom he assumed must surely be well into the interior—to return east until more forces could be collected. "If we lose you, My Lord, all is lost."[4] Miles had then turned around and attempted to intercept his employer lest he blunder into the opposition. Miles outdistanced his letter. According to John Allan, Selkirk was exhausted and asleep in his tent when Miles arrived, and so was not told of this news until the following morning. There is a suggestion here that the earl was not very well at this point. Selkirk's immediate response to the news was that Semple was too sensible to have provoked violence. Macdonell also reported that several Red River officials and settlers, including P.C. Pambrun, John Pritchard, John Bourke, Louis Nolin, John Spencer, and Donald McPherson, were all being held at Fort William. Most of these people had been eyewitnesses to the events at the Forks.

SEVEN OAKS

It would take months for contemporaries to reconstruct fully the events at Red River, and some aspects of the unfolding crisis have always remained shrouded in mystery. On 19 June at about 7 p.m., a man using a spyglass in the watch house at Fort Douglas spotted a party of armed men on horseback moving slowly across the prairie. "The half-breeds are coming, the half-breeds are coming," he shouted. The party apparently consisted of about sixty men of mixed descent, free Canadians, and First Peoples—accounts of the numbers varied from fifty to seventy—with those of mixed descent in the majority. It was led by Cuthbert Grant and Alexander Fraser. The horsemen would subsequently maintain that they were attempting to bypass Fort Douglas and the settlement, but there was nothing but open prairie behind them. They could have made a much wider sweep to the northwest had they wanted to ensure that they were avoiding trouble. The armed party had come up to the lots of the settlers, who were weeding potatoes in the fields, when Governor Semple asked for twenty volunteers from the fort to accompany him to meet the intruders. Six officers from the fort joined the makeshift platoon.

Semple was particularly concerned for the safety of the settlers in the fields, understandable given his earlier refusal to keep them sequestered in the fort. William Coltman, the commissioner who later investigated the Seven Oaks incident for the British government, was convinced that the governor's disagreements with Colin Robertson—Semple was now being proven wrong—aggravated Semple's lack of common sense and caution on this day.[5] The governor refused to wait for his small artillery force, assuring his people that he meant no battle. Several witnesses later reported that the governor had a paper that he intended to read to the intruders. On his way to meet the horsemen, Semple was informed that some settlers had been made prisoners. These actions were probably not ordered by the leaders of the horsemen. Sheriff Alexander Macdonell thought that these imprisonments irritated Semple, who marched with his party single file along the left bank of the Red River past a number of settlers' houses until he reached a bend in the river at what was called "Seven Oaks."[6] John Pritchard, one of the few survivors of the subsequent confrontation, insisted that Semple's group had no idea how numerous the other party was. Pritchard and others also claimed that the mounted party was dressed as Indian warriors in full war paint.[7]

What ensued was almost certainly a spontaneous eruption of violence between two armed forces psychologically prepared for trouble, rather than a deliberately planned incident of mass murder. At the bend in the river, dotted with tall oak trees, the well-armed horsemen surrounded the governor's men in a rough half-moon. Most testimony agreed that at this point a Canadian named Bouché or Boucher rode up to Semple and said something like "What do you want?" John Pritchard insisted that the question was asked in an "insolent tone," which may further have annoyed the governor. After a brief verbal exchange, Semple attempted to grab at either Boucher's gun or the reins of his horse. It is not clear whether Semple gave an order to fire, or who actually fired the first shot. The preponderance of testimony is that the first shot was fired by a settler. Since most of the surviving eyewitnesses were from the party of horsemen, this weight of testimony was not surprising and may not mean very much. In any event, a round of firing, most of it from Cuthbert Grant's men, followed the initial shot. In the battle that followed, the visitors had all the advantage. Most of the settlers were not soldiers and were unfamiliar with firearms, while their opponents— hunters and plainsmen—used them almost daily.

Semple was quickly wounded and several settlers killed. Semple's wound was in his thigh. He told Cuthbert Grant, to whom he pleaded for mercy, "I am not mortally wounded, and if you could get me conveyed to the fort, I think I should live." Grant promised to do so, but in the confusion of the fighting he did not remain with the governor. Grant soon lost control over his forces, who not only continued wildly firing their weapons but also ignored various attempts on the part of the settlers to surrender. Semple himself was fatally shot in the chest by an Aboriginal named Machicabaou. When the shooting finally ended, twenty-one settlers were dead, including a number of the settlement's officers and leaders. Only one member of the visiting party was killed. In a frenzy of blood lust, some of the settlers' bodies were mutilated and stripped of their possessions following the actual battle. It was this part of the incident at Seven Oaks that Lord Selkirk and his friends always regarded as "the massacre." One of the few settlers to escape was John Pritchard, who was physically protected by a Canadian named Lavigne, whom he had known when employed with the North West Company. Up to this point, the "war" in Red River had been conducted with little loss of life. Only a handful was involved in the post-battle slaughter. Nevertheless, the brutal behaviour would horrify the world beyond Red River, confirming in the minds of many the notion that those of mixed descent were little short of savages.

Events at the settlement did not end with the battle. At daybreak on the morning after Seven Oaks, acting governor Sheriff Alexander Macdonell attempted to rally his forces. Initially the remaining settlers agreed to defend Fort Douglas, and their defensive position was a strong one. With the assistance of the local Saulteaux, Sheriff Macdonell buried the dead. Later reports that mutilated bodies were left for weeks on the battlefield to be scavenged by dogs and coyotes were false. John Pritchard arrived with a message from Cuthbert Grant and Alexander Fraser demanding that the fort be surrendered, the settlers removed, and all property abandoned. Pritchard himself circulated a petition calling for capitulation. Feeling abandoned, Sheriff Macdonell negotiated safe passage for the settlers. He made a full inventory of all the public property at Fort Douglas and turned everything over to Cuthbert Grant, who received the goods as "Clerk to the North West Company, Acting for the North West Company."[8] As Nor'wester canoes converged on the settlement from all directions, Macdonell and the settlers were allowed to leave. Macdonell's party managed to get away with the documents intercepted by Colin Robertson at Fort Gibraltar. The documents were hidden by one of the females of the settlement under her skirts. The Nor'westers detained John Pritchard. This action persuaded Macdonell that John Pritchard was really a turncoat who had been spared at Seven Oaks to sow dissension in the settlement.

The wintering partners were obviously pleased by the course of events, but no direct evidence exists that they had either planned them or taken part in them.[9] A conflicting mass of testimony emerged from the trials of some of the leading participants at York, from the controversial pamphlets and books by the two contending parties, and from William Coltman's report on the fur-trade conflict—tabled as a Blue Book in the British Parliament in 1819. It demonstrates both the difficulty in assessing responsibility for Seven Oaks and in proving that the confrontation was a conspiracy on the part of the wintering partners of the North West Company or their leaders in Montreal.[10] When Lord Selkirk heard the news of Seven Oaks at the Sault, however, he was morally certain about responsibility. It belonged to the North West Company. Selkirk must have realized that his delays in the Canadas had helped make the disaster possible, but he took Miles Macdonell's report stoically and turned almost immediately to improvising a response.

SELKIRK'S RESPONSE: THE INVASION OF FORT WILLIAM

The principal component of Selkirk's plan was to take his party, including a large number of disbanded soldiers under the command of their former officers, to Fort William, the western headquarters of the North West Company. Here he would seek judicial examination of those who would be assembling shortly at the post for the annual meeting of the wintering partners. Evidence could be collected both on the general activities of the Nor'westers against the colony and on those leading to the death of Semple and the colonists. Although he held a magistrate's commission, Selkirk realized that as an interested party his investigations would be tainted. He therefore attempted to find an impartial magistrate to accompany him to Fort William. He asked John Askin, an Indian Department official and magistrate at Drummond's Island, but Askin answered he could not spare the time. He did provide Selkirk with a set of provincial statutes, a copy of Burns's *Justice of the Peace* (the standard manual of the day for magistrates), and a French Bible for taking oaths.[11] Selkirk also asked Charles O. Ermatinger, an independent trader and magistrate at the Sault, to go with him to Fort William. Ermatinger also begged off, although he helped Selkirk interview an Aboriginal man who had been accompanying Jean-Baptiste Lagimodière when he had been seized and stripped of his dispatches.[12]

Ironically enough, further details of Seven Oaks arrived at the Sault in the form of a letter from North West Company leader William McGillivray at Fort William. McGillivray had been born into poverty in the Highlands of Scotland and was adopted by his uncle Simon McTavish, who brought him into the North West Company in 1784. In 1804, he succeeded his uncle as head of the NWC, and was from the outset a fervent opponent of Selkirk and the HBC, saying "we cannot remain passive spectators to the violence used to plunder or destroy our property."[13] A self-made fur baron with an ambition to own large amounts of land, McGillivray was hardly likely to be sympathetic to Selkirk's pretensions. His letter reported that the settlement had been attacked by some Aboriginal people and people of mixed descent when no partner of the North West Company was within miles of the incident. McGillivray added that Robert Semple had been put to death despite having asked for mercy from Cuthbert Grant, a NWC clerk.[14] This news was the final straw. Apparently feeling that this attempt at impartiality would cover him given the urgency of the situation, Selkirk wrote Sir John Sherbrooke that he was proceeding to Fort William.[15] Miles

Macdonell was to take the canoe brigade to Sandy Lake and then proceed to the southern edge of the plains, south of the 49th parallel, to await instructions. If the Americans complained, Miles was to argue necessity and "wide differences of opinion as to the construction to be put on the Treaty of Peace" recently concluded.[16]

Not everyone in his party supported Selkirk's decision. A strong objection came, in writing, from John Allan, Selkirk's personal physician and companion on the expedition. Allan argued that the parties had come west on the understanding that they could be fed at the settlement. This was obviously now impossible. He added that both the American and British governments were likely to oppose "everything you may do or propose." Allan also pointed out the personal danger to Selkirk, emphasizing the difficulties even for a man in the best of health. "But in your Lordship's state of health, it would be almost surprizing if you survived it."[17] Allan's memorandum represents the first documentary indication that Selkirk's slowness in getting his relief expedition underway may have been caused by more than difficulties of organization. Although Allan was not precise about Selkirk's medical problems, they were clearly long term and life threatening, doubtless involving the consumptive condition that would ultimately kill him. Allan could not take into account the possibility of any remission of the disease, nor could he anticipate that the cool dry air of the west might be a positive benefit to a man in Selkirk's condition. Whatever the explanation, Selkirk was to thrive physically under the regimen that his doctor thought would destroy him, and serious illness would not recur until after his return to Canada more than a year later.

Selkirk and his party, now accompanied by a small military escort collected at Drummond Island, left the Sault on 2 August to canoe across Lake Superior. On 11 August Selkirk rejoined Captain Frederick Matthey and his party of disbanded De Meurons at Thunder Bay, fifteen miles east of Fort William. The twelve canoes of the Matthey brigade contained four former De Meuron officers and 100 former enlisted men, still wearing parts of their uniforms and still under military discipline. A day later, Selkirk reached the Kaministiquia River and camped in a tent a mile above Fort William, which was buzzing with activity. It was nearly time for the annual gathering—the rendezvous—of the North West Company. Business deliberations were designed to coincide with the arrival of the fur brigades from the west and the provisions brigades from the east. Fort William was not only occupied by a substantial number of NWC partners, but also by hundreds of voyageurs, employees, and Aboriginal people as well.

On August 13, John McNab, Captain D'Orsonnens, and Captain de Lorimier went to the NWC headquarters with nine soldiers, their weapons concealed. Calling for William McGillivray, the newcomers walked into the undefended fort through crowds of Nor'westers. They found McGillivray and handed him a note from Selkirk. The note said that as a magistrate Selkirk wanted to enquire into the causes of imprisonment of those being detained at Fort William. McGillivray denied that anyone was detained, but several of the prisoners later appeared at Selkirk's tent to swear affidavits about their treatment. McGillivray accepted the warrant "as a gentleman," requesting time to consult with wintering partners Kenneth McKenzie and John McLoughlin before appearing at Selkirk's tent. In a curious reversal of roles, the Nor'wester was playing the gentleman and Selkirk the ruffian. When the men of the North West Company appeared, Selkirk summarily arrested them. He then sent a party of twenty-five armed ex-soldiers commanded by their former officers back to the fort, carrying a search warrant. The Nor'westers tried to bar the gate, but the armed soldiers kept it open. A warrant for search was duly executed. A number of other partners were taken to Selkirk's tent and released on their word that no resistance or hostile moved would be taken. Once Selkirk had gained access to Fort William, he quickly discovered the prisoners who had been brought from Red River. P.C. Pambrun and John Pritchard insisted that they had been confined against their will, and Pritchard was actually in irons. From these men and others, Selkirk learned of hostile activities within the fort. Selkirk issued yet another warrant. A search found four cases of guns and forty fowling pieces loaded and primed. They had been concealed in a hayloft. Selkirk then discovered that the partners had used their paroles to empty their files and burn a number of documents. Deciding that the Nor'westers' word could not be trusted, the earl ordered the fort evacuated. His people occupied it and searched it, while he began the examination of witnesses.[18]

The absence of serious resistance to Selkirk's "invasion" requires a bit of explanation. A number of factors combined to paralyze the Nor'westers. The first factor was the element of surprise. The leaders of the North West Company at Fort William had expected that the news of Seven Oaks would induce Selkirk to turn back. Certainly nobody had expected him to go on the offensive. The second was that Selkirk was not really leading a simple party of prospective settlers to Red River. He was at the head of a small private army. Many of the soldiers were still wearing at least part of the uniforms in which they had been disbanded (allowing disbanded soldiers to keep the garments they were wearing was standard practice in the early nineteenth century). The soldiers were well armed and still under an informal military discipline. Selkirk's forces were only one-third as numerous as the total resident population of Fort William, if voyageurs and Aboriginal people were included, but they were properly commanded. The third factor was that Selkirk was a duly appointed magistrate operating within the bounds of a legality that the North West Company had never expected to have to confront. Every one in Fort William knew about the *Canada Jurisdiction Act*, which authorized magistrates appointed in the Canadas to operate in the West. But the Hudson's Bay Company usually eschewed such appointments, and, thus, normally only the Nor'westers acted as magistrates. As had been true in the Pemmican Proclamation business, the North West Company's members stood in awe of legal British authority. Operating without law as they did much of the time, the Nor'westers did not really understand about defying warrants. The ease with which Selkirk subdued the Nor'westers was the best proof possible of the accuracy of his continued insistence that a small military force authorized by government would easily quieten the Indian Territories. The North West Company had always assumed that Selkirk was an effete and ineffectual British "Milord" involved with a trading company of weaklings, while the earl had always assumed that his opposition were little more than bullies who had never been properly challenged. Fort William in 1816 demonstrated that Selkirk, rather than his opponents, had more accurately taken the measure of the enemy.

At Fort William was a building called the council room. Only partners were normally allowed to enter this room where the formal business of the North West Company was done. On 15 August in this room at the council table—in the presence of Captain Matthey, Captain Lorimier, Lieutenant Becher, constable McNab, Dr. John Allan, and former Red River sheriff John Spencer (who had been freed from confinement)—Lord Selkirk examined under oath the arrested partners. He kept notes of the examinations.[19] The Nor'wester partners denied having participated in the events at Red River. They insisted that they were not responsible for the conduct of either the wintering partners or their servants and did not have any means of controlling them. The partners maintained that they had no knowledge of property seized in Red River in 1815 and had given no rewards to any of the settlers, although some admitted they had given presents. William McGillivray allowed that Robert Semple had been killed at Seven Oaks but denied that he had been murdered. McGillivray did acknowledge that Cuthbert Grant was a clerk in the NWC service. Allan Macdonell confessed that he had Semple's double-barrelled gun and had brought it to Fort William. Most of the witnesses objected to Selkirk's use of the term "massacre" to describe Seven Oaks, altering the terminology to "battle" or "affair." Simon Fraser (of Fraser River fame) became so agitated by the examination that Selkirk suggested he retire to his room and prepare a declaration in his own handwriting. Partner Daniel McKenzie's examination was postponed until another day.

On 17 August, Selkirk wrote to Upper Canada's Solicitor General D'Arcy Boulton that he was sending to him "a Cargo of Criminals of a larger Calibre than usually came before the Courts at York," adding that evidence was mounting by the hour of "the most detestable system of villainy that was allowed to prevail in the British Dominions." It was not often, he noted, that "Acts of public justice are executed under circumstances like the present," with his 100 effectives surrounded by 300 members of the opposition, mainly "bastard Half-Breeds." He was addressing the warrants to Sandwich, but expected the chief justice of Upper Canada to deal with them himself and alter the destination if necessary.[20] The evidence Selkirk had collected was circumstantial. Twenty bales intended for the Red River department were found to contain suits of clothing; Selkirk was certain these were destined to reward those involved in Seven Oaks. In one of the NWC books was found a list of men who had received "habiliments" at Red River in June shortly after the battle. Names were ticked off. Thirteen names not ticked corresponded to the names on the clothing in the bales. In his enthusiasm over his easy victory, Selkirk forgot that he needed more than circumstantial evidence: he needed a smoking gun. In the short run, moreover, he had quite exceeded his authority as a magistrate.

Selkirk's lawyers in Montreal were well aware of the legal problems, and on the same day that Selkirk wrote to Boulton, Lady Selkirk in Montreal wrote to Sir John Sherbrooke, pleading again for government assistance for Red River. Lady Selkirk had received a letter from her husband written at the Sault, indicating that he intended to investigate the events of Red River at Fort William. That this letter was in Montreal by 17 August is a tribute to the swiftness of the canoe in the middle of summer. In her communication to Sherbrooke, Lady Selkirk's chief concern was that his authority in the West was inadequate for what needed to be done—and what he was doing. "All the magistrates for the Territories are equally parties interested," she noted, "& the Partners of the North West Company cannot be expected to offer themselves to justice."[21] What was needed was a show of proper authority. At Fort William Selkirk had been successful, but as Lady Selkirk was suggesting, his actual power as a magistrate was quite limited. Sherbrooke understandably refused to act. Lady Selkirk responded by suggesting that an impartial investigating team be sent. This was probably the genesis for the commission soon to be headed by William Coltman. Lady Selkirk quite rightly dreaded delay, she wrote, for "the necessary slow proceedings of Courts of Law, offered no remedy to such evils as now exist in that country."[22] Sherbrooke could only respond lamely that the lateness of the season and "various other causes too numerous to mention" made it impossible for him to act.[23] Sherbrooke's principal problem, of course, was his inability to find anyone in Montreal with a sufficient reputation for impartiality to serve as a credible head of a commission. The failure of governments on both sides of the Atlantic to impose their authority on the Indian Territories provided the best justification possible for Selkirk's unilateral and creative use of his power. Whether he could make this justification appear acceptable to the authorities was another matter.

Selkirk himself recognized that he had exceeded his authority by acting with force in a case in which he had a personal interest, and he attempted to justify himself in lengthy letters to Lieutenant Governor Gore and the attorney general York of Upper Canada. According to the earl, when he received news that his colonists had been "massacred by the Half Indian Servants of the North West Company"—the first public use of the term "massacre" to refer to the events of Seven Oaks—he had decided to visit Fort William "with a force capable of making the law respected." Unable to find a neutral magistrate to accompany him, he was forced to act himself. He asked Gore to lay aside the "scruples" that would have governed him "if I had been in a civilized and well regulated country." The proof of guilt was stronger than ordinarily necessary for arresting criminals, he maintained, and when the use of force became necessary Selkirk had employed it.[24] To the attorney general Selkirk sent the news that he had dispatched two Swiss officers east on 18 August in charge of eight arrested prisoners, mainly partners of the North West

Company.[25] While the wintering partners had all claimed innocence of events at Red River, pleading they had neither consented to nor approved the local actions, there were presents at Fort William that had been promised the "murderers" after the event. Claims that Semple had confronted a party of innocent brûlés without provocation were nonsense, for they had taken prisoners among the settlers. The expedition from its outset formed "a series of the most undisguised violence and aggression." Whether Selkirk could prove this assertion was a different question. Along with the prisoners, the earl had dispatched Archy McDonald to deliver papers and other evidence to the lawyers in Montreal.

From the outset, the legal difficulties of Selkirk's actions were perfectly plain, even to the earl himself. He had intervened in a situation in which he was himself involved, and employed force quite openly. Nevertheless, he expected to be supported by government because—as he observed to Sir John Sherbrooke on 23 August—the North West Company was "not to be restrained from crimes by anything less than a striking example of the Vengeance of the Law."[26] Even his legal adviser Samuel Gale, not often a great supporter of the earl's more extreme actions, later allowed that without the capture of Fort William, the full enormity of the Red River transactions would never have been known.[27] Selkirk also appreciated full well the problems of proving charges of conspiracy, one of the most difficult claims at law to support. But he defended such an approach to the Hudson's Bay Company legal counsel in Montreal, James Stewart, on the grounds that it was the only way to get all of the evidence in front of the public.[28] This observation suggests that, from the outset, Selkirk was at least as interested in public opinion as in justice. His basic assumption—that the behaviour of the North West Company was so extreme as to lead both government and the public to react against the Nor'westers once the "facts" were put before them—was not immediately confirmed, a possibility that apparently did not occur to the earl. Here perhaps was a principal disadvantage of being an interested party: an inability to access accurately the response of government or of the court of public opinion, especially in an unfamiliar colonial context. When William McGillivray arrived in Montreal under arrest, he immediately demanded to be released on bail, and bail was granted. Once freed, McGillivray angrily demanded of Sir John Sherbrooke that Fort William be returned to the North West Company. Sherbrooke was conciliatory and sympathetic. Whether Seven Oaks had changed anything was a matter of considerable uncertainty.

CHAPTER EIGHTEEN

More Overstepping
of Legality

WITH THOSE HE REGARDED as the principal culprits in the Seven Oaks business arrested and shipped east, Lord Selkirk turned to dealing with the North West Company's operations that his seizure of Fort William had temporarily halted. The remaining senior clerks at the post, J.C. McTavish and Jasper Vandersluys, pressed for permission to resume shipment of trade-goods west and peltries east without any resolution of the differences between Selkirk and the NWC. They argued that the larger issues could be settled only in the courts. On any consideration of fair practice, Selkirk should have conceded this point. But he had his hands on the North West Company's economic lifeline, and he was understandably reluctant to let go. He therefore insisted that there should be some indemnification for his losses suffered at the hands of the Nor'westers before he would release either goods or furs. He proposed an investigation and arbitration by two neutral parties at London of all acts of aggression by either the North West Company or himself for the past four years, with the principals liable for damages. The furs would be sent to the arbitrators at London as sureties, and until a decision was reached, the needs of his party would be met from NWC stock at Fort William at current prices.[1] The two clerks declined this proposal, which obviously would have left the earl in a commanding position.

In an unsent draft letter to Sir John Sherbrooke written at this point, Selkirk justified his actions in halting shipments. The goods heading west would have supplied a "band of Miscreant Halfbreeds" in a state of "nothing less than open rebellion against His Majesty's Government," while the furs were being held as a pledge for the restoration of his property and as an incentive for arbitration. The right of an injured party to take the property of a wrongdoer in order to obtain satisfaction was a principle of the English law, he maintained, although he admitted it was not often employed in "the well regulated parts of the Empire."[2] But in the West there was no regulation whatever, and Selkirk invoked William McGillivray himself in asserting that the only defence of property in the wilderness was retaliation. The earl obviously had second thoughts about this letter. The one eventually written to Sherbrooke on 3 September was even stronger in its defence of halting the western supplies, arguing that Red River was in a "state of rebellion," occupied by "Banditti, who avow their determination to set the laws of their Country at defiance."[3] But no mention was here made of either the furs or retaliation. Instead, Selkirk supported the appointment of a commission to sort out the controversy, insisting on his pleasure, "if the load of responsibility, under which I am now obliged to act, could be alleviated."

Meanwhile, reports originating at the Sault indicated that Selkirk was already beginning to lose the battle for public opinion in eastern Canada with which he was so concerned, as he had already lost the support of governments there. The canoes with Selkirk's prisoners had arrived at the Sault, but one of the canoes that carried NWC partner Kenneth McKenzie had capsized in a sudden storm on Lake Superior with all its passengers lost. The NWC would make much of this mishap, claiming that the canoe was overloaded and Selkirk's people failed to take proper precautions. Archy McDonald would find some of the victims on his way east and bury them. When McDonald reached the Sault, he was dismayed to discover that Simon McGillivray had already contrived to send an express canoe to Montreal with his version of Seven Oaks, the events at Fort William, and the canoe mishap.[4] Archdeacon John Strachan responded to the arrival of the surviving prisoners at York with a view of the controversy between Selkirk and the Nor'westers that was doubtless a common one in Canada. Strachan observed, "There is a great feeling here as it appears to be a mercantile quarrel and people have not sympathy with a Peer of Great Britain turning Fur Merchant and applying the power which an ample Inheritance gives him in destroying a trade which has given bread to them for two centuries."[5] Allowing that both sides had taken "great Liberties with Justice," Strachan opined that Selkirk had all the advantages.

John Strachan was no friend of Lord Selkirk. Earlier in the year he had published in London a fierce attack on Selkirk's emigration theories and colonization activities, not confining himself to Red River.[6] Strachan accused Selkirk of offering to his Highland settlers "generous" terms that "native Americans would never accept," adding that the earl was merely a land speculator "anxiously preparing an asylum in a distant corner of the earth" in case his country should fall to the enemy. When he turned to Red River, Strachan used an outdated and uncirculated prospectus for the colony in the earliest days of its planning. Strachan insisted that the title was insecure, the territory indefensible by the British authorities, the colony thoroughly isolated and unable to find a market for its produce, the land shamefully overpriced, and the settlers misled by "false and delusive" promises. Strachan concluded by predicting that the colonists would find themselves caught in the struggle between rival fur-trading companies, a position productive only of "melancholy events." He recommended that any in Britain tempted by Selkirk's offers come instead to Upper Canada, where they would receive free land and the protection of the law.

The effort by John Strachan was not the only publication about Red River circulating in the autumn of 1816. The contending parties had now begun a war of words in newspapers and pamphlets that would reach major proportions over the next few years. It was arguably the most extensive public controversy in British America since the days of the American Rebellion. Selkirk's own extended critique of the North West Company was by this time available on both sides of the Atlantic. His supporters, under the name of Archibald McDonald, had also published in London a brief account of the 1815 dispersal of the settlement as *Narrative respecting the Destruction of the Earl of Selkirk's Settlement upon Red River, in . . . 1815*. This account saw the dispersal of the settlement as a North West Company plot, rather than a voluntary withdrawal by discontented settlers. McDonald's name was also used to refute John Strachan's "pamphlet" in a series of letters to the editor of the *Montreal Herald,* later collected as *Reply to the Letter, Lately Addressed to the Earl of Selkirk, by the Hon. John Strachan, D.D., &c. Being Four Letters (reprinted from the Montreal Herald) Containing a Statement of Facts, Concerning the Settlement on Red River, in the District of Ossiniboia, Territory of the Hudson's Bay Company, Properly Called Rupert's Land*. The McDonald narrative in turn produced more letters to the editor of the *Montreal Herald,* which became *Communications from Adam*

McAdam, originally published in the Montreal Herald, in reply to letters inserted therein under the signature of Archibald Macdonald, respecting Lord Selkirk's Red River Settlement.

The McAdam work, in its annoyance and anger, was obviously responding to Selkirk's *Sketch of the Fur Trade,* although that publication was never mentioned by name. McAdam treated Selkirk as little more than an exploitative land-jobber and fur trader. He was well informed about the Selkirk family's radical past, however. At one point McAdam exclaimed, "Perhaps his Lordship in this age of revolution, having studied the fine spun dreams of Paris and Edinburgh on the rights of man, &c, &c, thinks the Red River a fit place for an experiment on those wild theories. It is certainly cut off from the rest of the world. I suppose, as soon as his Lordship has appointed his council and officers of state, and modelled his army, he will exclaim to the Sovereigns of Europe, behold a Government of Perfection!" This was one of the few places that suggested a utopian cast to Red River. By and large, however, McAdam presented the Nor'westers as innocent victims of a scheme that included the recruitment of "the discharged assemblage of men that compose the De Meuron regiment, whose tongues and dialects were so various, that scarce any ten of them understood [an]other ten." For McAdam, Selkirk had used "force of arms to seize the servants and effects of the British Merchants from Canada," driving them out from the west, and thus destroying "a vast extended commerce, dearly purchased, and upheld by innumerable hardships and dangers, and great risk of capital."[7]

At Fort William, Lord Selkirk and his associates were preparing yet another act of calculated aggression against the North West Company. Selkirk's people, headed by Dr. John Allan and Miles Macdonell, had been leaning heavily on Daniel McKenzie, the one North West Company partner remaining at Fort William. Initially they were looking for information about company intentions against Red River. His interrogators soon discovered that McKenzie was not well. He had to be allowed to make notes to himself over a period of several days in order to produce any coherent statement of his activities. He was fearful that he would be left holding the bag for Seven Oaks, and Selkirk's friends did not disabuse him of his concerns. From Montreal, Samuel Gale—Lord and Lady Selkirk's Canadian "man of business" and an experienced lawyer—wrote a desperate letter advising the earl to give up the furs, since he was in danger of "compounding for crimes."[8] Gale was the son of a Loyalist who had joined the Quebec bar in 1807. He was an active pamphleteer against Sir George Prevost during the War of 1812 and later put his pen into service on Selkirk's behalf. He would travel west to advise Selkirk in 1817. Infatuated with Lady Selkirk, Gale saw himself as her knight errant during his journey to the Indian Territories. Whether Selkirk would have paid any attention to Gale is an open question. But the warning did not arrive in time. Selkirk and McKenzie came to an agreement on 19 September to send the earl's grievances against the North West Company to two or more arbitrators chosen by the Lord Chief Justices in King's Bench and Common Pleas, Westminster.[9] The parties were to indemnify each other for damages, with a decision to be reached by 1 December 1819. This was a perfectly reasonable way to settle the dispute between his lordship and the Nor'westers, and it would later be recommended by the commission of investigation headed by William Coltman. Whether Daniel McKenzie was the appropriate person with whom to make this agreement was another matter entirely. He would subsequently repudiate the deal as soon as he was freed from Selkirk's hands, claiming inebriation, intimidation, and rough treatment.[10] Even more dubious was the consignment by McKenzie to Selkirk of all furs and the sale of all property at Fort William to the earl. In return Selkirk conveyed an estate worth £3000 yearly to be held in trust. Cash of fifty pounds was handed on 19 September to McKenzie to seal the arrangement.

By this point Selkirk had received mail forwarded from the east, and was probably now aware of his British financial difficulties. Moreover, his redeployment of men, some of whom were intended for the service of the Hudson's Bay Company, made him realize that not only was it impossible to separate his expenses from those of the company, but also that those of 1816 were probably "entirely lost."[11] Understanding that the various HBC thrusts into the Athabasca country had been disasters, he also ordered another year's reinforcements for this region from Montreal.[12] Meanwhile, Selkirk forwarded the documents in the McKenzie negotiations to his lawyers in Montreal, undoubtedly hoping to recover some of his expenses in the process. McKenzie was not a retired partner, he insisted, and was fully responsible. The earl admitted the papers had been drawn up without legal advice. The lawyers would be suitably appalled at Selkirk's actions.[13]

In October, on Daniel McKenzie's behalf, Miles Macdonell wrote to the wintering partners of the NWC, reporting the arbitration agreement and asking them to consign this winter's furs to a neutral party in London. By

English law, Miles argued, each partner had the right to act for the partner-ship at large. In this Miles was undoubtedly echoing Selkirk himself. Selkirk had no interest in breaking up the Athabasca trade, Miles insisted, but in allowing it to continue under the HBC charter, with those joining him "no longer . . . hewers of wood & drawers of water for the Nabobs of Montreal," but reaping proper profits that would enable them eventually to retire to a "comfortable assylum at Red River."[14] The wintering partners understand-ably ignored this letter.

Daniel McKenzie might not have been retired, but there was considerable question whether he was sufficiently in command of his mental facilities to understand fully what he had done, particularly given his later claims of bad treatment and intensive interrogation. In truth, being forced to dry out was probably the most severe pressure that could possibly be placed upon him, and Dr. Allan had advised against it. When Allan had pointed out that buying furs and goods from McKenzie might be viewed as misrepresentation, Selkirk replied, It would be absurd to abstain from doing anything merely to avoid being misrepresented by the NWCo. who had already misrepresented his best actions, and would invariably misrepresent his conduct however unim-peachable it might be. Selkirk went beyond this argument—that he might as well be hung for a sheep as a goat—when he wrote gleefully to one legal acquaintance in London, "I flatter myself that the step which I have taken, tho' perhaps unusual, is not so far out of the common path, as to be in any degree improper."[15] Indeed, had McKenzie been a more responsible figure, the agreement might well have been a stroke of genius. By it, Selkirk exposed the weakness of the corporate structure of the North West Company, and had not only completely disrupted the trade of the opposition, but also had taken it over. Even with all its limitations and weaknesses, the deal with McKenzie could be defended for the chaos it created in North West Company ranks, as an act of corporate guerrilla warfare, to be justified strictly in terms of its disruptive qualities. The chaos Selkirk created would take years to undo. It could be argued that the Nor'westers never did entirely recover from this action, particularly when it was used to justify the complete takeover of the NWC posts on the canoe routes between Fort William and Red River. Unfortunately, Selkirk apparently thought the agreement a legitimate busi-ness arrangement as well, although he was virtually alone in thinking it was a good idea.

Lord Selkirk spent a busy autumn in 1816, issuing orders to his forces in the field, with an eye to reconquering Red River, to opening the western trading routes to the HBC, and to uncovering further evidence of Nor'wester criminality. As part of his efforts, he despatched P.C. Pambrun, Michael McDonell, and William Laidlaw to Fond du Lac with warrants for the arrest of the partners residing there. The charge was the detention and robbery of Jean-Baptiste Lagimodière. Laidlaw returned to Fort William in early October with James Grant and William Morrison, who readily admitted the charge. They produced a letter from Archibald McLeod ordering them to do so. Grant said that he was in the council room when the packet of letters from Lagimodière was brought in, the seals still intact. No one was willing to be seen breaking them. The next days, however, the partners were reading them and handing them around. When one partner expressed surprise that the letters had been opened, another half jokingly suggested that perhaps they had been opened by mice. On 10 and 11 September, Selkirk dispatched two units of De Meurons up the Kaministiquia River. They were to rendezvous at Lac la Pluie under the command of Proteus D'Orsonnens, a De Meuron officer who would later become an administrator at Red River. Four weeks after his dispatch, D'Orsonnens reported that he had occupied Fort lac la Pluie in the name of the HBC, using warrants issued by Selkirk.[16] The De Meurons had been forced to break down the gate of the fort, but had met little resistance within. A number of Nor'westers had been put under arrest. Selkirk's aim to re-establish the Old Grand Portage route along the proposed international border and to control the canoe routes to the interior had now been achieved. Whether D'Orsonnens could carry out the earl's ultimate ambition—to send a winter expeditionary force to retake Fort Douglas at Red River—was another matter. To the Hudson's Bay Company's London Committee, Selkirk reported that he was making settlement headquarters at Lac la Pluie until Red River could be recaptured in the spring. He requested a change from the Winnipeg River to the 49th Parallel in his grant, since the Americans were claiming the latter as a western boundary.[17] Western surveys and boundaries were obviously on Selkirk's mind. Taking advantage of a late express to the Canadas, Selkirk wrote to his friend, the hydrographer William Fitzwilliam Owen, about these matters.[18] The earl noted that David Thompson's "survey on a large scale is hunting up in the great Hall of this Fort." Thompson's "neat drawing, the minuteness & apparent care bestowed on his plans" had impressed people, Selkirk asserted, but governments should not be deceived by a "piece of quackery." Everything on this survey was incorrect, he asserted.

By this time word of the disaster at Seven Oaks was in common circulation, and the earl's response at Fort William was quickly becoming known as well. An eyewitness account by John Pritchard was inserted by Selkirk supporters in the *Montreal Herald* of 12 October, and even those sympathetic to the North West Company were prepared to use his account as the basis of their own versions.[19] Some news of the events of the summer had reached England as well, for one of Selkirk's military friends wrote of reports of fresh disaster at Red River, adding "at no former period would it probably have been so easy to have directed the flood tide of emigration towards Assiniboia as at the present."[20] Obviously the thousands of Highlanders currently beginning to emigrate to Canada in the wake of the end of the war against Napoleon would hardly be tempted by Red River in its current uncertain state.

The reviewer of Selkirk's *A Sketch of the British Fur Trade*, which appeared in the October 1816 *Quarterly Review,* was remarkably up-to-date on news from the West, on recent developments in the struggle between the two trading companies, and on government attitudes.[21] Although Selkirk was "an amiable, honourable, and intelligent man," the review opened, and "his . . . not the deep-laid schemes of a sordid narrow-minded calculator, but the suggestions of an ardent imagination and a benevolent heart—such as are apt sometimes to overlook difficulties which it is not easy to overleap"—he had obviously overstepped the bounds in the present business. He had purchased stock in the Hudson's Bay Company and received a grant of land under its charter, which the law officers of the Crown did not approve. He had then interfered in the deadly feud between the North West Company and the Hudson's Bay Company without waiting for any support from the government. The reviewer in the *Quarterly Review* went on to admit that "the details of the extraordinary transactions which have urged his lordship to the strange steps he has taken are not yet fairly before the public." For his part, the reviewer could not believe that Selkirk would have taken Fort William and arrested Nor'westers under any authority, much less under a warrant issued by himself, given his "avowed political principles." But, the reviewer continued with his major point that the earl's work on the fur trade "fully prepared us— not only for transactions like that just mentioned, but—for any species of outrage and aggression." The reviewer was prepared to accept Selkirk's accusations against the North West Company, noting that if the facts were false, the Nor'westers would surely "feel it incumbent upon them to take immediate steps to wash away the foul stain cast upon them." Among all the controversial literature produced for the North West Company over the next few years, a refutation of *A Sketch of the British Fur Trade* would never be included. The *Quarterly Review* author doubted in 1816 that the Hudson's Bay Company was appreciably more honourable, fair and moderate, however, and thought the true different between the companies was in "the energy of the one and the apathy of the other." Selkirk did not intend to become a rival trader to the North West Company; he wanted a settlement of industrious farmers in the heart of the Indian Territories, a settlement that the reviewer suspected would in time engage in the fur trade. Unlike Sir Alexander Mackenzie's early work, Selkirk's book was less "a history, than a Bill of Indictment against the North-west Company—an angry attack on the provincial administration of justice—and a panegyric on the Hudson's Bay Company."

In the Canadas, Selkirk's enemies and the colonial authorities had been busy. Sir John Sherbrooke revoked the earl's commissions as magistrate and justice of the peace in the Indian Territories as part of a general process of cancellation of all commissions for the region. Instead, Sherbrooke appointed W.B. Coltman and John Fletcher as magistrates in the territories and as special commissioners to investigate the recent events in the West as well. William Bachelor Coltman had been born in England, but resided in Quebec from 1799. He operated with his brother as a merchant, and was not closely associated with the North West Company. His subsequent work as commissioner demonstrated that he had some legal background, although nothing is known of this side of his life. He did not claim to be a lawyer. He had been appointed an executive councillor of Lower Canada in 1812.[22] Coltman's junior colleague on the commission, John Fletcher, was also born in England and had made a considerable reputation as a brilliant attorney before coming suddenly to Canada in 1810. A whiff of unspecified scandal, probably connected with the excessive consumption of alcoholic beverages, surrounded him in the colony. Fletcher had a reputation for being eccentric and a drunkard. He had served as a militia officer during the War of 1812, and was compulsively fascinated with matters military. Like Coltman, he was not closely associated with the NWC, although there were rumours he had been occasionally employed by the

Nor'westers. Fletcher was apparently intended to provide legal expertise, but in the administration of the commission he never once advised Coltman.[23] At a time when Selkirk lost his commission and Coltman was appointed, a warrant was sworn against Selkirk at Sandwich in Upper Canada for forcible entry and detainment.[24] An Upper Canadian constable named Robinson, a former sergeant major, left Sandwich for Fort William with the warrant on 30 October, while Sir John Sherbrooke wrote to Lord Bathurst of the appointment of Messrs Coltman and Fletcher. The entire western territory was up in arms, asserted Sherbrooke, and both sides in the fur-trade struggle claimed they wanted the law properly administered in the region. He requested either more powers or men of "rank and talent" to investigate affairs in the West.[25] Sherbrooke did not know about Constable Robinson, although there was probably nothing he could have done about the warrant, which was issued in an Upper Canadian court.

While Sherbrooke was acting, the Montreal newspapers were full of invective. A series of letters appeared in the *Montreal Herald* between 20 August and 20 November 1816. "Mercator" was Henry McKenzie, a cousin of Sir Alexander McKenzie who managed Sir Alexander's Canadian property as well as that of Simon McTavish. He later became a partner in McTavish, McGillivrays and Company and the Michilimackinack Company.[26] These letters answered another series signed by "Manlius," who, according to Mercator, was a Selkirk "hireling paid by the yard." Initially intended to defend the North West Company interpretation of the Hudson's Bay Company charter, Mercator's letters developed into an ongoing commentary on events in the West as news of them reached Montreal. Seven Oaks became forgotten in the face of the evidence of Lord Selkirk's successful employment of force. Mercator's writings became more and more strident and full of personal invective against Selkirk. The earl was described in an early letter as a "canting pretended philanthropist" whose colony "originated in avarice, has been prosecuted by deception and fraud, and must end in disgracing the character of a British nobleman." Mercator certainly intended to hasten the disgrace along. In the letter of 15 November, Mercator labelled Selkirk "a lordly usurper, tyrant, and hirer of cut-throats, who in his closet, in cold blood, planned the starvation to death of 500 persons in the employ of the North West Company."[27]

At Fort William, Lord Selkirk received information of the murder of one of his former agents now employed by the Hudson's Bay Company. Owen

Keveny had been arrested in the fur-trade country on 16 August under a warrant issued by Archibald McLeod. He had been sent eastward to Fort William. The canoe in which he was travelling had turned back when word reached it that the fort had been captured. Keveny, who was quite ill, was killed by his escorts, one man named Mainville and the other Charles de Reinhard, the latter a former sergeant of the De Meuron regiment now in the employ of the North West Company. Keveny was an Irishman with a caustic tongue. He was probably murdered because his captors increasingly found him a burden. The murder of Keveny under arrest was thus fresh in Selkirk's mind when he too was presented with a warrant by Constable Robinson.

On 12 November Selkirk sent off a special express with letters to Lieutenant Governor Gore in Upper Canada and Sir John Sherbrooke in Quebec. To Sherbrooke he offered a vigorous defence of his conduct. Failing to forward the furs was an act he would chance with the courts, he wrote, since the trade that had collected them "under the guise of Commerce . . . is an organized system of repine, & a conspiracy against all other British Subjects, carried on by a daily repetition of robbery, with the occasional intervention of murder, whenever the interests of the concern appear to require it." A better one-sentence summary of his book on the fur trade could not have been written. In short, Selkirk argued, he had stopped a public nuisance. As for the arrangement with McKenzie, it was not a "leonine contract," but one made with a man sent by William McGillivray to manage the fur trade at Red River.[28]

To Gore he reported that a canoe had arrived at Fort William with two North West Company clerks accompanied by a man who claimed to be a constable with warrants for the earl's arrest. The warrant was irregular and full of perjuries and the man had no credentials. Since Selkirk could not conceive that Gore, for no reason, had ordered the arrest of one of his magistrates by a man without credentials, he decided to treat the man as an imposter and refuse to accompany him across Lake Superior under conditions probably "irregular & surreptitious." His determination to resist was increased by learning that the Nor'westers had sent a force of canoes to recover Fort William, "either by strategem or by force, by legal pretexts or open violence." Defending the legitimacy of his purchase of the fort itself, which he insisted was located on Crown land, he announced that he would not allow the North West Company to enter until a body of King's troops arrived to take it over.[29]

Whether Selkirk was being disingenuous in his protestations or quite sincerely believed the constable a fraud is not certain, but Mr. Robinson was quite genuine. A deposition about Selkirk's treatment of the Upper Canadian legal officer and his companions was sworn at York on 17 December. According to Robert McRobb, a clerk of the North West Company, when the small party of officials had arrived at Fort William, the constable had gone to Selkirk's room and made the arrest. He had subsequently also arrested Frederick Matthey and John McNab. The Upper Canadians were told by Matthey to depart the fort. They replied that he had no power to enforce his orders. Matthey allegedly answered "that he should then make use of the means in his power to enforce obedience to his orders." The law officers were then guarded by seven armed De Meurons until their forced departure from Fort William.

The perversion in the Indian Territories of the mechanisms of the law for partisan and private purposes had obviously gone too far and desperately needed to be reigned in. Governor Sherbrooke had revoked commissions in the West, but had not cancelled the legal powers of the governments of the Canadas under the *Canada Jurisdiction Act*. Lord Selkirk had in disobedience found a way to short-circuit the North West Company's abuse of legal warrants. He would always claim, with some legitimacy, that he might have lost his life had he allowed himself to be arrested. Unfortunately, his defiance of the authority of the Crown would prove the final straw in London, and he would become the chief target of the government's campaign to reassert itself in the West. There was considerable irony to the treatment about to be meted out to Selkirk. He had campaigned with government for years for the institution of proper law and order in the Indian Territories, warning of the dangers of not acting. When the government sat on its hands, Selkirk had taken the law into his own. For this he was about to pay a heavy price.

Selkirk was well ensconced in Fort William and was able to feel quite satisfied about his performance until the spring of 1817, when the early mails arrived. But the forces against him were growing in confidence, using every action he had taken as further evidence of his malevolence. His family and friends in eastern Canada were made aware over the winter of 1816–17 that the colonial governments in the Canadas were preparing to throw him to the wolves as soon as he returned to the east. Unbeknownst to the earl's people in North America, the British government had also turned against him. But the winter closure of communications with the east insulated Selkirk from the full force of the storm of censure rising against him. Until the spring, he could carry on as though he still had right on his side. There would even be a final triumph, as Proteus D'Orsonnens would lead a successful military operation that recaptured Fort Douglas in January of 1817.

Some indication of Selkirk's general thinking can be gleaned from a lengthy letter to Proteus D'Orsonnens at Lac la Pluie, penned in early December of 1816. He had heard rumours of government disapproval of his actions at Fort William, Selkirk wrote, but treated the warrant for his arrest as a trick and the man serving it an imposter. The letters he had subsequently received indicated that the evidence he had collected at Fort William was well regarded, and nothing was to be read into the revocation of all Indian Territory commissions, including his own. Still thinking in terms of offence, Selkirk then moved on to a discussion of "the old contests between the Engl Colonies & the French of Canada," in which winter marches had been frequent. It was impossible to reinforce D'Orsonnens, and for him to pull back would be a "retrograde" step. Since government intervention was not yet a reality and the wintering partners of the North West Company were getting desperate, the best step might well be to anticipate them by a winter march to Red River, to capture the artillery, and to disperse the rebels. Selkirk examined such an operation quite dispassionately. By concerting with the First Nations, it would be possible to march on snowshoes through the woods. The settlement could be restored only if Selkirk's forces were seen as superior. The earl concluded by observing that the pressure of business "has not allowed me to take as much part as I would wish in the social amusements of the party," and hoping that the boredom felt by his people could be altered by "some brilliant pictures . . . from Red R to revive them & warm their imaginations westward."[30]

Except in terms of having conceived the original idea, Selkirk had virtually no part in the military reconquest of Red River. Understandable concerns of those at Lac la Pluie about getting lost in the snowy winter conditions were unexpectedly obviated by the appearance of a qualified guide who knew well the territory between Lake of the Woods and the Red River. This guide was a man named John Tanner, who had lived among the First Nations for many years and was known as "the American."[31] Tanner had been captured as a child in Kentucky by a war party of Ottawas, and raised as an Aboriginal person at Michilimackinac. He had later followed his adoptive people to Lake of the Woods. Tanner no longer spoke English, although he had some memories of his childhood and wanted to visit his natural family. Like most of his band, he did not take kindly to the abusive treatment of the North West Company. He offered to guide an expedition to Red River in return for eventual conveyance to Michilimackinac, where he could begin the quest for his origins. A party of about fifty, including twenty-four De Meurons, set off on foot on 10 December. Each man had snowshoes, although not enough snow was yet on the ground to use them. Every two men were allotted a hand sledge to carry their baggage and Spartan rations of provisions. Three draught oxen were yoked to a sledge to carry two pieces of artillery brought from Fort William, and some cattle were driven ahead as well. A draught ox that injured itself on the ice of Lake of the Woods had to be killed and provided a welcome supply of fresh meat. West of Lake of the Woods, a small party of First Nations joined the expedition as scouts, and a party of Saulteaux welcomed the invaders at the LaSalle River. Fort Douglas was taken by surprise on an early morning on 10 January 1817.[32]

The reoccupation of Fort Douglas represented the high point of Selkirk's military adventuring. The governments in Canada and in Great Britain had finally bestirred themselves to become involved in the conflict in the Indian Territories. The activities of the Royal Commission headed by William Coltman would mark the beginning of a new phase in the fur-trade wars, one that would prove even more costly and debilitating for Lord Selkirk than the violence of the previous two years. Coltman himself had headed west not long after his appointment, but was unable to get further west than Nottawasagua, thus leaving Selkirk with a free hand until spring.[33]

CHAPTER NINETEEN

On the Defensive, 1817

DURING THE LONG WINTER of 1816–17, Lord Selkirk settled comfortably at Fort William. He sketched desultorily, read, wrote memoranda and letters to scattered correspondents, and waited for a spring that would bring the investigating commission headed by William Coltman and a backlog of letters from around the world. He tramped about the woods on snowshoes, later admitting he found it "on trial to be a much less formidable undertaking than I had imagined."[1] He worried about the progress of his wife's pregnancy. He had left Lady Selkirk in June, knowing only that she was expecting a child around the first of the year, but he could do nothing to help. The earl's mind continued to be active, as his correspondence over the winter demonstrated. He continued to think like a practical political economist. In one letter to Michael McDonell in Wisconsin, for example, he warned that the NWC would likely try to use American warrants against him.[2] He advised McDonell to sit tight and remember that his location was still territory disputed between the United States and Britain. In another letter to Donald McPherson, the earl enclosed extracts from three different books with directions for brewing beer from wild rice.[3] Presumably the books were in the library at Fort William. We can only wonder what other marvels that library contained, for no catalogue for it exists today. To Captain Antoine Graffenreid, at Lac la Pluie, Selkirk wrote that he had forwarded a keg of rum that had been rectified by Dr. Allan and Frederick Matthey to a higher alcoholic content for easier transport.[4] This shipment was apparently in response to a letter from Graffenried, who had set off earlier with twenty-two De Meuron soldiers and a handful of Canadians to reinforce La Pluie. The party had gotten lost in the woods. When their provisions were finished, Graffenried had reported, they were forced to boil and eat their snowshoes and one of the dogs with them. Finally finding food, Graffenried's men did "nothing but cook and eat all day." When they finally arrived at Lac La Pluie on 27 January 1817, the men found the fort stripped bare and virtually empty. Graffenried confessed "the want of liquor more than I could believe."[5]

One of the manuscripts on which Selkirk worked over the winter of 1816–17 was a lengthy historical analysis of the fur trade and the growth of competition in the West. Although written in the third person and passive voice, this account attempted to explain and defend his involvement in the trade.[6] It probably came as close as anything he ever wrote to revealing his mature thinking on the subject. The analysis was also, of course, a justification of his behaviour and actions in establishing Red River. Although undated, several internal references make clear that it was written after the Fort William occupation and almost certainly at Fort William. Selkirk began by emphasizing the failure of the servants of the Hudson's Bay Company to respond to the acts of violence of the North West Company, adding that they ignore their leaders not only in this respect but also in refusing to winter in some of the less favourable inland situations. The HBC was able to keep up a trade with the people of the plains, partly because they associated in larger bands harder to intimidate, partly because the company adhered to an ancient standard of trade that bore no relationship to modern realities and was very favourable to the Aboriginal people. This ancient standard still paid high prices for skins of animals abounding on the plains but which were practically useless in London. Expenses ran higher than income, and bankruptcy for the HBC was inevitable. The restoration of commercial viability was what interested Selkirk in the management of the company, he wrote. That restoration was important not only in financial terms, but also in terms of protecting the territorial rights of the HBC against the free traders. To restore energy, the HBC adopted a profit-sharing scheme for its employees, which probably would have succeeded in reinvigorating the company except for the lawlessness of the Nor'westers, who according to some observers seemed able to intimidate the "timid and phlegmatic" Orkneymen who dominated the factories in the west. Selkirk doubted that there was much good reason for accusing them of lack of courage. But the HBC wanted to recruit more aggressive servants from Ireland and the Highlands and Western Island of Scotland.

Selkirk emphasized that his plans for colonization fit in nicely with the plans of the directors of the HBC, not least because an increase in population would lead to the establishment of law and order through an effective judicature. Such a judicature would be challenged by the opposing fur traders in the courts. Eventually appeals to the Privy Council would settle the question of the charter. Moreover, a colony would provide a home for elderly and redundant servants of the HBC, many of whom had formed "connections with Indian women and reared numerous families," making them averse to leaving the region. The Red River country was selected as the place for colonization because the natural resources for provisions were extensive and the district "was of little consequence for the fur trade." This analysis was, of course, to ignore the importance of Red River to the Nor'westers as a provisioning centre for the canoe brigades. In any event, the governor and superintendent of the Northern Department were instructed to begin laying out lots in Red River and assigning them to suitable settlers. Unfortunately, William Auld did not follow through on his instructions, which included beginning settlement as well as introducing energy and economy into business dealings. Auld's failure to begin a colony at Red River led to Selkirk's taking upon himself the charge of forming the intended settlement on condition of an extensive land grant. The HBC directors felt that a settlement was crucial, but also knew that their plan of recruiting in Ireland and the Highlands was not working. Selkirk, through his acquaintances and reputation in the area, might be more successful. Selkirk agreed to undertake the management of this project.

The major opposition to the plan, wrote Selkirk, came initially from Sir Alexander Mackenzie. He and Selkirk had made some joint purchases of Hudson's Bay Company stock, but after the earl became involved in the management of the HBC, he discovered that Mackenzie's plans for a cooperation between it and the North West Company were intended to benefit only the Nor'westers. The earl refused any further dealings with him. After the grant had been sanctioned by the shareholders over the objections of men from the North West Company, Edward Ellice had a long conversation with Selkirk in which he described the nature of the opposition that would ensue. The wintering partners of the North West Company, Ellice argued, were men destitute of all moral principle who had operated for

years in the Indian country at a distance from all the restraints of law,
order, and the public opinion of society. They would not scruple at anything
to advance the affairs of their company. Selkirk was surprised that men of
such high principle as Ellice pocketed a share of the profits arising from the
crimes of such a set of ruffians without a qualm. It was hard to tell whether
the threats were serious, but recently discovered letters written in 1811 to
the partners at Fort William—and obviously uncovered by Selkirk in his
occupation—made it clear that prevention by any means was a serious
prospect. In any case, the threats meant that the first settlers needed to be
well armed and trained to military discipline. Those men, under the
command of Miles Macdonell, sailed from Stornoway only after much
opposition from the Nor'westers.

On 22 February, Selkirk reported to Lady Selkirk, "The most material
point that you will be anxious to know is Somebody is very well, and amusing
himself as well as can be expected in such a lonesome seclusion."[7] While the
earl was locked away in enforced and somewhat frozen isolation, both
private and public activity in less wintry climes such as London increased in
tempo. In England, Henry Goulburn at the Colonial Office responded to a
letter from HBC governor Joseph Berens—providing news of the "most
savage massacre" at Seven Oaks—by observing that the situation had
changed from a dispute of "conflicting claims of two Mercantile Companies" to one of the exchange of outrages that each imparted to the other. The
courts would settle the questions of culpability and jurisdiction in the Indian
Territories, wrote Goulburn, adding piously, "it being the only justification
of some of the late Acts committed.[8] A few days later, the London agents of
the North West Company proposed to the Hudson's Bay Company that
because of the "continuance of disputes and cabals in the Indian country," all
property and posts be restored without prejudice to the recovery of damages,
and the issues resolved by a competent tribunal in Britain. Had requests from
both sides for government intervention been met, they added, much of the
mischief could have been prevented.[9] This conciliatory attitude doubtless
reflected the damage that Selkirk's capture of Fort William had done and was
doing to the Nor'westers. Selkirk's actions had contributed to, and indeed
probably forced, the North West Company to look for cooperation with
their rivals to resolve the controversy in the backcountry.

The search for cooperation did not mean that the NWC gave up its own
efforts in the corridors of power. The deposition by Robert MacRobb

accusing Selkirk of resisting a legal warrant, sworn in Montreal in December of 1816, was in Lord Bathurst's hands in early February of 1817. It did not get there through official government channels, but through the connections between the London agents of the NWC and the Colonial Office. Simon McGillivray and his friends had sent six letters to Henry Goulburn between 1 January 1817 and early February. Earlier, on first learning of Selkirk's capture of Fort William at the head of a force of mercenary soldiers, the colonial secretary had urged the earl's return to Britain to substantiate the charges of murder he had made against those he had arrested.[10] He felt that justice could be done only by bringing the persons arrested by Selkirk home to Britain for trial.[11] He had also instructed the HBC that His Majesty's government wished the directors to order Selkirk home and to dismiss him if he failed to comply. The HBC directors replied that they had no control over Selkirk.[12] In response to this latest outrage by Selkirk, Bathurst wrote to Sir John Sherbrooke expressing his concern for Britain's commercial and political interests as a result of the earl's "admission of foreign influence over the Indian Territories," supposedly to end the violence that had too long prevailed. The colonial secretary wanted the two companies to cease their violence and to return captured property. Sherbrooke was to issue a proclamation in the name of the prince regent. By resisting the warrants for his arrest, Bathurst added, Selkirk had made himself doubly responsible to the law, and the government would enforce it against him. Sherbrooke was instructed in no uncertain terms to prefer an indictment against Selkirk and to arrest him, even if it were necessary to do so under the *Canada Jurisdiction Act*.[13] D'Arcy Boulton would write one of Selkirk's attorneys, James Woods of Sandwich, on 23 June that "the fact is I am under orders to prosecute his Lordship criminally on his return."[14] These pre-emptory instructions of Bathurst would influence the actions of colonial officials in Canada for several years, since they could be interpreted as an official repudiation of Selkirk's conduct. Sherbrooke was also instructed to inform Selkirk of the substance of his instructions, if not the actual text. For some reason, the Lower Canadian governor did not make a very good job of this communication.[15] Selkirk and his supporters learned the details of Bathurst's hostile orders only much later.

Why Bathurst responded with such vehemence to the accounts of Selkirk's behaviour presented to him by the North West Company has never been entirely clear. In principle it was certainly true that the British government could not condone a peer of the realm's leading a private army and resisting legal Crown warrants, especially one operating on both sides of an uncertain border between British America and the United States. But the response ignored the fact that the government had resolutely refused for years to intervene in the fur-trade dispute in order to bring some law and order into the Indian Territories. Moreover, no evidence exists that Bathurst waited to hear Selkirk's side of the story before acting. Selkirk's associates in London and Lady Selkirk in Montreal were certain that Henry Goulburn and probably Bathurst himself were entirely too friendly with Simon McGillivray, Edward "Bear" Ellice, and other NWC people in Britain. Lady Selkirk wrote her brother in April, "I fear the Colonial Office is even more the scene of North West influence than the Council here. Who could have believed that the mere scum of Scotland could have attained to this?"[16] Even more than her husband, Lady Selkirk's attitude toward the Nor'westers was one of class hostility, and her attitude toward the leading officials of the Colonial Office was one of disdain. She had supreme confidence that "one upright mind is more than a match for all the villains in the North West Company."[17] As for her brother, Andrew Colvile, he found "the prejudice against Selkirk at the Colonial Office makes it very hard work."[18]

It was certainly true that the NWC seemed to have much easier access to the ear of the ministry than did the officials of the Hudson's Bay Company, but what this meant is less certain. Whether the prejudice was against Selkirk or to the Hudson's Bay Company, a monopoly attempting to entrench itself, is another matter. The ease of access may simply have reflected the willingness of the NWC people to meet personally and informally with the Colonial Office people. The Hudson's Bay Company's correspondence with the Colonial Office certainly gives the impression of a reluctance to soil its hands over the fur trade business, probably because the HBC's position was always that the Nor'westers were upstarts who should not be recognized and taken seriously. In any event, some sort of special relationship obviously did exist among Goulburn, Bathurst, and the Nor'westers. In May, Simon McGillivray delivered personally to Sir John Sherbrooke a series of dispatches dealing with the confrontation with Selkirk and the Hudson's Bay Company, and, in his report to Goulburn of the delivery, took the opportunity to offer all sorts of unsubstantiated gossip and much procedural advice to the Colonial Office.[19]

Bathurst's reaction was probably simply visceral and ill-considered, ignoring the possibility that there might be another side to the story.[20] The colonial secretary may well also have been annoyed by a realization that Selkirk had forced the government's hand. For years Bathurst had resisted involving the British administration in the matter of the Hudson's Bay Company charter and in the question of jurisdiction in the territories claimed by the company. Law officers of the Crown had already been in discussion with the colonial secretary on these points.[21] He was now prepared to sponsor legislation defining the limits of HBC territory as the "mode most likely to prevent the recurrence of those mischiefs which had taken place."[22] To some extent, this determination reflected a recognition of some uncertainty over whether the British government had direct authority over the territory claimed by the HBC according to its charter. The HBC itself backed off a confrontation over the sovereignty question in the short run, agreeing that its people in North America would recognize the Coltman commission without prejudice to the larger issue.[23]

Lord Selkirk was away from Fort William when the first canoes arrived in March, containing letters from Lady Selkirk. She warned her husband that the "enemy" was not yet beaten, exclaiming, "For Heaven's sake be less sanguine, you really frighten me."[24] In another letter, she noted that the cost of Selkirk's activities was mounting rapidly. She added, "And it really will be little short of ruin if you go on with your own private funds. I acknowledge I cannot swallow the exchange of St. Mary's Isle for your kingdom on Red River."[25] Her concern was that Selkirk was fighting the Hudson's Bay Company's battles with his own money. Selkirk wrote to Miles Macdonell at Red River about the welcome news of the appointment of the commission on 20 March 1817. He noted that the commissioners' appointment might encroach on the jurisdiction of the charter, but it would be improper to stand on this objection. But in waiving it, one could still register a protest about the rights of jurisdiction.[26] A later canoe brought the official announcements about the commission chaired by William Coltman along with the revocation of all other commissions in the west. This canoe also brought a deputy sheriff, one William Smith, from Upper Canada to arrest Selkirk. The earl pointed out to Smith that all commissions west of the Sault had been revoked by government, although it was still not clear whether this action applied to warrants issued in the Western District of Upper Canada. It appears likely that Sir John Sherbrooke had intended such a revocation, but had failed to close all the loopholes in his proclamation. This was yet another illustration of the problems of exercising long-distance authority over the West. Selkirk would later complain to Lieutenant Governor Gore about the behaviour of Smith.[27] The deputy sheriff continued to hang around the fort, attempting to execute his warrants. Selkirk tried to throw him out, then placed him under armed guard within the fort, providing yet another illustration of resistance to authority.[28]

Others in Selkirk's entourage became unfortunately involved in this resistance. Smith complained in writing to A.B. Becher, who wrote to Selkirk as an "impartial person in the service of His Majesty" to enquire about the law officer's treatment.[29] Selkirk responded that with the appointment of the Coltman Commission came the revocation of all commissions of peace west of the falls of St. Mary.[30] Smith should have known about this revocation before proceeding, Selkirk insisted. No one would bother him were he not so insistent about executing his illegal writs. Smith would subsequently protest to Sir John Sherbrooke about his mistreatment at Fort William, adding that Selkirk's military escort had not only failed to respond to his appeals for assistance but had also rescued several individuals whom he had apprehended. Smith further noted that he carried a military order to Sergeant Pugh of the 37th (the non-com in charge of the military escort), which Pugh refused to receive until he had consulted Lord Selkirk. As Sir John Sherbrooke would observe to Selkirk of the sergeant, "the poor fellow has certainly been placed in a situation of great difficulty."[31]

In early April Selkirk learned of the reoccupation of Fort Douglas. A few days later, a rush of mail assured him that his family was flourishing in Montreal. A baby girl had been born to Lady Selkirk without incident on 4 January. She was named Katherine Jean and Lady Sherbrooke was the godmother. Fortunate it was that the news was so positive on the personal front and at Red River, for what Selkirk learned from his business correspondence was hardly very encouraging. Samuel Gale wrote that Selkirk's proposal to Vandersluy and McTavish were referred to in the press as an offer to "compound felonies & other crimes," and the arrangements with Daniel McKenzie were improper since he was not specifically authorized to do such business. Such transactions, Gale maintained, only provided pretext for further imputations. He advised Selkirk to return to Montreal unless the earl found it "expeditiously necessary" to remain with the commissioners heading west, and reported that the North West Company would probably attack both Fort William and York Factory in the spring.[32]

Selkirk's Montreal attorney, James Stuart, was even more brutal about the deal with McKenzie than Gale. Stuart, like Gale, was the son of a Loyalist. He was a graduate of King's College in Windsor, and one of the most skilled legal minds in the province. At this time he was one of the leaders of the Lower Canadian House of Assembly in its opposition to the governor of the province in the person of Sir John Sherbrooke. Selkirk and the Hudson's Bay Company seemed to fall naturally in with the colonial opposition to the elite oligarchy that ran the Canadas, while the North West Company seemed equally naturally to be a part of that oligarchy. No legal way existed to make the furs answerable for Selkirk's claims, Stuart insisted, and McKenzie could not bind his co-partners to arbitration, which was showing him more latitude as a partner than did either English or Canadian law. While the sale of goods could be claimed by Selkirk to be valid, Stuart frankly doubted its legitimacy, and he recommended leaving all remaining goods when he departed the fort. In conclusion, Stuart observed that the warrants against Selkirk were quite legal, and he could but hope that his client was beyond their reach by the time they were served, preferably re-establishing the power of government at Red River.[33]

Selkirk never expressed any regrets over defying the law officers of Upper Canada. However, in a chastened tone, Selkirk wrote his wife after receiving these letters:

> The consequences so naturally arising from my wretchedly ill-judged conduct in September, give room for bitter enough reflections, but on the other hand I have the cordial of knowing that my own love is safe and well, about which I have had many an anxious fit since New Year's Day. . . . I hope the letter I sent for Sherbrooke may have been of some use in apologizing for the measures I have so much reason to regret. Though it was but an imprudent avowal, I think it was better to take the responsibility frankly on myself than to attempt to evade it and hope that my letter would at least show that my error was rather an exception than specimen of my general conduct.[34]

Heeding Stuart's warning, he ordered only necessary supplies and his own goods packed for the journey west from Fort William. In letters to the commissioners, Selkirk apologized to them for not remaining at Fort William. He also apologized for exposing himself to misrepresentation "through my own imprudence" in dealing with Daniel McKenzie. He further noted that Messrs. Spencer and McNab were named in the warrants carried by Deputy Sheriff Smith, but the earl was certain that the commission would not sanction these documents.[35] On 1 May the Selkirk party— including manservant William, Captain de Lorimier, and William Laidlaw—left Fort William. Dr. Allan would follow later, confirming that Selkirk was feeling quite hale and hardy at this point. John McNab was left in charge of Fort William, with orders to hand it over to the commissioners or persons authorized by them. The canoe journey to Red River went exceptionally well, although not swiftly. To his wife, Selkirk reported, "I was never in better health, and in fact have enjoyed a vigour of health since I have been under my tent, such as I hardly knew when living in a house."[36]

Further correspondence catching up with Selkirk on his journey to Red River indicated that the North West Company was continuing to gain ground in the battle of public opinion. In Britain, John Halkett had earlier recognized the extent to which Selkirk was losing the press wars, and he had attempted to set forth the story of the harassment of the settlement in 1815 and 1816 in an anonymously written and privately printed pamphlet entitled *Statement respecting the Earl of Selkirk's Settlement of Kildonan, upon the Red River, in North America; its destruction in the years 1815 and 1816; and the massacre of Governor Semple and his Party.*[37] The discretion of private publication may have been self-defeating. Sir James Hall wrote to the publisher Blackwood that the pamphlet had been "circulated privately" and he had no extra copies.[38] Selkirk's old tutor and mentor Dugald Stewart wrote Lady Katherine Halkett, expressing great approval for this pamphlet. The old man wanted the work published under the author's name, openly admitting the relationship and friendship with Selkirk. Stewart continued:

> A friend of mine, who ranks very high at our bar, & on whose judgment I have great reliance (Mr. Thomas Thomson) has just left me. He had got the pamphlet in Edin'r late in an Evening, & was so irresistibly carried along with it, that he read it from beginning to end before he went to bed. It was with much pleasure I heard him add, that if all the facts in it should be substantiated by proper evidence, he had not the slightest doubt that Lord S. will obtain a complete triumph over his enemy.[39]

"Proper evidence" was the key phrase, of course. Halkett's pamphlet, like the Selkirk case generally, relied heavily on circumstantial evidence that strongly suggested but did not prove any conspiracy on the part of the Nor'westers. More ominously, Stewart added, Selkirk's "personal presence in London is, in my opinion, the most effectual Step; (perhaps the *only* effectual Step) to quash this formidable & atrocious opposition to his projects on the other Side of the Atlantic." Stewart was probably quite accurate in this assessment, although it was already too late to change policy in London, and Selkirk was desperately needed at his settlement. Whatever his location, Selkirk would not give in. As Lady Selkirk put it to Halkett a few months later, "I think we are all agreed that although we must weigh well whether the gain is worth the expense, yet if we are to be poor for three generations we must absolutely fight this out."[40] What was at stake, of course, was less Red River than Selkirk's honour and reputation.

While Selkirk headed for Red River, several parties from Lower Canada set off by canoe for the west in the spring of 1817. The Nor'westers had been collecting men all winter for what was widely rumoured to be a major attack on Selkirk's position at Fort William. A brigade sent in the autumn of 1816 had foundered in the gales of Lake Superior and had been forced to turn back. William McGillivray himself personally led the North West force from Lachine, which departed by the first canoes possible. McGillivray had plenty of incentive for his haste. Selkirk's forces were in occupation of the entire western canoe route from Lake Superior to Fort Douglas. The earl had seized and arguably purchased £100,000 worth of furs, the proceeds from which were absolutely essential to keep the North West Company solvent. To make matters worse, fur magnate John Jacob Astor was soon threatening to assert American rights south of the 49th parallel. Astor had already lost one struggle with the North West Company on the Pacific Coast when his trading post on the Columbia River, Fort Astoria, had been forcibly sold to the Nor'westers in 1812.[41] He was keen to renew the rivalry.

At about the same time, another party consisting of forty-eight De Meuron soldiers, forty-five of their wives, and fifty-five Canadian voyageurs—personally recruited by Lady Selkirk—also set off from Lachine. The voyageurs were intended to reinforce the Hudson's Bay Company in the Athabasca region, while the De Meurons were for the Red River settlement. Lady Selkirk wrote her brother, "I plume myself much on them as they are my throw entirely." They made, she thought, "a very effective addition to the Posse comitatis of Red River." The De Meurons were under the command of Archy McDonald. Their departure was delayed at Lachine by Commissioner Coltman, who was afraid that the De Meurons were heading off well armed, although the only guns they carried were eight cases of trade guns belonging to the Hudson's Bay Company. As a precaution, Lady Selkirk had a list of the entire cargo of the canoes sworn before a magistrate to avoid charges that they were carrying war stores. Nevertheless, Coltman ordered the Prince Regent's proclamation read to the entire company. When the reading was over, a Canadian in the HBC group stepped up to Coltman and asked, "Est ce tout, Monsieur?" Surprised, Coltman responded, "Oui, Monsieur." The Canadian answered, "Eh bien si cela est tout, vive Lord Selkirk." All the De Meurons took off their hats and cheered, "Vive Lord Selkirk!" Coltman took oaths from the entire expedition, and finally permitted it to depart. According to Lady Selkirk, "Archy in a fit of despair offered to undergo any punishment if they could find a single man to vary in the story; then they called in the sergeant, and the sergeant's wife, & examining them declared themselves satisfied, and our men went off in high glee."[42]

Lady Selkirk had also persuaded Samuel Gale to accompany the commissioners to the West. Gale was a small timid man. A bachelor in his thirties, he worshipped Lady Selkirk. The canoe journey to Red River, with John Pritchard accompanying him as his assistant, would be the great adventure of his life. William Coltman refused to admit Samuel Gale into his canoe, reported Lady Selkirk to her brother, but she had anticipated this and provided a canoe for the little lawyer, with "as many comforts as I could procure for my champion, and a little flag which he demanded with the arms and motto which had taken his fancy amazingly when he saw them on the seal." She added, "It is bad to go on, but worse to go back, that is all I can say." Gale was of value at the Sault, when the Selkirk expedition would be held up again, this time by Major John Fletcher, the other commissioner appointed by Sir John Sherbrooke, in a series of confrontations of comic-opera proportions, and it arrived at Red River very late in the year.[43]

At the Sault, Samuel Gale's canoe caught up with those of the commissioners. Major Fletcher objected to Gale's presence at the investigations, saying it did not seem proper to adopt suggestions or put questions "proceeding from an advocate when there was an advocate on one side only."[44] This attitude bothered Gale, for if the commissioners ignored him, there would be the appearance of legal counsel for Selkirk but not the reality. Major Fletcher was even more disturbed when he learned that Colonel Coltman was departing alone for Fort William, and had invited Gale to join him in his canoe. Before he left the Sault, Coltman asked Gale to join a dinner party to celebrate the king's birthday, adding, "I know of no better occasion of employing a jar of the Patent soup put up eighteen months ago in London & presented me by a fair lady before leaving Quebec."[45] The soup was opened and found in perfect order. It was quite palatable after some local whitefish was added to it. Gale learned that Major Fletcher was not going on immediately to Fort William, but was remaining behind with his soldiers. Gale was convinced that Fletcher's job was to delay and deter the De Meurons from joining Selkirk. In his cups, Fletcher later told a British officer (who told Gale) that Coltman had left to avoid being implicated in the proceedings, leaving Fletcher to "get through the affair as well as he could."

Even Samuel Gale had to admit that Major Fletcher's behaviour at Sault Ste Marie was ludicrous and would have been amusing had the stakes not been so high. "Sometimes the occurrences of the last fortnight have produced melancholy, at other times indignation, and at other times it has been impossible to avoid laughter."[46] Gale's reports of Fletcher's buffooneries were confirmed by depositions from British officers who were equally offended by them. Fletcher was a drunkard who consumed alcoholic beverages from morning to night but somehow managed to function. He was also a man fascinated and obsessed with military drill, in which he could engage with his little detachment for hours. According to Gale, "The spectacle was a little outre, to see a *Major* commanding and putting through their manual a dozen men half a dozen times a day."[47] Fletcher ingeniously combined these two penchants to frustrate and aggravate the party being led west by Archy McDonald. Samuel Gale recognized the danger perfectly well. If any of Selkirk's party lost their temper, Fletcher would have an excuse for further action. Gale advised McDonald's people to meet every act of aggression with Christian forbearance. He was prepared to allow that Colonel Coltman was a neutral, but obviously had considerable doubts about Major Fletcher.

Fletcher seized the eight cases of trading guns from the HBC canoes and refused to listen to Gale's legal objections. "I act *en militaire*," he proclaimed at one point.[48] As the Montreal lawyer well knew, Fletcher was quite correct in his assertion that "there were no great Chams of Tartary in this part of the world" but the commissioners, who "might do as they chose with anything."[49] On 9 June, Simon McGillivray arrived at the encampment. Lieutenant Moir described a meeting with McGillivray at Fletcher's tent. The Nor'wester was "armed with a pair of hair trigger duelling pistols, a fowling piece with a

Spanish barrel, and Egg's waterproof lock, and a coteau de chasse."[50] As for Major Fletcher, in the presence of Gale and McGillivray, he ostentatiously loaded his pocket pistols and his double-barrelled fowling piece with ball cartridge, three balls per cartridge. Although Gale insisted that there was no law prohibiting the Selkirk party from proceeding, they were not authorized to depart. Frustrated by the delays, Archibald McDonald wrote a letter of protest and announced his intention to proceed regardless. The major met Archy's canoes at the first portage with his detachment of soldiers, arms at the ready. He ordered the men to drop their packs and took McDonald into custody, subsequently releasing him. Not until 20 June were McDonald's canoes allowed to proceed to the entrance to Lake Superior. There they paused for several days before Fletcher allowed them to enter the Lake and proceed with him to Fort William. By this time, it was certainly too late to get any of the party to the Athabasca.

Whatever the intent of the commissioners, the effect of their actions was to allow the Nor'westers to re-enter Fort William uncontested. Not long after Selkirk's departure, Deputy Sheriff Smith had arrested John McNab and John Spencer.[51] He immediately demanded all the keys and was apparently joined by William McGillivray, who placed John McNab and John Spencer in adjoining apartments under the watchful eye of a constable. John Spencer reported that a guard accompanied the captives everywhere, even "to the necessary."[52] McGillivray admitted that he had no authority and denied that McNab was his prisoner, insisting that he had been committed under the authority of Deputy Sheriff Smith. In any event, McNab and Spencer were removed under custody from the fort on 2 June, while the Nor'westers got on with the task of assessing the damage done to the fort and the NWC by Selkirk's occupation. A few days later, McNab and Spencer met Commissioner Coltman heading west. On 13 June they reported to Samuel Gale and Major Fletcher at the Sault, on their way east to Sandwich to answer charges of having forcibly entered Fort William. On that same day, two NWC canoes arrived at Fort Lac la Pluie. Deputy Sheriff Smith advanced with a piece of paper in his hands, demanding admittance. When refused, he called for an axe. A number of Nor'westers cut their way into the fort. Those occupying it were sent packing.

On 20 June, the Selkirk entourage met North West Company partner Angus Shaw on the Red River. Shaw asked Selkirk whether he had seen the Red River proclamation by the Prince Regent, which ordered a mutual restitution of all property. Selkirk said he had not. Shaw said that he had come directly from England, where he had confidential meetings with His Majesty's ministers. He added that the proclamation he handed to Selkirk demonstrated that the HBC and Selkirk had no more right to the country than anyone else. Shaw demanded that Selkirk send an order to Bas de la Rivière to surrender the fort. Selkirk replied that he had already given such an order. Captain de Lorimier then informed Selkirk that Deputy Sheriff Smith was in the canoe with Shaw.[53]

Dr. Allan and Lord Selkirk, accompanied by Sergeant Pugh and his military escort, arrived at Fort Douglas on the evening of 21 June. Two days later, Lieutenant Graffenreid arrived from Bas de la Riviere. He had opened the gate on being shown the Prince Regent's proclamation by Angus Shaw and Deputy Sheriff Smith, he reported. The latter, claiming it his duty, had seized the furs of the HBC. On 24 June, Messrs Shaw and Smith also arrived at Fort Douglas. Smith was immediately arrested by Governor Macdonell as a disturber of the public peace. The next day, John Shaw requested an interview with Selkirk.[54] He demanded the return of the furs and other property of the NWC that had been in the fort when Captain D'Orsonnens had taken possession of it. Selkirk replied that Shaw could take everything that could be ascertained to belong to the NWC except two brass cannon, which would be delivered up to the king's commissioners. Shaw insisted that those of mixed descent were not under the control of the NWC. They were regarded by the Nor'westers as was any other band of Aboriginal people, he asserted. He extended this declaration to Cuthbert Grant, Alexander Fraser, and Roderick MacKenzie, and later told Selkirk that he considered his own son William as "merely an Indian."

On a more positive note, Selkirk met John Tanner at Fort Douglas. "The American" had spent the remainder of the winter and spring of 1817 hiding with the Aboriginal people from the wrath of the NWC before taking refuge with Selkirk's people. The earl was not only grateful to Tanner, but also quite fascinated with his story. He promised to assist the American to return to his relations and would keep his word. In his later memoir, Tanner related that Selkirk became "very impatient" waiting for Commissioner Coltman.[55] This was quite understandable, since Selkirk's reputation and the future of his settlement both depended on the commissioner's adjudication of the dispute and his eventual report. The impatience was not reduced by news coming to Selkirk from all quarters that the Nor'westers were behaving in their usual arrogant fashion. Nor was it helped by a letter from Sir John Sherbrooke, brought by an express, alluding to instructions for the due execution of the law that he received from the British government and was entrusting to the commissioners. Sherbrooke noted that the measures would seriously affect Selkirk, but he did not fully explain them, thus ignoring his explicit instructions from Lord Bathurst.[56] Selkirk would not learn the full details from Coltman, either. Unfortunately, Samuel Gale was not yet on hand to provide advice. Delayed by Major Fletcher, Gale was only making his way to Fort William during the period Selkirk anxiously awaited Coltman at Fort Douglas. Gale's experiences had already led him to believe that there was some kind of vendetta in operation against the earl. "Does it not seem probable that orders have been received from England for something like a hunt against the E of S thro the influence of the under friends of the NW's at home?" he asked in a letter to Lady Selkirk.[57] Gale would prove considerably less trusting of Commissioner Coltman than Selkirk himself.

Not surprisingly, Selkirk wrote to the commissioners from Fort Douglas on 28 June complaining that while he was complying with the injunctions of the proclamation, the NWC was engaged in new acts of aggression.[58] He also protested strenuously about the actions of "soi-distant" Deputy Sheriff Smith, "who has the effrontery to assume the powers of a magistrate in this territory." He concluded by insisting that the commission should be arranging the restitution rather than one party seizing "with the strong hand whatever they may pretend to claim as their own wherever they may have the power to enforce their claim." This would be the beginning of a long protracted series of disagreements between Commissioner Coltman and Selkirk over the role of the commission and the alleged favouritism shown to the NWC.

Colonel Coltman continued on majestically beyond Fort William towards Red River. He stopped briefly at Bas de la Riviére but took no action against the Nor'westers he found there. From the head of the Red River, he wrote a letter to Selkirk stating that he had come on in advance of the remainder of his party in hopes of being useful.[59] Coltman briefly outlined his plan of conduct. He emphasized that the Prince Regent's first objectives, as stated by Lord Bathurst, were the cessation of hostilities, the mutual restoration of all property, and the pacification of the country. Thus "the enquiry into & investigation of past offences will consequently stand last in point of time." The emphasis would be placed on measures for the future rather than considerations of the past. Such a strategy could hardly please Selkirk and his people, whose principal interest was legal retribution against those who had been harassing the settlement and the HBC for years. No mention was made in this letter about the instructions from Lord Bathurst to Governor Sherbrooke regarding the legal treatment of Selkirk. Coltman would later insist he merely kept his own counsel.

At the Forks, which he reached on 5 July, Coltman pointedly ignored Selkirk's salute and ordered his four canoes paddled about a mile above Fort Douglas. Here he pitched his tent and dined with partners of the NWC. The corpulent Coltman did break bread with Selkirk and his "gentlemen" the following day, successfully reassuring the earl that he was indeed impartial. Selkirk was considerably less convinced that the commissioner really understood the situation, however well disposed he might be. Selkirk tried to explain the problem, as he saw it, to Coltman in a letter of 7 July.[60] Most of the disorder resulted from the habit of the Nor'westers to take the law into their own hands. If Selkirk's people had responded in kind, it was because there was no alternative. The NWC had ignored the Prince Regent's injunction to abstain from violence in every case where they had the advantage, such as at Fort William and Lac la Pluie. Coltman would accomplish little if Selkirk's people and the HBC could "see no check put on outrages which have thus been committed almost under your eye." The Nor'westers needed a practical lesson about the impropriety of their conduct, which implied legal action against their excesses.

At the Forks, Lord Selkirk was quickly disabused of any hope he may have had that Colonel Coltman would move to investigate the outrages committed against his settlement in 1815 and 1816 by immediately calling witnesses and hearing testimony. Instead, the earl found himself haggling over the restoration of property and other matters he regarded as peripheral, while individuals who had played a leading role at Seven Oaks were allowed to come and go as they pleased. Worse still to his mind, he learned that Coltman in effect was granting immunity to most of the mixed-blood people in return for their evidence. Conscious of his heavy losses in the Athabasca district, Selkirk understandably wanted a simultaneous restoration of all property throughout the Indian country. Simon McGillivray insisted that restitution start immediately with Red River. Selkirk maintained that only property illegally seized should be returned, while the Nor'westers wanted everything included since to make inventories of what belonged to each company was a "manifest absurdity."[61] The NWC also insisted that all servants hired by either party while still under contract to the other be restored. This was actually a quite one-sided demand, since all the servants thus hired were defectors from the NWC. They included Frederick Heurter, a former De Meuron who had signed on with the Nor'westers but who claimed to be so horrified by their savage behaviour that he crossed over to the Hudson's Bay Company.[62] Coltman added insult to injury by refusing to take Heurter's evidence on the grounds that he had left the NW service and was not a neutral witness.

Both Selkirk and Coltman quickly discovered that their respective but conflicting high expectations for the commission were not to be met. If Selkirk had hoped for a full investigation of the violence in the west, Coltman had hoped that the termination of the immediate state of hostilities between the parties in his presence would end "the misconstructions of each other's proceedings so naturally arising out of the jealousies and suspicions incident to a state of hostility."[63] Instead, the commissioner found all the elements of the confrontation being continually played out in the negotiations themselves, making it increasingly unlikely that he could ever effect a genuine pacification. Selkirk blamed everything on NWC predilections for violence. The NWC, in its turn, insisted that the problem originated in the HBC's assumption of unwanted territorial rights and jurisdictions. If trade had not been interrupted, the fatal contests on the plains would never have occurred. In any case, only the NWC seemed to be getting what it wanted— a return to the status quo ante bellum—from Coltman's presence.

After many days of bargaining and the exchange of numerous letters frequently written in leaky tents by the various parties involved, Coltman had managed to arrange with Selkirk the return of all contested property to the NWC. Coltman and Selkirk exchanged over fifty letters and memoranda between July and September 1817, most of them in the first half of July. Selkirk fought fiercely to have the question of the property purchased from Daniel McKenzie adjudicated in the courts, but eventually surrendered the point. The order on restitution was signed by the parties on 15 July.[64] On that same day, Coltman reported in a letter to Sir John Sherbrooke that the proof was decisive that Selkirk obeyed "legitimate authority."[65] The earl had also demonstrated his peaceable intentions by his refusal to interfere with NWC canoes bound for the Athabasca, despite many rumours of violence committed against HBC traders in that western region. Coltman added that he was not clear whether Selkirk's reasons for refusing to obey the earlier warrants were "well founded," but "with his Lordship's views of the character and proceedings of his opponents, they were not unnatural, and must I think be allowed considerable weight in extenuation on a future bona fide surrender." Taken in conjunction with the commissioner's own refusal to recognize the authority of Deputy Sheriff Smith, this judgment went a long way to acquit Selkirk from charges of flaunting legal warrants. Unfortunately, this implicit exoneration would not be known for some time in either eastern Canada or in Great Britain.

Selkirk did not make much progress with the commissioner on the matter of legal action for earlier depredations against the settlement. Coltman did meet on 10 July with a delegation of Métis to retrace *in situ* the movements of 19 June 1816.[66] A few days later he had Peter Fidler draw up a map reflecting the testimony of the participants. In an affidavit sworn before Coltman, Fidler managed to make an editorial comment on his map and the Métis testimony, noting that there were no natural impediments to the mixed-blood party making a wider sweep around Fort Douglas than they had done.[67] Coltman also took many depositions from the Métis and Canadians. Samuel Gale would later complain that the commissioner allowed the witnesses long preambles of "mitigation and extenuation of the atrocities committed in Red River."[68] The Selkirk people were continually upset by Coltman's refusal to detain legally any of those involved in the violence. Both Selkirk and Captain D'Orsonnens offered to execute the warrants already outstanding against the culprits, but were refused by Coltman. The commissioner's rationale for this tolerance of lawbreakers was twofold. In the first place, he would not have had the cooperation of the Métis in his fact-finding investigations had he gone around arresting them, either before or after they had testified. In the second, he truly believed—and would repeat many times—that most of what had happened, while horrible, was not really actionable in the courts.

On 12 July Lord Selkirk asked Commissioner Coltman whether he would agree to meet with a delegation of local Indian chiefs, mostly of the Salteaux nation, but including several Cree leaders. Coltman was initially reluctant to do so in the absence of an official government interpreter, but Selkirk offered an ingenious solution involving two interpreters whose versions could be checked against each other.[69] The earl was anxious that Coltman learn the sentiments of the local Aboriginal people, so that exploitation of them could not be subsequently charged against him. He was also anxious that the commissioner witness their consent to a specific cession of a portion of their lands for agricultural settlement. Selkirk succeeded in getting Coltman to attend a two-day conference with a number of Aboriginal leaders from the Red River region who were at the Forks. He also managed to convince the commissioner to discuss with the chiefs the question of a land concession to the settlement. On 17 July, Coltman wrote to Selkirk, "It appears to me as far as I can see that the Indians wish the Settlement for their own advantage & would scarcely require any consideration for allowing to the Settlers an exclusive possession of a reasonable portion of land."[70] He added, "something will however perhaps be expected as the subject has been so much talked of & certainly an annual present seems best, as it is evident that the interests of the Colony would require the Indians' friendship to be ensured in this manner, even if they gave up their lands voluntarily." What Selkirk proposed was not a "Sale but a Gift." Instead of a large purchase price, he offered only a small annual present. The cession, the boundaries of which would be specified by the chiefs themselves, would thus be made "to shew in a more decided manner their sense of the Benefits likely to arise from agricultural settlements." He insisted the negotiations could not wait, as assembling so many leading men again would be difficult.[71]

Coltman promised to get the Aboriginal sentiments "faithfully recorded," but understandably wanted nothing to do with the negotiations concerning any deed of land. These negotiations were carried out independently on 18 July by Selkirk and a number of officers from the settlement with five of the Saulteaux and Cree chiefs who were attending the conference, including Peguis. In return for an annual quitrent of £200 of "good merchantable tobacco," the chiefs granted to the king—the exact terminology was "give, grant, and confirm"—an area extending six miles in all directions from Fort Douglas and Fort Daer, as well as land extending two miles from the banks on either side of the Red and Assiniboine rivers. This land was to "have and to hold forever" and was for the use of Selkirk and the settlers he established on these lands. Whatever other effects the transaction had or would have, it made clear that the resident Aboriginal people were in 1817 well disposed to Selkirk's settlement.[72] Selkirk's strategy of an Aboriginal gift, while enlightened in principle, may have been too complex for those involved to comprehend fully. Despite the existence of a written treaty providing for the cession of land signed by the chiefs, several of them would many years later insist that they had not actually sold their land, but only leased it for a limited number of years.[73]

Samuel Gale and his travelling companion Colonel Robert Dickson finally arrived at the Forks on 27 July. Gale arrived minus twenty volumes of law books, which were soaked in a canoe mishap and sent back to Quebec. Dickson was a former fur trader who had worked for the British government as Indian agent and superintendent, his salary paid out of the secret-service funds. He successfully raised First Nations warriors for the British during the War of 1812. The acquisition of his support by Selkirk and the Red River Settlement at this point seemed a considerable coup, although Dickson unfortunately had no financial sense whatever and would end up costing Selkirk a small fortune.[74] Coltman issued a public letter to the "respective proprietors, governors, factors, agents, servants or adherents of the Hudson's Bay and North West Companies."[75] The letter in many respects anticipated Coltman's ultimate findings on the dispute. It called for obedience to the Prince Regent's proclamation. It noted that one of the great legal questions of the dispute between the two companies related to whether the charter to the HBC had been earlier breached by non-use. It described the violence in the western territories as resulting from one party's assertion of the rights of the charter before they had been confirmed in the courts and the other's retaliation on principles of self-defence "in a country distant from the customary protection of the law," which was "a plea inadmissable by any government." Coltman's letter further observed that the proclamation "appears to treat these violences rather as acts of private hostility or war, than as robberies, felonies, or Murders, in the usual acceptation of these words, and it is fairly presumed that Judges and juries will hereafter be inclined to look upon them in a similar view." Those involved in the violence could look for lenity, said Coltman, if they had "not participated in deliberate murder or been the primary cause or instigators of the offences at large."

Despite the frequently annoying presence of the commission, Selkirk did succeed in putting his settlement back on its feet, particularly after the settlers had returned to the Forks on 19 July and after the arrival of Samuel Gale a few days later. Gale took over most of the detailed negotiation with Coltman, casting a suspicious eye on most of the commissioner's activities. Alexander Macdonell recorded the meeting between the founder and his people laconically: "About 11 o'clock forenoon he came to the Frog Plains and conversed with the settlers."[76] As well as arranging the treaty with the Aboriginals,

Selkirk allocated land for a church and a school. According to several eyewitnesses, he responded to the request of the inhabitants of this first parish in
Red River by naming it Kildonan. The earl also promised a Presbyterian
clergyman.[77] He announced that those loyal settlers who had suffered in the
recent depredations—twenty-four families—would have their land forever
free of any debt to him. Land surveys of Peter Fidler, which allowed farm lots
of 220 yards along the river and 1980 yards back from it, were confirmed by
the earl, and lots given to the De Meurons. Set aside for the Roman Catholic
Church were 10,000 acres of land, a substantial amount, given the nature of
the Aboriginal cession. Selkirk also negotiated with the HBC for the establishment of a company store at Fort Douglas.

The earl was under no illusions about what he had done. It was only a
beginning, virtually a fresh start from scratch. His presence and actions in the
summer of 1817 acquired the status of mythology in the settlement, as Alexander Ross would record in his history published nearly forty years later.[78]
But despite the potential exhilaration of dealing in person with his settlers,
Selkirk spent precious little time with them. His time at Red River was taken
up with negotiations with Colonel Coltman and the Nor'westers, and it was
soon necessary to return east to deal with a myriad of problems there. The
earl spent longer in Red River than he had at any of his previous colonization
sites, but he displayed little interest either in establishing rapport or in serving
as a leader. Selkirk fought unsuccessfully to prevent the Nor'Westers from
continuing to hold Fort Gibraltar within gunshot of the Forks. He argued to
Coltman that without the elimination of the NWC, it would be most prudent
to remove the settlers across the American boundary to Pembina, "where at
least they will not have to apprehend hostility from subjects of the same
Government and where if they be liable to be attacked it will not be considered an offence to be prepared for resistance."[79]

Samuel Gale accompanied commissioner Coltman to Bas de la Riviére in
mid-August. There the NW canoes for the western interior were stopped, the
prince regent's proclamation was read to the voyageurs and traders, and
some depositions were taken. Gale was not happy with the time spent
collecting information on what had happened in the Athabasca, arguing that
what had occurred earlier at Red River was "the cause and sole justification
for any of the measures at Fort William."[80] Coltman stayed up all night to
take the depositions, so as not to delay the brigades unnecessarily. Upon the
commissioner's return to Red River, a minor dispute pregnant with larger

implications blew up between Selkirk and the Nor'westers. By this point, the NWC was also represented by legal counsel, a Canadian lawyer named Henry McKenzie, who had the previous year in the press as "Mercator" castigated and insulted Selkirk.[81] Not surprisingly, Selkirk found McKenzie very offensive. The contretemps arose over the cutting of hay in an open and unenclosed meadow.[82] Coltman supported the NWC's right to occupy ground at Red River as part of his general support of the Nor'west refusal to acknowledge HBC charter rights, while Selkirk insisted that the claims of the Nor'westers subverted the settlers' security of title.[83] If Selkirk could not guarantee title to the land he was granting to his settlers, his enterprise was obviously in enormous trouble. This question would not be resolved until the merger of the two companies. In late August Selkirk was also forced to deal with the fur-trading part of the brigade that had come west in 1817 and had been delayed for so long by Major Fletcher at the Sault. He determined to winter the fur traders at Lac la Pluie rather than send them late in the year into the Athabasca, where they would probably have only experienced another disaster. But it meant that the proper restoration of property in the Athabasca and the resumption of competition in that region would not occur until 1818.

Commissioner Coltman was quite unsympathetic to Selkirk's plan to return to Canada through the United States, apparently feeling that he would be charged with having allowed the earl to escape out of the jurisdiction of the Crown.[84] Selkirk's advisors insisted that the earl ran the risk of being arrested and returned to Montreal in chains if he passed through NWC territory on his way east. They were probably right, since Miles Macdonell was arrested in August near Fort William and taken to Canada under heavy guard, and Selkirk no longer had the protection of an armed escort. Sergeant Pugh had finally opened his orders from Sir John Sherbrooke and found he was relieved from duty. Officially, Selkirk's reason for his decision was the need for canoes (and voyageurs to paddle them) to take witnesses to Montreal.[85] Selkirk's entourage would have consumed too many canoes needed for other purposes. Coltman eventually decided he did not have the authority to prevent the earl from his proposed American route. Instead, he tried deterrence, insisting upon a heavy bail for Selkirk and his Fort William associates, to guarantee that they would show up for court appearances in Canada. This bail—£6000 for Selkirk and two sureties of £3000 each, and half that amount for Dr. Allan, Captain Matthey, and

Captain D'Orsonnens—was of an unprecedented size. Selkirk and his attorney questioned Coltman's competence to exact such bail for offences allegedly committed within the jurisdiction of Upper Canada. Gale further complained of the legal absurdity of the process, in which "a magistrate for the Indian territory, for offences charged to have been committed in the Western District of Upper Canada, took bail for the appearance of the parties in the district of Montreal in the province of Lower Canada."[86]

The NWC made one final attempt at Selkirk's apprehension at Red River, attempting to use a deputy sheriff's assistant named Campbell to execute another warrant from Upper Canada. Even Commissioner Coltman thought this effort was "indecorous," but he was unable to persuade the Nor'westers to drop it. Campbell subsequently turned up in Selkirk's room at Fort Douglas with his warrant. The earl summoned Samuel Gale, complaining, "Here is a person who has been committing an assault and battery upon me in my own house."[87] Coltman was again summoned to deal with the matter, which was argued before him by Samuel Gale and the NWC lawyer Henry McKenzie. The commissioner eventually found the warrant was improper, thus apparently accepting Samuel Gale's argument that warrants issued for the Western District of Upper Canada were not valid at Red River. This ruling was not a judicial one and did not deal with the question of the legality of the Upper Canadian warrants at Fort William, which was in the Indian Territories. Campbell was charged with assault and battery and released on bail. His security was given in the amount of £500.

Despite the ruling by Coltman in the warrant business, Selkirk and his people would become increasingly critical of Coltman's performance at Red River as time went on. The taking of bail was only one of the principal subjects of their objection. Selkirk himself, who had held his temper with Coltman over most of the summer and continued to do so until his departure, later turned livid whenever he contemplated this affront to his honour, particularly when it was combined with a refusal on the commissioner's part to hold those acting for the NWC to a similar requirement.[88] Newspapers in Canada and Britain, in subsequently reporting the huge amount of the bail, often observed on the enormity of the crimes that must have brought it about. After Selkirk's return to Montreal, when he was able to recount the events of the summer to Lady Selkirk in detail, she wrote to her brother, "You cannot imagine anything like the turmoil, inconvenience, hardship and interruption at Red River, how Lord Selkirk kept his health through it all I cannot imagine; lodging food and clothing, what none of you could have endured. An umbrella planted over the table with the papers to keep them dry, the roof and the walls coming down in *puddings,* Lord Selkirk only escaped being wet in bed whenever rain fell. It must have been the spirit of contradiction that kept him in better health through all this, than he ever enjoyed in his life, at least for many years."[89] The meaning of Selkirk's acquiescence with Coltman's actions and orders would later become a subject of controversy. The earl was in the summer of 1817 in a difficult position. He had to obey the prince regent's proclamation, but he probably should have been more plain in writing that obedience was not acceptance of the justice of the commissioner's decisions.

As he prepared for departure, Selkirk wrote to his wife that the settlement was not fully back on its feet: "The N.W. are already beginning their intrigues again among the Highlanders. But the new Meurons promise well. . . . I think that Half breeds got a good fright from Coltman, & are too much in aware to venture again on such violent measures as last year. . . ." But, he added, "As we are thrown back into all the difficulties of the very first stage of a settlement, it is possible that discontents may arise amidst the unavoidable privations of that state of things."[90] On 9 September Lord Selkirk departed Red River, riding south on horseback. William Coltman left the Forks in the other direction two days later, with Samuel Gale and canoes full of witnesses not far behind. Gale's passage east was broken by continual controversy with the NWC at each of the stopping points before Lake Superior. At Lac la Pluie, for example, he found the Nor'westers and the HBC people arguing over the location of the HBC post. Although the NWC post was a mile and a half away, the Nor'westers insisted that they had always intended to build on the place chosen by the Bay's people. At Point Meuron, near Fort William, where the HBC was also building a post, he was told that the Nor'westers claimed all the lands adjacent to the Kaministiquia River for the purposes of trade. At Fort William, he found that Major Fletcher had drawn up depositions concerning Selkirk's proceedings there, allegedly allowing only facts to the disadvantage of Selkirk.

Samuel Gale became increasingly less sympathetic to William Coltman on his journey east, partly because he saw the amount of time the commissioner spent in convivial company with the Nor'westers, and partly because he had time to brood on the events of the summer. Sitting in his canoe for hours on end, Gale became persuaded that Coltman's insistence on benevolent neutrality was really designed to be quite detrimental to Selkirk and the HBC. As the little lawyer wrote Lady Selkirk from the Sault, Coltman "took it for granted that Government looked upon all parties in almost the same light, which he deemed likewise to be apparent from the Proclamation of the Prince Regent, and like a good subject he has labored to fulfil what he believes to be the wishes of Government."[91] Gale was scathing over the concept of "private war," saying "private war is not within the limits of my law, it is a species of offence which I do not rightly understand." To label arson and murder as private war was ridiculous. It was unusual, moreover, to establish before the investigation the nature of the crime that was the subject of the inquiry, he opined. He acknowledged that this was as much the result of the prince regent's proclamation as Coltman's efforts. Gale's conclusions from his ruminations were critical, for they helped determine the future course of the entire fur-trade controversy. He did not expect much vindication from Coltman or his commission. "I look for no justice save only what we can force from persons in power, through fear of disgrace," he wrote Lady Selkirk. Only publicity about the outrages of the Nor'westers would have any effect on the outcome of events. "Our cause is happily one which may be so managed as to excite sympathy and it should be our endeavour to create a universal interest. No set is so humble as to be unimportant, nor ought we to consider any so exalted as to be beyond our reach." The management of Canadian public opinion became for Gale the key to Lord Selkirk's ultimate vindication.

Selkirk was guided through the Sioux country by Colonel Dickson, riding to the St. Peter's River and carrying on by boat to the Mississippi, arriving in St. Louis on 27 October.[92] He was accompanied by Messrs Matthey, D'Orsonnens, Heurter, and Allan, all returning to face the Canadian courts for their actions at Fort William. Selkirk got held up at St. Louis until early November. He finally got horses and set out for Pittsburgh. The party bogged down in Vincennes, Indiana, in mid-month. Despite having spent much of the summer in leaky tents and a leakier Fort Douglas, despite much autumn bad weather and aggravation, Selkirk was able to report to his wife, "with all this somebody keeps his health perfectly."[93] A few days later, in Lexington, Kentucky, his group decided to continue via Virginia instead of Pittsburgh. On 16 December Selkirk was able to write Lady Selkirk that he had arrived in Washington, where he was well received by the American administration.[94]

During his stay in Washington, the earl arranged for legal assistance to protect his charter interests south of the 49th parallel, choosing a young lawyer named Daniel Webster as his agent. Three days after his arrival, he attended a state ball and was introduced by the British ambassador to John Quincy Adams, the American secretary of state.[95] Undoubtedly pursuing a conversation begun on that occasion, he wrote Adams on 22 December attempting to arrange a special status for Red River trade with the United States.[96] He reached New York on 28 December.

Several thousand miles on horseback had neither depressed nor exhausted Selkirk. He had obviously spent much of his time attempting to rethink his entire settlement operation. A letter to Andrew Colvile from New York the day of his arrival there was full of schemes for attracting American settlers to Red River. He emphasized:

> The plan of settling the country with Europeans only, must be abandoned; but (that point granted) facilities appear, that I had previously no idea of, & I believe that as a speculation it may turn out much beyond any ideas, that I ever entertained of it. The plan of the Prospectus will need some modification to suit it to Americans, but they are much more likely to go into the plan, than people of the old country. From the rapidity with which the Western country is filling up, we shall soon be within what the Yankees reckon such a moderate distance, that they will readily go to get good land cheap.[97]

The only hitch was getting the Americans to recognize his title south of the American border, he wrote. Selkirk had actually applied to the president of the United States for that recognition, but it would be denied in April 1818.[98] Lost entirely in these new plans was any hint of philanthropy. The new Red River was to be purely a land speculation. Given his many problems and expenses in Red River, certainly not yet over, Selkirk probably felt himself well within his rights in thinking purely in terms of recovering a substantial investment. But the position was disappointingly crass nevertheless, tending to confirm the complaints of his critics that Red River had only been a money-making operation, however mismanaged.

As he moved closer and closer to Canada, Lord Selkirk thought increasingly about the legal battles upcoming in the Canadas and to the public presentation of the evidence. Even his destination was a matter of some consequence and internally debated at some length.[99] Letters from Lady Selkirk and Samuel Gale reached him at Albany at the end of the year. Gale advised Selkirk that the charges at Sandwich included theft of guns from Fort William, a felony rather than a misdemeanour.[100] Selkirk could not return to Montreal until he resolved the issues at York and Sandwich. The earl decided to head to York. In his baggage, Selkirk remarked to his wife, were copies of the "Statement," doubtless the London reprint of John Halkett's pamphlet, still without the author's name on the title page but including "Observations" on a work commissioned by the Nor'westers and written by a young journalist named Samuel Hull Wilcocke. The Wilcocke pamphlet was entitled *A Narrative of Occurrences in the Indian Countries of North America, since the Connexion of the Right Hon. the Earl of Selkirk with the Hudson's Bay Company, and his Attempt to Establish a Colony on the Red River; with a Detailed Account of His Lordship's Military Expedition to, and Subsequent Proceedings at Fort William in Upper Canada.* "I have left a few at New York," he noted, "& sent 2 or 3 to Washington &c—& take three with me for distribution at York &c. The copies that are sent to you should be distributed as far as possible in Upper Canada, for it is there by Gale's account, that the misstatements of the NW Co. have had the most effect."[101] Selkirk now understood that he was losing badly the press war with the North West Company. He also appreciated that his reputation and the future of his settlement would be decided both in the press and in the courts.

CHAPTER TWENTY

Campaigning at Law, January to June 1818

L ORD SELKIRK AND HIS PARTY finally arrived in York in early January of
1818 "in high spirits from the hope of being soon on the way to
Montreal," but instead he found himself trapped in innumerable legal
complications. The news was disquieting. In a visit with D'Arcy Boulton,
Selkirk was told "of the orders he had received from Lord Bathurst to prosecute me criminally for the 'escape' (as it was called) from Dr. Mitchell's
warrant," adding that he might well have been arrested at York had not
William Coltman already taken bail for an appearance at Montreal.[1] Thus
Selkirk found himself embroiled with the Canadian courts, a process that
consumed virtually all his energy until his eventual return to England in
broken health at the end of the year. One earlier student of the courts business has remarked on the extent to which Selkirk's relations with Canadian
justice were "influenced by a kind of recurring and fatal enthusiasm,"
adding, "if deliverance by the Commissioners of Special Inquiry was illu-
sory, recourse to litigation was nothing less than fatal."[2]

Selkirk returned to Canada still in good health. Lady Selkirk, on his
return to Montreal in February of 1818, reported, "he is certainly looking
very well a good deal browned, and cheeks rounder, although not much
fatter altogether, and a look of active health very different from the languid
look he sometimes used to have, but I fear it will not last long, for already
the effect of scribbling and confinement is observable."[3] The progress of
consumption (or tuberculosis) was and is extremely difficult to predict. If the
outdoor life bought Selkirk a remission, perhaps Lady Selkirk was correct

that an indoor one of great tension would soon bring him down. In any event, Selkirk was sick in June, although he appeared to recover. By August he was complaining of feeling constantly tired and had begun spitting blood; by October he was clearly very ill. As Selkirk's health deteriorated during the course of 1818, Lady Selkirk, Dr. John Allan, and Samuel Gale increasingly took over command of the battle in the courts.

THE LEGAL BATTLES: AN OVERVIEW

More than a year of virtually non-stop legal activity produced suits, countersuits, and the expenditure of thousands of pounds by the parties involved.[4] For the enormous outlay of energy and money, the concrete results were puny to the point of absurdity. Three categories of legal action were carried out in 1818, two against Selkirk and his settlers and one against the North West Company's servants and associates. Among the first grouping of actions, those resulting from Lord Bathurst's dispatch, were charges against Selkirk of resisting arrest and committing a misdemeanour at Fort William. In the second grouping were charges brought by the North West Company against the settlers at Red River and against Selkirk by various legal officers for his treatment of them. In the third grouping were the indictments brought by Selkirk against the Nor'westers for various offences, including the murders of Robert Semple and Owen Keveny. In the end, one North West Company employee was convicted of the murder of Owen Keveny, but he was never punished. Several individuals were awarded damages for abuse done them by Selkirk, but this was in a civil case heard under curiously political conditions. In the criminal prosecutions against Selkirk for his treatment of Crown officers, the cases were dismissed. In the criminal prosecutions initiated by Selkirk for abusive actions, mainly committed in Red River, no one was ever convicted. The larger issues, particularly the claims by the Hudson's Bay Company under its charter, remained completely unresolved by the Canadian courts.

From the beginning, Selkirk had resolved upon conspiracy charges that his attorneys warned him would be difficult to sustain, in the hopes that such charges would force more documentation and evidence of North West Company malice in front of the public. While bringing the whole business home to England for trial would have been preferable, it was both practically and politically unworkable. Within this context, Selkirk appeared to have underestimated the obstacles his prosecutions had to overcome, in some ways curious given his own analysis of Canadian justice in his *Sketch of the Fur Trade*.

In the first place, the Canadian ruling classes held enormous power over the courts, a fact that Selkirk had noted in his book. He ought not to have been surprised at the difficulty in initiating and winning criminal proceedings against the North West Company and its employees, since those proceedings could only be begun and conducted by members of colonial governments who were close friends of the Nor'westers. When Selkirk and his family attended worship services at Montreal's St. Gabriel Street Church, as they occasionally did, he and Lady Selkirk must have sensed the extent to which they were regarded as outsiders and how close were the links between colonial officials and Nor'westers.[5]

The situation was only complicated by Lord Bathurst's ill-considered instructions to the colonial governments early in 1817. One historian expert on the trials has commented, "The harmful effect of this dispatch on the Earl's legal status is impossible to adjudge. Its effect could be traced with monotonous persistence through the maze of legal decisions."[6]

In the second place, the *Canada Jurisdiction Act* of 1803, which transferred criminal trials from the Indian Territory to the courts of the Canadas, was seriously flawed. The legislation simultaneously left gaping jurisdictional holes and produced curious overlaps, both of which could easily be manipulated by the lawyers on either side. Selkirk found himself being leapfrogged from one colony to another by his adversaries, who took full advantage of every opportunity to introduce countersuits. Proper legal counsel was hard to obtain, especially in Upper Canada, where the Nor'westers had hired all the available lawyers and the Law Society objected to allowing a lawyer to be brought up from Montreal merely to deal with Selkirk's legal business. Selkirk's chief Lower Canadian attorney, James Stuart, refused to expose himself to the humiliation of being refused admission to the Upper Canadian bar. The existence of the district around Fort William as an anomaly of imprecise jurisdiction did not help matters. The *Canada Jurisdiction Act* also meant that proceedings would be heard in two colonial judicial and legal systems, one of them originally French.

Behind these obvious problems were others less apparent. One was the difficulty of proving conspiracy in the courts, especially thousands of miles from the event. Indeed, many of the prosecutions were extremely abstract, even abstruse, in nature. They were essentially efforts to use the legal system for propaganda purposes. They involved attributing criminal motives to events much more easily understood as spontaneous.

The earl's efforts to convict the Red River settlers who left the colony in 1815 of felonious behaviour were as dubious as the Nor'wester prosecutions of the colony's officials in the pemmican business. Even without the manipulations of the Crown against Selkirk's attempted prosecutions, most if not all would probably have ended in either acquittal or hung juries.

Another problem was the reluctance of Canadian legal officers to allow Selkirk's lawyers to participate in the prosecutions they had brought, as would have occurred in England. Selkirk's people insisted that the Crown did not understand the cases his lawyers had constructed, and was not eager to pursue them in any case. The simple fact was that Crown officials in British America did not believe in private prosecutions. Moreover, they were ham-handed lawyers to boot, easy for a defence that had sympathy from the bench to outmanoeuvre. In this and other respects, the trials demonstrated that criminal proceedings in British America were not simply imitations of British justice. British America was not Great Britain. Selkirk's Canadian lawyers seriously contemplated pleading his privilege as a peer to escape from the Canadian court actions against him, for example, but were told by English counsel that in Canada Selkirk had "no privilege or rank but by courtesy."

Moreover, the court cases of 1818 were not simply about the law. They were also matters of high politics in both Upper and Lower Canada. The cases became inextricably intertwined with local political infighting. Given the Selkirk side's apprehension that colonial governments and officials were hand-in-glove with the Nor'westers, it was not surprising that the earl's people should seek support from the ranks of the political opposition to the elites. In Lower Canada, Selkirk's friends sought to identify with French-Canadian interests in the legislature, possibly aided by the political role of James Stuart, the Hudson's Bay Company's chief legal counsel. In Upper Canada, Selkirk had formed a firm if informal alliance with the developing popular opposition to the Family Compact, which in the period of the trials was associated with both the Scots-born critic Robert Gourlay and the American-born critic Barnabas Bidwell. This alliance was aided by the fact that Selkirk had long done his business in Upper Canada with the Lowland Scots, who were now employing Gourlay as a stalking horse in the province. The Lowlanders had joined with the American critics of the government, and only opposition lawyers were available in 1818 to be hired in Upper

Canada. The developing opposition critique in Upper Canada saw the influence of the North West Company in government circles as one more illustration of the conspiracy between Crown officials and anti-democratic forces in the province.

Lurking behind all the very real legal and political difficulties were two general overriding understandings. One was that what had happened in the West was beyond the law. The Indian Territory, despite the *Canada Jurisdiction Act*, was basically no man's land. Both sides had committed reciprocal atrocities in the absence of a proper legal structure. The situation was akin to some sort of cosmic struggle between feudal barons. The sooner the whole business was ended and peace restored, the better. This was certainly the view of William Coltman, the commissioner who had investigated the disputes in 1817. It was also the judgment of Upper Canada's Attorney General John Beverley Robinson, who explained to newly arrived Lieutenant Governor Sir Peregrine Maitland late in 1819:

> I always considered that the most correct view to be taken of the occurrences in the Indian Territories, arising out of the interference of rival interests, was to consider the violent and illegal acts, with one or two unhappy exceptions . . . as overt acts of a Conspiracy to ruin the adverse party, and for this reason that the evidence generally proved them to have been prompted not by the guilty motives which incite to these acts in a more civilized and controlled state of society, but by other objects, such as the desire of retaliation . . . or the hope of disarming an adversary by anticipating one expected act of violence by another.[7]

The second understanding was that the court cases were show trials, designed more for publicity purposes than for the achievement of true justice. "Heaping accusations upon each other in aggravated terms, and applying to them descriptions which do not belong to them is a prominent characteristic of this unhappy dispute," observed John Beverley Robinson.[8] Such a view was to some extent unfair. Both sides truly believed that the other had been guilty of great enormities that deserved punishment. In the case of Red River, there had been considerable loss of life. Selkirk and his supporters genuinely and legitimately sought legal retribution.

At the same time, public opinion was always an important consideration in the legal manoeuvring. Lord Selkirk was quite conscious that his credibility had taken quite a beating in the course of the conflict, and he sought a full exposure of events to vindicate his honour. The Selkirk forces took for granted that they and the Hudson's Bay Company started, at least in Canada, with public sympathy against them. From this perspective, the trials and their surrounding publicity—whatever the outcome—could only redound to the Selkirk/HBC advantage. The Nor'westers could be charged with a good many more serious criminal offences (including murder) than could the HBC and the settlers. From the North West Company perspective, much of the legal activity was purely defensive, designed to prevent Selkirk and the HBC from gaining too much advantage from their assumed position as innocent victims of NWC violence. The Nor'westers engaged in the typical tactic of attempting to find an equivalent "outrage" for every one that they had themselves committed.

Lord Selkirk might not have triumphed in the courts of the Canadas, but he would posthumously win the battle for public sympathy. In his lifetime, the earl never entirely appreciated that getting justice for his settlement, his settlers, and for himself was not part of anyone's agenda except his own. It was not central to the Coltman Commission, not central to the governments of the Canadas, not central to the courts, and certainly not central to the British government. At the same time, he and his advisors eventually managed to turn the failures in the Canadian courts to their advantage in the subsequent war of words. Undoubtedly the biggest mistake of the NWC in the dispute was to take too much advantage of its political connections in 1818 and 1819, persecuting its adversaries and evading prosecution itself. The Nor'westers thereby exposed themselves as easy targets for HBC propaganda presenting them as oppressive oligarchs, which helped Selkirk's people to win the battle of the press. The biggest mistake of government on both sides of the Atlantic was in not acting. The question ceased to be, What had happened in the West? It became, instead, Who was responsible for the failure to achieve any measure of justice for what had happened in the West? In the process, Lord Selkirk was transformed into an innocent victim, an honourable man attempting to gain justice for his people despite the best efforts of governments in both Britain and British America, overly sympathetic to the Nor'westers, to sweep matters under the rug. Selkirk himself argued this case most convincingly in a printed but unpublished work entitled "The Memorial of Thomas Earl of Selkirk to His Grace Charles Duke of Richmond," submitted to Richmond, the governor general of British America, late in 1818.[9]

Following the complicated legal proceedings is no easy matter. Bills of indictment were filed against most participants, and not all indictments resulted in prosecutions or court cases. Trials were removed from one province to another and postponed from one term to the next. Samuel Gale characterized the business as "perfect chaos," and he was very nearly correct. Nevertheless, it is possible to bring some order out of the confusion. For convenience, the court battles of 1818 (and a few in 1819 after Selkirk's departure from Canada) can be divided into three categories. First, there were the prosecutions encouraged by Lord Bathurst's memorandum. They were instituted against Selkirk and those who accompanied him into the interior. Second, there were the proceedings by Lord Selkirk and his people against the North West Company's employees and those held to be its accomplices. Third, there were the prosecutions instituted by the NWC against persons employed at or belonging to the Red River Settlement. For convenience's sake, each of these categories can be further divided into those occurring earlier in the sequence of events and those occurring later. The unfolding of the legal battles occurred against a background of other events. These included: the interventions, continued investigations, and eventual completion of the report of Commissioner William Coltman; increasing evidence of Selkirk's mortal illness; political events in the Canadas; and the agreement by the British and American governments on the joint occupation of the Oregon country.

THE EARLY PROSECUTIONS AGAINST SELKIRK AND HIS ASSOCIATES

Several Upper Canadian warrants had been obtained by the North West Company against Lord Selkirk for his actions at Fort William. His opponents had attempted on several occasions to execute these warrants at both Fort William and Red River. For his part, Selkirk had refused to accept them on-site on a variety of grounds, including his understanding that Fort William was not in Upper Canada. The earl and his leading associates had been forced by Commissioner William Coltman to supply an enormous bail to guarantee that they would answer charges involving them and their resistance in the courts of Lower Canada, the only venue in which the commissioner had jurisdiction. Selkirk and his legal advisors were so concerned about dealing with the Upper Canadian warrants that the earl (accompanied by Dr. John Allan and Proteus D'Orsonnens) rushed straight to York in Upper Canada upon their arrival from the United States at the end of 1818, instead of heading to Montreal to be reunited with his family and see the daughter born in his absence. Lady Jean and the children had to settle for second-hand accounts of Selkirk's successes from William, the earl's manservant, who had gone on to Montreal instead of to Sandwich, although, as she pointed out to her brother, Selkirk was generally so laconic that "I daresay I may give William's news without fear of his having antici-pated me."[10] William had certainly been most impressed with his employ-er's performance in the West.

Upon his arrival at York, Selkirk immediately called upon Chief Justice William Dummer Powell and then on Solicitor General D'Arcy Boulton in an attempt to sort out the legal complications. Powell was a Loyalist who was a bit of an outsider, not being part of the Simcoe coterie that had founded Upper Canada. He was a well-trained and experienced lawyer, if more than a bit pompous. Selkirk had met Powell on his Upper Canadian tour in 1804 and had done Powell a personal service in London a year later.[11] Doubtless he hoped for some reciprocation. The earl offered to surrender himself and give bail to answer the charges against him, but Powell claimed he could not interfere, since officially no charges were before him. A day later, Boulton informed Selkirk of the orders from Lord Bathurst, although he did not allow the earl to see the exact words used by the colonial secretary. Boulton further suggested that if the case were brought officially before him he would have to arrest Selkirk on a charge that was not bailable. The solicitor general suggested, apparently seriously, that Selkirk and his associates immediately flee to the United States to escape his jurisdiction.[12] Colin Robertson would later take similar advice and cross the border. Selkirk refused to take such a step at this time, arguing instead that he was already under a huge bail ordered by Coltman to answer these charges in the Lower Canadian courts. Boulton insisted that Coltman had no power to take such a bail, a position with which Selkirk privately concurred. But the two men agreed that the Coltman bail eliminated the need for Boulton to act. In reporting all this to his wife, Selkirk appeared genuinely surprised at the revelation of the Bathurst order.[13] Lady Selkirk was not so surprised. She and Samuel Gale had suspected something of the sort for nearly a year.

Having failed to resolve very much at York, Selkirk and his companions—accompanied by Boulton—headed off for Sandwich, the seat of the court of quarterly sessions for the Western District of Upper Canada that had issued the original warrant for felony. This was the warrant that Selkirk had refused to accept at Fort William. Local attorney James Woods objected to holding any trials in Sandwich, arguing that the situation was remote and that judges did not like to tarry there.[14] Woods was an extremely able lawyer who was nearly blind and infirm, not likely to be helpful to Selkirk beyond the Sandwich district. The earl took advantage of the visit to try to find out more about what had happened to his sheep after the American invasion in 1812 and to re-establish his settlement at Baldoon.[15] The Selkirk party found the session of the court just ended, but the chief magistrate obligingly called a special session. Sandwich was not far from Selkirk's former settlement at Baldoon, and he had a good deal of public sympathy in the district. One correspondent commiserated with the earl about a "confederacy yet more formidable than that of the N.W. Co. that of the Courts of law *alone* serve to convey clandestine persecution and force many of H.M.'s subjects out of the sphere of their allegiances."[16] Selkirk testified that the North West Company clerks had perjured themselves by saying that they had been shown no search warrant, and another affidavit by Jasper Vandersluys was produced that totally contradicted the one on which the warrant had been based. The court set this warrant aside and discharged the parties from it. So far so good.[17]

Unfortunately, the discharged warrant was not the only one that had been issued. Boulton produced another one charging Selkirk with committing a riot at Fort William and forcing the gates. Selkirk countered that he was acting as a magistrate and there had been unlawful resistance. He challenged Boulton to prove that the force used to carry out the arrests was excessive. The court insisted on witnesses, who were not present. Selkirk was put under bail—a small one—to answer these charges at the next meeting of the court. Boulton then brought forward yet another warrant, the one he was officially directed to prosecute. This one, the one ordered by Lord Bathurst, was for refusing to submit at Fort William to the original warrant for felony (already set aside by the court). Selkirk again explained his actions and the court demanded witnesses. Boulton insisted that the charge of resistance was not a bailable offence, but the court disagreed. Selkirk and his associates were bound over on a small recognizance on this charge, as well as on another of resisting in March 1817 the warrant served by Deputy Sheriff Smith. These indictments would hang around for several years before they were settled, with the Crown on several occasions postponing prosecution and on one occasion quashing an indictment, although

Selkirk had transported his witnesses to Sandwich at considerable expense.[18] Selkirk was finally discharged with a jury acquittal on 12 January 1819.[19] Lady Selkirk wrote to her husband while he was at Sandwich in 1818 that everyone seemed to have known of Lord Bathurst's dispatch but him, adding "never be taken in by a 'cordial reception' again, distrust everything that breathes, you may begin with me if you like, there are moments when I feel no confidence in any of the human race."[20]

With the Upper Canadian warrants seemingly dealt with, at least for the moment, Selkirk and his companions dashed off for Lower Canada to meet the recognizances that Colonel Coltman had demanded before they had left Red River. Here they stepped into a real legal quagmire. Coltman had required appearance at a court in Lower Canada for offences committed in Upper Canada. The attorney general of Lower Canada admitted that he could not institute proceedings for the alleged offences. But instead of discharging the recognizances, the attorney general moved for new ones guaranteeing that Selkirk would answer the same charges before a special court of oyer and terminer to be held in the upper province. The attorney general acknowledged that he took this action because of his interpretation of the Bathurst dispatch of 11 February 1817. Selkirk's lawyers argued unsuccessfully that this action was both illegal and vexatious, since the cases were already being heard in the Upper Canadian courts, where bail had been given in far lesser amounts. But in the end, Selkirk had not freed himself and his colleagues from Coltman's bail.[21]

COMMISSIONER COLTMAN'S INTERVENTION

While Selkirk and his lawyers were preparing their court cases against the Nor'westers, William Coltman continued in Canada the investigations and interrogations he had begun in Red River. Coltman had returned to Canada long before the earl, and it fell to Lady Selkirk to deal with him in the autumn of 1817. Lady Selkirk reported to her brother on the first of his visits.[22] She had been very nervous and was not sure how to receive him. As it worked out, George Garden and his wife were drinking tea with her when Coltman finally called. After the commissioner had left, she "played music to them to drive the big man out of my head and lay the evil spirit."[23] In subsequent meetings, Lady Selkirk allowed her hostility to Coltman to show through more than a bit, vigorously defending her husband and criticizing the commissioner on several occasions. She found the situation "quite sickening."[24] But the fat man had refused to take offence. In conversation he made clear that he regarded the murder of Robert Semple as an accidental encounter without felonious intent.[25] By this point Major Fletcher was entirely out of the picture, rumours circulating of investigations of his conduct at the Sault. Complaints had been registered not only by Samuel Gale, but also by several military officers stationed in the west. Fletcher would not sign the final report of the commission, and became virtually invisible in its proceedings.

In late January of 1818, after Lord Selkirk had made his first visit to Sandwich but before the opening in Lower Canada of the trials against the NWC and those connected with it, Commissioner William Coltman attempted to arrange an out-of-court agreement among the contending parties. By this time Coltman had finished the first draft of his report on the violence in the western territories, but had not yet submitted it to the authorities. From the beginning of his appointment, and certainly from his arrival at Red River, Coltman had taken the view that there was nothing to be gained from attempting to assess culpability in the conflict. He had made this clear to Lady Selkirk and to Selkirk's lawyers. Coltman in general viewed the violence in the West as beyond the capacity of courts to adjudicate. What was more important, he thought, was the restoration of stability for the sake of the settlement and the resumption of the western trade for the sake of the companies. As evidence of his eagerness to promote stability, Coltman assisted Samuel Gale and the Selkirk forces early in 1818 in arranging for the establishment of a western mission by the Catholic Bishop of Quebec.[26] This effort followed up on earlier initiatives by Lord Selkirk in 1816. Lady Selkirk used her wiles to help bring about Coltman's cooperation. The commissioner agreed with Gale that the presence of priests might well meliorate the present wildness of the Métis and the freemen, which could only work to the advantage of the Red River region. He went so far as to take a subscription list for the clergymen to the Nor'westers, who refused to subscribe on the grounds that "the premature establishment of an hierarchy in that quarter [Red River] would be both impolitic in its nature, and from its novelty *perilous* in its execution."[27] This mission was ultimately sanctioned by Lord Bathurst, who would have preferred a Protestant one but accepted its necessity.[28]

Coltman made his overtures about settlement of the fur-trade dispute through Colin Robertson, who appeared in Montreal to make his deposition before the commissioner at the end of January 1818. In their informal conversations before Robertson began officially testifying, Robertson later reported that he remarked that the best ways to secure peace in Red River were through the establishment of priests—a project by now set afoot—and the establishment of a hundred-mile cordon around the colony free from either trading company.[29] Coltman, who had been in continual contact with both sides since returning from Red River, responded that he thought the NWC would not disturb the colony again and might agree to abandon Red River altogether if Selkirk would cease the prosecutions currently pending. Robertson wondered how Selkirk was to be reimbursed for the two successive destructions of his colony. Coltman answered that he thought William McGillivray so tired of law that he might waive his demands for damages at Fort William and allow Selkirk damages for what had taken place at Red River. McGillivray thought, said Coltman, that Selkirk by now must realize he could make nothing of the charge of conspiracy. Minor prosecutions might be withdrawn, leaving the Crown to prosecute criminal cases at its discretion, especially the murder of Owen Keveny, which was distinctive from the other transactions in the Indian Territories. Robertson observed that the personal feelings of Lord Selkirk had to be taken into account. But Coltman remarked that expenses were enormous for proceedings at law, and Selkirk's feelings could be satisfied by allowing the government to decide the legal issues based on three reports: one by Selkirk, one by the NWC, and a third by the commissioner. Robertson asked whether he could communicate these thoughts to Selkirk. Coltman said yes, and repeated the substance of his statement. Robertson reported that Lord Selkirk had insisted that he could not drop the criminal charges and was averse to discussing matters verbally.[30]

Selkirk and Coltman exchanged letters in early February on matters relating to the earl's relations with the commissioner while in Red River and his complaints against Coltman's proceedings there. Coltman insisted that Selkirk's obedience to the Prince Regent's proclamation suggested that he was satisfied.[31] The commissioner brushed aside Selkirk's charge that he should have been told about Lord Bathurst's instructions. For his part, the earl insisted that his obedience to the proclamation was not meant to suggest any approbation of it, nor any abstention from attempting to obtain redress "at the proper time and place for any injustice which I might sustain."[32] Coltman continued to maintain that as a magistrate he should have been formally warned of Selkirk's dissent.[33] Selkirk argued that Coltman's commission and its extraordinary powers put him in an unusual position, writing if he agreed "to forbear for a time from urging my own rights, it would be very unfair if this should be interpreted into an acquiescence in the justice of the claims of my antagonists." He did not want it said that Coltman had acted with his acquiescence, but rather with his obedience to the injunction of the proclamation.[34] Although Selkirk could not know it, the main thrust of this disagreement with Coltman was also being discussed in the corridors of power in Whitehall at virtually the same time. The Hudson's Bay Company had memorialized Lord Bathurst on 4 February 1818, among other things complaining about the Coltman Commission. The Nor'westers had boasted that the prince regent's proclamation had been issued at their suggestion and that it signified government's forgiveness for the past, the memorial maintained. The governor of Canada, the HBC warned, would find that when the special commission closed its labours he would still need an impartial investigation. The memorial lamented that impartial people had not been sent from Britain.[35] Henry Goulburn replied that the acquiescence of both parties in the actions of the commissioners suggested that their work had been satisfactory to both contending parties.[36]

Later in February proposals in writing were exchanged between William McGillivray and Selkirk through the medium of Commissioner Coltman, who proposed that the HBC withdraw from the Athabasca and the NWC pay for the goods left there.[37] In return the NWC would withdraw from Red River, although it would continue to hold the upper part of the Assiniboine. Civil damages were to be submitted to intelligent merchants two for each side and, in case of a disagreement, to an umpire. Criminal charges were all to be waived.[38] For his part, Selkirk denied that he had anything to do with the Athabasca. He further insisted that any limitation of criminal prosecutions would, in his view, appear to compound the crimes. To the commissioner's apparent surprise, he subsequently reported to Lord Selkirk that his intervention had made matters worse.[39] He added that the NWC's terms for Red River were "so unreasonable that there is no hope of anything being done unless by the influence of government." The commissioner told Colin Robertson that "there was more difficulty than had been imagined in the way of the proposed arrangement."[40] Coltman added that he was sorry the matter could not be settled, since he was of the opinion that Selkirk might not have another opportunity for so advantageous an adjustment. However sensible an analysis of the situation Coltman might have made, he still had not appreciated the true nature of the controversy or the stubbornness of its chief protagonists. The NWC's chief concerns were to recover its monopoly of the Athabasca and to free itself from criminal prosecutions, although it was unwilling to give up completely on the Red River region. Selkirk's chief concerns were to protect his settlement and to obtain "justice" for those settlers who had been killed or otherwise abused by what he still regarded as an NWC conspiracy.

Coltman's involvement in these "negotiations" further confirmed Selkirk's suspicions that Coltman was really a tool of the NWC. As for Samuel Gale, he was convinced that "trumped-up" charges against Lord Selkirk were among the NWC's major weapons for forcing a settlement between the parties. The harshest critic of William Coltman was Lady Selkirk, who found him both biased and pompous.[41] Her brother Andrew Colvile agreed on the basis of her accounts that Coltman was "a consummate scoundrel."[42] As for Coltman's own assessment of his performance, he wrote John Allan in March that the dissatisfaction of both parties with his proceedings was proof of his success in maintaining impartiality.[43] Coltman and Selkirk had later negotiations over the possibility of a formal statement on the commissioner's part of his meeting at Red River with the chiefs of the First Nations.[44] The two men disagreed over what the chiefs had said about the confrontations between the settlers and the Métis.[45] The law officers of the Crown advised Coltman against signing anything as an agent of government.[46]

Trapped as he was in the throes of the Canadian legal system, Selkirk had to fight in absentia in 1818 for re-election to the House of Lords as a representative peer. His nephew Basil Hall met with the leading ministers, and was able to assure Selkirk that his legal difficulties would not by themselves serve as an obstacle to the support of government in the election.[47] Hall also reported that the government insisted that Selkirk be at home to stand for election in person, apparently little appreciating the difficulty of doing this given the enormous bail exacted by William Coltman to guarantee the earl's appearance in the Canadian courts. Selkirk's brother-in-law Sir James Montgomery served as his agent in circulating the discreet requests for support, writing simply that Selkirk's return from America had been delayed by his legal prosecutions against "various Persons" in Canada. Montgomery could hardly say that one of those "Persons" was Selkirk himself. The Duke of Buccleuch probably spoke for many of Selkirk's colleagues in the Scottish peerage when he wrote that despite his goodwill for Selkirk, "I must fairly confess, that his Lordship's constant absence from Britain, as also the probability of its increased continuance, precludes me from giving him my vote at the ensuing election."[48] Montgomery was unable to get the government's Scottish manager Lord Melville to lean heavily on his colleagues to vote for Selkirk.[49] Moreover, Melville probably sealed Selkirk's fate by ruling that since the earl was abroad and not on His Majesty's service he could not vote himself.[50] Montgomery had actually withdrawn Selkirk's name from consideration at the last minute, and Selkirk had gotten votes only from those unaware that he was not a candidate.[51] Selkirk took the defeat badly, convinced that the government had made it impossible for him to appear in person and then condemned him for his absence. He insisted with some legitimacy that his enemies interpreted the defeat as another sign of the government's hostility to his cause.[52]

THE PROSECUTIONS AGAINST
THE NOR'WESTERS CONTINUED

One of the major weaknesses of the *Canada Jurisdiction Act* was that it allowed venues to be transferred on the order of the governor general, but did not specify in detail the legal processes to be employed in so doing. The government of Lower Canada had argued in 1817 for a North American venue, but it also determined that while indictments could be generated in the province, it did not want—perhaps could not manage—to hold the actual trials. Thus Selkirk found the cases of those people he had arrested transferred to courts in Lower Canada, and also from Lower Canada to Upper Canada.[53] He spent innumerable hours trying to keep track not only of his witnesses but also of the accused, many of whom simply returned to the Indian Territory. Moreover, the two provinces disagreed over the legal instruments to be employed. Upper Canada would not accept the documents prepared and sent to it by Lower Canada executing the transfer. The Upper Canadian law officers, headed by John Beverley Robinson, insisted that the crimes to be tried had to be specified in detail. Many defendants were released in the process. Samuel Gale protested the policy of simply letting those arrested go, arguing with Robinson that "if the provisions of the act of George III, be really inadequate to the purposes of securing offenders who have committed crimes in the Indian territories, as you have supposed, the sooner their insufficiency is established by legal determinations the better for the ends of justice."[54] Transferring venues meant that witnesses had to be transported from one place to another at great expense and, given the distances involved, would often not be available to testify in all venues unless proceedings were carefully coordinated. Selkirk understandably wanted all the charges of crimes committed in the Indian Territories tried at the same place and at the same time, but he forgot that his interests were not the same as every one else's in the matter.

The Court of King's Bench in Montreal had proved quite incapable of dealing with almost any of the cases brought previously before it, since two of its justices declared their connections with the NWC in open court late in 1817 at a time when there were only three justices sitting. As a result, Sir John Sherbrooke issued a commission that in effect created a special court of oyer and terminer that opened at Montreal on 20 February 1818. This court quite promptly found a number of bills of indictment on evidence provided by the Selkirk forces. The total included bills of indictment against fifteen NWC partners, twelve NWC clerks, and fifteen lesser NWC servants for principals or accessories to murder; bills of indictment against two partners, six clerks, and others for arson; and bills of indictment against six partners, eleven clerks, and sixteen others for robbery. As well, another bill of indictment was found against twenty partners, eleven clerks, and twelve others for a conspiracy to destroy the Red River Settlement. Every individual sent east to Lower Canada under warrant of Selkirk was indicted with at least one offence. Indictments are not the same thing as convictions, of course, but the actions of this special tribunal should have got Selkirk off the hook as far as the Colonial Office was concerned. His activities at Fort William had, after all, resulted in "true bills." The special court was then forced to adjourn because of the opening of the Court of King's Bench.

Another parallel tribunal in Montreal opened on 21 February 1818 to deal with charges laid in warrants by the NWC against officers of the Red River Settlement in Red River. The NWC had used legal warrants from 1815 onwards for such purposes. Sheriff John Spencer and Governor Miles Macdonell were both arrested in the spring of 1815 under a warrant issued by Norman McLeod for breach of the peace, although not for seizure of pemmican. Spencer was held in custody for nearly a year at Fort William before he was released by the Earl of Selkirk. Left by Selkirk in charge of Fort William in the spring of 1817, he was rearrested when the NWC reoccupied the fort and was sent east in irons. As for Macdonell, he was in 1815 taken to Montreal, where he was again arrested on a felony warrant, this time for the pemmican. The NWC informed Lord Bathurst in London early in 1816 that legal opinion indicated that it was doubtful Spencer and Macdonell could be prosecuted further for their part in the pemmican affair, since they had acted under a misapprehension of authority without any felonious intent. The criminal warrants were not rescinded, however. Macdonell and Spencer both appeared in court in Montreal in 1816, but only to have their bail extended. Trial proceedings on the pemmican warrants finally occurred in September 1817, by which point both men had been served with warrants in other matters.

John Spencer had first appeared before the Court of King's Bench in Montreal in September 1817, and he was joined by Colin Robertson. Two justices of the court had declared their interest for the NWC, and said they could not proceed in the cases. Without a quorum, neither Spencer nor Robertson could receive a trial but simply had their recognizances again extended. The prisoners petitioned Sir John Sherbrooke for a commission of oyer and terminer, which was granted. This was the tribunal that opened on 21 February 1818. Seven bills against Spencer, Macdonell and Robertson were preferred before the Grand Jury of this court, but only one— against Robertson and others for pulling down Fort Gibraltar in 1816—was accepted. An attempted indictment against John Pritchard and two other settlers who had survived Seven Oaks was also dismissed; the charge being murdering the one Métis who had been killed that day. Pritchard fainted in the middle of his testimony, which, according to Lady Selkirk, had a great effect on the Grand Jury.[55] A subsequent session of the Court of King's Bench in Montreal indicted the Red River people under many of the same charges, however. On this occasion many of the grand jurors were connected to the NWC. The sheriff testified that he had been told that no fur-trade business would be done by this court, or he would not have summoned such a jury. Selkirk was unable to get the Lower Canadian law officers to drop the charges, and his people were required again to give bail to appear in court in September 1818. At this point the individuals involved protested their "perpetual recognizances," indicating a willingness to go to jail if they were not tried immediately. The charges were finally abandoned. In the end, all the criminal charges brought against Selkirk's settlers for the events of 1814 to 1816 were dismissed by magistrates, thrown out by grand juries, or abandoned by the law officers of the Crown.

One of Selkirk's people in March 1818 prepared an advertisement for the Montreal newspapers in the form of a comparison of the various bills of indictment found against members of the two parties. It reported:

Murders: **NWC 42, HBC 0.**
Arsons: **NWC 18, HBC 0.**
Burglaries: **NWC 9, HBC 0**
Robberies: **NWC 21, HBC 0**
Stealing in boats on a navigable river: **NWC 9, HBC 0**
Grand larcenies: **NWC 9, HBC 0**
Stealing in a dwelling house: **NWC 0, HBC 8**
Maliciously shooting: **NWC 6, HBC 1**
Riot and pulling down houses: **NWC 0, HBC 5**
Riot and false imprisonment: **NWC 0, HBC 3**
Assault & battery: **NWC 0, HBC 5**[57]

The scene now shifted to Quebec City, where the trial of Charles de Reinhart and Archibald MacLellan for the murder of Owen Keveny had been transferred from Montreal.[57] In Montreal, before the case opened, however, Attorney General Norman Uniacke had handed Lord Selkirk two hastily bundled lots of papers relating to the forthcoming business. Uniacke was the son of Nova Scotia's Richard J. Uniacke and was appointed attorney general of Lower Canada in 1808 through his father's influence.[58] In one of the bundles, Selkirk found in the handwriting of the advocate general a copy of a dispatch dated 11 February 1817 originally sent by Lord Bathurst.[59] This finally provided the text acted upon by various colonial officials. When Uniacke discovered that Selkirk had made a copy of this copy, he demanded it back. Selkirk refused to comply, although he initially told his wife he thought it unfairly obtained. Lady Selkirk thought differently. She hoped the original could be called for in the House of Commons so that the world could see how her husband had been treated in the colonies on the basis of a single affidavit by one Robert MacRobb. Sir John Sherbrooke felt it necessary to write to Lord Bathurst through Henry Goulburn, advising that the text of the dispatch had gotten into Selkirk's hands.[60] Since Bathurst had intended Selkirk to know its substance, he must have been surprised at the tone of Sherbrooke's dispatch, which merely confirmed that Sherbrooke's paralytic stroke, suffered on 6 February 1818, had rendered him ineffectual. The first trial of MacLellan and Reinhart was broken off in mid-hearing. In the process, MacLellan (and a number of other indicted individuals, including Cuthbert Grant) were released on bail and immediately departed the province. The dispersal of the prisoners meant that they might not all be present at the same time for trial, further complicating matters for the maintenance of witnesses.

At the beginning of the MacLellan/Reinhart trials for the murder of Owen Keveny, the law officers of the Crown in Lower Canada announced unexpectedly that they were solely responsible for the management of all the trials relating to offences committed in the Indian country. Selkirk's lawyers were surprised by this news.[61] They had been allowed to participate in the grand jury proceedings, and they thought they had an agreement with the attorney general for the trial of Reinhart that they would do most of the examining and cross-examining. Selkirk and his attorneys protested this decision in vain, pointing out that they had better command of the "facts and the evidence" than did the Crown's officers and a better familiarity with the colloquial French employed by many of the witnesses.[62] Selkirk complained in his memorial to the Duke of Richmond that the Lower Canadian law officers "were imperfectly acquainted with the language in which the trial was to be conducted, not ready in the use even of classical French, and not at all acquainted with the Provincial idiom of the Canadian peasantry and the technical phraseology used by the voyageurs."[63] Such arguments only aggravated these officers, who insisted that they were fully capable to conduct the prosecutions.[64] But the result, Selkirk observed, was that many witnesses were kept in the witness box for hours, while everyone tried to sort out what had been said.[65] Why the Lower Canadian legal officers took this step was never clear, although it seems likely that they disliked being treated as inferiors by Selkirk's legal team, who plainly saw them as incompetent blunderers. Selkirk's people understandably saw it as part of the conspiracy against them. In his preparations for this trial, as for others, Selkirk exhibited a desperation for convictions on any grounds. He wrote Samuel Gale, "It is of essential consequence to the peace of the interior to procure a *conviction,* upon any capital offence; and not to allow these miscreants to be discharged as innocent men, so that we should not neglect to bring against them charges for any description of felony which can be distinctly proved."[66]

William Coltman submitted his final report to Sir John Sherbrooke for transmission to Lord Bathurst in mid-May of 1818. With the report he supplied "a Statement of my own impressions as to the evidence I had

collected respecting the disturbances in the Indian Territories."[67] No
mention was made of Major John Fletcher, who did not sign the final
version. Sherbrooke sent the report and its extensive collection of documents to Bathurst on 16 May 1818.[68] As might have been expected, Coltman's overall analysis was that every one was to blame. He saw the HBC
as responsible for initiating the fur-trade war by attempting to enforce a
monopoly that had been allowed to fall into disuse. He was particularly
hard on Selkirk's agents at Red River, especially Miles Macdonell, for the
Pemmican Proclamation, which asserted a legal authority well beyond
anything tested in the courts. He also admitted that there was no evidence
that Selkirk had authorized such proceedings. As for the various outrages
carried out in the colony in 1815 and 1816, Coltman acknowledged that
here—as in the fur-trade war generally—the NWC had employed violence
and intimidation as a routine part of their daily lives. But after a detailed
discussion of all the available evidence in the Seven Oaks affair, he concluded
that it was an inadvertent explosion rather than a deliberate action.
Although he allowed that the mixed bloods were trying to intimidate the
settlers, they had not set out to murder them. Moreover, there was no
evidence that the NWC had ordered such depredations. Coltman added
that Selkirk had a sincere understanding of the law and his legal rights and
had never transgressed them. As for resolving the questions of how to
prevent the continuation of what had gone wrong in the West, however,
Coltman's report was singularly ineffectual. He called weakly for the
assumption of control of the Indian Territories by the Crown, but offered
no more specific remedies.

Recognizing that his report left some matters up in the air, commissioner
Coltman raised them in a separate letter to Sir John Sherbrooke written on
20 May.[69] He was particularly concerned to call the attention of government
to the settlers at Red River. He thought their interests best served by leaving
them under the protection of Lord Selkirk or the Hudson's Bay Company.
All classes in the Indian Territories, including Selkirk, had been quite obedient
to the commands of the prince regent. Selkirk made his restitutions of property while possessing a physical force capable of overwhelming any opposition, and he was obviously much irritated by the gratuitous violence with
which the Nor'westers reoccupied their posts, especially the destruction of a
field of barley at the Forks. The commissioner was also impressed with the
De Meuron soldiers, who engaged in no violence and on more than one

occasion helped prevent it. In this letter Coltman also described Selkirk's understanding of the yielding of obedience, as it was later explained to him by the earl, as reserving the right to obtain redress by applying to the Privy Council on the basis of a wrongful exercise of authority by the government of Lower Canada (which had issued Coltman's commission) within the bounds of the government of the Hudson's Bay Company. The commissioner had thus introduced the matter of territorial control and boundaries, although not in his report.

At the end of May Selkirk received a packet of letters from Prince Edward Island, a constituency that had probably not crossed his consciousness for some time. The island had developed considerably since the earl had transported his Highlanders there in 1803, thanks in large measure to his settlement project. Donald MacDonald Glenaladale wrote warning that Lieutenant Governor Smith had begun demanding and enforcing the payment of quitrents, those duties to the Crown that were attached to every land grant on the island. PEI was the only place left in North America where quitrents were ever collected, and Smith was using them partly as revenue so that he did not have to deal with an elected assembly and partly as a way of returning undeveloped land to the Crown. The island was coming up to the point where a resident proprietor could with proper management actually develop a decent estate, but Selkirk's lands had been managed by a succession of agents who did little, kept any revenue for themselves, and failed to make any proper report on their stewardship to the earl. The latest of these agents was William Johnston, PEI's attorney general, who had pocketed funds from a number of clients and was being pursued legally by several of them, a point tellingly made by several of the correspondents in this packet.[70] Glenaladale offered to pay Selkirk's quitrents if necessary while wondering why Selkirk's agent allowed the earl's property to be "exposed to rapine." A letter from Johnston himself announced the sale of Lot 10 and included a document containing heads of an agreement for its purchase by Island Acadians for £2000.[71] A final missive came from Thomas Halliday, complaining that William Johnston had still not given a proper land conveyance to either the old stonemason or to Mary Cochrane.[72] He reported that Mary could read and write well and was well advanced in arithmetic, but had no land set aside for her as promised by Lord Selkirk.

Both sides in the Keveny murder trials recognized their importance, and struggled to produce their own version of a verbatim report. The best local stenographer was reputed to be William Simpson, whom everyone assiduously courted. Simpson told Selkirk that his rates were five guineas per diem and seven pence half penny per hundred words for the copy, or 100 guineas for the duration of the job.[73] Selkirk contemplated bringing in a stenographer from New York for future assignments, but his friends were unable to find a decent candidate.[74] Dr. John Allan was put in charge of negotiating with Simpson and dealing with his easily bruised ego.[75] It was no easy task.[76] Simpson's initial notes were not regarded as sufficiently detailed to bring out the falsities in the NWC testimony at the Charles Reinhart trial and had to be supplemented by other material. Moreover, sensing a seller's market, Simpson's demands became increasingly extravagant. At the same time, he was very slow at producing final copy. Allan reported to Samuel Gale that Simpson was "the most unreasonable mortal alive."[77] He said Simpson would not accept a stipend of £300 pounds per year and all the profits of publication unless he was allowed to give away copies and received travelling expenses. Worse still, said Allan, "he talked highly of his rights as a Stenographer to publish whatever he pleased." At one point Lord Selkirk was forced to write a letter of apology to Simpson for communicating with him through Dr. Allan instead of personally.[78]

Allan became so frustrated with Simpson that he went to John Neilson's bookstore in Quebec and bought a book on stenography, hoping to teach himself the technique of shorthand writing.[79] He found it harder than anticipated. After a few days of practice, he reported he could write the Lord's Prayer in shorthand, but confessed "it occupies half the number of lines and about twice the time I can write it in my usual hand."[80] In the end, Samuel Hull Wilcocke—who probably prepared his own shorthand copy of the Reinhart/MacLellan trials—was able to bring his version out first as *Report of the trials of Charles de Reinhard and Archibald M'Lellan for murder, at a court of oyer and terminer, held at Quebec, May 1818.* Simpson's *Report at large of the trial of Charles de Reinhard for murder (committed in the Indian territories), at a court of oyer and terminer held at Quebec, May 1818, to which is annexed a summary of Archibald M'Lellan's indictment as an accessory* was not published until almost a year later. The two transcripts of the same trial mainly demonstrated how different the same original testimony could appear in partisan hands.

The separate trials of Reinhart and MacLellan ended in early June with the conviction of the De Meuron sergeant but the acquittal of the Nor'wester.

The defence, led by wily Henry McKenzie, had attempted to introduce the argument that a private war had existed between the two companies. John Allan reported on the arguments of Reinhart's counsel for a new trial. The major argument was that the *Canada Jurisdiction Act* gave the courts of Canada only such jurisdiction as was not cognizable by any other jurisdiction. Since a statute of Henry VIII provided a jurisdiction in England for treason and murder, these were not included in 43 George III.[81] Reinhart was sentenced to be hanged, but that sentence was not immediately carried out because of the uncertainty of the boundary line, which made reference necessary to the king in Council.[82] The De Meuron soldier never was punished. In the course of MacLellan's trial, the Chief Justice of Lower Canada (Jonathan Sewell) ruled that the western limits of Upper Canada were the same as those framed by the *Quebec Act* of 1774. Fort William and the Dalles—where Keveny had been killed—fell outside Upper Canada's limits in the Indian Territories.[83] William Coltman took the occasion of the MacLellan acquittal to reiterate that his earlier proposal for settlement was still a good one.[84] On the other hand, Samuel Gale wrote Lady Selkirk that the whole business only confirmed that the law "is rather a labyrinth of technicalities and subtleties whereby the guilty escape from punishment, than a direct and open path by which the innocent arrive at justice."[85] At this point, neither Gale nor the countess had yet seen the law at its worst.

CHAPTER TWENTY-ONE

Further Campaigning at Law,
June to November 1818

IN JUNE OF 1818, the two Catholic clergymen chosen by Lower Canada's Bishop J. O. Plessis for western service—fathers J.N. Provencher and Sévère Dumoulin—departed from Montreal for Red River. They were guided by Captain de Lorimier. Lord Selkirk had personally to assure Sir John Sherbrooke that Lorimier was not in the employ of either the earl or the Hudson's Bay Company, for officially this religious initiative was bipartisan.[1] The instructions to the missionaries were to "recall from barbarity and the disorders which are the consequence of it the Savage Nations dispersed over that vast Country."[2] The priests accompanied a party of French Canadian families recruited by Selkirk as settlers for Red River.[3] The little group travelled in a brigade consisting of seven canoes headed by Frederick Matthey, who had been appointed by Selkirk as superintendent at the settlement. Matthey had been almost entirely freed of the courts and Selkirk felt he needed someone responsible at Red River.[4] Commissioner Coltman supported Matthey's being allowed to head west because of his influence over the De Meurons.

The Nor'westers tried to upset Matthey's canoe at the Grand Calumet Portage but were not successful.[5] Matthey arrived at the Forks on 1 August. He directed his brigade to pass the Nor'westers in "the usual way, in line of Battle like a Squadron of Cavalry the flag in the center—the canoes within 1 or 2 yards of one another—paddling in perfect good time, on one good Voyageur Song only the female in their best attire most of them paddling." As Matthey observed, "the sight must have been very imposing and interesting to any christian eye—and so it appeared to be to every one on the quay except a few Partners and Clerks who saw us pass with quite different feelings." At Point Meuron his brigade met the eleven canoes of the North West Company's Red River brigade passing in the other direction:

> They were marching in the same order as we did taking the whole breadth of the River—on perceiving our flag of the White, they stopt within a gun shot of us—we continued our charge and Song, each canoe pointing to an interval in the other Brigade, so that we passed like Magic through their fleet, with a few hand shaking, and in very friendly manner their Voyageurs and Bois Brules were evidently touched at the sight of so many Canadian children and women.[6]

Matthey was probably correct in his assertion that the arrival of Canadian families suggested to the Nor'westers that the colony was more solid and established than they had previously realized.

The summer news from both the settlement and the west was encouraging. Colin Robertson reported Red River was prosperous: "The old Scotch Sentiment of Peace & Plenty is at last realised on the fertile plains of Ossiniboia." He added that "German Street appears to have been settled there ten years in place of ten months." The Highlanders were grumbling, but heavy crops soothed the complaints.[7] Alexander Macdonell confirmed the word of excellent crops, and William Laidlaw was pleased with the farm.[8] A list of names of settlers at Red River produced in August 1818 by Matthey showed 130 Scots, 26 Canadians, and 47 Meurons.[9] On another front, Colin Robertson subsequently wrote that he was returning to the Athabasca country with eighteen canoes.[10]

SELKIRK'S SUMMER

Selkirk spent the end of June and the beginning of July under the weather. A heavy cough had returned. He felt sufficiently better in early July to deal with his correspondence from Prince Edward Island. To William Johnston, he wrote a thank you for the information about the sale of Lot 10, adding that he would have appreciated as well some particulars of the state of his affairs on the island. He ordered Johnston to sort out the business of the land for Thomas Halliday, and reiterated that he wanted a general statement of his affairs "& of the pecuniary transactions which have passed thro your hands since the commencement of your agency."[11] In the letter to

Thomas Halliday, the earl made no mention of Halliday's paternity insinuations, but he did increase the land amounts both the stonemason and his ward would receive from 200 to 300 acres.[12]

A few days later Selkirk penned a memorandum on the Upper Canadian boundary question. He began with the claim of Charles de Reinhard's defence lawyer that Lake Winnipeg was within the jurisdiction of Upper Canada, a claim supported by discussion of the western limits of Canada in the *Quebec Act* of 1774. The earl observed that no mention had been made of northern limits, where the *Quebec Act* drew the boundary of Quebec "northward" to the territories of the Hudson's Bay Company. His Montreal lawyers opined that the HBC should petition the Privy Council on this point as an advantageous way to bring up a discussion of company rights under the charter. The question of the extent of the territorial grant would occur simply as a question between two adjoining colonies. There was clearly a need to counter a doctrine throwing large tracts of land included in the HBC charter to Upper Canada. Indeed, Selkirk concluded, "It appears to me that the Co. cannot now omit taking some such step for putting in their claim, without being held to abandon it."[13] This memorandum was subsequently sent to Sir John Sherbrooke.[14]

Selkirk also began gearing up for his defence in the courts of Upper Canada. He travelled by canoe and caleche with Samuel Gale from Montreal to Kingston in early July to catch the steamboat for York. He reported to Lady Selkirk that the canoe worked perfectly: "There is no more fatigue than in lying on the sofa—with the advantage of the air:—& on the whole I feel already decidedly better."[15] In the caleche he and Gale were protected from heavy rain by an awning and heavy cloaks, but the damp weather made the cough worse, he subsequently admitted to Lady Selkirk.[16] He had considerable difficulty in finding legal counsel in Upper Canada. Most of the best Upper Canadian lawyers, including John Beverley Robinson, had accepted fees from the NWC. Selkirk's Lower Canadian lawyers were not members of the Upper Canadian bar and were not likely to be allowed to become so. On recommendations from his Scottish friends in Upper Canada, Selkirk retained as one of his attorneys Daniel Washburn of Kingston, a known radical reformer, knowing full well that this action meant that he was really introducing Barnabas Bidwell into the cases.[17] The actual "feeing" of Washburn had been done by Dr. John Allan in early April.[18] Bidwell, an American who had been attorney general of Massachusetts and an ardent Jeffersonian, had come to Canada in 1810 to escape prosecution for malversation of funds. As an alien and a fugitive from justice, he was not a member of the Upper Canadian bar, although "the cleverest lawyer in the province," but worked as a law clerk in Washburn's office. On the eve of the War of 1812, he had become involved in a fierce controversy with John Strachan in the pages of the Kingston *Gazette*.

One of the tasks Bidwell took on in 1818 was to investigate the possibility of suing Strachan for libelling Selkirk in his pamphlet on emigration.[19] The problem here was twofold, Selkirk was advised. First, it was necessary to prove that Strachan was the author, and then that the pamphlet had been published in Upper Canada.[20] Neither Bidwell nor Washburn was in Sandwich in September of 1818, but the government must have been aware of their involvement in Selkirk's legal affairs. There were certainly rumours circulating of the possible lawsuit against Strachan, and Strachan himself had been privately advised of the possibility in early September of 1818. Thus, Selkirk had managed to associate his cause not only with Robert Gourlay but also with both the notorious "Alien Question"—revolving in part around Americans like Bidwell—and with the political opposition to Strachan, described by one Upper Canadian as "this meddling Scion of upstart clerical importance."[21] Both Gourlay and the "Alien Question" themselves were connected back to Selkirk's Scottish friends, who were land speculators anxious to be able to sell their lands to incoming American settlers. Indeed, Selkirk himself held Upper Canadian lands that he had been advised would be attractive only to Yankees.

At York, Selkirk managed to meet with Attorney General John Beverley Robinson. He discovered to his dismay that the transfer of jurisdiction between Lower and Upper Canada had not gone smoothly, and he urged against further delay to prevent more witnesses from returning home.[22] One problem, as he would subsequently write to Lower Canada's attorney general, was that Robinson was not happy with the catchphrase "all crimes hitherto committed" to describe all the cases not tried in Lower Canada. Upper Canada wanted the crimes to be specifically mentioned.[23] To his wife he reported that Robinson intended to continue with the prosecutions at Sandwich about the Fort William business, which depended upon what the earl thought were fairly stretched arguments about the outermost bounds of the colony.[24] As for his health, he felt better. "The coughing & expectoration seldom troubles me at night—but generally there is a fit in the morning, sometimes more sometimes less, but never so bad as usually at Montreal."[25]

Selkirk's health was clearly on his mind as he sat down back in Montreal in mid-August to write James Stewart in Halifax. He began by observing that he had been involved with "the perplexities of the law aggravated by every circumstance that could well be added to render them more irksome & vexatious." Why his health had been "indifferent" all summer was not clear, he wrote, unless the indifference was a product of a sedentary life and constant strain. "The fatigues & privations I met with in the Indian country I felt as nothing, & willingly would I undergo ten times as much to be out of the pettifogging atmosphere of this Province." The earl had employed Stewart previously as a disinterested outsider to deal with his business on Prince Edward Island, and he admitted he was spurred to write because of letters from the island showing his affairs in considerable disarray. He had been informed that his agent William Johnston was bankrupt, obliged to abscond from the sheriff, and had applied to his own use money he had received as agent for absentee proprietors. Johnston's situation probably explained why Selkirk had not heard from the agent for several years. The political state of the island was equally bad. James Stewart in Halifax would not necessarily know about current politics on PEI, and so Selkirk brought him up to date, demonstrating in the process that he knew quite a lot about what was going on there. The government's policy on the quitrents, which involved payment in cash on an island constantly short of that commodity, would destroy the land market. John MacDonald Glenaladale's son had offered to take over the agency, but he needed some more information about him. "When I saw him in England 3 or 4 years ago he was a mere stripling & did not lead me to think that he was likely to prove an able man of business." Selkirk confessed that he would like to dispose of his property on the island, which he still thought had considerable intrinsic value, on almost any terms. He was willing to pay a considerable premium to someone prepared to deal with it. If Stewart in opening this letter expected a romantic account of adventures, Selkirk concluded, he would be disappointed. He could not give an account of his travels "till I am washed clean of the mud of the law."[26]

Selkirk and his family sailed for Sandwich by steamer in late August of 1818, so that the earl and Captain Proteus D'Orsonnens could answer the charges laid against them in the Sandwich court. The earl was still recovering from his bout of illness. The family took the steamer *Charlotte* to Kingston, then the *Frontenac* to Niagara Falls, where they boarded the vessel *Walk on the Water,* which sailed the length of Lake Erie to Detroit. The leisurely voyage gave Selkirk's enemies plenty of time to mark his progress. James Woods of Sandwich had earlier warned that Detroit lawyers had been retained to harass the earl in the American courts, but this advice was either ignored or lost.[27] As the steamer landed on American soil, the sheriff of Wayne County boarded the vessel and served Selkirk with a writ issued on the complaint of Nor'wester James Grant, charging that the earl had caused his fur-trading post at Fond du Lac (in Wisconsin) to be pillaged of goods to the amount of $50,000.[28] The American authorities were slightly embarrassed by this act of legal harassment, and, with the assistance of a prominent local attorney, Solomon Sibley, Selkirk was quickly released on bail. When the case was subsequently tried, the judge dismissed it on the grounds that the writ had been improperly served on the Sabbath. His decision, based on citations from the Bible, Coke, Blackstone, and William Wilberforce, was in manuscript twenty pages long, and filled several columns in the Detroit newspapers. Samuel Gale would later write Lady Selkirk that one citation was from a statute book of Edward the Confessor.[29]

BACK IN THE COURTS AGAIN: THE SANDWICH EXPERIENCE
Freed from American custody, Selkirk was able to appear before the Sandwich court in September of 1818. Chief Justice Powell was himself on the bench. Here Selkirk began by answering the charge of resisting legal process at Fort William, the behaviour that had led to the Bathurst dispatch. Much contradictory evidence was heard, and this bill of indictment was thrown out by the Grand Jury.[30] Selkirk was finally legally vindicated. An Upper Canadian court had not sustained the charge to which Lord Bathurst had responded so angrily in early 1817. For Selkirk's supporters, this merely demonstrated the extent to which the colonial secretary had shot from the hip, acting on the basis of information from only one side in the dispute. In fairness to Bathurst, he had only insisted that Selkirk would be prosecuted, not that he be necessarily found guilty. The dispatch had emphasized "upon a true bill being found," and this had not occurred. The true meaning of Bathurst's original dispatch and this vindication of Selkirk was considerably obscured, however, by the actions at this point of Upper Canada's Attorney General John Beverley Robinson. These actions had precious little to do

with Lord Bathurst's instructions and a great deal to do with Upper Canadian politics in 1818.

In his earlier visit to Upper Canada in 1804, Selkirk had developed an understandable hostility to the elite, which ran the province like a little fiefdom. He had employed a member of this elite, Alexander Macdonell, as his agent at his Baldoon settlement. Macdonell proved both incompetent and unable to cut through the obstacles placed upon land development by the Upper Canadian bureaucracy, obstacles that Selkirk would write about in an untitled pamphlet in 1819.[31] Selkirk had naturally turned for assistance in 1804 to the critics of that elite bureaucracy, who also happened to be Lowland Scots from the earl's own region of Scotland around Dumfries. This cadre of Lowlanders included the Dickson brothers (Thomas and William), Thomas Clark of Niagara Falls, Robert Nichol, and Robert Hamilton. Clark especially was still selling land for Selkirk in the Thames River district.[32] By 1818, the elite had not changed their attitudes, although they now had a different leader in the person of Dr. John Strachan, the Aberdeen-born rector of the Anglican Church at York.

Strachan was connected by marriage with the NWC and, as early as 1815, had declared himself on Selkirk and Red River by writing a pamphlet denouncing Selkirk as an unscrupulous emigration promoter and his settlement as inimical to the interests of Upper Canada. Strachan was genuinely appalled by the stories he was told about Selkirk's recruiting in Sutherlandshire by the Highlanders who were carried by canoe to Upper Canada in 1815 after the NWC dispersal of the settlement. However, he might have appreciated a bit more that these people still had to make a case to justify their abandonment of Red River. He was equally appalled by the overstatements about the climate and fertility of the soil at the Forks that he found in a promotional brochure conveniently circulated in Canada by the NWC, even though it had never actually been published by Selkirk, who had quickly come to realize its excesses. By September of 1818, Strachan had heard that he would be taken to court for libelling Selkirk. The Selkirk people had found a Canadian version of Strachan's pamphlet. Strachan wrote the editor of the *Montreal Herald* for an affidavit that the republication of his pamphlet in Lower Canada occurred without his permission.[33]

Not only did Strachan have a long-standing hostility to Selkirk, but he also believed there was a close connection between the earl and Robert Gourlay, the latest critic of the Upper Canadian elite.[34] Gourlay, who was himself from the Dumfries area not far from Kirkcudbright and had come to Canada in 1817. He was encouraged by those same Lowlanders who were associated with Selkirk and who formed the backbone of the popular hostility to the elite in the legislative assembly. In early 1818 Gourlay had sent out his notorious thirty-one questions on the state of Upper Canada, and he had also published a letter in the *Niagara Spectator* blaming Seven Oaks in part on John Strachan's earlier pamphlet attacking Selkirk.[35] Gourlay spent most of the year 1818 escalating his critique of what was now emerging as the "Family Compact" and being systematically hounded in the Upper Canadian courts for his pains. By the time of Gourlay's third address to the people of Upper Canada in April 1818, which called for "a radical change of system in the government of Upper Canada," most of his earlier Scottish allies had disassociated themselves from his cause. The government had ordered Attorney General John Beverley Robinson to prosecute Gourlay at the first opportunity, and he was charged with seditious libel in several cases. The trials occurred in August in Kingston and in Brockville, and in both instances Gourlay was acquitted by the jury.

John Beverley Robinson was the son of an American Loyalist.[36] He had been literally brought up and educated by John Strachan at his boarding school in Kingston, and Strachan always regarded Robinson as his best pupil, still in some ways in tutelage to the master. According to Robinson's biographer, Strachan in 1816 had done his best to prejudice Robinson against Selkirk.[37] Robinson had spent much of the summer of 1818—when he was not prosecuting Robert Gourlay and attempting to keep the Americans out of Canada—closeted with Nor'westers preparing for the prosecutions of Selkirk. When the Grand Jury failed to find a true bill on the charge of resisting arrest, Robinson postponed the other charges he had pending. Instead he brought forward a bill of indictment that charged Selkirk and his companions with conspiracy to injure or destroy the trade of the NWC. This charge epitomized the Nor'wester case against Selkirk. Chief Justice Powell warned the attorney general against this strategy, pointing out the difficulty of proving conspiracy. But Robinson had forty NWC witnesses who could testify to Selkirk's behaviour at Fort William and elsewhere.[38] By this time William Coltman had issued his report, and Robinson was able to take advantage of its testimony. Unfortunately, the attorney general in this instance ignored Coltman's careful analysis, which was that there had been no conspiracy on either side.

Robinson was under considerable pressure from Lord Selkirk and his friends. Selkirk was still demanding action on the transferral of cases from Lower to Upper Canada, while both Gale and Dr. John Allan had their own causes to press. Gale wanted the attorney general to commence proceedings against Major John Fletcher for his behaviour at the Sault in June 1817.[39] As for Dr. Allan, he wanted the North West Company clerks Vandersluys and Mctavish prosecuted for perjury. They had declared in affidavits that Selkirk had feloniously stolen eighty-three fusils belonging to the North West Company. Robinson offered Allan a long explanation of why he did not act, but the surgeon was not persuaded.[40]

In the Sandwich courtroom, Robinson went so far as to propose that Simon McGillivray be admitted into the jury room and allowed to examine the witnesses. When this was denied, Robinson insisted on doing all the examination himself, on the grounds that the complexity of the testimony could not be made intelligible to the Grand Jury unless "properly marshalled." Two known NWC agents were on the Grand Jury, but Chief Justice Powell refused to order them to step down, saying he was sure they would withdraw if they thought it "proper."[41] Robinson took three days to examine witnesses. In the middle of the examinations, Lord Selkirk approached the bench and publicly complained about Robinson's poisoning of the jurors in private consultations. The Grand Jury then itself deliberated for several days, recalling several witnesses in the process and making clear that it was having trouble reaching a decision. The court met again on a Monday morning, with fifteen of the seventeen Grand Jurors assembled separately in the Grand Jury Room. Before the Grand Jury could report that they had been unable to find a true bill, Chief Justice Powell addressed the bar, complaining of the Grand Jury's conduct. He then declared the court adjourned *sine die*. Having recently lost two libel cases against Robert Gourlay, the Upper Canadian oligarchy could hardly afford another acquittal in a highly publicized political trial. Selkirk subsequently protested this action to the lieutenant governor of Upper Canada, writing: "My conduct has been misrepresented & my character traduced in the most infamous manner & by this mode of proceeding I have been deprived of the opportunity of exposing the calumnies against me." The earl further complained that the attorney general refused to act against Major Fletcher and declined to prosecute Vandersluys and McTavish. He pointed out that William Coltman had required a huge bail at Red River, and he had complied although not legally obliged to do so.

He had then come voluntarily to Upper Canada to answer the charges brought against him, and had met with nothing but harassment and disappointment.[42] A day later, Selkirk wrote to the Duke of Richmond that he had written a memorial about the conduct of certain officers of Lower Canada. It was prepared but still had to be copied out. He was sorry he could not deliver the memorial in person but had to leave it to agents.[43]

A printed version of the memorial, dated 21 October, was in circulation by February 1819, for Dr. John Allan from York reported that some people had commented that Selkirk should have brought it out earlier, before he left the country. This pamphlet was Selkirk's most complete effort to provide a perspective on the fur-trade war and his participation in it. Much of it was written before he became seriously ill and while he was still in complete intellectual command of the documentation. The narrative of events in the interior up to 1816 offered little that was new, although by this time Selkirk did appreciate that the mixed blood people (he used the terms "half-breeds" or "Bois Brûlés") were neither Aboriginal nor Canadian, but a separate group of people. At the same time, he denied that they were independent players, insisting that most were employed by the NWC. Selkirk struck out into fresh territory when he got to the appointment of William Coltman as commissioner of special enquiry. His account of his experiences with the Coltman Commission left it clear that he found Coltman part of the problem rather than part of the solution.

John Allan reported from York early in 1819 that some readers were unhappy that Selkirk had come down "too heavy upon poor unoffending Coltman, a good natured Laugh and Grow fat sort of person, who had no wish but to conciliate and tranquillize all parties." But the negative consequences of Coltman's inoffensiveness were exactly Selkirk's point. It allowed all those who had committed violence in the Indian territories to escape punishment. Coltman failed to arrest many he might have put in custody, and did not take testimony from many who should have been interrogated. The large bail Coltman exacted from Selkirk and his associates provided an added grievance. Selkirk continued his tale of woe by describing the difficulties he had experienced with the governments and law officers of the Canadas, apparently backed by the Colonial Office. He rehearsed the postponements and the changes of venue that made it impossible to prosecute properly those guilty of offences in the West. He concluded by making the point that would characterize all the later Selkirk publications. The issue was no longer the control of the fur trade, "but whether the British Government, does or does not afford protection to its subjects," and further, "whether to promote the sordid purposes of individual gain or illegal monopoly, murder may be systematically organized, and the blood of British subjects remain unatoned, because some of those who profit by it, are members of the Executive and Legislative Councils of Lower Canada, and reputed to be under the special protection of His Majesty's Government."

THE YORK TRIALS

A further blow for the Selkirk prosecutions came in October of 1818 at York. These trials had been several times postponed over the summer of 1818. In the dock were François Boucher and Paul Brown, charged with the murder of Governor Robert Semple.[44] Selkirk himself was not present, having returned to Montreal. Instead, Samuel Gale and Dr. John Allan observed the conduct of the trials by Upper Canada's law officers, John Beverley Robinson, assisted by Henry John Boulton. On the bench were Chief Justice William Dummer Powell, D'Arcy Boulton, and Mr. Justice Campbell. For the defence stood Samuel Sherwood and his brother Levius, both of Loyalist background and both highly experienced defence lawyers.[45] Both men had been earlier recommended to Selkirk by James Woods, but were probably already engaged.[46] Despite his inexperience at criminal prosecution, Robinson refused adamantly to take advice from Gale, who recommended that the charge be revised from the murder of Semple to the murder of Captain John Rogers. Gale argued that Semple's death was less clear-cut than that of Rogers, who was cut down while on his knees pleading for mercy. Robinson also rejected many of the legal instruments transferred from Lower Canada, thus weakening his case.[47]

Robinson was from beginning to end totally out-lawyered by Samuel Sherwood. Even before the attorney general had begun his opening statement, Sherwood was on his feet, asking for bail as a diversionary tactic. The attorney general had no sooner finished his opening account of Seven Oaks when Sherwood's real attack began. The Montreal lawyer insisted that Robert Semple was not a governor but "a Turkish Bashaw." Chief Justice Powell intervened. "Do let the trial go on," he told Sherwood, "he is not to be murdered though he was not a governor." As Robinson proceeded with his examination of witnesses, Sherwood used all the techniques of the successful defence lawyer. When he could not shake the witnesses' testimony

through cross-examination, he discredited them through *ad hominum* arguments whenever possible, in the process building an alternative case. Michael
Heden, who insisted that the two shots that killed Lieutenant Holte and Robert
Semple had come from the mixed-blood party, for example, was accused of
having improperly seized lands in Red River. The settlement was not a proper
one but only a thinly disguised trading post and a camp for hunters. The impli-
cation was that the mixed bloods had a legitimate case.

Sherwood finally unveiled his chief argument, which, like most of his
arsenal, had come from a careful perusal of the Coltman report. Red River
was in a state of private war such as had prevailed at the time of Edward I
between the earls of Hereford and Gloucester. What happened at Seven Oaks
was therefore not murder, but only a great riot, for which the mixed blood
people had considerable justification. Sherwood focused attention on the
question of who had fired the first shot, as if this were all that mattered.
Robinson in his turn failed to elicit from the witnesses evidence that no
matter who fired the first shot in this encounter, the mixed-blood men had
congregated looking for trouble, rigged out in war paint, fully armed, and
taking prisoners. The defence witnesses finished the job. Two provided an
unchallenged alibi for Paul Brown, and two others testified that Michael
Heden had told them, "we cannot blame the half-breeds, we fired first, and
if we had got the better we would have served the half-breeds the same." It
was a perfect way to close. Chief Justice Powell ordered Brown acquitted.
The jury itself acquitted Boucher in fifteen minutes, before the judges had
time to leave the courthouse. John Beverley Robinson later insisted that the
jury was composed of farmers who were ignorant of both parties and Red
River.[48] In a letter to Lady Selkirk, Samuel Gale provided his analysis of the
trial. "Relations, only on one side, of irritations caused at distant times and
at different places are produced combined and confounded together. Dates
are confused, hearsay is brought forward where facts are deficient, the
charges from the bench increase the confusion till all becomes perfect chaos.
In a case of doubt the jury are bound to acquit. It must certainly be a case of
doubt where all is unintelligible."[49]

The pattern of the Brown/Boucher trial was repeated in the trial of a
number of North West Company partners as accessories to the murder of
Robert Semple. The defendants included John Siveright, Alexander
Mackenzie, Hugh McGill, John McDonald, John McLaughlin, and Simon
Fraser. Judge Boulton, in his charge to the jury, observed that the only one of

the defendants against whom there was any evidence was John McLeod, but he had discovered to his surprise that McLeod was not in the dock. The problem with the Lower Canadian warrants was obviously to blame for the failure.[50] The same session of oyer and terminer that acquitted Brown and Boucher also tried John Cooper and Hugh Bennerman on charges of stealing cannon in a dwelling house of the Earl of Selkirk at Red River and putting its inhabitants in bodily fear for their lives. The law officers of the Crown prosecuted, and Mr. Sherwood represented the defendants. Attorney General Robinson insisted that the jury had nothing to do but decide on the innocence or guilt of the two men before the court. "It is, gentlemen, no matter where the crime has been committed, so that we prove it was within your jurisdiction that it was perpetrated." From the beginning of the cross-examinations, Sherwood ran rings around Robinson. He berated the attorney general for objecting to the line of questioning he was taking, and the chief justice had to intervene to rule that the defence had to confine themselves to questions put by the prosecution. Sherwood ridiculed the notion that the cannon were kept in a dwelling house, having been allowed to bring out through questioning that both pigs and sheep resided there as well as people. Sherwood insisted that what had been done was at most a mere trespass. In his charge to the jury, Mr. Justice Boulton agreed, labelling the present trial "another of the trials resulting from the misunderstanding, and a very unhappy misunderstanding it is, of these two rival companies." The defendants were unhappy and feared the cannon might be used to prevent them from leaving the colony. The jury returned a verdict of not guilty. The attorney general then explained that he had more cases to bring, but could not because of the defective instruments prepared in Lower Canada.

Attorney General Robinson subsequently admitted that despite the acquittals of all the parties in these trials, the evidence certainly justified Selkirk's actions in charging them and in bringing them to trial. "Twenty-one persons whom his Lordship had been instrumental in removing from their native Country had been miserably butchered in a distant land by their fellow subjects, for certainly I think no regard can be paid to the extraordinary claim set up by these half-breeds, to be considered an independent nation." But it was possible to argue against any premeditated design of the defendants through the evidence of the trial, a means of judging to which the Earl of Selkirk had not access. Had Selkirk's exercise of his powers of magistrate stopped here, observed Robinson, "I am sure the exercise of it would not have been too rigidly inquired into, even had it appeared to have been a little overstrained."[51]

THE LORD SELKIRK PERSECUTION BILL

The next scene in what Lord Selkirk regarded as persecution against him began in October of 1818 in the legislature of Upper Canada. Attorney General Robinson (and probably John Strachan) was convinced that both Selkirk and Robert Gourlay had escaped judicial punishment in the Upper Canadian courts because they had been tried in venues that were friendly to them. One of Selkirk's offences, later argued Robinson, was to try to evade justice by "raising the cry of oppression."[52] Use of judicial persecution in the courts to deal with individuals disliked by the Upper Canadian oligarchy was at its height at this point. Legislation in the form of the *Sedition Act* of 1804, never before used against a British subject, was available to employ against Gourlay. This gadfly would be ordered out of the province in January 1819; when he failed to comply he was put in jail to await trial. Robinson had to create new legislation to deal with the Earl of Selkirk, however. He introduced a bill into the House of Assembly that made it possible for trials of crimes and offences committed in the province but not committed "within the limits of any Township or County" to be tried in any judicial district of the province. Fort William was notoriously outside the limits of any township or county, and Selkirk's supporters immediately suspected that the legislation was directed against the earl, the more so when it was rumoured that the government would apply the legislation retroactively. Samuel Gale reported that, although the bill passed the assembly 10–5, one its opponents said that Selkirk should be thanked for his colonization rather than persecuted.[53] The opposition in the House of Assembly was unable to prevent passage of the legislation, which was unofficially named by its opponents "The Lord Selkirk Persecution Bill" because it was adopted before the rural representatives, especially those from the Western District, had arrived to attend. An act banning seditious meetings was passed at about the same time with equally little opposition.

Samuel Gale, as legal agent for an absent Selkirk, protested the legislation to the lieutenant governor of the province.[54] This legislation was never actually applied to Selkirk, however. It was amended the following year to make retroactive employment impossible, and Selkirk complained of the new act to the Privy Council in England. The earl asked that the Crown disallow the legislation. Its presence mainly serves to confirm the extent to which Selkirk was being treated in Upper Canada in the same way as other "enemies" of the government. Selkirk's offence had been his "pretended imperialism," while Gourlay had been guilty of "levelling" rabble-rousing. Such reactions and responses could only with difficulty be associated with the directions to Canadian officials from the Colonial Office. Daniel Washburn explicitly connected the legislation with the politics of the province, noting that it would be difficult to procure popular petitions against the act that were not "immediately construed into *Gourlayism* and represented as seditious by those who have the ear of the Government."[55] A law agent for Selkirk subsequently wrote to Lord Bathurst, asking to be informed as soon as the legislation reached the Colonial Office.[56] It apparently never did.

Apart from the persecution bill, the period of the autumn meeting of the Upper Canadian legislature was mainly distinguished by an assault on Samuel Gale by Archibald McLellan, who attacked the little lawyer several times with his stick. Gale made light of the business, claiming he could have avoided the blows had he not been recently so sick. "This is the first beating of the kind that has fallen to my lot," he reported ruefully to Lady Selkirk, although going to law meant "pocketing the affront."[57] McLellan was later sentenced to six months' imprisonment and a fine of £100 for his actions.[58]

By November it was clear that Selkirk was very sick. Because of his illness, because of the lack of success of the prosecutions, and because of the obvious need to deal with the government at home, Selkirk determined to return to Great Britain. Lady Selkirk was not at all keen about a return to London and to a political struggle. In a New York City hotel, on his way back to England, Selkirk had experienced another bout of coughing blood. He had been bled and sent to bed by a doctor. He reported this illness to his wife in a matter-of-fact manner, mentioning it only to explain why he had not attended a great soiree at the home of John Jacob Astor.[59] On 15 November, the countess replied to her husband that if his health would not stand the strain, and obviously she thought it could not, "for pity's sake make up your mind to let the wicked flourish." She offered instead to meet Selkirk at Red River, which obviously was better for his health and where he could govern his settlement.[60] But such an offer, even if seriously made, was too late.

CHAPTER TWENTY-TWO

Returning to Europe, 1818–1820

L EAVING LADY SELKIRK and his family behind in Montreal to tie up the loose ends of his business still remaining, Lord Selkirk was in Albany in early November on his way to New York City by steamboat. His head was clearly filled with economic worries. Although his estates in Kirkcudbright were doing somewhat better, his expenditures had been enormous over the past few years. The financial situation was still not yet fully reduced to a balance sheet, but obviously his outlays had more than exceeded his income by a substantial amount and would continue to do so for some unforeseeable length of time. As he would later explain to his London banker, "my honor is at stake in the contest with the NWC & in the support of the Settl't at RR." Until the settlement was out of danger and the falsehoods of the Nor'westers were exposed, "expenses must be incurred, which it is utterly impossible for me to avoid or to which it does not depend on me to put a limit." Those expenses "necessary for the accomplishment of the object must be submitted to, even tho they may go beyond my income."[1] On the steamboat he may have been a bit feverish. He fell in with an old American acquaintance, one whom he had first met in the Genesee country of New York on his first tour of North America. He spent the voyage pouring over a map and confiding to John Greig all his schemes for settling the Red River country and selling the American part. Greig, a fellow Scotsman from Moffat, had been part of the New York speculations of Sir William Pulteney, and he encouraged Selkirk to think about organizing a company to "purchase and settle that part on speculation," perhaps at about 6d. per acre.[2]

Selkirk worked out the details on paper, probably filling up part of his time on the ocean voyage back to England with the plans, and he forwarded the scheme to Greig on 2 December 1818, the day after his arrival in Liverpool. He knew that the British and the Americans had agreed on a western boundary line, but insisted that the speculation was still possible, since "in a question of private rights, it cannot be supposed that the [American] Administration, as such, would take any part, & as the individual members of Congress are in general well versed in Law, they will the more readily perceive how strong are the grounds of the right that I assert."[3] The notion that the part of his grant from the Hudson's Bay Company that ended up on the American side of the boundary would be accepted by the Americans was almost totally ludicrous, and while it was easy to understand his attempts to negotiate some agreement with the United States government about his land in 1817 and 1818, he had been firmly rebuffed at the highest levels. Selkirk's almost childlike enthusiasm for solving his economic problems through a public sale of stock in a company based on lands he did not really hold probably reflected the extent of his illness, and certainly was influenced by both his financial situation and the need to recover something from the wreckage of his North American ventures.

The departure of Lord Selkirk from Canada in November of 1818 brought to an end any serious efforts to bring Nor'westers to "justice" in the Canadian courts. Most of the initiative had come from Selkirk acting as a private prosecutor, and the law officials of the Canadas were happy to be done with the cases. Getting free of them was not as easy as it might seem, however. Selkirk and his lawyers had obtained a large number of indictments in several courts in Lower Canada. Many of the cases had been transferred to the court in Upper Canada, and most of the defendants in all the courts had paid their bail and returned to the west. There were legal hoops that had to be jumped through. The defendant would first have to reappear in the court that had granted him bail—and Selkirk's private prosecutions would either have to be withdrawn or dismissed—in order to achieve his absolute freedom. At least one court, the commission of oyer and terminer in Quebec City, resolutely refused to discharge any indictments that it had not issued. Selkirk's lawyers refused in his absence to appear to prosecute. The result was that indictments hung over the heads of many of the Nor'westers, especially the freemen and mixed-blood men, for years and years. Some of them—such as the murder indictment of Cuthbert Grant—may never have been formally discharged. Thus, the Selkirk campaign at law ended in confusion and uncertainty rather than with substantial court decisions. The legal campaign of the NWC against the HBC, on the other hand, continued through 1819 and 1820, shifting to actions dealing with the competition in the Athabasca region.

The immediate concerns of Selkirk on arriving in England included the Red River Colony and some reassurances for the wife of Robert Gourlay. Reports from Red River continued to be promising, but indicated that a firm hand was needed to keep the disparate interests in check. One candidate for governor was a Kirkcudbrightshire man named Captain Roxburgh, who had spent many years in mercantile enterprise in Canada. The people consulted by the earl gave him a mixed review. One correspondent thought Roxburgh might still be in debt to members of the North West Company. On another front, the earl wrote to James Woods at Sandwich in early January to make arrangements for shipping cattle to the settlement.[4] As for Mrs Gourlay, Andrew Maitland reported on 1 January 1819 from Edinburgh, "I called upon Mrs. Gourlay, & promptly told her that you did not anticipate any danger to her husband from what was past, provided he conducted himself with prudence & discretion in time to come. She seems fully aware of the sanguine & rash character of her husband."[5] Gourlay was not behaving very prudently. John Allan wrote Lady Selkirk in January of 1819 that Gourlay was currently rotting in prison because he refused to accept deportation from the province as an alien.[6] Allan later added, "Since he is down every sycophant is kicking at him."[7] Selkirk's sister Lady Isabella Douglas reported on her visit to Sir John Sherbrooke and his wife. Sherbrooke was still quite crippled, she wrote. He was not conducting business but was in contact with Lord Bathurst and the Duke of York. He advised that Selkirk's relations with the government not become a party matter.[8]

Back in London Selkirk was confined to his house and under the constant care of a physician, but was still working long hours at his desk. Diagnosing illness in the historical past is a difficult business at best. Selkirk had a recurrent cough from at least June of 1818, accompanied by various pulmonary problems. This was fairly certainly tuberculosis. But in London in 1819, he had another whole set of symptoms involving the nervous system that are hard to attribute to consumption. He was easily agitated by bad news, and the agitation prevented him from sleeping. His restless mind turned matters over constantly. This sounds like an emotional disorder, possibly the result of nervous strain. Recognizing that overwork, complicated by mental and emotional strain, was somehow part of Selkirk's health problem was easy. Getting him to slow down and relax was a different matter. He seemed totally driven by the need to vindicate himself from the aspersions cast upon him. The earl admitted that the correspondence from Lady Selkirk was so concerned about his health that he was surprised she had not left Montreal.[9] She would continue to run the North American branch of the family business until June, when she and the children would finally come home. Everyone in Montreal was impressed with the countess. J.W. Clarke wrote, "Lady Selkirk is justly esteemed a woman of uncommon cleverness and on all occasions so reasonable and amiable in her conduct that I cannot believe she could so warmly espouse the cause of her husband did she not believe him to be acting an honourable part, however outra he may be in his projects."[10] Men like Clarke would have been astounded could they have seen Lady Selkirk's private correspondence, in which she was if anything more committed and driven than her husband to bring the miscreants to justice.

From London, Selkirk involved himself in what John Halkett described as "a multiplicity of business."[11] He was still supervising the British end of his North American enterprise, including the recruitment of the 1819 contingent of servants for the Hudson's Bay Company required by his grant.[12] He was dealing, usually at long distance, with financial matters involving both his Kirkcudbright lands and his total estate. Agriculture had picked up by 1819, but his men of business still scrambled desperately to keep the Selkirk estate afloat, given the enormous outlays it had experienced both for Red River and the court trials. The bulk of the earl's time, however, was spent preparing a series of statements outlining his understanding of events in North America as well as defending his conduct and his "honour." He went so far as to research the opposition correspondence to the newspapers in 1811.[13] With John Halkett, he prepared a lengthy account of the legal battles that had resulted from Lord Bathurst's dispatch of 1817. Halkett had carried on a lengthy private correspondence with Earl Bathurst in the period from 1817 to 1819 that was highly critical of both the Colonial Office and the authorities in the Canadas, who, he maintained, were acting in response to what they thought were instructions from London. Those letters were now collected and printed as *Correspondence in the years 1817, 1818, and 1819, between Earl Bathurst and J. Halkett, Esq., on the subject of Lord Selkirk's settlement at the Red River in North America*. One of Halkett's major theses in the letters was that many of Selkirk's legal problems had originated with the order of 11 February 1817 from Bathurst to have the earl criminally indicted, which Selkirk had subsequently found out about only inadvertently. In this dispatch, Bathurst had prejudged the earl's behaviour at Fort William on the representations of a single interested party, thus setting in motion an entire series of subsequent injustices. Selkirk also drafted a lengthy account of his judicial adventures in Canada that would become *A Letter to Lord Liverpool*, submitted to the prime minister in March.

Bathurst's chief clerk Henry Goulburn attempted to answer the charge of prejudgment in a letter dated 9 February 1819, which was actually printed in the pamphlet.[14] It was Goulburn who was reputed to be good friends with the Nor'westers. Goulburn claimed that the initial order was only for an indictment and "no other Prosecutions against his Lordship" were ever directed. He attempted to divert attention from the issue by attacking "the manner in which Lord Selkirk obtained possession" of the text of the dispatch, and complained about inaccuracies in Selkirk's transcription. Halkett quite properly observed that any errors could hardly be Selkirk's, since he was never shown the original.[15] Even Goulburn realized that his answer did not deal with Halkett's point that the Canadian authorities found constant justification for their persecution of Selkirk in the 11 February order, which was never properly revealed to the earl. He spoke of several misapprehensions of what had passed, adding that although Halkett's letter "inculpates in a charge of prejudice and injustice towards Lord Selkirk all the high Official Authorities in Canada, many of whom cannot be suspected of having been misled by personal interest or partial affection." It "contains matter of much grave charge" that would have to be investigated by the governor general of Canada.

The final court cases resulting from Selkirk's personal activities in the west came in the spring of 1819 at the York Assizes, after the earl had gone home to continue the fight to clear his name. Selkirk had been again tried in Sandwich on 12 January 1819—in absentia—for an assault and false imprisonment of William Smith. Through his attorneys, the earl pleaded not guilty and was found not guilty by a jury.[16] Later in the month, in York, John Beverley Robinson acted on behalf of Deputy Sheriff William Smith and Daniel Mckenzie, who sued Selkirk in civil court for false imprisonment. Dr. John Allan was the only witness for the defence, and Robinson insisted that his testimony helped prove the charges.[17] While Selkirk's detention of

McKenzie may not have been criminal, it was clearly coercive, particularly when combined with the purchase from McKenzie. Much was made of this purchase of goods by a magistrate from a person he held as prisoner under a felony charge. John Beverley Robinson later wrote Sir Peregrine Maitland that Selkirk's invasion of Fort William "might have been justified by what appeared to him at the time," but he had acted as a magistrate in matters "affecting so nearly his personal interests and feelings."[18] Miles Macdonell was the person who actually did the coercion, although Selkirk was held to have authorized it. Chief Justice Powell told the jury that the only limitation upon its award was "the amount of the defendant's fortune." The jury found for the plaintiffs and awarded substantial damages.[19] The only property which Selkirk was known to hold in Upper Canada was attached for these awards, but they did not otherwise directly affect Selkirk or his estate.[20] The Selkirk people claimed that the account of this trial in the Montreal *Herald* was full of false statements by McKenzie and his lawyers, but was widely copied. According to Lady Katherine Halkett, it was a paragraph in a London newspaper "insidiously alluding" to the McKenzie trial that set the earl on his downhill path in terms of health. He was planning a libel action when another hemorrhage occurred, she wrote, and "from that time forward, we had nothing but anxiety, sorrow, labour of body, and heart break."[21]

At a subsequent session of oyer and terminer held at York on 22 February, Selkirk and all his major associates—Miles Macdonell, John Spencer, John Allan, Proteus D'Orsonnens, Frederick Matthey, Gustavus Fauché, Frederick de Graffenreid, John McNabb, Donald McPherson, Archibald McDonald, Jean Baptiste Chevalier de Lorimer, A.B. Becher, Louis Nolin, Jacques Chattellain, P.C. Pambrun, John Pritchard, John Bourke, Michael Heden, and Jacob Vitsche—were indicted, chiefly in absentia, for a conspiracy "to interrupt and abstract, and to put a stop to and ruin the Trade and business of certain persons trading under the name of the North West Company."[22] The oyer and terminer was held under the recent legislation allowing criminal proceedings resulting from crimes in the Indian Territories to be held in any court in Upper Canada. John Allan was the only person indicted who was actually present, and he put up a spirited defence, submitting a lengthy affidavit telling the entire Fort William story from his perspective. Attorney General Robinson said that he could not see the point of the affidavit, and Allan's attorney answered in three words several times repeated: "mitigation of bail." Bail was taken.

Allan described the entire incident to Lady Selkirk as representing a "New era in British Judicature" in which British legal rights were trampled upon by the state.[23] Perhaps not surprisingly, this business ended with Allan charged with assault following a visit to his quarters by the acting solicitor general armed with a cane.[24]

Allan was left to deal with this litigation virtually by himself. He had actually managed to find an Upper Canadian lawyer. George Ridout had attended John Strachan's school and was admitted to the bar in 1812 to look after Selkirk legal business in Upper Canada. The Ridout family was independent of the Upper Canadian oligarchy, and George's brother John had been killed in a duel with a prominent member of the Family Compact in 1817.[25] He would later be dismissed by Sir Francis Bond Head as "the most intemperate of my opponents." Samuel Gale was not much impressed with Ridout, claiming that he did not inspire respect.[26] With the acquisition of Ridout by the Selkirk people, however, Samuel Gale was finally freed from attending court as an observer. Selkirk was able to report to John Greig in March that the little lawyer was off to Washington to arrange for the American lands.[27] The object, Selkirk wrote to Gale, was to assure his settlers at Red River "a safe asylum & a regular Gov't on crossing the parallel of 49."[28]

The unexpected death of Lord Errol in early 1819 created a vacancy in the representative peerage of Scotland. Selkirk wrote to Lord Melville, the ministry's man in Scotland, announcing his intention to "offer myself as a Candidate." He added, "As my friends assure me, that my absence at the time of the late General Election was the only reason for the support of Government being withdrawn, I trust that no other candidate will be preferred on the present occasion."[29] The earl received some expressions of support. To Lord Hopetoun he confessed his unhappiness at the stigma of being turned out of the House of Lords in 1818. He noted that both Lord Melville and Lord Sidmouth had told him recently that they had not known about the Bathurst order of 11 February 1817, but this was not very reassuring. He found it hard to believe that Bathurst would take such a step "unless he had calculated that his colleagues took a very faint interest in the individuals whom he had resolve to persecute." Melville and Sidmouth both thought that the probability of his return to America would count against him at the poll.[30] Selkirk could hardly respond that he was really too ill to travel anywhere. Instead, he wrote Lord Sidmouth that if the government acted on his complaints, his visit to North America could be brief.[31] To his potential supporters, the earl insisted that he had originally gone to America through necessity and would return only to protect his tenantry and dependents. This action would not be a voluntary and permanent abandonment of his native land.[32] All these reassurances were not enough. Although his friends stood by him, Selkirk got only nineteen votes to twenty-nine for the opposition.[33]

In early March, Lord Selkirk attempted to deal with his Prince Edward Island business. By now he had heard from James Stewart in Halifax, who had suggested a potential agent. Writing to Stewart, the earl hoped to be able to wind up his affairs advantageously, or at least by "making the best of a bad bargain." In any case, he added, "I shall at all events . . . follow without hesitation the plan of disposing of my whole property in the Island as soon as it can be affected." He had heard bad reports of William Johnston while in Canada, and a long period without a report from the agent did not bode well.[34] A month later Selkirk wrote Stewart again. He had thought that Johnston had no proper authorization from him, but his solicitor had found a power-of-attorney that he did not remember signing. So it was necessary to execute a new power-of-attorney by which Johnston could be superseded.[35]

At about the same time, Selkirk became involved with the Colonial Office over the so-called "Selkirk persecution bill" passed by the Upper Canadian legislature late in 1818. In a letter to James Woods and Daniel Washburn, the earl reported that he had entered a caveat at the Colonial Office against the bill, which he understood had been passed without a suspending clause. The earl wrote to the prime minister, Lord Liverpool, requesting his intervention in these "extraordinary proceedings in Canada."[36] Liverpool agreed to transmit Selkirk's letter to Lord Bathurst, who responded that he had no such bill at the Colonial Office and could not act without it.[37] As it turned out, the panic about the Upper Canadian legislature had been both premature and misguided. Samuel Gale wrote Selkirk in early May that the information on the bill that he had supplied to Selkirk (and which Selkirk had included in his letter to Lord Liverpool) had been based on second-hand information.[38] When Gale actually saw the bill, he found it no worse than improper and inexpedient, and he doubted that it applied to Selkirk's case. This whole business provides a perfect example of how partisan politics in the Canadas translated into misunderstanding and how the assumptions of a concerted conspiracy on the part of the Selkirk forces could sometimes be misleading.

Virtually every day brought some new demand involving Red River. Robert Laidlaw wrote on behalf of his son William, managing Selkirk's farm near the Forks. He included news from William's letters about the progress of the crops. William needed farm workers, especially ploughmen. His father offered to recruit some. The earl was sympathetic, although he wrote he would rather hear directly from William himself.[39]

In March Lord Selkirk was too ill to deal with the unfortunate Mrs. McLean, a relic of the violence in Red River. Andrew Colvile conducted the negotiations. The lady had been waiting in London since November 1817 to apply personally to the earl for assistance.[40] Charles McLean had been part of the 1812 immigration to Red River, subsidized by Selkirk as a potential leader among the settlers. He had been injured in a cannon explosion in 1815, and then killed at Seven Oaks in 1816. Mrs. McLean, who had been accused by the fur traders at York Factory in 1812 of pocketing spoons from the dinner table, had been defended by Miles Macdonell. The case had damaged Miles's relationship with the traders. She had come after Seven Oaks to London, where Colvile offered her £100 and £20 per annum until Lord Selkirk could deal with her case personally. She had rejected this offer with indignation and only later accepted it, after she had tried the agents of the North West Company.[41] Colvile had little sympathy for Mrs. McLean. He indignantly denied that her husband was fighting for Lord Selkirk when he died, insisting that McLean was fighting for a farm that he himself valued at £2000. Selkirk could not admit such a claim as a matter of right, for Selkirk could not "be considered responsible for the consequences of crimes which it was not in his power to prevent." Mrs. McLean had been paid "a donation as commiseration of her misfortunes and distressed situation." The payment would be continued for the same reason.[42] Unmentioned anywhere in the correspondence was Andrew Colvile's realization that Mrs. McLean could not be allowed to wander around London claiming that Lord Selkirk did not properly look after his people in their time of need.

Lady Selkirk in March wrote to her husband that she had "by accident" come upon Lady Sherbrooke's letters regarding the Coltman report. The first one had been dated 21 May 1818, and it reported that Sir John had written to London that he had received an abstract of Coltman's report. It laid all high crimes and misdemeanours at the hands of the Nor'westers. In another letter a few days later, Lady Sherbrooke wrote that she had seen a small part of the report related to Lord Selkirk, "and in my opinion it is quite impossible to have made a statement more in Lord Selkirk's favour than he has done there, if it related to my husband I should feel perfectly satisfied with it, and look upon Mr. Coltman as one of my best friends."[43] By the end of March, Selkirk had pretty well decided to bring an end to the Montreal prosecutions and commit his energy to dealing with the British government. One of the considerations was his health. The doctors wanted to send him to a warmer climate. "How this is to be reconciled to other objects," he wrote his wife, "Heaven knows."[44] He had sent Lord Liverpool a copy of a printed letter and copies of correspondence between John Halkett and the Colonial Office on 19 March. The manuscript had obviously been finished between early February, when Selkirk had written Liverpool requesting his intervention, and mid-March, suggesting that Selkirk had remained active during this period. *A Letter to Lord Liverpool* was not intended for publication.[45] Indeed, Selkirk's lawyer, Alexander Mundell, cautioned: "No copy should be given to any person, but for a purpose necessary for the prosecution of the means of redress in a legal or constitutional manner—and that it may be impossible it can be said this is the publication of a Libel—in short the Printed Copies should be dealt with as written Copies."[46]

If the letter to Liverpool had been handled as Alexander Mundell had advised, it is doubtful it would have had much public effect. Apart from a possible later reaction by the government of Lower Canada, the memorial to the Duke of Richmond had little immediate effect in the Canadas. From Sandwich, Selkirk attorney James Wood wrote in March of 1819 that the memorial was "a most important tho' humiliating Document, and may *eventually* be productive of much advantage to the Inhabitants of these Provinces." William Berezy added that the pamphlet "has excited universal indignation in all its readers against the Oppression of the Settlement & the infamous Conduct of Mr. Coltman of the extent of which before I had no idea." But, he added, it would not lead to public protests against the regime. But the letter to Liverpool was not handled quite as circumspectly as Mundell would have wanted. The printing bill in May of 1819 indicated that 250 copies each of the Liverpool letter and the Halkett/Bathurst correspondence had been initially printed, and that a second edition of another 250 copies each had also been completed.[47]

Selkirk was appealing to Liverpool, he emphasized in his letter, because he could not get redress from the Colonial Department. The problem was "the unexampled misconduct of the Law Officers of the Crown, and other public functionaries in Canada; and the total perversion of justice which it has occasioned."[48] Selkirk began by observing that his settlement had originally been undertaken with Liverpool's approval. Unlike William Coltman, he began the narrative of the conflict with the determination of the Nor'westers to frustrate the settlement, which predated any of those acts fastened on by the North West Company as "the original cause of all the disturbances."[49] Selkirk had not yet seen the Coltman Report, and so this work was not a critique of it, although the earl had a pretty good idea of the approach Coltman would take. In this pamphlet, as in the Memorial to the Duke of Richmond, Selkirk seemed less interested in indicting the judicial systems of the Canadas or even the Colonial Office than in exposing the actions of the Commissioners of Special Inquiry as partial and unfair quite independently of the text of the final report. He concentrated particularly on William Coltman's actions in Red River that allowed many culprits to escape and the North West Company to cause much disruption to the settlement. As the earl pointed out toward the end of the pamphlet, he had submitted to Coltman's decisions in Red River, but at that time understood that the prince regent's proclamation pledged that a full investigation and adjudication of his rights could still occur. "That this pledge may at length be redeemed, is the principal object of the application which I now make to your Lordship."[50] What Selkirk wanted, he wrote, was a state inquiry by the king in Council into the Hudson's Bay Company charter, the adoption of measures to remedy the problems of government in the interior of British America, and a rigorous investigation of the extraordinary judicial proceedings in the Canadas. These were three separate and distinct questions, of course, and rather a lot to expect from any government.

One enthusiastic response to the printed letter to Lord Liverpool came from Selkirk's former mentor, Dugald Stewart. The old man wrote that this letter in combination with the published exchange of correspondence between John Halkett and Lord Bathurst "appears to me to make out so very strong a case as will render it impossible for any influence whatever to quash the investigation you solicit."[51] He called for a broad public distribution, exactly the opposite of what the legal advisors wanted. On 27 April—the very day that Dugald Stewart wrote so encouragingly—Lord Liverpool gave his answer to Selkirk's submissions. "As the subject of your Lordship's complaint does not come within my jurisdiction as first Lord of the Treasury," he wrote, "I do not see in what manner I can interfere in the present state of the business."[52] He suggested an appeal to the Colonial Secretary, who would in turn decide whether it would be brought to the Privy Council or cabinet. Once there, Liverpool noted, he would be obliged to give an opinion. What that opinion would be he did not specify.

About a month before Lord Liverpool had rejected Selkirk's appeal, the earl's former recruiting agent in the Highlands, Alexander Macdonald of Dalilia, wrote for the latest information on Red River. Macdonald had been a part of the venture when it could still be viewed as philanthropic. He observed:

> The Highland Proprietors are now becoming sensible of the justness of your enlightened remarks on the state of the population of that part of the Country, & they are now, when too late, so eager for the people emigrating, as they were formerly to throw obstacles in their way to prevent them, they find (as your Lordship predicted) that their Estates are consumed by a superabundant, increasing poor, useless, population, who have wasted the means at home that might formerly have enabled them to transport themselves to another quarter of the Globe, where they might be of Service to themselves & to our manufacturers at home, instead of starving & hanging now as a dead weight upon the industry of others.[53]

Dalilia's kind words may have been responsible for encouraging Selkirk to take pen in hand to revisit his earlier work on emigration and national settlement.

The result was two untitled pamphlets that were printed by J. Brettell but were never published.[54] In one of these productions, Selkirk rehearsed his early interest in Highland emigration, and his decision to experiment "at my own risk" with a venture to shift the destination of Highlanders from the United States to Canada. He emphasized that the Prince Edward Island emigration was conducted upon government insistence on a maritime destination, and did not really deal with his larger thinking about national colonization. For that he required an isolated region of great fertility and capable of immediate cultivation, and he corresponded with the government at length over the matter. The government had no desire to establish a new colony, and he was given the right to land grants in Upper Canada. After visiting Upper Canada, he determined that no individual could create a national settlement there. Since he could not follow out the views of colonization he had elaborated to the government, he established no large number of settlers in Upper Canada and only carried on a farm as an experiment.

One of the major problems with Upper Canada was regulations against ge land grants and the establishment of a province on what amounted to principles of agrarian equality. Selkirk pointed out in passing that this encouraged democratic sentiments, but his real concern was with settlement. The small land grants given out were capable of being assembled into tracts, but these tracts were scattered and interspersed with the property of others, making it difficult for a landowner to improve them. The reservations for the clergy and for schools further militated against improvement. Thus regulations introduced to prevent land jobbing were responsible for it. The system excluded men of capital from investing in Upper Canada. As a result, emigrants had landed in British America in recent years, but most had crossed to the American side, where they purchase land rather than receive it free or upon payment of the fees of office. They behave this way out of self-interest, argued Selkirk. They knew they would be helped by the proprietor who held the mortgage on the land, and they knew their property would increase in value from the growth in population. The earl's critique of Upper Canadian land policy anticipated that of Robert Gourlay in his *Statistical Account of Upper Canada, Compiled with a View to a Grand System of Emigration*, published in 1822. The similarity of the views of Selkirk and Gourlay was not surprising, given their overlapping confrontations with the official oligarchy in 1818. Selkirk was highly critical of emigration assisted by government, insisting that "men of capital" could do the job better and without expense to the government. But no one in government paid any attention to his concern to "excite the attention of Government to a more comprehensive view of the importance of peopling the British provinces in America, with the overflowings of our own population."[55]

Selkirk repeated here his insistence that the settlement of Red River was a consequence of his involvement with the Hudson's Bay Company. He pointed out to the directors of the HBC the value of a permanent agricultural settlement in their territories and the need for an asylum for servants of the company. The directors agreed, but did not think the company could afford it. He proposed to undertake the settlement at his own risk, providing he got enough land to repay him for his investment. The undertaking was begun, the earl insisted, with the larger view of emigration in mind. Obviously a person of "moderate fortune" could not execute on "the scale of a national measure," but perhaps a foundation could be laid upon which government might later build. And such would have occurred, if the settlement had not been so interrupted. All the natural advantages, Selkirk insisted, "have been more than realized by actual observation."[56] He had been unable to obtain justice for the settlers or for himself, Selkirk concluded, since "all ordinary means of redress have been exhausted in vain."[57] His appeal to the head of His Majesty's government resulted in a referral back to the Colonial Department that had abused him earlier. He was now appealing to the Legislature for redress.[58] Apart from the final section, Selkirk's pamphlet had sketched out a critique of Canadian land policy and offered a solution to it. What he really needed to do was fill out the sketch into a major study comparable to *Observations on the State of the Highlands of Scotland.*

Unfortunately, the earl's health was not up to any more major literary enterprises, as he acknowledged in the other pamphlet written and printed (but not published) in 1819. Here he could manage little more than a brief cannibalization and summary of his earlier work on emigration and the Highlands.[59]

While emigration across the Atlantic might be, as Alexander Macdonald suggested, extremely attractive to many Scots after the Napoleonic War had finally ended, Red River was still not a popular destination. In April Selkirk dealt personally with various matters concerning his settlement. He was already selling his Upper Canadian lands and hoping to dispose of his Prince Edward Island property as well. Robert Laidlaw wrote Selkirk early in the month to recount the troubles he was having with the people he had engaged to work on his son's farm. They had heard false and exaggerated reports of the country, climate, and inhabitants. They were told that Governor Semple had been murdered by Aboriginal people and were convinced they would have their throats cut within a week. Laidlaw had to threaten to hold them all to a large penalty if they did not fulfill their contracts.[60] William Anderson—who was negotiating financing to keep Selkirk solvent—reported from Edinburgh that the chief problem with the Laidlaw recruits was the clause in their contract binding them to defend Selkirk's property with courage and fidelity. This clause suggested the presence of danger. If it was struck and the condition omitted that these people could be dismissed at any time, Anderson thought most recruits would agree to go.[61] Selkirk refused to change the contract, arguing that yielding to unreasonable objections only caused later troubles. The power to dismiss was essential, although, given the expense of sending these people to Red River, he was unlikely to dismiss them frivolously. The terms "courage" and "fidelity" were useless in contracts, and could be scratched out, but it would be better to shame the men out of the objection. One man who seemed of particularly litigious disposition should be dismissed, he wrote, since he would be only a mischief.[62] Selkirk worried about grain seed that Laidlaw proposed to send, asking whether there was a species of red wheat that was hardier. All seeds should be packed in small casks.[63] He also sent letters looking for a Presbyterian clergyman and a medical man for his settlement. The inducements for the doctor were considerable. The cost of living was low, and money could be made in private practice beyond the £100 per annum in salary the earl was offering. One carpenter had remitted £90 sterling last year, wrote Selkirk.[64]

At the end of April, prospects for Red River took an upward turn. John Halkett decided to retire from his position in public service.[65] On 28 April, Selkirk wrote to Lady Selkirk that he hoped Halkett would go to Red River in his place. In order to encourage him, Selkirk decided to convey to his brother-in-law all the lands in his charter south of the 49th parallel. It would be up to Halkett to sell these lands.[66] Halkett would travel to North America in 1821 as an executor of Selkirk's estate. He would travel to Washington to try to arrange some sale of the American lands, and he did visit Red River in 1822, although he did not remain. Selkirk would later try to involve Robert Dickson in a purchase from the Sioux of some of these lands.[67]

The fairly extensive "private" circulation of the Liverpool letter and Halkett–Bathurst correspondence made an impact in some circles. After reading these works, Selkirk's brother-in-law Sir James Hall wrote of his indignation at the earl's treatment by governments on both sides of the water. He recommended a campaign "to draw the public attention toward it." One step would be the engagement at any expense of a young man named Henry Brougham, generally regarded to be the cleverest and most eloquent lawyer in the British Isles. The hiring of Brougham would quickly have publicized Selkirk's case.[68] In a follow-up letter, Hall advocated an attack on Lord Bathurst, writing "in what form I cannot pretend to say; but surely you have suffered enough and the constitution of this Kingdom has been sufficiently injured in your person to call for some punishment of him as a public man." Even if the attack were not successful, it would publicize Selkirk's case. Hall hoped that the earl would act with the "vigour which has already carried you through so many tremendous scenes."[69] Agreement as to the perfection of the case made out in these works came from another correspondent, who wrote, "Such a perversion of justice in one of our most important colonies, countenanced by a principal department of Government, with the interest it deserves from your connection with it, must be a subject that would engage the attention of Parliament."[70] Despite his illness, Selkirk determined to act. He wrote to his "friends" about orchestrating the business of bringing the matter to the attention of Parliament.[71] In a letter to Sir James Scarlett on 19 May, Selkirk wrote that his doctors had pushed him out of smoky London with orders not to meddle with business; he would retreat to Andrew Colvile's Langley Farm in the countryside outside the city. The earl should not even be writing a few lines to tell him that his brother-in-law Sir James Montgomery would move in the House of Commons on his case, probably bringing the question in the shape of a motion for papers.[72] What Selkirk was forced to omit from this letter was the information that a petition for relief from John Pritchard would be used by Sir James as the occasion for his motion. By the time Selkirk wrote, 250 copies of this petition had already been printed.[73] A day later he wrote a fairly lengthy letter in his own hand, probably to Proteus D'Orsonnens, offering "the state of my health" as an explanation to all those in the West who were expecting letters from him.[74] Selkirk wrote to Samuel Gale later in the month of the doctors' orders, observing, "Tho' it has not been possible to fulfill this literally & entirely, yet my absence even at this small distance from town has thrown back many things which ought to have been attended to." Among the loose ends were his American lands and the legal proceedings at York.[75]

Among the friends who rallied round Selkirk in 1819 were three of his old political allies from the anti-slavery days, William Smith, Zachary McAulay, and William Wilberforce. McAulay acknowledged his support (and that of Wilberforce) in a letter to Selkirk on 28 May, writing of the letter to Liverpool, "The narrative I have read with painful interest."[76] This letter undoubtedly cheered Selkirk up, for relations had been strained for years with Wilberforce, who did not approve of Selkirk's connections with the Hudson's Bay Company or actions in the West. A day later Selkirk wrote to George Garden about initiating an action for libel against the editor of the Montreal *Herald*, who had printed an account of the civil trial initiated by Daniel McKenzie. This was apparently the libel action referred to by Lady Katherine Halkett as bringing on the major hemorrhage that produced the final decline in Selkirk's health. We can therefore probably date the beginning of the last phase of Selkirk's illness at the end of May 1819. Before this point, Selkirk was clearly very sick, but still capable of considerable periods of energy and involvement in his affairs. The drafting of the letter to Liverpool and two other pamphlets—however cannibalized from earlier work—demonstrated his continued capacity. He had managed to keep up with his correspondence as well. After May the number of letters he wrote dwindled, and everything he wrote apologized for "the state of my health." The earl ceased to be a player in his life, but merely a passive victim of forces that had long since been set in motion.

The news on Selkirk's North American business was not very satisfying. The Laidlaw party finally set sail for the bay. Selkirk complained about Robert Laidlaw's lack of efficiency and economy.[77]

The Colonial Office continued to stonewall. In a letter to Henry Berens, governor of the Hudson's Bay Company, Henry Goulburn on behalf of Lord Bathurst denied that he had discouraged a judicial decision on the question of jurisdiction in the West. Bathurst would have investigated affairs in the Canadas already, Goulburn insisted, had he not information "from that quarter" that Berens had been misled as to the true situation. The Colonial Secretary certainly opposed the introduction of any military force to support territorial rights, "which, in the extent to which they are claimed, have not received any judicial sanction."[78] Berens replied that he and the Hudson's Bay Company were ready to test the validity and extent of the charter in any competent tribunal.[79] By this time Simon McGillivray had entered the lists, writing to Lord Liverpool on 2 June that he had only just seen Selkirk's privately circulated pamphlet and accompanying correspondence. To answer fully its falsehoods, McGillivray would have to offer Liverpool and the public a detailed counterstatement. The Nor'wester claimed that he was flattered to be opposed with "all the influence, the power, and the talents of the Earl of Selkirk." In the meantime, he was only surprised at Selkirk's appeal, given the fact that the North West Company case had made such an impression on Bathurst himself, the commissioners appointed to investigate the proceedings in the West, and the law officers of the Crown.[80] In the end, the Nor'westers riposted to Selkirk's appeal not by writing an answering pamphlet but by bringing actions against him in the Court of Common Pleas at Westminster.[81]

As if to provide additional graphic documentation of exactly the sort of thing that Selkirk was complaining about in terms of legal proceedings, the Lower Canadian government did eventually respond to his memorial. The Duke of Richmond wrote Selkirk on 22 May 1819 that he had now read the memorial and referred the earl to the law courts of the province since he could not act upon it.[82] A few days later, the Duke of Richmond's military secretary, Colonel John Ready, wrote James Stuart, Selkirk's legal advisor in Montreal, that the government would act on the memorial to convene a special court of oyer and terminer to try offences committed in the Indian Territories.[83] Stuart replied that it was too late. The principal criminals had been admitted to bail or had escaped to the Indian country. The witnesses had been dispersed. He suggested a lengthy postponement.[84] Ready replied that there was no need for postponement, since the court of oyer and terminer that had been opened in March of 1818 had been continued by adjournment and could easily reassemble.[85] Stuart was understandably astounded at this piece of information, that a court originally opened for the trial of the murderers of Owen Keveny had been regarded by the government as constituted to try all offences in the Indian Territory and was still open.[86] Had Selkirk known that the court of oyer and terminer could have been generally employed for other prosecutions, he would have used it, he emphasized. If the court had been continued, it was by secret adjournment. If the court were assembled now at short notice, Selkirk could not be expected to provide evidence and witnesses. Stuart could see in such proceedings "only a continuance of the abuse of the powers of Government, for the purpose of shielding from punishment the culprits under the protection of the North West Company." In a letter to Selkirk, Stuart emphasized that in his view, the proposed holding of the court was simply a way for the NWC to get clear of all remaining prosecutions. Selkirk could not have provided the evidence, and everyone's case would be dismissed. Despite Stuart's response to Ready, the court of oyer and terminer did meet in October 1819. It discharged all Nor'westers from all charges over which it had competence, but refused to issue general dismissals.

On the political front, correspondence of Maitland Garden & Auldjo, the Montreal-based agents of the Hudson's Bay Company, with the selfsame Colonel Ready, provided continued evidence of the failure of the colonial governments to deal with the fur-trade conflict in the West, particularly in the Athabasca country. The problem was at the trading post called Fort Wedderburn. On 11 October 1818, Colin Robertson was arrested by a party headed by Simon McGillivray and the "enforcer" Samuel Black that had confronted him at his dwelling. The charge was that the HBC man had brandished a pistol at the Nor'westers, and Robertson himself admitted that a pistol had mysteriously gone off in his pocket in the course of the scuffle. None of the HBC people came to Robertson's assistance, and he ended up in a NWC canoe on his way to Fort Chipewyan, where partner J.G. McTavish sheltered him from further intimidation. Robertson would spend the winter under confinement in a room connected to the post's privy. Maitland Garden & Auldjo wanted to dispatch a canoe with a warrant for Black's arrest, backed by the support of the government through the persons of several soldiers to serve the warrant.[87] Ready responded that the Duke of Richmond did not wish to use soldiers, and preferred instead to call upon some of the respected partners of the North West Company for their assistance and cooperation in serving the warrant.[88] The Montreal agents responded with incredulity. Richmond could not have been informed of the history of the business at issue. He could not simply refer to the Nor'westers. The arm of public authority had to be visibly extended to assert the execution of the law.[89] Richmond doggedly insisted that he could use military force only if the civil power had been forcibly resisted.[90] But, of course, there was no civil power in the Athabasca to be resisted, and what was being asked was that he introduce some.

Sir James Montgomery made his motion with regard to the petition of John Pritchard on 24 June 1819, calling for the tabling of the relevant Colonial Office papers on the Red River Settlement.[91] Debate was held on the motion that same day. Lady Selkirk arrived home from Montreal just in time to be present in the House of Commons for the speech and the debate. According to the diary of William Wilberforce, "Sir James Montgomery, Ellice, Scarlett, William Smith, Bennett, and Goulburn all did well in their several manners—Smith very acute, Montgomery singularly attic, simple, and clear. Ellice manly and strong."[92] Despite some misleading statements by Henry Goulburn, the motion carried easily. Goulburn had insisted that the question of the Hudson's Bay Company charter was already before the Privy Council when the case was still buried at the Colonial Office; Selkirk himself pointed out this inconsistency to Lord Bathurst in a letter on 16 July.[93] The house requested "copies of extracts of official communications which may have taken place between the secretary of state and the provincial government of Upper or Lower Canada, or to any complaints made of those proceedings by Lord Selkirk or the agents of the Hudson's Bay or the North-

West Companies," as well as the Coltman report. By this time it was really too late. Less than a week after the parliamentary debate, the earl wrote to a correspondent, "at present I am miserably weak, so that even such a letter as this is an exertion which I can hardly venture to undertake."[94]

The printing by Commons order of the Blue Book, *Papers Relating to the Red River Settlement,* was completed by 12 July 1819, less than three weeks after Sir James Montgomery had spoken in the House. This publication of the full record was probably as close to a vindication as Selkirk was likely to get in his lifetime. Those willing to plough through its folio-sized pages would discover that the earl had consistently acted as he had always insisted he had acted. He had demanded protection for his settlers, the Colonial Office had been slow to act, and the colonial governments had fumbled the ball. William Coltman's appended analysis of the fur-trade war was also in most respects sympathetic to Selkirk. The commissioner went to great pains to insist that Selkirk was always motivated by belief in the legality and righteousness of his actions, while the retaliation of the North West Company "exceeded all reasonable or lawful bounds of self-defence . . . as to render the proceedings of their party, beyond comparison, the most criminal." Given the complexity of his motives, Selkirk could really expect little more. On the eve of the formal release of the Blue Book, the Earl of Bathurst finally wrote to his Canadian governor general to request information on the court battles that had occurred over the past few years.[95]

A few days after the Blue Book appeared, Lord Selkirk roused himself to take pen in hand. He produced a relatively lengthy letter—given his physical state—to his old friend and ally William Wilberforce. It began, "I understand that you had an intention of expressing your sentiments; but that the turn which the debate took did not afford a good opportunity. I regretted this much at the time, being persuaded that even two or three sentences from you would have been of material service to our cause."[96] The earl continued that he hoped Wilberforce would take a lead in the business he had opened for the sake of the "Native Indians" who groaned under grievous oppression. He apologized for not consulting with Wilberforce at the time of his grant. He did not seek profit, Selkirk emphasized, but he admitted he coveted the influence implicit in such rights in a territory without civilization. The Hudson's Bay Company had done its best, but did not have enough political power to assert its jurisdiction successfully. Selkirk confessed that he had taken on "a task of too great magnitude for one individual," but added that he did not anticipate the difficulties. In his reply on 26 July, Wilberforce acknowledged the apology.[97] He promised to continue to follow Selkirk's case, "interesting indeed & deeply so it is on its own account & to every feeling mind, it must be rendered much more so, by the peculiar circumstances which belong to it." He was fully convinced, the great reformer added, that Selkirk's scheme had been undertaken out of humanitarian motives, with a view to the improvement and benefit of his fellow human creatures. Wilberforce continued that he knew that when pursuing a favourite object, men were sometimes led "into the use of means which they may afterwards see reason to disapprove. And this especially happens, when from the nature of the case, we are obliged to avail ourselves of the services of men, whose character we cannot scrutinize very nicely. Excuse me. if I say that I conceived such might be your situation." Neither of the two old collaborators had written unambiguously. Selkirk's "apology" was hedged with self-justification, and Wilberforce's acceptance of it was vaguely tinged with criticism. But the exchange probably satisfied both of them.

Selkirk may have been willing to accept Wilberforce's claim that his servants had failed him. Samuel Gale might have concurred. Gale always saw Miles Macdonell and Colin Robertson as the evil geniuses of Selkirk's downfall. But to put the responsibility on others would have been to delude himself. The major decisions had been his, and given the circumstances in which he found himself, they were reasonably good decisions for which no commander in the field need apologize. The dispatch of Lord Bathurst that caused so much difficulty would probably have been drafted whatever Selkirk had or had not negotiated with Daniel McKenzie. The seizure of Fort William, which had been the cause of Bathurst's negative reaction, was a real coup, well worth doing and the only way of gaining any advantage over unscrupulous adversaries. At about the same time as Selkirk and Wilberforce exchanged their correspondence, Robert Dickson wrote Lady Selkirk that he hoped the House of Commons would rise to do justice to Selkirk. But, he added, someday the world would know. "God is Just & Merciful and virtue must ever overcome vice."[98]

CHAPTER TWENTY-THREE

To the Death

I N JULY OF 1819, Lord Selkirk's mail for the first time contained lawyer's letters regarding the disposition of his estate. The earl was clearly putting his affairs in order. To James Wedderburn, Selkirk insisted that until his honour had been vindicated in the contest with the North West Company, he could not begin to limit his expenses. He tried to be careful, but, he wrote, he was not always successful. He hoped the struggle would soon end. He could then retire to St. Mary's Isle "and live on sixpence a day till I am out of debt."[1] Selkirk was now on a heavy diet of mercury and was "so miserably weak." A letter to George Garden in Montreal at the end of July dealt with Canadian legal business, including the verdicts obtained against him by Sheriff Smith and Daniel McKenzie at York. He needed better legal information in order to bring the matter back to England for appeal. Lady Selkirk was visiting her mother prior to going with Selkirk abroad, the earl wrote, where he hoped the climate would "set me up again."[2] In a subsequent letter to Judge Stewart in Halifax dealing with new complaints against his agent on Prince Edward Island, Selkirk reported his health slightly improved.[3] He and Lady Selkirk were leaving Daer at school but taking "the rest of our Caravan with us." The "caravan" included Selkirk's two daughters, but also a young medical man recently graduated from the University of Edinburgh. John Allan had recommended Dr. George William Lefevre, and Lord and Lady Selkirk found him more than acceptable. Lefevre's first impression of the earl was that he was almost dead, but the attending surgeon thought he might live some time longer. Unimportant items of business continued to consume what Dr. Lefevre described as "a mind which evidently could not remain a moment unoccupied."[4] Who would pay, for example, for the "Irish Union Bag Pipes" Miles Macdonell had ordered from Dublin?

By the middle of September the little "caravan" was on its way to Paris via Dover. Selkirk's illness and subsequent sudden departure from Britain in September 1819 left many matters unsettled and many loyal supporters unsatisfied. John Allan had arrived in London from Upper Canada to find only Andrew Colvile left minding the store, for example, while George Garden in Montreal and William Mure in Kircudbright, among others, had been unable to get answers to their pressing questions.[5] It was Lady Selkirk who wrote a subsequent letter to Miles rejecting his offer to return to Red River, saying that Selkirk "considers that your returning to Red River could not be beneficial to yourself & so far from advancing his interests might perhaps have a contrary effect."[6] The earl and his "caravan" made a slow journey to Paris, seldom starting before eleven a.m. and stopping at dinner. In six days they were in the French capital, arriving on 25 September. Selkirk reported to Earl Hardwicke (in a letter written by a third party) that the travelling had so far agreed with him, and he was feeling much better.[7] Dr. Lefevre knew better than to share in any such optimism. The party left Paris at the end of September, paused at Bordeaux, and fetched up at Pau, in the shadow of the Pyrenees. Selkirk seemed to respond favourably to the change of scenery. At Pau the rains suddenly arrived, and the locals were certain that winter had come. The Basques held up their hands and exclaimed, "Jesus! Qui diable vous a conseille de venir ici?"[8] Nevertheless, Lady Selkirk decided to stop for the winter, and without further ado took a house with a view overlooking the mountains and the Gave valley.

Whether Selkirk ever saw the letters from Red River written from the settlement in the late summer and early autumn of 1819 is not clear. One from Frederick Matthey told of a great HBC triumph over the Nor'westers.[9] The new spirit of the HBC was given further meaning by the actions of recently appointed HBC governor-in-chief William Williams at the Grand Rapid in June of 1819. Williams was not a professional fur trader. He had served previously in the East India Company and was a bluff sailor. He had been hired to give some backbone to the HBC in the West. Selkirk had forwarded various warrants issued by a grand jury in Lower Canada to Williams, who decided to use them. Williams expanded his warrants by issuing his own as a magistrate of Rupert's Land, although he had no authority for offences committed in the Athabasca. The governor visited Red River and organized a spring offensive in coordination with Captain Matthey. The HBC well knew that the best place to effect a capture of Nor'westers was at the Grand Rapid, and the idea had been discussed several times in the past although never pursued seriously. With twenty of Matthey's De Meurons among his party of thirty constables, Williams carefully planned the action. He mounted cannon on a barge and placed other artillery to control the bottom of the rapid. At the last moment he was reinforced by John Clarke and his men, who arrived at the Grand Rapid ahead of the Nor'westers. The unsuspecting Nor'westers walked down the banks of the Saskatchewan while their canoes shot the rapid—two miles in six minutes—and at the bottom they were, one by one, summarily arrested. The haul included partners John Duncan Campbell, Benjamin Frobisher, William Connolly, John McDonald (le Borgne), John Angus Shaw, John George McTavish, and William McIntosh, as well as a number of voyageurs.

Williams's arrests were for the most part of dubious legality. Only William Coltman's warrants were valid in Rupert's Land, and then only on the assumption that his powers as commissioner were still in effect. Most Canadian warrants did not work at the Grand Rapid, and certainly Williams had no right to issue warrants for crimes committed in the Athabasca. The arrests were in many ways an embarrassment to the HBC. They demonstrated a visible renewal of the earlier exchanges of legal harassment, and much was made of their illegality by the NWC. Worse still, Benjamin Frobisher died of exposure in the course of attempting to escape from his captors, becoming the second Nor'wester martyr to the fur-trade conflict. Shaw, McTavish, and Cameron were sent to England for trial, and were released, as had been Dugald Cameron earlier, for want of English court competence to try felonies committed in the HBC territories. Those Nor'westers subsequently brought for trial in Lower Canada were also released for want of prosecution. It could be argued—and was—that such behaviour was unfortunate at a point when the two companies were involved in negotiations toward a settlement.

Certainly the Grand Rapid business belied the claim of the HBC to be the passive and innocent victim of NWC aggression, as well as bringing into question the HBC claim for sole jurisdiction over the Indian Territories. An English legal opinion on the cases spoke of the need to concede a "concurrent jurisdiction over the Company's territory" to the courts of Canada. Samuel Gale tutted, and officially the London Committee of the HBC was quite critical of Williams. Gale insisted that the action was too strong for a legal manoeuvre and not strong enough for a military one. Fear that Williams would be arrested and taken out of the country for his actions would lead to the dispatch of George Simpson as "Locum Tenens" in February 1820.[10] At the same time, the arrests proved that the successful exercise of force was still the best strategy to employ in the interior of the continent.   Like the earlier Fort William occupation of 1816 by Lord Selkirk, the Grand Rapid arrests totally disorganized the NWC in the West. They also sent a message to the Athabasca, especially to the First Nations, that the HBC was still a force to be reckoned with. In the complex negotiations that led to the resolution of the fur-trade war, the events at Grand Rapid ultimately strengthened the HBC's bargaining position. It was certainly not the last act of legal retaliation in the fur-trade war, however, much less the last act of violence.

That same summer that saw the arrests at Grand Rapid also bore witness to another harbinger of change in the unorganized territories of British North America. A party led by John Franklin sailed on board the HBC's *Prince of Wales* from Gravesend.[11] It was sponsored by the British Admiralty with the goal of finding a navigable sea passage from the Atlantic to the Pacific Oceans across the polar north (the "Northwest Passage"). Franklin and other British naval officers had tried to cross the Arctic Ocean by ship in 1818, but had been turned back by pack ice. This new expedition would take an overland route. It had the full support of both trading companies, which had promised to give every assistance possible. Franklin and his party reached York Factory on 30 August 1819, then headed by boat to winter at the HBC's Cumberland House. Franklin and two companions then journeyed by snowshoe to Fort Chipewyan in January of 1819, where he expected the NWC to provide assistance. Franklin subsequently complained that neither company's people on the spot were totally helpful, failing to understand the transportation and provisioning problems that he faced. The party was subsequently met at Great Slave Lake by Nor'wester Willard Wentzel, who accompanied it along the Yellowknife River in the summer of 1820. This expedition marked the first occasion since the eighteenth century where the fur-trading companies were deliberately employed by British Imperialism for non-economic purposes. The companies were expected to set aside their competition for the moment in the interests of "science." This would hardly be the last time that the fur trade was harnessed to imperial ambitions.

While Selkirk was travelling to France, both fur-trading companies, as well as the earl himself, were reeling from the blows of the opposition and the escalating costs of maintaining the conflict. In the end, the winner was likely to be the party with the most dependable line of credit with the bankers. The HBC overdraft at the Bank of England was £75,000 in 1820, with unpaid bills representing an additional £30,000 of indebtedness. But the directors of the Bank of England had considerable confidence in the ultimate success of the HBC, despite its lack of government support. Maintaining the loyalty of those servants in the interior was also critical, and here the HBC also seemed more successful than its rival. The credit crisis and the loyalty one were closely connected for the NWC. Alexander Ross later insisted that the cost of the trials in the Canadas to the NWC was over £50,000, and for the most part the money was found by not paying the wintering partners such as himself. Dissension in the ranks of the NWC, which had been going on for years, reached another peak in the summer of 1819 at the annual meetings at Fort William. Many of the partners had been arrested at Grand Rapid on their way to this gathering. The firm was desperately short of working capital. William McGillivray tried to convince the wintering partners to promise continued support for McTavish, McGillivray and Company with only limited success. A few partners agreed to give their powers of attorney to McGillivray, but most did not. John McLoughlin actually proposed that the winterers approach the HBC to become their agent if the engagement of 1804, due to come up in 1822, could not be renewed. But the NWC was not dead yet. Despite the overall dissension and the disruptions caused by the HBC at the Grand Rapid, the Nor'westers confirmed their trading structure in the Athabasca, now clearly under HBC assault and missing several important figures who had been carried off by the opposing company. George Keith was continued in charge. Colin Robertson, who had been imprisoned by Keith at Fort Chipewyan, admired Keith's "firmness of character" and his refusal to waltz "to any tune the McGillivray's chose to strike up." Keith was to be assisted by Simon McGillivray and Samuel Black.

As a result of the Fort William gathering, Samuel Gale was approached informally about negotiations with the HBC by an unnamed wintering partner of the NWC, John McLoughlin, through third party George Moffatt.

Would the HBC supply goods to the wintering partners who could not get
their money from the Montreal houses? Gale thought it would be possible to
work with all but the worst criminals. In London, Andrew Colvile concurred
that most of the winterers were not involved in the disgraceful acts of the war,
although a few would have to be excluded. But Colvile did not see how the
HBC could act as a supplier to its competitors. His alternative was "that the
whole trade of these countries, both what is comprised within the territories
of the Company, and what is beyond its limits, is to form one concern, that a
certain number of the servants of the Company are to be joined with those
persons now wintering partners of the North West Company, and thus form
a united body of managers resident in the Hudson's Bay or interior country,
whose time and attention shall be wholly devoted to the management of the
trade of the concern."[12] Colvile recognized that this arrangement could not be
brought into effect until the termination of the present partnership of the
NWC in 1822, by which point the rights and privileges of the HBC under the
charter would have been determined either by the Privy Council or Parliament. But many of the old HBC servants were on the eve of retirement to Red
River, and there would be plenty of room for Nor'westers.

Further complicating matters was a report in early December 1819 from
Sir James Montgomery to Andrew Colvile of his meeting with Henry Goulburn on the Privy Council decision about the charter. There was no word,
Montgomery emphasized, although Goulburn urged the expediency of a
compromise, since the decision might be unfavourable to both sides. At the
same time, Goulburn thought the government might confirm any arrangement the parties made themselves.[13] Andrew Colvile in December of 1819
certainly preferred the possibility of a merger to the alternative he and Lord
Selkirk had been discussing for some months with Edward "Bear" Ellice,
under which Ellice would purchase the HBC stock held by Selkirk and his
friends at a liberal price, indeed, at their holders' own valuation.[14] Ellice was
the London agent for the NWC and an important Whig politician, who had
married in 1809 the youngest sister of the second Earl Grey.[15] Lady Selkirk
had long suspected his fine hand in the support of the Colonial Office for the
NWC. The arrangement would involve guarantees for the continuation of
the Red River settlement and the abandonment of all civil actions and
damage claims by the NWC. Lord Selkirk did not like this proposal, which
both he and Lady Selkirk saw as "merely a question between money and
principle."[16] The earl was unwilling to give in to what he described as "a set

of unprincipled miscreants" on the basis of an acquiescence in the equality of "faults on both sides."

From Selkirk's perspective, it was critical to prove that his settlement was "neither a wild and visionary scheme nor a trick and a cloak to cover sordid plans of aggression upon the property of others." This proof could come only through the ultimate success of the scheme, which he feared would not long be continued under the NWC. Selkirk also suspected Ellice's motives, particularly the assertion that his proposal was totally independent of the NWC. If so, where was the money coming from? It could be considered seriously, he thought, only if the HBC felt it could not hold out against the combined power of the NWC and the Colonial Office. For his part, wrote Selkirk in early January 1820 from France, "I am ready nevertheless to fight the battle, if the only alternative is to submit to injustice and dishonour."[17]

Tidying up the loose ends from the frantic years was not easy. From Pau, Lady Selkirk attempted to deal with Miles Macdonell without involving her husband. Macdonell had turned up in England in 1819 under his own steam, looking for a financial settlement. As far as she knew, the countess wrote her brother, Macdonell understood that his salary had ended when he surrendered himself to the Nor'westers in June 1815. Selkirk told him in March 1816 that he would not put him back in charge of Red River, and Macdonell agreed to offer his services for three years as a "volunteer" for the sake of revenge. The man felt so guilty in 1816 that the earl had not emphasized his failures, but this could not be construed to mean approval, she insisted. Lady Selkirk thought Miles could have his land (a large grant in Assinoboia) and an allowance of between £200 and £300, if he accepted the offer with cordiality.[18] As she had suspected, however, Macdonell was not disposed to go quietly. Back in Montreal he submitted his account to George Garden, including salary at £300 per annum from 1811 to December 1817, plus interest from 1812 to 1819. The total account amounted to £4475. This account was also forwarded to Andrew Colvile. In the covering letter, Miles noted he had given up a remunerative appointment as Sheriff of the Home District in Upper Canada to serve Selkirk in 1810, adding, "I am now many years older than I was then, thrown out of every situation, my property neglected and wasted in my absence, and have lost many friends by espousing and adhering to the interests of Lord Selkirk."[19] Colvile wrote back to Samuel Gale that Selkirk desired as amicable a settlement as possible with Miles, based on an adjustment of the account to the most reasonable terms possible.[20]

Macdonell was already overcompensated, Colvile opined. Andrew Colvile himself decided to offer William Laidlaw, who had left the farm at the settlement some months earlier, £200 for eighteen months service.[21] Laidlaw's father replied by expressing incredulity that his son's "faithful & troublesome services" should be met with a strict adherence to the original bargain.[22]

Lord Selkirk continued to be fixated by that part of his grant from the Hudson's Bay Company south of the 49th parallel. He wrote to Samuel Gale in a quandary about how to proceed. He was willing to give land away to get "a good steady class of people," but hesitated to give the land, since Americans were almost suspicious of something for nothing. He needed to establish a price, but how?[23] Robert Dickson had suggested New England settlers, but Dickson clearly had no head for business, as the matter of the cattle Lord Selkirk had authorized Robert Dickson to drive from the United States to the settlement clearly demonstrated. Selkirk had put an absolute limit of £5000 on the business and insisted delivery must be to Red River. Dickson had subsequently signed a contract with an American named Michael Dousman to deliver 120 head of cattle to Big Stone Lake, and a man named A.D. Stewart had purchased the contract from Dousman for $1100. Stewart had actually procured the cattle in Illinois and wintered them on the prairies. He complained that his wintering expenses were not part of the original contract, nor was the $1100 he had paid Dousman for it. The result was a whining letter from Stewart, but no sign of the cattle at the settlement.[24] After Selkirk's death, John Halkett would visit Washington to attempt (unsuccessfully) to save something from that part of the grant now in the United States.

By March of 1820 all Selkirk's business was being conducted by his wife and Andrew Colvile, mainly by the latter working out of London. In his villa in Pau, Selkirk was slowly wasting away, and the end was near. He barely had enough energy to be moved outside to admire the view, although he talked with Dr. Lefevre until the last about political economy and colonization. Colvile still had many loose ends to manage. He learned, for example, that Selkirk's Grand River lands had been detached by Sheriff Smith for the judgment given him against Selkirk, and he wrote to Thomas Clark to let the land be sold.[25]

On 8 April 1820 Lord Selkirk finally died peaceably at Pau. He was stretched out reading on a sofa when he experienced a heavy coughing fit. By the time the doctor got to him, he was dead. His wife described the last days to her sister-in-law: "Mercifully there is hardly any suffering except from weakness, perfect tranquillity of mind and inexhaustible patience." The earl was buried in the closest Protestant cemetery to Pau. It was at Orthez, perhaps forty kilometres away. His will was entered at Edinburgh on 28 April, only three weeks later. The estate's executors would be John Halkett, Andrew Colvile, Sir James Montgomery, and James Wedderburn. Their job would not be easy. Wrapping up the estate would take many years. The earl died £60,000 in debt. Much of his assets were in his North American lands and in Hudson's Bay Company stock.[26] The former especially still needed to be properly developed. As Andrew Colvile pointed out to Sheriff Alexander Macdonell in Red River, Selkirk's death made no difference to the administration of the settlement.[27]

Perhaps the best epitaph was pronounced on Selkirk by his wife. She wrote about a month after his death to Lady Katherine Halkett: "I feel confident if we have patience, he will receive ample justice, and when the North West Company are forgotten his name and character will be revered as they ought. For this I would wish to wait although it may be his grandchildren only who are likely to feel it."[28] In this hope she would be, at least to some extent, satisfied.

CHAPTER TWENTY-FOUR

Coda

THE DEATH OF LORD SELKIRK left in midstream his three great projects—the reinvigoration of the Hudson's Bay Company, the settlement of Red River, and the settlement of Prince Edward Island—very much up in the air. Satisfactorily resolving these projects took some time after his death. The Hudson's Bay Company was the first to be sorted out, with the merger of the two great fur-trading companies in 1821. Selkirk's death had probably made this resolution possible.

MERGER

The 1820 meeting of the wintering partners at Fort William was full of controversy.[1] The wintering partners again refused to renew their agreement with the merchants. Eighteen partners authorized John McLoughlin and Angus Bethune to travel to London in order to deal with the HBC on their behalf. The two men sailed for England in the autumn of 1820 on the same ship as Colin Robertson.[2] Andrew Colvile always insisted that, without the pressure from the wintering partners, the Nor'west leaders would never have come to terms. For his part, Simon McGillivray thought the parties were on the verge of an arrangement favourable to the Nor'westers when the winterers' representatives arrived in London.

The negotiations were far enough advanced by early January 1821 for John Halkett to outline a potential settlement in some detail to Lady Selkirk.[3] This was not the Gale-Moffatt plan, Halkett emphasized. Instead, the HBC would take on as regular partners most of the wintering agents of the NWC. Halkett did not much like it, because he still did not trust the Nor'westers. The entire business would be divided into 100 shares. Forty would go to the NWC wintering partners and HBC chiefs and factors, five would go to the London agents, twenty to the Montreal agents, twenty to the HBC, five to Selkirk for losses suffered, and ten as a contingency fund. A subcommittee of five would run the new concern, two from the NWC (Simon McGillivray and Edward Ellice) and three from the HBC. The scheme might work with honest men, he thought, but the Nor'westers were not of such character. Without honesty, in five years the NWC would control the company, charter and all, he warned. A few days later, Andrew Colvile further reported on the arrangement to Lady Selkirk.[4] It was to last for twenty-one years. What Colvile described was not appreciably changed from the one discussed by Halkett, but Colvile was far more jubilant, writing, "We retain the power of management and get paid for our stolen goods, and they kiss the rod in both respects." (William McGillivray would subsequently write of the agreement, "We have made no submission. We met and negotiated on equal terms."[5]) Lord Selkirk would get at least £5000 per annum in dividends, beginning in 1823. Colvile and Simon McGillivray had worked out the final terms in half an hour, Colvile wrote. Colvile's exultation was a bit premature, for the deal subsequently came unstuck on several occasions. Part of the problem involved the demands of the NWC, part the resistance of some directors of the HBC, including John Henry Pelly. Among the debated issues was the place of Colin Robertson in the new company. Pelly wished him to be the leading Chief Factor; the NWC wanted him excluded altogether. On 26 March 1821, the parties finally signed a formal agreement.[6] Lord Selkirk would probably have opposed it, for it made no provisions for the settlement at Red River nor for his honour.

The Colonial Office was easy to win over to the new arrangement, which had the great advantage of including all of the previous antagonists.[7] "An Act for regulating the Fur Trade and establishing a Criminal and Civil Jurisdiction within certain part of North America" passed Parliament on 2 July 1821. It permitted the King to grant exclusive trading privileges for twenty-one years in all parts of North America not part of the lands previously granted the HBC or embodied in a province. This act tacitly recognized the HBC charter and equally tacitly insisted that the Athabasca, Mackenzie, and Peace basins, the Pacific Slope, and the fur-trading territory north and east of the Canadas were not part of the territorial grant to the HBC in 1670. A clause reserved American rights west of the Rockies. Courts were authorized throughout the western territories. Lord Bathurst on 5 December 1821 granted to the HBC and to three partners of the NWC (William and Simon McGillivray and Edward Ellice) a twenty-one year monopoly licence in North America. The new company was, in the end, a coalition rather than a true merger.

Although satisfactory negotiations at the top, sanctioned by the British government, were obviously vital to peace in the fur trade, they did not entirely settle the business. The biggest remaining problem was the wintering partners of the NWC, whose acceptance of the new arrangement was absolutely essential. The dissenting winterers, of course, had hoped to deal directly with the HBC. Instead, the negotiations had been shanghaied in London by the merchants of the NWC. Rather than becoming partners in a loose trading association now supplied with goods by the HBC, the NWC winterers found themselves about to become profit-sharing employees of a much more centrally organized monopoly than had ever previously existed. Without the Nor'west traders, the new company could not succeed. Members of the new company set out in the summer of 1821 to sell the resident fur traders of both companies on the advantages of the new organization. Simon McGillivray travelled to Montreal with Nicholas Garry, the only bachelor serving on the HBC committee, to try to settle the business. Garry, accompanied by William and Simon McGillivray, headed west by canoe for Fort William, where the three men would meet with the bulk of the winterers of both companies at the annual summer gathering. Here the traders would be introduced to the "Deed Poll," the document that set out the terms of the agreement between the two companies and that those who would remain with the new company would have to sign within eighteen months of 26 March 1821. Here the traders would be informed of the forty shares (out of a total of 100) in the current trade to be set aside for the wintering partners, the chief factors, and the chief traders. These shares were neither in the HBC itself nor in the land of trading. The forty shares would be further divided into eighty-five parts. Twenty-five chief factors would get two shares each. Twenty-eight chief traders would get one share each. Seven shares would be held for retiring servants.[8]

The meeting at Fort William in July of 1821 was an astonishing gathering. We are fortunate to have a vivid account of its beginning by John

Todd.[9] At one level, there was great rejoicing that the many years of bitter rivalry were finished. At another level, there was bound to be much unhappiness over the terms offered to the winterers and traders. And at yet a third level, of course, men who had fought bitterly with one another for years would now have to cooperate. When a bell summoned this group of men to dinner on 10 July, wrote Todd, they stood around on the floor of the mess hall, uncertain about how to seat themselves. It was George Simpson who stepped into the breach with tact and dexterity, concentrating on the pacification of the Nor'westers. A few of the former rivals shook hands and embraced one another, while others continued to glare at the opposition. Eventually all were seated and the dinner was begun. Simon McGillivray and Nicholas Garry would go on together from Fort William to the chief posts of the HBC to explain the new arrangement. The meeting went on to arrange the administration of the trade. Not surprisingly, the Nor'westers got most of the key positions. At the same time, Fort William was abandoned as a central supply depot in the fur trade, to be replaced by the forts at the bay. The bay—connected directly with England—would become the North American entrepot for the trade. In this sense the HBC had triumphed. The HBC had also seen its people appointed as chief North American administrators. William Williams (thoroughly detested by the Nor'westers) became governor of the Southern Department, while George Simpson took over the Northern Department, which ran most of the fur trade.

Not everything went totally smoothly. Later in 1821, John Halkett visited North America on behalf of the Selkirk estate. Halkett, of course, had been one of the most effective of the Selkirk pamphleteers, and he was cordially detested by many Nor'westers for what he had said of them in print. On 18 October, Halkett was met outside a Montreal hotel by Alexander (Greenfield) Macdonell and threatened with a horsewhip. Halkett had a writ issued against the Nor'wester, but took the precaution of carrying a set of primed pistols. Later that same evening, Jasper Vandersluys (he of the Fort William affidavit) resumed the attack, again with a whip. Halkett fired his pistols and wounded Vandersluys, who subsequently charged him in court with "intent to kill."[10] As Halkett's presence demonstrated, the Selkirk estate still controlled Red River. The Selkirks also had five shares of the 100 shares of stock in the company.

The Selkirk interests may well have come out better in the end than the McGillivrays' and their creditors. In March of 1821, the McGillivrays had drawn a document that promised compensation for loss of income by the wintering and retired partners of the NWC in 1821 and 1822, in return for release of all claims on the outfits of these years. Simon apparently negotiated the signing of this document at the time of his 1821 visit to North America. McTavish, McGillivrays and Company was continued in 1822 as McGillivrays, Thain and Company to settle the affairs of the old firm and its debts, including the compensation paid for the release. At a creditors' meeting in 1825, Simon McGillivray declared a suspension of payment of debts. In 1827 Simon insisted that the creditors had earlier benefitted from the merger, which allowed the wintering partners to become chief traders and factors in the HBC and the retired partners to realize returns on their NWC property.[11] A letter to the *Canadian Courant* in 1830 argued that none of the receipts of McGillivrays, Thain and Company had ever been made tangible to the creditors, however. A composition of 13s. 4d in the pound was apparently offered in 1830, but whether it was accepted is not known. The decline in the fortunes of the McGillivrays meant that any notion of equality between the HBC and the North West agents, such as that represented by equal representation on the Joint Committee of Management, went by the boards. The Nor'westers gradually became subsumed into the corporate structure of the HBC.

The complex details of rationalizing the merger on the ground would take some time to complete. Many posts, often deliberately set next to one another, would have to be closed. George Simpson was put in charge of the department that supervised most of the fur trade; William Williams was placed in charge of the department dominated by the Red River Settlement. Simpson calculated that twice as many traders were available as were needed. Only a few of the main combatants from the NWC—men like Alexander (Greenfield) Macdonell and Duncan Cameron who were at the centre of the violence—were excluded in advance from the new company. Many others were persuaded to retire. Some went to the Canadas. Some, especially HBC employees and their mixed-blood families, were encouraged to remove at company expense to Red River, where they received lots of land. Many traders were in effect forced out of the country or into retirement by Simpson's placement of them in the new scheme of things. Lesser employees simply were not given new contracts. In 1821, at the time of the merger, there were 1983 company employees. By 1825 there were 827 remaining, and their wages had been reduced substantially as well. Simpson's ruthless domination of the fur trade confirmed that in the end, the HBC had indeed won the peace, if not the war.[12]

THE SETTLEMENT

For the Red River Settlement, the period between 1819 and 1826 falls into two parts: a period of development and one of benign neglect.[13] Lord Selkirk before 1821 and the executors of his estate after his death made some serious efforts to develop the settlement and to increase its population. The development process reached its height in 1821 with the expenditure of thousands of pounds on a project to transplant Swiss settlers to the plains of the West.[14] With the failure of the Swiss operation, the Selkirk executors began to attempt to run the settlement without spending money on it, in the hope that it would eventually prosper. Benign neglect seemed to be working, at least until the flood of 1826. After the devastation of the flood, the estate did little for Red River until its sale in 1835 to the Hudson's Bay Company for £30,000. The payment was chiefly to extinguish title, for little else of Selkirk's vision was still to be found except a handful of Scots settlers on the Red River north of the Forks.

PRINCE EDWARD ISLAND

Despite the flourishing of Selkirk's settlements on Prince Edward Island, he had not received a farthing in revenue from them at the time of his death, and, indeed, had never received a detailed report on their progress. In 1819, Judge James Stewart in Halifax had recommended Halifax attorneys Charles and Samuel Fairbanks to replace William Johnston as Selkirk's agent on the island.[15] Samuel Fairbanks made a visit to PEI in 1819 and was taken on an extensive tour of the estate by Johnston, who proudly reported to Selkirk that his settlers were most independent and prosperous of any on the island.[16] Fairbanks reported in 1819 on Selkirk's estate there in quite favourable terms, and in a subsequent letter to the estate in the summer of 1820 he observed that settlers wishing to make payments either did so in kind or in a "currency peculiar to the Island" that was almost impossible to exchange for use off of it.[17] Hence it was almost impossible to remit funds from the island to the Selkirk estate. By inference, Lord Selkirk could profit from his island lands only by living on the island. Fairbanks also noted that Angus MacAulay had several lawsuits pending in the island courts when Selkirk died. One related to a libel suit resulting from somehow allowing the earl's letter to McDonald of Tracadie to get into McAulay's hands. "The iniquitous course of proceedings adopted in these cases, and which I am sorry to say was overlooked or sanctioned by the Chief Justice," and would have caused trouble had the earl not died. McAulay had great influence with the settlers and he continued to be troublesome.[18] William Johnston made a desperate appeal to Andrew Colvile to be allowed to remain in charge of the Selkirk lands, promising to reform. Colvile accepted Johnston's declarations of better performance, probably because the Fairbanks agency—administered as it was from off-island— was likely to become expensive.[19] In 1823 Colvile angrily removed Johnston again from his post, pointing out that he had not met his promises. There were still no regular accounts and no remittances.[20] There is considerable evidence that plundering of the timber on Selkirk lands continued for many years.

The loss of the original family papers makes it almost impossible to follow the development of the Selkirk estate until 1833, when William Douse was appointed agent by the sixth Earl of Selkirk, who by now had reached his majority.[21] Douse was a native of Wiltshire who had emigrated to the island in the 1820s. He initially used the Selkirk agency to supplement his income, but gradually the agency became his principal employment. Although we do not know many of the details of his administration, Douse was well known on the island for issuing long-term leases and making decent arrangement for purchase of land. He was not able to control outlaw timbering on Selkirk lots. Whether his management produced much income for the sixth earl is not known. Douse used his agency as a powerful political weapon, basing a long career in the island assembly on the strength of voters from the Selkirk estate. Rumours claimed that he coerced tenants into voting for him, but these charges were never confirmed. Douse was a confirmed opponent of escheat. Over the years he obviously sold off a substantial percentage of the Selkirk lands, which had at one time totalled 110,000 acres, since in 1860 the remaining Selkirk lands—62,059 acres—were sold to the province for a very reasonable price of £6586 sterling.

Despite his long involvement and continued investment in both Red River and Prince Edward Island, to the point of virtual bankruptcy, Lord Selkirk's North American investments were not in the end very profitable.

ENDNOTES

Chapter 1

1 Glasgow history.

2 Andrew Hook and Richard B. Sher, eds., *The Glasgow Enlightenment* (East Linton: Tuckwell, 1995).

3 Quoted in Annand Chitnis, *The Scottish Enlightenment: A Social History* (London: Croom Helm, 1967), 160.

4 *The Defects of a University Education* (London: E. Dilly, 1772), 9.

5 Caroline Robbins, *The Eighteenth-Century Commonwealthman: Studies in the Transmission, Development and Circumstance of English Liberal Thought from the Restoration of Charles II until the War with the Thirteen Colonies* (Cambridge, MA: Harvard University Press, 1959).

6 Quoted in David McElroy, *Scotland's Age of Improvement: A Survey of Eighteenth-Century Literary Clubs and Societies* (N.p: Washington State University Press, 1969), 13.

7 Quoted in Michael Joyce, *Edinburgh: The Golden Age 1769–1832* (London: Longman's Green, 1951), 14.

8 Douglas Young, *Edinburgh in the Age of Sir Walter Scott* (Norman, OK: University of Oklahoma Press, 1965).

9 Ibid., 48–49.

10 Quoted in ibid., 114.

11 This paragraph is based on J.E. Handley, *The Agricultural Revolution in Scotland* (Glasgow: Burns, 1963); J.E. Handley, *Scottish Farming in the Eighteenth Century* (London: Faber and Faber, 1953); R H. Campbell, "The Scottish Improvers and the Course of Agrarian Change in the Eighteenth Century," in L.M. Cullen and T.C. Smout, eds., *Comparative Aspects of Scottish and Irish Economic and Social History 1600–1900* (Edinburgh: Donald, 1977).

12 Ibid., 298.

13 Ian Donnachie and Innes MacLeod, *Old Galloway* (London: Newton Abbot David and Charles, 1974); M. Sloan, *Galloway* (London: N.p., 1908); Alexander Trotter, *East Galloway Sketches* (Castle-Douglas, 1901).

14 Donnachie and MacLeod.

15 The best source for these family details is John Philip Wood, *The Peerage of Scotland by Robert Douglas* (Edinburgh: Arnold Constable, 1813), 2:478–491. The Selkirk sketch was written by the fifth Earl himself.

16 Ibid.

17 This case has produced a substantial primary and secondary literature, of which the most useful are: A. Francis Steuart, ed., *The Douglas Cause* (Toronto: Canada Law Book, 1909), and Lillian De La Torre, *The Heir of Douglas* (New York: Knopf, 1953). But see also "Collection of Papers in the Process of Reduction of the Service of Archibald Douglas," National Library of Scotland (NLS), 8273.

18 Quoted in Steuart, ed., *The Douglas Cause*, 22.

19 Michael W. McCahill, "The Scottish Peerage and the House of Lords in the late Eighteenth Century," *Scottish Historical Review* 51 (1972): 172–196; William Robertson, *Proceedings Relating to the Peerage of Scotland from January 16, 1707 to April 29, 1788* (Edinburgh: Bell and Bradfute, 1790).

20 Ibid.

21 Lord Selkirk to John Paul Jones, 9 June 1778, Selkirk Papers, United States Naval Academy, Annapolis, Maryland.

22 Ibid.

23 The latest biography is by Evan Thomas, entitled *John Paul Jones* (New York: Simon and Schuster, 2004).

24 Samuel Eliot Morrison, *John Paul Jones: A Sailor's Biography* (London: Faber and Faber, 1960), 7.

25 Selkirk to John Halkett, 1813, quoted (from manuscripts later destroyed in a fire) in John Perry Pritchett, *The Red River Valley 1811–1849: A Regional Study* (New Haven and Toronto: Yale University Press, 1942). Pritchett had done research for his book at St. Mary's Isle in the 1930s. He did not preserve his notes, however.

26 Lady Selkirk to the Countess of Morton, 15 May 1778, Selkirk Papers, U.S. Naval Academy.

27 The letter is reprinted in full in Morrison, *John Paul Jones,* 148–150.

28 Ibid.

29 This letter is also reprinted in full in Morrison, 151–154.

30 Quoted in George Bryce, *Manitoba: Its Infancy, Growth, and Present Condition* (London: J. Low, Marston, Searle, and Rivington, 1882).

Chapter 2

1 Karl F.C. Miller, ed., *Henry Cockburn's Memorials of His Times* (Chicago: Chicago University Press, 1974), 11.

2 Irene Parker, *The Dissenting Academies in England* (New York: Octagon Books, 1969).

3 See William McCarthy and Elizabeth Kraft, eds., *Anna Laetitia Barbauld: Selected Poetry & Prose* (Athens, GA: University of Georgia Press, 2001); Anna Letitia Le Breton, *Memoir of Mrs. Barbauld, including Letters and Notices of Her Family and Friends* (London: N.p., 1874).

4 Mrs. Barbauld to William Taylor, 10 April [1784], reprinted in Betsy Rodgers, *Georgian Chronical: Mrs Barbauld and Her Family* (London: Metheun, 1958), 206.

5 See, for example, Thomas Dundas to Henry Erskine, 1 January 1784, reprinted in Alexander Fergusson, *The Honourable Henry Erskine, Lord Advocate for Scotland* (Edinburgh and London: W. Blackwood, 1882), 194. For Dundas's role in Scottish politics at this time, see John Dwyer and Alexander Murdoch, "Paradigms and Politics: Manners, Morals and the Rise of Henry Dundas, 1770–1784," in *New Perspectives on the Politics and Culture of Early Modern Scotland,* ed. John Dwyer et al. (Edinburgh: John Donald, 1982), 210–248.

6 Dwyer and Murdoch, "Paradigms."

7 Christopher Hibbert, *King Mob: The Story of Lord George Gordon and the Riots of 1780* (London: Longmans, Green, 1958).

8   *The Rolliad: Probationary Odes and Political Miscellanies* (London: J. Ridgeway, 1795), 167.

9   Lord Selkirk to Countess of Morton, 6 March 1784, Scottish Record Office (SRO), GD 150/2378.

10 Lord Selkirk to Lord Camden, 3 June 1784, National Library of Scotland Ms 3420/171.

11 Fergusson, *Henry Erskine,* 196 ff; Lord Selkirk to Lord Morton, 23 May, 7 June 1785, SRO GD 150/2378.

12 Lord Selkirk to William Cullen, 4 October 1785, Thomas-Cullen Papers, University of Glasgow Library.

13 Helen I. Cowan, "Selkirk's Work in Canada: An Early Chapter," *Canadian Historical Review* 9 (1928): 299–308.

14 A.J. Youngson, *The Making of Classical Edinburgh, 1750–1840* (Edinburgh: Edinburgh University Press, 1966); Douglas Young, *Edinburgh in the Age of Sir Walter Scott* (Norman, OK: University of Oklahoma Press, 1965); Michael Joyce, *Edinburgh: The Golden Age 1769–1832* (London: Longman's Green, 1951).

15 Annand C. Chitnis, *The Scottish Enlightenment: A Social History* (London: Croom Helm, 1967); Gladys Bryson, *The Scottish Inquiry of the Eighteenth Century* (Princeton, NJ: Princeton University Press, 1945); R.H. Campbell and Andrew S. Skinner, eds., *The Origins and Nature of the Scottish Enlightenment* (Edinburgh: John Donald, 1982).

16 Quoted in Roy Porter, *The Creation of the Modern World: The Untold Story of the British Enlightenment* (London: Norton, 2000), 183.

17 6th Earl of Selkirk to Dr. George Bryce, 2 May 1881, Bryce Papers, Public Archives of Manitoba (PAM); Class books of University of Edinburgh, University of Edinburgh, Edinburgh, Scotland.

18 This paragraph is based on a study of university records and lecture notes of the time surviving in various Scottish repositories.

19 Lord Selkirk to Lord Morton, 12 September, 25 September, 30 September, 7 October, 29 October 1786, SRO GD/2378.

20 Lord Selkirk to William Hall, 27 October 1786, SRO GD 2061/457. For James Hall, see V.A. Eyles, "Sir James Hall Bt. (1761–1832)," *Endeavour* 20 (1961): 210–216, and his "The Evolution of a Chemist: Sir James Hall Bt.," *Annals of Science* 9 (1963): 153–182.

21 George Davie, *The Democratic Intellect: Scotland and her Universities in the Nineteenth Century,* 2nd ed. (Edinburgh: Edinburgh University Press, 1964), 275.

22 Liam McIlvanney, *Burns the Radical: Poetry and Politics in Late Eighteenth-Century Scotland* (East Linton, NJ: Tuckwell, 2002), 15–67.

23 Hans Hecht, *Robert Burns: The Man and His Work,* 2nd ed. (London: W. Hodge, 1950), 90–91.

24 Burns citation.

25 Charles Elphinstone Adam, ed., *View of the Political State of Scotland in the Last Century* (Edinburgh: D. Douglass, 1887), 195.

26 Fourth Earl of Selkirk to Earl of Buchan, 15 September 1788, NLS, Miscellaneous Papers, MS 4239, f9.

27 Ibid., 344.

28 Thomas Douglas to William Clerk, 28 September 1787, SRO GD 18/5540.

29 John Perry Pritchett, *The Red River Valley 1811–1849: A Regional Study* (New Haven and Toronto: Yale University Press, 1942), 19. According to Pritchett, there was at St. Mary's Isle a notebook kept by Thomas during his student days, as well as two French diaries kept in 1792. These obviously have not survived.

30 John Gibson Lockhart, *The Life of Sir Walter Scott* (London: J.M. Dent, 1959), 1: 1–60.

31 Ibid., 1: 169–170n.

32 See, for example, Scott to Lady Selkirk, 26 February 1808, NL Acc 6110; Scott to Lady Katherine Halkett, 10 June 1819, Bryce Papers, PAM. This latter letter is a convoluted apology for Scott's inability to support his old friend publicly.

33 Basil William Douglas, "Petition and Complaint of the Right Honourable Basil William Douglas, 23 December 1789," British Museum (BM) Law and Parliamentary Tracts, 518 113.

34 Alexander Lord Saltoun, *Thoughts on the Disqualification of the Eldest Sons of the Peers of Scotland, to Sit from that Country to Parliament* (London: T. Cadell and John Robson, 1788), 155.

35 *History of the Speculative Society of Edinburgh from its Institution in M.DCC.LXIV* (Edinburgh: N.p., 1845); Speculative Society Minutes (1775–1800), Edinburgh University Library (EUL).

36 Quoted in David D. McElroy, *Scotland's Age of Improvement: A Survey of Eighteenth-Century Literary Clubs and Societies* (N.p.: Washington State University Press, 1969), 111.

37 *History of the Speculative Society,* 28.

38 *History of the Judicial Society of Edinburgh* (N.p.: 1875), 26–27.

39 Speculative Society of Edinburgh Minutes, III, UEL.

40 Thomas H.D. Mahoney, ed., *Reflections on the Revolution in France/Edmund Burke* (Indianapolis, IN: Bobbs-Merrill, 1955), xxi.

41 Speculative Society Minutes.

42 Lord Belcarres et al to Earl of Buccleuch, 28 March 1790, SRO GD 224/579.

43 [Alexander Mackenzie], *A View of the Political State of Scotland at the Late General Election* (Edinburgh: Ainslie 1790), 236–7.

44 Roy H. Browne, ed., *The Burke-Paine Controversy: Texts and Criticism* (NY: Harcourt Brace and World, 1963).

45 Speculative Society Minutes, EUL.

Chapter 3

1   V. A Eyles, "The Evolution of a Chemist: Sir James Hall Bt." *Annals of Science* 9 (1963): 153–182.

2   Simon Schama, *Citizens: A Chronicle of the French Revolution* (NY: Knopf, 1989), 77.

3   D. McKie, Antoine Lavoisier: Scientist, Economist, Reformer (NY: Collier Books 1952).

4   Hall journal, NLS.

5   Quoted in David Garrioch, *The Making of Revolutionary Paris* (Berkeley and Los Angeles: University of California Press, 2002), 286.

6   La Rochefoucauld would later in the 1790s make a tour of North America, and his account of the journey would be quoted by the 5th Earl of Selkirk in his study of the fur trade of Canada.

7   Quoted in Emma Rothschild, *Economic Sentiments: Adam Smith, Condorcet, and the Enlightenment* (Cambridge, MA: Harvard University Press, 2001), 161.

8   Reprinted in Bumsted, ed., *Collected Writings of Lord Selkirk* (Winnipeg: Manitoba Historical Society, 1984), 1: 86–99.

9   Hall journal, NLS.

10 Lord Daer to the 4th Earl of Selkirk, Selkirk Papers, United States Naval Academy.

11 Hall journal, NLS.

12 Albert Mathiez, *The French Revolution* (NY: Russell and Russell, 1962), 77–79.

13 Hall journal, NLS.

14 Jack Fruchtman, Jr., *Thomas Paine: Apostle of Freedom* (NY and London: Four Walls Eight Windows, 1994).

15 Henry Collins, ed., *Thomas Paine Rights of Man* (Harmondsworth, England: Penguin 1969).

16 Hall journal, NLS.

17 Ibid.

18 Collins, ed., *Thomas Paine Rights of Man,* 17.

19 Fruchtman, 240.

20 E.P. Thompson, *The Making of the English Working Class* (Harmondsworth, England: Penguin, 1970), 103 ff.

21 Ibid.

22 Hall journal, NLS.

23 Ibid.

24 *The Edinburgh Evening Courant,* 15 October 1791.

25 James Dunfermline, *Lieutenant-General Sir Ralph Abercromby, K.B. 1793–1801: A Memoir by his Son* (Edinburgh: Edmonston and Douglas, 1861), 36.

26 Ibid., 37.

27 Miller, Karl F.C., ed., *Henry Cockburn's Memorials of His Times* (Chicago: Chicago University Press, 1974), 83.

28 John Bushby, 3 May 1792, SRO GD 51/198/14/2.

29 Quoted in Thompson, *The Making,* 19.

30 British Museum Add. Mss. 27811 (Place Collection), f. 15.

31 Henry Meikle, *Scotland and the French Revolution* (NY: A.M. Kelley, 1969), 79.

32 Quoted in ibid., 82.

33 Thomas Douglas to Dunbar Douglas, 2 May [1792], Boulton Papers, Public Archives of Ontario (OA).

34 Lord Selkirk, *Observations on the Present State of the Highlands of Scotland* (London, 1805), reprinted in *The Collected Writings of Lord Selkirk,* 109.

35 Quoted in Meikle, 83.

36 Ibid.

37 Thomas Douglas to Dunbar Douglas, 16 November 1792, quoted in Chester Martin, *Lord Selkirk's Work in Canada* (Toronto: Oxford University Press, 1916), quoting manuscripts subsequently destroyed.

38 Quoted in Meikle, 95.

39 Reprinted as Appendix A in Meikle, 239–273.

40 *The Caledonian Mercury,* 15 December 1792.

41 Ibid.

42 Meikle.

43 *The Caledonian Mercury,* 15 December 1792.

44 Quoted in Meikle, 251.

45 Lord Daer to Charles Grey, 17 January 1793, reprinted in P. Berresford Ellis and Seumes Mac A'Ghobhainn, *The Scottish Insurrection of 1820* (London: Gollancz, 1970).

46 Quoted in Meikle, p. 251.

47 Ibid.

48 Dugald Stewart to Archibald Allison, January 1793, reprinted in Sir William Hamilton, ed., *The Collected Works of Dugald Stewart* (Edinburgh: N.p., 1858), 10: cxxxv–cxxxvi.

49 Information on the Hamiltons comes from Colin Simpson, *Emma: The Life of Lady Hamilton* (London: Bodley Head, 1983).

50 John Syme to Alexander Cunningham, 3 August 1793, reprinted in Robert T. Fitzhugh, *Robert Burns The Man and the Poet: A Round, Unvarnished Account* (London and NY: W.H. Allen, 1971), 365–369, especially p. 368.

51 Burns to George Thomson, ca. 30 August 1793, in *The Letters of Robert Burns,* ed. G. Ross Roy, 2nd ed. (Oxford: Oxford University Press, 1985), 2: 235–6; Fitzhugh, 369.

52 Lord Selkirk to Thomas Douglas, 14 July 1793, quoted in Martin, 16.

53 Ibid.

54 Meikle, 153.

55 Ibid., 142–146.

56 *Gentleman's Magazine,* May 1795.

57 Malcolm Nicolson, "The Continental Journeys of Andrew Duncan junior," <http://www.repe.ac.uk/library/continental_journey/journey5.html>.

58 Quoted in Martin, 18.

Chapter 4

1 Rosalind Mitchison, *Agricultural Sir John: The Life of Sir John Sinclair of Ulbster, 1754–1835* (London: Bles, 1962), 137–158.

2 Lord Daer to [Sir John Sinclair], 28 January 1798, SRO RH4/49/2.

3 *Annals of Agriculture,* XXVI, 435.

4 Istvan Hont and Michael Ignatieff, "Needs and Justice in the *Wealth of Nations:* An Introductory Essay," in *Wealth and Virtue: The Shaping of Political Economy in the Scottish Enlightenment,* eds. Hont and Ignatieff (Cambridge: Cambridge University Press, 1983), 13–26.

5 [Thomas Malthus], *An Essay on the Principle of Population, as it Affects the Future Improvement of Society, with Remarks on the Speculations of Mr. Godwin, M. Condorcet, and Other Writers* (London: N.p., 1798).

6 Mitchison, *Sir John Sinclair,* 178.

7 See J.M. Bumsted, ed., *Collected Writings of Lord Selkirk* (Winnipeg: Manitoba Historical Society, 1984), 1: 86–99.

8   A.A. Cormack, *Poor Relief in Scotland* (Aberdeen: N.p., 1923); Charles Stewart Loch, "Poor Relief in Scotland: Its Statistics and Development, 1791–1891," *Journal Royal Statistical Society* 61 (1898): 271–370.

9   T.C. Smout, *A History of the Scottish People 1560–1830* (London: Fontana, 1985), 263.

10 Bumsted, ed., *Collected Writings*, 94.

11 Ibid., 96.

12 Ibid., 98–99.

13 For the controversy over the estate, see the undated memorandum of Helen Hall, SRO GD 206/4/62.

14 SRO RD 3/338, 170–180.

15 *Valuation Roll of the Stewartry of Kirkcudbright as Made Up by the Commissioners of Land Tax for the Said Stewartry, 14th June 1799* (Dumfries: R. Jackson, 1800).

16 Helen I. Cowan, "Selkirk's Work in Canada: An Early Chapter," *Canadian Historical Review* 18 (1928): 299–308; and her *Charles Williamson: Genesee Promote, Friend of Anglo-American Rapprochment* (Rochester, NY: Rochester Historical Society, 1941).

17 "Selkirk's Work," 303.

18 Lord Selkirk to Sir Alexander Gordon, 28 December 1799, Ewart Library, Dumfries.

19 Minutes of Kirkcudbright Council, 28 December 1799, Hornel Library.

20 Dugald Stewart Diary of tours in England and Scotland, 1797–1803, UEL, Dc 8.178, 8.

21 Diary of Sir James Hall, October 1801, SRO GD 206/II/315/13.

22 Ibid.

23 For further details, see my *The People's Clearance: Highland Emigration to British North America 1770–1815* (Edinburgh: Edinburgh University Press; and Winnipeg: University of Manitoba Press, 1984), 83–107.

24 See my "Highland Emigration to the Island of St. John and the Scottish Catholic Church, 1769–1774," *Dalhousie Review* 58 (1978): 511–527.

25 This analysis was advanced by "A Highlander" in *The Present Conduct of the Chieftains and Proprietors of Lands in the Highlands of Scotland* (Edinburgh: N.p., 1773), first published in 1773. Selkirk was familiar with this work.

26 Andrew Mackillop, "*More Fruitful than the Soil: Army, Empire, and the Scottish Highlands* (East Linton, NJ: Tuckwell Press, 2000).

27 Stephen Brumwell, *Redcoats: The British Soldier and War in the Americas, 1755–1763* (Cambridge: Cambridge University Press, 2002).

28 M.W. Flinn, "Malthus, Emigration and Potatoes in the Scottish North-West, 1770–1870," in *Comparative Aspects of Scottish and Irish Economic and Social History 1600–1900*, eds. L.M. Cullen and T.C. Smout (Edinburgh: Donald, 1973), 47–64.

29 Quoted in *The People's Clearance*, 85.

30 For general background on kelping, see Malcolm Gray, "The Kelp Industry in the Highlands and Islands," *Economic History Review*, 2nd ser., 4 (1951): 197–209; Gray, *The Highland Economy, 1750–1850* (Edinburgh: Edinburgh University Press, 1957); James Hunter, *The Making of the Crofting Community* (Edinburgh: Donald, 1976), passim; A.J. Youngson, *After the Forty-Five: The Economic Impact on the Scottish Highlands* (Edinburgh: Edinburgh University Press, 1973), esp. 134–140. See also my "The Rise and Fall of the Kelping Industry of the Highlands," forthcoming in a book on archaeology in the Hebrides by the University of Sheffield Press.

31 "State of Emigration from the Highlands of Scotland," NLS 35.6.18.

32 Bishop John Chisholm to Reverend Charles Maxwell, 20 November 1801, Scottish Catholic Archives (hereafter SCA), Blairs Letters.

33 Copy of a letter from the Lord Advocate to the Rev'd Mr. Rattray, 31 October 1801, SCA Blairs Letters.

34 Bishop John Chisholm to Reverend Charles Maxwell, 25 January 1802, SCA Blairs Letters.

35 "Memorial of the Earl of Selkirk Relative to the Security of Ireland," February 1802, Selkirk Papers National Archives of Canada (hereafter SPNAC), vol. 52, 13893–7.

Chapter 5

1 "Conversation Lord P," SPNAC, vol. 52, 13902.

2 Selkirk to Lord Pelham, 3 April 1802, and "Observations Supplementary to a Memorial Relative to the Security of Ireland," Public Record Office [hereafter PRO], Kew Gardens, London, CO 42, vol. 330, ff. 169–177.

3 Sir Alexander Mackenzie, *Voyages from Montreal, on the River St. Lawrence, through the Continent of North America, to the Frozen and Pacific Oceans, in the Years 1789 and 1793* (London: T. Cadell Jr. and W. Davies, Cobbett and Morgan, and W. Creach, 1801), lxi–lxvi.

4 John Fraser to Simon McTavish, 6 August 1802, Hudson's Bay Company Archives (HBCA), F 3/2/62.

5 Selkirk to Lord Pelham, 4 April 1802, PRO CO 42/330/144–145.

6 SRO RD 2.285/156–166.

7 Selkirk, 10 June 1802, SPNAC, 14263; "Instructions for Irish Recruiting," SPNAC, 14256–14257.

8 Selkirk to Hobart, 6 July 1802, SPNAC, vol. 52, 13840–1. For the whole correspondence, see SPNAC, vol. 52, and PRO CO 42, vol. 330.

9 Hobart to Selkirk, 30 July 1802, SPNAC, vol 52, 13851–2.

10 Selkirk to Lord Napier, 12 July 1802, EUL Laing Mss., ii, 416.

11 Selkirk to Adam Gordon, 21 August 1802, PRO CO 42/330/185–6.

12 Selkirk to Lord Hobart, 21 August 1802, PRO CO 42/330/185–6.

13 Dugald Stewart to Selkirk, 1802, SPNAC, 13903–13906.

14 Advertising poster dated 22 October 1802, SRO GD 112.61/1.

15 Burns Itinerary and Expenses, SPNAC, 14308–14323; Selkirk's instructions to Burn, SPNAC, 14266–14268; Selkirk to Burn, 25 September 1802, SPNAC, 14265.

16 "William Burn," DCB, V, 125–127.

17 A. Macdonell to Lord Pelham, 1802, SRO RH 2/4/87.

18 Ibid.

19 Father Alexander Macdonell, "Page from the History of the Glengarry Highlanders," Ontario Archives, Macdonell Papers, 1–20.

20 Gerald Craig, *Upper Canada: The Formative Years 1784–1841* (Toronto: McClelland and Stewart, 1963), 64–65.

21 Ibid.

22 For the Canadian Regiment, see my *The People's Clearance: Highland Emigration to British North America, 1770–1815* (Edinburgh: Edinburgh University Press, 1984), 155–187.

23 Macdonell, "Page," 17.

24 Kathleen Toomey, *Alexander Macdonell: The Scottish Years 1762–1804* (Toronto: Canadian Catholic Historical Society, 1985), 147. For Macdonell, see also J. E. Rea, *Bishop Alexander Macdonell and the Politics* (Toronto: Ontario Historical Society, 1974); Hugh Joseph Somers, "The Life and Times of the Honorable and Rt. Rev. Alexander Macdonell, unpublished doctoral dissertation, Catholic University of America, 1931.

25 Macdonell, "Page," 17.

26 [Edward S. Fraser], "On Emigration from the Scottish Highlands and Isles," unpublished manuscript in NLS; Alexander Mackenzie, *History of the Macdonalds and Lords of the Isle* (Inverness: A.W. Mackenzie, 1881); Malcolm Macqueen, *Skye Pioneers and 'the Island'* (Winnipeg: Stovel, 1929), 65–69.

27 [Fraser], "On Emigration," 37.

28 [Fraser], "On Emigration," 137.

29 Colonel A. Macdonald of Boisdale to Robert Brown, 1 December 1802, SRO Lennoxlove Muniments, Robert Brown Papers, Bundle 15.

30 William Porter to Colin Mackenzie, 27 December 1802, SRO GD 9/166/23. See also Roderick McNeil to Robert Brown, 22 November 1802, NRA, Brown Papers, Bundle 15.

31 [Fraser], "On Emigration," 38–40.

32 William Porter to John Mackenzie, 27 December 1802, SRO GD 9/166/23.

33 Selkirk to Lord Hobart, 30 November 1802, SPNAC, 13845–6.

34 Sir James Hall to Lord Seaforth, 4 December 1802, SRO GD 46/17/10.

35 Helen Hall Memorandum, SRO GD 206/4/62.

36 Ibid.

37 Ibid.

38 SRO RD 3/338/170–180.

39 *Farmer's Magazine*, February 1803, 42.

40 Alexander Irvine, *An Inquiry into the Causes and Effects of Emigration from the Highlands and Western Islands of Scotland, with Observations on the Means to be Employed for Preventing It* (Edinburgh: N.p., 1802), passim.

41 Edward Fraser to Lord Seaforth, 30 December 1802, SRO GD 46/17/21.

42 Selkirk to James Stewart, 16 January 1803, SRO GD 128/36/4.

43 Ibid.

44 Ibid.

45 W. Robertson to Mr. Pallister, 31 January 1804, SRO GD 38/2/45; Robertson to Duke of Athol, SRO GD 38/2/45.

46 *Edinburgh Review, or Critical Journal*, 1 (1803), 61–63.

47 Selkirk to Rt. Hon. Henry Addington, 1 February 1803, SPNAC, 13853–13855; Selkirk to Lord Hobart, 9 February 1803, SPNAC, 13856–7; Selkirk to Addington, 10 February 1803, SPNAC, 13858.

Chapter 6

1   See my *Land, Settlement, and Politics on Prince Edward Island* (Kingston and Montreal: McGill-Queen's University Press, 1987).

2   Memorandum, 4 April 1802, CO 226/18/11-17.

3   "Observations upon the Plan for a Composition," CO 226/19/703-5.

4   Council Minutes, Whitehall, 6 April 1802, CO 226/18/215-7.

5   John Macdonald to John Sullivan, 23 April 1802, CO 226/18/231-2; John Hill to Sir, 14 October 1802, CO 226/18/321-4.

6   John Stewart to Alexander Ellice, March 17, 1803, NLS Ellice Papers, E96/6-7. The quitrents owing on the lots totalled £876.13.4 as of 1 May 1803, according to an undated memorandum in SPNAC 15101-2.

7   John Cambridge to Alexander Ellice, 10th month 17 1803; Ibid, E96/16.

8   [George William Lefevre], *The Life of a Travelling Physician* (London: Longman's 1843), 1: 24.

9   I am indebted to Professor John Flint of Dalhousie University for this suggestion.

10 "Notes by Marchioness of Stafford of Conversation with Lord Selkirk, 18 March and 13 April, 1813," in *Papers on Sutherland Estate Management 1802–1816*, ed. R.J. Adam (Edinburgh: Scottish Record Office, 1972), 1: 143.

11 Lord Haddington to Earl of Morton, 19 May 1807, SRO GD 150/2382.

12 For Stewart, see F.L. Pigot, *John Stewart of Mount Stewart* (Summerside, PEI: The Author, 1973).

13 See my *The People's Clearance: Highland Emigration to British North America, 1770–1815* (Edinburgh: Edinburgh University Press; Winnipeg: University of Manitoba Press) especially 55–82 and 238–241.

14 See my *Land, Settlement and Politics.*

15 Donald Steel to Ranald Macdonald, 16 September 1802, SRO GD 248/659.

16 Edward S. Fraser to Lord Seaforth, 30 April 1803, SRO GD 46/17/23.

17 For further details, see *The People's Clearance,* 129–154.

18 For such an interpretation, see K.A. Walpole, "The Humanitarian Movement of the Early Nineteenth Century to Remedy Abuses on Emigrant Vessels to America," *Transactions of the Royal Historical Society,* 4th ser., 4 (1931): 197–224.

19 This work has been reprinted in my *Collected Writings of Lord Selkirk,* 1 (Winnipeg, 1984).

20 Selkirk to John Stewart, 3 May 1803, PAPEI 3744.

21 Selkirk memorandum dated April 16, 1803, reprinted in Malcolm Macqueen, *Skye Pioneers and the Island* (Winnipeg: Stovel, 1929), 15.

22 Abstract cash book Jas Williams, SPNAC, 14877.

23 See, for example, Customs Board to Tobermory Collectors, 14 June 1803, SRO CD 4/2/77; Board of Customs to Tobermory Collectors, 16 June 1803, SRO CE 74/2/7.

24 Printed by Patrick C.T. White, ed., *Lord Selkirk's Diary 1803–1804: A Journal of his Travels in British North America and the Northeastern United States* (Toronto: Champlain Society, 1958).

25 Ibid., 5.

26 Quoted in DCB, V, 775.

27 See, for example, Selkirk to MacAulay, 2 September 1803, reprinted in Malcolm A. Macqueen, *Hebridean Pioneers* (Winnipeg: Henderson Directories, 1957), 14.

28 Selkirk Diary, 7–8.

29 Ibid, 10.

30 Ibid.

31 Ibid., 29.

32 For Williams, see DCB, VI.

33 Selkirk Diary, 35.

34 For MacAulay, see DCB, VI, 412–15.

35 Selkirk to Captain John MacDonald, quoted in DCB, VI, 414.

36 Selkirk Diary, 20.

37 "Drafts on Ransom M & Co to J. Williams 1803/4," SPNAC, 14888–14890.

Chapter 7

1 It has been published as *Lord Selkirk's Diary 1803–1804: A Journal of His Travels in British North America and the Northeastern United States,* edited with an introduction by Patrick C.T. White (Toronto: Champlain Society, 1958).

2 The published version of the diary bears the heading "DIARY I/ AUGUST 5TH, 1803 TO OCTOBER 3RD, 1803, THE MARITIMES," although the first entry for the text is on 3 August.

3 Diary, 45.

4 An earlier reference while on PEI spoke of "talking my best Gaelic" to four lads from Ross-shire. Diary, 17.

5 Ibid., 49.

6 Ibid., 57.

7 For Burke, see DCB, V, 123–5.

8 Ibid., 67.

9 Ibid., 74.

10 Ibid., 271–272.

11 Ibid., 79.

12 Ibid., 83.

13 Ibid., 85.

14 Ibid., 91.

15 J. Guillamard to Alexander Hamilton, Gower St. [London], 22 February 1803, reprinted in *The Papers of Alexander Hamilton,* ed. Harold C. Syrett, 25 (New York: Columbia University Press, 1979), 88.

16 For biographical studies of Hamilton, see Jacob E.Cooke, *Alexander Hamilton* (NY: Scribner's, 1982), and Forrest Macdonald, *Alexander Hamilton: A Biography* (NY: Norton, 1979). For his thinking, consult Gerald Stourzh, *Alexander Hamilton and the Idea of Republican Government* (Stanford, CA: Stanford University Press, 1970).

17 See Alan Karras, *Sojourners in the Sun: Scottish Migrants in Jamaica and the Chesapeake 1740–1800* (Ithaca, NY: Cornell University Press, 1992) and David Dobson, *Scots in the West Indies, 1707–1857* (Westminster, MD: Clearfield, 2002).

18 Diary, 92.

19   Letter is reprinted in Syrett, ed. Hamilton's papers.

20   Ibid., 93.

21   Ibid., 96.

22   Helen I. Cowan, *Charles Williamson, Genesee Promoter, Friend of Anglo-American Rapprochment* (Rochester, NY: Rochester Historical Society, 1941).

23   For modern analyses of the early years of American politics, consult Richard Buel, Jr., *Securing the Revolution: Ideology in American Politics, 1789–1815* (Ithaca, NY: Cornell University Press, 1972); William Nisbet Chambers, *Political Parties in a New Nation: The American Experience, 1776–1809* (NY: Oxford University Press, 1966): Joseph Charles, *The Origin of the American Party System: Three Essays* (NY: Harper and Row, 1961).

24   This argument is repeated by Manning J. Dauer, *The Adams Federalists* (Baltimore: Johns Hopkins Press, 1983).

25   Diary, 128.

26   All the quotations on the next few pages are from *Lord Selkirk's Diary*.

27   B.A. Parker, "Thomas Clark: His Business Relationship with Lord Selkirk," *Beaver,* outfit 310 (Autumn, 1979): 50–58.

28   See Gerald Craig, *Upper Canada: The Formative Years 1784–1841* (Toronto: McClelland and Stewart, 1963); F.C., Hamil and T. Jones, "Lord Selkirk's Work in Upper Canada: The Story of Baldoon," *Ontario History* 57 (1965): 1–12.

29   Quoted in DCB, VIII, 857.

30   Selkirk to Burn, 19 November 1803, SPNAC, 14291.

31   Diary, 145.

32   Ibid., 153.

33   For Macdonell, see DCB VII, 554–556.

34   General P. Hunter to Selkirk, 24 December 1803, SPNAC, 14108–14110.

35   Selkirk to George Chisholm, 22 December 1803, reprinted in Hazel Mathews, *The Mark of Honour* (Toronto: University of Toronto Press, 1965), 146.

36   Instructions to William Burn, December 1803, SPNAC, 14278.

37   SPNAC, 14130.

38   Miles Macdonell to John Macdonell, 6 April 1804, reprinted in A.G. Morice, "Sidelights on the Careers of Miles Macdonell and His Brothers," *Canadian Historical Review,* 10 (1929): 308–332.

39   Diary, 199.

40   Ibid., 208.

41   Ibid., 217.

42   Ibid., 202.

43   Ibid., 217.

44   Ibid., 220.

45   Ibid., 233.

46   Ibid., 239.

47   Ibid., 258.

48   For the Hamilton-Burr feud, see Roger Kennedy, *Burr, Hamilton, and Jefferson* (NY: Oxford University Press, 2000).

49   Diary, 324.

50 Notes on agreements with employees, SPNAC, 14653–655.

51 Diary, 326.

52 Selkirk Papers, vol 4, 105–108.

53 SPNAC, 14653–5.

54 Selkirk to General Hunter, 30 August 1804, SPNAC, 14114–14119.

55 Report of Upper Canada Executive Council, 18 September 1804, SPNAC, 14121–14122.

56 Selkirk to Alexander McDonell, Halifax, 6 November 1804 (rough notes), SPNAC, 14536–7.

57 The best studies of Baldoon are A.E.D. MacKenzie, *Baldoon: Lord Selkirk's Settlement in Upper Canada* (London, ON: Phelps Pub., 1978) and F.C. Hamil and T. Jones, "Lord Selkirk's Work in Upper Canada," 1–12. Neither really asks any critical questions, much less answers them.

58 See, for example, the detailed plans for the home farm at Baldoon in SPNAC, 14628–14652.

59 Diary, 351–352.

60 Ibid., 354.

Chapter 8

1 Holden Furber, *Henry Dundas: First Viscount Melville 1742–1811: Political Manager of Scotland, Statesman, Administrator of British India* (Oxford: Oxford University Press, 1931), 149 ff.

2 Dugald Stewart to Francis Horner, 8 June 1805, *Works* (1858 edition), 10: cxxxviii.

3 A. McDonell to Selkirk, 25 September 1804 (received 22 November 1804), NAC MG 24/I8/9/2–4; A. McDonell to Selkirk, 8 November 1804 (received 14 January 1805), NAC MG 24/I8/9/6–7.

4 Selkirk to General Hunter, 1 February 1805, SPNAC, 14123–24.

5 A. McDonell to Messrs LeRoy, Bayard & McEwer, NY, 4 May 1805, NAC, MG 24/I8/9/17–18.

6 Proposal to the Rt. Hon. Earl Camden, 4 February 1805, for Settlement on Mohawk Lands, Grand River, Upper Canada, SPNAC, 14125-14129.

7 Selkirk to Lord Camden, 14 February [1805], SPNAC, 14171–4.

8 H. M. Buchanan to Robert Brown, 23 May 1805, SRO, Lennoxlove Muniments, bundle 28.

9 *The Critical Review, 3rd* ser., 5 (1805): 366–378.

10 *Scots Magazine,* 67 (1805): 609–616.

11 The *Edinburgh Review,* 7 (1805): 186–202; Francis Horner to Sir James Mackintosh, 25 September 1805, in Leonard Horner, ed., *Memoirs and Correspondence of Francis Horner, M.P.* (London: J. Murray, 1843), 1: 312–313.

12 *Farmer's Magazine,* 5 (1805): 483–490.

13 Robert Adam, ed., *Papers in Sutherland Estate Management, 1802–1816* (Edinburgh: Scottish Record Office, 1972), 2:39.

14 See my "Another Look at the Founder: Lord Selkirk and Political Economy," in *Thomas Scott's Body and Other Essays in Early Manitoba History* (Winnipeg: University of Manitoba Press, 2000), 37–56.

15 Selkirk to William Pitt, 29 July 1805, SPNAC, 13926; "Outlines of a Plan for the Settlement & Security of Canada 1805," SPNAC, 13919-26.

16 Representation by the Earl of Selkirk to William Pitt, 25–26 July 1805, SPNAC, 14130-36.

17 See my "The Rise and Fall of the Kelping Industry in the Western Ilses," in Keith Branigan, ed., *From Clan to Clearance: History and Archaeology on the Isle of Barry c. 850–1850 A.D.* (Oxford: Oxbow Books, 2005), 123–138.

18 Selkirk to Earl of Morton, 3 October 1805, SRO GD 150/2382; Selkirk to Lord Napier, 3 October 1805, EUL Laing Mss ii 461 (Napier Papers).

19 The Earl of Keltie to Baron Napier, 20 October 1805, SRO GD 124/15/1707.

20 Alex Murray to Archibald Constable, 8 October 1805, quoted in John Reith, *The Life and Writings of Rev. Alex Murray* (Dumfries: J. Maxwell & Son, 1903), p. 174.

21 A. McDonell to Selkirk, 28 July 1805 (received 18 October 1805), McDonell Papers, NAC 9/29–31.

22 A. McDonell to Selkirk, 3 August 1805 (received 19 October 1805), McDonell Papers, NAC 9/31–6.

23 Selkirk to A. McDonell, 2 November 1805, SPNAC, 14546–14555. This letter was signed "Y'r aff'te fr'd Selkirk," one of the few instances in Selkirk's lengthy correspondence of such an expression.

24 Dr. the Right Honble the Earl of Selkirk by LeRoy Bayard & McEvers, 12 October 1805, SPNAC, 14693.

25 Alexander Mundell to Selkirk, 30 November 1805, SPNAC, 14901.

26 James Williams to General Fanning, 4 August 1805 (received early December 1805), SPNAC, 14898–14900.

27 "Prince Edward Island Statement, 1806," SPNAC 13966–13972.

28 Ibid.

29 Robert Brown, *Strictures and Remarks on the Earl of Selkirk's Observations on the Present State of the Highlands of Scotland* (Edinburgh: Abernathy and Walker, 1806); *Eight Letters on the Subject of the Earl of Selkirk's Pamphlet on Highland Emigration, As They Lately Appeared under the Signature of AMICUS in One of the Edinburgh Newspapers* (Edinburgh: Longman, Hurst, Rees, and Lorne, 1806); Anon., *Remarks on the Earl of Selkirk's Observations on the Present State of the Highlands* (Edinburgh: John Anderson, 1806).

30 *Monthly Review,* 5 (1806): 411–419; *Critical Review,* 3rd ser., 8 (1806): 374–378; *Farmer's Magazine,* 6 (1806): 241–248.

31 See Peter Jupp, *Lord Grenville 1759–1834* (Oxford: Oxford University Press, 1985), esp. 345–412.

32 A.D. Harvey, "The Ministry of All the Talents: The Whigs in Office, February 1806 to March 1807," *Historical Journal,* 15 (1972): 619–648.

33 Lady Bessborough to Lord Granville, 15 March 1806, in *Lord Granville Leveson Gower (First Earl Granville) Private Correspondence 1781 to 1821.* ed. Catania Countess Granville (London: Murray, 1916), 2: 184; Charles James Fox to Anthony Merry, 7 March 1806, PRO FO 115/13; Beckles Willson, *Friendly Relations* (Boston: Little Brown 1934), 53.

34 SPNAC, 13927-13936.

35 Selkirk to William Clerk, 30 April 1806, SRO GD 18/3297.

36 Selkirk to Sir John Stippisley, 22 March 1806, British Museum (BM) Add. Mss., 37849, ff. 290–291.

37 Ibid.

38 Selkirk to William Windham, {June 1806], BM Add. Mss. 37884, ff. 11–24.

39 Copy Letter to Lord Auckland per Board of Trade, 12 April [1806], "Granting Lands in North America," SPNAC, 13937, 13949.

40 Selkirk to William Clerk, 30 April 1806, SRO GD 18/3297.

41 See *A Letter to the Peers of Scotland by the Earl of Selkirk* (London, 1807), reprinted in my *The Collected Writings of Lord Selkirk* (Winnipeg: Manitoba Historical Sociey, 1984), 1: 241–258.

42 Ibid.

Chapter 9

1   Selkirk to James Stewart, 3 July 1806, SPNAC, 14908-14913.

2   Ibid.

3   Selkirk to Lord Auckland, 4 July 1806, CO 226/21/174–5; John Stewart, *An Account of Prince Edward Island* (London: Winchester and Sons, 1806), vi–vii and *passim.*

4   J.M. Bumsted, *The People's Clearance: Highland Emigration to North America* (Edinburgh: Edinburgh University Press, Winnipeg: University of Manitoba Press, 1984).

5   Selkirk to Lord Castlereagh, 30 August 1806, CO 42/342/187.

6   Alexander Macdonell to Selkirk, 13 April 30, May 1806, NAC MG 2418, vol. 9, 56–84. Selkirk would have received these letters over the summer of 1806.

7   Selkirk to Macdonell, 30 October 1806, SPNAC, 14564–14566.

8   Selkirk to Henry Erskine, 12 September 1806, cited in Alexander Fergusson, *The Honourable Henry Erskine: Lord Advocate for Scotland* (Edinburgh and London: W. Blackwood 1882), 457n.

9   Lord Kinnaird to Lord Napier, 25 October 1806, EUL: Laing Mss., ii, 461.

10 See, for example, Selkirk to Lord Napier, 25 October 1806, SRO GD 26/13/198/4/1.

11 Grenville to Earl of Leven and Melville, 27 October 1806, SRO GD 26/13/198/4/1.

12 On Burr, see Thomas Perkins Abernathy, *The Burr Conspiracy* (NY: Oxford University Press, 1954).

13 Selkirk, "Observations on S. America [1806] delivered to Windham & to Lord Grenville," SPNAC, 13950-13965, reprinted with introduction and notes by John Perry Pritchett in "Selkirk's View on British Policy Towards the Spanish-American Colonies, 1806" *Canadian Historical Review* 24 (1943): 381–396.

14 Grenville to Selkirk, 15 November 1806; ibid., 396.

15 Selkirk, "Memorial on Irish Emigration transmitted to Lord Sidmouth, 19 November 1806, SPNAC, 13874–92.

16 *Caledonian Mercury,* 6 December 1806.

17 Minutes of Meeting of the Peers of Scotland, 5 December 1806, SRO GD 150/2382.

18 Roger Anstey, *The Atlantic Slave Trade and British Abolition, 1760–1810* (London: Macmillan, 1975).

19 *Parliamentary Debates,* 5 February 1807, 666–667.

20 Ibid., 667–668.

21 William Wilberforce to Lord Muncaster, 11 February 1807, quoted in *The Life of Wilberforce in Five Volumes,* ed. Robert and Samuel Wilberforce (London: J. Murray, 1838), 3: 294.

22 John Pollock, *Wilberforce* (London: Constable, 1977), 210–212.

23 Ibid.

24 Archibald Constable diary, entry of 16 March 1807, quoted in Thomas Constable, ed., *Archibald Constable and his Literary Correspondents* (Edinburgh: Edmonston and Douglas, 1873), 1: 108–109.

25 Selkirk, Memorial to Lord Grenville, 1807, SPNAC, 14149–14153.

26 Selkirk, Observations on *Emigrant Regulation Act,* 22 February 1807, sent to Lord Sidmouth, SPNAC, 13973–13976.

27 Selkirk to Lord Holland, 13 March 1807, SPNAC, 13977–13982. Scholars have recognized that the western boundary of the Purchase was not clear, but have not much discussed the northern boundary or the British rights. See Herman Binger, *The Louisiana Purchase and Our Title West of the Rocky Mountains* (Washington: N.p., 1890); John Keats, *Eminent Domain: The Louisiana Purchase and the Making of America* (NY: Charterhouse, 1973).

28 *A Letter to the Peers of Scotland by the Earl of Selkirk* (London, 1807), reprinted in *The Collected Writings of Lord Selkirk,* ed. J.M. Bumsted (Winnipeg: Manitoba Historical Society, 1984), 1.

29 Earl of Morton to Selkirk, 26 December 1806, SRO GD 150 2382; Lord Torphichen to Selkirk, 14 January 1807, EUL, Laing Mss., ii, 461.

30 Torphichen to Selkirk, 14 January 1807.

31 *A Letter to the Peers of Scotland.*

32 John Fraser to James Stewart, 8 November 1806, SPNAC, 14918–14920.

33 A. Macdonell to Selkirk, 17 December 1806, NAC MG 24 18, vol. 9, 72–78.

34 Selkirk to Alexander Macdonell, 8 April 1807, SPNAC, 14567.

35 Selkirk to Duke of Buccleuch, 30 April 1807, SRO GD 224/579; Selkirk to Earl of Morton, 29 April 1807, SRO GD 150/2382.

36 Duke of Buccleuch to Lord Melville, 8 May 1807, EUL: Laing Mss., ii, 461.

37 Lord Napier to Duke of Buccleuch, 10 May 1807, SRO GD 224/579.

38 Lord Haddington to Earl of Morton, 19 May 1807, SRO GD 150/2382.

39 General Election, 9 June 1807, EUP: Laing Mss., ii, 461.

40 *Gentleman's Magazine* 77 (1807): Part I, 575.

41 Sir John Fortescue, *The County Lieutenancies and the Army 1804–1814* (London: Macmillan, 1906).

42 Harvey, "The Ministry of All the Talents: The Whigs in Office, February 1806 to March 1807," *Historical Journal* 15 (1972): 627–629; Richard Glover, *Peninsula Preparation: The Reform of the British Army 1795–1809* (Cambridge: Cambridge University Press, 1963), 214–254.

43 The bill is summarized in Fortescue, *A History of the British Army* (London: Macmillan, 1910), 6: 79–83.

44 Reprinted in Bumsted, ed., *The Collected Writings of Lord Selkirk 1799–1809* (Winnipeg: Manitoba Historical Society, 1984), 259–288.

45 See, for example, Alexander Macdonell to Selkirk, 30 June 1807, NAC MG 24 18, vol. 10, 8–10.

46 Lord Auckland to Lord Grenville, 14 November 1807, Dropmore Mss., IX, p. 144.

47 See, for example, *Edinburgh Advertiser* (28 November 1807); *Gentleman's Magazine* 77 (1807): Part 2, 1171.

Chapter 10

1 James Stewart to Selkirk, 19 May 1807, SPNAC, 14923.

2 Lady Helen Hall to Jean, Lady Hunter, 3 January 1803, Hall of Dunglass family letters, photocopies at NLS.

3 James Stewart to Selkirk, 13 June 1807, SPNAC, 14925; James Williams to Stewart, 20 May 1807, SPNAC, 14926–14928; "State of the Sale of Lands upon the Earl of Selkirk's Estate, Prince Edward Island North America Nov'r 1807," SPNAC, 14862–14869.

4 Lucille Campey, *The Silver Chief: Lord Selkirk and the Scottish Pioneers of Belfast, Baldoon, and Red River* (Toronto: Natural Heritage Books, 2003), 49. Campey is wrong in her suggestion that all the money was lost on the island.

5 James Williams to Selkirk, 16 November 1807, SPNAC, 14932–14943; Williams to Selkirk, 1 December 1807, SPNAC, 14945–14952.

6 A grant of 30,800 acres on the Grand River was recorded to Selkirk on 17 November 1807; Ontario Archives RG 1 C-III-7, vol. 6.

7 Selkirk to Lord Leven, 8 January [1808], SRO GD 26/13/197.

8 Ibid.

9 Selkirk to James Williams, 15 April 1808, SPNAC, 14953; Selkirk to Williams, 2 May 1808, SPNAC, 15103–15105.

10 SPNAC, 1–3.

11 Glyndwr Williams, "The Hudson's Bay Company and the Fur Trade: 1670–1870," *The Beaver* (Autumn, 1983): 43–44; Barry Gough, *First Across the Continent: Sir Alexander Mackenzie* (Toronto: McClelland and Stewart, 1998).

12 Joseph Irving, *Book of Eminent Scotsmen* (Paisley: Gardner, 1881), 466.

13 Observations by Lord S., July 1808, SPNAC, 14161–14168.

14 Alexander Murray to Mr. Constable, 3 August 1808, in T. Constable, ed., *Archibald Constable and his Literary Correspondents* (Edinburgh: Edmonston and Douglas, 1873) 1: 273–275.

15 Ibid.

16 Ibid.

17 Selkirk to Francis Gore, 31 March 1809, PRO CO 42/349/64–66.

18 Selkirk to A. Mundell, 11 March 1809, McGill University Library.

19 For Cartwright, see F. D. Cartwright, ed., *The Life and Correspondence of Major Cartwright* (London: N.p., 1826), especially 1: 392–393.

20 Patrick White, ed., *Lord Selkirk's Diary 1803–1804: A Journal of His Travels in British North America and the Northeastern United States* (Toronto: Champlain Society, 1958), 86.

21 John Pearson, *Review of Lord Selkirk's Objections to a Reform in the Representation of the People: In a Letter to John Cartwright, Esq. from John Pearson, Esq.* (London: J. Johnson, 1809).

22 Ibid., 1, 6, 10.

23 The biography is the one by John Morgan Gray, *Lord Selkirk of Red River* (Toronto: Macmillan, 1964).

24 See my "Thomas Halliday, Mary Cochrane, the Earl of Selkirk, and the Island," *The Island Magazine* 18 (1986): 27–32.

25 Thomas Halliday to Selkirk, 18 March 1818, 4680–83.

26 Quoted in John Morgan Gray, *Lord Selkirk of Red River*, 52.

Chapter 11

1 Quoted in E.E. Rich, *The History of the Hudson's Bay Company 1670–1870, vol. 2, 1763–1870* (London: Hudson's Bay Record Society, 1959), 259.

2 See A.S. Morton, *A History of the Canadian West to 1870–71: Being a History of Rupert's Land (the Hudson's Bay Company's Territory); and of the North-West Territory (Including the Pacific Slope)*, 2nd ed. (Toronto: University of Toronto Press, 1973), especially 518–524; E.E. Rich, *The Fur Trade and the Northwest to 1857* (Toronto, 1967); E.E. Rich, *The History of the Hudson's Bay Company 1670–1870, vol. 1, 1670–1763* (London: Hudson's Bay Record Society, 1958).

3 E.E. Rich, ed., *Colin Robertson's Correspondence Book, September 1817 to September 1822* (Toronto: Champlain Society, 1939), xxi–xxii.

4 Consult Murray G. Lawson, *Fur: A Study in English Mercantilism, 1700–1775* (Toronto: University of Toronto Press, 1943); Harold A. Innis, *The Fur Trade in Canada: An Introduction to Canadian Economic History* (Toronto: University of Toronto Press, 1999).

5 Arthur J. Ray and Donald Freeman, *"Give Us Good Measure": An Economic Analysis of Relations between the Indians and the Hudson's Bay Company before 1763* (Toronto: University of Toronto Press, 1978).

6 Selkirk to MacDonald, 6 December 1809, SPNAC, 14967–14976.

7 MacDonald to Selkirk, 3 May 1810, SPNAC, 15006-9.

8 Selkirk to Miles Macdonell, 6 December 1809, PAC MG19 E4, 52.

9 For Auld, see DCB, VI, 17–18.

10 For Robertson, see DCB, VII, 748–752.

11 Rich, ed., *Robertson's Correspondence*, xxiv–xxvi.

12 Selkirk to Miles Macdonell, 10 February 1810, NAC MG18 E4, 56.

13 Selkirk, "HBCo 1810/Scross Observations Wollaston's Plan," SPNAC, 16–28; see also his "HBC, 1810/Cross Plan New System," SPNAC, 9–15, and "HB 1810 Feb/Scroll Resolutions new System" SPNAC, 29–37.

14 "HBC 1810 Scroll observations Wollaston's Plan."

15 "HBC 1810/Feb/Scroll Resolutions new System."

16 Rich, ed., *Robertson's Correspondence*, xxxiii–xxxiv; Morton, *A History*, 531–532.

17 Rich, *The Fur Trade and the Northwest*, 205–207.

18 Rich, ed., *Robertson's Correspondence*, xxxiii–xxxiv; Morton, *A History*, 531–532.

19 Memorandum by Selkirk, SPNAC, A27, 1–22.

20 Maria Edgeworth to Mrs. Barbauld, 1 August 1810, reprinted in Betsy Rogers, *Georgian Chronical: Mrs. Barbauld and Her Family* (London: Metheun, 1958), 200.

21 John MacDonald to Selkirk, 23 April 1810, SPNAC, 14981–15005.

22 James Williams to Selkirk, 14 August 1810, SPNAC, 14963–14966.

23 Some notion of the information available in Britain on the western interior at this time is discussed by Eric Ross in his book *Beyond the River and the Bay: Some Observations on the State of the Canadian Northwest in 1811 with a View to Providing the Intending Settler with an Intimate Knowledge of that Country* (Toronto: University of Toronto Press, 1970).

24 Committee minutes, 6 February 1811, HBC Archives, A1/50.

25 Memorandum by the Earl of Selkirk, SPNAC, A27, 1–22. This was probably written at Fort William over the winter of 1816/17.

26 Committee minutes, 6 March 1811, HBC Archives, A1/50.

27 "April 1811/Lumbr HB/Calculations per Christie & Co," SPNAC, 38–39; *The Inverness Journal and Northern Advertiser,* 19 April 1811.

28 DCB, VI, 413–415.

29 Affidavit, Selkirk v. Spraggon, 27 February 1811, Public Archives of Prince Edward Island (PAPEI), Supreme Court Papers.

30 DCB, V, 861–2.

31 Marjorie Wilkins Campbell, *The North West Company* (Vancouver: Douglas and McIntyre, 1983).

32 Samuel Gale to Lady Selkirk, September 1817, SPNAC 4097–4113.

33 Marjorie Wilkins Campbell, *Northwest to the Sea: A Biography of William McGillivray* (Toronto: Clarke Irwin, 1975).

34 Reprinted in *The Collected Writings of Lord Selkirk, vol. 2, 1811–1820,* ed. J.M. Bumsted (Winnipeg: Manitoba Historical Society, 1987), 47–110.

35 Minutes of General Court, 22 May 1811, HBC Archives, A1/50; "Minute by Miles Macdonell of threats by Sir A. McKenzie vs RRS, 22 May 1811, SPNAC, 1925.

36 Minutes of General Court, 30p May 1811, HBC Archives, A1/50.

37 Ibid.

Chapter 12

1 McTavish Fraser & Co., Inglis Ellice & Co., Alex MacKenzie to William Mainwaring, 3 June 1811, SPNAC, 199–201.

2 *The Inverness Journal and Northern Advertiser,* 21 June 1811. This newspaper circulated widely in the towns of the Highlands of Scotland.

3 See my detailed "The Affair at Stornoway, 1811," *The Beaver* (Spring 1982): 52–58.

4 Miles Macdonell to Selkirk, 1 October 1811, SPNAC, 40–57.

5 William Auld to Selkirk, October 1811, SPNAC, 58–64; Auld to Wedderburn, 3 October 1811, SPNAC, 65–88.

6 See, for example, Selkirk to Dr. Marcet, 21 October 1811, Small Collection, NLS 3649, ff. 17–18.

7 Copy of a letter from Selkirk to Thomas Clark, n.d., University of Western Ontario Library, 4378.

8 For more details, see my "The Loyal Electors," *The Island Magazine,* 7 (1980): 8–14.

9 A. Lean to Selkirk, 14 March 1812, HBC Archives, A5/5.

10 Selkirk to Miles Macdonell, 24 March 1812, SPNAC, I, 291. The American declaration of war on Great Britain a few months later would completely alter the situation, of course.

11 Quoted in Chester Martin, *Lord Selkirk's Work in Canada* (Toronto: Oxford University Press, 1916), 90–91, referring to manuscript material subsequently lost in the St. Mary's Isle fire.

12 Ibid., quoting lost manuscripts.

13 Minutes of Committee, 29 April 1812, HBC Archives, A1/50.

14 Ibid.

15 Selkirk to Alexander Mundell, BM 31897, f. 24.

16 Macdonell Papers, PAC MG 24 18, vol. 35, 108.

17 Alexander MacDonald to Archibald McDonald, 14 May 1812, SPNAC, 289–291.

18 Miles Macdonell to Selkirk, SPNAC, 344–63.

19 For another assessment of Miles, see DCB, VI, 440–444.

20 Selkirk to William Auld, 18 June 1812, SPNAC, 383–404.

21 Selkirk to William Hillier, 18 June 1812, SPNAC, 405–410.

22 Selkirk to Auld, 18 June 1812.

23 Selkirk to Miles Macdonell, 20 June 1812, SPNAC, 405–410.

24 E.E. Rich, *The Fur Trade and the Northwest to 1857* (Toronto: McClelland and Stewart, 1967), 205–207.

25 Selkirk to Miles, 20 June 1812.

26 HBC Archives, E8/8, ff. 116–168.

27 HB Obs'a to Ld Liverpool, 11 July 1812, SPNAC, 14007–14009.

28 Irish Catholic Proposition to Lord Liv., 11 July 1812, SPNAC, 13983–13986.

29 Selkirk, "Spain—Suggestions to Ld. Sid—August 1812," SPNAC, 13995–14006.

30 Selkirk, "Irish Catholic Church arrang'ts proposed to N. Vansittart," 28 August 1812, SPNAC, 139987–13993.

31 Lord Melville to Lord Buccleuch, SRO GD 224/579.

32 Selkirk to Lord Leven and Melville, 3 October 1812, SRO GD 26/13/200/6.

33 Selkirk to Lord Buccleuch, 13 October 1812, SRO GD 224/579; Buccleuch to Selkirk, 22 October 1812, SRO GD 224/579; Selkirk to Buccleuch, 24 October 1812, SRO GD 224/579.

34 Lord Napier to Lord Melville, 10 November 1812, SRO GD 51/197/47.

35 "A Statement of Losses Sustained by the right Honourable Earl of Selkirk on Account of the Americans under the Command of Cap't Forsyth coming to Baldoon and Township of Dover and County of Trent," University of Western Ontario Regional Collection, 4378.

36 Miles Macdonell to Selkirk, 4 July 1812, SPNAC, 413–419.

37 Testimony relative to Mutinies &c., 6 July 1812, SPNAC, 420–428; Minutes of Langston's Conduct, 1812, SPNAC, 438–440.

38 Miles Macdonell to Selkirk, 11 August 1812, SPNAC, 443–450.

39 Owen Keveny to Selkirk, 8 September 1812, SPNAC, 460–472.

40 Donald Gunn, letter 3 in Donald Gunn and Charles Tuttle, *A History of Manitoba* (Ottawa: MacLean, Roger, 1880).

41 William Auld to Selkirk, 12 September 1812, SPNAC, 477–501.

42 Committee minutes, 11 January 1812, HBC Archives, A1/50.

43 Ibid.

Chapter 13

1   For the Canadian Regiment, see John Prebble, *Mutiny* (London: Penguin, 1975), and my *The People's Clearance: Highland Emigration to British North America 1770–1815* (Edinburgh: Edinburgh University Press; Winnipeg: University of Manitoba Press, 1982), 155–187.

2   Selkirk to Alexander MacDonald of Dalilia, 23 January 1813, University of Edinburgh Library.

3   "Regiment Proposal 17 February 1813 to Ld Bathurst," SPNAC, 14032–37. See also my "Lord Selkirk's Highland Regiment and the Kildonan Settlers," *The Beaver* (Autumn 1978): 16–21.

4   "Act to repeal 43 George III c 56," British Library 31897, ff 25–26.

5   "Observations by Duke of York on Proposal Reg't, 6 March 1813, SPNAC, 14090–14091.

6   Selkirk to Bathurst, 9 March 1813, SPNAC, 14065–14072.

7   Quoted in Eric Richards, *The Leviathan of Wealth: The Sutherland Fortune in the Industrial Revolution* (London: Routledge and Kegan Paul, 1973), 178.

8   Ibid., 173.

9   Ibid.

10 Ibid., 175.

11 Countess of Sutherland to Sir Walter Scott, 22 October 1811, NLS MS 3881 f. 89.

12 Quoted in Richards, *Leviathan of Wealth*, 179.

13 Quoted in Ibid.

14 Ibid.

15 Ian Grimble, *The Trial of Patrick Sellar* (London: Routledge and Kegan Paul, 1962). See also Donald MacLeod, *History of the Destitution in Sutherlandshire* (Edinburgh: N.p., 1841); and John Prebble, *The Highland Clearances* (London: Secker and Warburg, 1963).

16 James Armour to William McDonald, 22 February 1813, SPNAC, 14088–14089.

17 Richards, *Leviathan of Wealth*, 180.

18 "Notes of the Marchioness of Stafford of conversations with Lord Selkirk 18 March and 13 April 1813,"in R.J. Adam, ed., *Papers on Sutherland Estate Management 1802–1804*, 2 vols. (Edinburgh: Scottish Record Office, 1972), 1: 142–144.

19 "Memo Mr. McD," SPNAC, 14041; "Queries by Sergeant Macdonald and answers thereto by Lord Selkirk with respect to the Sutherland Highlanders' Settlement in North America: 1813," *Sutherland Papers*.

20 Selkirk, "Modifications on Proposal Reg't," 6 April 1813, SPNAC, 14092.

21 *Sutherland Papers*, 1: 143–144.

22 Colonel Torrens to Selkirk, 14 April 1813, SPNAC, 14043–14044.

23 Selkirk to Lord Bathurst, 13 April 1813, SPNAC, 14037–14042.

24 Selkirk to Lord Bathurst, 21 April 1813, SPNAC, 14056–14057.

25 Selkirk to Marquis of Stafford, 24 April 1813, *Sutherland Papers*.

26 William Young to Earl Gower, n.d., *Sutherland Papers*.

27 Dugald Gilchrist to Marchioness of Stafford, 11 May 1813, *Sutherland Papers*.

28 Ibid.

29 William Young to Marchioness of Stafford, 11 May 1813, *Sutherland Papers*.

30 William Young, quoted in Richards, *Leviathan of Wealth*, 181.

31 Donald Gunn and Charles Tuttle, *A History of Manitoba* (Ottawa: MacLean, Roger, 1880), 90.

32 "Copies of receipts taken from the Originals at York 9 May 1816," Strachan Letter Book, Ontario Archives. The pamphlet was titled *A Letter to the Right Honourable the Earl of Selkirk on his Settlement at Red River near Hudson's Bay* (London: Longman, Hurst, Orme and Brown, 1816).

33 Gunn published his account first in a letter to the *Nor'-Wester* newspaper in 1869, and then in his *History of Manitoba*, 68ff.

34 Gunn and Tuttle, *History of Manitoba*, 91.

35 For McDonald, see Jean Murray Cole, *Exile in the Wilderness: The Life of Chief Factor Archibald McDonald, 1790–1853* (Don Mills: Burns & MacEachern, 1979).

36 Selkirk to Miles Macdonell, 5 June 1813, SPNAC, 629–646.

37 Selkirk to Miles Macdonell, 12 June 1813, SPNAC, 650–669.

38 Selkirk to Miles Macdonell, 14 June 1813, SPNAC, 682–88.

39 For example, Abel Edwards to Selkirk, 10 July 1813, SPNAC, 748–754.

40 Miles Macdonell to Selkirk, 17 July 1813, SPNAC, 764–794.

41 William Auld to Andrew Wedderburn, 16 September 1813, SPNAC, 843–865.

42 Miles Macdonell to Selkirk, 17 July 1813.

43 Miles Macdonell to Selkirk, 10 September 1813, SPNAC, 843–865.

44 Joseph Howse to Selkirk, 24 September 1813, SPNAC, 871–874.

45 William Auld to Selkirk, 26 September 1813, SPNAC, 836–842.

46 Owen Keveny to Miles Macdonell, 2 February 1814, SPNAC, 886–897.

Chapter 14

1 "Notes on the Pemmican Affair," probably by Selkirk, 1814, SPNAC, 886–897.

2 Proclamation, 8 January 1814, SPNAC, 916–18.

3 George Holdsworth to Miles Macdonell, 25 January 1814, SPNAC, 920–22.

4 John Wills to Miles Macdonell, 25 January 1814, SPNAC, 949–959.

5 Miles Macdonell to William Auld, 4 February 1814, SPNAC, 949–959.

6 "Paper on Abolition of Slave Trade and African Reform," SPNAC, 14015–14024.

7 Untitled paper on European Affairs, SPNAC, 14174.

8 Gregory Dowd, *A Spirited Resistance: The North American Indian Struggle for Unity, 1745–1815* (Baltimore: Johns Hopkins University Press, 1992).

9 "Scroll Copy—American Treaty—W Inds—1814", SPNAC, 14010–14014.

10 Miles Macdonell to Agents NWC, 8 March 1814, SPNAC, 967–71.

11 William Auld to Miles Macdonell, 13 March 1814, SPNAC, 971–980.

12 William Auld to William Hillier, 8 April 1814, SPNAC, 991–995.

13 HBC to Thomas Thomas, April 1814, SPNAC, 1327–1375.

14 Selkirk to Miles Macdonell, 12 April 1814, SPNAC, 1006–1062.

15 Selkirk to Miles Macdonnell, 15 April 1814, SPNAC, 1054–1060.

16 William Auld to Miles Macdonell, 15 April 1815, SPNAC, 1054–1060.

17 Miles Macdonell to William Auld, 25 April 1814, SPNAC, 985–989.

18 William Auld's advice, 13 May 1814, SPNAC, 1083–1089.

19 Miles Macdonell to John Wills, 20 May 1814, SPNAC, 926–27.

20 John Wills to Miles Macdonell, 21 May 1814, SPNAC, 928.

21 Miles Macdonell to John Wills, 22 May 1814, SPNAC, 929–30.

22 Minute of a Conference with Mr. Wills, 23 May 1814, SPNAC, 931.

23 Hudson's Bay Company to Thomas Thomas, 18 May 1814, SPNAC, 1308–1326.

24 Committee minutes, 18 May 1814, HBC Archives, A1/50.

25 Archibald McDonald to Selkirk, 22 May 1814, SPNAC, 1092–1124.

26 Quoted in Jean Murray Cole, *Exile in the Wilderness: The Life of Chief Factor Archibald McDonald, 1790–1853* (Don Mills: Burns and MacEachern, 1979), 18.

27 Donald Gunn and CharlesTuttle, *A History of* Manitoba (Ottawa: MacLean, Roger, 1880), 100.

28 Selkirk to Miles Macdonell, 28 May 1814, SPNAC, 1127–32.

29 Report of Mr. Sheriff Spencer, 30 May 1814, SPNAC, 932.

30 J.M. Bumsted, *Dictionary of Manitoba Biography* (Winnipeg: University of Manitoba Press, 1999).

31 One Isabel Gunn, a female disguised as a male, had earlier been posted to Pembina by the HBC and had given birth to a child there.

32 Duncan Cameron et al. to Miles Macdonell, 18 June 1814, SPNAC, 939.

33 Miles Macdonell to North West Company, 17 June 1814, SPNAC, 940–41.

34 Duncan Cameron et al. to Miles Macdonell, 16 June 1814, SPNAC, 942.

35 Miles Macdonell to North West Company, 17 June 1814, SPNAC, 943.

36 John McDonald et al to Miles Macdonell, 18 June 1814, SPNAC, 945–946.

37 Miles Macdonell to North West Company proprietors, SPNAC, 947.

38 John McDonald et al to Miles Macdonell, 18 June 1814, SPNAC, 948.

39 William McGillivray to John Pritchard, 23 July 1814, SPNAC, 1162–4.

40 Miles Macdonell to Selkirk, 24 July 1819, SPNAC, 1176–1181.

41 Selkirk to Miles Macdonell, 9 July 1814, PAC, MG E4, 101–103.

42 Gunn and Tuttle, 105.

43 Archibald McDonald to Selkirk, 24 July 1814, SPNAC, 1170–1175.

44 Gunn and Tuttle, 106.

45 Miles Macdonell to Selkirk, 25 July 1814, SPNAC, 1183–1203.

46 *Journal of a Voyage on the North West Coast of North America during the Years 1811, 1812, 1813 and 1814 by Gabriel Franchère*, ed. W. Kaye Lamb (Toronto: Champlain Society, 1969), 180.

47 Marjorie Wilkins Campbell, *The North West Company* (Vancouver: Douglas and McIntyre, 1983), 211.

48 Alexander Macdonell to John McDonald, 5 August 1814, SPNAC, 1207–1211.

49 Abel Edwards Report on Miles Macdonell, August–September 1814, SPNAC, 1207–1211.

50 Miles Macdonell to Selkirk, 9 September 1814, SPNAC, 1215–26.

51 Lord Selkirk, "William Hillier, Notes of his narrative of M. Macdonell Cond'n at YF Aug end, December 1814," SPNAC, 1504–1505.

52 Thomas Thomas to Selkirk, 9 September 1814, SPNAC, 1240–41.

53 Thomas Thomas to Selkirk, 20 September 1814, SPNAC, 1235–41.

54 Colin Robertson to Selkirk, 5 October 1814, HBC Archives A10/1.

55 John Macdonell to John McNab, 10 October 1814, SPNAC, 1245–9.

56 Colin Robertson to Selkirk, 29 October 1814, SPNAC, 1252–55.

57 John Pritchard to Colin Robertson, 11 October 1814, SPNAC, 1259–61.

58 Miles MacDonell Notice of Eviction, 21 October 1814, NAC, RG4, B46, vol. 1; SPNAC, 1250–1.

59 Sir James Hall Diary, SRO, GD 206/11,315/15.

60 Selkirk to A. Edwards, n.d., SPNAC, 513–4; Abel Edwards to Selkirk, December [1814], SPNAC, 518–9.

61 Selkirk to Colin Robertson, 6 December 1814, SPNAC, 1280–82.

62 Selkirk, "Ossiniboia," reprinted in Bumsted, ed., *The Collected Writings of Lord Selkirk, vol. 2 1810–1820* (Winnipeg: Manitoba Historical Society, 1988), 10.

63 Ibid., 15.

64 Ibid., 16–17.

65 William Auld to Selkirk, n.d. but December 1814, SPNAC, 510–12.

66 Selkirk to Colin Robertson, SPNAC, 1284–5.

67 Selkirk to Miles Macdonell, SPNAC, 1286–89.

Chapter 15

1 James Smith to Duncan Cameron, 24 December 1814, SPNAC, 1292–1293.

2 Duncan Cameron to Donald Livingston and Hector McEachern, 19 January 1815, SPNAC, 1740–1743.

3 Alexander Colvile to Messrs. Maitland Gordon & Auldjo, 4 January 815, HBC Archives, A5/5.

4 Joseph Berens to Lord Bathurst, 10 February 1815, NAC, RG4, B46, vol. 1.

5 Selkirk to Governor &c of HBC, 14 February 1815, SPNAC, 1914–1919.

6 Committee Minutes, 1 February 1815, HBC Archives, A1/51.

7 HBC Committee minutes, 17 February 1815, HBC Archives, A1/51.

8 "Statement 1815," NAC RG4 B46, vol. 1.

9 See my "Untitled Pamphlet on Indian Education" in *Collected Writings of Lord Selkirk* (Winnipeg: Manitoba Historical Society, 1988), 2: 1–7.

10 Selkirk to Lord Bathurst, 3 March 1815, SPNAC, 1476–1483.

11 Extract A. Macdonell to John Siveright, 16 February 1815, SPNAC, 1864–1865.

12 John McLeod's narrative, 18 February 1815, SPNAC, 1586–1589.

13 D. Cameron to Hector McEachern and Donald Livingston, 10 March 1815, SPNAC, 1744–1745.

14 Extract A. Macdonell to J.D. Cameron, 13 March 1815, SPNAC, 1864.

15 Lord Bathurst to Selkirk, 11 March 1815, NAC, RG4, B46, vol. 1.

16 Extract John Siveright to James Taitte, 16 March 1815, SPNAC, 1815.

17 Extracts Selkirk to Maitland Garden & Auldjo, NAC, RG4, B46, vol. 1.

18 Duncan Cameron to James Grant, 22 March 1815, SPNAC, 1865.

19 Selkirk to Miles Macdonell, 23 March 1815, SPNAC, 1492–1503.

20 William Auld to Mr. Thomas, 29 March 1815, SPNAC, 1508–1514.

21 Committee minutes, 5 April 1815, HBC Archives, A1/51.

22 DCB, 749–751.

23 See DCB, V, 750–752.

24 Proclamation, 18 June 1815, SPNAC, 6037.

25 Memorial of Mrs. McLean, March 1819, SPNAC, 6045–6047.

26 *Papers relating to the Red River Settlement . . . 1819* (London: House of Commons, 1819), 46.

27 See, for example, Extract A. MacDonell to Messrs Dun & Doug'l Cameron, 17 April 1815, SPNAC, 1868–1869.

28 George Holdsworth to Miles Macdonell, 23 April 1815, SPNAC, 1529–1530.

29 John Strachan to William McGillivray, Strachan Letterbook 1812–1836, Ontario Archives. This letter is misdated in *John Strachan: Documents and Opinions*, ed. J.H.L. Henderson (Toronto: McClelland and Stewart, 1969), 55–56, as 1813 rather than 1815.

30 Committee minutes, 3 May 1815, HBC Archives, A1/51.

31 Colin Robertson to A. Colvile, 19 May 1815, SPNAC, 1531–1533.

32 General Court minutes, 19 May 1815, HBC Archives, A1/51.

33 Memorial to Bathurst, HBC Archives, A9/8.

34 Joseph Berens to Earl Bathurst, 8 June 1815, HBC Archives, A10/1.

35 J. Harvey to William McGillivray, NAC RG4, B46, vol. 1.

36 Maitland, Garden & Co. to Harvey, 12 June 1815, NAC, RG4, B46, vol. 1.

37 William McGillivray to Lt. Colonel Harvey, 24 June 1815, NAC, RG4, B46, vol. 1.

38 See particularly, Chester Martin, *Lord Selkirk's Work in Canada* (Toronto: Oxford University Press, 1916), 80–87; John Morgan Gray, *Lord Selkirk of Red River* (Toronto: Macmillan, 1963), 98–115; A.S. Morton, *A History of the Canadian West to 1870–71: Being a History of Rupert's Land . . .* 2nd ed. (Toronto: University of Toronto Press, 1973), 567–572. For a North West Company perspective, see Marjorie Wilkins Campbell, *The North West Company* (Vancouver: Douglas and McIntyre, 1983), 211–212.

39 The only contemporary eye-witness account—obviously biased—is in Miles Macdonell to Selkirk, 20 June 1815, SPNAC, 1561–1571.

40 This interpretation is largely the one advocated by Margaret McLeod and W.L. Morton in *Cuthbert Grant of Grantown* (Toronto: McClelland and Stewart, 1974), 23.

41 Miles to Selkirk, 19 September 1815, SPNAC, 1698–1710.

42 See Martin, *Lord Selkirk's Work,* 87 fn.

43 William McGillivray to Lt. Col. Harvey, 6 July 1815, NAC RG4 B46, vol. 1; Extract Simon McGillivray to Arch'd McGillivray, 2 July 1815, SPNAC, 1868.

44 Lt. Col. J. Harvey to Messrs. Maitland, Gordon & Auldjo, 12 July 1815, NAC, RG4, B46, vol. 1.

45 E.E. Rich, ed., *Colin Robertson's Correspondence Book, September 1817 to September 1822* (Toronto: Champlain Society, 1939), llxiii–lxvi.

46 William McGillivray, "Statement Relative to the Settlers from the Red River," 15 August 1815, SPNAC, 1620–1625.

47 J.D. Cameron to Duncan Cameron, 21 August 1815, SPNAC, 1464–1466.

48 Sir F. Robinson to Sir G. Drummond, 22 August 1815, NAC, RG4, B 46, vol. 1.

49 Selkirk, *A Sketch of the British Fur Trade, 1815* in *The Collected Writings of Lord Selkirk, 1810–1820*, ed. J.M. Bumsted (Winnipeg: Manitoba Historical Society,1988), 54.

50   Ibid., 81.

51   Selkirk to Edward Roberts, 21 August 1815, HBC Archives, A10/1.

52   Hudson's Bay Company Committee to Selkirk, 21 August 1815, SPNAC, 1631–1632.

53   For the musical instruments, see Jno. Broadwood & Sons to Mr. Roberts, 26 August 1815, HBC Archives, A10/1; for the instructions, examine "Copy Instructions to Lord Selkirk respecting any Treaty with the N.W. Co.," 30 August 1815, ibid.

54   Selkirk to John McDonald, 1 September 1815, SPNAC, 1638–1651.

Chapter 16

1   Robert Semple to Colin Robertson, 5 September 1815, SPNAC, 1652–1654.

2   New settlers to A. McDonell, 5 September 1815, SPNAC, 1658.

3   Semple's observations, SPNAC, 1659–1666.

4   Robert Semple, Sundry Observations, Appendix 2, September 1815, SPNAC, 1667–1682.

5   Journal kept at Fort Douglas by Colin Robertson, September–October 1815, SPNAC, 1711–1726.

6   A copy of this petition does not seem to have survived.

7   Semple to Hudson's Bay Company, 20 September 1815.

8   Henry Goulburn to Governor, HBC, 14 October 1815, SPNAC, 1815–1816.

9   "General List of Settlers Inrolled for Canada under the Government Regulations at Edinburgh 1815," NAAC MG 11 c.c. 385, vol. 2.

10   John Campbell to Lord Bathurst, 14 October 1815, quoted in John Perry Pritchett, *The Red River Valley, 1811–1849: A Regional Study* (New Haven and Toronto: Yale University Press, 1942), 34.

11   Selkirk to Sir Gordon Drummond, 11 November 1815, NAC, RG4, B46, vol. 1.

12   John Macdonell to William J. Macdonell, 16 November 1815, reprinted in John Perry Pritchett, and Murray Horowitz, eds, "Five Selkirk Letters," *Canadian Historical Review* 22 (1941): 163.

13   Marjorie Wilkins Campbell, *Northwest to the Sea: A Biography of William McGillivray* (Toronto: Clarke, Irwin, 1975), 151.

14   Selkirk to J. Berens, 18 November 1815, SPNAC, 1939–1945.

15   W. H. Robinson to Sir Gordon Drummond, 25 November 1815, NAC, RG4, B46, vol. 1.

16   For another view of these negotiations, quite hostile to Selkirk, see Campbell, *Northwest to the Sea,* 151–153.

17   Conversations with Jo. Richardson, 10 December 1815, no. 1, SPNAC, 217–221.

18   NWCo Boundary Proposals, 12 December 1815, SPNAC, 222–226.

19   Sketch of Heads for an Agreement for a General Participation in the Indian Trade between the Hudson Bay Company and the North West Company, 12 December 1815, SPNAC, 227–231; Selkirk, "Observations on NWCo. Proposal Coalition HB," December 1815, SPNAC, 232–233.

20   That Selkirk had not expected to be talking with the North West Company calls into question Marjorie Campbell's assertion that he was waiting in his newly rented house for William McGillivray and his partners "to call on him with explanations of their defence at the Red River." (Campbell, *Northwest to the Sea,* 151.)

21   Selkirk to A. Colvile, 19 December 1815, HBC Archives, A10/1.

22 Robert Semple to Selkirk, 20 December 1815, SPNAC, 2718–2734.

23 NWC to Selkirk, 27 December 1815, SPNAC, 252–255.

24 Henry Goulburn to Governor, HBC, 29 December 1815, SPNAC, 1840–1841.

25 Selkirk to Andrew Colvile, 6 January 1816, HBC Archives, A10/1.

26 Ibid.

27 A. Colvile to Bathurst, January 1816 (draft); A. Colvile to Bathurst, n.d. but January 1816, HBC Archives, A10/1.

28 John Halkett to J. H. Pelly, 10 January 1816, HBC Archives, A10/1.

29 DCB, VIII, 351–353.

30 Halkett to Pelly, n.d., but January 1816, HBC Archives, A10/2.

31 A. Colvile to Selkirk, 24 January 1816, SPNAC, 2001–2003.

32 Selkirk, Memo, Examination RRs, January/February 1816, SPNAC, 2004–2043.

33 Capt. Fr. Mathey to Selkirk, 12 février 1816, SPNAC, 2143–2146.

34 Selkirk to Sir Gordon Drummond, 11 March 1816, SPNAC, 2081–2083.

35 Sir G. Drummond to Selkirk, 15 March 1816, SPNAC, 2084–2086

36 Robertson to Selkirk, 12 August 1816, SPNAC, 2508.

37 Colin Robertson to A. McDonell, 19 March 1816, SPNAC, 2493.

38 Extracts from the letters of the proprietors and clerks of the N.W. Co. found in their Winter's northern express &c 19th March 1816 at Forks Red River, SPNAC, 1870–1890.

39 Ibid.

40 Peter Fidler, "A Narrative of the re-establishment, progress, and total destruction of the Colony in Red River 1816, with a concise account of the conduct and proceedings of the N.W. Co. in their effecting it," SPNAC, 2509–2531.

41 James Sutherland to Robert Semple, 22 March 1816, SPNAC, 2098–2100.

42 R. Semple to Duncan Cameron, 31 March 1816, SPNAC, 2140–2142.

43 See E. E. Rich, ed., *Colin Robertson's Correspondence Book, September 1817 to September 1822* (Toronto: Champlain Society, 1939).

44 Ibid.

45 R. Semple to C. Robertson, 12 April 1816, SPNAC, 2180.

46 P. Fidler to Semple, 1 April 1816, SPNAC, 2147–2151; James Sutherland to Peter Fidler, 2 April 1816, SPNAC, 2161–2163.

47 P. Fidler to Semple, 7 April 1816, SPNAC, 2173–2174.

48 Semple to P.E. Pambrun, 12 April 1816, SPNAC, 2179.

49 Sir Gordon Drummond to Selkirk, 23 March 1816, SPNAC, 2109–2110.

50 Selkirk to Sir Gordon Drummond, 25 March 1816, SPNAC, 2103–2104.

51 Clarke to Selkirk, 26 March 1816, SPNAC, 2111–2112; see also Chief Justice Thomas Scott to Selkirk, 22 March 1816, SPNAC, 2067.

52 Selkirk to Thomas Vincent, 30 March 1816, SPNAC, 2128–2132.

53 Selkirk to Colin Robertson, 30 March 1816, SPNAC, 1894–1898.

54 Selkirk to C.O. Ermatinger, 30 March 1816, SPNAC, 2122–2123.

55 DCB, VIII, 481–482.

56 Selkirk to M. Duplessis, 8 April 1816, SPNAC, 2164–2165.

57 Selkirk to Sir Gordon Drummond, 4 April 1816, SPNAC, 2166–2168.

58 J. Berens to Selkirk, 5 April 1816, SPNAC, 2169–2172.

59 For Mure (d. 1823), see DCB, VI, 531–534.

60 John Mure to Selkirk, 13 April 1816, SPNAC, 2184–2186.

61 Sir Gordon Drummond to Selkirk, 17 April 1816, SPNAC, 2337–2338.

62 Selkirk to Drummond, 16 April 1816, SPNAC, 2139–2141.

63 Drummond to Selkirk, 20 April 1816, SPNAC, 2242–2243.

64 John Halkett to Selkirk, 17 April 1816, SPNAC, 2242–2243.

65 Selkirk to Sir G. Drummond, 23 April 1816, SPNAC, 2243–2248.

66 Sir G. Drummond to Selkirk, 25 April 1816, SPNAC, 2248–2249.

67 Sir G. Drummond to Selkirk, 27 April 1816, SPNAC, 2218.

68 Selkirk to Sir G. Drummond, 29 April 1816, SPNAC, 2223–2224.

69 Selkirk to John Mure, 1 May 1816, SPNAC, 2227–2228.

70 Maitland, Garden & Auldjo to Hudson's Bay Company, 3 May 1816, HBC Archives, A10/1.

71 John Mure to Selkirk, 4 May 1816, SPNAC, 2229–2230.

72 Sir Gordon Drummond to Selkirk, 14 May 1816, SPNAC, 2249.

73 Selkirk to Major General John Wilson, 6 May 1816, SPNAC, 2333–2336.

74 Selkirk to Gore, 10 May 1816, SPNAC, 2250.

75 Selkirk to Captain Steiger, 23 May 1816, SPNAC, 2279–2282.

76 On the armaments, see, for example, Robert Murray to Thomas Clark, 10 May 1816, SPNAC, 2253–2254, and Selkirk to D. Graham, 11 May 1816, SPNAC, 2261–2264.

77 Peter Fidler to Robert Semple, 11 May 1816, SPNAC, 2265–2268.

78 For Grant, see DCB, VIII, 342–344, and Margaret MacLeod and W.L. Morton, *Cuthbert Grant of Grantown* (Toronto: McClelland and Stewart, 1974).

79 James Sutherland's Narrative, SPNAC, 1951ff.

80 Peter Fidler, "A Narrative of the re-establishment, progress, and total destruction of the Colony in Red River 1816, with a concise account of the conduct and proceedings of the N.W. Co. in their effecting it," SPNAC, 2509–2531.

81 *Robertson's Correspondence Book*

82 Miles Macdonell to Selkirk 25 May 1816, SPNAC, 2307–2308.

83 Selkirk to J. Berens, 24 May 1816, SPNAC, 2287–2291.

84 Selkirk to HBC Committee, 23 May 1816, SPNAC, 2283–2287.

85 W. Mure to Selkirk, 25 May 1816, SPNAC, 2304–2306.

86 Thomas Coutts & Co. to Selkirk, 5 June 1816, SPNAC, 2328.

87 Fidler narrative.

88 *Robertson's Correspondence Book*.

89 Ibid.

90 General Order for Escort, 29 May 1816, SPNAC, 2313.

91 Selkirk to William Smith, 17 June 1816, SPNAC, 2339–2340.

92 Selkirk to Lord Melville, 17 June 1817, SPNAC, 2341.

93 Selkirk to Sir John Sherbrooke, 17 June 1816, SPNAC, 2342–2347.

94 DCB, VI, 716.

95 Ibid.

Chapter 17

1   Eric W. Morse, *Fur Trade Canoe Routes of Canada Then and Now* (Ottawa: Queen's Printer, 1969), 71–75.

2   For Lorimier, see DCB, VII, 516–517.

3   See Sian Bumsted, "Lady Selkirk and the Fur Trade," *Manitoba History,* 38 (Autumn–Winter 1999/2000).

4   Miles Macdonell to Selkirk, 7 July 1816, SPNAC, 2403–2405.

5   For the full text of the Coltman report, see "A general Statement and Report relative to the disturbances in the Indian Territories of British North America, by W.B. Coltman, Special Commissioner for enquiring into the offences committed in the said Indian Territories, and the circumstances affecting to same," in *Papers Relating to the Red River Settlement,* 12 July 1819, 152–251.

6   Alexander Macdonnell to Selkirk, 13 September 1816, SPNAC, A27, 320A.

7   John Pritchard's account is in his letter to Selkirk, 22 August 1816, SPNAC 2597–2619. Peter Fidler's "Narrative" is in SPNAC, 2509–2531.

8   SPNAC, A27, 320Sa–Sb.

9   The most detailed historical reconstruction of Seven Oaks is by Margaret MacLeod and W.L. Morton in their *Cuthbert Grant of Grantown* (Toronto: McClelland and Stewart, 1974), which in its footnotes lists the principle sources. See also Lyle Dick, "The Seven Oaks Incident and the Construction of a Historical Tradition, 1816 to 1970," *Journal of the Canadian Historical Association* 2 (1991): 90–114, and Robert Coutts and Richard Stewart, eds., *The Forks and the Battle of Seven Oaks in Manitoba History* (Winnipeg: Manitoba Historical Society, 1994).

10 For the contemporary literature, see W.S. Wallace, "The Literature Relating to the Selkirk Controversy," *Canadian Historical Review,* 13 (1932): 45–50.

11 Selkirk to John Askin, 26 July 1816; John Askin to Selkirk, 27 July 1816, SPNAC, 2445–2446.

12 Selkirk to Sir John Sherbrooke, 29 July 1816, SPNAC 1590–1592; see also DCB, VI, p. 236.

13 DCB, VI, 454–457.

14 William McGillivray to John Johnstone, SPNAC, 2454–2459. Selkirk's memorandum of this letter, written 17 July 1816, is in SPNAC, 2423–2424.

15 Selkirk to Sir John Sherbrooke, 29 July 1816, SPNAC, 1590–1592.

16 Selkirk, Instructions to Miles Macdonell, 28 July 1816, SPNAC, 2451–2453.

17 John Allan to Selkirk, 31 July 1816, SPNAC 2463–2467.

18 John McNab's account of arrests at Fort William, 17 August 1816, SPNAC, 2541–2545. See also *Account of the Transactions at Fort William, on Lake Superior, in August 1816, by Mr. Fauché, late Lieutenant of the Regiment De Meurons, Who Accompanied the Earl of Selkirk to Settle at the Red River Colony in North America* (n.p., n.d., but 1817). This little pamphlet is not listed in Wallace's bibliography of the writings in the Selkirk controversy.

19 Statements by North West partners under examination at Fort William, SPNAC 8919–8936.

20 Selkirk to D.A. Boulton, 17 August 1816, SPNAC, 2551.

21   Jean Selkirk to Sir John Sherbrooke, 17 August 1816, SPNAC, 2552–2554. Lady Selkirk subsequently journeyed to Quebec to argue her case in person, and it was on this visit that she became friendly with the Sherbrookes, who admired her courage.

22   Jean Selkirk to Sherbrooke, 22 August 1816, SPNAC, 2557–2558.

23   Sir John Sherbrooke to Lady Selkirk, 24 August 1816, SPNAC, 2559.

24   Selkirk to Lieutenant Governor Gore, 21 August 1816, SPNAC, 2567–2576.

25   Selkirk to AG, 21 August 1816, SPNAC, 2577–2583.

26   Selkirk to Sir John Sherbrooke, 23 August 1816, SPNAC, 2620–2622.

27   Samuel Gale to Lady Selkirk, 8 August 1817, SPNAC, 3929–3934.

28   Selkirk to James Stewart, 24 August 1816, SPNAC, 2623–2626.

Chapter 18

1   McTavish and Vandersluys to Selkirk, 26 August 1816, SPNAC, 2633–2634; Selkirk to McTavish and Vandersluys, 27 August 1816, SPNAC, 2635–2637.

2   Selkirk to Sir John Sherbrooke (not sent), 28 August 1816, SPNAC, 2643–2645.

3   Selkirk to Sir John Sherbrooke, 3 September 1816, SPNAC, 2653–2655.

4   Archibald McDonald to Selkirk, 1 September 1816, SPNAC, 2651–2652.

5   John Strachan to Judge Campbell, 6 September 1816, Strachan Letter Book, Ontario Archives.

6   John Strachan, *A Letter to the Right Honourable the Earl of Selkirk on his Settlement at Red River Near Hudson's Bay* (London: Longman, Hurst, Orme, and Brown, 1816).

7   *Communications from Adam McAdam, Originally Published in the Montreal Herald . . .* (Montreal: W. Gray, 1816), 17–18, 34, 57.

8   Samuel Gale to Selkirk, 11 September 1816, SPNAC, 2702–2704.

9   Agreement between Selkirk and Daniel McKenzie, Fort William, 9 September 1816, SPNAC, 2811–2818.

10   Protest of Daniel McKenzie, 11 November 1816, SPNAC, 2914.

11   Selkirk to Hudson's Bay Company, 24 September 1816, SPNAC, 2711–2717.

12   Selkirk to Maitland & Auldjo, 25 September 1816, SPNAC, 2773–2778.

13   Selkirk to James Stuart, 8 October 1816, SPNAC, 2786–2790.

14   Copy Miles Macdonell to Wintering Partners NWCo, October 1816, SPNAC, 2779–2785.

15   Selkirk to Sir Ld Gibbs, 10 October 1816, SPNAC, 2806.

16   D'Orsonnens to Selkirk, 8 October 1816, SPNAC, 2791–2799.

17   Selkirk to HBC Committee, 1 November 1816, SPNAC, 2897–2898.

18   Selkirk to Captain Owen, 1 November 1816, SPNAC, 2895–2896.

19   *Montreal Herald,* 12 October 1816; Angus Shaw to James Fraser, 14 October 1816, SRO, GD 45/3/17.

20   General Dunlop to Selkirk, 14 October 1816, SPNAC, 2834–2838.

21   *Quarterly Review,* 16, 31 (October 1816): 129–144.

22   For Coltman's biography, see DCB, VI, 166–168.

23   For Fletcher's biography, see DCB, VII, 300–301.

24   James Wood to Attorney General, Upper Canada, 25 October 1816, SPNAC, 2860–2863; Andrew William Cochrane to Selkirk, 28 October 1816, SPNAC, 2873.

25   Sir John Sherbrooke to Bathurst, 11 November 1816, SPNAC, 3120–3123.

26 DCB, VI, 468–469.

27 *Montreal Herald,* 9 October, 30 October, 15 November 1816. These letters were reprinted in 1817 as a pamphlet entitled *The Communications of Mercator, upon the Contest between the Earl of Selkirk and the Hudson's Bay Company, on one Side, and the North West Company on the other* (Montreal: W. Gray, 1817).

28 Selkirk to Sir John Sherbrooke, 12 November 1816, SPNAC, 2918–2922.

29 Selkirk to LG Gore, 12 November 1816, SPNAC, 2915–2917.

30 Selkirk to Captain D'Orsonnens, 2 December 1816, SPNAC, 2938.

31 For a biographical sketch, see DCB, VII, 844–845. Most information on Tanner comes from his own reminiscences, *A Narrative of the Captivity and Adventures of John Tanner,* ed. Edwin James (NY: G and C and H Corvill, 1830).

32 For a detailed narrative of the recapture, see Miles Macdonell to Selkirk, 6 March 1817, SPNAC 3233–3251.

33 W. Coltman to Selkirk, 28 December 1816, SPNAC, 3023–3026.

Chapter 19

1   Selkirk to Lady Selkirk, 23 April 1817, SPNAC, A27, 399E.

2   Selkirk to Michael McDonell, 21 February 1817, SPNAC, 3183.

3   Selkirk to Donald McPherson, 22 February 1817, SPNAC, 3183.

4   Selkirk to Graffenried, 5 March 1817, SPNAC, 3213.

5   Graffenried to Selkirk, 3 February 1817, SPNAC, 3110–3116.

6   Memorandum by the Earl of Selkirk, SPNAC, A27, 1–22.

7   Selkirk to Lady Selkirk, 22 February 1817, SPNAC, A27, 399A–D.

8   Henry Goulburn to Joseph Berens, 16 January 1817, SPNAC, 3058–3059.

9   Copy letter Ellice and McGillivray to HBC, to sign jointly and send to Lord Bathurst, 22 January 1817, SPNAC, 3083–3085.

10 Lord Bathurst to Sir John Sherbrooke, 17 January 1817, *Papers Relating to The Red River Settlement: Return to An Address from the Honourable House of Commons to His Royal Highness the Prince Regent, Dated 24th June 1819* (London: House of Commons, 1819), hereafter 1819 Blue Book, 66.

11 Bathurst to Sherbrooke, 17 January 1817.

12 J. Berens to Bathurst, 6 February 1817, CO 42/177/182–4.

13 Extract, Lord Bathurst's Dispatches, 11 February 1817, SPNAC, 3117–3119.

14 Boulton to Woods, 23 June 1817, SPNAC, 3644.

15 Sir John Sherbrooke to Selkirk, 3 May 1818, SPNAC, A27, 398G–J, which does not summarize the dispatch very well at all.

16 Lady Selkirk to Andrew Colvile, 27 April 1817, SNAC, A27, 398M 2.

17 Lady Selkirk to Lord Selkirk, 7 May 1817, SPNAC, A27, 398M, 1–4.

18 Colvile to Lady Selkirk, 6 February 1817, SPNAC, A27, 390M, 3.

19 Simon McGillivray to Goulburn, 27 May 1817, CO 42/177/260ff.

20 For another interpretation arguing that the Colonial Office was not hostile to Selkirk, see F.L. Barron, "Victimizing His Lordship: Lord Selkirk and the Upper Canadian Courts," *Manitoba History,* 7 (Autumn 1984): 4–22. Barron argues that the trouble was entirely the responsibility of the colonial oligarchies in their interpretation of Bathurst's dispatch.

21 Samuel Shepherd to Bathurst, 16 January 1817, CO 42/178/183–5.

22 J. Berens to Bathurst, 6 February 1817, CO 42/177/182–4.

23 See Alexander Mundell to A. Colvile, 19 April 1817, HBCA A10; and Joseph Berens to Bathurst, 1 May 1817, SPNAC, 3398. Selkirk advocated the same strategy in a letter to the Governor and Committee of the HBC dated 23 April 1817, SPNAC, 3358–60.

24 Lady Selkirk to Selkirk, SPNAC, A27, 390F.

25 Lady Selkirk to Selkirk, "Hogmanay," 1816, SPNAC, A27, 390H.

26 Selkirk to Miles Macdonell, 20 March 1817, SPNAC, 3296–3297.

27 Selkirk to Gore, 17 April 1817, SPNAC 3290–3291.

28 Ibid. See Smith to Selkirk, 31 March 1817, Ontario Archives.

29 Alexander Becher to Selkirk, 27 March 1817, SPNAC 3440–3441.

30 Selkirk to Becher, 27 March 1817, SPNAC 3307–3308.

31 Sherbrooke to Selkirk, 15 May 1817, SPNAC, A27, 398M 4–398F.

32 Samuel Gale to Selkirk, 28 December 1816, SPNAC, 3023–3026.

33 James Stuart to Selkirk, 20 January 1817, SPNAC, 3042–3054.

34 Selkirk to Lady Selkirk, 23 April 1817, SPNAC, HBCT, 399d–411.

35 Selkirk to the Commissioners, 28 April 1817, SPNAC, 3365–3372.

36 Selkirk to Lady Selkirk.

37 London: J. Bretell, 1817.

38 Blackwood MSS, NLS, MS 4002, ff 141.

39 Dugald Stewart to Lady Katherine Halkett, 30 March 1817, NLS, MS 546, ff. 24–27.

40 Lady Selkirk to John Halkett, 12 June 1817 in Chester Martin, Lord Selkirk's Work in Canada (Toronto: Oxford University Press, 1916), quoting lost manuscripts, p. 159n.

41 J.J. Astor to Selkirk, 23 May 1817, SPNAC, 3441–3442. For Astor, see K.W. Porter, John Jacob Astor, Business Man, 2 vol. (NY: Russell and Russell, 1966). For Astoria, consult James Ronda, Astoria & Empire (London and Lincoln: University of Nebraska Press, 1990).

42 Lady Selkirk to Colvile, 19 May 1817, SPNAC, A27, 414ff. The cheering story was picked up by Simon McGillivray, who reported it to Henry Goulburn. See McGillivray to Goulburn, 27 May 1817, CO 42/177/260.

43 See my Fur Trade Wars: The Founding of Western Canada (Winnipeg: Great Plains Publications, 1999), 181–183.

44 Gale to Lady Selkirk, 3 June 1817, SPNAC, A27, 423–438.

45 W. B. Coltman to Gale, 4 June 1817, SPNAC, 3529.

46 Gale to Lady Selkirk, 15 June 1817, SPNAC, A27, 470.

47 Gale to Lady Selkirk, 13 June 1817, SPNAC, A27, 438–444.

48 Ibid.

49 Memorandum by Lieut. Moir, 37th Regiment, SPNAC, A27, 455–465.

50 Ibid., 463.

51 John McNab affidavit, 30 May 1818, SPNAC, 3438.

52 John Spencer to Selkirk, 31 May 1817, SPNAC, 3490–3493.

53 Selkirk to the Commissioners, 28 June 1817, SPNAC, 3615–3621.

54 Ibid., A27, 413A–413F.

55 John Tanner, *A Narrative of the Captivity and Adventures of John Tanner during Thirty Years Residence among the Indians in the Interior of North America* (New York: G. and C. and H Corville, 1830).

56 Selkirk to Gale, 3 July 1817, SPNAC, A27, 497–501.

57 Samuel Gale to Lady Selkirk, 4 July 1817, SPNAC, 3660–3667.

58 Selkirk to the Commissioners, 28 June 1817, SPNAC, 3615–3621.

59 W. B. Coltman to Selkirk, 4 July 1817, SPNAC, 3657–3659.

60 Selkirk to Coltman, 7 July 1817, SPNAC, 3674–3680.

61 Selkirk, "Remarks on the Restitutions ordered by the Proclamation," 11 July 1817, SPNAC, 3717ff.; Simon MacGillivray to William Coltman, 12 July 1817, SPNAC, A27 511–514.

62 Heurter's story was subsequently published in *Narratives of John Pritchard, Pierre Chrysologue Pambrun, and Frederick Damien Heurter, Respecting the Aggressions of the North West Company, against the Earl of Selkirk's Settlement upon Red River* (London: J. Bretell, 1819).

63 Coltman to Selkirk, 11 July 1817, SPNAC, 3727–3728.

64 Order on restitution, 15 July 1817, SPNAC, 3792–3797.

65 Coltman to Sherbrooke, 15 July 1817, SPNAC, A27, 526a–526b.

66 William Smith, "Record of a visit to the route whereby the Metifs or halfbreeds and others proceeded past Fort Douglas near the Forks of the Red River," SPNAC, 3798ff.

67 Deposition of Peter Fidler, 4 August 1817, SPNAC, 3906–3909.

68 [Samuel Gale letter], *Notices on the Claims of the Hudson's Bay Company and the Conduct of its Adversaries* (Montreal: William Gray, 1817).

69 Selkirk to Coltman, 14 July 1817, SPNAC, 3777.

70 Coltman to Selkirk, 15 July 1817, SPNAC, 3812.

71 Selkirk to Coltman, 17 July 1817, SPNAC, 3809–3811.

72 Indian treaty, 18 July 1817, SPNAC, 3824–3825.

73 See my *The Red River Rebellion* (Winnipeg: Great Plains Publications, 1994).

74 For Dickson, see DCB, VI, 209–211.

75 Coltman to respective proprietors, governors, factors, agents, servants or adherents of the Hudson's Bay and North West Companies, 27 July 1817, SPNAC, A27, 523–526.

76 Journal of Alexander Macdonell, SPNAC, 18168–18175.

77 George Bryce, *Manitoba: Its Infancy, Growth and Present Condition* (London: J. Low, Marston, Searle, and Rivington, 1882), 256.

78 Alexander Ross, *The Red River Settlement: Its rise, Progress and Present State . . .* (London: Smith, Elder, 1856), especially Chapter 4.

79 Selkirk to Coltman, 23 August 1817, SPNAC, 3974.

80 Gale to Selkirk, 15 August 1817, SPNAC, A27, 550–553.

81 See DCB, VI, 468–469.

82 H. McKenzie and James Leith, claim for land at RR, 22 August 1817, SPNAC, 3962–3964.

83 Selkirk to Coltman, 24 August 1817, SPNAC, A27, 561–563.

84 Coltman to Gale, 6 September 1817, SPNAC, A27, 572–576.

85 Selkirk to Coltman, 7 September 1817, SPNAC, A27, 578–579.

86　Samuel Gale to Lady Selkirk, September 1817, SPNAC, A27, 582–601.

87　Ibid.

88　For a full illustration of Selkirk's critique of Coltman, see "The Memorial of Thomas Earl of Selkirk to His Grace Charles Duke of Richmond," reprinted in Bumsted, ed., *Collected Writings of Lord Selkirk* (Winnipeg: Manitoba Historical Society, 1988), 2: 110–197.

89　Lady Selkirk to Andrew Colvile, 23 February 1818, SPNAC, A27, 750–755.

90　Selkirk to Lady Selkirk, 7 September 1817, reprinted by John Perry Pritchett in *Canadian Historical Review*, 17 (1936): 406–407.

91　Samuel Gale to Lady Selkirk, 23 October 1817, SPNAC, A27, 610–618.

92　According to George Bryce, who had examined the Selkirk papers at St. Mary's Isle, "There is treasured up still a small note-book, an itinerary of his journey from the Red River colony." *Manitoba*, 261. That notebook no longer survives.

93　Selkirk to Lady Selkirk, 15 November 1817, CHR.

94　Selkirk to Lady Selkirk, 16 December 1817, CHR.

95　Charles Francis Adams., ed., *Memoirs of John Quincy Adams,* IV (Philadelphia: J.B. Lippincott, 1875), 29 (19 December 1817).

96　Selkirk to John Quincy Adams, CHR, 17, 421–423.

97　Selkirk to A. Colvile, 28 December 1817, CHR.

98　John Scott to Selkirk, 21 April 1818, SPNAC, 4824.

99　Selkirk to Lady Selkirk, 31 December 1817, CHR.

100　Gale to Selkirk, 25 December 1817, SPNAC, A27, 639ff.

101　Ibid.

Chapter 20

1　Selkirk to Lady Selkirk, 10 January 1818, CHR.

2　Gene Gressley, "Lord Selkirk and the Canadian Courts," *North Dakota History*, 24 (1957): 89–105, esp. 94.

3　Lady Selkirk to Andrew Colvile, 13 February 1818, SPNAC, HBCT, 740–741.

4　As well as Gressley's article above, see F.L. Barron, "Victimizing His Lordship: Lord Selkirk and the Upper Canadian Courts," *Manitoba History* 7 (Autumn 1984): 14–22.

5　Robert Campbell, *History of the St. Gabriel Street Church* (Montreal: W. Drysdale, 1887), 308.

6　Gressley, "Lord Selkirk," 94.

7　John Beverley Robinson to Sir Peregrine Maitland, 29 November 1819, Ontario Archives, J.B. Robinson Papers.

8　Ibid.

9　Reprinted in J. Bumsted, ed., *Collected Writings of Lord Selkirk* (Winnipeg: Manitoba Historical Society, 1988), 2: 110–197.

10　Lady Selkirk to Andrew Colvile, 6 January 1818, SPNAC, A27, 700–704.

11　For a biography, see W.B. Riddell, *The Life of William Dummer Powell: First Judge of Detroit and Fifth Chief Justice of Upper Canada* (Lansing, MI: Michigan Historical Commission, 1924). See also DCB, VI, 605–613.

12　Memorandum by Doctor Allan, Montreal, 12 Februrary 1818, SPNAC, 4042–4052.

13　Selkirk to Lady Selkirk, 10 January 1818, SPNAC, A27, 645–649.

14 James Woods to Miles Macdonell, 3 January 1818, SPNAC, 4828–4830.

15 Selkirk to John Brown, 18 January [1818], University of Western Ontario library.

16 T. Smith to Selkirk, January 1818, SPNAC, 4400–4402.

17 Selkirk to Lady Selkirk, 17 January 1818, CHR, p. 418.

18 J.B. Robinson to William Elliot, 21 September 1818, SPNAC, A27, 851.

19 Certificate of Western District, 12 January 1819, SPNAC, A27, 903; John Allan to Lady Selkirk, 12 January 1819, SPNAC, 5720–5723.

20 Lady Selkirk to Selkirk, 21 January 1818, SPNAC, A27, 704–707.

21 Selkirk, *Memorial to the Duke of Richmond,* in Bumsted, ed. *Collected Writings,* 182.

22 Lady Selkirk to Andrew Colvile, 19 November 1817, SPNAC, A27, 660–677.

23 Ibid.

24 Lady Selkirk to Colvile, 6 January 1818, SPNAC, A27, 677–690.

25 Lady Selkirk to Colvile, 19 November 1817, SPNAC, A27, 660-677.

26 For the correspondence of this negotiation, see Samuel Gale to William Coltman, 1 January 1818, SPNAC, 4303–44305; Coltman to Sir John Sherbrooke, 5 January 1818, SPNAC, 4331–4332; Coltman to Gale, 5 January 18, SPNAC, 4333; Coltman to Gale, 15 January 1818, SPNAC, 4343–4346; also consult Grace Nute, ed., *Documents Relating to Northwest Missions 1815–1827* (Saint Paul, MN: Minnesota Historical Society, 1942), 3–150; J. O. Plessis, authority for mission to Red River, 20 April 1818, SPNAC, 4816–4821.

27 William Coltman to Samuel Gale, 23 January 1818, SPNAC, 4386–4388.

28 Sir John Sherbrooke to Lord Bathurst, 29 April 1818, CO 42/178/181–2. Bathurst minuted this dispatch.

29 Colin Robertson Affidavit, 27 May 1818, SPNAC, 4462–4466.

30 Ibid.; Selkirk to Committee of Hudson's Bay Company, 14 February 1818, SPNAC, 4536.

31 Coltman to Selkirk, 3 February 1818, SPNAC, 4469–4470.

32 Selkirk to Coltman, 5 February 1818, SPNAC, 4508–4510.

33 Coltman to Selkirk, 10 February 1818, SPNAC 4521–4523.

34 Selkirk to Coltman, 12 February 1818, SPNAC, 4526–4528.

35 Memorial of HBC to Bathurst, 4 February 1818, SPNAC, 4471–4501.

36 Henry Goulburn to J. Berens, 13 February 1818, SPNAC, 4502–4503.

37 W. Coltman to Selkirk, 10 February 1818, SPNAC, 4455–4463.

38 Negotiations with NWC per Coltman, Feby 1818, SPNAC, 4455–6.

39 Coltman to Selkirk, 18 February 1818, SPNAC, 4538–4540.

40 Colin Robertson Affidavit.

41 Lady Selkirk to Andrew Colvile, 23 February 1818, SPNAC, A27, 750–755.

42 Colvile to Lady Selkirk, 3 April 1818, SPNAC, A27, 780a.

43 Coltman to John Allan, 18 March 1818, SPNAC, 4669–4671.

44 Draft Certificate for Coltman, 28 March 1818, SPNAC, 4718–4722; Mem'l 28 March 1818 to Coltman Process Verbal of Indian Council, SPNAC, 4723.

45 Coltman to Selkirk, 29 March 1818, SPNAC, A27, 719–720.

46 George Pyke to Coltman, 1 April 1818, SPNAC, A27, 721–722.

47 Basil Hill to Selkirk, 30 January 1818, SPNAC, 4393–4395.

48 Duke of Buccleuch to Sir James Montgomery, 16 May 1818, SRO, 51/197/64.

49 Sir James Montgomery to Lord Melville, 20 May 1818, SRO, GD 51/197/64.

50 Lord Melville to Lord Hume, 15 June 1818, SRO, GD 51/197/70.

51   Selkirk circular re peerage election, 1 February 1819, SPNAC, 5862–5863.

52   Selkirk to Lord Hopetoun, 2 February 1819, SPNAC, 5860–5861.

53   Selkirk to J.B. Robinson, 8 April 1818, SPNAC, 4778–4782.

54   Samuel Gale, *Notices of the Claims of the Hudson's Bay Company and the Conduct of its Adversaries* (Montreal: William Gray, 1817).

55   Lady Selkirk to Andrew Colvile, 27 February 1818, SPNAC, A27, 756.

56   Enclosed in Lady Selkirk's letter of 26 March 1818, SPNAC, A27, 766.

57   See [Samule Hull Wilcocke], *Report of the trials of Charles de Reinhard and Archibald M'Lellan for murder, at a court of oyer and terminer, held at Quebec, May 1818* (Montreal: James Lane and Nahum Mower, 1818) and William Simpson, *Report at large of the trial of Charles de Reinhard for murder (committed in the Indian Territories), at a court of oyer and terminer held at Quebec, May 1818, to which is annexed a summary of Archibald M'Lellan's indicted as an accessory* (Montreal: N.p., 1819).

58   For Uniacke, see DCB, VII, 872.

59   Lady Selkirk to Andrew Colville, 19 March 1818, SPNAC A27, 758–761.

60   Sir John Sherbrooke to Henry Goulburn, 28 March 1818, CO 42/178/113–114.

61   Selkirk to Lady Selkirk, 26 March 1818, SPNAC, A27, 766.

62   Selkirk to Sir John Sherbrooke, 30 March 1818, SPNAC, 4728–4737.

63   "Memorial to the Duke of Richmond, in Bumsted, ed., *Collected Writings,* 188.

64   N.F. Uniacke to Selkirk, 16 May 1818, SPNAC, 4883–5; Charles Marshall to Mr. Cochrane, 21 May 1818, SPNAC, A27, 777–780.

65   "Memorial to the Duke of Richmond."

66   Selkirk to Samuel Gale, 23 May 1818, McCord Museum, M2984.

67   Coltman to Sherbrooke, 14 May 1818, CO 42/178/208–223.

68   Sherbrooke to Bathurst, 16 May 1818, CO 42/178/206.

69   Coltman to Sherbrooke, 20 May 1818, SPNAC, A27, 724a–724f.

70   For Johnston, see DCB, VI, 360–361.

71   William Johnstone to Selkirk, 31 March 1818, SPNAC 4739–4741; Heads of an agreement, 31 March 1818, SPNAC 19145–19147.

72   See Chapter 10, infra.

73   W.S. Simpson to Selkirk, 20 May 1818, SPNAC, 4942.

74   Selkirk to Dr. S. Kennedy, 4 June 1818, SPNAC, 4970–4971.

75   Selkirk to John Allan, 2 June 1818, SPNAC, 4311–13; John Allan to Samuel Gale, 2 June 1818, SPNAC, 4959–4962.

76   Selkirk to John Allan, 3 June 1818, SPNAC, 4968–4969, reporting on Simpson's demands.

77   J. Allan to Gale, 9 June 1818, SPNAC, 4992–4996.

78   Selkirk to Simpson, 20 June 1818, SPNAC, 5068.

79   John Allan to Lady Selkirk, 22 June 1818, SPNAC, 5069–5072.

80   Ibid, 24 June 1818, SPNAC, 5080–5081.

81   John Allan to Gale, 3 June 1818, SPNAC, 4964–4966.

82   John Allan to Selkirk, 5 June 1818, SPNAC, 4974–4975.

83   Sewell had earlier made this point in a letter to A.W. Cochrane on 4 May 1818, SPNAC, 4862–4863, responding to Selkirk's attempt to get the trial transferred to Great Britain because of jurisdictional uncertainty. See also Selkirk to JB Robinson, 4 June 1818, SPNAC, 4972–4973.

84 Coltman to John Allan, 25 June 1818, SPNAC, 5087–5088.

85 Samuel Gale to Lady Selkirk, 26 and 27 May 1818, SPNAC, A27, 794–796.

Chapter 21

1   Sherbrooke to Selkirk, 11 June 1818, SPNAC 5009; Selkirk to Sherbrooke, 13 June 1818, SPNAC, 5021.

2   Instructions to Provencher and Dumoulin, 20 April 1818, SPNAC, 4822.

3   List of crews and passengers intended for the RR settlement, 15 June 1818, SPNAC 5027–5030.

4   Captain Matthey to Mr. Coltman, 17 June 1818, SPNAC A27, 808–809; Selkirk to Coltman, 19 June 1818, SPNAC A27, 810.

5   Matthey to Selkirk, 10 July 1818, SPNAC, 5151–5160.

6   Matthew to Selkirk, 1 August 1818, SPNAC, 5226–5236.

7   Colin Robertson to Selkirk, 18 July 1818, SPNAC, 6182–6183.

8   Alexander Macdonell to Selkirk, 20 July 1818, SPNAC, 5188–5200; William Laidlaw to Selkirk, 22 July 1818, SPNAC, 5206–5219.

9   List of settlers, August 1818, SPNAC, 5237.

10 Colin Robertson to Selkirk, 7 August 1818, SPNAC, 5249–5252.

11 Selkirk to William Johnston, 4 July 1818, SPNAC, 5140–5141.

12 Selkirk to Thomas Halliday, 4 July 1818, SPNAC, 5139.

13 Memorandum, July 6th, 1818, SPNAC, 5148–5149.

14 Selkirk to Sherbrooke, 10 July 1818, SPNAC, 5150.

15 Selkirk to Lady Selkirk, 6 July 1818, SPNAC, 5147.

16 Selkirk to Lady Selkirk, 10 July 1818, SPNAC A27, 814–817.

17 For Bidwell, see DCB, VI, 54–59. For a recommendation, see Roderick McKay to _____, 1 April 1818, SPNAC, 4750–4752.

18 John Allan to Dr. Robertson, 4 April 1818, SPNAC, 4759.

19 Selkirk to Daniel Washburn, 16 April 1818, SPNAC, 4800–4801.

20 George Ridout to Selkirk, 22 April 1818, SPNAC, 4825–4827.

21 Roderick McKay to _____, 1 April 1818, SPNAC, 4750–4752.

22 Selkirk to J.B. Robinson, 14 July 1818, SPNAC, 5172–5174.

23 Selkirk to N. Uniacke, 14 August 1818, SPNAC 5280–5281.

24 Selkirk to Lady Selkirk, 16 July 1818, SPNAC, A27, 817–821.

25 Ibid., 5175–5176.

26 Selkirk to James Stewart, 14 August 1818, SPNAC, 5273–5279.

27 James Woods to John Allan, 27 March 1818, SPNAC, 4714.

28 William L. Jenks, "The Earl of Selkirk in Michigan Courts," *Michigan Magazine of History,* 12 (1928): 662–668.

29 Samuel Gale to Lady Selkirk, 24 October 1818, SPNAC, A27, 851–858.

30 Return to Bill of Indictment at Sandwich Asseizes, 7 September 1818, SPNAC, 5357.

31 See Chapter 22.

32 Thomas Clark to Selkirk, 2 February 1818, SPNAC, 4467–4468.

33 John Strachan to Mr. Gray, editor, Montreal Herald, 8 September 1818, Ontario Achives, Strachan Papers, Letterbook, 1812–1836.

34   For Gourlay, see Lois Darroch Milani, *Robert Gourlay, Gadfly: Forerunner of the Rebellion in Upper Canada 1837* (Thornhill, ON: Ampersand Press, 1971).

35   James Woods to John Allan, 27 March 1818, SPNAC, 4714.

36   Patrick Brode, *Sir John Beverley Robinson: Bone and Sinew of the Compact* (Toronto: Osgood Society, 1984).

37   Ibid., 45.

38   Ibid., 47–48.

39   Gale to Robinson, 9 September 1818, SPNAC, A27, 839–840. For Fletcher's behaviour, see Chapter 19 infra.

40   Robinson to Allan, 12 September 1818, SPNAC, A27, 843–846; Allan to Robinson, 16 September 1818, SPNAC, A27, 846–850.

41   Ibid., 48.

42   Selkirk to Sir Peregrine Maitland, 21 October 1818, SPNAC 5421–5427.

43   Selkirk to the Duke of Richmond, 22 October 1818, SPNAC, 5428.

44   For trial reports, consult [Samuel Hull Wilcocke, ed.], *Report of the Proceedings connected with the Disputes between the Earl of Selkirk and the Northwest Company, at the Assizes, held in York in Upper Canada, October 1818* (Montreal: [James Lane and Nahum Mower], 1819); and Andrew Amos, *Report of Trials in the Courts of Canada, Relative to the Destruction of the Earl of Selkirk's Settlement on the Red River* (London: J. Murray, 1820). Both these were partisan publications. Wilcocke's contained a preface blaming Selkirk for delaying the trials, while Amos, an experienced English court reporter, was horrified by the proceedings in general.

45   For Levius Sherwood, see DCB, VII, 794–796.

46   James Woods to Selkirk, 31 January 1818, SPNAC, 4396–4399.

47   Gene Gressley, "Lord Selkirk and the Courts," *North Dakota History* 24 (1957): 97.

48   Robinson to Sir Peregrine Maitland, 29 November 1819, Robinson Papers, Ontario Archives.

49   Gale to Lady Selkirk, 24 October 1818, SPNAC, A27, 851–858.

50   *Report of the Proceedings . . . Held at York,* 214–215.

51   Robinson to Maitland, 29 November 1819.

52   Ibid., l.

53   Ibid.

54   Copy Gale to Sir Peregrine Maitland, 29 October 1818, SPNAC, 5484–5486.

55   Daniel Washburn to Samuel Gale, extract, 1819, SPNAC, 5682–5683.

56   Selkirk Law Agent to Lord Bathurst, 5 February 1919, SPNAC, 5893–5897.

57   Samuel Gale to Lady Selkirk, 30 October 1818, SPNAC, A27, 862–872.

58   Dr. Allan to Lady Selkirk, 3 March 1819, SPNAC, A27, 893.

59   Selkirk to Lady Selkirk, 7 November 1818, SPNAC, A27, 882–883.

60   Lady Selkirk to Selkirk, 15 November 1818, SPNAC A27, 885–887.

Chapter 22

1   Selkirk to J. Wedderburn, 1819, SPNAC, 5772.

2   Selkirk to Lady Selkirk, 9 November 1818, Ontario Archives. For the Pulteney settlement, see Helen I. Cowan, *Charles Williamson: Genesee Promoter, Friend of Anglo-American Rapprochment* (Rochester, NY: Rochester Historical Society, 1941).

3   Selkirk to John Greig, 2 December 1818, Ontario Archives. See also Selkirk's "Sketch American Scheme," Ontario Archives.

4   Selkirk to James Woods, 9 January 1819, SPNAC, 5705–5708.

5   A. Maitland to Selkirk, 1 January 1819, SPNAC, 5688–5689.

6   John Allan to Lady Selkirk, 12 January 1819, SPNAC, 5720–5723.

7   John Allan to Lady Selkirk, 1 February 1819, SPNAC, 5766.

8   Lady Isabella Douglas to Selkirk, 5 January 1819, SPNAC, 5692–5694.

9   Selkirk to George Garden, 23 January 1819, SPNAC, 5741.

10 J.W. Clarke to William Dummer Powell, 12 November 1818, Powell Papers, Toronto Public Library.

11 Halkett to Lord Bathurst, 30 January 1819, SPNAC, 5776–5853.

12 James Wedderburn to Selkirk, 13 January 1819, SPNAC, 5733–5736.

13 John Macdonald to Selkirk, 27 January 1819, SPNAC, 5755–6.

14 Henry Goulburn to Halkett, 9 February 1819, SPNAC, 5854–5856.

15 Halkett to Bathurst, 11 February 1819, SPNAC, 5856–58567

16 John Allan to Lady Selkirk, 12 January 1819, SPNAC, 5720–5723.

17 Dr. Allan to Colvile, 25 January [1821], SPNAC, 5744; John Allan to Lady Selkirk, 31 January 1819, SPNAC, 5724–5730.

18 Robinson to Maitland, 29 November 1819, Robinson Papers, Ontario Archives.

19 John Allan to Lady Selkirk, 3 March 1819, SPNAC, A27, 893.

20 Thomas Clark to Maitland Garden & Auldjo, 14 November 1819, 6567–6568.

21 Lady Katherine Halkett to Lady Selkirk, 1819, quoted in Chester Martin, *Lord Selkirk's Work in Canada* (Toronto: Oxford Univeristy Press, 1916), 165.

22 Certification of indictment, 1 March 1819, Liverpool Papers, BM Add. Mss. 38368, f 2375.

23 John Allan to Lady Selkirk, 3 March 1819, SPNAC, 5975–5981.

24 Lady Selkirk to Selkirk, 26 March 1819, SPNAC, A27, 894.

25 DCB, X. 618–619.

26 Gale to Lady Selkirk, July 1819, SPNAC, 6394–6402.

27 Selkirk to John Greig, 27 March 1819, 6020–6021.

28 Selkirk to Gale, 27 March 1819, SPNAC, 6022.

29 Selkirk to Melville, 28 January 1819, NLS GD 51/197/73.

30 Selkirk to Lord Hopetoun, 2 February 1819, SPNAC 5860–5861.

31 Selkirk to Lord Sidmouth, 4 February 1819, SPNAC, 5890–5892.

32 Selkirk to Lord Napier, 24 February 1819, SPNAC, 5943–5944.

33 Selkirk to Lady Selkirk, 29 March 1819, SPNAC, 6028; *Caledonian Mercury,* 20 March 1819.

34 Selkirk to James Stewart, 6 March 1819, SPNAC, 5985–5987.

35 Selkirk to Stewart, 6 April 1819, SPNAC, 5984.

36 Selkirk to Earl of Liverpool, 8 February 1819, SPNAC, 5909–5914.

37 Bathurst to Selkirk, 15 February 1819, SPNAC, 5915.

38 Gale to Selkirk, 9 May 1819, SPNAC, A27, 895–899.

39 Selkirk to Robert Laidlaw, 1 March 1819, SPNAC, 5971–5972.

40 Archibald Campbell to Selkirk, 17 March 1819, SPNAC, 6038–6039.

41 Colvile to Archibald Campbell, 6 April 1819, SPNAC, 6048–6055.

42 Colvile to Campbell, 10 July 1819, SPNAC, 6056.

43 Lady Selkirk to Selkirk, 14 March 1819, SPNAC, A27, 893A.

44 Lord Selkirk to J.S., 29 March 1819, SPNAC, 6028.

45 It is reprinted in Bumsted, ed. *Collected Writings of Lord Selkirk* (Winnipeg: Manitoba Historical Society, 1988), 2: 204–230.

46 Alexander Mundell to Selkirk, 21 April 1819, SPNAC, 6106–6107.

47 John Bretell Printer to Selkirk, 20 May 1819, SPNAC, 6203–6205.

48 Bumsted, *Collected Writings,* 205–206.

49 Ibid., 210.

50 Ibid., 224.

51 Dugald Stewart to Selkirk, 27 April 1819, SPNAC, 6127–6129.

52 Lord Liverpool to Selkirk, 27 April 1819, SPNAC, 6132–6133.

53 Alexander Macdonald to Selkirk, 26 March 1819, SPNAC, 6009–6010.

54 Reprinted in Bumsted, *Collected Writings,* 2: 248–273.

55 Ibid., 264.

56 Ibid., 266–267.

57 Ibid., 270.

58 Ibid., 271. Concluding at this point dates the completion of this pamphlet as June 1819.

59 Untitled pamphlet reprinted in Bumsted, *Collected Writings,* 2: 232–246.

60 Robert Laidlaw to Selkirk, 10 April 1819, SPNAC, 6069–6072.

61 William Anderson to Selkirk, 13 April 1819, SPNAC. 6079–6084.

62 Selkirk to William Anderson, 16 April 1819, SPNAC, 6092–6094.

63 Selkirk to Robert Laidlaw, 17 April 1819, 6101–6103.

64 Selkirk to J. Wardrop, 16 April 1819, SPNAC, 6095–6096.

65 John Halkett to Lord Binning, 22 April 1819, Liverpool Papers, BM Add Mss 38276, f 310.

66 Selkirk to Lady Selkirk, 28 April 1819, SPNAC, 6146–6147; Copy Draft Deeds J. Halkett, 29 April 1819, SPNAC, 6148.

67 Selkirk to Robert Dickson, 21 May 1819, SPNAC, 6208–6212.

68 Sir James Hall to Selkirk, 30 April 1819, SPNAC, 6149–6151.

69 Ibid.; 3 May 1819, SPNAC, 6156–6158.

70 Dugald Bannatyne to Selkirk, 12 May 1819, SPNAC, 6186–6188.

71 Selkirk to Lord Arch'd Hume, 14 May 1819, SPNAC, 6190.

72 Selkirk to Scarlett, 19 May 1819, SPPNAC, 6202.

73 John Brettell Printer to Selkirk, 20 May 1819, SPNAC, 6203–6205.

74 Selkirk to _____, 20 May 1819, Robert Logan Papers, Public Archives of Manitoba, MG2/C23.

75 Selkirk to Gale, 20 May 1819, SPNAC 6245–6247.

76 Zachary McAulay to Selkirk, 28 May 1819, SPNAC, 6244–6245.

77 Selkirk to Colvile, 18 May 1819, SPNAC, 6195–6196

78 Henry Goulbourn to Governor of HBC, 18 May 1819, SPNAC, A27, 944–945.

79 Berens to Bathurst, 9 June 1819, SPNAC, A27, 945–947.

80 Simon McGillivray to Lord Liverpool, 2 June 1819, Liverpool Papers, BM Add Mss 38380, 19–21.

81 Selkirk to Alexander Garden, 29 June 1819, SPNAC, A27, 900–902.

82 Duke of Richmond to Selkirk, 22 May 1819, SPNAC, A27, 905–906.

83 Colonel Ready to Mr. Stuart, 22 May 1819, SPNAC, A27, 906–907.

84 Stuart to Ready, 25 May 1819, SPNAC, A27, 907–910.

85 Ready to Stuart, 28 May 1819, SPNAC, A27, 910–911.

86 Stuart to Ready, 9 June 1819, SPNAC, A27, 912–915.

87 Maitland, Garden & Auldjo to Colonel Ready, 17 June 1819, SPNAC, A27, 923–927.

88 Ready to Maitland, Garden & Auldjo, 24 June 1819, SPNAC, A27, 927–928.

89 Maitland, Garden & Auldjo to Colonel Ready, 29 June 1819, SPNAC, A27, 931–932.

90 Ready to Maitland, Garden & Auldjo, 10 July 1819, SPNAC, A27, 933–934.

91 Sr. James Montgomery, *Substance of the Speech of Sir James Montgomery, Bart., in the House of Commons, on the 24th of June, 1819, on bringing forward his motion relative to the Petition of Mr. John Pritchard of the Red River Settlement* (London: J. Brettell, 1819). A handwritten note on one copy of this item reads "Not published."

92 Robert Isaac Wilberforce and Samuel Wilberforce, *The Life of William Wilberforce / In Five Volumes* (London: J. Murray, 1838), 5: 27.

93 Selkirk to Bathurst, 16 July 1819, SPNAC, 6313–6316. A letter from Bathurst on 28 July confirmed that the case had now been submitted to the Privy Council. Bathurst to Selkirk, 28 July 1819, SPNAC, 6367–6368.

94 Selkirk to George Garden, 29 June 1819, SPNAC, A27, 900–902.

95 Bathurst to Duke of Richmond, 10 July 1819, Powell Papers, Toronto Public Library.

96 Selkirk to Wilberforce, 22 July 1819, SPNAC, 6338–6342.

97 Wilberforce to Selkirk, 26 July 1819, SPNAC, 6361–6365.

98 R. Dickson to Lady Selkirk, 21 July 1819, SPNAC, 6332–6335.

Chapter 23

1 Selkirk to James Wedderburn, 1819, SPNAC, A27, 923.

2 Selkirk to George Garden, 29 July 1819, SPNAC, 6369–6371.

3 Selkirk to Judge Stewart, 4 August 1819, SPNAC, 6432–6433.

4 [George William Lefevre], *The Life of a Travelling Physician* (London: Longman's, 1843), 1: 23.

5 John Mure to Selkirk, 12 August 1819, SPNAC, 6445–6471

6 Lady Selkirk to Miles Macdonell, 29 August 1819, SPNAC, 6453–6464.

7 Selkirk to Hardwicke, 25 September [1819], Hardwicke Papers, BM Add Mss. 35652, f. 268.

8 *Life of a Travelling Physician*, 36.

9 Frederick Mathey to Selkirk, 2 August 1819, SPNAC, 6406–6423.

10 See E.E. Rich's introduction to his edition of *Journal of Occurrences in the Athabasca Department by George Simpson, 1820 and 1821, and Report* (Toronto: Champlain Society, 1938).

11   C. Stuart Houston, ed., *Arctic Artist: The Journal and Paintings of George Back, Midshipman with Franklin, 1819–1822* (Montreal and Kingston: McGill-Queen's University Press, 1994); Paul Nanton, *Arctic Breakthrough: Franklin's Expeditions, 1819–1847* (London: Clarke Irwin, 1971). For a modern life of Franklin, consult Martyn Beardsley, *Deadly Winter: The Life of Sir John Franklin* (Annapolis, MD: Naval Institute Press, 2002).

12   Colvile to Gale, 24 December 1819, SPNAC, A27, 968–973.

13   Sir James Montgomery to Colvile, 2 December 1819, SPNAC, A27, 967.

14   Selkirk to Colville, 11 December 1819, SPNAC, A27, 966a–966g.

15   For Ellice, see James M. Colhart, "Edward Ellice and North America," PhD dissertation, Princeton University, 1971.

16   Ibid.

17   Selkirk to Colvile, 8 January 1820, SPNAC, A27, 973A–973F.

18   Lady Selkirk to Colvile, 22 January 1820, SPNAC, A27, 978–984.

19   Miles Macdonell to Colvile, 1 February 1820, SPNAC, A27, 975–977.

20   Colvile to Gale, 19 February 1820, SPNAC, A27, 986–989.

21   Colvile to Robert Laidlaw, 5 February 1820, SPNAC, 6695–6696.

22   Robert Laidlaw to Selkirk, 10 February 1820, SPNAC 6697–6701.

23   Selkirk to Gale, 24 January 1820, SPNAC, 6659–6665.

24   A.D. Stewart to Selkirk, 30 January 1820, SPNAC, 6891–6893.

25   Colvile to Clark, 30 March 1820, SPNAC, 6793–6794.

26   SPNAC, A27, between pages 699 and 700.

27   Colvile to Alexander Macdonell, 25 May 1820, SPNAC, 6872–6881.

28   Lady Selkirk to Lady Halkett, 15 May 1820, SPNAC, A27, 1005A.

Chapter 24

1   Marjorie Campbell, *The North West Company* (Vancouver: Douglas and McIntyre, 1983), 254–75.

2   See the sketch of John McLoughlin in DCB, VIII, 575–581.

3   John Halkett to Lady Selkirk, 10 January 1821, SPNAC, A27, 1018–1023.

4   Andrew Colvile to Lady Selkirk, January 1821, SPNAC, A27, 1024–1026.

5   Quoted in DCB, VI, p. 456.

6   E.E. Rich, *The History of the Hudson's Bay Company, 1670–1870* (London: Hudson's Bay Record Society, 1956–1959), 2: 384. 400.

7   Ibid.

8   Ibid.

9   Madge Wolfenden, ed., "Career of a Scotch Boy," *British Columbia Historical Quarterly* 18 (1954): 133–238.

10   For Halkett's own account of the incident, see J. Halkett to Earl of Dalhousie, 19 October 1821, SRO GD 45/3/17.

11   See "Thomas Thain," DCB, VI, 764–766.

12   John Galbraith, *The Hudson's Bay Company as an Imperial Factor, 1821–1869* (Toronto: University of Toronto Press, 1957).

13 In general, see my *Trials and Tribulations: The Red River Settlement and the Emergence of Manitoba 1811–1870* (Winnipeg: Great Plains Publications, 2003).

14 For the Swiss business, consult my "The Swiss and Red River, 1819–1826," in *Thomas Scott's Body and Other Essays on Early Manitoba History* (Winnipeg: University of Manitoba Press, 2000), 57–76.

15 Selkirk to James Stewart, 6 March 1819, SPNAC, 5985–5987. For Charles Fairbanks, see DCB, XI, 308–309.

16 William Johnston to Selkirk, 21 August 1819, SPNAC, 6456–6452.

17 Samuel P. Fairbanks to _____, July 1820, SPNAC, 19153–19156.

18 In one of his last dealings with the island in 1819, Lord Selkirk had written to James Stewart that he knew "the Soil of the Island is abundantly productive of falsehood & calumny." Selkirk to James Stewart, 6 March 1819.

19 A. Colvile to Messrs Charles and Samuel Fairbanks, 7 December 1820, SPNAC, 19161.

20 A. Colvile to William Johnston, 12 April 1823, SPNAC, 19169–19170.

21 DCB, IX, 222–224.

BIBLIOGRAPHY

Manuscripts

British Museum, London
    Add Mss 27811 (Place Collection)
    Add Mss 31897
    Add Mss 35652 (Hardwicke Papers)
    Add Mss 37849
    Add Mss 37884
    Add Mss 38368-80 (Liverpool Papers)
    Dropmore Mss.

Ewart Library, Dumfries
    Lord Selkirk to Sir Alexander Gordon, 1799

Hornel Library, Kirkcudbright
    Lord Daer letters
    Minutes of Kirkcudbright Council, 1799

Hudson's Bay Company Archives, Winnipeg
    A1
    A5
    E8
    F3

McCord Museum, Montreal
    Lord Selkirk to Samuel Gale, 23 May 1818

McGill University Library
    Selkirk to A. Mundell, 11 March 1809

National Archives of Canada
    Selkirk Papers
    MacDonell Papers
    RG 4

National Library of Scotland, Edinburgh
    Ms 3420
    Ms 3881
    Ms 8273 ("Collection of Papers in the Process of the Reduction of the Service of
    Archibald Douglas")
    Ms 10787 (Davidson and 4th Lord Selkirk correspondence)
    Acc 6110
    E96 (Ellice Papers)
    Sir James Hall Journal
    Small Collections

Public Archives of Manitoba, Winnipeg
    Bryce Papers
    Robert Logan Papers

Public Archives of Ontario, Toronto
    Boulton Papers
    Macdonell Papers
    RG 1
    John Strachan Letter Book
    John Beverley Robinson Papers
    Selkirk Correspondence

Public Archives of Prince Edward Island
    Ms 3744
    Supreme Court Papers

Public Record Office, London
    CO 42
    CO 226
    FO 115

Scottish Catholic Archives, Edinburgh
    Blairs Letters

Scottish Record Office, Edinburgh
    CD 4
    CE 74
    GD 18 (Sir John Clerk of Penicuik Papers)
    GD 26 (Leven and Melville Papers)
    GD 38
    GD 45 (Dalhousie Papers)
    GD 46
    GD 51
    GD 112
    GD 128
    GD 150
    GD 206 (Hall of Dunglass Papers)
    GD 224
    GD 248

GD 2061
GD 2378
RD 3
RH 2
RH 4 (Sinclair Papers)
Lennoxlove Muniments, Robert Brown Papers

Sutherland Papers, St. Andrew's University, St. Andrew's, Scotland

United States Naval Academy, Annapolis, Maryland
Selkirk Papers

University of Edinburgh Library, Edinburgh
Class Books of the University of Edinburgh
Dugald Stewart Diary of Tours in England and Scotland, 1797-1803
Laing Mss
Mic. M. 1206 (Speculative Society Minutes, 1775-1800)
Archibald Macdonald of Dalilia Papers

University of Glasgow Library, Glasgow
Thomas-Cullen Papers

University of Western Ontario Library
Regional Collection 4378

Contemporary Printed

Account of the Transactions at Fort William, on Lake Superior, in August 1816, by Mr. Fauché, late Lieutenant of the Regiment De Meurons, who Accompanied the Earl of Selkirk to Settle at the Red River Colony in North America. N. p., n. d. [1817].

Amicus [probably James Gordon of Craig]. *Eight Letters on the Subject of the Earl of Selkirk's Pamphlet on Highland Emigration, as They Lately Appeared under the Signature of AMICUS in One of the Edinburgh Newspapers.* London: Longman, Hurst, Rees, and Lorne, 1806.

Amos, Andrew. *Report of Trials in the Courts of Canada, Relative to the Destruction of the Earl of Selkirk's Settlement on the Red River; with Observations.* London: J. Murray, 1820.

Anon. *The Defects of a University Education.* London: E. Dilly, 1772.

Anon. *Remarks on the Earl of Selkirk's Observations on the Present State of the Highland.* Edinburgh: John Anderson, 1806.

Annals of Agriculture, 26.

Boucher, François. *Relations donnée par lui-même des évènements qui ont eu lieu sur le territoire des sauvages depuis le mois d'octobre 1815, jusqu'au 19 juin 1816, époque de la mort de Mr. Semple, avec les détails de son long emprisonment, jusquà son jugement.* Montreal: N. p., 1819.

Brown, Robert. *Strictures and Remarks on the Earl of Selkirk's Observations on the Present State of the Highlands of Scotland.* Edinburgh: Abernathy and Walker, 1806.

Caledonian Mercury, The. 15 December 1792; 6 December 1806, 20 March 1819.

Cartwright, F.D., ed. *The Life and Correspondence of Major Cartwright.* London: N. p., 1826.

Chappell, Lt. Edward. *Narrative of a Voyage to Hudson's Bay in His Majesty's Ship Rosamund.* London: J. Mawman, 1817.

Critical Review, 3rd ser., 5 (1805), 366–378; 3rd ser., 8 (1806): 474–78.

Douglas, Basil William. "Petition and Complaint of the Right Honourable Basil William Douglas, 23 December 1789." *British Museum Law and Parliamentary Tracts.*

Edinburgh Advertiser, 28 November 1807.

Edinburgh Evening Courant, 15 October 1791.

Edinburgh Review, or Critical Journal, 1 (1803), 7 (1805), 186–202.

Farmer's Magazine, 3, February 1803; 5 (1805); 6 (1806), 241–8.

Fergusson, Robert, Junior, of Craigdarroch. *The Proposed Reform of the Counties of Scotland Impartially Examined . . . .* Edinburgh: Elphinston Balfour, 1792.

[Gale, Samuel]. *Notices on the Claims of the Hudson's Bay Company and the Conduct of its Adversaries.* Montreal: William Gray, 1817.

Gentleman's Magazine, May, 1795; 1807.

[Halkett, John, ed]. *Correspondence in the years 1817, 1818, and 1819, between Earl Bathurst and J. Halkett, Esq., on the Subject of Lord Selkirk's Settlement at the Red River in North America.* London: J. Brettell, 1819.

[Halkett, John]. *Postscript to the Statement Respecting the Earl of Selkirk's Settlement Upon the Red River.* Montreal, n. p., 1818.

[Halkett, John]. *Statement Respecting the Earl of Selkirk's Settlement of Kildonan, upon the Red River in North America, Its Destruction in the years 1815 and 1816; and the Massacre of Governor Semple and His Party.* London: J. Brettell, 1816.

[Halkett, John]. *Statement Respecting the Earl of Selkirk's Settlement of Kildonan, upon the Red River in North America, Its Destruction in the years 1815 and 1816; and the Massacre of Governor Semple and His Party, with Observations upon a Recent Publication, Entitled "A Narrative of Occurrences in the Indian Countries," &c.* London: J. Brettell, 1817.

"Highlander, A." *The Present Conduct of the Chieftains and Proprietors of Lands in the Highlands of Scotland.* Edinburgh: N. p., 1773.

Inverness Journal and Northern Advertiser, 19 April 1811, 21 June 1811.

Irvine, Alexander. *An Inquiry into the Causes and Effects of Emigration from the Highlands and Western Islands of Scotland, with Observations on the Means to be Employed for Preventing It.* Edinburgh: N. p., 1802.

Journal of a Voyage on the North West Coast of North America during the Years 1811, 1812, 1813 and 1814 by Gabriel Franchère. Edited by W. Kaye Lamb. Toronto: Champlain Society, 1969.

McAdam, Adam. *Communications from Adam McAdam, Originally Published in the Montreal Herald, in Reply to Letters Inserted Therein Under the Signature of Archibald Macdonald, Respecting Lord Selkirk's Red River Colony.* Montreal: W. Gray, 1816.

MacDonald, Archibald. *Narrative respecting the Destruction of the Earl of Selkirk's Settlement upon Red River . . . in 1815.* London: J. Brettell, 1816.

_____. *Reply to the Letter, Lately Addressed to the Earl of Selkirk, by the Hon. and Rev. John Strachan, D.D., &c. Being Four Letters (Reprinted from the Montreal Herald), Containing a Statement of Facts, Concerning the Settlement on Red River, in the District of Ossiniboia, Territory of the Hudson's Bay Company, Properly Called Rupert's Land.* Montreal: W. Gray, 1816.

Macdonell, Alexander Greenfield. *A Narrative of Transactions in the Red River Country: from the Commencement of the Operations of the Earl of Selkirk, till the Summer of the Year 1816.* London: B. M'Millan, 1819.

Mackenzie, Alexander. *A View of the Political State of Scotland at the Late General Election.* Edinburgh: J. Ainslie, 1790.

Mackenzie, Sir Alexander. *Voyages from Montreal on the River St. Lawrence, through the Continent of North America, to the Frozen and Pacific Oceans, in the Years 1789 and 1793.* London: T. Cadell Jr. & W. Davies, Cobbett and Morgan, and W. Creach, 1801.

M'Kenzie, Daniel. *A Letter to the Rt. Hon. the Earl of Selkirk in Answer to a Pamphlet Entitled "A Postscript in Answer to the Statement Respecting the Earl of Selkirk's Settlement on the Red River in North America."* Sandwich: N. p., 1818.

[Malthus, Thomas]. *An Essay on the Principle of Population, as It Affects the Future Improvement of Society, with Remarks on the Speculations of Mr. Godwin, M. Condorcet, and Other Writers.* London: N. p., 1798.

Mercator [Henry McKenzie]. *The Communications of "Mercator" upon the Contest between the Earl of Selkirk and the Hudson's Bay Company on One Side, and the North West Company on the Other.* Montreal: W. Gray, 1817.

Montgomery, Sir James. *Substance of the Speech of Sir James Montgomery, Bart., in the House of Commons, on the 24th of June, 1819, on Bringing Forward His Motion Relative to the Petition of Mr. John Pritchard, of Red River Settlement.* London: J. Brettell, 1819.

Montreal Herald, 28 August, 9 October, 12 October, 30 October, 15 November, 20 November 1816. [The "Mercator" letters of Henry McKenzie].

Monthly Review, 5 (1806), 241–248.

Narratives of John Pritchard, Pierre Chrysologue Pambrun, and Frederick Damien Heurter, Respecting the Aggression of the North West Company, Against the Earl of Serkirk's Settlement Upon Red River. London: J. Brettell, 1819.

Observations upon the Papers Laid before the House of Commons, Relating to the Red River Settlement. London: N. p., 1820.

Papers Relating to the Red River Settlement: Viz: Return to An Address from the Honourable House of Commons to his Royal Highness the Prince Regent Dated 24th June 1819; for Copies or Extracts of Official Communications Which May Have Taken Place between the Secretary of State and the Provincial Government of Upper or Lower Canada, or to Any Complaints Made of Those Proceedings by Lord Selkirk or the Agents of the Hudson's Bay or the North-West Companies; Also for Copies or Extracts of the Reports Made by the Commissioners of Special Inquiry, Appointed to Inquire into the Offenses Committed In the Indian Territory so Far as can be Made Public without Prejudice to the Public Service, or to Judicial Proceedings Now Pending in Canada. London: House of Commons, 1819.

Pearson, John. *Review of Lord Selkirk's Objections to a Reform in the Representation of the People: In a Letter to John Cartwright Esq. from John Pearson, Esq.* London: J Johnson, 1809.

Quarterly Review, 16, 31 (October 1816), 129–144.

Robertson, William. *Proceedings Relating to the Peerage of Scotland from January 16, 1707 to April 29, 1788.* Edinburgh: Bell and Bradfute, 1790.

Rolliad, The: Probationary Odes and Political Miscellanies. London: J. Ridgway, 1795.

Saltoun, Alexander Lord. *Thoughts on the Disqualification of the Eldest Sons of the Peers of Scotland, to Sit from that Country to Parliament.* London: T. Cadell and John Robson, 1788.

Scots Magazine, 67 (1805), 609–616.

Selkirk, Lord. *A Letter Addressed to John Cartwright, Esq. of the Committee at the Crown and Anchor on the Subject of Parliamentary Reform.* London: 1809. Reprinted in *The Collected Writings of Lord Selkirk,* edited by J.M. Bumsted, I, 359–366. Winnipeg: Manitoba Historical Society, 1984, 1988.

_____. *A Letter to the Earl of Liverpool, 1819.* London: 1819. Reprinted in *Collected Writings,* II, 205–230.

_____. *A Letter to the Peers of Scotland by the Earl of Selkirk.* London: 1807. Reprinted in *Collected Writings,* I, 242–259.

_____. *The Memorial of Thomas Earl of Selkirk, ca 1819.* Montreal: 1819. Reprinted in *Collected Writings,* II, 111–204.

_____. *Observations on the Present State of the Highlands of Scotland.* London: 1805. Reprinted in *Collected Writings,* I, 101–241.

_____. *On the Necessity of a More Effectual System of National Defence, and the Means of Establishing the Permanent Security of the Kingdom.* London: 1808. Reprinted in *Collected Writings,* I, 290–358.

_____. "Ossiniboia, ca. 1815." In *Collected Writings,* II, 9–46.

_____. *A Sketch of the British Fur Trade, 1815.* London: 1816. Reprinted in *Collected Writings,* II, 48–110.

_____. *Substance of the Speech of the Earl of Selkirk, in the House of Lords, Monday, August 10, 1807, on the Defence of the Country.* London, 1807. Reprinted in *Collected Writings,* I, 260–289.

_____. "Untitled Pamphlet on Indian Education, ca. 1814." In *Collected Writings,* II, 1–8.

_____. "Untitled Pamphlet on Poor Relief." In *Collected Writings,* I, 86–99.

_____. "Untitled Pamphlet, 1819." In *Collected Writings,* II, 233–248.

_____. "Untitled Pamphlet, ca. 1819." In *Collected Writings,* II, 249–273.

Simpson, William S. *Report at Large of the Trial of Charles de Reinhard for Murder (Committed in the Indian Territories) at a Court of Oyer and Terminer Held At Quebec, May 1818, to Which is Annexed a Summary of Archibald M'Lellan's Indictment as an Accessory.* Montreal: N. p., 1819.

Stewart, John. *An Account of Prince Edward Island.* London: Winchester and Sons, 1806.

Strachan, John. *A Letter to the Right Honourable the Earl of Selkirk on His Settlement at Red River Near Hudson's Bay.* London: Longman, Hurst, Orme, and Brown, 1816.

Tanner, John. *A Narrative of the Captivity and Adventures of John Tanner during Thirty Years Residence among the Indians in the Interior of North America*. New York: G. and C. and H. Corvill, 1830.

To the Right Honorable Henry Earl Bathurst, One of His Majesty's Principal Secretaries of State, . . . The Memorial of Messrs. M'Tavish, Fraser, and Co. and Messrs. Inglis, Ellice, and Co. (London, N. p., 1816).

Valuation Roll of the Stewartry of Kirkcudbright as Made Up by the Commissioners of Land Tax for the Said Stewartry, 14th June 1799. Dumfries: R. Jackson, 1800.

[Wilcocke, Samuel Hull]. *A Narrative of Occurrences in the Indian Countries of North America, since the Connexion of the Right Hon. the Earl of Selkirk with the Hudson's Bay Company, and His Attempt to Establish a Colony on the Red River: with a Detailed Account of His Lordship's Military Expedition to, and Subsequent Proceedings at Fort William in Upper Canada*. London: B. Macmillan, 1817.

[_____]. *Report of the Proceedings at a Court of Oyer and Terminer Appointed for the Investigation of Cases from the Indian Territories, Held . . . at Quebec . . . 21 October 1819*. Montreal: William Gray, 1819.

[_____]. *Report of the Proceedings Connected with the Disputes Between the Earl of Selkirk and the North West Company, at the Assizes, held in York in Upper Canada, October 1818*. Montreal: [James Lane and Nahum Mower] 1819.

[_____]. *Report of the trials of Charles de Reinhard and Archibald M'Lennan for Murder, at a Court of Oyer and Terminer, Held at Quebec, May 1818*. Montreal: James Lane and Nahum Mower, 1818.

[_____]. *The Trial of John Cooper and Hugh Bennerman*. Montreal: N. p., 1819.

Wood, John Philip. *The Peerage of Scotland by Robert Douglas*. 2 vols. Edinburgh: Archibald Constable, 1813.

Later Printed Books

Abernathy, Thomas Perkins. *The Burr Conspiracy*. New York: Oxford University Press, 1954.

Adam, Charles Elphinstone, ed. *View of the Political State of Scotland in the Last Century*. Edinburgh: D. Douglass, 1887.

Adam, R.J., ed. *Papers on Sutherland Estate Management 1802–1816*. Edinburgh: Scottish Record Office, 1972.

Adams, Charles Francis, ed. *Memoirs of John Quincy Adams*, IV. Philadelphia: J.B. Lippincott and Co., 1875.

Anstey, Roger. *The Atlantic Slave Trade and British Abolition, 1760–1810*. London: Macmillan, 1975.

Beardsley, Martyn. *Deadly Winter: The Life of Sir John Franklin*. Annapolis, MD: Naval Institute Press, 2002.

Begg, Alexander. *History of the North-West*. 3 vols. Toronto: Hunter and Rose, 1894.

Binger, Herman. *The Louisiana Purchase and Our Title West of the Rocky Mountains*. Washington: N. p., 1890.

Brode, Patrick. *Sir John Beverley Robinson: Bone and Sinew of the Compact*. Toronto: Osgoode Society, 1984.

Browne, Roy B., ed. *The Burke-Paine Controversy: Texts and Criticism.* New York: Harcourt, Brace and World, 1963.

Brumwell, Stephen. *Redcoats: The British Soldier and War in the Americas, 1755–1763.* Cambridge: Cambridge University Press, 2002.

Bryce, George. *The Life of Lord Selkirk: Colonizer of Western Canada.* Toronto: Musson Book Co., [1912].

_____. *Mackenzie, Selkirk, Simpson.* Toronto; Morang, 1910.

_____. *Manitoba: Its Infancy, Growth, and Present Condition.* London: J. Low, Marston, Searle, and Rivington, 1882.

_____. *The Romantic Settlement of the Pioneers of Manitoba.* Winnipeg: Russell, Long, 1909.

Bryson, Gladys. *The Scottish Inquiry of the Eighteenth Century.* Princeton, NJ: Princeton University Press, 1945.

Buchan, James. *Crowded with Genius: The Scottish Enlightenment; Edinburgh's Moment of the Mind.* New York: Perennial, 2004.

Buel, Richard, Jr. *Securing the Revolution: Ideology in American Politics, 1789–1815.* Ithaca, New York: Cornell University Press, 1972.

Bumsted, J.M., ed. *The Collected Writings of Lord Selkirk.* 2 vols. Winnipeg: Manitoba Historical Society, 1984, 1988.

_____. *Dictionary of Manitoba Biography.* Winnipeg: University of Manitoba Press, 1999.

_____. *Fur Trade Wars: The Founding of Western Canada.* Winnipeg: Great Plains Publications, 1999.

_____. *Land, Settlement, and Politics on Prince Edward Island.* Kingston and Montreal: McGill-Queen's University Press, 1987.

_____. *The People's Clearance: Highland Emigration to British North America, 1770–1815.* Edinburgh: Edinburgh University Press; Winnipeg: University of Manitoba Press, 1984.

_____. *The Red River Rebellion.* Winnipeg: Great Plains Publications, 1994.

_____. *Thomas Scott's Body and Other Essays on the Early History of Manitoba.* Winnipeg: University of Manitoba Press, 2000.

_____. *Trials and Tribulations: The Red River Settlement and the Emergence of Manitoba 1811–1870.* Winnipeg: Great Plains Publications, 2003.

Campbell, Marjorie Wilkins. *The North West Company.* Vancouver: Douglas and McIntyre, 1983.

_____. *Northwest to the Sea: A Biography of William McGillivray.* Toronto: Clarke, Irwin, 1975.

Campbell, R.H., and Andrew S. Skinner, eds. *The Origins and Nature of the Scottish Enlightenment.* Edinburgh: John Donald, 1982.

Campbell, Robert. *History of the St. Gabriel Street Presbyterian Church.* Montreal: W. Drysdale, 1887.

Campey, Lucille H. *The Silver Chief: Selkirk and the Scottish Pioneers of Belfast, Baldoon, and Red River.* Toronto: Natural Heritage Books, 2003.

Chambers, William Nisbet. *Political Parties in a New Nation: The American Experience, 1776–1809.* New York: Oxford University Press, 1966.

Charles, Joseph. *The Origin of the American Party System: Three Essays.* New York: Harper and Row, 1961.

Chernow, Ron. *Alexander Hamilton.* New York: Penguin Books, 2003.

Chitnis, Annand. *The Scottish Enlightenment: A Social History.* (London: Croom Helm, 1967.

Cockburn, Henry. *Journal of Henry Cockburn.* 2 vols. Edinburgh: Edmonston and Douglas, 1874.

Cole, Jean Murray. *Exile in the Wilderness: The Life of Chief Factor Archibald McDonald, 1790–1853.* Don Mills: Burns and MacEachern, 1979.

Collins, Henry, ed. *Thomas Paine Rights of Man.* Harmondsworth, England: Penguin 1969.

Constable, Thomas, ed. *Archibald Constable and His Literary Correspondents.* Edinburgh: Edmonston and Douglas, 1873.

Cooke, Jacob E. *Alexander Hamilton: A Biography.* New York: Scribner's, 1982.

Cormack, A.A. *Poor Relief in Scotland.* Aberdeen: N. p., 1923.

Coutts, Robert, and Richard Stewart, eds. *The Forks and the Battle of Seven Oaks in Manitoba History.* Winnipeg: Manitoba Historical Society, 1994.

Cowan, Helen I. *Charles Williamson: Genesee Promoter, Friend of Anglo-American Rapprochment.* Rochester, NY: Rochester Historical Society, 1941.

Craig, Gerald. *Upper Canada: The Formative Years 1784–1841.* Toronto: McClelland and Stewart, 1963.

Cullen, L.M., and T.C. Smout, eds. *Comparative Aspects of Scottish and Irish Economic History 1600–1900.* Edinburgh: Donald, 1977.

Daniells, Roy. *Alexander Mackenzie and the North West.* London: Oxford University Press, 1969.

Dauer, Manning. *The Adams Federalists.* Baltimore: Johns Hopkins Press, 1983.

Davie, George. *The Democratic Intellect: Scotland and Her Universities in the Nineteenth Century.* 2nd ed. Edinburgh: Edinburgh University Press, 1964.

De La Torre, Lillian. *The Heir of Douglas.* New York: Knopf: 1953.

Devine, T.M. *The Tobacco Lords: A Study of the Tobacco Merchants of Glasgow and Their Trading Activities, c. 1740–1790.* Edinburgh: Donald, 1975.

Dictionary of Canadian Biography. Toronto: University of Toronto Press, 1965 ff.

Dobson, David. *Scots in the West Indies.* 2 vols. Westminister, MD: Clearfield, 2002.

Donnachie, Ian, and Innes MacLeod. *Old Galloway.* London: Newton Abbott David and Charles, 1974.

Dowd, Gregory. *A Spirited Resistance: The North America Struggle for Unity, 1745–1815.* Baltimore: Johns Hopkins University Press, 1992.

Dugas, Georges. *L'Ouest Canadien: Sa Découverte par le Sieur de la Vérendrye. Son Exploitation par les Compagnies de Traiteurs jusqu'à l'année 1822.* Montreal: Cadieux and Dermer, 1896.

Dunfermline, James. *Lieutenant-General Sir Ralph Abercromby, K.B. 1793–1801: A Memoir by His Son*. Edinburgh: Edmonston and Douglas, 1861.

Dwyer, John, et al., eds. *New Perspectives on the Politics and Culture of Early Modern Scotland*. Edinburgh: John Donald, 1982.

Ellis, P. Beresford, and Seumes Mac A'Ghobhainn. *The Scottish Insurrection of 1820*. London: Gollancz, 1970.

Fergusson, Alexander. *The Honourable Henry Erskine, Lord Advocate for Scotland*. Edinburgh and London: W. Blackwood, 1882.

Fitzhugh, Robert. *Robert Burns the Man and the Poet: A Round, Unvarnished Account*. (London and New York: W. H. Allen, 1971.

Fortescue, Sir John. *The County Lieutenancies and the Army, 1804–1814*. London: Macmillan, 1906.

Fortescue, Sir John. *A History of the British Army*. Vol. 6. London: Macmillan, 1921.

Fruchtman, Jack, Jr. *Thomas Paine: Apostle of Freedom*. New York and London: Four Walls Eight Windows, 1994.

Furber, Holden. *Henry Dundas: First Viscount Melville 1742–1811: Political Manager of Scotland, Statesman, Administrator of British India*. Oxford: Oxford University Press, 1931.

Galbraith, John. *The Hudson's Bay Company as an Imperial Factor, 1821–1869*. Toronto: University of Toronto Press, 1957.

Garrioch, A.C. *First Furrows: A History of the Early Settlement of the Red River Country; Including that of Portage la Prairie*. Winnipeg: Stovel, 1923.

Garrioch, David. *The Making of Revolutionary Paris*. Berkeley and Los Angeles: University of California Press, 2002.

Glover, Richard. *Peninsula Preparation: The Reform of the British Army 1795–1809*. Cambridge: Cambridge University Press, 1963.

Gough, Barry. *First Across the Continent: Sir Alexander Mackenzie*. Toronto: McClelland and Stewart, 1998.

Granville, Catania Countess, ed. *Lord Granville Leveson Gower (First Earl Granville) Private Correspondence 1781 to 1821*. vol. 2. London: Murray, 1916.

Gray, John Morgan. *Lord Selkirk of Red River*. Toronto: Macmillan, 1964.

Gray, Malcolm. *The Highland Economy, 1750–1850*. Edinburgh: Edinburgh University Press, 1957.

Grimble, Ian. *The Trial of Patrick Sellar*. London: Routledge and Kegan Paul, 1962.

Gunn, Donald, and Charles Tuttle. *History of Manitoba*. Ottawa: MacLean, Roger, 1880.

Hamilton, Sir William, ed. *The Collected Works of Dugald Stewart*. Vol. 10. Edinburgh: N. p., 1858.

Handley, J.E. *The Agricultural Revolution in Scotland*. Glasgow: Burns, 1963.

_____. *Scottish Farming in the Eighteenth Century*. London: Faber and Faber, 1963.

Hecht, Hans. *Robert Burns: The Man and His Work*. 2nd ed. London: W. Hodge, 1950.

Henderson, J.L.H., ed. *John Strachan: Documents and Opinions*. Toronto: McClelland and Stewart, 1969.

Hibbert, Christopher. *King Mob: The Story of Lord George Gordon and the Riots of 1780.* London: Longman's, Green and Co., 1958.

Hill, Robert. *Manitoba: History of its Early Settlement, Development and Resources.* Toronto: W. Briggs, 1890.

History of the Judicial Society of Edinburgh. N.p., 1875.

History of the Speculative Society of Edinburgh from its Institution in M.DCC.LXIV. Edinburgh: N. p., 1845.

Hont, Istvan, and Michael Ignatieff, eds. *Wealth and Virtue: The Shaping of Political Economy in the Scottish Enlightenment.* Cambridge: Cambridge University Press, 1983.

Hook, Andrew, and Richard B. Sher, eds. *The Glasgow Enlightenment.* East Linton, NJ: Tuckwell, 1995.

Horner, Leonard, ed. *Memoirs and Correspondence of Francis Horner, M.P.* London: J. Murray, 1843.

Houston, C. Stuart, ed. *Arctic Artist: The Journal and Paintings of George Back, Midshipman with Franklin, 1819–1822.* Montreal and Kingston: McGill-Queen's University Press, 1994.

Hunter, James. *The Making of the Crofting Community.* Edinburgh: Donald, 1976.

Innis, Harold A. *The Fur Trade in Canada: An Introduction to Canadian Economic History.* Toronto: University of Toronto Press, 1999.

Irving, Joseph. *Book of Eminent Scotsmen.* Paisley: Gardner, 1881.

Joyce, Michael. *Edinburgh: The Golden Age 1769–1832.* London: Longman's Green, 1951.

Jupp, Peter, *Lord Grenville 1759–1834.* Oxford: Clarendon, 1985.

Karras, Alan. *Sojourners in the Sun: Scottish Migrants in Jamaica and the Chesapeake 1740–1800.* Ithaca, NY: Cornell University Press, 1992.

Keats, John. *Eminent Domain: The Louisiana Purchase and the Making of America.* New York: Charterhouse, 1973.

Kennedy, Roger. *Burr, Hamilton, and Jefferson.* New York: Oxford University Press, 2000.

Lawson, Murray G. *Fur: A Study in English Mercantilism, 1700–1775.* Toronto: University of Toronto Press, 1943.

Le Breton, Anna Letitia. *Memoir of Mrs Barbauld, Including Letters and Notices of Her Family and Friends.* London: N. p., 1874.

[Lefevre, George William]. *Life of a Travelling Physician.* 2 vols. London: Longmans, 1843.

Lockhart, John Gibson. *The Life of Sir Walter Scott.* London: J.M. Dent, 1957.

MacBeth, R.G. *The Selkirk Settlers in Real Life.* Toronto: W. Briggs, 1957.

McCarthy, William, and Elizabeth Kraft, eds. *Anna Laetitia Barbauld: Selected Poetry & Prose.* Athens: University of Georgia Press, 2001.

Macdonald, Forrest. *Alexander Hamilton: A Biography.* New York: Norton, 1979.

McElroy, David. *Scotland's Age of Improvement: A Survey of Eighteenth-Century Literary Clubs and Societies.* N. p.: Washington State University Press, 1969.

McIlvanney, Liam. *Burns the Radical: Poetry and Politics in Late Eighteenth-Century Scotland.* East Linton, NJ: Tuckwell, 2002.

MacKenzie, A.E.D. *Baldoon: Lord Selkirk's Settlement in Upper Canada*. London, ON: Phelps Pub., 1978.

Mackenzie, Alexander. *History of the Macdonalds and Lords of the Isle*. Inverness: A. W. Mackenzie, 1881.

McKie, D. *Antoine Lavoisier: Scientist, Economist, Reformer*. New York: Collier Books 1952.

McKillop, Andrew. *More Fruitful than the Soil: Army, Empire, and the Scottish Highlands*. East Linton, NJ: Tuckwell Press, 2000.

McLeod, Donald. *Gloomy Memories of the Highlands of Scotland*. Glasgow: Thompson, 1857.

_____. *History of the Destitution in Sutherlandshire*. Edinburgh: N.p., 1841.

McLeod, Margaret, and W.L. Morton. *Cuthbert Grant of Grantown*. Toronto: McClelland and Stewart, 1974.

Macoun, John. *Manitoba and the Great North-West: The Field for Investment, the Home of the Emigrant, Being a Full and Complete History of the Country*. Edinburgh: T.C. Jack, 1882.

Macqueen, Malcolm A. *Hebridean Pioneers*. Winnipeg: Henderson Directories, 1957.

_____. *Skye Pioneers and 'The Island.'* Winnipeg: Stovel, 1929.

Mahoney, Thomas H.D., ed. *Reflections on the Revolution in France/Edmund Burke*. Indianapolis: Bobbs-Merrill, 1955.

Martin, Chester. *Lord Selkirk's Work in Canada*. Toronto: Oxford University Press, 1916.

Mathews, Hazel. *The Mark of Honour*. Toronto: University of Toronto Press, 1965.

Mathiez, Albert. *The French Revolution*. New York: Russell and Russell, 1962.

Meikle, Henry. *Scotland and the French Revolution*. New York: A.M. Kelley, 1969.

Milani, Lois Darroch. *Robert Gourlay, Gadfly: Forerunner of the Rebellion in Upper Canada 1837*. Thornhill, ON: Ampersand Press, 1971.

Miller, Karl F.C., ed. *Henry Cockburn's Memorials of His Times*. Chicago: Chicago University Press, 1974.

Mitchison, Rosalind. *Agricultural Sir John: The Life of Sir John Sinclair of Ulbster, 1754–1835*. London: Bles, 1962.

Morrison, Samuel Eliot. *John Paul Jones: A Sailor's Biography*. London: Faber and Faber, 1960.

Morse, Eric W. *Fur Trade Canoe Routes of Canada Then and Now*. Ottawa: Queen's Printer, 1969.

Morton, A.S. *A History of the Canadian West to 1870–71: Being a History of Rupert's Land (the Hudson's Bay Company Territory); and of the North-West Territory (Including the Pacific Slope)*. 2nd ed. Toronto: University of Toronto Press, 1973.

Nanton, Paul. *Arctic Breakthrough: Franklin's Expeditions, 1819–1847*. Toronto: Clarke Irwin, 1971.

Nute, Grace, ed. *Documents Relating to Northwest Missions, 1815–1827*. Saint Paul, MN: Minnesota Historical Society, 1942.

Parker, Irene. *The Dissenting Academies in England*. New York: Octagon Books, 1969.

Pigot, F.L. *John Stewart of Mount Stewart*. Summerside, PEI: The author, 1973.

Pollock, John. *Wilberforce*. London: Constable, 1977.

Porter, K.W. *John Jacob Astor, Business Man*. 2 vols. New York: Russell and Russell, 1966.

Porter, Roy. *The Creation of the Modern World: The Untold Story of the British Enlightenment*. London: Norton, 2000.

Prebble, John. *The Highland Clearances*. London: Secker and Warburg, 1963.

_____. *Mutiny*. Harmondsworth: Penguin 1975.

Pritchett, John Perry. *The Red River Valley 1811–1849: A Regional Study*. New Haven and Toronto: Yale University Press, 1942.

Ray, Arthur J., and Donald Freeman. *"Give Us Good Measure": An Economic Analysis of Relations between the Indians and the Hudson's Bay Company before 1763*. Toronto: University of Toronto Press, 1978.

Rea, J. E. *Bishop Alexander Macdonell and the Politics of Upper Canada*. Toronto: Ontario Historical Society, 1974.

Rendall, Jane. *The Origins of the Scottish Enlightenment*. London: Macmillan, 1978.

Rich, E.E., ed. *Colin Robertson's Correspondence Book, September 1817 to September 1822*. Toronto: Champlain Society, 1939.

Rich, E.E. *The Fur Trade and the Northwest to 1857*. Toronto: McClelland and Stewart, 1967.

_____. *The History of the Hudson's Bay Company, 1670–1870*. 2 vols. London: Hudson's Bay Record Society, 1959.

_____., ed. *Journal of Occurrences in the Athabasca Department by George Simpson, 1820 and 1821*. Toronto: Champlain Society, 1938.

Richards, Eric. *The Leviathan of Wealth: The Sutherland Fortune in the Industrial Revolution*. London: Routledge and Kegan Paul, 1973.

Riddell, W. B. *The Life of William Dummer Powell: First Judge at Detroit and Fifth Chief Justice of Upper Canada*. Lansing, MI: Michigan Historical Commission, 1924.

Robbins, Caroline. *The Eighteenth-Century Commonwealthman: Studies in the Transmission, Development and Circumstance of English Liberal Thought from the Restoration of Charles II until the War with the Thirteen Colonies*. Cambridge, MA: Harvard University Press, 1959.

Rodgers, Betsy. *Georgian Chronical: Mrs. Barbauld and Her Family*. London: Methuen, 1958.

Ronda, James. *Astoria & Empire*. London and Lincoln, NE: University of Nebraska Press, 1990.

Ross, Alexander. *The Red River Settlement: Its Rise, Progress and Present State, with Some Account of the Native Races and its General History to the Present Day*. London: Smith, Elder, 1856.

Ross, Eric. *Beyond the River and the Bay: Some Observations on the State of the Canadian Northwest in 1811 with a View to Providing the Intending Settler with an Intimate Knowledge of the Country*. Toronto: University of Toronto Press, 1970.

Rothschild, Emma. *Economic Sentiments: Adam Smith, Condorcet, and the Enlightenment*. Cambridge, MA: Harvard University Press, 2001.

Roy, G. Ross, ed. *The Letters of Robert Burns*. Oxford: Oxford University Press, 1985.

Schama, Simon. *Citizens: A Chronicle of the French Revolution*. New York: Knopf, 1989.

Schofield, F.H. *The Story of Manitoba*. 3 vols. Winnipeg: S.J. Clarke, 1913.

Schwoerer, L.G. *"No Standing Armies!" The Antiarmy Ideology in Seventeenth-Century England*. London: Johns Hopkins University Press, 1974.

Simpson, Colin. *Emma: The Life of Lady Hamilton*. London: Bodley Head, 1983.

Sloan, M. *Galloway*. London: N. p., 1908.

Smout, T.C. *A History of the Scottish People 1560–1830*. London: Fontana, 1985.

Steuart, Francis, ed. *The Douglas Cause*. Toronto: Canada Law Book, 1909.

Story, Norah. *The Oxford Companion to Canadian History and Literature*. Toronto: Oxford University Press, 1957.

Stourzh, Gerald. *Alexander Hamilton and the Idea of Republican Government*. Stanford, CA: Stanford University Press, 1970.

Syrett, Harold C., et al. *The Papers of Alexander Hamilton*. Vol. 25. New York: Columbia University Press, 1979.

Thomas, Evan. *John Paul Jones*. New York: Simon and Schuster, 2004.

Thompson, E.P. *The Making of the English Working Class*. Harmondsworth: England, Penguin, 1970.

Thornton, Robert Donald. *James Currie/The Entire Stranger & Robert Burns*. Edinburgh and London: Oliver and Boyd, 1963.

Toomey, Kathleen. *Alexander Macdonell: The Scottish Years 1762–1804*. Toronto: Canadian Catholic Historical Society, 1985.

Trotter, Alexander. *East Galloway Sketches*. Castle-Douglas: Adam Rae, 1901.

Western, J. R. *The English Militia in the Eighteenth Century: The Story of a Political Issue*. London: Routledge and Kegan Paul, 1965.

White, Patrick C. T., ed. *Lord Selkirk's Diary 1803–1804: A Journal of His Travels in British North America and the Northeastern United States*. Toronto: Champlain Society, 1958.

Wilberforce, Robert, and Samuel Wilberforce, eds. *The Life of Wilberforce/In Five Volumes*. London: J. Murray, 1838.

Willson, Beckles. *Friendly Relations*. Boston: Little Brown, 1934.

Young, Douglas. *Edinburgh in the Age of Sir Walter Scott*. Norman, OK: University of Oklahoma Press, 1965.

Youngson, A.J. *After the Forty-Five: The Economic Impact on the Scottish Highlands*. Edinburgh: Edinburgh University Press, 1973.

_____. *The Making of Classical Edinburgh 1750–1840*. Edinburgh: Edinburgh University Press, 1966.

Later Printed Articles

Barron, F. L. "Victimizing His Lordship: Lord Selkirk and the Upper Canadian Courts." *Manitoba History* 7 (Autumn, 1984): 14–22.

Bumsted, J. M. "Highland Emigration to the Island of St. John and the Scottish Catholic Church, 1769-1774." *Dalhousie Review* 58 (1978): 511–27.

_____. "Another Look at the Founder: Lord Selkirk and Political Economy." In Bumsted, *Thomas Scott's Body and Other Essays in the Early History of Manitoba*, 37–56.

_____. "Thomas Halliday, Mary Cochrane, the Earl of Selkirk, and the Island." *The Island Magazine* 18 (1986): 27–32.

_____. "The Affair at Stornoway, 1811." *The Beaver* (Spring, 1982): 52–58.

_____. "The Loyal Electors." *The Island Magazine* 7 (1980): 8–14.

_____. "Lord Selkirk's Highland Regiment and the Kildonan Settlers." *The Beaver* (Autumn, 1978): 16–21.

_____. "The Swiss and Red River, 1819–1826." In Bumsted, ed., *Thomas Scott's Body*, 57–76.

Bumsted, Siân. "Lady Selkirk and the Fur Trade." *Manitoba History* 38 (Autumn/Winter 1999/2000).

Campbell, R.H. "The Scottish Improvers and the Course of Agrarian Change in the Eighteenth Century." In L.M. Cullen and T.C. Smout, eds. *Comparative Aspects of Scottish and Irish Economic History 1600–1900*. Edinburgh: Donald, 1977.

Cowan, Helen I. "Selkirk's Work in Canada: An Early Chapter." *Canadian Historical Review* 9 (1928): 299–308.

Dick, Lyle. "The Seven Oaks Incident and the Construction of a Historical Tradition, 1816 to 1970." *Journal of the Canadian Historical Association* 2 (1991): 90–114.

Dwyer, John, and Alexander Murdoch. "Paradigms and Politics: Manners, Morals and the Rise of Henry Dundas, 1770–1784." In John Dwyer, et al., *New Perspectives*.

Eyles, V.A. "The Evolution of a Chemist: Sir James Hall Bt." *Annals of Science* 9 (1963): 153–182.

_____. "Sir James Hall Bt (1761-1832)." *Endeavour 20* (1961): 210–216.

Flinn, M.W. "Malthus, Emigration and Potatoes in the Scottish North-West, 1770–1870." In L.M. Cullen and T.C. Smout, eds., *Comparative Aspects*.

Gray, Malcolm. "The Kelp Industry in the Highlands and Islands." *Economic History Review*, 2nd ser., 4 (1951): 197–209.

Greenwood, F. Murray, and Barry Wright. Canadian State Trials. 2 vols. Toronto: Osgood Society for Canadian Legal History, University of Toronto Press, 1996.

Gressley, Gene. "Lord Selkirk and the Canadian Courts." *North Dakota History* 24 (1957): 89–105.

Hamil, F.C., and T. Jones. "Lord Selkirk's Work in Upper Canada: The Story of Baldoon." *Ontario History* 57 (1965): 1–12.

Harvey, A.D. "The Ministry of All the Talents: The Whigs in Office, February 1806 to March 1807." *Historical Journal* 15 (1972): 619–648.

Hay, Douglas, and Francis Snyder. "Using the Criminal Law, 1750–1850: Policing, Private Prosecution, and the State." In *Policing and Prosecution in Britain, 1750–1850*, edited by Douglas Hand and Francis Snyder, 3–54. Oxford: Clarendon House, 1989.

Henderson, Anne. "The Lord Selkirk Association in Rupert's Land." *Manitoba Pageant* 7, 3 (April 1962).

Hont, Istvan, and Michael Ignatieff. "Needs and Justice in the *Wealth of Nations:* An Introductory Essay." In *Wealth and Virtue: The Shaping of Political Economy in the Scottish Enlightenment,* edited by Istvan Hont and Michael Ignatief, 13–26. Cambridge: Cambridge University Press, 1983.

Jenks, William L. "The Earl of Selkirk in Michigan Courts." *Michigan Magazine of History* 12 (1928): 662–668.

Kolish, Evelyn, and James Lambert. "The Attempted Impeachment of the Lower Canadian Chief Justices, 1814–1815." In Greenwood and Wright, *Canadian State Trials.* 1 (Toronto, 1996): 450–87.

Loch, Charles Stewart. "Poor Relief in Scotland: Its Statistics and Development, 1791–1891." *Journal Royal Statistical Society* 61 (1898): 271–370.

McCahill, Michael. "The Scottish Peerage and the House of Lords in the Late Eighteenth Century." *Scottish Historical Review* 51 (1972): 172–196.

Morice, A. G. "Sidelights on the Careers of Miles Macdonell and His Brothers." *Canadian Historical Review* 10 (1929): 308–32.

Nicolson, Malcolm. "The Continental Journeys of Andrew Duncan junior." <http://www.repe.ac.uk/library/continental_journey/journey5.html>.

Parker, B.A. "Thomas Clark: His Business Relationship with Lord Selkirk." *Beaver* outfit 310 (Autumn, 1979): 50–58.

Pritchett, John Perry, and Murray Horowitz, eds. "Five Selkirk Letters." *Canadian Historical Review* 22 (1941): 159–167.

Pritchett, John Perry. "A Selkirk Letter." *Canadian Historical Review* 17 (1936): 406–407.

_____. "Selkirk's View on British Policy towards the Spanish-American Colonies, 1806." *Canadian Historical Review* 24 (1943): 381–396.

_____. "Selkirk's Return from Assiniboia via the United States to the Canadas, 1817–18." *Mississippi Valley Historical Review* 33 (1945): 399–418.

Thomas, L.G. "Historiography of the Fur Trade Era." In Richard Allen, ed., *A Region of the Mind: Interpreting the Western Canadian Plains.* Regina: Canadian Plains Research Centre, University of Saskatchewan, 1975.

Wallace, W.S. "The Literature Relating to the Selkirk Controversy." *Canadian Historical Review* 13 (1932): 45–50.

Walpole, K.A. "The Humanitarian Movement of the Early Nineteenth Century to Remedy Abuses on Emigrant Vessels to America." *Transactions of the Royal Historical Society,* 4th ser., 14 (1931): 197–224.

Williams, Glyndwr. "The Hudson's Bay Company and the Fur Trade: 1670–1870." *The Beaver* (Autumn, 1983).

Wolfenden, Madge, ed. "Career of a Scotch Boy." *British Columbia Historical Quarterly* 18 (1954): 133–238.

Wright, Barry. "The Gourlay Affair: Seditious Libel and the Seditions Act in Upper Canada, 1818–19." In Greenwood and Wright, eds. *Canadian State Trials.* 1: 487–504.

Unpublished Works

Barron, F.L. "The York Trials of 1818: Lord Selkirk and John Strachan." M.Phil. thesis, University of Waterloo, 1970.

Bumsted, J.M. "Rise and Fall of the Kelping Industry in Scotland, 1750–1920." Forthcoming in a book about archaeology in the Hebrides by Sheffield University Press.

Colhart, James. "Edward Ellice and North America." Ph.D. diss., Princeton University, 1971.

[Fraser, Edward S.]. "On Emigration from the Scottish Highlands and Isles." NLS.

Robertson, John. "The Improving Citizen: Militia Debates and Political Thought in the Scottish Enlightenment." D. Phil. thesis, University of Oxford, 1980.

Somers, Hugh Joseph. "The Life and Times of the Honorable and Rt. Rev. Alexander Macdonell D.D." Ph.D diss., Catholic University of America, 1931.

INDEX